Economic Challenges in Higher Education

A National Bureau
of Economic Research
Monograph

Economic Challenges in Higher Education

Charles T. Clotfelter,
Ronald G. Ehrenberg,
Malcolm Getz, and
John J. Siegfried

The University of Chicago Press

Chicago and London

CHARLES T. CLOTFELTER is professor of public policy studies and economics at Duke University. RONALD G. EHRENBERG is the Irving M. Ives Professor of Industrial and Labor Relations and Economics at Cornell University. MALCOLM GETZ is associate professor of economics and associate provost for information science and technology at Vanderbilt University. JOHN J. SIEGFRIED is professor of economics at Vanderbilt University.

The University of Chicago Press, Chicago 60637
The University of Chicago Press, Ltd., London

© 1991 by The University of Chicago
All rights reserved. Published 1991
Printed in the United States of America

00 99 98 97 96 95 94 93 92 91   5 4 3 2 1

ISBN 0–226–11050–8

Library of Congress Cataloging-in-Publication Data

Economic challenges in higher education / Charles T. Clotfelter . . . [et al.].
        p. cm.—(A National Bureau of Economic Research monograph)
    Includes bibliographical references and index.
    1. Education, Higher—Economic aspects—United States.   2. College attendance—United States.   3. Student aid—United States.   4. College teachers—United States—Supply and demand.   5. College costs—United States.   I. Clotfelter, Charles T.   II. Series.
LC67.62.E25   1991
338.4′737873—dc20   91-23330
                                                                         CIP

Relation of the Directors to the
Work and Publications of the
National Bureau of Economic Research

1. The object of the National Bureau of Economic Research is to ascertain and to present to the public important economic facts and their interpretation in a scientific and impartial manner. The Board of Directors charged with the responsibility of ensuring that the work of the National Bureau is carried on in strict conformity with this object.

2. The President of the National Bureau shall submit to the Board of Directors, or to its Executive Committee, for their formal adoption all specific proposals for research to be instituted.

3. No research report shall be published by the National Bureau until the President has sent each member of the Board a notice that a manuscript is recommended for publication and that in the President's opinion it is suitable for publication in accordance with the principles of the National Bureau. Such notification will include an abstract or summary of the manuscript's content and a response form for use by those Directors who desire a copy of the manuscript for review. Each manuscript shall contain a summary drawing attention to the nature and treatment of the problem studied, the character of the data and their utilization in the report, and the main conclusions reached.

4. For each manuscript so submitted, a special committee of the Directors (including Directors Emeriti) shall be appointed by majority agreement of the President and Vice Presidents (or by the Executive Committee in case of inability to decide on the part of the President and Vice Presidents), consisting of three Directors selected as nearly as may be one from each general division of the Board. The names of the special manuscript committee shall be stated to each Director when notice of the proposed publication is submitted to him. It shall be the duty of each member of the special manuscript committee to read the manuscript. If each member of the manuscript committee signifies his approval within thirty days of the transmittal of the manuscript, the report may be published. If at the end of that period any member of the manuscript committee withholds his approval, the President shall then notify each member of the Board, requesting approval or disapproval of publication, and thirty days additional shall be granted for this purpose. The manuscript shall then not be published unless at least a majority of the entire Board who shall have voted on the proposal within the time fixed for the receipt of votes shall have approved.

5. No manuscript may be published, though approved by each member of the special manuscript committee, until forty-five days have elapsed from the transmittal of the report in manuscript form. The interval is allowed for the receipt of any memorandum of dissent or reservation, together with a brief statement of his reasons, that any member may wish to express: and such memorandum of dissent or reservation shall be published with the manuscript if he so desires. Publication does not, however, imply that each member of the Board has read the manuscript, or that either members of the Board in general or the special committee have passed on its validity in every detail.

6. Publications of the National Bureau issued for informational purposes concerning the work of the Bureau and its staff, or issued to inform the public of activities of Bureau staff, and volumes issued as a result of various conferences involving the National Bureau shall contain a specific disclaimer noting that such publication has not passed through the normal review procedures required in this resolution. The Executive Committee of the Board is charged with review of all such publications from time to time to ensure that they do not take on the character of formal research reports of the National Bureau, requiring formal Board approval.

7. Unless otherwise determined by the Board of exempted by the terms of paragraph 6, a copy of this resolution shall be printed in each National Bureau publication.

(Resolution adopted October 25, 1926, as revised through September 30, 1974)

Contents

Acknowledgments

This book is a product of the National Bureau of Economic Research program on the economics of higher education. It discusses three major economic issues facing higher education in the United States and attempts to do so in a form that will be accessible to noneconomists. In writing the book, we have benefited from the advice, assistance, and support of many people. We would like to single out a few of them for special thanks.

Several people and organizations generously provided data and other unpublished material. Alan Fechter and his staff at the National Research Council prepared numerous tabulations of unpublished data; Michael Olivas and William Bowen provided extensive materials; and Michael McPherson and the National Center for Higher Education Management Systems provided data sets and processed data. For helpful discussions and comments on earlier drafts, we are grateful to Gary Barnes, William Becker, James Belvin, Rudolph Blitz, William Bowen, Paul Brinkman, Philip Cook, Sal Corallo, Martin Feldstein, T. A. Finegan, W. Lee Hansen, Robert Hauser, Stephen Hoenack, William Jenkins, Thomas Kane, Hirschel Kasper, Charlotte Kuh, Michael McPherson, Thomas Mortenson, Emmett Miller, Michael Olivas, Michael Rothschild, Harold Shapiro, Lawrence J. White, Hao Zhang, and several anonymous reviewers for the NBER and University of Chicago Press. One part of the NBER program on higher education has been a working group that has been meeting periodically at the Bureau's offices in Cambridge, Massachusetts. That group has provided many useful discussions and comments related to this project.

We would like to thank Linda Knopp, Panagiotis Mavros, Emmett Miller, Dan Rees, Caroline Siegfried, Tom Shirkey, Michelle Stevens, Jane Farley Terrell, and Hao Zhang for their contributions to this project as research assistants. And we are grateful to Marshall Adesman, Patricia Dickerson, Maria Hall, Lynne Miller, Beth Shulman, Carole Stern, and members of the NBER staff for their valuable assistance in manuscript preparation. In addition, Emmett Miller's 1990 senior thesis at Vanderbilt University served as an informative pilot project in the development of Part III of the book.

We are grateful to the Andrew W. Mellon Foundation, which has provided financial support for this book and the NBER higher education project. In addition, we have received research support from Duke University, Cornell University, Vanderbilt University, and the National Science Foundation. However, the views expressed in the book do not necessarily reflect those of any of these organizations.

Introduction

Higher education profoundly affects the economy, society, and culture of this country. Whether viewed as engines of economic growth, keepers of the keys to culture, or tools of credentialism, colleges and universities are powerful, important, and pervasive forces, a fact attested to by the attention that scholars have paid to them over the years. American higher education is often held up as a model for the world—in marked contrast to popular contemporary views of American elementary and secondary schooling. Higher education is seen as vital to the country's continued growth and ability to compete in an increasingly international market.[1] The technological gap between the United States and other countries is narrowing, spawning a demand for increased creativity and flexibility in the American economy. Although the main responsibility of higher education historically has not been to prepare students for specific jobs, the percentage of students who major in the liberal arts has plummeted in the 1970s and 1980s as the percentage majoring in professionally oriented areas has soared.[2]

The last two decades have been a turbulent period for American higher education, marked by profound demographic shifts, episodes of high inflation, gyrating salaries, and significant changes in the nation's economy. Enrollments have risen markedly, increasing by 49 percent from 1970 to 1988 (U.S. Department of Education 1989, table 163, p. 181), and new federal programs to provide aid to college students have been initiated. During the 1970s, tuition increases in both public and private colleges lagged behind inflation, only to accelerate in the 1980s as the rate of inflation slowed. Between the academic years 1970–71 and 1987–88, the average annual rate of increase in tuition and fees at public colleges and universities exceeded the rate of

1. For a concise statement of this point, see Newman (1985).
2. See Bowen and Sosa (1989), and also Table 7.1 and Chapter 11, n. 2, below.

1

inflation by 0.8 percent, and for private institutions the difference was 2.1 percent.[3] Critics have bitterly denounced these price increases, citing them as evidence not only of inefficiency but also of institutional greed and irresponsibility.[4]

This period has also witnessed dramatic changes in the academic labor market, marked by substantial reductions in hiring of new Ph.D.s in many fields. But as we enter the 1990s there is evidence that surpluses will again give way to shortages in a number of academic fields (Bowen and Sosa 1989). As a result of developments in the 1970s and 1980s, however, the numbers of American graduate students in several disciplines, particularly technical fields, have declined dramatically just when demand promises to rebound, generating concern about our capacity to serve all capable college students in the future.

Among the prominent issues in current discussions about higher education, three are especially noteworthy and amenable to economic analysis. These issues constitute the themes for the three parts of this book. The first is the demand for undergraduate places in colleges and universities. Among the notable features of this market are the relatively large size of the expenditure on a college education compared to other items in the family budget, the participation of both students and their parents in decisions about college, limited knowledge about alternative suppliers, and an elaborate application and selection process. In recent years, the prices faced by households in this market have risen markedly. At the same time, governments, by means of student aid programs and state subsidies, are able to influence these prices. What are the economic forces affecting demand in this market? In particular, what is likely to be the effect of rising tuitions and government policy on the level and composition of this demand? Are minorities and the poor participating to a greater or lesser extent over time?

The second issue addressed is supply in the academic labor market. Projections of supply and demand for faculty sometimes rely on simple assumptions about supply, owing to our ignorance of the factors that determine whether a person engages in graduate work, how long he or she spends completing that training, and the probability that a nonacademic career will ultimately be chosen. Is the supply of Ph.D.s likely to increase? If so, in what fields will it increase, and what will be its quality? Can Ph.D.s currently employed in the nonacademic sector be induced to move to the academic sector? More generally, will academe experience a shortage of Ph.D.s?

3. The average inflation rate over the period was 6.5 percent. The average rate of increase in tuition and fees was 7.3 percent in public institutions and 8.6 percent in private ones. These calculations are based on U.S. Department of Education (1989, table 258) and Council of Economic Advisers (1991, 351). The average consumer price index (CPI) for each pair of years was used.

4. See, e.g., William Bennett, "Our Greedy Colleges," *New York Times,* 18 February 1987, p. A31; "Colleges: A Machine with No Brakes," *Washington Post Weekly,* 21–27 August 1989; Chester Finn, "Trying Higher Education: An Eight Count Indictment," *Change* 16 (May/June, 1984): 29–33, 47–51.

The third issue is the rising cost of a college education. When costs rise faster than inflation, both the efficiency and the objectives of colleges and universities come under scrutiny. Why have these increases occurred? Have they been accompanied by lower student/faculty ratios? Are they due to deliberate actions on the part of institutions or to forces beyond the control of administrators? Questions such as these provide the motivation for this book.

The "Market" for Higher Education: A Brief Description

Economists are accustomed to viewing the provision of any good or service in terms of the concepts of demand (describing the behavior of households and individuals), supply (describing the conduct of firms), and market (describing the interactions of supply and demand). While it is obvious that the provision of higher education is far too complex to fit into the neat categories of textbook economics, these constructs can nevertheless be useful when peculiarities characterizing a specific market are taken into account. It is natural therefore to begin our treatment of these three issues with a thumbnail sketch of the "market," noting especially its unusual features. We first provide some summary measures of the size and growth of the market for higher education; we then discuss diversity, decentralization, firm organization, and finance.

Size and Growth

In 1987, there were about 3,400 institutions of higher education enrolling some 12.3 million students.[5] Adding up all expenditures on higher education yields a total $130 billion in 1988–89. As shown in Table 1, this amount is about two-thirds of the total spent on elementary and secondary schooling, an impressive amount considering that the full-time equivalent enrollment of colleges and universities is only one-fifth of that at lower levels.[6] Furthermore, the growth in expenditures for colleges and universities has been considerably more rapid than that for elementary and secondary schools, reflecting in large part an explosion in enrollments. Between 1929–30 and 1988–89, total enrollments in colleges and universities increased more than tenfold. Over that period, expenditures on higher education also grew rapidly, from 0.6 to 2.7 percent of GNP, but not in proportion to enrollments. Expenditures for elementary and secondary schools rose from 2.4 to 4.1 percent of GNP over this period, during which time precollege enrollments increased by 60 percent.[7]

Diversity

What do career counseling, computerized reference services, planetarium shows, seminars on literary criticism, televised football games, high-energy

---

5. For the data, see Table 2 below.

6. U.S. Department of Education (1989, 9, 180). Enrollment figures are based on 1987.

7. Enrollments in 1929–30 and 1988–89 were, respectively, 28.3 and 45.4 million for grades K–12 and 1.1 and 12.8 million for colleges and universities (U.S. Department of Education 1989, 10).

Table 1   Expenditures of Educational Institutions (dollar amounts in billions)

	Elementary and Secondary Schools		Colleges and Universities			
	Amount($)	% of GNP	Public($)	Private($)	Total($)	% of GNP
1929–30	2.49ᵃ	2.4	.29	.34	.63	.6
1939–40	2.52ᵃ	2.8	.39	.37	.76	.8
1949–50	6.25	2.4	1.43	1.23	2.66	1.0
1959–60	16.71	3.4	3.90	3.24	7.15	1.4
1969–70	43.18	4.5	16.23	9.04	25.28	2.6
1979–80	103.16	4.1	41.43	21.03	62.47	2.5
1988–89	199.10	4.1	85.50	45.80	131.40	2.7

Sources: U.S. Department of Education (1989, table 26, p. 30); U.S. Council of Economic Advisers (1990, table C-1, p. 264).
Note: GNP is for beginning year.
ᵃEstimated from information on public expenditures, using ratio of public to total expenditures in 1949–50 and 1959–60.

physics experiments, fast-food operations, lectures on introductory psychology, advice on agricultural pest control, weight lifting, teacher training, and orchestra rehearsals have in common? The answer, of course, is that they are all among the many activities of colleges and universities. As suggested by the variety of these activities, the service called "higher education" is in reality an amalgam of qualitatively different outputs, produced in a wide assortment of settings.[8]

The diversity of American higher education is manifested in the aims of its institutions, the activities in which they engage, and the accomplishments of their students and faculty. Founded for reasons as different as training clergy, producing teachers, and serving the general population of individual states, colleges and universities in this country have evolved into several distinct types of institutions. A relatively small number of well-known universities embrace research as their essential, if not primary, responsibility. They account for a disproportionate share of the country's Ph.D.s, federal grants, and articles published in academic journals. Other universities place comparatively less emphasis on research while still maintaining some doctoral programs. Many of the state universities have active public service programs, including agricultural extension services, the provision of consumer information, medical services, and industrial extension services that assist employers. In contrast to these larger institutions, the mostly private liberal arts colleges specialize in basic undergraduate education in the arts and sciences, emphasizing the process of student-faculty interaction. One other group of four-year colleges is the so-called comprehensive institutions. By and large, they serve

8. Where services are necessarily produced in conjunction, they are called "joint products." Nerlove (1972) has argued, e.g., that teaching and research are joint products of universities.

students within a limited geographic area and tend to offer a higher percentage of professional programs than the research universities or the liberal arts colleges. Rounding out the array of higher education institutions are the two-year colleges, which are used by some as a stepping-stone to a four-year college and by others as a means of obtaining basic training in job-related skills.

One widely recognized scheme for describing the variety of institutions in higher education is a classification system developed by the Carnegie Foundation for the Advancement of Teaching. The purpose of the system is to group institutions according to their primary mission, and it uses such criteria as enrollment, number and type of degrees awarded, and amount of federal research support to make distinctions. Ten categories defined in this system are listed in Table 2, along with short descriptions of each.[9] The usefulness of this classification scheme lies in its grouping together of institutions that are similar in mission and, to some extent, size. But the consideration of this or any other classification of institutions of higher education should begin with the realization that these groupings are far from distinct. Just as institutions in different classes share many of the same characteristics, there is also much diversity among institutions that are grouped together.

The individual institutions differ enormously. In size, they range from the gargantuan state universities with enrollments over 40,000 to intimate colleges with only a few hundred students. Over the last decade, some have grown at rates of more than 15 percent per year (e.g., Hawaii Pacific College, the University of Alaska at Juneau), while others have suffered enrollment declines in excess of 10 percent annually (e.g., Gratz College).[10] In purpose, they range from such clearly delineated objectives as religious education and the great books approach to the almost all-encompassing aims of the large state universities. Of the latter, the University of North Carolina is illustrative. According to its official mission statement, "The mission of the University is to serve all the people of the State, and indeed the nation, as a center for scholarship and creative endeavor. The University exists to expand the body of knowledge; to teach students at all levels . . . ; to improve the condition of human life through service and publication; and to enrich our culture."[11]

9. In addition to the first nine categories listed in Table 2, the Carnegie classification system also contains categories for free-standing professional schools and specialized institutions (e.g., independent medical and law schools, seminaries, and institutions with exclusively graduate-level programs). This is an extremely heterogeneous group and includes relatively few institutions that offer undergraduate degrees. We generally group them together as specialized institutions or ignore them in what follows.

10. Calculations cover the period 1978–79 to 1987–88. For a description of the data, see Part III.

11. "Mission Statement of the University of North Carolina at Chapel Hill" (*Record of the University of North Carolina at Chapel Hill,* April 1989). Reflecting on the multiplicity of purposes and traditions that influence the modern "multiversity," Kerr (1982, 18) gives this not entirely tongue-in-cheek assessment: "A university anywhere can aim no higher than to be as British as possible for the sake of the undergraduates, as German as possible for the sake of the graduates and the research personnel, as American as possible for the sake of the public at large—and as confused as possible for the sake of the preservation of the whole uneasy balance."

Table 2   Enrollment in Institutions of Higher Education in the United States, 1976 and 1987

Type of Institution	Enrollment (000s)		% Change in Enrollment, 1976–87	No. of Institutions		% Change in Number, 1976–87	Share of Enrollment in 1987	% of Students Enrolled in the Category in Public Institutions in 1987
	1976	1987		1976	1987			
Total	**11,165**	**12,301**	**10.2**	**3,072**	**3,389**	**10.3**	**100.0**	**76.9**
Doctorate-Granting	**3,056**	**3,429**	**12.2**	**184**	**213**	**15.8**	**27.9**	**77.4**
Research University I	1,144	1,579	38.0	51	70	37.3	12.8	79.7
Research University II	803	630	−21.5	47	34	−29.8	5.1	85.9
Doctorate-Granting I	805	680	−15.5	56	51	−8.9	5.5	72.8
Doctorate-Granting II	304	540	77.6	30	58	96.7	4.4	66.9
Comprehensive Universities and Colleges	**3,170**	**3,303**	**4.2**	**594**	**595**	**1.2**	**26.9**	**72.0**
Comprehensive I	2,628	2,971	13.1	381	424	12.1	24.2	76.7
Comprehensive II	542	332	−38.7	213	171	−18.3	2.7	29.2

Liberal Arts Colleges	531	584	10.0	583	572	-3.3	4.7	7.5
Liberal Arts I	154	214	39.0	123	142	1.6	1.7	2.3
Liberal Arts II	377	370	-1.9	460	430	-4.6	3.0	10.5
Two-Year Institutions	3,978	4,518	13.6	1,146	1,367	19.4	36.7	94.1
Specialized Institutions	416	467	12.3	559	642	15.0	3.8	28.1

Sources: Carnegie Foundation for the Advancement of Teaching (1987, tables 1, 2, 4); Carnegie Foundation for the Advancement of Teaching (1989).

Note: Carnegie classes are defined as follows: *Research Universities I*: Institutions that offer a full range of baccalaureate programs, award at least 50 Ph.D. degrees annually, and receive at least $33.5 million of federal research support annually; *Research Universities II*: Same criteria as Research Universities I, except these institutions receive between $12.5 and $33.5 million annually in federal research support; *Doctorate-Granting Universities I*: Institutions that offer a full range of baccalaureate programs and award at least 40 Ph.D. degrees annually in five or more disciplines; *Doctorate-Granting Universities II*: Institutions that offer a full range of baccalaureate programs and award at least 20 Ph.D. degrees annually in one discipline or at least 10 Ph.D. degrees in three or more disciplines; *Comprehensive Universities and Colleges I*: Institutions that enroll at least 2,500 students, award at least half their baccalaureate degrees in two or more professional disciplines, such as engineering or business administration, and also offer graduate education through the master's degree; *Comprehensive Universities and Colleges II*: Institutions that enroll between 1,500 and 2,500 students, award at least half their degrees in two or more professional disciplines, and, in many cases, offer graduate education through the master's degree; *Liberal Arts Colleges I*: Primarily highly selective undergraduate colleges that award more than half their baccalaureate degrees in the arts and sciences; while not a criterion, almost all these institutions enroll fewer than 3,000 students annually and have limited, if any, graduate programs; *Liberal Arts Colleges II*: Less selective liberal arts colleges and smaller comprehensive type universities and colleges with annual enrollment of less than 1,500; because of the mixture of liberal arts colleges and comprehensive institutions, we sometimes label this category "Other-Four-Year Colleges" in the chapters that follow; *Two-Year Institutions*: Institutions that offer certificate or degree programs through the associate of arts level and (with few exceptions) offer no baccalaureate degrees; this category includes "freshman and sophomore" branch campuses of some large state universities (e.g., Penn State), specialist technical and vocational colleges, and free-standing institutions offering associate of arts degrees; *Specialized Institutions*: Institutions that offer at least half their degrees in a single specialized field; this category includes freestanding theological seminaries, medical schools, teachers colleges, and institutions offering other professional degrees.

The diversity of our colleges and universities ranges into the production process as well. Large doctorate granting universities tend to employ graduate teaching assistants to help with undergraduate instruction. Many comprehensive institutions and less selective liberal arts colleges frequently use part-time faculty to teach courses, while the highly selective liberal arts institutions rely almost exclusively on full-time faculty for instructional purposes. The teaching load and responsibilities of the faculty vary too. At institutions where the faculty are expected to engage in extensive research and scholarship, faculty rarely teach more than four courses annually. At the elite private liberal arts colleges, teaching loads range from four to six courses per year, while faculty at comprehensive institutions and less selective liberal arts colleges often teach eight or more courses per year.

What occurs inside classrooms also varies across institutions. The student/faculty ratio, which affects the pedagogical strategies available to an instructor, is quite different at different institutions, ranging from above 50 to 1 at several dozen four-year colleges and universities to under 10 to 1 at some private institutions. Certainly, the amount of individual attention, dialogue, and feedback on written assignments, all elements of the learning process, must differ when the student load varies by a factor of five to one.

Institutions also differ, obviously, in geographic location. A college education in the traditional American sense is a product that one purchases at the point it is provided. Mail-order and telecommunicated higher education has never been an important part of the college experience in America. And seldom do colleges move, although some do offer classes in various locations.

The diversity of experiences available from American colleges and universities means that comparisons are, at best, hazardous. Prices can be expected to vary significantly when the product mix differs so much. During a period of a shrinking college-age population, as America has been experiencing, it is natural to see institutions reaching out to less traditional students and competing on the basis of their differences. The effect of this enormous product differentiation on market behavior and performance is ambiguous. A market in which many services are purchased together (e.g., cognitive development, sorting, screening, social development, entertainment, and job placement) and not sold directly makes it difficult to assess value. Information about quality is difficult to assemble and evaluate, which in turn may affect the average level and variation of quality offered.

Product differentiation also spawns non-price competition among colleges and universities, competition that has increased noticeably in the last decade. Cardboard boxes full of slick brochures touting the advantages of various colleges and universities are no longer limited to the closets of outstanding high school athletes. It is now commonplace for high school seniors (and many juniors) who score well on college entrance examinations to be courted aggressively by colleges.

The enormous diversity of goals, quality, and teaching methods found in various institutions makes it difficult to assess changes in the American higher education sector. For example, shifts in enrollment from one type of institution to another can easily be mistaken for systematic changes in all institutions. To ease the interpretation of data, in this volume we frequently subdivide the higher education sector into smaller groups of institutions; while each still offers unique characteristics, we believe that these groups are more homogenous. We have elected, for the most part, to use three significant differences among the institutions: mission, control, and size. The Carnegie classification system (see Table 2) is one widely recognized way of dividing institutions. Most recently revised in 1987, this scheme is useful for distinguishing among colleges and universities with quite distinct goals, and we use it as the basis for organizing several presentations of data on institutions.

The market for higher education is strongly shaped by government action at a variety of levels. Over three-fourths of college students are in institutions directly operated by some level of government, from ubiquitous community colleges to pinnacle land-grant campuses. Students at both public and private institutions receive direct financial support in the form of federal and state grants, institutional scholarships, loans, subsidized work-study jobs, Reserve Officer Training Corps programs, and several state grant programs. Federal grants provide significant support for research in agriculture, health, science, and other fields. The prominent role played by the states reflects the decentralized federal character of government in the United States. Many states operate more than one system of higher education, with separate finance and governance structures for community colleges, comprehensive universities, and doctoral level campuses. To a significant degree, then, higher education is a function of government, and federalism promotes diversity within the public sector.

Yet the private sector persists and, in many cases, thrives. Any list of the country's oldest and most prestigious institutions will contain many that are private. The most selective liberal arts colleges are almost all private. Many private institutions have strong religious or ethnic heritages that make them distinctive. The private institutions retain an important place in higher education in America. There are even a few institutions like Cornell and Temple that combine public and private control.

Finally, there are obvious differences between institutions that enroll 40,000 or more students and the many (at least 600) that enroll fewer than 1,000. Table 2 summarizes the distribution of enrollments according to the Carnegie classification scheme. In 1987, about 77 percent of students enrolled in higher education were in public institutions, with this percentage ranging from 7.5 in liberal arts colleges to 94.1 in two-year institutions. Over one-quarter of all students were enrolled in research and doctorate-granting institutions and a similar number in comprehensive institutions, while over one-third (many of these part-time students) were enrolled in two-year institutions. Liberal arts colleges, which in 1987 represented almost 17 percent of institutions or higher education, enrolled less than 5 percent of students that year.

Table 2 also highlights changes in the share of enrollments of the various categories. Between 1976 and 1987, enrollments in institutions of higher education grew by about 10 percent in the United States. However, enrollments in some categories grew substantially faster, while enrollments in other categories actually declined significantly. These enrollment changes are due to changes in enrollment within existing institutions, the birth and death of institutions, and shifts in institutions between Carnegie categories. Many institutions used the loose academic labor markets of the late 1970s and early 1980s as an opportunity to upgrade their faculty and start or expand graduate programs. This shift in function is reflected in the 16 percent increase in the number of research and doctorate-granting institutions, compared to the 1 percent increase in comprehensive institutions and the 3 percent decline in liberal arts colleges.

Characteristics of institutions vary widely across institutional categories. Table 3 illustrates the variability on five dimensions—average full-time enrollment, percentage of students enrolled part-time, percentage of students who already have four-year degrees, average full-time-equivalent student to full-time faculty ratio, and average educational and general expenditures per full-time-equivalent student. The ten Carnegie categories have been condensed into six for the purpose of this table (specialized institutions are excluded).

There is great variation in all five criteria reported in Table 3. Research universities average almost 20,000 students per campus, while the typical college in the Other-Four-Year category is smaller than many urban high schools. The selective liberal arts colleges (Liberal Arts I) enroll primarily full-time students. The other institutions all have a large number of part-time students, but for different reasons. The Research and Doctoral institutions' part-time students include graduate and postbaccalaurate professional students, while the part-timers at Comprehensive and Two-Year colleges are more commonly undergraduates. Graduate education is concentrated at the Research and Doctoral universities, but expenditures per student are highest at the Research and Liberal Arts I institutions. Not only are selective liberal arts colleges very expensive, but their costs are growing the fastest of any classification of institutions. Table 3 also shows that the ratio of full-time-equivalent students to full-time faculty varies considerably across categories of institutions, from a low of 14 at the selective liberal arts colleges to 27 at two-year colleges. At the institutional level, there is even more variation in student/faculty ratios, which range from a low of about 10 to several dozen institutions above 50. There are obviously different approaches to teaching implied by the variation in this central relationship in higher education—that between student and instructor.

Table 3   Characteristics of Colleges and Universities by Carnegie Classification, 1987–88

Type of Institution	Sample Size	Average FTE[a] Enrollment	% of Students Who Are Part-Time	% of Students Who Are Post Baccalaureate	Average 1987-88 E&G[b] Expenditures per FTE Student	Sample Size for Student/Faculty Ratio Calculation	Average FTE Students per FT Faculty[a]
Research	90	18,948	23.5	20.7	13,093	87	19.0
Doctoral	96	9,576	32.8	17.4	8,561	88	20.5
Comprehensive	522	4,307	36.2	11.3	6,815	485	20.7
Liberal Arts I	131	1,451	12.2	4.0	12,858	122	13.9
Other Four-Year[c]	353	784	27.7	4.5	8,095	306	16.7
Two-Year	853	2,373	64.9	.0	4,747	716	27.0
All	2,045	3,601	42.5	9.6	8,123	1,804	20.9

Source: Computation by authors based on the sample of 2,045 institutions used in Part III of this volume.

[a]Full-time-equivalent (FTE) students = full-time students + ⅓ part-time students; full-time (FT) faculty does not include any part-time faculty.

[b]Educational and general (E&G) expenditures include expenditures for instruction, public service, libraries, computers, deans, student services (admissions, registrars, health, and recreation), institutional support (presidents and provosts, accounting and finance, fund-raising and security), plant operations, unrestricted scholarships, and interest on accumulated debt and exclude restricted scholarships (e.g., Pell grants) and externally sponsored research (in 1987–88 dollars).

[c]Liberal Arts II.

Non-Price Rationing

Unlike the competitive market visualized in textbooks, the market for higher education does not reach equilibrium through the adjustment of market prices. In the language of economics, the market does not "clear."[12] There are important capacity constraints, some of which the governing bodies of institutions place on themselves. Where the number of applicants desiring places exceeds the number of places the institution is willing to offer, the places are rationed through an admissions and selection process. Fewer than half the institutions in American higher education are "selective" in the sense of turning away more than one-third of their applicants. But, within the group of most selective institutions, this process takes on great importance, not only for the institutions and the applicants, but also for society in general.

Decentralization

In comparison to those in other developed countries, the system of colleges and universities in the United States is relatively decentralized, with 50 separate state regimes and hundreds of private institutions run by self-perpetuating boards of trustees. Bok (1986) argues that this decentralization is a central characteristic of American higher education and that it encourages competition, innovation, and diversity. As Rosovsky (1990) points out, one manifestation of this decentralization is a national admissions process in which several thousand offices are making admission decisions independently. Similarly, decisions regarding the allocation of research funds are also decentralized, although to a lesser extent, owing to the smaller number of funding sources. Decentralization also means that we have a less monolithic higher education establishment than do most other developed countries. One illustration of this, noted by Fallows (1990, 17–18), is the fact that only two of the seven American presidents since 1960, Kennedy and Bush, graduated from an elite private institution, while all Japanese leaders graduated from a single college, the University of Tokyo.

The internal organization of colleges and universities is also characterized by decentralization. Instead of the hierarchical structure typical of corporations, universities are staffed by semiautonomous faculty members with few specific duties. In the words of Coleman (1973), the university is an "institutional anachronism" whose governing structure is based on the concept of community and whose administrators face a constant challenge of management without having much control over their faculty members' time.[13]

Financing

The higher education industry shares an important institutional characteristic with the health sector—the people who receive the service usually pay

---

12. For a formal discussion of market clearing in higher education, see Abowd (1977).

13. There are also more than the usual number of principal-agent problems since it is not altogether clear who the principal is or what the objective function of the institution is. For a discussion, see James (1990).

little, if anything, out of their own pockets. In the health industry, medical insurance provides third-party payments covering most expenditures. Few people purchase higher education insurance (although some prepaid college education plans have an insurance element to them). But students, who usually have a lot to say about whether and where they will attend college, only rarely pay the full bill. The difference is made up by contributions from state and federal governments, taxes forgone by local governments, payments from parents (which may have some cost to students if they reduce other gifts and bequests from parents to students), income from gifts and endowments, and subsidies from other (e.g., charitable) organizations.

As outlined in the first part of this volume, federal and state governments subsidize the costs of students' attendance in a number of ways. Direct appropriations from state governments to public institutions permit relatively low tuitions to be charged to all students attending public institutions. Some states also provide grants to residents who attend in-state institutions, subsidized loans for students, and payments to private institutions for each degree that they grant. At the federal level, undergraduate aid is provided in the form of need-based grants, subsidized loans, and subsidized employment. Aid is also provided under various entitlement programs, such as veterans benefits and through direct support of the five service academies.

Thus, the primary consumers of the education experience—the students—rarely pay the entire bill. Although distortions can arise whenever the decision makers do not confront all costs directly, these so-called third-party payment problems are not likely to be as serious in the market for higher education as they are in the health industries because students shoulder a good share of the cost of attending college, in the form of earnings that are forgone in order to matriculate.

Purpose and Outline of This Volume

The three major concerns of this volume—undergraduate enrollments, the supply of academics, and costs—lend themselves to economic analysis and in fact have generated significant scholarly attention. Much of the resulting research is not, however, easily accessible to noneconomists. It is therefore one objective of this volume to present findings from the economics literature in a form that can be understood by noneconomists. Another objective is to present and discuss data that are relevant both to these findings and to public policies affecting higher education. Most of these data are presented in the form of tables or figures; technical references to econometric estimates are relegated to notes or appendices. Finally, each part of the book attempts to highlight the implications of the data and other findings discussed, both for the higher education industry and for public policies affecting it.

Part I of the volume focuses on the demand for undergraduate places, with special attention to the effects of changes in tuition and financial aid on that demand. Demand is measured in terms of both the overall size of enrollments and their composition. Chapter 1 introduces the topic by comparing American college enrollments to those in other countries. It then examines the components of recent enrollment changes in this country over a period during which the size of the 18-year-old population began to decline. Chapter 2 presents a statistical portrait of undergraduate enrollment, beginning with aggregate measure of enrollment growth. It notes the rising proportion of women and part-time students among undergraduates. It then considers in some detail who goes to college, what kinds of colleges they attend, their progress toward completion, and the implications of these patterns for the racial and economic composition of undergraduate student bodies.

Chapter 3 turns to economic models of education to explain recent trends in enrollment. It presents evidence on three trends occurring during the 1980s that affected demand for higher education: the dramatic turnaround in the financial returns from college training, the rapid rise in college costs, and the bulging of the income distribution at the top. In considering demand for undergraduate places, it is important to keep in mind the difference between selective colleges, which experience excess demand for their places, and non-selective institutions, which do not. Chapter 4 examines the role of financial aid, beginning with a brief description of the programs and their methods of awarding aid. The chapter then traces the changes that have taken place over the last decade in these programs and discusses their likely effect on both the numbers and the composition of undergraduate enrollments. Chapter 5 first presents a summary of the major changes over the period 1979–87 that affected aggregate demand. It then turns to the question of whether the economic disparity between those who do and those who do not attend college has been growing over time. It concludes with a review of some of the important unanswered questions related to the demand for undergraduate places.

Part II of the volume focuses on academic labor supply. Projections of forthcoming shortages of Ph.D.s abound. For example, one major book recently concluded that by the late 1990s there will be large shortages of faculty in the arts and sciences and that these shortages will be especially large in the humanities and social sciences, where there may be as few as seven candidates for every ten faculty positions (Bowen and Sosa 1989).

Economists typically define shortages as arising when, at the prevailing salaries in an occupation, demand exceeds supply (Ehrenberg and Smith 1991, chap. 2). As long as salaries are free to rise, shortages will eventually be eliminated. Still, there is concern over potential shortages of doctorates in academe, for two reasons. First, many observers believe that academic institutions may not possess the resources to increase faculty salaries enough to eliminate these shortages. Second, the time it takes graduate students to complete doctoral degrees is sufficiently long that, even if new graduate enrollments were to increase in response to an increase in salaries, the supply of new doctorates would not begin to rise until a number of years later. Thus, if shortages do materialize in the future, they may persist for a number of years.

Among the policies proposed to avert these projected shortages are increased financial support for graduate students and the shortening of the time it takes graduate students to complete their degrees. Yet evidence on the magnitudes of likely supply responses to such proposed changes is actually quite scanty. Part II of this volume reviews the academic literature and available data, from a wide range of sources, to summarize what we know about academic labor supply and what we need to know to make informed policy decisions.

Chapter 6 begins with a description of how estimates of projected shortages arise and summarizes the issues one must address before deciding if policy interventions are required. The remainder of this chapter presents some background data on the academic labor market and new Ph.D. production in the United States. Chapter 7 describes a schematic model of academic labor supply and indicates the underlying trends since 1970 in a number of variables that contribute to projections of shortages of faculty. In Chapter 8, a general model of occupational choice and the decision to undertake and complete graduate study is sketched. This framework, available data, and the prior academic literature are then used to address students' choices of college majors, decisions to undertake and complete graduate study, decisions on the time it takes to complete Ph.D. programs, and decisions on choices of sectors of employment for new and experienced Ph.D.s. Chapter 9 addresses issues relating to the age structure of the faculty and retirement policies and minority and female representation in academe. Chapter 10 considers whether a shortage of American Ph.D.s would really matter or could be eased by increased reliance on foreign students trained in the United States, faculty currently employed in foreign institutions, and faculty without doctorates. It also briefly summarizes the implications for both future research needs and public policy.

Part III of the volume considers costs. Because there are no accurate measures of "output" from colleges and universities, conclusions about productivity can only be inferred from indirect evidence. This section of the volume thus focuses primarily on costs. Chapter 11 outlines six possible explanations for the rapidly rising costs in higher education: better-quality service, more expensive inputs, inherently low productivity growth, faculty and administrators' self-interest maximization, poor management, and increased government regulation. The possibilities are examined with financial data from 2,045 colleges and universities covering the period 1978–79 to 1987–88. The institutions are distinguished on the basis of their mission, control, size, and enrollment growth.

Chapter 12 examines the various categories of expenditures made by colleges and universities during the 1980s. Instruction accounts for about half of all current expenditures. Expenditures per student have increased at a rate of 2.8 percent per year over and above the general rise in prices. They rose fastest in the period 1983–84 to 1985–86. The most rapidly increasing categories of expenditures are scholarships funded internally, student services (e.g., recruiting, record keeping, health, and recreation), and institutional support (president, provost, finance, accounting, public relations, fund-raising, and campus security). Expenditures per student increased much faster at selective private liberal arts colleges than at any other type of institution. Overall costs per student are rising much faster at private than at public institutions. Cost inflation is even worse if expenditures are compared to the number of degrees awarded.

Chapter 13 examines cost trends on the basis of institutional size and the rate of change of enrollment. Institutions whose enrollments declined during the 1980s experienced a much larger surge in costs than those institutions with stable or growing enrollments. Four-year institutions with stable enrollments are used to evaluate scale economies in private colleges and universities. There is evidence of overall size advantages only for private research universities and for less selective private liberal arts colleges.

Instructional costs are decomposed in Chapter 14. Different types of institutions have quite different ratios of instructional expenditures to total expenditures, full-time faculty salaries to instructional expenditures, average salary levels per full-time faculty member, and students per faculty member. Over the period 1978–79 to 1987–88, noninstructional costs have increased faster than instructional costs. Within instructional costs, the faster growth has been in categories other than full-time faculty salaries (e.g., fringe benefits, part-time faculty, support staff, equipment, and supplies). Faculty salaries have gained on inflation over the period, and the number of students per faculty member has increased modestly. The most dramatic differences across institutions occur in the ratio of full-time faculty to instructional expenditures, suggesting that colleges and universities differ markedly in the way they combine resources to produce "education." Chapter 14 concludes by evaluating the possible explanations for rising costs presented in Chapter 11.

The three parts of this volume yield three perspectives on the challenges facing higher education in the United States in the 1990s. First, the growth of aggregate enrollments, which defied adverse demographic trends during the 1980s, is likely to cease during the first half of the decade and then resume in the second, owing in both instances to changing demographics. Second, as enrollments rebound in the second half of the decade, increased demand for faculty may induce higher salaries and a variety of adjustments in the supply of faculty. Third, cost per student may increase rapidly when the demand for higher education is damped and may slow when demand recovers and enrollments increase. Even given these broad generalizations, however, one must consider the great diversity of mission, scale, control, location, and heritage of the colleges and universities. Some institutions will be growing even as others are declining, some will experience decreases in student-faculty ratios while others see them increase, and costs per student in dollars of constant purchasing power will decline for some even as they are rising for others. All three parts consider how higher education, in all its diversity, adapts to changing circumstances.

I Demand for Undergraduate Education

Charles T. Clotfelter

1   Size and Significance

Among the major functions of higher education, none touches more people directly than undergraduate education. By the late 1980s, there were more than 11 million undergraduate students in U.S. colleges and universities, and over one-fifth of the population between the ages of 25 and 29 had completed at least four years of college. Although the effects of college training are still not well understood, there is strong evidence that college training affects not only the potential economic productivity of graduates but also personal attitudes and values (see, e.g., Hansen 1970; and Solmon and Taubman 1973). The demand for undergraduate education raises important issues at two levels, issues related to the aggregate level of college enrollment and to its composition (particularly by racial and socioeconomic group).

At the aggregate level, the demand for higher education is important most obviously to the higher education industry itself since enrollments are a principal determinant of total revenues available to colleges and universities. But this demand has much broader significance, in part because of the scale of the enterprise and the extent of the economic resources that it represents. A major portion of the economic cost of undergraduate training takes the form of productive work that students would have been engaged in had they not been enrolled, measured roughly by their forgone earnings while in college. To the extent that college training does increase productivity, there are obviously important economic implications of the demand for college places, for both individuals and society. This issue has taken on a significance in recent years reminiscent of the post-Sputnik period, as debate has increasingly focused on the ability of the nation's education system to prepare young workers for technical positions in industries facing stiff international competition.[1] From the

---

1. Newman's (1985) book is a good example of this line of argument. Projections of labor requirements such as those periodically published by the Department of Labor also indicate a growing need for college-trained labor. See, e.g., "Demand for College-Educated Workers May Outstrip Supply in 1990's," *Chronicle of Higher Education*, 3 January 1990, p. A2.

standpoint of public policy, perhaps the biggest question concerning aggregate demand is whether the size of college enrollment is socially optimal or whether it needs to be increased by way of government subsidy. Some observers believe that the benefits of higher education go beyond those enjoyed by the students themselves and that such external benefits constitute an important justification for public subsidies (see, e.g., Nerlove 1972). This view would lend support both to government-financed student aid programs and to the low-tuition policies of most state higher education systems. Others believe, however, that most of the benefits of higher education accrue to the students themselves, thus weakening the case for across-the-board subsidies.[2]

Not only is the size of enrollments important, but so is their economic and demographic composition. Because of the strong association between college training and lifetime earnings, the distribution of college training is closely linked to the distribution of income. Whether this strong association arises because college training makes students more productive or merely because a college degree is a recognizable and lucrative credential, college remains an extremely important avenue for the attainment of status and wealth.[3] Despite an increase in college participation among traditionally underrepresented groups, there continues to be concern that a large share of the benefits of higher education goes to a relatively small group of students (Newman 1985, 24). In particular, attention has been focused on the comparatively low college enrollment rates of minority students. One issue raised by these concerns is the whole question of preferential treatment in admission, including both affirmative action policies and institutional practices such as preferences toward children of alumni.

Another important issue is financial aid and the pricing of public higher education. In this connection, the policy debate is often framed using two terms that express widely accepted aims of public policy: students should have "access" to some form of higher education regardless of their income, and all applicants qualified to be admitted to an institution should have the "choice" of enrolling there regardless of the cost. Both these aims appear to be threatened by trends over the last decade, including increases in college tuitions and declines in the relative importance of federal scholarships. At the same time, questions have been raised regarding the effectiveness of existing financial aid programs. These doubts in turn have stimulated the discussion of proposals for new kinds of aid programs, some of which would tie aid to student performance.

The purpose of this first part of the present book is to examine the demand for undergraduate enrollments, focusing on both the aggregate level of demand and the composition of that demand by economic and demographic group. The remainder of this chapter sets the stage for this examination by, first, comparing college enrollments and financing in the United States to

---

2. For a statement of this argument, see Schultz (1972).

3. For a discussion of the importance of education in determining status, see, e.g., Sewell and Hauser (1975, 15).

those in other countries and, second, presenting the basic data on recent trends in undergraduate enrollments. Chapter 2 presents data on what is known about patterns and trends in college enrollments in the United States. It examines differences by race, sex, and economic position. It also distinguishes between initial enrollment and continued enrollment in various types of postsecondary educational institutions. Chapter 3 discusses issues raised in the economics of demand for undergraduate education, reviewing models of demand and evidence relevant to judging the usefulness of those models. It looks in particular at the rebound in the economic return to college that occurred in the 1980s and at the rise in college costs during the same period, and it reviews empirical research related to the effect of college costs on demand. It also discusses two aspects of supply that distinguish the market for higher education, both of which affect the way that demand is translated into enrollments. These are the recruitment of students and the admissions process, the importance of which differs widely among institutions. Chapter 4 deals with student financial aid programs, describing how they operate and how they have evolved over the last two decades. The chapter then considers the effects of student aid on demand. The final chapter considers all the major factors affecting demand for undergraduate places. It focuses first on aggregate enrollments in the period 1979–87, then looks at recent changes in the composition of demand, and ends with a brief discussion of implications and unanswered questions.

1.1 Demand in Comparative Perspective

Counting students in both two-year and four-year programs, college enrollment rates observed in the United States are high relative to those in other developed nations. Because systems of education differ by country, it is difficult to compare rates of college enrollment across countries. A useful comparison can be made, however, by looking at enrollment rates by age. Table 1.1 makes such a comparison. In the United States, and in most of the countries shown, 17-year-olds are still in secondary school. At this age, 89 percent of Americans are enrolled, far more than the 49 percent in Britain, but still less than the near-universal enrollment observed in West Germany. By age 20, only about 36 percent of Americans are enrolled in school. Most are students in institutions of higher education, though other postsecondary schools, such as technical institutes, account for some enrollment. At this age, the United States again ranks near the top among the countries shown, but its rate is not the highest. By age 23, school enrollment is definitely confined to a minority in all these countries. The U.S. rate of 16 percent is again among the highest.[4]

These rates illustrate one way in which the United States differs from other

4. It should be noted that different ways of classifying educational institutions can lead to different conclusions regarding relative enrollment rates. Clark (1985, 295) reports, e.g., the following rates of enrollment in higher education: Japan, 86 percent; the United States, 75 percent; France, 26 percent; Sweden, 21 percent; the United Kingdom, 20 percent; and West Germany, 20 percent.

Table 1.1   Emrollment Rates, Selected Countries, Selected Ages, 1986–87
                   (percentage of age group enrolled, both full- and part-time)

	Age		
	17	20	23
Canada	78.5	36.3	13.9
Denmark	75.4	36.4	21.8
France	79.7	28.1	10.0
Germany, West	99.7	36.6	16.8
Greece	58.7	29.0	10.3
Ireland	64.7	17.6	3.7
Japan	90.5	a	a
Netherlands	78.3	31.9	13.7
Sweden	83.0	9.5	12.5
Switzerland	83.1	30.2	15.0
United Kingdom	49.3	23.8	a
United States	89.0	35.7	16.2
Yugoslavia	66.3	47.3	10.1

Source: Organization for Economic Cooperation and Development, *Education in OECD Countries, 1986–87* (Paris, 1989), tables 4.2, 4.3, pp. 81, 83.
[a]Not available.

developed countries in the institutional structure of education. Secondary schools in Japan and most Western countries control the flow of students into the higher education system by means of either exit examinations, such a those used in Japan, or systems of specialized secondary schools, such as those in France. Secondary schools in the United States, by contrast, are for the most part comprehensive, and successful completion of high school virtually guarantees admission into some college or university. According to Clark (1985), the democratic values that have created support for the comprehensive school also contribute to pressure to reduce dropouts in high school. The result is a large and diverse outpouring of high school graduates with little specialized training, some of whom are not well prepared for college work. And the concern about "access" of minority groups and the poor to education is not confined to high school.

The system of higher education in the United States is distinguished from those in other industrialized countries by the importance of private nonprofit institutions. This does not mean, however, that American college students do not receive substantial government subsidies; they do, as is illustrated in Table 1.2, which compares the costs of and sources of support for undergraduate education in five countries. The first column gives estimates for the per-student total cost of college education in each country. The remaining columns show the estimated distribution of sources to cover those costs for each of two comparable income groups. In general, the distributions for the United States are distinguished by the relatively large shares borne by students and their

Table 1.2   Estimated Costs of Higher Education in Five Countries and Sources
                   of Funding, Low-Income and Middle-Income Families, 1985–86

| | | Share of Total Costs Borne (%) | | | | | |
| | Annual Cost (U.S. dollars) | Low Income | | | Middle Income | | |
		Family	Public	Institution	Family	Public	Institution
Britain	3,280	6	94	0	71	29	0
West Germany	4,398	42	58	0	86	14	0
France	2,016	17	83	0	85	15	0
Sweden	4,217	55	45	0	62	38	0
United States:							
Average public	5,314	38	62	0	89	11	0
Average private	9,659	36	47	18	65	19	17
High-cost private	15,000	31	33	36	51	15	33

Source: Johnstone (1986, 148, 150). For sources and definitions of income levels, see the notes
to the original figures.
Note: Family share includes contributions by students and parents.

parents. Also noteworthy is the support provided by private institutions in the
United States, much of which is derived from private donations.

1.2 The Resilience of College Enrollments

The recent history of college enrollments in the United States presents one
striking fact: despite a decline in the number of 18-year-olds in the population
that began after 1979, college enrollments continued to increase throughout
the 1980s. As shown in Figure 1.1, undergraduate enrollments increased by
almost 60 percent between 1969 and 1987 at the same time that the number of
young people in the traditional college age group was, in turn, rising and
falling. This is an empirical puzzle that invites exploration. However, the
track record of demand projections in this area makes it clear that existing
models are as yet far from perfect. To illustrate the difficulty of projecting the
demand for higher education, Table 1.3 compares two forecasts of undergraduate enrollments, made in the early 1970s, with the subsequent actual levels.
Based largely on the demographic changes noted above, Cartter's forecast
showed an 18 percent increase in full-time enrollments between 1973 and
1980, followed by a decline to 1985. Freeman's model, which also accounted
for the effects of a decline in the economic returns to college training, predicted even less growth. As it turned out, of course, both sets of projections
were too low. Especially surprising was the continued increase after the demographic downturn began in 1980.

Because the surprising strength of demand for undergraduate education is
one of the empirical questions that motivates the present study, it is helpful to
begin by examining the components of this demand. Given the demographic

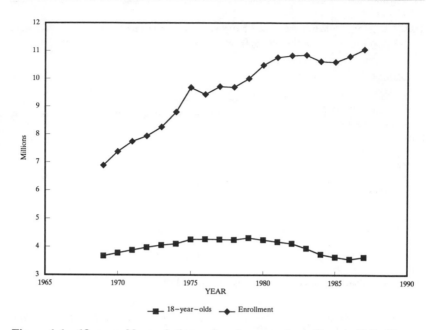

Figure 1.1   18-year-old population and underground enrollment, 1969–87.
Sources: Enrollment: U.S. Department of Education (1989, table 158, p. 177). Population:
U.S. Bureau of the Census, *Current Population Reports*, Series P-25, *Estimates of the
Population of the United States by Age, Sex and Race: 1969*, No. 519 (1974), table 1, p. 16;
1970–79, No. 917 (1982), table 1, p. 8; *1980–87*, No. 1045 (1990), table 1, p. 41.

downturn shown in Figure 1.1, only two things could be responsible for the
continued rise in undergraduate enrollments in the 1980s. Either the enrollment rates for those in the traditional college-going age group had to increase,
or the enrollments of older people had to increase. It turns out that increases
of both kinds occurred. In order to show the contribution of each more pre-

Table 1.3   **Two Forecasts and Actual Levels of FTE Undergraduate Enrollment,
Two- and Four-Year Institutions, as Percentage of 1973 Enrollment,
Selected Years, 1975–1990**

	Cartter	Freeman	Actual
1973	100	100	100
1975	103	101	114
1980	118	111	118
1985	113	105	120
1987	a	a	124
1990	111	106	a

Source: McPherson (1978, 249); U.S. Department of Education (1989, tables 148, 158, 162).
Full-time equivalents for undergraduate enrollments were obtained by applying to part-time
undergraduate enrollments the ratio for each year of full-time equivalents less full-time enrollments to part-time enrollments calculated for total college enrollments and adding the result to
full-time undergraduate enrollments. The ratios ranged from 0.344 in 1980 to 0.377 in 1975.
aNot available.

cisely, it is necessary to look at changes in enrollments for specific subgroups of the population. One by-product of this approach is that it joins the analysis of aggregate enrollments with that of enrollment composition.

College students were divided into 18 demographic groups defined by sex, race, and age, as shown in Table 1.4. Data on full-time and part-time undergraduate enrollment taken from the Current Population Survey were combined to yield estimated full-time-equivalent enrollments (FTE) for each group. Over the decade 1976–86, total FTE undergraduate enrollments in-

Table 1.4 Changes in Population and Undergraduate Enrollments, 1976–86, by Sex, Race, and Age

Sex, Race, and Age	% Change in Population	Change in Enrollment:			
		Due to Population Change	Due to Change in Enrollment Rate	Total	As % of 1976 Enrollment
Male:					
White:					
18–24	−4.2	−114.7	89.5	−25.2	−1.0
25–34	30.6	93.5	−138.4	−44.9	−10.1
35+	18.4	18.7	−6.1	12.6	11.7
Black:					
18–24	12.5	31.6	−34.5	−3.0	−1.0
25–34	55.4	25.8	−29.7	−3.9	−5.1
35+	22.0	6.1	6.4	12.4	58.9
Other:					
18–24	81.6	63.6	1.0	64.5	83.9
25–34	131.5	20.0	−2.8	17.2	95.2
35+	135.3	3.0	1.3	4.4	463.8
Female:					
White:					
18–24	−5.4	−141.6	171.2	29.5	1.2
25–34	27.3	100.8	110.2	211.0	81.3
35+	16.9	43.2	87.4	130.6	77.6
Black:					
18–24	8.5	31.1	−.8	30.3	8.2
25–34	50.3	31.8	3.1	34.9	58.0
35+	26.4	9.4	8.9	18.3	68.8
Other:					
18–24	64.9	57.1	33.8	90.8	167.6
25–34	102.8	11.7	3.8	15.5	205.8
35+	134.8	4.7	−2.1	2.6	46.6
Total	15.8	295.7	302.0	597.7	8.4

Source: Author's calculations based on tabulations from the October Current population Survey for 1976 and 1986, provided by Thomas Kane.

Note: Population figures exclude those in military service (for the method of decomposition, see text). FTE enrollments are the sum of full-time enrollments and one-third of part-time enrollments.

creased by some 598,000, or 8.4 percent.[5] To see how changes in each group contributed to this overall result, enrollment changes were split into two components. One portion, which measures the effect of population change, represents the change that would have occurred if the enrollment rate had been constant (at its 1986 level) and only the group's population had changed. The other portion, showing the effect of changes in the college enrollment rate, is the change in enrollment that would have taken place if population had remained constant over the period and only the enrollment rate had changed.[6] Of the 18 groups, only male and female whites in the 18- to 24-year age group declined in population over the period. Because of the large size of these groups, their declines would have resulted in a significant drop in enrollment—some 256,000. However, population growth in the other 16 groups was responsible for increases in college enrollment that would have more than offset this decline. All together, about half the total increase in college enrollments over this period can be attributed to population changes, despite the declining number of young whites.

The other half of the increase in college enrollments can be attributed to the effects of changing enrollment rates. Although rates increased in only 11 of the 18 groups, those among white women increased markedly. Owing to the large number of white women, these increases had a tremendous effect, by themselves representing an increase of about 369,000 in total enrollments.[7] There were also significant increases among young white males and young females in the residual racial group. Offsetting these increases were drops in enrollment rates among white males aged 25–34 and among black men under 35.[8] As a result of the changes in population and enrollment rates shown in Table 1.4, the composition of students over the age of 24 increased from 25 to 31. By 1986, women had become the majority of college students, rising from 49 to 53 percent of the total. And, although not shown in the table, more and more college students were studying part-time, with their share rising from 28 to 33 percent. The nonwhite share of enrollments rose slightly, from 14 to 15 percent, reflecting an increase not among blacks but among other nonwhites.

5. The corresponding increase in total undergraduate enrollments was 1.1 million. Over the period, full-time enrollments increased from 6,266,000 to 6,611,000 and part-time enrollments from 2,439,000 to 3,197,000.

6. Since enrollment is equal to the product of population and the enrollment rate, the change in any group's enrollment can be expressed as the sum of (1) the 1986 enrollment rate multiplied by the change in population and (2) the 1976 population multiplied by the change in the enrollment rate.

7. The FTE enrollment rate for white women increased 6.7 percent for the 18 to 24-year age group and 37 percent for the 25- to 34-year age group.

8. It is possible that part of the decline in enrollment rates among men over this period could be explained if there were a bulge in enrollments in 1976 of Vietnam veterans on the GI Bill. In fact, the percentage of undergraduates under 35 who were male declined rather steadily between 1970 (when it was 58 percent) and 1980 (48 percent), after which it showed no trend (U.S. Bureau of the Census 1990, table A-6). It is nevertheless possible that this effect may be important in explaining the drop in the rate for young blacks.

The strength of the demand for undergraduate education shown by these data is one of the facts that motivates Part I of this book. In the following chapters, data are presented showing that college costs increased in real terms during the 1980s and that student scholarship aid did not keep pace. Despite these factors and the decline in the number of young people in the traditional college age group, undergraduate enrollments increased. What does this experience imply about the likely effects of continued price increases? What effect do student aid programs and other public policies have on demand? Another set of questions relates to the composition of these enrollments. Are enrollments among poor and minority students following the general trend and increasing? What is the effect of tuition increases and changes in student aid on the college-going behavior of these groups? Thus, the remaining chapters in Part I will examine both aggregate demand and components of that demand.

2   Patterns of Enrollment and Completion

The first step in examining the demand for undergraduate college education is to describe patterns and trends in enrollments. It is not just initial enrollments that are of importance, however. Because educational attainment, not enrollment per se, is by far the most important "output" of higher education, it is necessary to consider what happens after students first enroll. The demand for college therefore must consider both college-going and college-completing behavior. The purpose of this chapter is to establish the basic facts concerning both of these, to be used as a foundation for the following chapters, which focus on demand and the role of financial aid policy.

As a starting point, Table 2.1 offers a snapshot of undergraduate enrollments in 1988, broken down by age, type of institution, and full-time/part-time status. Of the 10.6 million undergraduates enrolled in that year, almost two-thirds were in four-year institutions. Those in the two-year colleges tended to be older (almost 40 percent were 25 or older) and were more likely to be enrolled part-time. A tabulation such as this is helpful in thinking about who the "typical" college student is. When one thinks of college students, the most common image may be that of a young person who is studying full-time at a four-year college, but this image is in fact representative of only about half of all undergraduates. In 1988, about 18 percent of undergraduates were enrolled full-time at two-year colleges, while 32 percent were enrolled part-time at both two- and four-year colleges. The tabulations presented in this chapter generally do not reflect all three of these distinctions at the same time. For example, data on total enrollments typically lump together full-time and part-time students. Some series distinguish between two- and four-year institutions, while others do not, and so on. Thus, it is useful to keep in mind a rough idea of the distribution suggested in Table 2.1: two-year institutions enroll about one-third of all college students, and another third are part-timers.

Table 2.1   **Undergraduate Students by Type of Institution, Age, and Attendance Status, 1988**

	Four-Year College or University	Two-Year College	Total
Number enrolled (in millions):			
14 to 24 years old	5.2	2.3	7.5
(% full-time)	(91)	(67)	(84)
25 years and over	1.6	1.5	3.1
(% full-time)	(39)	(23)	(31)
Total	6.8	3.8	10.6
% distribution:			
Full-time	50.5	17.9	68.4
Part-time	13.3	18.3	31.6
Total	63.8	36.2	100.0

Source: U.S. Bureau of the Census, *Current Population Reports,* Series P-20, *School Enrollment—Social and Economic Characteristics of Students: October 1988 and 1987,* No. 443 (1990), table A.

Going beyond these broad classifications, this chapter examines distinctions of demography, race, and economic status, and it focuses on both the size and the composition of the college-going population. Section 2.1 examines college enrollments in historical perspective, noting their impressive growth and several important changes in their composition. The rise of public institutions, particularly the growth of two-year community colleges, has transformed the nature of college demand dramatically during this century. Perhaps the most prominent change, however, has been the steady increase in the numbers of female students, though the growing importance of part-time status is also evident. Changes in the size and composition of the population will contribute to shifts in enrollment, holding changes in enrollment rates constant. In particular, the continued decline in the 18- to 24-year-old population implies a reduction, albeit a milder one, in total enrollment. Following more general population trends, college enrollments are likely to become still older on average and to have an increasing proportion of nonwhites.

The remainder of this chapter focuses on the economic and demographic composition of college enrollments. Section 2.2 shows that there are dramatic differences in enrollment patterns by economic status. Both the probability of entering college and the probability of completing college rise with family income and socioeconomic status as well as with measured aptitude. Among higher education institutions, there is an unmistakable pecking order, with a comparatively small number of highly selective institutions enrolling a disproportionate number of high-achieving and affluent high school students. More generally, such students are also more likely to enroll in four-year than in two-year institutions. One result of these patterns is that the student bodies of colleges differ dramatically in racial composition and income distribution. Section 2.3 examines the progress of students once enrolled. The chance of completing a four-year degree program differs greatly depending both on the type of institution initially enrolled in and on economic status. The chapter ends with a brief concluding section.

2.1 Enrollments over Time

2.1.1 Historical Patterns of Growth

In the fall of 1988, there were some 13.1 million Americans enrolled in institutions of higher education. This figure represents a historical peak. In fact, the growth in college enrollments in this country over the last century has been little short of phenomenal. Table 2.2 gives information on total enrollments from the 1869–70 school year up to 1988–89. Over this period, during which the country's population grew at an average annual rate of 1.5 percent, the number of students enrolled in colleges grew at an average annual rate of 4.8 percent.[1] One benchmark useful for measuring the relative growth of enrollments is the population aged 18–24, which approximates the traditional college-age population. Over the period shown, total enrollments increased from about 1 percent to over 49 percent of the size of this age group.

One clear result of this expanded enrollment has been a steady rise in the level of educational attainment in the population. This increase has been especially sharp for Americans born after World War I. As Table 2.3 shows, the median number of years of schooling for the population increased from 10.3 in 1940 to 12.8 in 1988. The rise in college completion has been much more dramatic. In 1940, the percentage of 25- to 29-year-olds (those born between 1921 and 1925) who had finished four or more years of college was 5.9. This increased about 2 percentage points in the 1940s, 3 in the 1950s, 5 in the 1960s, and 6 in the 1970s, to stand at 22.1 percent in 1980. During the 1980s, both the growth of college enrollments and college attainment have slowed down. The annual rate of enrollment growth dropped to 1.1 percent, and the percentage of 25- to 29-year-olds who had completed college rose only slightly, to 22.7 percent. Also worth noting is the convergence in the education levels of whites and blacks. By 1988, there was little difference by race in the median years of schooling. The percentage of whites with four years of college continued to exceed that of blacks by a large margin, but the growth in the black percentage has been more rapid.[2]

1. The population of the United States grew from 39.9 million in 1870 to 248.2 million in 1989 (United States Bureau of the Census, *Historical Statistics of the United States* [Washington, D.C.: U.S. Government Printing Office, 1960], 7; and U.S. Bureau of the Census, *Current Population Reports*, Series P-25, *State Population and Household Estimates: July 1, 1989*, No. 1058 (1990).

2. There has been continual progress in educational attainment rates for both blacks and whites in the United States over the past century. Smith (1984, 689), e.g., reports the following percentages of black and white males, respectively, with more than 12 years of schooling for selected cohorts: 1886–90, 3.3 and 9.8; 1926–30, 12.1 and 26.7; and 1946–50, 27.5 and 44.4. Although

Table 2.2   **Enrollment in Institutions of Higher Education, 1970–86**

	Fall Enrollment (1000s)[a]	% of Population 18 to 24 Years Old
1869–70	52	1.1
1879–80	116	1.6
1889–90	157	1.8
1899–1900	238	2.3
1909–10	355	2.9
1919–20	598	4.7
1929–30	1,101	7.2
1939–40	1,494	9.1
1949–50	2,659	16.5
1959–60	3,640	22.3
1969–70	8,005	32.6
1979–80	11,570	39.7
1988–89	13,116	49.2

Sources: U.S. Bureau of the Census, *Historical Statistics of the U.S.*, Series H700-715 (Washington, D.C.: U.S. Government Printing Office, 1960), p. 383; U.S. Department of Education (1989, table 147, p. 166); U.S. Bureau of the Census, *Current Population Reports,* Series P-20, *School Enrollment—Social and Economic Characteristics of Students: October 1988 and 1987,* No. 443 (1990), table A-8.

[a]From 1869–70 to 1949–50, numbers are for degree credit resident enrollment. For 1959–60 and 1969–70, the comparable figures were 3,216 and 7,545, respectively. Thus, the growth between 1949–50 and 1959–60 in degree credit enrollment was 21 percent.

Table 2.3   **Trends in Educational Attainment by Race, Persons 25–29, 1940–88**

	Median Years of School Completed			% with Four or More Years of College		
	All	White	Black	All	White	Black
1940	10.3	10.7	7.0	5.9	6.4	1.6
1950	12.0	12.2	8.6	7.7	8.2	2.7
1960	12.3	12.3	9.9	11.1	11.8	4.8
1970	12.6	12.6	12.1	16.3	17.3	6.0
1980	12.9	12.9	12.6	22.1	23.7	11.4
1988	12.8	12.9	12.7	22.7	23.5	12.3

Sources: U.S. Department of Education (1989, table 8, p. 15); U.S. Bureau of the Census, *Statistical Abstract of the United States* (Washington, D.C.: U.S. Government Printing Office, 1990), table 215, p. 133.

Behind the dramatic growth in college enrollments lie several fundamental changes in the nature and function of American higher education. Colleges of the nineteenth century were anything but broadly representative of the general population. According to Veysey (1973), their primary functions were to pro-

---

the rate of growth in black attainment rates was larger, the percentage difference between the two rates actually grew over this period. It is possible, therefore, that increases over time in attainment may have increased rather than decreased the black-white difference in attainment over some periods.

mote Christianity and to teach classical subjects in a disciplined manner. In addition, he argues, "an unstated but very real aim was the maintenance of a numerically tiny social elite against the hostile pressures of Jacksonian egalitarism" (p. 1). A central function of colleges was to train teachers, ministers, and other professionals. Normal schools, many of which offered only two years of instruction, were the primary institution for accomplishing the first function. These normal schools evolved into the state colleges and gradually added two more years to their offerings. By 1920, as shown in Table 2.4, there were slightly more than a thousand institutions offering undergraduate education, and almost all these offered four-year programs.

The years since 1920 have witnessed rapid growth in public institutions, especially two-year community colleges. Since 1920, the number of four-year institutions has doubled, reflecting growth in the number of both public and private colleges and universities. The number of two-year colleges, however, exploded in the 1920s, in the 1930s, and then again after 1960. These two-year colleges became a keystone to the educational policy of states and localities and now constitute a large part of the higher education offerings in this country. From 1963 to 1987, a period in which enrollments in four-year institutions doubled, the number of students in two-year colleges increased by a factor of five and a half (U.S. Department of Education 1989, 168). There has been greater growth in the public sector than in the private. Since 1950, the number of public institutions has doubled, while the number of private insti-

Table 2.4   **Number of Undergraduate Institutions, 1920–88**

School Year Ending:	Four-Year Colleges and Universities			Two-Year Colleges		
	Total	Public	Private	Total	Public	Private
1920[a]	989	[b]	[b]	52	10	42
1930[a]	1,132	[b]	[b]	277	129	148
1940[a]	1,252	[b]	[b]	456	217	239
1950[a]	1,327	344	983	524	297	227
1960[a]	1,422	367	1,055	582	328	254
1970[a]	1,639	426	1,213	886	634	252
1980[a]	1,863	464	1,399	1,112	846	266
1986[a]	1,915	461	1,454	1,240	865	375[c]
1986[d]	2,029	566	1,463	1,311	932	379[c]
1988[d]	2,135	599	1,536	1,452	992	460[c]

Sources: 1920–40: U.S. Bureau of the Census, *Historical Statistics of the United States*, Series H689-699 (Washington, D.C.: U.S. Government Printing Office, 1960), 382–93; 1950–88: U.S. Department of Education (1989, table 19.6, p. 217).

[a]Excluding branch campuses.

[b]Not available.

[c]Reflects increase in number of accredited trade and technical schools. See U.S. Department of Education (1989, table 196n).

[d]Including branch campuses.

tutions increased by only half that rate. Measured by the size of enrollments, public institutions have increased their share of total college enrollments from 49 percent in 1950 to 78 percent in 1970, at which level it has remained during the 1980s.[3]

Community colleges are worthy of special attention, owing to their size and spectacular growth. On the one hand, they have been hailed as "democracy's colleges," especially because the option of transferring to four-year institutions following successful completion of the associate degree allows those of modest means to have an affordable option for attaining a college degree. Yet these same institutions have also been attacked as tools of the ruling class, functioning to keep the children of the working class out of four-year college classrooms.[4] Given this contrast in views, it is important to examine how community colleges fit into the overall enrollment patterns in higher education.

2.1.2   Female and Part-time Students

Two trends evident in the 10-year comparison shown in Chapter 1—the rising importance of women and part-timers—are among the most significant long-term changes in college enrollments in the postwar period. There has been no more striking trend in college enrollments since World War II than the steady rise in participation by women. As shown in Table 2.5, the growth in the number of college students of both sexes has been dramatic. After the postwar GI Bill bulge, the number of men enrolled in college increased from 1.5 million in 1950 to 6.0 million in 1988 (before 1972, students 35 and older were not counted), at an average growth rate of 3.7 percent. Yet the growth in female enrollments has outstripped this rate by a wide margin—from 0.7 million in 1950 to 7.2 million in 1988, for an average annual rate of 6.3 percent.[5] Outnumbered by men two to one in 1950, women now constitute the majority of college students. It is not difficult to find parallels for this increased participation in the rising status of women in the labor market and increases in female labor force participation. An interesting component of the change in college enrollment that may also complement these other changes is the shift in the age distribution of female college students. In the postwar period, a sizable majority of female students were comparatively young, probably reflecting both earlier high school graduation and the larger percentage who attended college for only two years. While the percentages of male and female students under 20 have converged over time so that there is now little difference by gender to be observed, there has been and continues to be a significant

3. The percentage of college students enrolled in public-controlled institutions was 49.4 in the fall of 1949; 59.9 in 1959; 73.7 in 1969; and 78.1 in 1979 and 1987 (U.S. Department of Education 1973, 74; U.S. Department of Education 1989, 167).
   4. For a statement of the latter thesis, see Karabel (1972).
   5. U.S. Bureau of the Census, *Current Population Reports,* Series P-20, *School Enrollment—Social and Economic Characteristics of Students: October 1988 and 1987,* No. 443 (1990), table A-4.

Table 2.5   College Students by Sex and Age, October of Selected Years

	Number (in thousands)			% Under 20 Years Old		% 35 and Over	
	Total	Male	Female	Male	Female	Male	Female
Students 14–34:							
1947	2,311	1,687	624	25	61		
1950	2,175	1,474	701	32	63		
1960	3,570	2,339	1,231	36	56		
1970	7,413	4,401	3,013	34	46		
1972	8,313	4,853	3,459	31	42		
1980	10,180	5,025	5,155	29	33		
1988	10,937	5,223	5,714	27	32		
Students 14 and over:							
1972	9,096	5,218	3,877	29	38	7	11
1980	11,387	5,430	5,957	27	29	7	13
1988	13,116	5,950	7,166	24	25	12	20

Source: U.S. Bureau of the Census, Current Population Reports, Series P-20, School Enroll-ment—Social and Economic Characteristics of Students: October 1986, No. 429 (1988), table A-4, p. 83.

difference between the percentages who are 35 and older. In 1988, 20 percent of the women enrolled in college—full- and part-time—were 35 or older, as compared to just 12 percent of the men. This increase in later school enrollment among women could well reflect delays in education due to household formation and child rearing.

A second trend is the increasing importance of part-time enrollment. The ratio of part-time to total college enrollment increased from 32 percent in 1970 to 41 percent in 1980 to 43 percent in 1987 (U.S. Department of Education 1989, 167). This increase corresponds to the trend noted by Hauser (1990, 5) for young people to pursue employment and schooling at the same time. The increase in part-time enrollment also corresponds to an increase in the number of older students, most of whom are presumably employed or have families before they undertake part-time college work.

2.1.3   Enrollment by Minority Groups

Because of the importance of race in matters of public policy, including education policy, trends in college enrollment by race and ethnic group are prominent facts to be considered in any description of the demand for college education. A diminishing but persistent vestige of America's history has been large disparities in educational attainment between whites and blacks, and these have certainly included differences in the portion of adults with college degrees. As Table 2.3 above shows, the black-white gap in median years of schooling has practically disappeared, falling from 3.7 years in 1940 to 0.2 years in 1988. However, the difference in the percentage finishing four years of college has remained sizable. In 1940, 6.4 percent of whites aged 25–29

Table 2.6   Percentage Distribution of College Students Age 3–34, by Race and
                     Ethnicity and Attendance in Public Institutions, Selected Years

	1955	1965	1975	1985	1988
Enrollments as % of total:					
White	93.5	93.7	87.8	85.9	84.5
Nonwhite	6.5	6.3	12.2	14.1	15.5
Total	100.0	100.0	100.0	100.0	100.0
Detail:					
Black	a	a	9.8	9.7	10.2
Hispanic[b]	a	a	4.2	5.3	6.0
% in public institutions:					
White	64.3	67.1	79.0	76.4	79.0
Nonwhite	55.5	76.0	83.0	81.6	80.4
Total	63.7	67.7	79.4	77.1	79.2

Source: U.S. Bureau of the Census, *Current Population Reports,* Series P-20, *School Enrollment—Social and Economic Characteristics of Students: October 1988 and 1987,* No. 443
(1990), table A-2.
[a]Not available.
[b]Persons of Hispanic origin may be of any race.

had completed at least four years of college, compared to only 1.6 percent of
blacks. Since then, there has been steady progress in college attainment, but
even today the percentage of blacks who complete four years of college remains smaller than that of whites. In 1960, the rates for whites and blacks
were 11.8 and 4.8 percent, respectively; in 1988, the corresponding rates
were 23.5 and 12.3 percent.

These figures on attainment reflect in part a steady increase in the number
of blacks enrolled in college. Between 1955 and 1988, the number of nonwhites enrolled in college increased over tenfold, while the number of whites
enrolled quadrupled over the same period.[6] Combined with the desegregation
of the 1960s and 1970s, these enrollment trends have transformed the composition of most colleges and universities. Table 2.6 summarizes some of
these changes. Overall, nonwhites have grown from 6.5 percent of all students
in 1955 to 15.5 percent in 1988. Blacks now constitute about two-thirds of the
nonwhite total. The percentages of both racial groups enrolled in public institutions have grown over the period, but the growth for nonwhites has been
especially rapid. The proportion of nonwhites attending public institutions
rose from slightly over half in 1955 to four-fifths in 1988, probably reflecting
the desegregation of public institutions in the South. Because the nonwhite
population is growing at a faster rate than the white population, the prospects
are good for continued increases in the percentage of college students who are

6. Ibid., table A-2.

Table 2.7   College Enrollment Rates of 18- to 24-Year-Olds by Race/Ethnicity, 1967–88

	Enrollment as % of 18- to 24-Year-Olds				Enrollment as % of High School Graduates 18–24			
	All	White	Black	Hispanic	All	White	Black	Hispanic
1967	25.5	26.9	13.0	a	33.7	34.5	23.3	a
1968	26.0	27.5	14.5	a	34.2	34.9	25.2	a
1969	27.3	28.7	16.0	a	35.0	35.6	27.2	a
1970	25.7	27.1	15.5	a	32.7	33.2	26.0	a
1971	26.2	27.2	18.2	a	33.2	33.5	29.2	a
1972	25.5	26.4	18.1	13.4	31.9	32.3	27.1	25.8
1973	24.0	25.0	16.0	16.0	29.7	30.2	24.0	29.1
1974	24.6	25.2	17.9	18.1	30.5	30.5	26.6	32.3
1975	26.3	26.9	20.7	20.4	32.5	32.4	32.0	35.5
1976	26.7	27.1	22.6	19.9	33.1	33.0	33.5	35.8
1977	26.1	26.5	21.3	17.2	32.5	32.2	31.5	31.5
1978	25.3	25.7	20.1	15.2	31.4	31.1	29.7	27.2
1979	25.0	25.6	19.8	16.6	31.2	31.2	29.5	30.2
1980	25.6	26.2	19.2	16.1	31.6	31.8	27.6	29.8
1981	26.2	26.7	19.9	16.7	32.5	32.5	28.0	29.9
1982	26.6	27.2	19.8	16.8	33.0	33.1	28.0	29.2
1983	26.2	27.0	19.2	17.2	32.5	32.9	27.0	31.4
1984	27.1	28.0	20.4	17.9	33.2	33.7	27.2	29.9
1985	27.8	28.7	19.8	16.9	33.7	34.4	26.1	26.9
1986	27.9	28.3	21.9	17.6	34.0	34.1	28.6	29.4
1986[b]	28.2	28.6	22.2	18.2	34.3	34.5	29.1	30.4
1987	29.6	30.2	22.8	17.6	36.4	36.6	30.0	28.5
1988	30.3	31.3	21.1	17.0	37.3	38.1	28.1	30.9

Sources: U.S. Department of Education (1989); and U.S. Bureau of the Census, *Current Population Reports,* Series P-20, *School Enrollment—Social and Economic Characteristics of Students: October 1988 and 1987,* No. 443 (1990), table A-7, pp. 180–85.

Note: To illustrate the variability of these estimates, the approximate standard errors for the percentages of 18- to 24-year-olds for 1988 are 0.5 for whites, 1.1 for blacks, and 1.2 for Hispanics. See U.S. Bureau of the Census, *Current Population Reports,* Series P-20, *School Enrollment—Social and Economic Characteristics of Students: October 1988 and 1987,* No. 443 (1990), app. C.

[a]Not available.

[b]The Census Bureau changed its methods of classification and estimation after 1986. Estimates using the revised methodology for 1986 are given on this line.

nonwhite. In 1985, nonwhites accounted for 20.5 percent of all births, and blacks alone accounted for 16.2 percent.[7]

An issue that has received considerable attention in recent years, and one that has raised alarm in policy circles, is the apparent decline in the college enrollment rate among blacks and Hispanics since the mid-1970s.[8] Table 2.7

7. U.S. Bureau of the Census, *Statistical Abstract of the United States* (Washington, D.C.: U.S. Government Printing Office, 1988), 60.

8. See, e.g., "Fewer Blacks on Campus," *Newsweek,* 29 January 1990, p. 75.

summarizes these trends by showing college enrollment rates for all 18- to 24-year-olds and for those in that age group who are high school graduates. Although there are drawbacks to both these measures, they provide two easily understood metrics for reflecting trends in enrollment.[9] For whites, there is in each series a slight dip during the 1970s, but the enrollment rates by 1988 were at their all-time highs. For blacks and Hispanics, however, enrollment rates hit peaks in 1975 or 1976 and quickly fell, leveling off after about 1978. The only minority enrollment rate that regained its previous high is that for 18- to 24-year-old blacks in 1987, but the change in Census methodology adopted in 1986 probably accounts for all that difference.

These trends in minority enrollment rates have been a source of much concern. Some have pointed to them as an indication that financial aid programs have failed in their objective of opening up college to traditionally disadvantaged groups. These trends can also be seen within a larger context of the deteriorating social and economic conditions experienced by minorities, especially blacks. A report issued in 1990, for example, claimed that young black males were more likely to be under the control of an institution of the criminal justice system (prison, jail, probation, or parole) than to be enrolled in college.[10] The enrollment trends also complement recent reports of a growing gap between whites and blacks in health and life expectancy.[11] However, Hauser (1990) argues that the declines in black enrollment rates cannot be explained by changes in income. And not all trends point toward a widening racial gap. There is evidence that black-white differences in measured achievement have been shrinking. The gap between white and black average reading scores on the National Assessment of Educational Progress (NAEP) given to 17-year-olds fell from 53 points in 1975 to 21 points in 1988.[12]

2.1.4   Implications of Demographic Changes

If there has been one constant over the past thirty years, it has been that college enrollment rates have continued to change. As we have seen, models attempting to predict enrollment rates have had only limited success. Before examining in more detail differences in enrollment rates and economic models

9. One drawback of these two measures is that those who graduate from college before the age of 25 and stop attending college have the effect of lowering the college enrollment rate. Hauser (1990, 18) points out several other problems: because these measures are based on a large population, they are not very sensitive to year-to-year changes in the enrollment of high school graduates; they reflect high school graduation rates as well as college enrollment rates; and they are not sensitive to the rate of progress and part-time nature of enrollment. Another imperfection in these data is the exclusion of active military personnel. How this conclusion affects the resulting measures is unclear, but some effect is not unlikely since minorities are overrepresented in the military.

10. Robert Hauser, in personal correspondence, has criticized this claim, noting that the age group covered (20–29) excludes many college students and that college graduates are ignored. For a discussion of this finding, see Hauser (1990, 4).

11. "Health Report Shows Racial Gap Widening," *Raleigh News and Observer,* 23 March 1990, p. 3A.

12. The standard deviation of these scores was approximately 40 points (see Smith and O'Day 1990, table II and p. 18).

Table 2.8   Enrollment Rates by Race, Age, and Sex, 1988

	Male	Female
White:		
16–17	1.7	3.1
18–24	31.4	31.2
25–34	6.2	7.2
35+	1.4	2.5
Black:		
16–17	1.1	4.8
18–24	18.0	23.8
25–34	5.2	7.2
35+	1.4	2.3
Other nonwhite:		
16–17	1.7	7.3
18–24	46.5	37.4
25–34	22.1	8.3
35+	3.1	1.9

Source: See Table 2.9 below.

used in explaining such differences, it is useful to consider the implications of a set of changes that are comparatively easy to predict, namely, population shifts. Using current enrollment rates, it is possible to use population projections to produce a set of predicted enrollments. Projections of this sort should then be seen as estimates of future enrollments based on the assumption that enrollment rates remain constant. To calculate the projections, the population was divided into 24 groups, by sex, age, and race. Projected future enrollments were calculated by applying the 1988 college enrollment rate for each group to projections of the size of each group. The 1988 enrollment rates are shown in Table 2.8. Needless to say, the recent past gives ample reason to believe that enrollment rates will not, in fact, remain constant. The rates for those 35 and older have been rising steadily, for example. However, the simple approach used here has the virtue of producing projections that can be easily interpreted and are the result only of predicted changes in the size and composition of the population.[13]

Projections were made for five-year intervals from 1990 to 2010; these are summarized in Table 2.9. Crucial to the determination of college enrollment is the size of the population in the traditional college-going age group. As noted above, the number of 18-year-olds in the United States has been projected to decline by about 25 percent between 1980 and 1992. This decrease

13. Between 1986 and 1988, some of these enrollment rates changed markedly. For example, the rates for whites aged 18–24 increased from 28.9 to 31.4 percent for males and from 27.8 to 31.2 percent for females. Part of these increases is due to changes in Census methodology for tabulating enrollments (see U.S. Bureau of the Census, *Current Population Reports,* Series P-20, *School Enrollment—Social and Economic Characteristics of Students: October 1988 and 1987,* No. 443 (1990), p. 190).

Table 2.9   **Projected College Enrollments, 1990–2010, Based on 1988 Age-, Race-, and Sex-Specific Enrollment Rates (enrollments in millions)**

Total Enrollment	18–24 Population as % of 1988	Enrollment		% of College Students Who Are:			FTE Enrollment[a]	
		Total	As % of 1988	Black	Other Nonwhite	35+	Total	As % of 1988
Actual:								
1988	100	13.1	100	10.1	5.3	16.6	9.5	100
Projected:								
1990	102	13.4	103	10.4	5.7	17.2	9.7	102
1995	94	12.9	99	10.9	6.7	19.8	9.2	97
2000	98	13.2	101	11.2	7.5	21.1	9.4	99
2005	105	13.8	105	11.3	8.2	21.3	9.9	104
2010	106	14.1	107	11.6	8.6	21.8	10.0	106

Source: Author's calculations based on Census population projections and 1988 enrollment rates by age, sex and race. U.S. Bureau of the Census, *Current Population Reports,* Series P-25, *Projections of the Population of the United States, by Age, Sex and Race: 1988 to 2080,* No. 1018 (1989), and Series P-20, *School Enrollment—Social and Economic Characteristics of Students: October 1988 and 1987,* No. 443 (1990), table 1.

[a]Based on age- and sex-specific rates for part-time enrollment in 1986 (U.S. Department of Education 1989, 169). For these calculations, part-time enrollees are assumed to be equivalent to one-third of a full-time enrollee, and the rates used for age 16–17 are based on the observed rates for ages 14–17.

is evident in the projected size of the population aged 18–24, which is predicted to drop by about 6 percent between 1988 and 1995 but which will then rebound. Projected total enrollments increase after 1995, slightly exceeding the 1988 level again by 2000 and continuing to increase to 14.1 million by 2010. The composition of college enrollments will change as well, with growing proportions of students who are nonwhite and who are 35 or older. When measured in terms of FTE enrollments, the growth of enrollments is slightly less, owing to the projected increase in part-time study.

2.2   Who Goes to College?

A useful first step in considering the demand for college is to document existing patterns of college enrollment. Enrollments can be related to such categories as sex, age, race, aptitude, and economic class. In fact, each of these categories can produce clear relations when compared to college enrollment one at a time, and such simple correlations are one useful way of describing the population of college students. However, a fuller picture may be obtained by examining these patterns when other things are held constant. For this reason, some of the findings in this section apply to the relations between college enrollment and two or more variables at a time, either through regression analysis or through tabular presentations. This section begins by focusing on how college enrollment relates to characteristics of students; it then considers how these patterns lead to differences among the student bodies of various kinds of institutions.

2.2.1 Characteristics of Students

Socioeconomic Status

Viewed from the perspective of the economics of education, probably the most revealing characteristic of college students is their economic class. Both college enrollment and educational attainment are strongly associated with parents' income and social status. Table 2.10 illustrates this correlation for college enrollment in 1988. It shows the percentage of dependents aged 18–24 enrolled in college by family income. For all such dependents, this percentage rises steadily with income, from 18 percent for those families with incomes under $10,000 to 59 percent for those families with incomes of $50,000 or more. It is also apparent that this positive income effect applies generally to whites, blacks, and those of Hispanic origin, although the smaller sample for the latter two groups makes for less precise estimates of percentages. Table 2.10 can also be used to compare enrollment rates for the three racial and ethnic groups at given income levels. Looking across rows at dependents from the same income class shows that the rates for whites consistently exceed those for blacks and Hispanics. Holding family income constant therefore reduces, but does not eliminate, differences in enrollment rates associated with race and ethnicity.

The association between college enrollment and economic status is worth exploring in detail. Not only is this relation basic to our understanding of the social and economic effects of higher education, but it is also central to the

Table 2.10	College Enrollment by Family Income, 1988 (percentage of dependent family members 18 to 24 years old enrolled in college)			
Family Income	Total	White	Black	Hispanic
Under $10,000	17.9	18.8	13.9	14.6
$10,000–$14,999	26.8	27.4	24.1	16.1
$15,000–$19,999	31.5	32.0	26.9	30.6
$20,000–$24,999	35.5	38.6	21.2	32.6
$25,000–$34,999	39.2	41.0	26.6	29.3
$35,000–$49,999	47.0	47.7	41.6	43.8
$50,000 and over	58.7	59.2	49.5	47.9
Not reported	41.9	40.7	40.5	6.5
Total	41.7	44.2	26.9	26.5

Source: U.S. Bureau of the Census, *Current Population Reports,* Series P-20, *School Enrollment—Social and Economic Characteristics of Students: October 1988 and 1987,* No. 443 (1990), table 15. To illustrate the variability of these estimates, the approximate standard error of the enrollment rate for dependents with family incomes from $35,000 to $49,999 is 1.8 percentage points for whites, 5.2 for blacks, and 6.5 for Hispanics. Calculations are based on eq. 4 in app. C of the report.

Table 2.11   **College Enrollment by Socioeconomic Status, Sex, and Type of Institution, High School Classes of 1961, 1972, and 1982 (percentage enrolled in college)**

Type of Institution and Socioeconomic Quartile	Males			Females		
	1961	1972	1982	1961	1972	1982
Four-year:						
Lowest	23	20	24	22	20	24
Second	33	23	29	28	21	33
Third	40	29	39	32	27	41
Highest	53	42	55	48	44	62
Two-year:						
Lowest	7	12	15	6	13	18
Second	7	18	19	7	17	21
Third	8	19	22	6	17	25
Highest	11	15	20	12	14	22

Source: Clowes, Hinkle, and Smart (1986, 126).

evaluation of public policies designed specifically to weaken that correlation. Does this association differ by type of institution? What has been the effect of financial aid programs on it? Has it grown weaker or stronger over time? The first of these questions is addressed in the present chapter, while the other two are taken up in later chapters.

From its beginnings in this country, college was popularly viewed as the meeting place of the affluent. Although certainly not accurate in all particulars, this perception was by and large correct. Few from the working classes attended college in the nineteenth century. According to Veysey (1965, 271), while some colleges were quite exclusive as to social position, few enrolled anything close to a cross section of the population: "The undergraduate population of the turn of the century seems remarkably homogeneous: a parade of Anglo-Saxon names and pale, freshly scrubbed faces." Even the emerging public institutions tended to enroll children of upper- and middle-income families. A survey of the occupations of fathers of Michigan students in 1902, for example, showed six times as many businessmen as mechanics, craftsmen, and skilled laborers put together (Veysey 1965, 291–92).

Modern surveys have made it possible to be more precise in relating social and economic position to college enrollment. Table 2.11 presents data on college enrollment and socioeconomic status for students who were high school seniors in 1961, 1972, and 1980.[14] The measure of socioeconomic status is a statistical composite based on family income, parents' education, father's occupation, and household possessions. There are two advantages of using this

14. Although Clowes, Hinkle, and Smart (1986) label the most recent class as 1982, their description of the data (p. 122) indicates that their figures are based on the class of 1980.

measure as an alternative to reported family income: its components are correlated to permanent income, and it is typically available for a larger portion of the samples than is income.[15] Rates of college enrollment in the fall of the given years are broken down by sex and type of institution.

Looking first at four-year institutions, the figures clearly indicate that enrollment rises with socioeconomic status, supporting the strong income correlation shown above. Roughly speaking, those in the top quartile of socioeconomic status are slightly more than twice as likely to be enrolled in a four-year college than those in the lowest quartile, and this relation did not change over the two decades covered by the tabulation. The only important qualification to this generalization arises from the increase in enrollments of women over the period in the upper three quartiles. Beginning at rates below those of men in 1961, women were enrolling at rates as high or higher than those of men in every quartile by 1980. This is just one reflection of the overall surge in female enrollments, but one dimension of it was an apparent increase in the socioeconomic disparity in enrollment rates in 1980.

An equally important aspect of the association between college enrollment and socioeconomic status shown in Table 2.11 is the marked difference in patterns between four-year and two-year institutions. Among the latter, a positive correlation between status and enrollment again appears, but the differences are quite a bit less than with the four-year institutions. In general, students from the top quartile were less than twice as likely to enroll in two-year colleges as those from the bottom. If enrollments for both types of institutions were combined, of course, the resulting enrollment rates would be strongly correlated with socioeconomic status, as are the four-year rates. The figures in the table also reflect the rapid growth of two-year colleges over the period, with rates generally doubling. In the process of growth, two-year institutions have in effect specialized in lower-income students. While four-year enrollment rates of students from the lowest quartile have remained roughly constant over the period, the two-year rates for this group have more than doubled.

Aptitude

Another characteristic of students that has not been mentioned is aptitude, which is often measured by standardized test scores. Ignoring for the moment the question of whether standardized tests are biased or whether they measure the appropriate traits, few would dispute the proposition that a student's potential for gaining from college training depends on his or her ability and

15. Using data for the 1980 base year questionnaire, each of the five components of the socioeconomic status variable was converted to a standardized variable with a mean of zero and a standard deviation of one. The composite variable was then formed as the simple average of nonmissing components. Of the 11,995 persons in the High School and Beyond sample (see n. 18 below), this variable is available for 11,130 of them. Of those not included, 495 were not surveyed in the base year, and 370 had insufficient data to form the measure. Tabulations of family income against the socioeconomic status variable show that the two are highly correlated.

Table 2.12   **Enrollment in Four-Year and Two-Year Institutions, by Academic Preparedness and Socioeconomic Status, High School Class of 1980, Fall 1980 (percentage enrolled in college, fall 1980)**

Type of Institution, Sex, and Aptitude Score Quartiles	Socioeconomic Status Quartiles		
	Lowest	Middle two	Highest
Four-year institutions:			
Men:			
Lowest	4.6	5.9	11.6
Middle two	18.1	22.4	34.7
Highest	34.0	59.9	65.3
Women:			
Lowest	7.1	10.2	13.2
Middle two	19.0	27.1	50.6
Highest	52.6	58.8	81.6
Two-year institutions:			
Men:			
Lowest	4.5	6.7	19.1
Middle two	11.1	17.0	21.9
Highest	12.4	15.5	8.0
Women:			
Lowest	9.8	11.6	18.5
Middle two	15.2	20.3	24.7
Highest	12.0	17.1	7.9

Source: Peng (1983, tables 4, 5).

academic training. In addition, while colleges have sometimes had explicit policies favoring certain applicants on the basis of race or social class, aptitude has virtually always been one criterion for admission. For these reasons, one would expect to see an association between measured aptitude and college attendance, and, indeed, that is what is observed.

Table 2.12 illustrates this association for students in the high school class of 1980. The test scores used for classification in the table are based on short standardized tests similar to the Scholastic Aptitude Test (SAT). The table shows how enrollment rates classified by sex, socioeconomic status, and type of institution differ according to scores on a standardized achievement test. Enrollment in four-year colleges is strongly associated with test scores, with those scoring in the top quartile at least five times as likely to enroll as those in the bottom quartile. But the table also shows that the previously noted effects of sex and socioeconomic status do not disappear when measured aptitude is taken into account. Particularly striking is the strong association that remains between four-year enrollment rates and socioeconomic status. Also noteworthy is the 16 percentage point difference in enrollment rates between men and women in the highest socioeconomic and test score quartiles.[16]

16. The standard error of the difference in these two percentages is approximately 4.9 percentage points.

The effect of measured aptitude on enrollment in two-year colleges is decidedly more ambiguous. While those scoring in the middle two quartiles are more likely to enroll, in most cases the enrollment rate drops off in the highest test quartile. It is also interesting to see how socioeconomic status and test score interact. For those below the top test score quartile, the two-year college enrollment rates rise with social class, but this is not the case for those scoring in the top quartile. For example, among men whose test scores fell into the top quartile, the percentage enrolling in two-year colleges dropped from 15.5 in the middle socioeconomic group to 8.0 in the top quartile. Clearly, these declines in two-year enrollment rates among those in the top socioeconomic and aptitude quartiles reflect their high rates of enrollments in four-year institutions. Enrollment rates based on both two-year and four-year institutions show strong positive correlations to both socioeconomic status and test scores.

As clear as the association between achievement test scores and college enrollment is, the interpretation of that association is a complex issue indeed. Tests such as the SAT have been criticized as being culturally biased, in favor of middle- and upper-income students and against minority students (see, e.g., Fallows 1980). They are certainly highly correlated with income (see, e.g., Bishop 1977, 291; Baird 1984, 378; or Nairn et al. 1980, 201). Nairn et al. (1980) argue that the SAT contains a two-pronged class bias: an inherent bias in the test questions themselves and an advantage obtained from pretest coaching, which he argues increases scores. A survey reported in 1979 showed that 41 percent of students who had received coaching had family incomes over $30,000 while only 17 percent of those who had not received coaching had family incomes over $30,000 (Nairn et al. 1980, 98). According to Nairn et al., the observed high correlation between family income and measured aptitude overstates the relation, if any, between income and achievement potential. Racial differences in achievement scores are subject to much the same argument. It is relevant to note in this connection that, when test scores are held constant, blacks show higher rates of enrollment in four-year colleges than whites.[17]

Other Influences

Having looked separately at how college enrollment correlates to several different kinds of variables, it is useful to conclude by asking about the joint effect of the entire set of variables. In their model of college-going behavior, Manski and Wise (1983, 79–80) present regressions explaining the probability that a student will apply to college, the quality of the college (measured by the average SAT score of its students), and the probability that the student will be admitted. The estimated effects of student attributes in these equations pro-

---

17. For those scoring in the top quartile, e.g., 71 percent of blacks attended four-year institutions compared to 63 percent of whites and 51 percent of Hispanics (see Peng 1983, 14).

vide an interesting comparison to the data presented above. Two variables that have consistently positive and significant effects in all three of these equations are SAT score and high school grades. In addition, the following variables have positive and significant effects on both the probability of applying to college and college quality: parents' income, parents' education, being a leader in high school, and being an athlete. Blacks had a higher probability of applying to college, other things being equal, but the quality of the schools they applied to was lower in the South and higher outside the South.

2.2.2 Type of Institution

To answer more completely the question of who goes to college, it is necessary to go beyond the two-year/four-year distinction. As the introduction to this volume stresses, higher education in the United States is nothing if not diverse, and one manifestation of this diversity is the existence of a number of quite distinct kinds of undergraduate institutions. This diversity among institutions of higher education exists within a larger set of post–high school options, some of which offer training quite similar to that available in some colleges. One way of summarizing these options is given in Table 2.13, which is based on High School and Beyond, a national survey that followed a sample of high school sophomores and seniors for six years.[18] This table summarizes the enrollment decisions of the high school class of 1980 in the fall of that year. Students are divided into four racial and ethnic groups and further separated by socioeconomic quartile. Students of Hispanic descent were classified as Hispanic regardless of race and are not included in any other grouping. Several kinds of college enrollment options are specified, including two-year versus four-year and part-time versus full-time. In addition, four-year colleges are split up into three categories: highly selective, other public, and other private. The highly selective group includes 85 institutions with median freshman SAT scores of 575 or more or median ACT scores of 28 or more in 1980.[19] The table also shows enrollment in vocational programs and military enlistment as two alternatives to college enrollment.

The table's bottom row shows that, in October 1980, 44 percent of the entire cohort were enrolled in college, 4 percent were enrolled in vocational programs, 2 percent were in the military, and the remaining 50 percent were not enrolled in any postsecondary program. Of those in college, 2 percent were in one of the selective colleges, and 19 percent were in other public and 8 percent in other private four-year programs as full-time students. The pro-

18. The High School and Beyond survey covered about 60,000 high school sophomores and seniors in about 1,000 schools in the spring of 1980 and at two-year intervals to 1986. The National Center for Education Statistics has published numerous descriptions of the data. For example, see National Center for Education Statistics, *Contractor Report: High School and Beyond 1980 Senior Cohort First Follow-Up (1982), Data File User's Manual* (Washington, D.C., May 1983).

19. These institutions were categorized as "most competitive" or "highly competitive" in *Barron's Profiles of American Colleges* (1980, x, xi). Most of the institutions included were private.

Table 2.13   Enrollment by the High School Class of 1980 by Demographic Group, October 1980

Racial/Ethnic Group and Socioeconomic Status Quartile	2-Year Full-Time	4-Year Public, Full-Time	4-Year Private, Full-Time	4-Year Selective, Full-Time	Vocational	4- or 2-Year, Part-Time	Military	High School Graduate, Not Enrolled	Not High School Graduate	% of All Seniors
Hispanic:										
Lowest	6	6	2	1	4	3	2	74	2	4.4
Second	14	9	2	0	4	3	3	64	0	2.2
Third	13	8	4	4	3	9	2	54	3	1.7
Highest	20	24	10	4	3	3	2	35	0	1.0
Other:										
Lowest	17	6	4	3	6	6	3	55	0	.6
Second	15	7	3	1	1	6	5	61	0	.5
Third	19	24	2	3	4	6	4	37	1	.6
Highest	17	40	8	11	1	6	1	14	1	.6
Black:										
Lowest	6	13	3	0	3	2	5	65	2	5.3
Second	7	16	6	0	3	2	4	61	2	2.3
Third	10	23	11	1	2	1	3	48	1	1.6
Highest	12	26	12	2	1	4	0	42	1	1.0
White:										
Lowest	8	9	4	0	6	2	2	68	2	14.6
Second	11	14	5	0	6	4	3	54	1	20.1
Third	14	22	8	1	4	4	2	44	1	21.4
Highest	11	31	14	5	3	5	1	29	0	22.2
Total	11	19	8	2	4	4	2	49	1	100.0

Source: Calculations based on High School and Beyond.

Note: The unweighted sample size for these percentages, from the lowest to the highest socioeconomic status groups, are as follows: Hispanic: 1,115, 452, 333, and 211; other: 119, 94, 111, and 114; black: 1,047, 455, 314, and 183; white: 958, 991, 1,044, and 1,138, for a total of 8,679. Standard errors, calculated as the square root of $P(1 - P)/N$, where P is the calculated percentage and N is the sample size, are generally on the order of 1 or 2 percentage points. For example, the standard error of the 13 percent estimate for third-quartile Hispanics going full-time to four-year public institutions is 1.5; the comparable percentage for third-quartile whites is 1.3.

portion enrolled in two-year programs was 11 percent. Turning to the entries for the separate demographic groups yields a detailed picture of enrollment rates that roughly correspond to the broad relations noted above. Most prominently, enrollment in four-year institutions generally increased with socioeconomic class. In terms of percentage differences in rates, the increases tended to be sharpest in the case of the highly selective colleges. Among students from the top socioeconomic quartile, 5 percent of whites and 11 percent of the residual class (which includes students of Asian descent) were enrolled in these selective institutions; at the same time, these institutions enrolled very few students from the lowest socioeconomic quartile. The patterns for two-year institutions and part-time college enrollment are considerably flatter. The biggest observed difference by socioeconomic group was among Hispanics, with the enrollment rate in two-year colleges rising from 6 to 20 percent from the bottom to the top socioeconomic quartile. These figures support the impression gained above of a much less pronounced class-defined pattern of enrollments in two-year, as opposed to four-year, institutions.[20] Because the table does not control for aptitude, the patterns it shows reflect to some extent the existing correlation between aptitude and socioeconomic status.

Table 2.13 also presents several comparisons by race that are useful to note. Probably the most important is that, if socioeconomic status is held constant, there is little apparent difference in college enrollment rates between blacks and whites in the two largest categories of full-time students in four-year institutions. However, Table 2.13 does reveal white-black disparities in four categories: highly selective, two-year, part-time, and vocational institutions. In each of these cases, the rate for whites equals or exceeds the corresponding rate for blacks in each socioeconomic quartile. As between non-Hispanic whites and Hispanics, there are similar disparities in vocational rates and in the two largest four-year college rates. Finally, the rates for the residual racial group are anomalous, with those in the highest socioeconomic quartile showing the highest enrollment rates for selective and other public four-year colleges and for two-year colleges. In considering these findings, it is useful to emphasize that these tabulations are based on only one cohort and that there may be changes in these patterns over time.

One obvious way that differences in enrollments show themselves is in the makeup of student bodies. Differences in enrollment rates at the individual level translate into differences in composition among institutions. These differences among types of colleges and universities are illustrated in Table 2.14

20. These findings are consistent with statistical studies of college choice. For example, in a regression equation excluding measures of student performance and expectations, Hearn (1988, 72) finds that college cost tended to rise with parents' education and family income, to fall with family size, and to be lower for Hispanics. In an expanded model, however, tested ability, high school grades, high school track, and educational expectations were all found to be significant; of the remaining variables, only mother's education and the indicator for blacks were significant, the latter taking on a positive sign.

Table 2.14   Income Level and Racial/Ethnic Composition of College Freshmen, by Type of Institution, Fall 1988 (percentage of freshmen)

	Estimated Parental Income		Racial/Ethnic Group(%)[a]		
	Below $15,000	$75,000 & above	White	Black	Hispanic
All institutions	11.7	16.1	83.2	9.5	3.2
Four-year colleges:					
Public	11.9	11.1	80.7	16.0	1.6
Private nonsectarian	8.4	26.2	80.9	13.1	1.6
Protestant	11.8	17.0	84.9	12.3	1.1
Catholic	9.4	21.5	88.3	3.9	4.9
Universities:					
Public	7.8	21.0	84.9	6.1	2.9
Private	5.2	37.7	84.3	4.4	2.5
Predominantly black colleges:					
Public	31.0	4.7	1.9	97.0	.4
Private	23.4	9.4	.6	99.0	.5
Two-year colleges:					
Public	16.5	8.6	83.0	7.0	5.3
Private	13.2	17.7	87.0	8.0	2.1

Source: Astin et al. (1988, 47–48).

[a]The percentages generally do not sum to 100 because some students may fall into two classes and some into none of them.

by comparing data on racial composition and reported family income of freshmen. The affluence of student bodies differs greatly among institutions of different kinds, with the percentage of freshmen from families with incomes of $75,000 and over ranging from a low of 5 percent in predominantly black public colleges to a high of 38 percent in private universities. The percentages of low-income students tend to vary inversely. Racial composition also differs among these institutional types. The predominantly black colleges stand out in this regard, of course, but there are important differences among the other categories as well. Whites predominate in Catholic and private two-year colleges, while, among predominantly white institutions, blacks are most heavily represented in public colleges. Hispanic students have their largest representation in public two-year colleges, a finding that is probably affected by the wide coverage offered by California's system of community colleges. Of course, the differences among individual institutions are greater than those among types of institutions.

2.3   After Matriculation

Most of the reasons why we are interested in undergraduate enrollment do not have to do with enrollment per se but rather with the outcomes of college education. Therefore it is important to go beyond the question of who goes to college to a consideration of the transitions following enrollment. One issue that has received a great deal of attention among policy analysts of higher education is that of college dropouts, and many studies have been conducted exploring the determinants of what is called "persistence to degree." As is the case with college enrollment, differences by race and socioeconomic group in rates of college completion have important implications for public policy.

A useful starting place for an empirical understanding of transitions after enrollment is the point made at the beginning of the previous section: only a minority of college students fits the stereotype of the full-time college student who enrolls immediately after high school graduation and proceeds to finish in four years. As an illustration, of those high school graduates in the class of 1982, only 13 percent had completed four years of college by 1986.[21] The percentage of students finishing in four years differs widely among institutions. In the state of North Carolina, for example, the four-year completion rates for students who entered in 1985 ranged from 87 percent at Duke and 59 percent at the University of North Carolina's Chapel Hill campus to 9 percent at Winston-Salem State and 6 percent at Fayetteville State.[22] Of those who do not complete degrees in the initial four years, some will finish later, and others will never in fact graduate with a college degree. College degree attainment thus requires leaping over three distinct hurdles: high school graduation, college enrollment, and completion. By the time all is said and done, only about 30 percent of those in recent college-age cohorts will receive four years of college training (see Table 2.15 below). For one cohort coming of college age in the 1970s, about three-fourths finished high school, about three-quarters of those graduates enrolled in college, and about half those who entered college completed a degree.[23] For the young population as a whole, therefore, dropping out is relatively commonplace at both the high school and the college levels.

Table 2.15 presents one way of summarizing students' progress toward college graduation. It shows, for whites and blacks, the educational attainment of several different cohorts of high school graduates in the fall of 1986. For example, for the high school class of 1982, the table indicates that about 57 percent of whites and 50 percent of blacks were enrolled or had completed at least one year of college four years after high school graduation. The percentages of those who had completed four years of college, however, were only about 15 and 4, respectively. College completion rates tend to rise with the older cohorts, indicating delayed college going, though there are of course

21. U.S. Bureau of the Census, *Current Population Reports,* Series P-20, *School Enrollment— Social and Economic Characteristics of Students: October 1986,* No. 429 (1988), table 8, p. 27.

22. Katie Mosher, "Path to Degree Taking Longer in UNC System," *Raleigh News and Observer,* 16 February 1990, p. A1.

23. These percentages are based on Jackson's (1988, 18) illustration using the cohort born in 1957.

Table 2.15   Years of College Completed by High School Graduates, October 1986

Race and Year of High School Graduation	Proportions of High School Graduates							Conditional Probabilities of:	
	Completed 1 Year or Now Enrolled	< 1; Not Enrolled	By Number of Years Completed					Completing 2 Years, Having Completed 1 Year	Completing 4 Years, Having Completed 2 Years
			< 1; Now Enrolled	1	2	3	4+		
White:									
1986	56.2	43.8	54.8	.8	.2	.1	.3	a	a
1983–85	54.4	45.6	7.2	24.6	15.3	6.2	1.0	.48	a
1982	56.7	43.3	2.7	12.3	14.0	13.0	14.5	.77	.35
1981 or earlier:									
Under 26 years old	52.9	47.1	1.9	9.3	11.9	5.6	24.0	.82	.58
26–28	51.5	48.5	1.8	8.5	10.6	4.8	25.7	.83	.63
29–34	55.9	44.1	1.2	9.3	11.8	4.2	29.6	.83	.65
Black									
1986	39.5	60.5	35.4	2.9	1.3	a	a	a	a
1983–85	48.6	51.4	9.1	25.0	11.0	2.8	.8	.37	a
1982	50.1	49.9	2.7	15.4	13.8	14.2	3.7	.67	.12
1981 or earlier:									
Under 26 years old	46.7	53.7	1.8	10.5	13.6	9.5	11.0	.76	.32
26–28	44.7	55.3	2.6	9.2	12.7	6.1	14.3	.78	.43
29–34	49.4	50.6	1.2	9.4	15.2	6.6	16.9	.80	.44

Source: U.S. Bureau of the Census, *Current Population Reports*, Series P-20, *School Enrollment—Social and Economic Characteristics of Students: October 1986*, No. 429 (1988), table 8, pp. 28–29.

aNot calculated owing to small base.

differences among cohorts when compared at the same age.[24] The last two columns of Table 2.15 give proportions that may be interpreted as conditional probabilities. The first shows the probability that a high school graduate who had finished one year of college had also completed a second. These rates rise as the ages of the cohorts increase and reach roughly 80 percent for both whites and blacks for the oldest cohort, although the rates for blacks tend to lag behind those for whites. The last column gives the probability that a person who had completed two years of college would also have completed four years. These rates also rise with age, reflecting the time needed to complete degrees, but they are markedly different for whites and blacks. For the oldest cohort, this conditional probability for blacks is only two-thirds that for whites. It is this second conditional probability that is the most important explanation for the large gap in four-year completion between the races, given the similarity of initial enrollment rates.

Another way to describe college students' progress toward completion is by examining the careers of individual students over time, which can be done with panel data. Using one such data set, the National Longitudinal Survey (NLS), Manski and Wise (1983) examined patterns of college enrollment of a sample of young people over a five-year period following their high school graduation in 1972. While their data refer to years in which students are enrolled full-time and not to degree completion, their findings provide strong support for the relative rarity of immediate and continuous full-time enrollment leading to a degree. Table 2.16 summarizes some of these findings. The top half of the table shows that only about one-quarter of whites and about 15 percent of blacks could be characterized by the traditional pattern of immediate, full-time enrollment. Although a majority of each race/sex group enrolled full-time in at least one year following high school graduation, relatively few enrolled in college for four straight years after high school. These findings suggest that many students work while they pursue college study. According to Manski and Wise (1983, 44), a quarter of those enrolled in two-year and vocational programs were working full-time. Since these data are based on years of enrollment, four years of enrollment do not necessarily imply completion of a degree. In fact, Manski and Wise (p. 51) report that 26 percent of those who were enrolled for the first four years and 71 percent of those enrolled for all five years did not receive bachelor's degrees.

The bottom part of Table 2.16 focuses on those who attended college for at least two years right after high school. While these rates are much higher than those for continuous four-year enrollment, still only a minority of high school students enrolled for even two years immediately after high school. As with the percentages for continuous four-year enrollment, the rates for whites exceed those for blacks. The bottom row in the table gives the proportion of

---

24. Table 5.3 below compares rates of enrollment and completion for several cohorts at the same ages.

Table 2.16   **Patterns of Full-Time Postsecondary Enrollment, High School Class of 1972, Fall 1972–76 (percentage of all high school seniors)**

	White		Nonwhite	
	Male	Female	Male	Female
Continuous enrollment for at least four years immediately following high school	26	22	14	15
Enrolled full-time at least one year, some other pattern	40	38	42	47
Never enrolled	35	40	44	39
Total	100	100	100	100
Detail:				
Continuous enrollment for at least two years immediately following high school	40	36	28	30
Portion of the above who were enrolled at least four years all together	70	66	59	55

Source: Calculations based on Manski and Wise (1983, 48).

those enrolling immediately for two years who went on to enroll full-time for another two years between 1974 and 1976. Corresponding to the conditional probabilities shown in Table 2.15, the rates for blacks are lower than those for whites, the difference being about 10 percentage points.

There is in fact a considerable body of research on dropouts, as illustrated by a review of the research on the subject by Tinto (1975). Studies show that college dropouts, as compared to those who remain in school, tend to have lower grades and to have parents with less education and lower incomes. Historically, males have been less likely to drop out than females. Studies have also shown that students who have higher levels of interaction with faculty and other students are less likely to leave school, but such interaction is most likely a function of many of the same factors that influence the probability of dropping out. To what extent dropout rates should constitute a source of concern is another question. According to Stampen and Cabrera (1986, 28), rates of attrition from college have remained fairly stable for at least a century, except during major wars. And, as Manski (1989) has argued, an increase in the number of dropouts from college is not necessarily a bad thing. Enrollment, he argues, is one important way a person has of obtaining information about his or her suitability for college training, and increases in enrollment may well lead to increases in the number of dropouts.

One significant feature of the process that extends from enrollment to completion—and includes dropping out as one option—is the heterogeneity that exists among institutions. Not only can students enroll or drop out, but they can also enroll part-time or transfer from one type of institution to another. Historically, one of the principal aims of two-year colleges has been to provide a stepping-stone between high school and four-year institutions, although their success in this regard has been questioned (see, e.g., Karabel 1972). The armed forces have also marketed themselves as an avenue for training and further education following service. It is difficult to appreciate the connection between enrollment and attainment without considering the variety of institutions among which high school graduates have to choose and the possibilities of transferring among them.

One way of summarizing the interactions among various postsecondary activities is given in table 2.17, which tracks the progress of the high school class of 1980 from the fall of 1980 to their highest level of educational attainment by the spring of 1986. Ignoring differences among demographic groups, the table shows the probability that a young person in a given enrollment category in the fall of 1980 would obtain a degree or attain a certain level by 1986. Fall 1980 activities for the high school class of 1980 are divided into the nine categories given above in Table 2.9. Another nine possible states of attainment or activity are defined for 1986. Where students attained more than one of the indicated states—for example, a vocational certificate and a two- or three-year degree—the state to the left was used for classification. From the perspective of those interested in college attainment, the first four of these states are especially important—the three groups of bachelor's recipients and those who are enrolled full-time in four-year institutions, who have a high average likelihood of completing degrees as well.

In terms of obtaining bachelor's degrees, the table shows two things: relatively high completion rates for those who enroll in four-year institutions right after high school and relatively low rates for those who do not. The table indicates, for example, that a student who was enrolled full-time in a four-year public institution in the fall of 1980 had a 0.48 probability of having earned a degree from such an institution by 1986 and a 0.01 and a 0.03 chance of obtaining a degree from a highly selective or other private four-year institution, respectively—in other words, a slightly better than even chance (0.52) of obtaining a bachelor's degree within five and a half years. The chances were higher (0.71 and 0.61, respectively) for those who enrolled initially in highly selective or other private institutions, suggesting the existence of demographic differences in completion rates. Far below those completion rates were the ones for students who initially enrolled in college as part-time students (0.18) or as full-time students in two-year institutions (0.21), though in both these cases a significant share of students were enrolled full-time in four-year institutions in 1986, suggesting that eventual completion rates would be higher.

One thing that the table makes clear is the importance of being enrolled in some college program immediately after high school. For the students who were not, very few had obtained bachelor's degrees by 1986. In particular,

Table 2.17   Educational Attainment Six Years after High School: Transition Probabilities from Fall 1980 States to Spring 1986 States (entries show the probability a person in 1980 state will attain given 1986 state)

1980 Enrollment Status	1986 Attainment Status								
	Graduate, Selective 4-Year	Graduate, Other Public 4-Year	Graduate, Other Private 4-Year	Enrolled, 4-Year, Full-Time	2- or 3-Year Degree	Vocational Certificate	Some Post-secondary	High School Only	Not High School Graduate
Enrolled in two-year, full-time	0	.18	.03	.07	.20	.09	.43	0	0
Enrolled in four-year public, full-time	.01	.48	.03	.06	.07	.04	.33	0	0
Enrolled in four-year private, full-time	.01	.12	.48	.04	.06	.04	.26	0	0
Enrolled in four-year selective, full-time	.63	.02	.06	.05	.01	.03	.21	0	0
Enrolled in vocational program	0	.01	0	.03	.19	.28	.48	0	0
Enrolled in four- or two-year, part-time	.01	.12	.05	.05	.12	.12	.52	0	0
Military	0	.01	0	.02	.04	.27	.26	.40	0
High School graduate, not enrolled	0	.05	.02	.03	.05	.12	.29	.44	0
Not high school graduate	0	0	0	0	.03	.07	.19	.30	.41

Source: Calculations based on High School and Beyond.

Table 2.18   Conditional Probabilities of Receiving a Bachelor's Degree by Spring
                    1986, High School Class of 1980, by Fall 1980 Enrollment Status and
                    Population Group

| | Fall 1980 Enrollment (full-time) | | | |
| | Two-Year College | Four-Year Institutions | | |
		Public	Private	Selective
All	.20	.51	.61	.71
Male	.26	.53	.56	.68
Female	.16	.49	.66	.74
White	.22	.54	.65	.72
Black	.08	.32	.37	.45
Upper SES	.27	.57	.65	.74
Lower SES	.12	.39	.51	.55

Source: Calculations based on High School and Beyond.

neither the military nor vocational schools offered promising paths to a college degree, at least within the five-and-a-half-year period covered by the survey, although they did often lead to vocational certificates. In fairness, military service necessarily entails some delay in completing postsecondary
education, but remarkably few of those who began in the military had finished
even a two-year degree program by 1986. Entry into a handful of selective
institutions was even more restrictive: virtually the only route to a degree from
one of these colleges was through immediate enrollment in one.

As might be guessed from the data discussed earlier in this section, transition probabilities such as these differ by race and economic status. These differences tend to compound the differences that exist in enrollment rates to
produce attainment patterns that are strongly correlated to these demographic
variables. Table 2.18 examines differences in several key transition probabilities, those indicating the chance of obtaining a degree from some four-year
institution by 1986 for those students who were enrolled full-time in college
in 1980. Those enrolled in two-year institutions in 1980, for example, had a
20 percent probability of obtaining a bachelor's degree by 1980, which corresponds, rounding aside, to the sum of the first three columns of Table 2.17.
As Table 2.18 makes clear, there are large differences in probabilities between
whites and blacks as well as between students in the upper two quartiles of
socioeconomic status and those in the lower two. No matter which type of
college is considered, black students and those from lower socioeconomic
backgrounds have lower probabilities than others of obtaining a bachelor's
degree within five and a half years of initial enrollment.[25] The factors asso-

25. Anderson (1984, 14) found that, among blacks alone, those in predominantly black institutions had higher completion rates than those who were not. This difference became insignificant,

Table 2.19   **Educational Attainment in 1986, High School Class of 1980, by Demographic Group (percentage of each race/ethnic/socioeconomic status group that had graduated or were enrolled)**

Racial/Ethnic Group and SES Quartile	Graduates of 4-Year Institutions			Enrolled in 4-Year, Full-Time	Graduate of 2- or 3-Year Program
	Selective	Other Public	Other Private		
Hispanic:					
Lowest	0	4	1	2	8
Second	0	9	2	2	11
Third	2	7	2	4	5
Highest	1	17	6	13	6
Other:					
Lowest	0	12	3	4	14
Second	3	16	5	2	12
Third	6	19	3	9	10
Highest	9	28	6	12	10
Black:					
Lowest	0	8	2	3	6
Second	0	7	3	3	6
Third	0	13	6	6	8
Highest	3	20	8	4	6
White:					
Lowest	0	7	2	2	5
Second	0	10	4	4	10
Third	1	19	6	4	9
Highest	5	27	12	6	7

Source: Calculations based on High School and Beyond.
Note: SES refers to socioeconomic status, as defined in High School and Beyond.

ciated with college completion are further analyzed in Chapter 4 in the examination of the effects of various financial aid programs.

The resulting patterns of attainment are illustrated in Table 2.19, using the 1986 levels for 1980 high school graduates. Degree attainment in all three types of four-year institutions rises with socioeconomic status. Particularly striking is the near absence of low-socioeconomic-status students among the graduates of highly selective institutions. If these colleges in fact produce a sizable portion of the leaders in various sectors of the economy, it is clear that few young people from poor families are making their way into this elite. Differences by race are less pronounced once socioeconomic status is controlled for, though there is still a gap evident in degrees from public four-year institutions between Hispanic and black young people on the one side and other nonwhites and whites on the other.

---

however, when other factors were held constant, including the student's grade point average, whether the student lived on campus, and whether the student knew a faculty member who could write a letter of recommendation for him or her.

Table 2.20   **Selected Demographic Characteristics by Educational Attainment in 1986**

Educational Attainment in 1986	% of Those in Each Attainment Group Who Were Members of Selected Groups		
	Low-SES Black	Low-SES White	High-SES White
Graduate, selective four-year	0	0	68
Graduate, other public four-year	3	7	40
Graduate, other private four-year	2	5	48
Enrolled, four-year, full-time	4	7	34
Two- or three-year degree	4	9	19
Vocational certificate	6	15	15
Some postsecondary	7	14	21
High school only	6	27	6
Not high school graduate	9	32	0
Total	5	15	22

Source: Calculations based on High School and Beyond.
Note: SES refers to socioeconomic status quartile as defined in High School and Beyond.

Another way of looking at these resulting patterns of attainment is to observe the composition of the cohort of graduates from each type of institution, as shown in Table 2.20. Among graduates of very selective colleges and universities, fewer than 1 percent were from the bottom quartile of socioeconomic status, black or white, while 69 percent were top-quartile whites. Other public and private four-year colleges had some low-socioeconomic-status representation among their graduates, but in both cases over 40 percent of their graduates were high-status whites. The pattern was much the same for those still enrolled full-time in four-year institutions. Comparing these percentages to the percentage of these three groups in the entire high school class of 1980, it is clear that high-status whites were greatly overrepresented among four-year college graduates and that the poor were underrepresented.

2.4 Summary

Growth and inequality have been two distinguishing characteristics of college enrollment in the United States. The total number of college students has grown almost without pause for the last century, and this growth has continued in the most recent decade despite a decline in the number of 18-year-olds in the population. Since 1950, this growth has been accompanied by increases in the proportion of women, part-time students, and older students. During these recent decades of growth, the institutional landscape of higher education has been transformed by the expansion of public colleges and universities, especially the two-year community colleges. The growth in college enrollment has been both result and cause of the steady advance in educational attainment in the population. The percentage of those 25–29 who had finished four or more years of college increased from 6 in 1940 to 23 in 1988.

College enrollments are also marked by inequality—that is to say, inequality of composition rather than inequality of access, although remnants of the latter may exist as well. High school graduates face markedly different probabilities of attending college, depending on their aptitude and socioeconomic status. Among college choices, there are also important distinctions between highly selective undergraduate institutions, other four-year institution, and two-year colleges. The economic and racial composition of colleges in each of these classes often differs markedly, ranging from a handful of affluent and predominantly private institutions to the equally small number of historically black colleges and the vast collection of blue-collar community colleges. The overall growth in enrollments noted above has in effect utilized and created the division of labor evident in these institutional differences: the public institutions, especially the two-year colleges, have opened college to those of modest means. Initial enrollment does not guarantee completion, however, and there is evidence that completion rates also differ by race and socioeconomic status, even controlling for the type of institution. Still, whatever differences in enrollment and completion exist, they appear to be considerably smaller than those that would have been observed in the first half of the century, before the enormous growth in total enrollments.

3   Explaining the Demand

What can economic models contribute to an understanding of the college enrollment patterns we observe? The aim of this chapter is to go beyond the basic facts of enrollment presented in Chapter 2 in order to seek explanations based on existing models in the economics of education. In the language of economics, the process of enrollment is seen as a manifestation of demand by potential students and their families for the service called college training. (However, this parallel is not exact in that students must also contribute their own time as an input to the "production" process; thus, they become instruments of supply as well.) Enrollment then is equivalent to the quantity demanded of this service. But, as is the case in markets for other goods, the amount demanded will also depend on aspects of supply, and it is important to recognize these factors as well as those that affect only demand. In the market for undergraduate education, one especially important aspect of supply is "non-price rationing," or mechanisms other than the fluctuation in price that bring demand and supply into balance. The most prominent form of such rationing is selective admissions policies.

Section 3.1 discusses the application of economic models of demand to the case of undergraduate education. It notes that the benefits of higher education may come in monetary or nonmonetary forms. The monetary benefits, which arise from the increased earnings associated with college, provide the basis for a clear set of implications linking relative earnings and college demand. Section 3.2 examines evidence useful for judging the explanatory power of the economic model of demand. In particular, it presents information on the relative earnings of high school and college graduates and on the cost of attending college. Evidence from empirical studies of enrollment is also reviewed, and the estimated effects of economic return, cost, and other variables are noted. Section 3.3 considers two important aspects of supply in this market that influence the amount and distribution of demand—admissions and recruitment. It focuses particularly on the criteria used in determining who is admitted and the likely effect of this process on demand. There is a brief concluding section.

3.1   Economic Models of Demand

Over the years, economists have demonstrated that almost any human activity is susceptible to analysis in terms of the formalistic concepts of microeconomics, and college training is no exception. According to economic models, people enroll in college because they believe it will do something for them. Although it is not necessary to be certain what the actual effects are in order to be able to analyze or predict behavior, it is helpful to have a notion of what goes on during the time a student is enrolled in college. Most economic models are based on the underlying assumption that education, including college education, enables students to become more productive workers. An alternative view is that colleges function primarily by identifying the most able young people rather than by transforming anyone. It is necessary to consider both these points of view in any assessment of the demand for undergraduate places. Before proceeding to these issues, however, several preliminary questions need to be addressed.

3.1.1   Issues in Applying Economic Models of Demand

In applying conventional economic models to the demand for undergraduate education, it helps to be clear on some basic questions of definition. At least three such questions are worth considering. First, how is demand in this market measured? The most obvious measure is enrollment, which can be differentiated by full-time and part-time status. An aspect of enrollment at the individual level is its timing. How long after high school do young people wait before enrolling, and do they drop out for spells after first enrolling? Another aspect of demand—one that is probably more useful than enrollments for judging demand at many institutions—is the number of applications. This measure, along with the prices that students and their families are willing to pay, serves as one metric for determining whether there has been an increase in the demand for places in highly selective colleges. Quality is another aspect in measuring the amount demanded. Few would argue that the quality of a year's enrollment is the same for all institutions, but there are no widely accepted measures of it. The use of expenditures to aggregate quantity purchased has a long history in empirical demand analysis, but this approach does not seem very promising in the case of higher education, primarily because public institutions charge tuitions that are designed to be artificially low. Another reason for caution is the diversity in "output" among institutions. What is produced at the typical community college, for example, is markedly different in many respects from what is provided by many four-year liberal arts colleges.[1]

A second question of definition is, Who are the demanders in this market? Certainly, the students themselves are, as long as they are willing participants. Because students typically must sacrifice employment opportunities to attend college, they pay an implicit cost in terms of forgone earnings. In the case of independent adults considering whether to attend college, the conventional model of consumer and product seems to fit. But it would be unrealistic not to include the parents as active consumers as well in the large number of cases in which they pay for the bulk of the out-of-pocket expenses for dependent students.

Third, how well informed are these consumers about the service they are purchasing? A common assumption underlying most simple models of demand is that consumers possess reasonably complete information about the goods and services they consume as well as about prices. Yet it is manifestly clear that this assumption is not very realistic in some markets, especially where the good or service is technically complicated or where for some other reason judgments of quality are difficult. Certainly, college education falls into this category, but it is not obvious that it is any more difficult to compare the quality of colleges than it is to compare the quality of automobiles or television sets, for example. There are consumer magazines that publish assessments of complex consumer items, including automobiles. Similarly, a number of different guidebooks publish information on colleges and universities. Controversy has surfaced in recent years, however, regarding one news magazine's attempt to provide a ranking of the best colleges, with college officials denouncing the exercise as a "travesty."[2]

3.1.2 What Explains the Demand?

Economic models of higher education, like those explaining any voluntary activity, rest on individual comparisons of benefits and costs. It is convenient to identify benefits of two kinds—the monetary return in the form of higher earnings available to graduates and other, nonmonetary benefits. As to the first, it is widely believed that college training will increase an individual's lifetime earnings potential. No more succinct statement of this view is available than that reported by Henry Adams ([1918] 1946, 305–6). As a member of the Harvard faculty in the 1870s, Adams asked one of his students what he intended to do with his college education. The student replied, "The degree of Harvard College is worth money to me in Chicago."

---

1. For a study of what characteristics of colleges are thought to be important indicators of quality by high-ability students and their parents, see Litten and Hall (1989).
2. Deirdre Carmody, "Ranking of 'Best Colleges' Rankles Many Educators," *New York Times,* 25 October 1989, p. 23. For the rankings referred to in this case, see *U.S. News and World Report,* 16 October 1989.

In the economics literature, this view finds expression in the theory of human capital, which envisions the prospective student as making the decision about whether to enroll in college in the manner any investor evaluates a potential investment. The costs of the investment, which include the earnings that would be forgone during college, are weighed against the likely returns, which come in the form of increased earnings. Such a student invests up to the point at which the marginal benefit of another unit of education no longer exceeds its cost.[3]

That college graduates usually earn more than nongraduates is clear. Exactly why this is so is another question. The explanation normally associated with the human capital model is that college training makes a person more productive and thus able to command a higher wage in the labor market. An alternative view is that colleges and universities function primarily to sort or screen high school graduates, identifying the ones with the most ability. According to Arrow (1973), higher education can be seen as providing a two-part filter enabling society to select able people—one part the selection of applicants and the other the failing out of the those who perform poorly. The emphasis in this model is selection rather than any enhancement in productivity. A college degree becomes a credential, one helpful in obtaining increased earnings but one more or less unrelated to any training that might occur during college.[4]

Students and their families may also derive nonmonetary benefits from college. One can think of many reasons to desire college training that are unrelated to future employment prospects, ranging from increased appreciation for literature or geological formations to the social and recreational activities available to students on most college campuses. At one level, these nonpecuniary motives for enrolling in college are no different from the preferences that underlie the consumption of most goods and services. There is, of course, no accounting for tastes. Taken to one extreme, the motives underlying college enrollment may be something close to an imperative of social class. Among some groups in society, the notion that a child would not go to college is almost heresy, no matter what the monetary return. For these demanders, "that ancient and honorable degree"[5] of bachelor of arts or science amounts to a minimum level of acceptable education. From recreation to social class requirements, considerations such as these are usually lumped together as "consumption" aspects of college. They constitute no less a valid foundation for

3. For discussions of the human capital model as applied to education, see Becker (1964) or Freeman (1986). For a recent review and discussion of the demand for higher education, see Becker (1990).

4. A corresponding change, according to this point of view, has been an increase in the credential requirements of jobs corresponding to the increase in the number of people with college degrees. Fallows (1985, 55) cites surveys that indicate a marked increase since the Depression in the percentage of employers who require a college degree.

5. Words taken from the traditional conferring of bachelor's degrees by the dean of arts and sciences at Duke University.

the demand for college than the desire for increased future earnings, and they are assumed to be part of measured demand.[6]

With regard to monetary benefits, the economic model of demand provides a clear empirical implication: a given person will tend to invest in more education as the economic payoff increases. According to the model, an increase in the earnings differential between high school and college graduates will tend to increase the amount of college training demanded. An increase in the college earnings advantage, whether it were attributable to screening or to the productivity effects of college training, would still enhance the attractiveness of going to college from the student's perspective. From society's point of view, however, it is important to know the extent to which education-related earnings differential can be attributed to the training itself. Because college students on average tend to have higher measured ability than those who do not go on beyond high school, only a portion of the observed earnings differential can be attributed to college training. Most statistical studies have concluded that this portion is relatively large, with no more than about 15 percent of observed differences being due to factors other than education, but a recent study by Behrman et al. (1980) suggests that nonschool factors are much more important.[7]

Another important set of implications of the economic model of demand relates to the costs of education and the role of capital market imperfections. According to that model, an increase in college costs will decrease college enrollment. An increase in the level of tuition, for example, would be expected to decrease the demand for higher education. Another reason for high costs is imperfection in the capital market arising from the ignorance, risk, and lack of collateral that are inherent in the market. The increased cost of capital caused by these problems would also tend to decrease the amount of education demanded (see, e.g., Becker 1964; or Nerlove 1972). This problem may be especially severe for high school graduates from low-income families, who tend to have much less ready access to capital than their more affluent counterparts. In the presence of these imperfections, the human capital model predicts that equally able students from the former group will be less likely to go to college than those from the latter. Adding to the disparity created by differential access to capital, disadvantaged students may also simply face more risk, owing to discrimination or a more volatile return to education. According to one survey, the percentage of respondents who think higher education is a good investment rises with income.[8]

6. For an extended discussion of the demand for education, see Freeman (1986, 367).

7. Their estimates imply that, when family background, including genetic effects, is held constant, the estimated effects of schooling on earnings fall by as much as two-thirds (Behrman et al. 1980, 28).

8. For a discussion of these survey results, and for an elaboration of this argument, see Mortenson, (1990, 33–34, 28). Mortenson also notes (pp. 43ff.) that low-income individuals may be more risk averse. Both these factors would explain a reluctance on the part of low-income families to use loans to finance college.

3.2   Evidence

Economic theory suggests that the demand for undergraduate places should be affected by the potential economic reward from attending college, the cost of attending college, and other factors that might influence the "consumption" aspects of college. This section presents two kinds of evidence on such influences relevant to the demand for undergraduate places. The first is evidence on broad trends in the variables thought to be important. The second kind of evidence comes from statistical studies intended specifically to analyze the demand for college. The section begins by focusing on the two most prominent sets of factors, economic returns and costs. Then it turns to a consideration of other factors that appear to be important in explaining the demand for undergraduate places.

3.2.1   The Economic Payoff of Attending College

In 1987, college graduates earned half again as much as high school graduates and also experienced less unemployment than others in the labor force. Among men aged 25–34, college graduates earned an average of $34,485, while those who had completed only high school earned an average of $22,990. As noted above, not all this earnings premium can be attributed to education itself, but enough of can be to cause the economic payoff to be seen as a major determinant of demand. As noted below, statistical studies show that college enrollment usually goes up when the economic payoff goes up. This consideration thus assigns a central role to the labor market in the determination of the demand for higher education.

The story of the last two decades of changes in relative earnings in the United States has been one of bust and boom for college graduates. During the 1970s, the relative earnings of college graduates declined markedly, apparently as the result of large increases in the supply of college graduates. In Table 3.1, the college earnings advantage is measured by the percentage difference by which average earnings for college graduates exceeded that for high school graduates. This measure is distinct from the rate of return, which is calculated below. As shown in Table 3.1, the college earnings advantage fell between 1970 and 1979, from 42 to 29 percent for men and from 45 to 37 percent for women, prompting the suggestion that the country may have "overinvested" in college training.[9] By around 1980, however, labor market conditions—a slowing in the growth of new graduates and continued increases in the demand for educated workers—had combined to reverse this decline. As a result, the college earnings advantage rose again, eventually exceeding the previous peak differentials observed around 1970 (see, e.g., Murphy and Welch 1989). Table 3.1 also shows that college graduates have enjoyed considerably lower rates of unemployment than those with less education, further contributing to the apparent economic advantage of college.

9. For discussions of the overinvestment question, see Becker (1964) or Freeman (1975a).

Table 3.1   **Earnings and Unemployment by Educational Attainment, 1970, 1979, and 1987**

	1970	1979	1987
Mean earnings (ages 25–34):[a]			
Men:			
High school graduates ($)	8,999	16,537	22,990
Some college ($)	10,398	17,829	25,534
College graduates ($)[b]	12,779	21,324	34,485
College earnings advantage (%)[c]	42	29	50
Women:			
High school graduates ($)	5,629	10,563	16,237
Some college ($)	6,409	12,244	19,331
College graduates ($)[b]	8,171	14,494	25,329
College earnings advantage (%)[c]	45	37	56
Unemployment rate (ages 25–64):			
All	3.3	4.4	5.7
High school graduates	2.9	4.4	6.3
Some college	2.9	3.5	4.5
College graduates[b]	1.3	2.1	2.3

Sources: U.S. Bureau of the Census, *Current Population Reports,* Series P-60, *Money Income of Households, Families and Persons in the United States,* No. 80 (1971), table 49; No. 129 (1981), table 52; and No. 162 (1989), table 35; Bureau of Labor Statistics, Bulletin no. 2340 (Washington, D.C.: U.S. Government Printing Office, August 1989), table 67.

[a]Year-round, full-time workers.

[b]Four or more years of college.

[c]Percentage diffenence between mean earnings for college over high school.

To see how the relative earnings of college graduates changed year by year, Figure 3.1 shows data over time for both the college enrollment rate for 18- to 24-year-olds and the college–to–high school earnings ratio for men aged 25–34. According to the later series, the college earnings advantage reached a peak in 1969, fell thereafter, reaching its nadir in 1980, and finally rose again, exceeding its previous high during the 1980s. The figure also shows the unemployment rate for those aged 20–24; this rate climbed fairly steadily until 1982, after which it receded somewhat.

From the perspective of an individual who is contemplating whether to attend college, these changes in relative earnings could loom large. To illustrate the effect of these changes in a format made familiar by the human capital model, Table 3.2 summarizes calculations of the financial payoff from attending college as viewed from the perspective of a high school graduate in each of three years. In the spirit of similar calculations of the returns to schooling (see, e.g., Becker 1964; or Freeman 1975a), the individual is assumed to compare (1) the lifetime earnings stream of the average high school graduate to (2) a four-year investment in college followed by the lifetime earnings of an average college graduate. Calculations such as these are meant to be illustrative rather than realistic, in that they implicitly assume that an individual

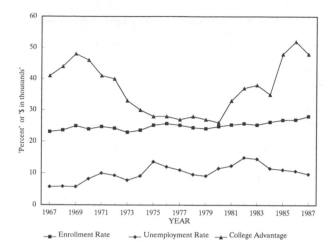

—■— Enrollment Rate   —♦— Unemployment Rate   —▲— College Advantage

Figure 3.1   College enrollment, unemployment, and college earnings advantage, 1967–87.

Sources: Total undergraduate enrollment: estimated, as 86.0 percent of total enrollment in institutions of higher education (the ratio for 1969 and 1970), from U.S. Department of Education (1989, table 148, p. 167 [for 1965–68], and table 158, p. 177 [1969–88]). 18–24 population: U.S. Bureau of the Census, *Current Population Reports*, Series P-20, *School Enrollment—Social and Economic Characteristics of Students: October 1986*, No. 429 (1988), table A-8. Unemployment rate: U.S. Bureau of Labor Statistics, *Labor Force Statistics Derived from the Current Population Survey, 1948–87*, Bulletin no. 2307 (Washington, D.C.: U.S. Government Printing Office, August 1988), table A-31. College–to–high school earnings advantage: unpublished estimates, provided by Richard Freeman and McKinley Blackburn, of the ratio of the average income of men with 16 years of schooling to that of men with 12 years of schooling, full-time year-round workers aged 25–34.

knows with certainty the alternative earnings streams open to him or her in the future.[10] In addition, the entire college versus high school earnings differential is assumed to be due to additional schooling; to the extent that this is not true, of course, the calculated returns to college are overstated. On the other hand, if college training increases the nonmarket incomes of graduates, the calculated returns will be understated. Private returns take into account costs and benefits relevant to the individual: out-of-pocket tuition and other costs and increases in after-tax earnings. Social returns are based on resource costs of education, using average costs, and increases in total output, measured by before-tax earnings. Table 3.2 summarizes investment outcomes in both of two conventional forms: as a present discounted value (using a discount rate of 2 percent) and as an internal rate of return.[11] All amounts are expressed in 1988 dollars.

10. One way such uncertainty could be reflected would be to use a discount rate that approximates the rate of return to risky assets rather than a risk-free rate. Alternatively, the earnings differentials themselves could be adjusted, with no change to the discount rate.

11. The internal rate of return is defined as that discount rate that makes the discounted present value equal to zero.

Table 3.2   Calculated Returns to College Training Based on Average Earnings
                   by Age, Sex, and Education

	1970	1979	1987
Present value of investment (1988 dollars)[a]:			
Private			
Men	244,600	202,400	267,900
Women	124,100	86,300	144,700
Social:			
Men	315,700	287,700	363,500
Women	139,300	103,400	185,400
Rate of return:			
Private:			
Men	8.6	7.5	9.6
Women	7.6	6.5	8.5
Social:			
Men	8.3	7.3	9.1
Women	6.6	5.6	7.8

Sources: U.S. Bureau of the Census, *Current Population Reports,* Series P-60, *Money Income of Households, Families and Persons in the United States,* No. 80 (1971), table 49; No. 129 (1981), table 52; and No. 162 (1989), table 35; U.S. Internal Revenue Service, *Statistics of Income—Individual Income Tax Returns* (Washington, D.C.: U.S Government Printing Office, 1970), table 1, p. 7, and (1979), table 1.1, p. 9; *SOI Bulletin* (Spring 1989), Fig. M, p. 14; U.S. Bureau of the Census, *Statistical Abstract of the United States* (Washington, D.C.: U.S. Government Printing Office), *1980,* p. 308; *1981,* p. 328; *1982–83,* p. 259; *1988,* pp. 270, 341; *1989,* p. 315; U.S. Department of Education (1989, 168, 281, 300).

[a]Present values were calculated in constant dollars using a 2 percent discount rate for a person age 18 who expected to work through age 64 and who is considering attending college full-time between ages 19 and 22. Expected earnings were based on mean money income of year-round full-time workers with high school only and four or more years of college, by sex, for four age groups: 25–34, 35–44, 45–54, and 55–64. Workers under 25 were assumed to earn the average for the 25–34 age group. Private returns were calculated after federal income, social security, and state income taxes. Average federal income tax rates were calculated according to income level. A single average state income tax rate was calculated for the nation for each year. For the three years, the social security tax rates were 0.048, 0.0715, and 0.0715. The calculated average state income tax rates were 0.014, 0.022, and 0.027. Private returns account for the direct cost of college by using the average tuition, room, and board for all colleges and universities. The social returns were calculated using before-tax incomes and estimates of the average educational and general expenditures per full-time-equivalent student. The 1985–86 average, adjusted for inflation, was used for 1987. In current dollars, average costs (tuition, fees, room, and board) were $1,635, $2,809, and $5,510 in the three years. The figure for 1970 was calculated as the weighted average of tuition, fees, room, and board of all public and private college institutions, using enrollments as weight.

For both men and women, the calculations indicate that college is a good investment: the present values are positive, and the rates of return exceed comparable real rates that borrowers generally face. Of course, the force of this conclusion is blunted to the extent that measured earnings differences overstate the pure effect of additional education. What is most important about the table, however, is the pattern of change in the measured returns over time, a pattern whose shape depends little on the assumption one makes about the independent effect of schooling on earnings differentials. The central message of Table 3.2 is the decline in the measured return from 1970 to 1979 and its subsequent rebound. Despite real increases in college tuitions, noted below, the changing labor market conditions illustrated here and in Table 3.1 increased the attractiveness of college training as a purely financial investment. Calculations of both private and social returns support this conclusion.

How has the return to college education differed by sex and race? Table 3.2 suggests that calculated returns based entirely on average earnings differentials yield substantially higher returns for men than for women, though the differentials appear to have narrowed between 1979 and 1987. Table 3.3 examines changes in percentage earnings differentials by sex and race between 1969 and 1987. For the years shown, the college earnings advantage was lowest in either 1974 or 1980 for each of the four groups. The recent improvement in the earnings advantage has been the greatest for black males (from 28 to 90 percent) and the least for black females (from 82 to 92 percent in 1984, followed by a fall to 89 percent in 1987). Supporting these conclusions, Murphy and Welch (1989, 20) find similar patterns over time when workers are classified by years of experience. The increase in the college earnings advantage from the late 1970s to the late 1980s has been widespread.

There is persuasive evidence that earnings differentials such as these exert an important influence on college enrollments. Freeman (1986) cites results from five time-series studies for the United States, all of which imply that increases in the college earnings advantage lead to increases in college enrollment. Referring to his own estimates, Freeman (1975a, 304) states, "The major factor determining enrollments of college graduates in the period under study was the state of the labor market." Estimates of the implied elasticity of enrollment with respect to earnings for college graduates range from 0.7 to 1.8. Studies using cross-sectional data also support the importance of earnings differentials. Bishop's (1977, 297) analysis of the college enrollment

Table 3.3   College Earnings Advantage by Sex and Race, Selected Years
(percentage difference in mean incomes of college graduates and high school graduates, 25 years and older)

	Male		Female	
	Black	White	Black	White
1969	48	59	93	67
1974	28	46	85	58
1980	38	57	82	66
1984	73	67	92	79
1987	90	77	89	86

Source: U.S. Bureau of the Census, *Current Population Reports,* Series P-60, *Money Income of Households, Families and Persons in the United States,* No. 75 (1970), table 47; No. 101 (1976), table 58; No. 132 (1982), table 51; No. 151 (1986), table 33; No. 162 (1989), table 35.

choices of 20,000 high school juniors in 1960 yielded the expected effect, but only for those in the middle two ability quartiles. Analyzing a sample of World War II veterans, Willis and Rosen (1979) found that predicted earnings gains had a significant effect on the decision to attend college. In addition, some limited support of the model was provided by a study by Fiorito and Dauffenbach (1982) of undergraduates' choices of major field.[12]

Despite the support that empirical studies have given this particular implication of the economic model of demand for higher education, projections based on estimated models have not succeeded in predicting future enrollments. For example, Freeman's model implied that, as a result of the decline in the rate of return to college training, college enrollments would increase by only 5 percent between 1973 and 1985—in fact, however, they increased by 20 percent (see Table 1.3). A more extreme example is given by a model developed by Dresch (1975), which reflects both the demand for college places, as a function of relative earnings, and the labor market's response to changes in the supply of educated workers. On the basis of the anticipation that increases in the number of college graduates would drive down their salaries, thus reducing the incentive for high school graduates to go to college, the model projected a 33 percent decline in college enrollments between 1970 and 2000, a drop far greater than anything that appears to be likely in 1990.[13] Another question is raised by the failure of enrollment among black males to follow the strong increase in the college earnings advantage for them, shown in Table 3.3. It should be quickly noted that the validity of models can never be judged solely by the accuracy of their predictions since other variables not accounted for in the equation could well change over time. But these results do certainly argue for caution in the use of such models.

3.2.2 Costs

A second major factor in the demand for undergraduate education that would figure prominently in most economic models is cost. The most obvious costs are of course the tuition and fees paid by students and their families, but economists have been quick to point out that there are important implicit costs as well, in the form of forgone earnings. As with the earnings data above, it is useful both to document recent changes in costs and to review evidence regarding their effect on demand. That college tuitions have been rising in recent years is a fact that has been reported widely. To provide some perspective on this increase, Table 3.4 summarizes data on college costs for selected academic years between 1959–60 and 1987–88. The cost figures shown do

---

12. In their analysis of trends in enrollments in the arts and sciences, Turner and Bowen (1990) suggest that students may be more sensitive to job prospects in bad economic times than in prosperous periods.

13. As summarized in Table 2.9, projections to 2000 based on the assumption of a continuation of 1988 enrollment rates imply an increase in 19 percent over the 1976 total of 11.1 million (see also Table 2.8).

not account for scholarships, a point that is discussed below. Averages, all expressed in 1988 dollars, are shown separately for universities, other four-year institutions, and two-year colleges and are further split between public and private. The top section of the table combines tuition, required fees, room and board; the second section shows only tuition and required fees. A comparison of these two sections shows why an emphasis on tuition alone may be misleading. Both the differences between public and private institutions and changes in costs over time in public institutions appear to be smaller when room and board are included.

Focusing on the more inclusive measure of costs, Table 3.4 clearly shows

Table 3.4   **Trends in College Costs (amounts in constant 1988 dollars)**

	School Year						
	1959–60	1964–65	1969–70	1974–75	1979–89	1984–85	1987–88
Tuition, room, and board:[a]							
Public:							
All	3,277	3,568	3,668	3,437	3,108	3,747	3,960
University	3,521	3,947	4,153	3,870	3,571	4,287	4,680
Other four-year	2,918	3,256	3,461	3,426	3,156	3,868	4,060
Two-year	2,250	2,396	2,900	2,944	2,616	3,086	3,160
Private:							
All	6,047	7,162	7,714	7,483	7,052	9,018	10,390
University	6,798	8,270	8,903	8,963	8,458	11,262	13,220
Other four-year	5,699	6,798	7,379	6,940	6,748	8,630	9,970
Two-year	4,141	5,464	6,077	5,697	5,385	6,820	6,790
Ratio of private to public (all)	1.3	2.0	2.1	2.2	2.3	2.4	2.6
Tuition:[a]							
Public:							
All	799	913	985	950	837	1,068	1,160
University	939	1,119	1,302	1,317	1,206	1,524	1,750
Other four-year	623	841	933	985	950	1,228	1,320
Two-year	316	372	543	609	510	642	690
Private:							
All	3,173	4,086	4,674	4,655	4,494	5,844	6,820
University	3,705	4,871	5,516	5,748	5,471	7,523	8,770
Other four-year	2,934	3,842	4,476	4,297	4,336	5,646	6,670
Two-year	1,739	2,636	3,153	3,006	2,960	3,832	3,910
Ratio of private to public (all)	4.0	4.5	4.7	4.9	5.4	5.5	5.9
Tuition, room, and board as % of family income:							
All public	14.6	13.7	12.2	11.4	10.3	12.3	12.3
All private	26.9	27.4	25.6	24.8	23.4	29.6	32.3

Sources: U.S. Department of Education (1989, table 258); U.S. Department of Education (1969, table 120); U.S. Bureau of the Census, *Statistical Abstract of the United States* (Washington, D.C.: U.S. Government Printing Office, 1988), table 700.

[a]Includes required fees. In-state tuitions and fees are used for calculations.

that college costs have risen, in real terms, over the nearly three decades covered by the table. Costs at both public and private institutions rose from their
1959–60 levels and then fell again in the late 1970s, in the case of public
institutions almost to their previous levels.[14] During the 1980s, however, the
trend in costs has been all upward. Costs have increased in every institutional
category, ranging from 21 percent for public two-year colleges to 56 percent
for private universities. For the latter group of institutions, this increase
amounts to a remarkable 5.7 percent annual growth rate in costs, over and
above tuition.

These are the increases that served to focus public attention on college costs
during the 1980s, creating a mini-firestorm of debate over the management of
colleges and universities, as discussed in Part III. Such increases have a different relevance in the current section. Namely, what do they imply for college
enrollments? One way to begin answering that question is to relate the increases to a measure of capacity, such as family income. The last two rows in
Table 3.4 do this. Using this yardstick, the increases in college costs, at least
on the public side, look less ominous. The average cost for public institutions
in 1987–88 was actually a smaller percentage of median family income (12.3
percent) than it was in 1959–60, though it is higher than it was at the beginning of the 1980s. For private institutions, the recent steep increases have
pushed the cost-to-income ratio to unprecedented heights, reaching almost
one-third in 1987–88. One aspect of the changes in college costs made clear
by this table is the relative cost of public and private institutions. Based on
tuition, room, and board, costs at private institutions exceeded those at public
institutions by about 30 percent in 1959–60, but they have been at least
double the public figure since then. In the most recent year shown, the average
private cost was 2.6 times the average public cost, and the ratio for universities was 2.8.

The figures shown in Table 3.4 fail to reflect economic costs in at least two
respects. First, the figures measure only the "sticker price" of college; they do
not reflect the price discount implicit when institutions award scholarships out
of internal funds. Aggregate financial data on the ratio of scholarships and
fellowships from unrestricted funds to tuition and fees can be used to approximate the size of this discount. In 1979–80, the average discount calculated in
this way was 6.7 percent for public institutions and 8.2 percent for private. By
1984–85, the discounts had diverged, with the public rate falling to 6.6 percent and the private rising to 11.0. Taking these discounts into account would
modify the trends shown in Table 3.4 only slightly, however. For example,
netting out the discount implies that the private-public ratio of costs was 2.2
in 1979–80 and 2.3 in 1984–85, instead of 2.3 and 2.4, respectively.[15] The

14. The overall average cost for public institutions in 1979–80 is lower than the comparable
average in 1959–60 only because of an increase in the share of two-year enrollment; the average
cost for each of the three types of institutions actually increased over the period.

15. Calculations of the ratio of scholarships and fellowships from unrestricted funds to tuition
and fees from students are based on U.S. Department of Education (1989, 293–94, 302–3).

Table 3.5   The Economic Cost of College: Some Illustrations
                    (1988 constant dollars)

	1969–70	1974–75	1979–80	1984–85	1987–88
Forgone earnings:[a]					
Male	15,480	14,937	13,619	12,909	12,925
Female	9,177	9,011	8,677	9,077	9,128
Tuition, room, board, and forgone earnings:					
Public university:					
Male	19,632	18,807	17,189	17,195	17,605
Female	13,330	12,881	12,248	13,364	13,808
Private university:					
Male	24,383	23,900	22,076	24,170	26,145
Female	18,080	17,974	17,135	20,339	22,348
Ratio, private/public:					
Male	1.2	1.3	1.3	1.4	1.5
Female	1.4	1.4	1.4	1.5	1.6
Tuition and forgone earnings:					
Public two-year college:					
Male	16,022	15,546	14,129	13,551	13,615
Female	9,720	9,620	9,187	9,719	9,818

[a]Calculated as three-fourths (to reflect the proportion of the calendar year taken up by school) mean earnings for full-time, year-round workers, aged 25–34 for high school graduates multiplied by one minus the unemployment rate for high school graduates in the labor force, reduced by 20 percent to reflect income and payroll taxes.

effects of scholarships and other financial aid on demand are discussed in more detail in Chapter 4.

Perhaps the more important shortcoming of the cost figures shown in the table is that they ignore the forgone earnings of attending college. It is useful to ask whether looking at costs using the broader economic concept changes the conclusions one draws from the recent history of college tuition hikes. Table 3.5 attempts to broaden this perspective by adding forgone earnings to produce a measure of total college costs over time.[16] Despite the refinements used in defining it, the measure of forgone earnings employed here is still quite crude, based as it is on market-wide averages. As is evident from the table's first two rows, forgone earnings for males have exceeded those for females over the nearly 20-year period covered by the table, though this gap has narrowed. For a student of either sex, however, it is clear that forgone earnings make up a significant share of total costs. For a male attending a private university in 1987–88, for example, forgone earnings represent just under half total costs; for a female attending such an institution, forgone earn-

16. For the purpose of Table 3.5, forgone earnings are defined somewhat more exactly than for the calculations used for the rates of return in Table 3.2, whose calculations were intended to parallel those of Freeman (1975a). Forgone earnings are here defined as three-quarters of mean high school earnings for workers 25–34, the three-quarters reflecting the proportion of the calendar year taken up by school, adjusted by the applicable unemployment rate and taxes.

ings amount to about 40 percent. Owing to the rapid increase in private tuitions, the share of forgone earnings in total costs has of course fallen for those attending private institutions, but it remains a significant portion.

One implication of measuring costs using this broader concept is that the relative cost disadvantage of private institutions evident in Table 3.4 is substantially reduced. Whereas a comparison using out-of-pocket costs shows that private universities are 2.8 times as expensive as public ones, for example, the inclusion of the forgone earnings measure used here reduces the ratio to 1.5 for men and 1.6 for women. These higher private costs do not necessarily imply that the rate of return to private college education is less than that to the public alternative, however, since the earning advantage may differ as well.[17] For comparison, Table 3.5 also presents the opportunity cost of attending a public two-year institution on the assumption that there would be no additional room and board costs. In this case, forgone earnings become by far the dominant portion of total costs.

Numerous statistical studies have examined the effect of changes in tuition and other costs on college enrollment, and the expected negative sign has been generally found. Two of these studies, by Radner and Miller (1975) and Manski and Wise (1983), illustrate the complex methodological issues that must be addressed in assessing the effect of costs or other variables on college choice. Both these studies use a model that explicitly recognizes the fact that high school graduates have several discrete options, including different kinds of colleges as well as not enrolling at all. They conclude in general that the probability of college attendance is negatively related to college costs. A review of 25 studies, by Leslie and Brinkman (1987), yielded a consensus effect, measured as the decline in the college enrollment rate for a $100 increase in tuition, of 0.7 percentage points. The median among the estimates produced by 10 studies cited by McPherson (1978) yields approximately the same value. Based on the corresponding mean values, this coefficient translates to an elasticity of about -0.7.[18] The conclusion that tuition exerts a negative effect on college enrollment is also confirmed in recent research based on the analysis of individual behavior (see, e.g., Ehrenberg and Sherman 1984; or Schwartz 1986).

Two questions of special importance are whether financial aid has an opposite (and equal) effect on enrollment and whether this tuition effect differs according to the income level of the student. The evidence regarding the first question tends to support the symmetry of tuition and financial aid effects, though the coefficients are not always equal in absolute value.[19] Obviously,

17. Ehrenberg (1989) provides evidence of a comparative earnings advantage for graduates of law schools of private universities. Earnings equations presented by James et al. (1988) suggest that higher financial returns are associated with attendance at selective institutions.

18. If the enrollment rate is 33 percent and average tuition in units of $100 is 34.2 ($3,400), the elasticity would be -0.73.

19. For the clearest test of these effects, see Manski and Wise (1983, 112ff.).

this finding is important in any assessment of the likely effects of financial aid programs. As for variation in the tuition effect by income, most studies that address it suggest that low-income students are most responsive to changes in tuition.[20]

Despite the high degree of consensus in statistical studies regarding the effect of college costs on demand, the recent experience of many selective institutions seems to belie this finding. Applications to the nation's most prestigious colleges and universities appear to have increased at the same time as tuitions were rising at unprecedented rates. Over the period 1981–88, for example, applications to Harvard increased by 7 percent while Harvard's tuition and fees rose by 27 percent in real terms, and applications to Williams rose by 18 percent at the same time as its cost rose by 31 percent. These are by no means unrepresentative examples. Could it be that demand for undergraduate places at some institutions is not affected by cost? Or are these increases in applications merely an artifact of a broader increase in the average number of applications submitted per individual?

In order to assess the effect of changes in college costs on applications to selective institutions, I examined information on tuition and fees and applications for a sample of 24 selective colleges and universities for the years 1981–88. By comparing rates of tuition increase among schools, it was possible to determine whether unusually large increases were associated with declines in applications relative to an institution's historical level. Regressions estimated for this sample gave absolutely no indication that tuition increases exerted a negative effect on the number of applications an institution receives. Nor was an institution's "yield" rate—the percentage of accepted applicants who matriculate—influenced by tuition increases.[21] For this group of colleges, over this period at least, it appears that demand was quite insensitive to price. This finding is certainly at variance with the price sensitivity observed in numerous statistical studies. The most reasonable explanation is that demand for places in the most highly selective colleges and universities is, at least within the range of tuitions observed in the 1980s, unlike the demand for college places in general. The relatively high proportion of students at such institutions who are receiving aid may explain some of this insensitivity to price; institutional

20. See, e.g., Radner and Miller (1975, 66) and Leslie and Brinkman (1987, 198). For a contrary finding, see Ehrenberg and Sherman (1984, 218), who find a smaller elasticity for the poor than for other applicants.

21. Two basic regressions were estimated to explain applications and yield. One equation, in which the logarithm of the number of applications was the dependent variable, included dummy variables for each year and institution as well as the institution's tuition and lagged tuition, both measured in constant dollars. The coefficients on the tuition variables (standard errors in parentheses) were 0.72 (0.44) and 0.54 (0.51), respectively. Although neither was significant at the 5 percent level, an F-test showed that they were when taken together, suggesting that tuition might actually exert a *positive* effect on applications to these institutions. This might be the case if price were taken to be a signal of quality. The second equation used the change in the logarithm of applications as the dependent variable and produced coefficients of -0.07 (0.42) for the change in tuition and 0.84 (0.50) for the change in lagged tuition, the latter coefficient being significantly different from zero at the 10 percent level. Similar equations using the yield rate as the dependent variable produced insignificant coefficients for the tuition variables.

pledges to meet full need reduce or eliminate the net marginal cost of tuition increases for these students.

3.2.3   Income

There is no more common variable to be found in empirical studies of demand than income: for most commodities, the amount consumed increases with the income available to the consuming unit. In the case of college enrollment, however, the effect of income is not so straightforward. In the human capital model, family income does not itself appear as a factor in the decision to invest in college. Only to the extent that the payoff from investing in college or a student's access to capital increases with family income does this model suggest that a student's family income may be associated with demand. It is not easy to think of reasons why at least the first of these should be the case. It is far easier to imagine why the nonpecuniary component of demand for college might increase with income. To the extent that college can be viewed as one (expensive) form of family consumption, purchased for a variety of reasons that may include prestige, a positive income elasticity is not a surprising thing to find. College is in fact a highly income-elastic commodity. As shown in Chapter 2, the propensity to enroll in college rises with family income. Studies of the demand for higher education, using various measures for demand, likewise indicate a consistently positive income effect.[22] Among those who enroll, there is abundant evidence that average expenditures on college rise with family income (see, e.g., Hearn 1988; and Astin, various years). Expensive, highly selective colleges also tend to enroll comparatively affluent students.

There is reason to believe that the demand for college by the families of these upper-income students may have experienced a surge during the 1980s. Incomes for households at the top of the income distribution grew rapidly. Between 1977 and 1987, the average income of households in the top fifth of the income distribution increased in real terms by 12.5 percent, compared to just 2.8 percent for households below them.[23] In addition, the effect of these income trends on consumption was bolstered by cuts in federal income taxes and increases in the value of major household assets. The federal income tax cuts of 1981 and 1986 both reduced the tax burdens of many high-income taxpayers. Households in the upper half of the income distribution also experienced increases in net worth owing to a strong stock market and sharply increasing house values.[24]

22. See, e.g., Galper and Dunn (1969), Spies (1978), Bishop (1977), Corman (1983), and Schwartz (1986). The income effect becomes more complicated as various college alternatives are considered. Radner and Miller (1975), e.g., examine nine different types of colleges. The income effect on attendance is consistently positive only for the three classes of high-cost institutions (p. 64).

23. U.S. Bureau of the Census, *Current Population Reports*, Series P-60, *Money Income of Households, Families, and Persons in the U.S.*, No. 162 (1989), Table 12.

24. See, e.g., Richard W. Stevenson, "Housing Prices Expected to be Sluggish in the 90's," *New York Times*, 6 April 1990, p. A1.

One apparent result of these favorable trends among the affluent was an increase in the demand for high-cost colleges. Because the number of places at these colleges is more or less fixed, this apparent surge in demand was not marked by a rise in enrollments. Instead, its manifestations include an increase in the number of applications to highly selective colleges, increasing difficulty in obtaining admission, and the rise in demand for courses that coach students for taking standardized tests.[25] Another manifestation may be the increase in tuition at these institutions: a shift in demand where supply is fixed produces an increase in the market-clearing price. Although the prices charged are below that market-clearing level, as indicated by the continuance of excess demand, this apparent shift in demand has certainly allowed institutions in this submarket to increase prices without adverse effects.

3.2.4   Other Influences on Demand

Among the variables that have been found to explain college enrollment, at least three others are worth noting in particular: perceived quality of the institution, availability or proximity, and the military draft. These are in addition to the personal characteristics noted in Chapter 2, such as parents' education, measured aptitude, and high school grades, which also show up consistently as important factors explaining college enrollment.

Perceptions of Quality

Although the proposition would be widely accepted that consumers' evaluations of the quality of various colleges affect demand, the process by which consumers form their evaluations is not at all self-evident. One recent study that looked at this question showed that high-ability students most often saw as indicators of quality a large variety of courses, small classes, and well-equipped laboratories and libraries, while their parents placed greatest stress on faculty who teach as well as do research (Litten and Hall 1989, 313).[26]

---

25. For a discussion of the possibility that many families are "buying up" by turning to more expensive colleges, see Edward B. Fiske, "Private Colleges Flourish Despite Forecasts That They Will Shrivel Away," *New York Times*, 7 September 1988, p. B8. For other indications of increasing demand for these institutions, see, e.g., Deirdre Carmody, "Better Students Finding Colleges Reject Them," *New York Times*, 20 April 1988, p. B11, and "Coaching Courses for S.A.T.'s Show Sharp Rise," *New York Times*, 28 September 1988, sec. 2, p. 14.

26. As noted earlier in this chapter, one of the most prominent recent attempts to measure quality has been the rankings of colleges published by *U.S. News and World Report*. One interesting question related to these rankings is whether they have had any effect on demand. I examined this question for the sample of 24 prestigious colleges and universities that was analyzed above in connection with the effect of tuition on demand. The magazine's first ranking, published in November 1983, listed 17 of the 24 as being among the top 20 universities and liberal arts colleges in the country ("Rating the Colleges," *U.S. News and World Report*, 28 November 1983, pp. 41–48). Regressions explaining both applications and yield rates for the larger sample of institutions showed no indication that being included in these rankings had any effect on demand. For a description of the sample and the estimated equations, see text and n. 21 above. The equation used here is the same except that it adds a dummy variable for those institutions listed in the *U.S. News* ranking.

Some statistical studies have used an institution's average SAT score as a measure of perceived quality. Manski and Wise (1983, 18–19) found that the probability of a student's choosing an institution rose with this measure up to a point and then declined when the institution's average score exceeded the student's own score by more than 100 points.

Proximity

Over the last three decades, the tremendous expansion of public institutions, particularly the two-year community colleges, has markedly increased the availability and proximity of colleges. One way of seeing how this expansion affected the availability of higher education, viewed from the perspective of potential students, is to look at the percentage of 18- and 19-year-olds who lived in a county containing a college or university. In Illinois, for example, this percentage increased from 76 percent in 1950 to 92 percent in 1986. In New York, the corresponding increase was from 89 to 97 percent.[27] These figures illustrate the increased ease of attending an institution of higher education. It has been the expansion of community colleges and, to a lesser extent, state colleges that has been largely responsible for this increased availability, and the geographic distribution of the student bodies in these institutions bespeaks their largely local character. In the fall of 1989, for example, 70 percent of those attending North Carolina's community colleges lived in the same county where the college was located, and another 19 percent lived in an adjacent county.[28]

Despite the historic association between enrollment growth and increasing geographic accessibility of college, the evidence is far from overwhelming that accessibility actually leads to higher rates of college enrollment. Bishop (1977, 296) took his findings on cost effects from the early 1960s to imply that locating a college centrally within a community or establishing a four-year college where none had previously existed would increase the probability that a young person would enroll in college. However, studies that examined more directly the influence of proximity on college enrollment do not imply a

27. Calculations were made for four states. Similar changes in the percentages from 1950 to 1986 were also observed in the two other states: Delaware, from 80 to 100 percent, and North Carolina, from 53 to 92 percent. Counties containing colleges or universities were identified for the 1949–50 and 1985–86 academic years using Office of Education, Federal Security Agency, *Education Directory: Higher Education* (Washington, D.C.: U.S. Government Printing Office, 1949); and U.S. Department of Education, Office of Educational Research and Improvement, *Education Directory: Colleges and Universities, 1985–86* (Washington, D.C.: U.S. Government Printing Office, 1986). Corresponding populations were taken from the U.S. Bureau of the Census, *General Characteristics of the Population* (Washington, D.C.: U.S. Government Printing Office, 1953, 1983). I am grateful to Michael Dieffenbach for his assistance in obtaining this information.

28. Figures are for students in college transfer programs in community colleges (*Statistical Abstract of Higher Education in North Carolina, 1989–90* [Chapel Hill: University of North Carolina, April 1990], 36–38). Comparable percentages of undergraduate students from the same county were 23 percent for the University of North Carolina system and 17 percent for private colleges and universities.

strong effect. Although having a college nearby will affect the chance of attending that college, it generally does not have a large effect on the chance of attending any college.[29]

Military Draft

Although the military draft is not at present a consideration for potential college students, it certainly has been a major factor in the past. In their time-series analysis of the demand for higher education, Galper and Dunn (1969) show that enrollments have been affected by both the growth in the size of and discharges from the armed forces. The latter, along with the funding provided by the GI Bill, propelled many veterans into colleges following World War II and the Korean War. The effect of the size of the military and the existence of the draft itself was a function of draft policies toward students. Student deferments available in the 1960s appear to have boosted college enrollments.[30] Bishop (1977, 301) found that high school students in districts with the greatest draft pressure were more likely to enroll in college than were others.[31] The overall college enrollment rate climbed steadily during the Vietnam buildup of the late 1960s, although this was also a period in which the economic payoff from college training was also increasing.[32]

3.2.5   Summing Up

Two principal implications arising from economic theories of demand for college are that enrollments will be affected by the economic return available to graduates and by the net cost of attending college. There is considerable evidence that both of these influences are empirically important, although there are exceptions, such as the apparent price insensitivity of those applying to highly selective private institutions. A thorough statistical analysis of the effect of recent trends on the demand for higher education is beyond the scope of this part, but the general rise in enrollment rates is at least consistent with the implications of the economic model, in that the college earnings advantage has grown, as has the unemployment rate for young people. An analysis of

29. Both Anderson, Bowman, and Tinto (1972) and Weiler (1986) conclude that the effect of proximity is small.

30. Statements to this effect are found in Riesman (1980, 8) and the 1960 annual report for the selective service. The latter stated, "Many young men would not have pursued higher education had there not been a Selective Service program of student deferment" (quoted in Bishop 1977, 301).

31. Draft pressure was defined as the ratio of draft physicals to the stock of men classified as eligible for service. This measure differed among states because of differences in classification policies.

32. The size of the U.S. military force in Vietnam grew from 184,000 in 1965 to a peak of 536,000 in 1968, declining to less than 25,000 in 1971. The percentage of 18- to 24-year-olds enrolled as undergraduates rose from 22.1 in 1965 to 24.9 in 1969, falling to 22.9 in 1973. (*Sources:* see the legend to Figure 3.1; and U.S. Bureau of the Census, *Statistical Abstract of the United States* [Washington, D.C.: U.S. Government Printing Office], table 355 [1964], table 383 [1968], table 397 [1970], table 540 [1975], and table 598 [1977]; U.S. Department of Education [1989, table 148 (p. 167) and table 158 (p. 177)].)

recent trends would also have to take into account the apparent influence of the rise in relative incomes among the most affluent households.[33]

3.3 Rationing and Recruitment

Colleges and universities engage in two important activities that are designed to affect the size of their enrollments and the quality of their matriculants. Although these two functions are quite distinct from one another and may even appear to work at cross-purposes, the responsibility for both within a given institution typically resides in the same administrative office. The first function, evocative of the stern-faced gatekeeper, is the selection of candidates for admission. Often the source of anxiety among aspiring students, this is the traditional function of college admissions offices. In recent years, however, the prospect of a decline in the 18-year-old population has spurred institutions to devote more attention to a second function, recruitment. In the language of economics, the first constitutes a form of non-price rationing, while the second is simply marketing—the supplier's attempt to influence the demand curve.

33. As a means of suggesting the likely influences on demand, I used the data presented in Figure 3.1 to estimate an equation explaining the overall college enrollment rate for the period 1966–87. The explanatory variables included the unemployment rate for 18- to 24-year-olds, the size of the American military force in Vietnam, the mean real household income and the mean income of households in the top quintile, a weighted average of real tuition and fees in colleges and universities, and the college earnings advantage. The tuition and fees measure was a fixed-weight average of average public and private tuitions and fees, with the weight for public being 0.75, which approximates the average public share of enrollments over the period. Only three of these variables were statistically significant, and each had estimated effects in the expected (positive) direction; these were the unemployment rate, the size of the military forces in Vietnam, and the average income for households in the top quintile. The remaining variables had estimated coefficients that were very small in relation to their standard errors.

The basic estimated equation (t-statistics in parentheses) was

$$\text{ENR} = 1.54 + 0.414 \text{ UNEMP} + 0.00659 \text{ MILITARY} - 0.005 \text{ CEA} +$$
$$(0.2)(2.8)(2.3)(0.1)$$
$$0.000373 \text{ TOP5MINC} - 0.00026 \text{ MINC} + 0.00016 \text{ TRB}, \quad R^2 = 0.83$$
$$(2.1)(0.5)(0.2)$$

where ENR is the college enrollment rate, UNEMP is the unemployment rate for those 20 to 24 years of age, MILITARY is the size of the U.S. military force in Vietnam in thousands, CEA is the college earnings advantage, TOP5MINC is the real mean income for households in the top quintile of the income distribution, MINC is the real mean household income, and TRB is a weighted average of real tuition, room, and board for public (weighted 0.75) and private (0.25) institutions. (*Sources:* see Figure 3.1). When CEA was dropped from the equation, it became possible to derive estimates using the period 1965–88. In this equation, the mean household income variable (MINC) was negative and significant, with the other variables that had been significant and positive remaining so. The finding of a significant effect for the unemployment rate is consistent with the human capital model, though the insignificance of the earnings advantage is not. The significance of the top quintile average income is interesting, especially in light of the lack of significance for average household income. This finding is consistent with the view of higher education as a consumption good with a high income elasticity. Because of its high level of aggregation, however, this equation offers little more than suggestive evidence on the importance of these variables and certainly does not provide an adequate test of the economic model of demand.

At the outset, it must be admitted that there is little empirical research on how the admissions function affects demand. To be sure, some empirical studies of demand include such measures of selectivity as the average SAT scores for institutions (see, e.g., Radner and Miller 1975; and Manski and Wise 1983), but little is known about the effect of rationing places on the total demand for college or how the process influences the composition of demand. Even if the effects of such rationing are not fully understood, it seems useful at least to note its importance in this market. Few other important classes of consumer expenditures are subject to such rigorous non-price rationing. Furthermore, the admissions and recruitment functions have implications for public policy with regard to institutional preferences toward applicants of certain groups. It seems likely, for example, that affirmative action policies have increased the number of minority students in selective colleges and universities, yet these policies remain the subject of continuing debate. In 1990, the Education Department suggested that scholarships designated for minority students might be forbidden.[34] Another policy that may affect the composition of student bodies is the preferential treatment that many institutions give to children of their alumni.[35] Although their effects cannot necessarily be quantified, forms of non-price rationing such as this deserve to be noted.

3.3.1   College Admissions Policies

Difference in Selectivity

Probably the most important descriptive statement that can be made about admissions policies in American colleges is that there exists tremendous diversity in the degree of selectivity of institutions. At one end of the spectrum are the handful of highly selective colleges and universities that offer admission to only a fraction of their applicants, most of whom are quite talented and accomplished. At the other end are a large number of institutions with more or less open admissions policies. The degree to which selectivity differs among institutions is clearly illustrated by a 1983 survey that asked college administrators to characterize their institutions' admissions policies, summarized in Table 3.6. If "open admissions" is defined as admitting any high school graduate, the table shows that over 90 percent of the public two-year colleges surveyed and almost half the private two-year institutions had open admissions policies. Among the four-year colleges and universities in the sample, 28 percent of the public and 18 percent of the private institutions had open admissions. In contrast, there were very few two-year colleges and relatively few four-year institutions that could be characterized as highly selec-

---

34. At the time this was being written, it was not clear whether this restriction would be put in place. See Michel Marriott, "Colleges Basing Aid on Race Risk Loss of Federal Funds," *New York Times,* 12 December 1990, p. A1.

35. For a comment on such preferential treatment, see Jerome Karabel and David Karen, "Go to Harvard, Give Your Kid a Break," *New York Times,* 8 December 1990, p. 17.

Table 3.6   Selectivity by Type of Institution (percentage of institutions)

	Two-Year		Four-Year	
Degree of Selectivity	Public	Private	Public	Private
Any individual wishing to attend will be admitted	41.8	3.0	2.0	1.5
Any high school graduate will be admitted	48.9	46.5	26.0	16.1
The majority of individuals who meet qualifications will be admitted	8.6	47.5	60.6	62.9
Only a limited number of those who meet the qualifications will be admitted	.7	3.0	11.4	19.5
Total	100.0	100.0	100.0	100.0
Number of institutions responding	419	106	403	779

Source: Survey of financial aid administrators at 2143 institutions in Van Dusen and Higginbotham (1984, 4, 44).

tive. Administrators at only about 200 of the 2,143 colleges in the sample said that they rejected a majority of qualified applicants.

Differences in degree of selectivity may also be observed in the wide variation in percentage of applicants accepted for admission. For example, of the 48 four-year colleges and universities in North Carolina in 1988–89, only five admitted fewer than half those who applied for admission. These five accounted for 29 percent of total applications received by all four-year institutions but only 16 percent of total acceptances. By contrast, there were 27 institutions that accepted 70 percent or more of their applicants; these accounted for 28 percent of total applications and 40 percent of all acceptances.[36] Although figures such as these certainly indicate that selectivity differs greatly among institutions, it should also be noted that the acceptance rate is by no means a perfect measure of selectivity. The degree of self-selection among applicants surely differs among institutions, as does the practice of submitting multiple applications. Where state colleges offer an effective guarantee to high school students who meet certain requirements, for example, there is little point for students not meeting those requirements to apply, nor is there reason for qualified students wishing to go there to apply elsewhere. A consequence of this self-selection, on top of the large percentage of nonselective schools, is that most students are admitted to their first choice among the

36. Calculations based on *Statistical Abstract of Higher Education in North Carolina, 1989–90* (Chapel Hill: University of North Carolina, April 1990), tables 67–68, pp. 137–40.

colleges to which they apply. In 1989, 69 percent of all freshmen reported that the college they were attending was their first choice.[37]

The clear differences in selectivity among institutions suggest a simplified model of demand and supply in which there are just two kinds of institutions: "nonselective" and "selective." The former follow an open admissions policy, accepting all candidates they deem qualified, while the latter reject at least some qualified applicants. It seems reasonable to assume that, over the period relevant for analysis, the size of the student body that can be accommodated by any institution is limited by the size of its staff and plant. Each institution is assumed to enroll all qualified applicants, charging a constant price, until this capacity constraint is reached. The left part of Figure 3.2 illustrates the supply and demand curves for a representative nonselective college under these assumptions. For the nonselective college, enrollment is given simply by the intersection of its supply curve and the demand curve for that institution's places. Enrollment in such an institution might be influenced by the tuition it charges or by other factors that affect demand, such as the economic payoff for college training.

In the case of the selective college, by contrast, there is excess demand at the prevailing price. In the right part of Figure 3.2, the graph for the selective college shows that there are A_3 qualified applicants willing to enroll at the price being charged but that there is room for only A_2. The difference between these two figures is the number of students who must be rejected and is thus an indication of the institution's relative degree of selectivity. While the same factors might affect the demand for a selective college, the results of shifts in demand are not the same. Since enrollment is by definition fixed, shifts in demand have no effect on the number of applicants accepted.[38] What then will be the effect of such shifts? If this were a market in which prices adjusted so as to bring supply and demand into balance, the effect of an outward shift in demand would be an increase in the price. But most of the evidence that we have about the higher education market suggests that suppliers do not charge such market-clearing prices. While the possibility remains that colleges enjoying excess demand might choose to raise their prices at the expense of some degree of selectivity, the policy of selectivity itself suggests that colleges do not charge as much as they might otherwise be able to.[39] Excess demand is the sine qua non of selectivity.

Criteria for Admission

If price is not used to ration demand for places in the selective colleges, what kind of non-price rationing is employed? By what criteria are the scarce positions allocated to aspiring entrants? History offers examples of a number

37. *Chronicle of Higher Education,* 24 January 1990, p. A3.
38. For the purpose of this model, the otherwise important issue of variation in yield rates is ignored. These applicants should be thought of as applicants who will attend if offered admission.
39. The degree of selectivity may, of course, influence demand.

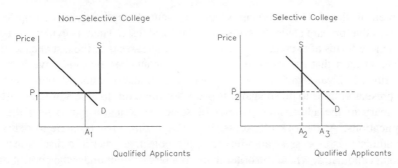

Figure 3.2   Supply and demand for places: selective and nonselective colleges.

of possible forms of non-price rationing, ranging from queues, lotteries, and elaborate rationing systems to bribes and the use of other forms of influence over the allocation process. Comparing this list to what we know about the process of college admissions serves to emphasize the allocation mechanisms that are usually *not* employed by colleges. The notion of first come first served plays little role in admissions, although most institutions do impose deadlines for applications. Nor is random choice normally employed (which is not to deny that a coin may occasionally be tossed behind the closed doors of an admissions committee during the last hours of decisions rounds).

Most striking in this enumeration of unutilized rationing mechanisms is perhaps the virtual absence of bribes and the insignificance of many forms of economic and political influence. In his eloquent brief for the private selective university, Rosovsky (1990, 71) makes this point forcefully: "The system is not corrupt: pull, personal influence, bribery—buying your way into Yale or Duke—are inconsequential factors." A distinction may be in order here. At some institutions, certainly some private ones, children of the rich and powerful may sometimes enjoy higher probabilities of admission than they would have if they had not been well born. Such favoritism is defended by appeal to the possibility of future benefits to the institution that might flow from a favorable decision. But decisions based on threats, bribes, or other quid pro quo agreements are rare indeed.

This set of circumstances makes the acceptance letter to a selective college an unusual commodity. Although valuable—with a theoretical "market price" that may be far in excess of its sticker price—it can be neither traded nor bid for. For other commodities with high income elasticities, such as automobiles and vacation homes, the rising incomes of the affluent in the last decade have had their predicted effect on demand. Strong demand is also reflected in the prices of assets in fixed supply, such as land. But places in selective colleges have been one desirable commodity whose supply has increased little and whose price remains below what it would be in an unconstrained market. In these circumstances, there are limits on what additional income can do to raise the chances of a child's acceptance into a prestigious college. One possibility is to enroll the child in a private secondary school; another is to sign up for courses that prepare students to take standardized tests. There is evidence that both these forms of expenditure have enjoyed increases over the last decade.[40]

The criteria that *are* used in selecting applicants can be (and have been) described in great detail (see, e.g., Boyer 1987), and it is not the purpose of the present volume to do so again. It is useful, however, to give a broad-brush summary of the admissions policies of selective colleges and to note their implications. At the risk of excessive simplification, it is possible to define the admissions process as an effort to apply objective criteria to discriminate among candidates, where the criteria are to a large extent under the control of the institution. This process focuses on two sets of characteristics of applicants: those that are closely related to the student's educational achievement or promise and those that are not.

Included in the first group are both the familiar academic traits, as reflected by high school grades, essays, recommendations, and standardized test sores, and the educationally relevant characteristics that may be evident in a student's participation in some extracurricular activities. Needless to say, institutions differ in how they define, measure, and weigh these characteristics. But two general points can be made. First, most admissions officers are on the lookout for "well-rounded" students (see, e.g., Boyer 1987, 36–37). Second, virtually all selective colleges pay attention to standardized test results, though the questions of how much weight these scores receive and ought to receive are matters of continuing debate.[41] Boyer (1987) argues for a decrease in emphasis on such tests, largely on the basis of a series of interviews with admissions directors. He reports that only one of the 29 admissions directors interviewed listed standardized test scores as the most important criterion for admission to their institution, and 62 percent of those interviewed said that the absence of the tests would have had little or no effect on the composition of their accepted class (p. 34). But these findings are weak evidence indeed for the proposition that standardized tests are unimportant in admissions. Boyer also reports that scores often cause students to adjust their sights, applying to less selective colleges if their scores are not as high as they expected. Such sorting among candidates could well increase the homogeneity of a given college's applicant pool, making it less important for admissions officers to use scores to differentiate among candidates.

The second set of characteristics used by admissions officers to select students are those more or less unrelated to a student's academic or other educational development. These may include characteristics of the student, such as

40. Between 1970 and 1987, enrollment in non-Catholic private secondary schools increased by 81 percent at the same time that the total enrollment in secondary schools fell by 9 percent (U.S. Department of Education 1989, 62, 68).

41. A recent attack on the use of standardized tests in college admissions came from Fallows (1980). For a discussion of the use and usefulness of standardized test results in admissions decisions, see Klitgaard (1985).

his or her race, religion, or region or whether he or she is an athlete who has been recruited to play on a college team. Or they may be characteristics of the student's parents, with preference often being extended to children of alumni or faculty and sometimes to children of wealthy or important people with no institutional connection. Preferences of the first kind are common. Some colleges give preferential treatment, for example, to applicants from underrepresented regions. Certainly, many athletes receive preferential treatment at the colleges and universities that compete seriously in the heavily televised sports. Race and religion, of course, have long been used as bases of discrimination, and many colleges in the United States explicitly discriminated on the basis of race into the 1960s.[42] At present, the two most important issues regarding the use of race as a basis for admissions are affirmative action policies and racial quotas. Affirmative action is a widely accepted practice, defended as a means of both compensating for past injustices and adding to the diversity of college student bodies.[43] In contrast, no college would admit to using quotas, a device that some charge has been employed against applicants of Asian descent.[44] Other preferences, such as those to children of alumni, appear to be widely accepted,[45] while the suggestion that children of the wealthy may be favored is troubling to many.

It is far easier to describe college admissions criteria in general terms than it is to determine their aggregate effect on patterns of enrollment. Admissions policies are difficult to observe or to quantify, and the whole process of admissions is variegated and decentralized, with each institution running its own operation. Still, there do appear to be common tendencies across institutions in admissions policies, and it is useful at least to consider their possible effects. Two questions arise in particular. The first has to do with the emphasis placed on standardized tests and especially their effect on the allocation of educational resources in the precollege years. As noted above, standardized tests have become an important factor in the process of matching students to colleges, and they have been used increasingly by public school systems to assess school performance. Such tests affect the allocation of resources to the extent that their administration displaces classroom work and students and teachers spend time preparing to take the test. An independent panel recently reported that elementary and secondary students are given about 127 million standardized tests a year, or approximately three tests per child per year. There

42. In 1970, the Legal Defense Fund of the National Association for the Advancement of Colored People brought suit against ten states (Arkansas, Florida, Georgia, Louisiana, Maryland, Mississippi, North Carolina, Oklahoma, Pennsylvania, and Virginia), charging that they operated segregated state systems of public higher education. During the next two decades, the federal government pursued the desegregation of public systems, in part by requiring these states and eight others (Alabama, Delaware, Kentucky, Missouri, Ohio, South Carolina, Texas, and West Virginia) to submit desegregation plans (*Chronicle of Higher Education*, 5 July 1990. p. A1).

43. For a defense of considering race in admissions decisions, see, e.g., Bowen (1977).

44. See, e.g., Robert Lindsey, "Colleges Accused of Bias to Stem Asians' Gains," *New York Times*, 19 January 1987, sec. 1, p. 10.

45. For an exception, see n. 35 above.

is also concern that secondary school teachers may be spending too much time focusing on standardized tests.[46] While these tests and the adjustments they engender are certainly important, it is unclear if they contribute to or detract from overall educational achievement.

A second question that arises about the effects of admissions policies, including the use of standardized tests, is whether the process taken as a whole produces an unintended bias against poor and minority applicants. The question of whether the tests are culturally biased is one that has long been debated. As was noted in Chapter 2, there is a strong association between SAT scores and income. Beyond any biases inherent in standardized tests, it is possible that other admissions practices favor the affluent. Certainly, the preference given to children of alumni, who surely have incomes higher than the average applicant at most institutions, has this effect. Moreover, Lewis and Kingston (1989) have argued, without much evidence, that preferences given to athletes and residents of underrepresented regions have a similar bias, as does the preference for "all-around" students. Over against these general policies, with their uncertain effects, is an explicit policy maintained by almost all colleges that admissions decisions are to be made independent of a student's financial need. A survey in 1983 revealed that more than 94 percent of private colleges maintained such a "need-blind" admissions policy, as did over 98 percent of public colleges (Van Dusen and Higginbotham 1984, 79).

3.3.2   Recruitment

As discussed in business schools, "marketing" is a function that is engaged in by any firm that sells a product. It encompasses such decisions as product design, pricing, and promotion. By this definition, colleges and universities have long engaged in marketing, including promotion. Harvard College distributed printed brochures to recruit students as early as 1643,[47] and there are few colleges operating today without a supply of handsome promotional booklets to send out to prospective students. But promotion takes other forms as well, including visits by admissions officers to secondary schools and college-night programs, special weekends when prospective students are invited to campus, and appeals by way of direct mailings. The last of these has been a form that has apparently grown in importance in recent years, thanks to computer technology and a ready supply of prospect lists. The organizations that administer standardized college entrance tests routinely sell lists of students who take the tests along with other information the students provide. Often by hiring other firms specializing in identifying prospects, colleges can customize these lists in a variety of ways to suit its particular needs—all stu-

46. See Jean Evangelauf, "Reliance on Multiple-Choice Tests Said to Harm Minorities and Hinder Reform; Panel Seeks a New Regulatory Agency," *Chronicle of Higher Education*, 30 May 1990, p. A1.
47. Edward B. Fiske, "In the Campaign to Attract Applicants, College Brochures Are Often a Glossy Foot in the Door," *New York Times*, 11 October 1989, p. 21.

dents from the Southwest who score above 1300, for example. Colleges can then send information with personalized letters to prospective high school students.[48]

Articles about the college recruiting function suggest that it has assumed a more important role in recent years as the number of new students has leveled off, but there is no objective information on the amount or nature of recruiting available with which to verify the existence of a trend.[49] Nor is there evidence on which institutions are spending the most on recruiting, although most of the examples given in newspaper accounts are for relatively nonselective private colleges. Similarly, there is some evidence that colleges and universities are spending more money to improve the appearance of their campuses and to provide more amenities to students, all of which would fall into the traditional definition of marketing through product design.[50] However, it is again difficult to know how widespread such actions are or whether their importance has in fact increased in recent years.[51]

3.4 Summary

At least two kinds of motives underlie the demand for undergraduate education. One of these, the desire for higher earnings, plays a prominent role in economic models of demand for education, but there is nothing in these models that necessarily excludes nonmonetary motives from consideration as well. In support of the economic model is considerable evidence that college enrollment rises with an increase in the expected economic return from obtaining a degree. The earnings advantage enjoyed by college graduates over high school graduates fell during the 1970s, but it reversed course in the 1980s. The improving prospects for college graduates is one likely explanation for the continued strength of enrollment through the 1980s. There remain some unanswered questions, though, and one is why the very strong increase in the college advantage for males was not accompanied by increases in their college enrollment rates.

48. One company advertises that its service "will help you yield far more successful results from each dollar and minute you devote to your admissions/recruitment process" (advertisement in the *Chronicle of Higher Education,* 20 September 1989, p. A39; see also Riesman 1980, 110).

49. For example, Robin Wilson ("College Recruiting Gimmicks Get More Lavish as Competition for New Freshmen Heats Up," *Chronicle of Higher Education,* 7 March 1990, p. A1) states, "In their zeal to attract students, more and more colleges are courting prospective freshmen with lavish parties, glossy videotapes, and expense-paid weekends." "Madison Avenue Intersects with College Avenue" (*New York Times,* 9 April 1989, sec. 4A, p. 7) contains a similar statement about the rising importance of recruiting: "Increasingly, many lesser-known colleges and universities feeling the pinch of declining applicant pools are resorting to clever and expensive marketing ploys to attract applications."

50. See, e.g., Michele Collison, "In Buyer's Market, Colleges Turn to Posh Dorms and Fast Food to Lure Students," *Chronicle of Higher Education,* 20 September 1989, p. A37, which offers examples of amenities ranging from fast-food courts to expanded athletic facilities to cable television.

51. For available information on the changing pattern of expenditures of colleges and universities, see Part III.

A second implication arising from economic theory—and this applies to demand for whatever reason—is that the amount demanded will be adversely affected by increases in the cost of attending. Again, there is considerable empirical support for this implication, most of it based on analyses of cross-sectional data, though demand for places in highly selective institutions seems to be an exception to this general rule. In the two decades leading up to 1980, the cost of college generally fell, and the increasing number of institutions simply made college easily accessible to more high school graduates. However, the 1980s saw rapid increases in the real costs of attendance, with more rapid increases occurring in private institutions.

Although it is not at all clear how the admissions process should be fit into an integrated model of demand, it seems important at least to consider its role in shaping enrollments. Institutions differ enormously in their selectivity. While there are a few colleges and universities whose standards of admission would effectively bar most high school graduates from enrolling, many institutions accept virtually any applicant with a high school degree. Enrollment at institutions in the latter group is determined simply by the rate of tuition and the demand curve for places. But enrollment in selective institutions is limited by an institutionally set cap; increases in the number of applicants who desire admission beyond that point merely add to the administrative burden of selecting an entering class. It follows that selective institutions charge less than the theoretical market price for their product. In light of the strong and growing demand for places at selective institutions, it remains an interesting question as to why those institutions have not raised tuitions even more than they have. Another unanswered question of interest is the larger one of how the admissions and recruitment functions have affected the actual composition of college enrollments.

4   Financial Aid and Public Policy

"Is higher education in the United States to be limited to those with wealth?" So begins a 1946 report sponsored by the American Council on Education (Sharpe et al. 1946, iii). Such a statement sounds quaint today, in light of the tremendous increase in college enrollment that has taken place over the four and a half decades since it was written. But the sentiment underlying it has surely not disappeared. Although over half of all high school graduates now attend college and over one-fourth receive bachelor's degrees, there has continued to be widespread concern about the role of higher education in promoting the long-held social goal of equal opportunity. Disparities in average enrollment rates of different income and racial groups such as those documented in Chapter 2 serve as a reminder that, here as elsewhere, equality remains elusive. Many would agree with Behrman, Pollak, and Taubman (1989, 416) that a principal reason for these disparities is unequal access to the means of financing a college education. The concerns about equity that underlie the question quoted above still exist, but they are expressed in an idiom that reflects the expansion of college attendance. The widely accepted policy aim of "access" provides an unequivocally negative answer. The companion aim, "choice," is equally bold, suggesting that a student's financial position should not stand in the way of entering any college to which he or she can be admitted.

This chapter examines these policies and programs and assesses their effect on undergraduate enrollment. The issue of public support for college students has assumed unusual importance in recent years. Among the reasons for this increased importance are the unprecedented increase in college costs during the 1980s, the restrictions on domestic spending in federal budgets, the growing importance of student loans relative to grants, the widespread perception that some financial aid programs, especially loans, are not working well, and an apparent increase in colleges' use of scholarships not based on financial need. These conditions raised concerns that the middle class might find it impossible to afford many private colleges and universities and that many low-income students might find it impossible to attend college at all.

Section 4.1 describes existing financial aid programs in the United States, including the system by which the financial need of students is determined as well as the process by which various forms of aid are combined. Section 4.2 examines the recent history of financial aid programs. It describes how the composition of aid has changed over time, with loans assuming an increasingly important role. A change of smaller proportions has been an increase in scholarships not based on financial need. Section 4.3 examines the distribution of the benefits of these programs and their effect on behavior. Of particular importance is how the different forms of aid affect enrollment and completion. Section 4.4 deals with the incidence and effects of state higher education, particularly the policy of setting low tuitions at state institutions. Section 4.5 summarizes the chapter and discusses recent financial aid proposals.

4.1   The Financial Aid System

Financial assistance to undergraduates comes in several different forms: as explicit payments, which may be gifts, grants, loans, or guaranteed work, or as subsidies that take the form of reduced tuition costs. "Financial aid" usually refers to explicit payments that come from outside a student's family, and by far the most important source of such aid is the federal government. There are dozens of separate federal programs that provide student aid to college students. Housed in a variety of agencies and operated according to different sets of criteria, these programs have been likened to a Rube Goldberg contraption. In 1985, David Stockman's Office of Management and Budget described federal financial aid as "a shotgun approach that has indiscriminantly sprayed assistance at students regardless of income" (Doyle and Hartle 1985, 8, 9). Whether or not this is so, the array of federal programs does appear bewildering at first glance. Thus, an important first step in understanding how financial aid works is to describe the current system. It is also important to examine in some detail the operation of and rationale behind the method of financial need assessment that is a central part of that system.

4.1.1   Sources of Aid

Perhaps it is easiest to visualize the operation of the current financial aid system from the perspective of a financial aid officer on a college campus. On the basis of information provided by an applicant or a current student, this officer first calculates the student's financial "need" and then puts together a "package" of financial aid sources in an effort to meet that calculated need. "Need" is defined as the difference between (1) the total costs of attending that institution (principally, tuition, fees, room, board, books, and transportation) and (2) an amount representing the expected contribution from the student and the student's parents, which is calculated using a standardized formula based on the family's financial resources (financial aid officers are given the discretion to adjust this calculation on the basis of other information). For a student who is financially independent, the calculation must be modified.[1] One straightforward but important implication of this method of calculation is that, for any given student, the calculated amount of need rises with college cost. The methodology employed in this calculation and its implications are discussed in more detail below.

The second step after determining the amount of aid that is required to cover the student's costs is to assemble a package consisting of one or more sources of financial aid. The administrator begins by assigning grant funds from any federal and state entitlement programs for which the student is eligible. The most important of these are Pell grants (formerly Basic Educational Opportunity Grants [BEOG]), a federal program aimed at lower-income students. This program was the largest source of federal grants in 1988–89. In order to limit the program's costs, Pell grants are limited to a percentage of total costs or to a maximum dollar amount (in 1988–89, 60 percent or $2,200) (Mortenson 1988b, 28).

If costs exceed both the grants to which the student is entitled and the calculated amounts for family contributions, the financial aid officer then turns to other sources of aid. Three of the largest federal programs, together referred to as campus-based aid because they are awarded by the campus financial aid officer, are Supplemental Educational Opportunity Grants (SEOG), College Work Study (CWS), and Perkins loans (formerly National Direct Student Loans [NDSL]). Each is intended to provide a different form of aid for financially needy students. Unlike Pell grants, the SEOG program can cover all costs, including the full amount of tuition; thus, the amount awarded under the SEOG program is more sensitive to tuition differences among institutions than is the amount under the Pell program. Perkins loans, drawing on revolving funds assigned to institutions, are heavily subsidized, carrying a very low interest rate (5 percent in 1990) and a repayment that is deferred until after a student has graduated. The CWS program provides subsidies for student employment.

Measured by the dollar amount of aid offered, the largest federal student aid program is the Stafford Student Loans (formerly Guaranteed Student Loans [GSL]). These loans, guaranteed by the government but issued by banks, also allow students to defer repayment until after graduation, and they carry favorable interest rates, though higher than the Perkins loans. Originally

1. In general, for a student to be classified as independent, he or she must live with parents no more than six weeks out of the year, must not be claimed as a dependent on parents' tax returns, and must not receive more than $750 a year from parents. As with other aspects of the need calculation, however, the ultimate determination lies with the financial aid official (Johnstone 1986, 134).

devised as an unsubsidized loan program for middle-income students, these loans have become a major source of federal subsidy for many low-income students. Of the remaining federal programs, State Student Incentive Grants (SSIG) involve a one-to-one match of state need-based grants, and the remaining general loan programs involve considerably less subsidy than the Perkins and Stafford programs. There also exist special programs to aid certain students, including assistance for veterans and Reserve Officer Training Corps scholarships.[2]

It is important to point out the sources of the subsidies implicit in these loan programs. Because it must eventually be repaid, a loan of $1,000 is not worth as much to a borrower as a grant of the same amount. But loans such as those offered in the major federal student loan programs do contain subsidies that are worth something. They carry below-market interest rates and allow students to postpone repayment while they are in school, thus making the real cost of repayment (the present monetary value of payments) less than the original amount of the loan. This difference is the loan's implicit subsidy, and the size of the subsidy depends on the terms of the loan.[3] On the basis of these terms, the subsidy implicit in the major student loan programs has been calculated to be in the range of 30–50 percent of the face value of the loan.[4]

If the various federal and state sources that have been added to the student's package do not cover costs, the difference can be made up with institutionally awarded aid. A college itself can offer a student financial aid—the source might be endowed scholarship funds, earmarked gifts, or current fund revenue. When the source is the last of these, a college ends up effectively offering a price discount to the student. Though they are typically not employed in public institutions, discounts account for up to one-third of gross tuition revenue in private institutions (McPherson, Schapiro, and Winston 1989b, 254). Such price discounting raises at least two relevant issues. When the price discounts are part of a need-based financial aid calculation such as that described here, they have been likened to a Robin Hood form of redistribution, with the wealthy paying a high price and the needy paying a low price. Not only can this use of internal funds present a public relations challenge for colleges, but

2. For discussions of financial aid programs, see, e.g., Hauptman (1982), St. John and Byce (1982), Lee (1985), Gladieux and Lewis (1987), or Gladieux (1989).

3. The present monetary value is defined as the sum of $M_t/(1 + r)^t$, where M_t is the repayment in year t, and r is the market interest rate (as opposed to the interest rate specified on the loan). This sum is roughly equivalent to the loan amount that a bank would pay in exchange for a commitment to receive the same future repayments on the same schedule. The lower the loan's interest rate, and the more distant the repayments, the less the present value is.

4. On the basis of the assumption of one and a half years in college plus the half-year grace period after graduation, a ten-year repayment, and a discount rate of 10 percent, Johnstone (1986, 124) calculates that the present value of the loan obligation is about 75 percent of the face value of the loan, for a subsidy of 25 percent. A discount rate of 12 percent yields a subsidy rate of 33 percent. Lengthening the period before repayment begins significantly increases the subsidy, however. On the basis of a 10 percent interest rate and three years in school, Hauptman (1982, 29–30) calculates subsidy rates of over 50 percent. After August 1988, Stafford Loans carried an interest rate of 8 percent for loans of up to four years and 10 percent for those of five or more years.

it will also affect the institution's ability to raise general revenue since a portion of any tuition increase must be recycled back to students receiving financial aid. One way an institution could cut these costs would be to reduce the number of students receiving aid. Though it has occasionally been adopted, this policy is frowned on in the higher education community, and the most prestigious colleges and universities make "need-blind" admission standard policy.[5] Another, more likely response to budget restrictions is simply to reduce the amount of need covered, allowing students to fend for themselves for the remaining unmet need.

Institutional price discounting raises a second issue in connection with scholarships that are not based on financial need. Concern has been raised that no-need scholarships will take away funds that would otherwise have been used for need-based financial aid. There is some evidence that no-need scholarships are being used increasingly by colleges who see them as a tool for recruiting good students.[6] One fear is that, instead of digging into general revenues to support needy students, private institutions will deal with the scarcity of financial aid funds by denying admission to at least some of their applicants who require aid.

A survey of public and private colleges in 1984 gives a useful picture of how the various sources of financial aid were utilized in the 1980s. On the basis of several hundred thousand student records, Miller and Hexter (1985a, 1985b) identified the most common financial aid packages at public and private colleges for several income classes. Table 4.1 illustrates their findings for students in the $7,000-$15,000 income class; it shows that the most common package in 1984–85 at both public and private colleges was one that included a Pell grant, some form of federal campus-based aid (SEOG, CWS, or Perkins loan), and a state grant as well as a family contribution. For each of the sources shown, the average amount awarded to students in private colleges exceeded that to those in public colleges, with the percentage difference being the least in the case of the Pell grant. Perhaps the most striking aspect of these two typical packages is that neither one covers all the estimated costs of attendance; in the case of the private college, the aid package covers only 65 percent. This lack of full coverage in fact characterizes the two most common packages at private colleges in both the low-income groups studied. Under these circumstances, it is not clear how these students make ends meet, as the

5. According to Sharpe (1933, 696), Yale deviated from this policy during the depression, announcing that it would admit only as many needy applicants as existing financial aid funds would allow for. A survey of financial aid officers in 1983 showed that almost all institutions follow a need-blind approach in admissions (Van Dusen and Higginbotham 1984, 35).

6. See, e.g., Haines (1984). The 1983 survey of financial aid officers revealed that most institutions, public and private, award some scholarships without regard to need. The percentage of institutions offering such scholarships ranged from 72 for two-year private colleges to 85 for four-year private institutions. Among the latter group, 51 percent of those who offered no-need scholarships said that their main justification was as recruitment rather than as a reward for previous achievement (Van Dusen and Higginbotham 1984, 31, 33), although institutions could certainly have a combination of motives in making these awards.

Table 4.1   The Most Common Financial Aid Packages at Public and Private
                   Colleges, 1984–85, Students with Family Incomes from $7,500 to
                   $15,000 (figures in dollars)

Public colleges:	
Average cost	4,572
Source of aid (average award):	
Family contribution	864
Pell grant	1,187
Federal campus-based aid	1,138
State grant	587
Aid total	3,776
Private colleges:	
Average cost	8,379
Source of aid (average award):	
Family contribution	1,163
Pell grant	1,273
Federal campus-based aid	1,510
State grant	1,487
Aid total	5,433

Source: Miller and Hexter (1985, 22–23).

Note: Aid packages are the most common for students surveyed. Cost of attendance includes tuition, fees, books, room, and board and other expenses allowed by the institutions; average cost is for students with this package.

authors note.[7] Possibilities include cutting costs, obtaining additional assistance from family members, or working for more hours or at a higher rate of pay than is assumed in the financial aid package. Stampen, Reeves, and Hansen (1988, 122), examining a sample of public college students, show that the last of these, additional student earnings, had the effect of reducing by about half the percentage of working students with unmet need.

To give an idea of how often various sources of financial aid are used, Table 4.2 shows the percentage of freshmen in each of three incomes classes who received assistance from each of twelve different funding sources. The great majority of these students relied on earnings or family resources for at lest some portion of their college expenses. Among the grant categories listed, Pell grants were utilized most by students with family incomes under $22,000, but students with higher family incomes were most likely to receive a grant made by their college. At all income levels, the most commonly used loan program was the GSL/Stafford federal guaranteed loan program. A curious aspect of this table is that, with the exception of Pell grants, the students in the second income category showed higher rates of utilization of every

7. As Miller and Hexter note, the students receiving these packages did not have GSL/Stafford loans to make up the uncovered amount. Among the eight packages for low-income students that were summarized in the study, the percentage of total costs covered ranged from 65 to 75 for students in private colleges and from 83 to 101 for those in public colleges (see Miller and Hexter 1985a, 22–24 and app. B).

Table 4.2   Percentage of Freshmen Receiving Aid by Source and Parents' Income, 1986

	Parents' Income[a]		
Source	Under $11,000	$11,001–$22,000	Over $22,000
Parent	52	72	76
Own savings	39	57	54
Employment	37	51	34
Any family	70	88	87
BEOG/Pell grant	34	28	9
SEOG	9	11	3
State grant	15	20	10
Institutional grant	15	24	16
Other private grant	5	8	6
Any grant	45	55	32
GSL/Stafford	21	36	21
NDSL/Perkins loan	7	11	5
College loan	3	5	4
Other loan	3	5	4
Any loan	27	45	28

Source: Unpublished tabulations by Thomas G. Mortenson based on data from surveys of freshmen conducted by the Cooperative Institutional Research Program.

[a]Tabulations were based on income as a percentage of the poverty threshold. In 1988 dollars, the 1986 poverty threshold for a family of four was $11,000. See Congressional Budget Office, *Trends in Family Income: 1970–1986* (Washington, D.C., February 1986), table B-3, p. 104; and U.S. Council of Economic Advisors (1990, 359).

other form of aid. Assuming that these self-reported rates are to be believed, there are at least three possible explanations for the difference: the tendency of low-income students to attend low-cost colleges reduces their calculated need, criteria other than need result in fewer low-income students being awarded aid, or low-income students are simply less likely to apply for aid for which they would be eligible.

4.1.2 Assessment of Need

In 1987, Congress mandated the use of a standardized method for determining how much a student or a student's parents would be expected to contribute toward total college costs.[8] Now referred to as the Congressional Methodology, it was merely an updated version of the so-called uniform methodology that had been developed and used over the previous 30 years by the College Scholarship Service, an arm of an association of colleges and universities

8. The methodology is used for GSL/Stafford loans, CWS, and NDSL/Perkins loans. Eligibility for Pell grants is based on a separate formula, and SSIG funds are awarded according to rules determined by each state (College Scholarship Service, *CSS Need Analysis: Theory and Computation Procedures* [New York: College Board, 1989], p. 3.1; and Lee 1985, 13).

called the College Board. Before 1950, the financial aid that was awarded by colleges was distributed largely on an ad hoc, case-by-case basis. Those with need applied for aid, but colleges seldom collected financial data on a systematic basis. In particular, it was quite exceptional for a college to collect and use information on family income in determining awards. It was not unusual for academic merit to figure into such awards as well.[9] Not only did this system lack a mechanism for determining aid to needy students, but there was growing concern among private institutions that the awarding of financial aid sometimes turned into a bidding war for attractive applicants.

It was therefore perhaps not surprising that the established private colleges and universities who led the movement to standardize need assessment would also favor coordination among institutions in determining financial aid packages.[10] Thus, in the early 1950s, the institutions in the College Board decided to adopt a standardized methodology for calculating financial aid offers. This system entailed four basic components: (1) the centralized collection of personal financial information from applicants and their families; (2) a standard formula that would calculate expected family contribution as a function of income, net worth, and other family characteristics; (3) the pointed omission of academic merit as an acceptable criterion for financial aid awards; and (4) the sharing of information among institutions about financial aid packages. The last function was accomplished in part by regular meetings of college officials to compare the packages being offered to individual students, such as the group of representatives from selective colleges known as the Overlap Group.[11] It was this effort to coordinate the awarding of financial aid that became the focus of an antitrust investigation in 1989.[12]

Although it has changed in its particulars, the formula for calculating a family's expected contribution has retained the basic shape it took when it was created in the 1950s. It resembles a progressive tax on income and wealth. Included in the concept of discretionary income that is the "tax base" for this calculation is after-tax income that exceeds a specified set of necessary expenditures and a percentage of net worth beyond a specified allowance for retirement. Table 4.3 illustrates the calculation of the expected contribution

9. Sharpe et al. (1946, 24) summarize the philosophy of financial aid this way: "Colleges should attempt to select from the admitted group those students who need aid and who, according to the criteria applied at admission, are superior to the admitted group as a whole. The selection factors should be those used at admission plus relative financial need."

10. According to Sharpe et al. (1946, 29), "The award of financial assistance should be, in so far as possible, a coordinated enterprise among colleges of similar type and of similar student clientele. . . . deliberate 'competitive bidding' for students—also undue 'shopping-around' by candidates—should be discouraged."

11. For a brief history of the creation of the College Scholarship Service and the origins of the Overlap Group, see College Scholarship Service, *CSS Need Analysis: Theory and Computation Procedures* (New York: College Board, 1986), 4–7.

12. See, e.g., Gary Putka, "Do Colleges Collude on Financial Aid?" *Wall Street Journal,* 2 May 1989, p. B1; and Scott Jaschik, "Investigation into Tuition Fixing Spreads; 55 Institutions Now Say They Are Targets," *Chronicle of Higher Education,* 4 October 1989, p. A1.

Table 4.3   Calculation of Parents' Contribution under Congressional
                   Methodology, 1989–90: Three Hypothetical Families (in dollars)

	Family		
	A	B	C
Income before taxes	15,000	30,000	60,000
Net Worth	5,000	60,000	200,000
Other children in college	0	0	0
Parents' contribution for student	0	2,454	15,901
Change in parents' contribution caused by:			
$1000 increase in income	0	+ 290	+ 470
$1000 increase in net worth	0	+ 35	+ 56
Another child in college	0	− 1,227	− 7,950

Source: Author's calculations and College Scholarship Service, *CSS Need Analysis: Theory and Computation Procedures* (New York: College Board, 1989).

Note: The table embodies the following assumptions. Average tax rates, including federal income, federal payroll, and state income for the three families, are 25, 28, and 42 percent , respectively. Each family has four members. Age of older parent is 45.

by the parents of a dependent student, using hypothetical families at three income levels. On the basis of the specified assumptions regarding net worth, the family making the near-median income of $30,000 would be expected to contribute $2,454 toward a child's college costs. This amount is of course an arbitrary determination, and many parents doubtless believe that it is excessively burdensome. According to the formula, a family making twice that income is expected to contribute over $15,000, while a family with half that income is expected to contribute nothing. The table also shows the effect of incremental increases in income or net worth. In family B's case, additional income is "taxed" at a rate of 29 percent, and additional net worth faces a rate of 3.5 percent.[13] The last line in the table shows the effect of having a second child in college: the expected contribution is divided between the two. Although the assessment of need is complicated by other issues, such a the evaluation of independent students and contributions from dependent students, the basic message to be taken from this table is that the uniform methodology embodies a sharply progressive tax on a family's income and net worth.[14]

This uniform methodology is now a basic part of federal financial aid policy. Its use has had at least two important effects on the shape of student aid subsidies. First, among institutions of similar cost, it causes subsidies to favor

13. The tax on net worth is the product of a 12 percent conversion rate for net worth into available income followed by the 29 percent tax on adjusted available income that is part of a progressive rate schedule. For such a family, the disincentive working against saving that exists in the income tax is added to by this implicit tax. In addition, because consumer durables are not counted as assets in the calculation of net worth, there is an incentive to purchase such durables before applying for aid.

14. Largely because it is an amalgam of both stock and flow concepts, Barnes (1977, 23) calls the uniform methodology "haphazard, inequitable, and logically indefensible."

the poor, owing to the progressive nature of the need-assessment formula. Second, because calculated need increases with the cost of attendance, the methodology guarantees that students attending expensive institutions will receive more aid than similar students attending inexpensive institutions. Devised by relatively high-price private institutions, this methodology has the effect of channeling a significant portion of federal student aid towards expensive private institutions. According to Johnstone (1986, 116), the existence of this system makes it possible for private institutions to raise tuition without fear of pricing out its needy students. Whether, as some have suggested, financial aid programs actually encourage tuition increases is unclear.[15] In any case, by helping students have the "choice" of attending high-price institutions, existing federal financial aid can be seen as part of a political compromise in which public policies encourage the continued existence of both private and public institutions.[16]

4.2 The Changing Composition of Student Aid

Between the early 1960s and the late 1970s, the nature and scope of student financial aid were significantly altered. The total amount of student aid in constant dollars increased tenfold between 1963 and 1980. Such evidence as exists also suggests that there was a corresponding increase in the proportion of students receiving some form of financial aid, particularly during the 1970s. For example, two national surveys showed that the portion of high school seniors who received some form of financial aid offer from a college or university increased from 24 percent in 1972 to 36 percent in 1980 (Jackson 1988, 19). A survey of private institutions indicated a similar increase among enrolled students: from 44 percent in 1970 to 53 percent in 1980 and 59 percent in 1987.[17]

The driving force behind this transformation was the creation and expansion of federal financial aid initiatives. Most of the existing federal programs are products of the last 25 years. The Higher Education Act of 1965, passed in the heady days of the Great Society, created two major programs that have constituted the backbone of federal student aid—the Basic Educational Opportunity Grants (now Pell grants) and the Guaranteed Student Loans (now Stafford loans)—and expanded two more existing programs—College Work-Study and National Direct Student Loans (now Perkins loans).[18]

Table 4.4 provides an overview of the changing composition of student aid from the 1963–64 school year to 1988–89. Loans are measured by the dollar

15. For a discussion of the "Bennett hypothesis" that increases in aid lead to increases in tuition, see McPherson (1988) and McPherson, Schapiro, and Winston (1989a, 1989b).

16. Doyle and Hartle (1985, 8) suggest this in arguing that the cuts in student financial aid proposed by the Reagan administration threatened to undermine this compromise.

17. Survey of 1,069 private institutions by the National Institute of Independent Colleges and Universities (Jean Evangelauf, "Private-College Spending of Student Aid Found Up Sharply in 1980's," *Chronicle of Higher Education*, 16 May 1990, p. A1).

18. For a description of this legislation, see Hearn and Wilford (1985).

Table 4.4 Student Financial Aid (constant 1988 dollars)

	1963–64	1970–71	1975–76	1977–78	1979–80	1980–81	1981–82	1982–83	1983–84	1984–85	1985–86	1986–87	1987–88	1988–89
Federally supported programs:														
Generally available aid:														
BEOG/Pell grants	0	0	2,060	3,100	4,082	3,427	2,992	2,964	3,316	3,453	3,922	3,716	3,894	4,460
SEOG	0	409	442	476	543	528	471	420	429	426	451	432	436	393
SSIS	0	0	44	117	124	111	100	91	71	87	84	79	78	73
CWS	0	692	649	916	970	948	812	754	811	734	721	679	561	706
NDSL/Perkins loans	441	735	1,011	1,201	1,053	996	755	732	810	771	773	824	838	859
Income-contingent loans						0	0	0	0	0	0	0	5	4
GSL/Stafford loans	0	3,095	2,786	3,391	6,397	8,901	9,305	7,965	8,623	9,272	9,156	8,991	9,482	9,168
Supplemental loans for students						0	21	96	172	252	291	499	1,851	2,071
Parent loans for under-graduate students						4	74	150	203	278	270	331	523	635
Subtotal	441	4,930	6,990	9,199	13,168	14,914	14,529	13,171	14,437	15,273	15,668	15,551	17,769	18,369
Specially directed aid:														
Social security	0	1,521	2,403	2,674	2,586	2,703	2,598	899	261	40	0	0	0	0
Veterans	259	3,418	9,191	5,271	2,967	2,464	1,758	1,662	1,364	1,141	933	842	795	743
Military	162	195	213	203	269	291	306	330	358	379	380	393	375	372
Other grants	35	49	139	160	186	175	138	104	74	68	74	72	77	80
Other loans	0	128	99	82	68	89	142	265	312	372	409	340	305	300
Subtotal	456	5,314	12,045	8,392	6,076	5,721	4,940	3,260	2,367	2,001	1,796	1,647	1,553	1,494
Total federal aid	893	10,241	19,036	17,591	19,244	20,635	19,468	16,430	16,803	17,272	17,466	17,198	19,322	19,863
State grant programs	216	720	1,077	1,322	1,284	1,150	1,199	1,233	1,314	1,391	1,441	1,546	1,565	1,642
Institutionally awarded aid	1,160	2,942	3,155	3,116	3,076	2,958	2,924	3,073	3,422	3,667	4,039	4,378	4,750	5,156
Total federal, state, and institutional aid	2,269	13,903	23,269	22,028	23,605	24,741	23,591	20,736	21,539	22,331	22,945	23,122	25,638	26,661

Sources: College Entrance Examination Board (1989, 6, 13); Gillespie and Carlson (1983); and *Chronicle of Higher Education*, 6 September 1989, p. A31.

Note: Conversion to constant dollars is based on the consumer price index for the calendar year in which the school year began.

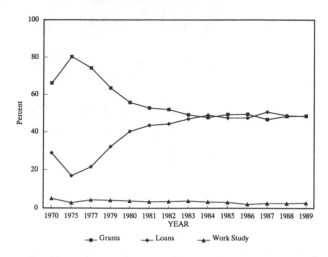

Figure 4.1   Percentage distribution of student aid, 1970–71 to 1989–90.
Sources: Gillespie and Carlson (1983, table 6); and *Trends in Student Aid* (1989, table 4).

amount of loan commitments, and all dollar amounts in the table are expressed in 1988 dollars. In 1963–64, half of all aid was provided by colleges and universities, 40 percent came from federal programs, and the rest came from states. The federal role grew markedly thereafter, with federal programs accounting for 74 percent of all aid in 1970–71 and 82 percent in 1975–76. Federal aid reached a peak, in both share and absolute amount, in 1980–81, after which it tended to decline.

Probably the most important development over this period—and one that has been noted often by those who analyze student financial aid—is the change in the composition of federal aid. Grants have been declining in importance while loans have been increasing. The most prominent reason for this shift has been the rapid growth in the federal government's biggest guaranteed loan program, the GSL/Stafford loans. Because of the dominance of federal aid, this shift has resulted in a redistribution of all student financial aid, as illustrated in Figure 4.1. All loans, again measured by the face value of loan commitments, increased as a share of all aid from 29 percent in 1970–71 to 49 percent in 1988–89. Because work-study funds decreased only slightly, virtually all the increased significance of loans came at the expense of grants, whose share fell from about two-thirds to a half.

As noted above, the actual subsidy value of loans is less than their face value. Therefore, actual value of federal aid programs has declined much more than the totals shown in Table 4.4 would indicate. The small 3.7 percent decline in total federal aid between 1980–81 and 1988–89 shown in the table resulted from the combination of a 30.5 percent increase in loans and a 35.9 percent decline in grants and college work-study. If loans were valued at half their face value, the total amount of federal aid would have declined by 14.7

percent.[19] Applying this correction to the total aid distribution shown in Figure 4.1 results in a less precipitous rise in the importance of loans. By that method of calculation, the share of loan aid increased from 17 percent in 1970–71 to 32 percent in 1988–89.

Lying behind these broad trends were the demise of one major program and changes in others. A major source of federal grant aid was the provision in 1965 for grants to dependents of social security recipients. At its peak, this source supplied almost as much grant aid as the Pell program, but it has since been eliminated. Another major grant program, GI Bill benefits for veterans, declined in the late 1970s as the number of eligible Vietnam veterans diminished. While these two major programs were shrinking, other sources of federal grant aid taken together experienced only modest growth. In particular, the growth of Pell grants was constrained by annual adjustments in the formula used for determining awards. Although the formula was briefly liberalized following the 1978 Middle Income Student Assistance Act (MISAA), the long-term effect of these adjustments was to keep individual grant amounts from growing as fast as college costs.[20] One reason for the tightening of the Pell formula was a significant increase in the share of Pell grants going to students in proprietary vocational schools. Between 1980–81 and 1985–86, the share of total Pell funds going to such students rose from 12 to 22 percent. Even though total Pell funding increased by 14 percent over that period, as reflected in Table 4.4, the amount received by college and university students increased by less than 1 percent.[21] At the same time as funding for grants was stagnating, there was a boom in federal guaranteed loans, especially the GSL/Stafford program. This increase appears to be the result both of the 1978 MISAA legislation and the sharp increase in market interest rates from 1979 to 1981, which made the program's low rates very attractive.[22]

In order to get a fuller appreciation of the effect of these changes, it is necessary to look at how they affected students in different income classes.

19. From Table 4.4, grants plus college work-study (measured in millions of 1988 dollars) totaled $10,644 and $6,827, respectively, in 1980–81 and 1988–89, while loans were $9,991 and $13,036.

20. Mortenson (1988b) provides a detailed analysis of changes in the Pell formula and illustrates their effects by calculations for students in eight hypothetical sets of circumstances over the period 1973–74 to 1986–87.

21. In 1980–81 and 195–86, respectively, the percentage of Pell funds going to students by sector was 29 and 22 for private nonprofit colleges and universities, 19 and 19 for public two-year, 41 and 37 for public four-year, and 12 and 22 for proprietary. By contrast, the percentage distribution of federal campus-based funding by sector remained essentially the same, with a 1 point increase in the percentage going to private nonprofit institutions and a 1 point decrease in the percentage going to public four-year institutions (*Trends in Student Aid* 1989, 12). McPherson (1988a, 14) attributes the increase in the proprietary share to a supply response by that industry.

22. The interest rate on GSL loans was 7 percent until 1980, when it was increased to 9 percent (Hauptman 1982). The prime rate rose from 6.8 percent in 1977, to 9.1 in 1978, to 12.7 in 1979, to 15.3 in 1980, to 18.9 in 1981 (U.S. Council of Economic Advisers 1977–81). For a discussion of MISAA, see Gladieux and Lewis (1987, 4–7).

Tables 4.5 and 4.6 provide two complementary views of the recent period. Table 4.5 shows average amounts of federal aid that college freshmen reported receiving for the school years beginning in 1974, 1980, and 1984 (on the basis of information presented in McPherson 1988a). Students were divided into five constant-dollar income classes on the basis of their reports of parents' income. In all income classes but the lowest, total federal aid increased sharply between 1974 and 1980, showing the effect of the 1978 MISAA legislation, and then declined again between 1980 and 1984. Average Pell grants, which were largest in the lowest two income classes, peaked in 1980 and then declined sharply over the next four years. Federal loans, by contrast, increased at the two lowest income levels over both years. In the second income class, for example, the share of loans (counted at face value) rose from 64 percent of all federal aid in 1974 to 77 percent in 1984. For students with incomes above $36,280, loans grew from 1974 to 1980 but then declined over the succeeding four years.[23]

Table 4.6, based on the same annual survey, shows the percentage of freshmen who reported receiving any support from various sources. In this table, students were divided by parents' income into classes defined in terms of percentages of the government-defined poverty threshold. Expressed in 1988 dollars, that threshold was $11,000 in 1982, making the income class limits $11,000 and $22,000. Like the previous table, Table 4.6 indicates a surge in the utilization of federal aid between 1978 and 1980. The jump in utilization is especially sharp for Pell grants by the second income class and for GSL/Stafford loans by all income classes. Table 4.6 also shows a decline in the percentage of students with Pell grants after 1980, reflecting the tightened eligibility requirements and also an increase in the use of GSL/Stafford loans for those in the lowest two income classes. Between 1978 and 1986, the proportion of students with below-poverty incomes who received any grant changed little, while the proportion among those with higher incomes increased. The explanation for this divergence appears to be in the increase in grants by institutions to those above the poverty threshold. Remarkably, these data suggest that those in the lowest income class were less likely to receive any grant than those in the next higher class, a fact that may be explained by cost differences in the institutions attended by these two groups. In contrast to grants, the proportion with loans increased markedly over the period for all income classes, approximately doubling. These data support the general conclusion that an increasing proportion of college students are borrowing to finance their educations.[24]

23. These survey data suggest that the average college student received 11 percent less in loans in 1984 than in 1980, which would seem to be consistent with the increase in aggregate federal loans shown in Table 4.4 of 10 percent (from $9,991 to $10,944 million) only if the proprietary share of such loans also increased significantly.

24. For a review of the evidence on the increase in borrowing and in loan burdens, see Hansen (1987).

Table 4.5   **Federal Aid per Student, Freshmen in Higher Education, by Income, 1974, 1980, and 1984 (amounts in 1988 dollars)**

Income and Aid Source	Year		
	1974	1980	1984
18,140 or less:			
Pell	1,025	1,072	775
Loans	628	720	1,083
Other	238	241	149
Total	1,890	2,033	2,006
18,140–36,280:			
Pell	305	484	270
Loans	651	1,038	1,150
Other	69	123	80
Total	1,023	1,645	1,500
36,280–54,420:			
Pell	105	172	60
Loans	437	1,056	811
Other	16	45	29
Total	559	1,273	900
54,420–90,700:			
Pell	78	78	24
Loans	325	931	448
Other	13	16	7
Total	415	1,025	479
90,700 or more:			
Pell	27	31	15
Loans	136	740	258
Other	5	7	5
Total	169	778	278
All:			
Pell	294	394	241
Loans	513	945	844
Other	65	94	62
Total	873	1,433	1,146

Source: McPherson (1988a, table 2, p. 6).

Note: Amounts shown for loans are face value. Base for calculations includes students with and without aid.

Table 4.6   Percentage of Freshmen Receiving Aid from Selected Sources, 1978–86

Aid Category and Parents' Income as % of Poverty Threshold[a]	Year				
	1978	1980	1982	1984	1986
Pell grants:					
0–100	37	49	37	33	34
101–200	24	44	32	28	28
200+	7	14	10	6	9
Institutional grants:					
0–100	11	13	12	15	15
101–200	16	17	16	22	24
200+	8	10	10	15	16
Any grant:					
0–100	48	60	49	45	45
101–200	47	63	53	52	55
200+	23	32	28	29	32
GSL/Stafford loan:					
0–100	6	14	19	21	21
100–200	9	21	29	33	36
200+	6	21	17	20	21
Any loan:					
0–100	14	25	28	28	27
101–200	22	37	40	43	45
200+	12	31	25	27	28

Source: Unpublished tabulations by Thomas G. Mortenson based on data from surveys of freshmen conducted by the Cooperative Institutional Research Program.

[a]Expressed is 1988 dollars, the income class intervals implied by the poverty threshold for a family of four in 1982 ($11,000 in 1988 dollars) were $11,000 or less, $11,001–$22,000, and over $22,000. The intervals are roughly the same for the other years (Congressional Budget Office, *Trends in Family Income: 1970–1986* (Washington, D.C., February 1988), table B-3, p. 104; and U.S. Council of Economic Advisers (1990, 359).

One other trend worth noting is the increase in aid given by colleges and universities out of their own funds. Table 4.4 shows that such aid increased by a factor of two and a half between 1963–64 and 1970–71 and has since increased at an annual rate of about 3 percent in real terms. As noted above, the growth in this form of aid has raised fears that it may represent a shift of resources away from need-based financial aid.[25] In order to examine the effect of institutional aid in recent years, Table 4.7 presents data comparing average grants received by freshmen at different income levels. Grants are divided into federal and all other, the most important source of which is institutional. Like the previous two tables, Table 4.7 exhibits an increase in federal aid in 1980 resulting from MISAA, followed by a decline in the next four years. What is striking about this table is the pervasive increase in average grants from other

25. Baum and Schwartz (1988c, 127) cite survey evidence showing that one-fifth of institutional discretionary aid awarded by colleges is not based on need.

Table 4.7   **Average Grant Aid per Student by Type, Freshmen at Private Institutions, by Income, 1974, 1980, and 1984 (in 1988 dollars)**

Income	Year		
	1974	1980	1984
18,140 or less:			
Federal	1,618	1,649	1,108
Other	922	1,384	1,413
18,140–36,280:			
Federal	590	887	483
Other	795	1,428	1,486
36,280–54,420:			
Federal	207	368	152
Other	388	1,139	1,166
54,420–90,700:			
Federal	143	147	51
Other	267	639	711
90,700–more:			
Federal	33	49	25
Other	87	285	412
All:			
Federal	490	640	365
Other	551	1,056	1,096

Source: McPherson (1988a, table 3, p. 12).

Note: Base for calculations includes students with and without aid. Federal grants are sum of BEOG/Pell and SEOG grants. Other grants include state, external, and institutionally funded grants.

sources and, especially, the large percentage increases of such grants in the higher income classes. Between 1980 and 1984, for example, the average grant from nonfederal sources received by a student in the highest income class increased by 45 percent, compared to an increase of 11 percent for the next highest class and increases of 4 percent or less for the bottom three classes. Such findings are consistent with an increase in the importance of no-need scholarships.

4.3   The Effect of Financial Aid

What effect does financial aid have on students? One effect is distributional: student financial aid clearly makes a difference in the financial situations of many students and their parents. The $27 billion of student financial aid distributed in 1988–89 undoubtedly made it possible for many families to spend less of their own resources for college expenses and for many students to enjoy a higher standard of living than they would have otherwise. A second kind of effect, probably more important than the first, is behavioral. Does financial aid increase the probability that a student will enroll in college and, once enrolled, graduate? Does aid affect applicants' choices among colleges? Do different forms of aid have different effects? An assessment of the effect of financial aid on the demand for undergraduate college places requires considering both these effects. Regarding distribution, it is important to be clear about what the actual incidence of financial aid programs has been, particularly in light of the evidence noted above that changes in federal aid programs in the 1970s had the effect of shifting aid from low- to middle-income classes. Recently, Newman (1985) has warned of deleterious effects of increased reliance on loans and has advocated aid programs that carry a requirement to perform service. According to Newman, loans are undesirable because of what he sees as their harmful effects on persistence, student career choices, and values. In this section, the distributional and behavioral effects of student aid are considered in turn.

4.3.1   The Incidence of Aid

As previous discussion has made clear, the bulk of student financial aid comes from programs whose aim is to provide assistance on the basis of financial need. A basic question to start with is whether the actual distribution of aid is consistent with this need-based objective. The available evidence points to an affirmative answer: actual aid packages decrease with a student's financial well-being and increase with college costs.[26] It is important to note that this definition of need does not guarantee that more aid will be directed toward low-income students. If more affluent students attend more expensive colleges, as they do on average, calculated "need" does not necessarily fall with income. In fact, the amount of aid does tend to fall with a student's family income. Data from freshmen surveys, such as are presented in Table 4.5, show this negative correlation with income, as do tabulations for 1980 and 1983 based on the High School and Beyond survey (Lee 1987, 13). But there are exceptions to this general rule, as shown, for example, in Table 4.2 above.

Criteria besides need also shape the distribution of financial aid. In particular, aid awards tend to increase with ability. Tabulations based on the High School and Beyond sample for 1983 by Lee (1987, 18) showed, for example, that college students in the top quartile of measured ability received aid that averaged more than double that reported by students in the bottom quartile.[27] Although federal formulas admit no criteria besides need, the positive association between aid and ability probably arises as a result of the tendency of high-ability students to attend more expensive colleges and of the inclusion of achievement as an explicit criterion in many nonfederal aid programs.

Despite its generally redistributive nature, student aid has undergone significant changes in recent years, and these certainly affect its incidence. As noted

---

26. See, e.g., Schwartz (1986, 110), Lee (1987, 13), or Stampen and Cabrera (1988, 41). In accordance with the uniform methodology, Schwartz finds that aid also rises with the number of siblings an applicant has.

27. Schwartz (1986, 110) finds a similar relation for public grants.

above, aid, especially at the federal level, has changed in distribution and in composition. For several years following MISAA in 1978, there was a marked but temporary increase in aid to middle-income students. The composition of federal aid changed after 1980, with loans increasing and grants declining. The 20 years between 1970 and 1990 offer several turning points in the shape of federal financial aid policy—a surge in aid to the poor, followed by a redistribution to the middle class, followed in turn by a return toward previous patterns but with an increasing reliance on loans rather than grants.

4.3.2 Effects on Enrollment

One need look no further than the post–World War II GI Bill for clear evidence that financial aid programs can have a large effect on college enrollments. Largely as a result of the college benefits offered by this program, male enrollments in the United States doubled between 1945 and 1947, and, by the 1947–48 academic year, payments under the program accounted for one-quarter of all educational and general income received by colleges and universities.[28] Current financial aid programs, by contrast, have aims as well as effects that are surely more diffuse than those of the postwar GI Bill, and thus it is not surprising that discerning the effect of these newer programs has not been a simple matter. Numerous statistical studies, most of them employing cross-sectional data on individual students, have been undertaken to assess the effect of various student aid programs on enrollment rates, choice of college, and persistence toward completion of degree requirements. Such studies typically control for variables such as parents' education and income, ability, sex, and race, among other characteristics. Leslie and Brinkman (1988) undertook an extensive survey of these statistical studies. They found that the general conclusion arising from this body of research is that financial aid has a significant effect on college enrollments and that this effect is strongest at low income levels. But, conclude the authors, "In all likelihood, the aid effects are relatively weak compared to factors known to be important, such as parents' education" (p. 136).

Several studies in this literature are particularly noteworthy. Each employs cross-sectional data based on massive surveys of students, and each produces estimates of behavioral models that imply that student financial aid programs have a large effect on college enrollment decisions. In their study based on the 1972 National Longitudinal Survey, Manski and Wise (1983) focus specifically on the effect of the BEOG/Pell grant program on college enrollments, presenting a simulation indicating what enrollments would have been in 1979 had the program not existed. This simulation suggests that the program made the greatest difference for students in the lowest income group (less than

---

28. Rivlin (1961, 64–70) provides a description of the Servicemen's Readjustment Act of 1944, the "GI Bill of Rights." For discussions of the effect of the GI Bill on the demand for higher education, see Galper and Dunn (1969) or Bishop (1977). For commentary on its importance in opening opportunities for education, see Berhman, Pollak, and Taubman (1989).

$27,500 in 1988 dollars). Without the program, college enrollments in that income class would have been some 27 percent less, according to the estimated model. The program made less difference in the middle and upper income classes—enrollments would have been 9 and 2 percent less, respectively. Virtually all these increases were in two-year institutions.[29] Using the same data, Blakemore and Low (1985) examined the likely effects of several policy changes, including a 30 percent cut in all scholarships. Again, the simulated enrollment effects are rather large, with predicted declines on the order of 5 percent. Schwartz (1986), employing the more recent High School and Beyond data, found that government grants significantly affected college enrollments, but only at low and middle incomes. For students whose parents had incomes of $21,500 (in 1988 dollars), for example, his estimates imply that the elimination of such grants would lower the probability of enrollment from 0.63 to 0.57; grants have little effect at income levels above $36,000, in 1988 dollars (Schwartz 1986, table 3, p. 113).

In apparent contradiction to research findings such as these, Hansen's (1984) examination of trends in aggregate enrollment rates suggested that financial aid had little effect. Reasoning that the federal initiatives in student financial aid during the 1970s should have stimulated the enrollment of low-income students relative to that of more affluent students, he compared the relative college enrollment rates by income group at the beginning of the decade and then again near the end of it. Specifically, he calculated enrollment rates for those below the median income and for those above it; the comparisons were based on computations of averages for 1970 and 1971 and for 1978 and 1979. Since the major federal aid programs of the 1970s were directed toward needy students, he reasoned, their expansion should have raised the enrollment rates of the low-income students relative to the high-income students. However, he found no evidence of this. Instead, the college enrollment rates of those below the median changed little or declined in comparison to the rates for those above the median. These findings appeared to pour cold water on hopes that financial aid programs would be able to erase some of the income-related disparities in college enrollment rates.

Owing in large part to its policy implications, this study has generated a great deal of debate,[30] so it is worth briefly considering the findings and their interpretation. One question that arises is whether these findings represent the facts fairly or whether they are merely the result of some statistical quirk. Although some have suggested modification in Hansen's methodology, his findings have been generally confirmed by subsequent research.[31] A second

29. In fact, the simulations suggest that enrollments in four-year institutions are slightly higher in the absence of the program. The largest effects are seen to be in two-year colleges and vocational schools (see Manski and Wise 1983, 124). In 1988 dollars, the threshold for their highest income class is about $35,400.

30. Hearn and Wilford (1985, 4–2) and McPherson (1988a, 5n), e.g., refer to the controversy surrounding Hansen's study.

31. On this point, see McPherson (1988a, 5n).

question is whether the empirical comparisons represent a good test of the effect of student aid on needy students. McPherson (1988a) points out that Hansen's second point of observation comes during the shift of federal aid toward middle-income students resulting from MISAA in 1978.

In light of these two points, it is instructive to plot the trend in enrollment rates throughout the 1970s and into the 1980s to see if the 1978/1979 observation was an aberration. Table 4.8 presents calculations based on Hansen's methodology for the years 1970–88.[32] The first three columns are based on data for families with dependents 18 to 24 years old. The next three columns present calculations for individuals in the same age group who were not married with a spouse present; most but not all of these are dependents, so data on income generally reflect family income of parents.[33] The third and sixth columns present ratios of enrollment rates for those below the median income to those above, and the movements in these ratios are quite similar over the period shown. During the 1970s, these rates showed little trend, which is consistent with Hansen's comparison of 1970/71 and 1978/79. After that period, however, the table shows a decline in both ratios between 1978 and 1983. This period witnessed the simultaneous deterioration in rates at low incomes and an improvement at above-median incomes, possibly reflecting the redistribution of student aid funds that accompanied the passage of MISAA in 1978. Since 1983, the rate based on families changed little, while that based on dependents increased slightly. Similar findings were obtained by Mortenson and Wu (1990), who calculated enrollment rates by income quartile over time. They concluded that the difference in rates between low- and high-income young adults has increased over time. By showing a relative deterioration in the enrollment rates among lower-income young people over the same period when grants were being cut and increased aid was directed to the middle class, these data are at least consistent with the hypothesis that student aid has had an effect, albeit a perverse one, on college enrollments.

A third question that arises in connection with Hansen's finding has to do with the interpretation of the statistical studies whose results appear to be contradicted. Based as they are on models that are estimated from cross-sectional data, the simulations of policy effects such as those discussed above embody the important implicit assumption "other things equal." These models would predict that an infusion of new funds into financial aid such as occurred in the 1970s would increase college enrollments, assuming that other influences on demand did not change. Needless to say, this assumption is hardly ever satisfied in real life. As we have seen, the demand for college places is

32. There is one minor difference in methodology. Whereas Hansen divided his samples in half, using the median income for the families of dependents 18 to 24 years old, the figures in Table 4.8 are based on dividing each year's sample by the median family income in that year.

33. Over this period, the percentage of financial aid recipients who were classified as financially independent of their parents was increasing. How this change affects the figures in Table 4.8 or their interpretation is not clear, but this is a trend that seems likely to affect the distributional effect of these aid programs as well as the measurement of their effect.

Table 4.8   **College Enrollment Rates, Above and Below the Median Family Income, 1970–88**

	% of Families with Members Aged 18–24 with One or More Enrolled in College Full-Time			% of Dependents Aged 18–24 Enrolled in College[a]		
	Below Median Income	Above Median Income	Ratio	Below Median Income	Above Median Income	Ratio
1970	27.9	52.4	.53	27.5	51.8	.53
1971	26.9	50.4	.53	26.8	49.9	.54
1972	26.8	49.3	.54	26.9	47.6	.57
1973	25.0	47.8	.52	24.8	46.4	.53
1974	23.7	45.4	.52	25.1	45.4	.55
1975	26.5	48.9	.54	27.6	48.5	.57
1976	25.8	49.7	.52	26.9	50.5	.53
1977	25.1	47.7	.53	26.2	48.5	.54
1978	25.1	44.7	.56	25.8	45.4	.57
1979	23.7	44.3	.53	25.1	45.0	.56
1980	23.8	46.0	.52	24.9	46.7	.53
1981	24.2	46.7	.52	24.9	46.6	.53
1982	22.2	46.3	.48	23.0	46.7	.49
1983	22.0	46.9	.47	22.4	47.3	.47
1984	23.1	48.4	.48	23.7	48.8	.49
1985	22.7	47.8	.47	23.9	48.1	.50
1986	22.9	48.3	.47	25.0	49.0	.51
1987	b	b	b	27.2	52.0	.52
1988	b	b	b	26.7	51.3	.52

Source: Calculations based on data in U.S. Bureau of the Census, *Current Population Reports,* Series P-20, *School Enrollment—Social and Economic Characteristics of Students* (various years). Columns 1 and 2 are based on tables entitled "College Attendance of Primary Family Members 18 to 24 Years Old by Family Income, Race and Hispanic Origin" (table 12 in the 1986 report). Columns 4 and 5 are based on tables entitled "Enrollment Status of Primary Family Members 18 to 24 Years Old" (table 15 in the 1988 report).

Note: Percentages in this table have standard errors of about 1 percentage point or less. For example, the estimated standard errors for the percentages in 1986 in columns 1 and 2 are 0.8 and 1.1, respectively. For columns 4 and 5, they are 0.7 and 0.9.

[a]Includes all primary family members aged 18–24, other than those who were married with a spouse present. In 1988, 93 percent of these were dependents.

[b]Not available. In 1987 and 1988, questions referred to dependent family members only.

affected not only by financial aid but also but such factors as the relative earnings advantage of college graduates, the family incomes of prospective students, and tuitions. Only a statistical study that accounted for the effects of influences such as these would be satisfactory in assessing the independent effect of financial aid. A step in this direction is an analysis by McPherson and Schapiro (1991) of variations both over time and among groups within the population. They analyze highly aggregated data on enrollments by sex of students in three income groups for a period of 10 years, divided into public and private institutions. Their estimated equations support the hypothesis that net costs exert a negative effect on the enrollment of low-income students but not on that of affluent students. Given the highly aggregated nature of the data and the omission of measures of economic return to college, however, these results remain suggestive rather than conclusive.

4.3.3   Other Effects

Besides its effect on overall enrollments, financial aid may influence the choice of institution enrolled in and whether a student already enrolled drops out. Research on choice of institution generally shows that the amount of grant aid has similar but opposite effects from those of tuition: increasing aid will raise the probability of enrolling a given student.[34] While these results are probably most useful for institutions considering how to structure their tuition and financial aid packages, research on choice of institution does have a significant implication for public policy. If aid is an effective demand-generating device, then need-based aid has the potential of encouraging needy students to apply to expensive colleges, thus blunting the existing tendency toward income homogeneity in college choice. In a study that examined whether high school students applied to one of a group of 63 highly selective institutions, Spies (1978) found evidence consistent with this effect. For students who were not seeking financial aid, the probability of applying to one of these colleges increased with income; for those seeking aid, however, there was little variation with income.[35]

As for the decision to stay in college, among the factors that have been found to be important are gender, race, age, and academic performance, both in high school and in college.[36] In addition, most research indicates that financial aid increases the chance of continuing in college. By removing or minimizing the financial reasons why a student might drop out, financial aid appears to put aid recipients on an equal footing with nonrecipients. A study by Stampen and Cabrera (1986) illustrates this finding. When several background

34. For a review of statistical studies on this question, see Leslie and Brinkman (1988, 156–63). For a study focusing on the effect of tuition and financial aid on enrollment at one institution, see Ehrenberg and Sherman (1984). In their study of the higher education benefit that existed as part of the social security program, Ehrenberg and Luzadis (1986) look at several dimensions of behavior, including choice of institution as measured by cost. Their findings suggest that this benefit induced families sending their children to private institutions to spend more, to contribute more, and to have the student work less.

35. See Spies (1978, 37–38). It is possible, however, that this result may arise from simultaneity, in that low-income students not planning to apply to an expensive college would be less likely to apply for aid in the first place.

36. See, e.g., Stampen and Cabrera (1986, 1988), Moline (1987), and Leslie and Brinkman (1988, 173ff.). As an extension of this research, I examined the college completion (by 1986) of a sample of about 3,000 students who had been enrolled full-time in the fall of 1980. Completion rates rose with income and measured ability. They were high for students originally enrolled in selective colleges or other private colleges and lower for those who started off in two-year colleges. Blacks had lower graduation rates than whites, although they were more likely to have finished at least two years of college.

variables were held constant, the neediest financial aid recipients experienced dropout rates similar to those receiving no aid (p. 32).

An important question is whether the form of the aid matters in the decision to drop out of or remain in college. Most studies appear to suggest that grants and work-study are more favorable to continued enrollment than loans.[37] However, Ehrenberg and Sherman (1987) found that college students who were employed, especially in jobs off campus, had higher dropout rates. Using the High School and Beyond sample, I examined a sample of 3,008 students who were full-time freshmen in 1980 to see if their initial financial aid packages were associated with whether they graduated within five and a half years. Separate equations were estimated by race and family income level. Three variables measured the financial aid packages: the logarithm of grants, the logarithm of loans, and whether the student received college work-study. Grants were associated with higher graduation rates for three groups of students: high-income (family incomes of $25,000 or more in 1980) whites, low-income blacks, and high-income other nonwhites. Loans were associated with higher graduation rates for low-income whites. College work-study was not significant in any of the equations. The positive effects estimated for loans agree with other findings and seem especially noteworthy in the case of low-income blacks. It is also interesting that loans did not have a significant negative effect in any of the equations. Results such as these may be subject to sample selection bias, however, in that students themselves applied for and accepted aid of different types.[38]

Of the types of aid whose effects on students are important for the consideration of student aid policy, none has received the degree of scrutiny that loans have. The growing importance of loan finance during the 1980s has been a source of intense concern among those interested in higher education policy. Not only is there a fear that the use of loans may "overburden a generation," but there is also concern about the effect of loans on enrollment and persistence rates, especially among minority students, on career choices, and on student attitudes (see Hansen 1987; and Newman 1985). That borrowing increased during the 1980s is widely recognized. Certainly, the aggregate amount of loan commitments shown in Table 4.4 indicates a substantial increase. The number of students taking out loans also rose sharply. The number of loans to undergraduates in Illinois, for example, more than doubled between 1975 and 1985. The number of GSL borrowers in Pennsylvania colleges and universities tripled between 1974–75 and 1983–84 (Hansen 1987, 9–10). By 1983, 59 percent of all full-time college seniors, and two-thirds of those in private institutions, had accumulated some debt (Hansen and Rhodes 1988, 107). Yet it is not clear that the magnitude of the accumulated debt is "excessive." In 1986, the average indebtedness after four years, among those

---

37. For statements on the superiority of loans and work-study, see Jensen (1984, 124), Leslie and Brinkman (1988, 174), and Stampen and Cabrera (1988, 31).

38. For a description of this estimation, see the appendix to this chapter.

at four-year institutions who borrowed anything, was $6,685 for students in public institutions and $8,950 for those in private. Despite the sharp rise in borrowing, the resulting loan burdens still do not appear to be excessive, except in a very small percentage of cases (Hansen 1987, 6, 37; Hansen and Rhodes 1988). Nor is there persuasive evidence that loan finance adversely affects persistence or significantly influences career plans (Voorhees 1985, 26; Hansen 1987, 33).

There is concern, however, about the effect of loan finance on the enrollment behavior of low-income students. Household surveys indicate that people's expressed willingness to borrow for educational expenses rises with income. A Federal Reserve Board survey in 1983, for example, found that the percentage of respondents who said they would be willing to borrow for educational expenses was over 80 percent in every income class over $14,300 (in 1988 dollars), while the percentage willing to do so was less than 80 percent in every income class below $12,000.[39] A survey of parents of high school seniors in 1980 asked whether the family was unwilling to go into debt to pay for schooling. Among parents with incomes over $43,000 (in 1988 dollars), 29 percent said they would be unwilling; among those with incomes below that, 40 percent expressed unwillingness (Olson and Rosenfeld 1984, 465). It has been argued that such reluctance is rational for minority groups that have historically been the object of discrimination, given the uncertainties that such circumstances lend to the calculation of the economic return to education (Mortenson 1990; Hauser 1990, 30–31). Whatever the rationale, such reluctance appears to be a factor worth considering in any assessment of the effect of financial aid on undergraduate enrollments. Adding to the importance of this consideration is the apparent high rate of growth in loan burdens among low-income students. Data collected for GSL indebtedness among undergraduates in Pennsylvania colleges showed the largest increases in debt in lower income classes. As a result, whereas average debt burdens generally increased with income in 1984, they actually tended to decrease with income in 1989 (Mortenson 1990, 19–22).

4.4   State Policies

As important as the role of the federal government has been in providing financial assistance to college students, it would be impossible to gain a fair impression of U.S. public policy to encourage college attendance without considering the role of the states. State policies directly affect the demand for undergraduate places in two ways—through their institutional support of public institutions and through state student aid programs. The most visible manifestation of the first is the vast infrastructure of colleges and universities that the states, and to a lesser extent local governments, have built up. As was

39. A similar survey in 1977 produced the same pattern, with the cutoff income at $9,000 rather than $12,000 (see Mortenson 1988a, 16–17).

noted in the previous chapter, the proximity of colleges influences enrollment; thus, the rapid expansion of state systems of higher education during the 1960s and 1970s, featuring the construction of hundreds of new two-year colleges, had an undeniable effect on college going. But a more significant aspect of this institutional support is the ongoing low-tuition policy followed in all the states. To compensate for the relatively small tuition revenues, the states provide direct appropriations to public institutions. Thus, institutional aid is directly tied to the price faced by students.

States also pursue a second set of policies—student aid programs closely resembling the federal programs discussed above. Partly as a result of the State Student Incentive Grant (SSIG) program, under which the federal government matches state need-based grants on a one-to-one basis, all the states operate at least some grant program. Recipients may include students at private as well as public institutions. All together, state grant programs amounted to $1.6 billion in 1988–89, or about one-quarter of the amount of federal grants awarded in that year (see Table 4.4). A number of states have also developed college savings plans using tax-exempt bonds, and a few states offer a form of prepaid tuition. The success of the latter appears to rest largely on whether the interest earned on funds deposited by parents into state accounts will be subject to federal income tax.[40]

Of these two types of state policies, the first is clearly the more important. The rest of this section examines the size, incidence, and effects of the states' institutional support of public colleges and universities.

The subsidy to students in the form of low tuitions at public colleges and universities appears to be larger than all federal student aid even when federal loans are valued at their face value. One rough measure of the aggregate amount of state subsidies to students is the difference between state appropriations to public institutions ($28.1 billion in 1985–86) and tuition received ($9.4 billion)—$18.6 billion. The total for federal student aid in that year was $15.9 billion (U.S. Department of Education 1989, 293, 302; *Trends in Student Aid* 1989, 6). As a result of state subsidies, the tuition paid by students in public colleges and universities usually covers a much smaller share of total costs than is the case in private institutions. To see just how much smaller a share, consider as a measure of spending on items directly related to students total educational and general expenditures minus expenditures on research and public service. At private institutions in 1985–86, tuition payments covered 44 percent of these costs, while at public institutions they covered only 22 percent.[41] The extent of public subsidies differs among states, as suggested by the variation in tuition levels. As shown in Table 4.9, tuition for in-state

40. For descriptions of state plans, see McGuinness and Paulson (1990); James Barron, "Pay-now, Learn-Later Plan Proves Popular in Michigan," *New York Times,* 12 August 1988, sec. 1, p. 8; and Andi Rierden, "Tax-Exempt College Bonds Planned," *New York Times,* 2 April 1989, sec. 23, p. 4.

41. Totals for 1985–86 from U.S. Department of Education (1989, 293–94, 302–3).

Table 4.9   **Average Undergraduate In-State Tuition at Public Four-Year Institutions: Highest, Lowest, and National Average, 1986–87($)**

National average	1,414
Highest five states:	
Vermont	2,942
Pennsylvania	2,496
New Hampshire	2,190
Virginia	2,070
Ohio	1,982
Lowest five states:	
Texas	885
North Carolina	818
Wyoming	778
Oklahoma	757
District of Columbia	634

Source: U.S. Department of Education (1989, table 259, p. 283).

students ranged from $634 in the District of Columbia and $757 in Oklahoma to $2,496 in Pennsylvania and $2,942 in Vermont.

From the perspective of college students, the subsidy implicit in low tuitions combines with explicit financial aid assistance to reduce the cost of attendance. Using information on individual students from the High School and Beyond survey, Lee (1987) estimated the average size of these components of subsidy for three types of institutions in 1983, as shown in Table 4.10. An institutional subsidy was calculated for each student as the difference between the per-student expenditures at that student's college (calculated from separate financial data for individual institutions) and the amount of tuition paid. The total subsidy enjoyed by a student is the sum of this institutional component and the amount of financial aid received. The table's first row shows the average expenditure per student for the institutions attended by those in the sample in 1983. Looking first at four-year institutions, the figures show that average expenditure at private institutions was about $2,200 more than that at public institutions but that the difference in average tuitions was about $3,200. While students at both types of institution received a subsidy—measured by the difference between average expenditures and tuition—the size of this subsidy was substantially greater in public four-year institutions.

When information on students' sources of financial aid is considered, however, this advantage disappears. Where loans are valued at 30 percent of their face value, the average student at a private institution received over twice that received by the average student at a public institution. It is interesting to note, however, that average financial aid in the public institutions is very close to their average tuition. Adding financial aid to the subsidies provided by institutions yields total subsidies of about $5,600 for private and $5,100 for public four-year institutions. The third column of the table gives corresponding information for public two-year colleges, showing much lower per-student ex-

Table 4.10   Sources of Subsidy by Type of Institution, 1983($)

	Type of Institution		
	Private Four-Year	Public Four-Year	Public Two-Year
A. Instructional and educational expenditures per student[a]	7,292	5,073	2,448
B. Tuition	4,394	1,230	584
C. Institutional subsidy (A − B)	2,898	3,843	1,856
D. Financial aid per student[b]	2,707	1,226	538
E. Total subsidy (C + D)	5,605	5,069	2,394

Source: Lee (1987, pp. 4–5, 6, and table 13).

[a]Includes expenditures for instruction, public service, academic support, student services, institutional support, operation and maintenance of plant, and transfers. Excludes expenditures on research, scholarships, and auxiliaries.

[b]The subsidy value of loans is assumed to be equal to 30 percent of face value.

penditure levels, tuitions, and financial aid.[42] The resulting institutional subsidy and total subsidy are only about half those offered by four-year public institutions. As the figures in this table make clear, the subsidies offered by state and local governments in the form of low tuitions have a substantial effect on the net cost of college attendance. While average financial aid at public colleges virtually matched average tuition in 1983, there remained a sizable tuition-aid gap in the private sector.[43]

What is the distributional incidence of these state subsidies? In a widely cited study of the public higher education system in California, Hansen and Weisbrod (1969) concluded that they were decidedly weighted toward upper-income households. This conclusion results from two basic facts concerning the pattern of subsidies offered by states and the relation of college attendance to income. First, as discussed above, states offer a subsidy in the form of education whose value exceeds the price charged, and the value of this subsidy is greater for four-year institutions than for two-year colleges. Hansen and Weisbrod found a similar pattern for California in the 1960s. The second fact leading to this result is that college attendance rises with income, and attendance at four-year institutions is especially concentrated among high-income households. Data presented by Hansen and Weisbrod (1969, table 5) for 1964 show, for example, that families with incomes over $20,000 ($76,400 in 1988 dollars) accounted for about 4 percent of all families in the

42. As Lee (1987, 20) notes, however, the subsidies for two-year institutions are most likely understated relative to those for four-year institutions because total enrollments, rather than full-time equivalent enrollments, were used for calculations.

43. Lee (1987, table 13) performed similar calculations for 1980 and found that average aid in that year exceeded tuition for those enrolled in public institutions. Similarly, using aggregate data, Hansen and Stampen (1987, table 5) find that financial aid exceeded tuition payments in 1980–81 but not in 1984–85.

state, 7 percent of those with children in two-year colleges, 8 percent of those with children in four-year state colleges, and 18 percent of those with children in the University of California. Although some portion of differences such as these result from differences in family life cycle—families with college-age children are typically near their peak lifctime earnings—the utilization of state subsidies for higher education clearly rises with income level.[44] Despite the egalitarian notions and rhetoric that are often associated with low public tuitions, therefore, they do not actually favor the poor.

Besides these distributional consequences, what effect do state subsidies of higher education have? One obvious consequence of the long-standing state policies of construction and subsidy has been to create a public sector of higher education. What is not obvious is whether this active public role has increased total enrollments and resources in higher education compared to what they would have been otherwise. Peltzman (1973) addressed this issue by viewing public higher education as an in-kind subsidy. State governments in effect provide a certain amount of higher education at a below-market price, but in this model consumers can obtain more than this amount (college education of higher quality) only by going to the private alternative and paying the higher price. Such a subsidy results in an increase in overall enrollment, but the effect on aggregate expenditures on higher education is not obvious. Faced with the two available alternatives, a consumer in theory might choose to purchase either more or less higher education. Peltzman's empirical work suggests that state subsidies increase the total expenditures on higher education but that most government spending simply substitutes for expenditures that would have been made otherwise in the private sector.[45]

State subsidies to public institutions constitute the single most important public policy affecting undergraduate student enrollment. Their aggregate value exceeds that of all federal student aid programs. By lowering the cost of college, in terms of both reduced tuitions and lower average transportation costs, the policy has had the effect of increasing college enrollments. Although the size of average subsidies increases with income, it seems likely that the largest effect on enrollments has been at middle and lower income levels, for it is students in these income classes who have participated most in the boom in community college enrollments. Beyond these aggregate effects on enrollment, there appears to be little research on the effects of state subsidies on specific behavior such as continuation of enrollment. This may simply be the result of the pervasiveness of the policy itself and the difficulty in linking variations in it to specific behaviors.

44. For further discussion of Hansen and Weisbrod's study, see, e.g., Pechman (1970) and Hartman (1970).
45. Peltzman's (1973, 19) estimates, based on two-stage least squares regressions explaining public and private expenditures on higher education in each state, imply that, in the absence of state subsidies, "expenditures would be three-fourths to five-sixths those of present total expenditures, and enrollment would be two-thirds to three-fourths of the present total."

4.5   Summary and Policy Options

In concluding this discussion of public policies affecting college enrollment, it is useful to summarize existing policy and to note some of the proposals for change that have been discussed in recent years.

Current public policy in this area consists of two major parts, one not obviously more important than the other. There is a state part consisting of across-the-board subsidies made available to college students attending publicly supported institutions, most of them on the state level, and there is a federal part composed of the major student financial aid programs. By all appearances, state policies have a pervasive effect on both the allocation of resources in higher education and the distribution of benefits. Because of these policies, a substantial percentage of undergraduates in the United States attend colleges operated by a state or local government. The largest subsidies made available in this way go to the middle class, although state and local construction and support of two-year colleges have greatly expanded college opportunities for low-income students in the past 30 years. As a result of state subsidies, high school seniors have the choice of applying to colleges in either of two distinct sectors—a generally high-priced private one and a lower-cost public one. The coexistence of these two sectors sets the stage for federal student aid policy, serving as both precondition and objective.

The array of federal aid programs is often denigrated for its complexity and apparent haphazard construction, with programs working at cross-purposes and with unintended consequences. While these descriptions could probably be used to characterize public policy in any number of areas, contradictions do not appear to be especially numerous in the area of student financial aid. Not only has the basic structure of federal student aid programs enjoyed rather widespread and sustained support, but existing policies appear to be consistent with two basic objectives that are by no means necessarily incompatible. One, arising out of widespread support for the ideal of equal opportunity, is to provide financial support for low-income students who are willing to work and borrow and who otherwise qualify for admission. This is the aim of "access" and is embodied in such programs as the BEOG/Pell and the SEOG grants, work-study, and the heavily subsidized NDSL/Perkins loans.

The second aim, "choice," is inextricably bound up with the existing two-sector structure of U.S. higher education. As in other federal programs touching higher education, student aid policy pays special attention to the requirements of high-cost college and universities. By basing awards on need, aid formulas have a built-in escalator clause that produces bigger awards for those who enroll in high-cost colleges. Although federal aid for students comes largely in the form of direct financial assistance to the students themselves rather than institutional support, the design of the aid has very important implications for the well-being of institutions. "Evenhandedness" is achieved in federal aid programs by offsetting state subsidies. As a further manifestation of this choice objective, the federal government has been sensitive to the predicament of middle-class students, and this sensitivity appears to have been the original motivation in creating the major student loan program, the GSL/Stafford loans.

What might have remained a neat access/choice policy of grants for the poor and loans for the middle class was undermined in the 1980s by reductions in congressional appropriations. In the best budget tradition of putting off outlays to the "out-years," Congress reduced grant programs and substituted loans in their place so that, by 1988–89, 49 percent of the federal student aid dollars awarded was in the form of loans. This shift has raised concerns about debt burdens, loan defaults, and adverse enrollment effects, especially among minority students.

Proposals to reform federal financial aid extend from marginal modifications of existing programs to the creation of altogether new programs.[46] Starting at the modest end, one obvious possibility is to increase the funding of the federal grant programs so that they would cover a greater portion of the college costs now being met with borrowing. One way of doing this would be to reduce or eliminate the grant funds going to students at proprietary schools, but such a remedy would obviously be opposed vigorously. Another way of increasing the amount of aid given to the poor, without increasing total expenditures, would be to change the formula used for needs analysis, making the implicit tax schedule more progressive. Among those students currently receiving aid, this change would increase calculated need for those with lower incomes and decrease it for those with higher incomes. However, this increase in implicit marginal tax rates would tend to worsen any existing incentive problems now associated with financial aid.

Another idea that would involve a relatively incremental modification of the current system is to change the way aid is packaged over a student's college career. The idea would be to front-load grants into a student's early years of study, allowing loans to finance the bulk of need after that. It is thought that this approach might overcome reluctance especially among minority students to borrow for college before they are confident that they will obtain a degree. However, it is unclear what effect a policy change of this kind would have on the already lower completion rates of minority students. A further argument for the approach is that it would reduce the loan default rate by reducing loans to those most likely to default, those just starting college.[47] A related idea is to restrict grants to students in the traditional college-going age group, letting

46. For discussion of policy options in student aid, see Charles F. Manski, "the Coming Debate on Postsecondary Student Aid Policy," *Focus* 2 (Winter 1988–89): 1–5; Janet S. Hansen, "Student Financial Aid: Old Commitment, New Challenges," *College Board Review* 152 (Summer 1989): 26–31; Thomas J. DeLoughry, "1991 Reauthorization of Higher Education Act Is Viewed as Opportunity for Major Change in Federal Student Aid," *Chronicle of Higher Education*, 2 May 1990, p. A21; and Hauptman (1990b, esp. chaps. 2, 3).

47. See Edward Fiske, "Are Colleges Winning—or Even Fighting—the Battle to Recruit More Minority Students?" *New York Times*, 25 April 1990; Thomas DeLoughry, "1991 Reauthorization of Higher Education Act Is Viewed as Opportunity for Major Change in Federal Student Aid," *Chronicle of Higher Education*, 2 May 1990. p. A21; and Hansen (1987).

older students, who presumably have better employment possibilities, rely on loans.

A second broad class of possible reforms seeks to increase the amount of grant money available to students, especially those with low incomes, by creating new programs that carry new conditions. One proposal with numerous variants is to institute some sort of volunteer or national service requirement as a condition for receipt of aid. This would be in effect a nonmilitary version of the GI Bill program. Whether such a program would take the place of all existing grant programs, effectively making service a precondition for receiving federal grant aid, or whether this would be an add-on to existing programs would be one of the questions that such a proposal would face if it were to be considered seriously.[48] Another direction for new grant programs has been suggested by the example of a philanthropist who promised an entire class of inner-city school children that he would finance their college educations if they would finish high school. A New York State program patterned after this approach provides scholarship funds to supplement Pell grants.[49] Proposals for similar programs include other requirements, such as not using drugs and avoiding criminal conviction. Still other proposals suggest that loans might be forgiven under certain conditions, such as graduation or taking a teaching position.[50]

Another idea for providing low-income students a new source of finance for college goes instead in the direction of fewer conditions. As proposed by Haveman (1989), the government would provide all young people with personal capital accounts that could be drawn on for a limited number of uses, including education expenses, the purchase of a house, or medical bills, at the discretion of the individual.

Finally, there has also been discussion of various means by which students and their families could more easily finance their own college expenses. One set of ideas focuses on family saving before a child enters college, by means of tax-sheltered accounts similar to Individual Retirement Accounts. While such savings plans appear to be popular with taxpayers, they are expensive and would be of little help to low-income families.[51] A way that college costs could be pushed into the future would be through income-contingent loans. Similar to a plan initiated by Yale during the 1970s, such loans would require a student to pay a fixed percentage of his or her future income for a certain

48. For a discussion of youth service proposals, see Goldie Blumenstyk, "State Leaders Are Wary of Federal Efforts to Link Student Aid to Volunteer Service," *Chronicle of Higher Education,* 22 March 1989, pp. A1, A20.

49. Ibid.

50. For descriptions of programs modeled after Eugene Lang's philanthropy, see Susan Diesenhouse, "Harvest of Diplomas for Boston Poor," *New York Times,* 24 May 1989; Goldie Blumenstyk, "State Leaders Are Wary of Federal Efforts to Link Student Aid to Volunteer Service," *Chronicle of Higher Education,* 22 March 1989, pp. A1, A20; and "Proposal Seeks to Help Needy Pay for College," *Raleigh News and Observer,* 26 June 1990, p. 2B.

51. See Scott Jaschik, "Higher-Education Officials Applaud Federal Efforts to Use Tax Code to Encourage Families to Save Money," *Chronicle of Higher Education,* 3 January 1990, p. A17.

number of years. Depending on their incomes, some students would end up paying more than they would under a conventional loan, and others would pay less.[52] If the reluctance of low-income families to undertake debt is the fear that repayment might be impossible, the shift to income-contingent repayment might well induce a higher percentage of such students to enroll in college.

There appears to be, unfortunately, little hard evidence on the likely effect of proposals such as these. This is hardly surprising in light of the difficulty of assessing the effects even of currently operating financial aid programs. In addition, we know little about how colleges and universities respond to financial aid programs—for example, by modifying their admissions standards, recruiting strategies, or financial aid packaging. However, the body of empirical research that already exists on the demand for undergraduate places provides a reasonable first step in the evaluation of proposals. If the sum total of grant aid continues to decline in real terms as it has during the past decade, the net cost of college is likely to keep increasing, pushing down the demand for places.

Appendix
Analysis of Financial Aid and College Completion

An analysis of the effect of financial aid on college completion was undertaken using a sample, taken from the High School and Beyond survey, consisting of those who were full-time college students in the fall of 1980. Those reporting unusually high tuitions (more than twice the average tuition at private universities) or financial aid amounts (more than twice the average tuition and fees at private universities) were dropped from the sample. Tuition and fees figures for 1980–81 were based on U.S. Department of Education (1989, table 258, p. 282).

Table 4A.1 gives the full set of estimated coefficients for probit equations explaining the completion of two and four years of college. These equations show clearly the strong effect of both income and measured ability. In addition, those who were initially enrolled in selective institutions or other private four-year institutions had higher completion rates than those in public four-year institutions, whose students in turn had higher rates than those who began in two-year colleges. Three variables were used to measure the form of financial aid: the logarithm of grants, the logarithm of loans, and whether the student received college work-study. In the aggregated equations in Table

---

52. Income-contingent loans were proposed by Friedman (1962). For discussions of such programs, see Gladieux and Lewis (1987, 8); and Robert D. Reischauer, "The Bizarre War on 'Stars,'" *New York Times*, 17 October 1988.

Table 4A.1   Probit Regressions Explaining Completion of Two and Four Years of College by Spring 1986 among Those Who Were Enrolled Full-Time in Fall 1980 (*t*-statistics in parentheses)

Independent Variable	Equation and Dependent Variable		Independent Variable	Equation and Dependent Variable	
	4.1, Completed Two Years	4.2, Completed Four Years		4.1, Completed Two Years	4.2, Completed Four Years
Family income, 1980:			Type of college, fall 1980:		
$7,000–$11,999	.073	.007	Selective	.699	.454
	(.8)	(.1)		(3.3)	(2.6)
12,000–15,999	.034	−.012	Other private	.436	.333
	(.4)	(.1)	four-year	(6.1)	(4.9)
16,000–19,999	.058	.077	Two-year	−.265	−.486
	(.7)	(.8)		(4.6)	(7.7)
20,000–24,999	.291	.330	Financial aid,		
	(3.4)	(3.7)	fall 1980		
25,000–37,999	.417	.352	Log of grant	.021	.029
	(4.5)	(3.7)	amount	(2.6)	(3.3)
38,000 or more	.479	.587	Log of loan	−.009	.0003
	(4.8)	(5.8)	amount	(.9)	(.0)
Ability quartile:			= 1 if college	.076	.064
Second	.266	.247	work-study	(.9)	(.8)
	(3.5)	(2.9)	Intercept	−.714	−.995
Third	.505	.437		(7.5)	(9.7)
	(6.9)	(5.5)			
Highest	.700	.664	Sample size	3,008	3,009
	(9.2)	(8.3)	Mean of	.550	.365
Race/ethnicity:			dependent		
Hispanic	.072	.007	variable		
	(1.1)	(.1)	Log of	−1,871.2	−1,756.8
Black	.159	−.167	likelihood		
	(2.3)	(2.3)	function		
Other nonwhite	.775	.179			
	(6.5)	(1.6)			
Male	.143	−.026			
	(2.9)	(.5)			
	(*continued*)				

Source: Sample was High School and Beyond.

4A.1, the grant variable is positive and significant, and the other two variables are statistically insignificant.

To see how these financial aid effects might differ among groups within the population, separate equations of the same form were estimated for twelve income and racial/ethnic groups. The estimated coefficients of the aid variables from these equations are shown in Table 4A.2. Grants were associated with higher graduation rates for three groups of students: high-income (family

Table 4A.2   Estimated Effects of Freshman Financial Aid on Probability of College Gradution by Spring 1986 among Those Who Were Full-Time Students in Fall 1980

Racial/Ethnic Group and Family Income[a]	N	% Graduating	Financial Aid Variable		
			Logarithm of Grant Amount	Logarithm of Loan Amount	= 1 if College Work-Study
White:					
Low	420	33	.030	.055*	.077
Middle	564	41	−.014	.006	.247
High	545	51	.070*	−.014	−.475
Black:					
Low	285	25	.092*	−.019	−.061
Middle	163	25	.048	.003	.158
High	68	43	.072	−.050	−.763
Hispanic:					
Low	267	25	−.017	.029	.524
Middle	188	37	.008	−.054	.667
High	106	37	.020	−.172	−2.079
Other nonwhites:					
Low	46	30	.045	−.127	1.484
Middle	52	37	.037	−.432	2.940
High	48	52	.217*	−.267	.054

Source: Sample was High School and Beyond.
[a]Income classes, in 1980 dollars, were as follows: low: under $16,000; middle: $16,000–$24,999; high: $25,000 and over.
*Significantly different from zero at the 5 percent level.

income $25,000 or more in 1980) whites, low-income (under $16,000) blacks, and high-income other nonwhites. Loans were associated with higher graduation rates for low-income whites. College work-study was not significant in any of the equations. The positive effects estimated for loans agree with other findings and seem especially noteworthy in the case of low-income blacks. It is interesting that loans do not have a significantly negative effect in any equation.[53] Estimates such as these suggest that the form of aid does matter and that cuts in grants, especially for those at lower income levels, could well have had the effect of discouraging continuation in school. The declines in four-year completion among blacks might well have resulted in part from the cuts in grant funds. Combined with evidence that aid affects initial enrollment choices, estimates such as these point to the retrenchment in financial aid as one likely culprit in explaining the divergent enrollment trends cited above.

53. Results such as these may be subject to sample selection bias in that students themselves applied for and accepted aid of different types.

5   Implications of Recent Enrollment Trends

Undergraduate education is not only one of the preeminent missions of higher education, it is also one of the most important activities engaged in by young people. It influences their economic productivity, social standing, and personal growth. In this country, college places are allocated among the eligible participants through the interaction of supply and demand. Supply in this market consists of several thousand largely independent institutions, many of which are operated by state and local governments. Some of these institutions limit the size of their enrollments, but most open their doors to all applicants who can meet certain academic qualifications and pay the stated tuition. To a large extent, then, total enrollment is determined by demand.

This chapter is divided into three sections. Section 5.1 considers aggregate demand, focusing on changes that have occurred in recent years both in enrollment and in the factors that are thought to influence demand. Section 5.2 turns to the other major question motivating this part of the book, namely, the composition of demand. It examines changes in the characteristics of college students over the last two decades in light of the influences that might have been responsible for those changes. There is a brief concluding section.

5.1   Recent Changes in Aggregate Enrollments

It is not hard to see why the demand for higher education might be a subject of concern to those interested in either education or its economic consequences. The rapidly escalating costs of operating colleges and universities, which are discussed in Part III, have been passed on in the form of tuition increases, especially in private institutions, and the magnitude of these increases has raised the specter of qualified college applicants, particularly those with low incomes, being priced out of higher education altogether. At the same time, the federal student aid programs that might otherwise have been expected to soften the blow of these cost increases were gradually pared down as a part of the larger budget tightening that occurred in the 1980s. Demand was buffeted by one further change that was especially disconcerting to college administrators, namely, the decline in the number of 18-year-olds. Remarkably, in spite of these trends, college enrollment not only held steady during the 1980s but increased.

Table 5.1 summarizes the major quantifiable changes that influenced demand for undergraduate places in the last decade, focusing specifically on changes between 1979 and 1987, or between the 1979–80 and 1987–88 school years. Row 1 shows the decline in the number of young people in the traditional 18- to 24-year-old college age group—9 percent. The number of 18-year-olds decreased even more—by 16 percent. This demographic downturn was accompanied by two other changes that reduced demand. The first of these was a dramatic transformation in the mix of student financial aid—the

Table 5.1   Student Aid, Costs, Income, and Enrollments, 1979 and 1987 (dollar values in 1988 dollars)

	1979	1987	Percentage Change
Number of 18–24-year-olds (1,000's)	30,048	27,336	−9
Student aid per FTE ($):			
Federal grants	1,456	708	−51
Federal loans	1,018	1,627	+60
Other	722	873	+21
Total subsidy value (loans valued at 50 percent)	2,687	2,395	−11
Tuition, fees, room and board ($):			
Public	3,108	3,960	+27
Private	7,052	10,390	+47
College earnings advantage (%):			
Men	29	50	+72
Women	37	56	+51
Mean household income ($):			
All households	36,363	38,081	+ 5
Top quintile households	75,818	83,207	+10
Undergraduate FTE enrollment (1,000's)	7,386	7,991	+ 8
Enrollment rate, 18 to 24-year-olds (%):			
Below median income	25.1	27.2	+ 8
Above median income	45.0	53.0	+16

Sources: 18- to 24-year-olds: National Center for Education Statistics; *Projections of Education Statistics to 2000* (Washington, D.C.: U.S. Government Printing Office, 1989), table A4; aid: Table 4.4; costs: Table 3.4; income: U.S. Bureau of the Census, *Current Population Survey,* Series P-60, *Money Income of Households, Families and Persons in the United States: 1987,* No. 162 (1989), table 12; earnings advantage: Table 3.1; FTE enrollment: U.S. Department of Education (1989, 177), estimated with part-time enrollments weighted one-third; enrollment rates: Table 4.3.

Note: FTE = full-time-equivalent student.

decline in federal grants and the emergence of loans as a major source of support. Owing largely to the demise of the social security education benefit, the decline in GI Bill payments, and the stagnation of other grant programs, the average value of federal grants per student contracted by half over this comparatively short period. Federal loan programs grew rapidly, but even this growth, combined with increases in other sources of student aid, was not sufficient to maintain the overall subsidy value of student aid over this period. If loans are valued at half their face value, the average amount of student aid from all sources per full-time-equivalent student declined by 11 percent. The decline in the amount of aid available to college students was even more severe than this, however, because of the rising share of federal funds going to students in proprietary schools.

The next two rows of the table show the other adverse development affecting demand during this period: the rapid increase in cost of attendance. Cost of tuition, fees, room, and board rose 27 percent in real terms at the average public institution and 47 percent at the average private one. Whether or not the increases for this particular period represent attempts by institutions to catch up with past price increases, these were the costs faced by students and their families during these years. On the basis of what can be inferred from the extensive empirical work on the demand for undergraduate places, price increases of this magnitude combined with the deterioration in the real value of student aid should have exerted a decidedly negative influence on demand over this period.

But other forces were at work pushing demand up. One of these was a dramatic turnaround in the comparative earnings of college graduates. Strong demand for college-trained workers greatly increased the college–high school earnings differential, seemingly erasing fears of only a decade before that we might be producing too many college graduates. By 1987, the average male college graduate was earning 50 percent more than comparable high school graduates; for females, the difference was 56 percent. A second trend boosting demand for college was the continued increase in personal income. The income of the average household grew in real terms by 5 percent over this period. More important, the income of households in the top 20 percent of the income distribution—those most likely to send their children to college, especially to private institutions—increased by 10 percent, reflecting the growing bifurcation occurring in the nation's income distribution.

Not only did enrollment rates increase, but total enrollments and full-time-equivalent enrollments also increased, this in the face of a falling number of young people in the traditional college age group. The continued increase in college enrollments during the last decade appears to be the result of strongly conflicting forces, with rising family incomes and dramatically improved earnings prospects as the primary explanations for the continued strong demand for college. There are, of course, a host of other, unmeasured factors that could help explain this continued strength in demand. A college degree could be increasingly seen as a requirement for social acceptance, for example; this would be consistent with evidence that undergraduate education is a "normal" good the demand for which will continue to increase as long as real incomes rise. But for the most part the record of the last decade is remarkable for the failure of the undeniably negative forces of demography, rising costs, and shrinking grant funds to pull down the total demand for undergraduate education.

Future directions in the forces affecting demand for places are, of course, notoriously difficult to assess, as are the likely effects of implementing new public policies. If the past decade is any guide, however, it seems unlikely that the factors that have been responsible for the sustained enrollment growth of the 1980s will continue to work in the way that they have. While incomes may continue to grow in real terms, the earnings advantage of college graduates seems unlikely to continue increasing at the rate it has, if at all. The demographic projections suggest that the size of the traditional college age population will hit bottom in the mid-1990s and then recover. What happens to enrollment rates and enrollments, however, appears to depend on the two factors that have been the drag on demand during the 1980s: cost and student aid. Sustained increases in real costs will decrease demand, other things being equal. Whether they occur and whether student aid programs adjust to offset their effects remain the questions that will determine the future direction of undergraduate enrollments.

5.2   Changes in Who Goes to College

College attendance is strongly correlated with economic position. Yet, as the discussion of financial aid policy in Chapter 4 makes clear, the ability of low-income students to attend college continues to be a widely accepted measure of the effectiveness of financial aid policy in the United States. With the general increase in college costs and the decline in grants, many observers have feared that lower-income students would lose ground in college enrollment. In light of the importance of these issues for public policy, it is useful to look specifically at recent trends in the composition of college students and relative enrollment rates. This section examines both trends in enrollment by income and socioeconomic status and trends in college completion rates by race.

5.2.1   Income and Socioeconomic Status.

The last row of Table 5.1 repeats information presented in Chapter 4 on the relative enrollments of students from families above and below the median income. Demand over this recent period appears to have been stronger among households with above-average incomes. The enrollment rate for those above the median income increased by 16 percent, compared to just 8 percent for those below the median.

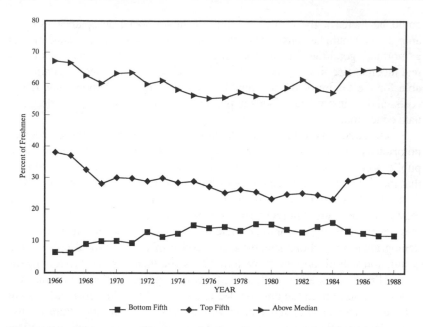

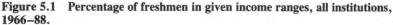

Figure 5.1   Percentage of freshmen in given income ranges, all institutions, 1966–88.
Source: Calculated from data contained in Astin et al. (selected years).

In order to examine trends in the composition of students over a larger time period, data from the annual surveys of freshmen conducted by the Cooperative Institutional Research Program were analyzed. Begun in 1966, this national survey includes a series of factual and attitudinal questions, among which is parental income. Although there are obvious drawbacks to relying on college students' estimates of their parents' income, trends in this measure appear to be a useful indicator. Whatever biases exist in the responses would appear to be more or less constant over time. For better or worse, this survey offers the best source of comparable income data on college students over time.[1]

Figures 5.1–5.3 present information on the distribution of parental income for freshmen in various types of institutions for the years 1966–88. In Figure 5.1, responses for all college freshmen are summarized using the percentage of students with parental income below the twentieth percentile of family incomes for the year, above the median family income, and above the eightieth percentile of family income. Because these income levels typically did not

1. One problem in making comparisons over time may occur when the number and width of income categories in the survey are changed from one year to the next. For example, in 1985, the survey readjusted its income classes, increasing the number of possible classes above $50,000 from two to five and decreasing the number below $10,000 from four to two. If students have a tendency to favor classes in the middle at the expense of those at the extremes, this change may have had the effect of increasing the average reported income.

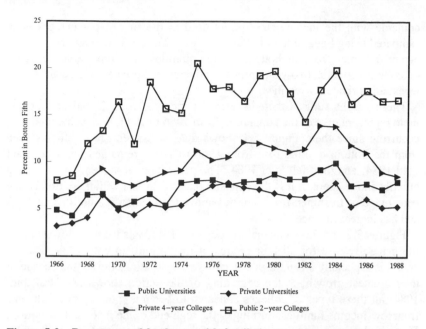

Figure 5.2   Percentage of freshmen with family income in bottom income quintile, by type of institution, 1966–88.
Source: See Figure 5.1.

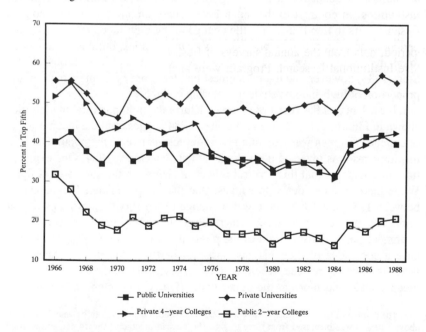

Figure 5.3   Percentage of freshmen with family income in top income quintile, by type of institution, 1966–88.
Source: See Figure 5.1.

coincide with the income-class limits used in the survey, percentages were estimated using linear interpolation. Figures 5.2 and 5.3 compare the percentage of freshmen from the bottom and top quintiles, respectively, at four types of colleges: public two-year, private universities, private nonsectarian colleges, and private universities.

These graphs suggest that, in terms of income, college students became more representative of the population from 1966 to 1984, with some reversion occurring since then. Figure 5.1 shows that the percentage of all freshmen from the bottom quintile rose from 1966 to 1975, remained fairly constant until 1984, and then fell after 1984. The percentage of students from the top quintile shows more or less the opposite pattern. In line with these trends, the percentage of freshmen from families above the median fell until about 1980 and has increased since 1984.

Figures 5.2 and 5.3 show that the portion of students from the lowest quintile generally rose for all four groups of institutions up until 1984. The increase is especially steep for public two-year institutions during the decade of their greatest growth, at the beginning of the period shown. At least until 1984, all these types of colleges appeared to become more open to students from low-income families. Turning to the high end of the income distribution, Figure 5.3 gives a graphic illustration of the concentration of relatively affluent students in universities and private four-year colleges: freshmen from the top quintile account for at least 40 percent of the total in all three types of institutions, in contrast to the much lower share among community college freshmen. As to trend, there is little change in the high-income share over the period among students in public and private universities, but this share tended to fall in private four-year and public two-year colleges, at least through 1984. Since 1984, however, the figures suggest that there has been an increase in the proportion of high-income students entering college.

It is evident that the year 1984 marked a turning point in several of the series shown in Figures 5.1–5.3. Trends through 1984 suggest that the income status of college freshmen was becoming more representative of the population, but this impression is reversed if one looks at the years since 1984. One explanation, of course, is that this reversal reflects a change in the survey or sample. While there is no evidence to suggest that the sample changed significantly between 1984 and 1985, there was a change in the survey questionnaire that might account for the noticeable increase in the family incomes reported by freshmen, particularly in light of the possibility that many freshmen may not have a good idea of their parents' income. In 1985, the income categories were significantly revised, resulting in fewer categories at the lower end of the income scale and more at the upper end.[2] If, say, freshmen unsure of their

2. The number of income classes below $15,000 was reduced from six to three, and the number above $40,000 was increased from three to six. The median income of the 14 categories listed rose from $20,000 to $35,000, by far the largest increase in any revision of the survey from 1966 to 1988. (Median income increased from $12,500 in 1969, to $16,250 in 1970, to $20,000 in 1979, and to $35,000 in 1985.)

family's income tended to mark answers close to the middle of the categories available, this change in the survey questionnaire could have resulted in an increase in the percentage of students indicating high family incomes.

In order to test for this possibility and more generally to provide another check on these income figures, I looked at changes in father's education, another measure of social class that should be correlated to family income but that is known with considerable certainty and is not subject to the category effect noted above. It is possible to calculate from the survey the proportion of freshmen whose fathers had completed college. Of course, education levels in the population have been rising over time, so looking only at the proportion of freshmen with college-educated fathers would not give any information on the relative social standing of college students. To be revealing, this proportion must be compared to that of the population at large. A convenient measure of relative social standing by this metric is the ratio of the odds of a man being college educated to the odds of a freshmen having a college-educated father. This ratio can be interpreted as the relative college enrollment rate of children of non-college-educated fathers, compared to the enrollment rate of those with college-educated fathers.[3] A change in this relative enrollment rate would have much the same implication as a change in the relative income position of college graduates—namely, a change in the relative social and economic standing of college students.

Table 5.2 shows this relative enrollment rate for all college freshmen and for freshmen at two-year colleges and private and public universities, along with the corresponding percentages of fathers of freshmen who were college graduates and the percentage of men 25 and older who had finished four years of college. The general increase in educational attainment in the male population and among fathers of freshmen over the period is quite evident. The relative enrollment rate of children of non-college graduates implied by these figures tended to fall over the period. For all freshmen, for example, the college enrollment rate for the children of non-college graduates in 1966 was 47 percent that of the children of college graduates. Mirroring the patterns of the income distributions shown above, this relative enrollment rate rose to 50 percent in 1984 and then fell to 43 percent. The changes shown for public and private universities more clearly indicate an increase in exclusivity. Only in

---

3. Let P be the proportion of men 25 and older in the population who are college graduates (defined here as those with four or more years of college). Let E be the college enrollment rate for those with fathers who are college graduates, let rE be the rate for those whose fathers did not finish college. Let X be the proportion of college freshmen whose fathers are college graduates. If N is the total number of young people who might otherwise be college freshmen, there are EPN freshmen whose fathers finished college and $rE(1 - P)N$ freshmen whose fathers did not. Therefore,

$$X = EPN/[rE(1 - P)N + EPN].$$

Rearranging terms yields an expression for the relative enrollment rate for those whose fathers are not college graduates:

$$r = [P/(1 - P)]/[X/(1 - X)].$$

Table 5.2   One Measure of the Social Class of College Freshmen, Selected Types
                   of Institutions, Selected Years

| | % of Males 25 and Over with Four or More Years College | % of College Freshment Whose Fathers Completed College | | | |
| | | All Institutions | All Two-Year | Universities | |
				Public	Private
1968	13.3	24.5	13.3	30.9	44.8
		(47)	(100)	(34)	(19)
1972	15.4	a	a	a	a
1976	18.6	33.4	23.5	45	55.9
		(46)	(75)	(28)	(18)
1980	20.8	35.5	24.1	47	60.8
		(48)	(83)	(30)	(17)
1984	22.9	37.2	25.1	49.1	65.3
		(50)	(89)	(31)	(16)
1988	24.0	42.5	29.1	54.7	69.9
		(43)	(77)	(26)	(14)

Source: U.S. Bureau of the Census, *Current Population Reports*, Series P-20, *Educational Attainment in the U.S.: March 1981 and 1986*, No. 428 (1988), table 12; U.S. Department of Education (1989, table 9); and Astin et al. (selected years).
Note: Relative college enrollment rates for children of non-college graduates are in parentheses.
ªNot available.

the case of public two-year colleges do these relative enrollment rates appear not to correspond to the income figures shown above. Figure 5.4 shows the relative enrollment rates for four-year institutions for all the years for which data were available. There are declines evident in all three series after 1983 and a longer decline in private universities before that.

The evidence on income and parental education presented here suggests no dramatic transformation in the relative economic and social standing of college students. In the main, college students have been and continue to be relatively affluent and to come from families with above-average educational attainment. But there have been subtle changes over time. During the late 1960s and early 1970s, there were increases in the proportion of freshmen from lower-income families, especially in the two-year public colleges. However, there appears to have been something of a reversal in the most recent decade, with college enrollment among those in the bottom part of the income distribution slipping relative to those at the top.

5.2.2 Trends in College-Completion Rates

Although there has been a great deal of discussion about recent trends in college enrollment rates, particularly regarding the declines in rates for minorities since 1976, relatively little attention has been paid to trends in the rates at which enrollees progress toward completion of degree requirements. As emphasized above, the rate of attainment depends not only on the rate of

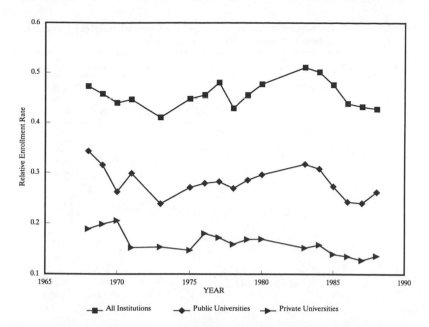

Figure 5.4   Relative college enrollment rates: those without vs. those with college-educated fathers, by type of institution, 1966–88.
Source: See notes to Table 5.2.

enrollment but also on the rate of completion for those who have enrolled. In particular, as Table 2.15 above shows, a large portion of the observed racial differences in college attainment can be attributed to differences in the rates of progression for those who have enrolled. In trying to understand the components of recent changes in attainment, therefore, it is important to look beyond enrollment rates and examine trends in college completion.

By using published Census data on college enrollment, it is possible to follow successive cohorts of high school graduates to examine their enrollment behavior and their college completion rates. Table 5.3 examines four loosely defined cohorts, each comprising three successive years' high school graduates, broken down by race and sex. The percentage of each cohort of graduates who were enrolled in college or the percentage who had completed four years of college are given for three points: one to three years after graduation, five to seven years, and 8–10 years. For example, the table shows that 27.4 percent of white males who had graduated in the years 1970–72 had completed four years of college by 1977 (five to seven years after graduation); by 1980 (8–10 years after graduation), 30.4 percent of the cohort had finished four years. When the data are grouped in this way, differences between cohorts over time can be distinguished from differences within the same cohort over time.

Looking first at white males, there is little trend in the enrollment rate one

Table 5.3   **College Enrollment and Four-Year Completion Rates by Race for Four Cohorts of High School Graduates**

Race, Cohort, % Enrolled in College, and % Who Had Completed Four or More Years of College	Years after Graduation					
	Male			Female		
	1–3	5–7	8–10	1–3	5–7	8–10
White:						
Classes of 1970–72:						
% enrolled	41.7	19.4	10.8	32.9	14.5	9.0
% 4 +	.6	27.4	30.4	.5	23.8	26.5
Classes of 1975–77:						
% enrolled	39.3	17.5	9.8	35.0	13.6	9.9
% 4 +	.5	25.3	27.3	.8	21.5	25.9
Classes of 1979–81:						
% enrolled	43.6	15.8	a	40.6	14.0	a
% 4 +	.9	22.5	a	.8	25.4	a
Classes of 1983–85:						
% enrolled	43.2	a	a	42.4	a	a
% 4 +	1.1	a	a	.8	a	a
Black:						
Classes of 1970–72:						
% enrolled	37.5	21.1	14.5	26.8	15.8	7.9
% 4 +	.5	12.0	18.9	.4	16.7	17.2
Classes of 1975–77:						
% enrolled	34.9	16.3	7.7	34.7	16.0	11.3
% 4 +	.6	11.1	14.3	.5	13.8	16.9
Classes of 1979–81:						
% enrolled	33.1	15.8	a	34.6	13.7	a
% 4 +	1.0	11.6	a	.8	10.5	a
Classes of 1983–85:						
% enrolled	33.4	a	a	34.2	a	a
% 4 +	.4	a	a	1.1	a	a

Source: U.S. Bureau of the Census, *Current Population Reports*, Series P-20, *School Enrollment—Social and Economic Characteristics of Students*: *October 1973*, No. 272; *October 1977*, No. 333; *October 1978*, No. 346; *October 1981 and 1980*, No. 400; *October 1982*, No. 408; *October 1985 and 1984*, No. 426; and *October 1986*, No. 429 (1988)—tables entitled "Year of High School Graduation for Persons 16 to 34 Years Old by Educational Attainment, Enrollment Status, Sex, and Race."

Note. Each report gives data on enrollment and completion rates for cohorts graduating in years (*t* denotes the year of the report) (*a*) *t*, (*b*), *t* - 1 to *t* - 3, and (*c*) *t* - 4 and three cohorts graduating in years *t* - 5 and before with ages (*d*) under 26, (*e*) 26–28, and (*f*) 29–34. If high school graduates are assumed to be 18 in the October following the year of their high school graduation, the last three cohorts correspond to the following years: (*d*) *t* - 5 to *t* - 7, (*e*) *t* - 8 to *t* - 10, and (*f*) *t* - 11 to *t* - 16. Cohorts *b*, *d*, and *e* all comprise three years' worth of graduates and thus can be compared over time. For example, the graduating classes of 1970–72 appear as group *b* in the 1973 report, group *d* in 1977, and group *e* in 1980. Illustrative approximate standard errors for the following estimates for males are given below for the classes of 1979–81. For the percentage enrolled one to three years after graduation, they are 1.2 (for the estimate of 43.6) for whites and 3.4 (for 33.1) for blacks. For the percentage with four or more years five to seven years after graduation, they are 1.0 (22.5) for whites and 2.2 (11.6) for blacks. For an explanation of these approximations, see app. C in the 1986 *Current Population Reports*, Series P-20, noted above.

aNot available.

to three years after high school, but there is a decline at five to seven years. Completion rates appear to decline over time, with the percentage having finished after five to seven years dropping from 27 to 23 from the first to the third cohorts. White females show a positive trend in one- to three-year enrollment rates, rising from 33 to 42 percent of high school graduates. While enrollment rates for white males were almost always higher than they were for white females, the completion rate for females overtook and surpassed that for males in the 1979–81 cohort.

The patterns for blacks contrast with those of whites in several respects. Although the smaller sizes for blacks result in substantially more variability (standard errors for these estimates are on the order of 2–3.5 percentage points), it seems clear that there are important differences in both the levels and the trends in these rates. For black males, the differences are the most striking. Estimates of all three of the college enrollment rates fell for the first three cohorts, although this decline is only about the size of the standard error in the one- to three-year case. Especially noticeable is the fall in the 8–10 year enrollment rate from 14.5 percent in the first cohort to 7.7 in the second. For black females, there are two contradictory trends: an increase in the one- to three-year enrollment rate between the first and second cohorts and a decline in the completion rate at five to seven years, which may be erased at 8–10 years. These figures are consistent with a gap between the educational attainment of black males and females.[4] When viewed in conjunction with the widely cited enrollment rates such as those in Table 2.7 above, information such as this yields a much cloudier picture of black progress. Whereas, on the basis of the historically high enrollment rates for blacks, the mid-1970s might otherwise be viewed as the time of greatest achievement, the figures here cast doubt on the subsequent success of those enrollees in completing bachelor's degrees. Increases in enrollment were apparently not matched by increases in the number of graduates.

In order to examine these puzzling trends more closely, Table 5.4 presents information on enrollment and progress toward completion by year. In this table, progress is measured by the percentage of roughly three high school graduating classes to complete a certain number of years of college five to seven years after high school.[5] Information is given for whites and blacks for the year 1973–86. The columns marked "(4)" in the table give the proportion of high school graduates who had completed four years of college five to seven years following their graduation from high school. Also shown are three components of this probability: in the columns marked "(1)" the probability that a member of these cohorts would have finished a year of college; in the columns marked "(2)," the probability of finishing two years having com-

4. See, e.g., Lee A. Daniels, "Experts Foresee a Social Gap between Sexes among Blacks," *New York Times,* 5 February 1989, p. 5.

5. More precisely, each cohort is composed of those who had graduated from high school at least five years before and were under 26 years old. For those who graduated from high school at age 18, this would imply the inclusion of 23- to 25-year-olds.

Table 5.4   Completion Probabilities for One, Two, and Four Years of College, Five to Seven Years after High School Graduation, 1973–86, by Race

	White				Black			
	(1)	(2)	(3)	(4)	(1)	(2)	(3)	(4)
1973	.507	.807	.615	.252	.401	.735	.437	.132
1974	.521	.807	.614	.258	.397	.751	.570	.170
1975	.534	.793	.621	.263	.401	.752	.492	.149
1976	.544	.788	.616	.264	.458	.725	.494	.164
1977	.537	.791	.600	.255	.411	.688	.514	.146
1978	.525	.795	.582	.243	.446	.766	.467	.160
1979	.509	.807	.581	.239	.445	.731	.470	.153
1980	.491	.811	.572	.228	.435	.748	.455	.148
1981	.496	.818	.582	.236	.445	.756	.437	.147
1982	.500	.811	.575	.233	.466	.701	.387	.127
1983	.500	.819	.595	.244	.443	.723	.380	.122
1984	.497	.810	.569	.229	.432	.736	.400	.127
1985	.511	.811	.582	.241	.395	.745	.352	.104
1986	.509	.817	.579	.241	.445	.763	.322	.110

Source: U.S. Bureau of the Census, *Current Population Reports*, Series P-20, *School Enrollment—Social and Economic Characteristics of Students: October 1973*, No. 272; *October 1974*, No. 286; *October 1975*, No. 303; *October 1976*, No. 319; *October 1977*, No. 333; *October 1978*, No. 346; *October 1979*, No. 360; *October 1981 and 1980*, No. 400; *October 1982*, No. 408; *October 1983*, No. 413; *October 1985 and 1984*, No. 426; *October 1986*, No. 429 (1988); and *October 1988 and 1987*, No. 443 (1990)—tables entitled "Year of High School Graduation for Persons 16 to 34 Years Old by Educational Attainment, Enrollment Status, Sex, and Race."

Note: Figures are for those who graduated five or more years before the sample date and are under 26 years old. Columns contain the following information: (1) probability of completing one year of college; (2) probability of completing two years having completed one; (3) probability of completing four years having completed two; and (4) probability of completing four years, i.e., (1) × (2) × (3).

pleted one year; and in the columns marked "(3)," the probability of finishing four years having completed two. The product of the last three is, by definition, equal to the probability of completing four years. By thus splitting up the completion rate, it is possible to examine trends in the components of college attainment.

The one-year completion rates show that, for most years during this period, a majority of white high school graduates had finished at least one year of college five to seven years after finishing high school; the rates among blacks were somewhat less. There is little trend in this rate among whites, but there is some improvement in the rate for blacks beginning in 1976. Once students had completed one year, the chances of completing a second year were quite good, roughly 80 percent for whites and 75 percent for blacks. There is a slight upward trend in this rate for whites but no trend for blacks.

The most striking change shown in the table is in the conditional probability of completing four years having finished two. While there is a slight decline in the rate for whites, that for blacks shows a marked decline. Comparing the average conditional probabilities for the first three and the last three years shown, the rate for whites declined from 0.62 to 0.58, or 6 percent. Over the same period, the average rates for blacks dropped from 0.50 to 0.36, or 28 percent. This decline signals a significant deterioration in educational attainment by blacks. Precisely why it has occurred is not clear from these figures, of course. The decline could be the result of higher dropout rates or merely a lengthening of the time to degree, manifested, for example, in an increasing tendency to study part-time.

The data presented in this section suggest a growing gap in the enrollment and completion rates of students in the upper and lower portions of the income distribution. The evidence on this is by no means unambiguous, nor is the shift of monumental proportions, but it is perceptible. Such a trend would be consistent with the hypothesis that rising tuitions and falling grant funds have differentially discouraged low-income and minority students from enrolling and remaining in college. It could also be explained to some extent by the strong income growth among the affluent. If it continues to be observed, this trend certainly poses important questions for public policy. Exactly what the access and choice objectives imply for relative enrollment rates is a political determination, but this apparent change in outcomes could add to the current interest in reevaluating student aid programs. At the same time, it has been pointed out that not all the observed trends are necessarily undesirable. For example, an increase in a given group's dropout rate could be the natural consequence of an increase in its rate of college entry, with some of the new entrants simply making the economically efficient choice not to pursue college.[6] However, to the extent that recent trends have arisen because low-income students are facing more imposing financial barriers to college attendance, the implications for policy may be quite different.

5.3 Questions for Research

As is evident from the discussion in this part, research on the demand for college has left a number of important questions unanswered. In concluding, it is appropriate to mention some of these. There are at least three sets of questions that call for further research. The first set can be thought of as basic questions of fact. For example, evidence has been presented above that there has been a divergence in enrollment rates for those above and below the middle of the income scale, but the evidence would have to be judged as circumstantial at best and needing further confirmation. To the extent that this is the case, however, it seems important to investigate how these changes are being felt by type of institution. Are the differences in economic status between public and private institutions growing? Is there a tendency for high-

6. According to Manski (1989), enrollment can be seen as a decision to experiment with college, and for some people dropping out may be the optimal decision. Reducing the number of dropouts is therefore not necessarily an improvement.

aptitude students to become more concentrated in a relatively small number of selective institutions?[7]

There are other questions that relate simply to the interpretation of published data. For example, Census data on school enrollment exclude those on active military duty. Since minority groups are overrepresented in the military and the military itself probably represents the major source of financial support for college training among those enlisted, the exclusion of this group may bias the statistics on college enrollment by race. Another widely recognized problem of interpretation relates to those students who, for the purpose of financial aid calculations, elect to be treated as independent of their families. The portion of students in this group has been growing over time, and this trend may confound statistics on financial aid in ways not now recognized. One other example has to do with interpretating the finding that a declining percentage of those who enroll in college are completing within five to seven years after their high school graduation. One possibility is that college students are simply taking longer to complete their degrees, not only by enrolling part-time, but also by taking more courses. Such a tendency not only would explain the observed drop in completion rates but may also have contributed to some of the increases in enrollment rates.

A second set of unanswered questions has to do with explaining the demand for undergraduate places. One clear need is to build on the existing economic models of demand that incorporate economic returns to college as well as price and income effects. During the 1980s, there were significant changes in several factors thought to be important in demand, including the college earnings advantage, college costs, and the composition of financial aid. It would be interesting to see how well such models account for the differences in college enrollment between men and women during the 1980s. They might also be used to explain the observed trends in college completion. In extending the research on demand, it seems important to pay more attention to the distribution of demand by type of institution. Changes in the aggregate enrollment rate are felt differently in four-year institutions than in two-year colleges, and so on. The substitutability among types of college has been reflected in models of individual choice, but the implications for aggregate enrollments have not been put together. One illustration of the importance of such interactions is the possibility of perverse effects from changes in federal student aid programs. It is possible, for example, that cuts in aid to middle-class students could induce such students to switch from private to public colleges, taking places that would otherwise have been occupied by low-income students.[8]

A third set of questions bridges the gap between demand and supply. How

---

7. For an examination of the latter question, see Cook and Frank (1991).

8. This possibility is suggested by Thomas Mortenson's assessment of changes he observed in Illinois in the 1980s. An accompanying feature was an increase in the admissions standards in public institutions, presumably brought about by the increase in applications from able students (McPherson 1988a, 14).

do colleges and universities respond to changes in demand and in public policy affecting demand? Several avenues of action are open to institutions, including admissions standards, recruitment, efforts to prevent students from dropping out, and, for private institutions, price changes. The question of how the selective institutions, who are facing excess demand for their places, set their prices has been discussed, but the process is not well understood. It appears at least that these institutions are not acting like profit maximizers in this regard. Institutional behavior not related to price has received little systematic study. Yet it may be quite important in determining who graduates, who enrolls, and who applies to college, and to what kind of college. It is evident that questions of this sort will provide an interesting and important research agenda on the demand for higher education.

II Academic Labor Supply

Ronald G. Ehrenberg

6　　　Projections of Shortages

6.1　An Overview of the Study

Projections of forthcoming shortages of Ph.D.s abound. A major book coauthored by a former president of Princeton University, who is now president of a major foundation, is announced to the world in a front-page story in the *New York Times* (Bowen and Sosa 1989; Fiske 1989). The book concludes that by the late 1990s there will be large shortages of faculty in the arts and sciences and that these shortages will be especially large in the humanities and social sciences, where there may be as few as seven candidates for every ten faculty positions. A National Science Foundation internal staff report projects a substantial shortfall in science and engineering doctorates starting in 1994 (National Science Foundation 1989a). A National Research Council committee projects substantial shortages of biomedical doctorates by the year 2000 (National Research Council 1990). These projections all lead the president of the American Association for the Advancement of Science to talk about the need for immediate corrective actions (Atkinson 1990).

Economists typically define shortages as arising when, at the prevailing salaries in an occupation, the quantity of labor demanded exceeds the quantity of labor supplied (Ehrenberg and Smith 1991, chap. 2). As long as salaries are free to rise, shortages will eventually be eliminated. Concern over potential shortages of doctorates in academe occurs both because academic institutions may not possess the resources to increase faculty salaries substantially, and because, even if they do, the time it takes graduate students to complete doctoral degrees is sufficiently long that an increase in graduate enrollments in response to a salary increase would increase the supply of new doctorates only many years later. Thus, if shortages do materialize in the future, they may persist for a number of years.

Among the policies proposed to avert these projected shortages are increased financial support for graduate students and the shortening of the time it takes graduate students to complete their degrees. Yet, as is indicated below, empirical evidence on the magnitudes of likely supply responses to such proposed changes is actually quite scanty.

How these estimates of shortages are arrived at can be illustrated by briefly summarizing Bowen and Sosa's (1989) projection model of the demand and supply in the arts and sciences for faculty with doctorates. At the risk of simplifying, their analysis proceeds as follows. First, they use data on the current age distribution of faculty and estimates of departure rates (to nonacademic jobs, retirement, and death) by age to project the replacement demand for faculty each year. Quite strikingly, they show that plausible changes in retirement behavior that might be induced by the abolition of mandatory retirement have only small effects on replacement demand.

Next, data on population trends and age-specific college enrollment rates are used to project college enrollments, and data on trends in enrollment by major are used to project enrollments in the arts and sciences. Data on trends in student/doctoral faculty ratios (which have been decreasing) and assumptions about whether these ratios are likely to rise or fall in the future are then used to project how changes in enrollment will translate into changes in the demand for new faculty with doctorates.

As shown below, while the number of Ph.D.s granted by U.S. universities has been roughly constant in recent years, nonacademic job opportunities are increasingly available to new Ph.D.s. In addition, new Ph.D. recipients are increasingly citizens of foreign countries who are temporary residents in the United States, and these new doctorates' probabilities of obtaining employment in the United States are low.[1] Projections of future academic labor supply are made on the basis of these trends and projections of the number of college graduates. Supply and demand forces are then integrated and the projections of future shortages obtained. Even Bowen and Sosa's most "optimistic" set of assumptions lead to projections of a 43 percent underproduction of new doctorates in the arts and sciences as a whole and a 66 percent underproduction in the humanities and social sciences during the period 1997–2002 (Bowen and Sosa 1989, table 8.5).

As noted by Bowen and Sosa, their projections of the supply side of the academic labor market, which are typical of those used in other studies, are based on a number of simplifying assumptions and "avowedly rough judgments" (Bowen and Sosa 1989, p. 166). Similarly, some of their proposed policy remedies, such as increasing financial aid for graduate students and shortening the time it takes students to receive degrees, are made without presenting any evidence on the likely magnitude of supply responses to these changes. As such, this part of the book reviews the academic literature and

---

1. These probabilities depend on foreign students' desired employment, academic employers' desires to hire foreign students, and U.S. immigration policies. I return to this point later.

available data (from a wide range of sources) to summarize what we know about academic labor supply and what we need to know to make informed policy decisions. Among the issues to be addressed are the following.

1. Why is the proportion of U.S. college graduates completing doctoral programs today substantially lower than it was 20 years ago? Does this reflect a changing relative financial attractiveness of employment opportunities for people with doctorates or simply a limitation over the last decade in academic employment opportunities? How and why has the distribution of undergraduate majors across fields changed, and how has this affected enrollments in doctoral programs? Has the quality of Ph.D. students declined in recent years?

2. Why has there been a growing lag between college graduation and entry to doctoral programs and a lengthening in the time students require to complete such programs? Do undergraduate loan burdens influence the former and financial support for graduate students and postgraduate job opportunities influence the latter? Do these factors also influence the proportion of graduate students who are studying part-time?

3. Why has the proportion of graduate students accepting postdoctoral appointments prior to permanent employment been rising? Would a shortage of Ph.D.s reduce the proportion of students accepting these appointments, and would a reduction in this proportion increase new applicants to graduate study?

4. Why has the proportion of new Ph.D.s choosing employment in the nonacademic sector increased? Is academe currently losing its best new Ph.D.s to the nonacademic sector? If shortages of new Ph.D.s materialize, will improved job opportunities and increasing wages in academe relative to the nonacademic sector induce more new Ph.D.s to enter the academic sector, more experienced nonacademic Ph.D.s to enter or reenter the academic sector, or fewer experienced academic Ph.D.s to leave the academic sector?

5. How will the changing age structure of faculty influence faculty productivity? How will the uncapping of mandatory retirement affect the academic labor supply?

6. Why are minorities and women underrepresented in academe? What policies may lead to increased representation of these groups?

7. Should (and can) American universities seek to increase employment of foreign students who receive their Ph.D.s here? Should (and can) they increase their employment of American and foreign-born academics currently employed in foreign universities?

8. Would a "Ph.D. shortage" really matter? That is, which institutions are likely to be "hurt" by a shortage of Ph.D.s? Are faculty at these institutions currently major contributors to our stock of research, the production of new Ph.D.s, or the production of undergraduates who go on to Ph.D. study? Could the Ph.D. shortage be averted by the use of more faculty without doctorates? Is there any evidence that a substitution of faculty without for faculty with

doctorates would lead to a reduction in the quality of undergraduate instruction?

The plan of this study is as follows. In the remainder of this chapter, some background data are presented on the academic labor market and new Ph.D. production in the United States. Chapter 7 describes a schematic model of academic labor supply and indicates the underlying trends since 1970 in a number of variables that contribute to projections of shortages of faculty. In Chapter 8, a general model of occupational choice and the decision to undertake and complete graduate study is sketched. This framework, available data, and the prior academic literature are then used to address students' choice of college majors, decisions to undertake and complete graduate study, decisions on the time it takes to complete Ph.D. programs, and decisions on choices of sectors of employment for new and experienced Ph.D.s. Chapter 9, addresses issues relating to the age structure of the faculty and retirement policies as well as minority and female representation in academe. Finally, Chapter 10 considers whether a shortage of American Ph.D.s would really matter and/or could be eased by increased reliance on foreign students trained in the United States, faculty currently employed in foreign institutions, and faculty without doctorates. It also briefly summarizes the implications of the study for both future research needs and public policy.

6.2   Background Data on the Academic Labor Market

In 1987, approximately 722,000 faculty were employed at institutions of higher education in the United States, and about 64 percent of these were full-time employees (Anderson, Carter, and Malizio 1989, table 104). These faculty were employed at over 3,000 different institutions. Table 6.1 presents some background data on their distribution in a recent year across various Carnegie Foundation categories of institutions.[2]

As the table shows, doctorate-granting institutions represent slightly more than 6 percent of all institutions of higher education (col. 2); however, they employ 40 percent of full-time faculty (col. 3). In contrast, undergraduate liberal arts colleges and two-year institutions, which in turn represent about 17 and 40 percent of all institutions, employ only 7 and 20 percent, respectively, of full-time faculty. While the vast majority of faculty at four-year institutions are full-time, more than half of all faculty at two-year institutions are part-time employees (col. 4).

Columns 5 and 6 make clear that not all faculty have doctorates. At major doctorate-granting universities, on average less than two-thirds of full-time faculty have doctorates, while, at selective liberal arts colleges (Liberal Arts I institutions), this number rises to over three-quarters. In contrast, only 12 percent of full-time faculty at two-year colleges have doctorates, and part-

2. These categories were described in this volume's introduction.

Table 6.1   Faculty Employment in Institutions of Higher Education in the Late
                   1980s in the United States

Institution Type	(1)	(2)	(3)	(4)	(5)	(6)
Total	**3,389**					
Doctorate Granting	**213**	**.062**	**.40**			
Research University I	70	.021	.22	.77	.65	.29
Research University II	34	.010	.07	.82	.58	.20
Doctorate Granting I	51	.015	.06	.69	.64	.20
Doctorate Granting II	58	.017	.05	.73	.65	.18
Comprehensive	**595**	**.176**	**.26**			
Comprehensive I	424	.125	.23	.66	.54	.14
Comprehensive II	171	.050	.03	.66	.51	.15
Liberal Arts	**572**	**.169**	**.07**			
Liberal Arts I	142	.042	.03	.77	.72	.28
Liberal Arts II	430	.127	.04	.63	.50	.17
Two-Year Institutions	**1,367**	**.403**	**.20**	.43	.12	.03
Specialized Institutions	**642**	**.189**	**.05**	.58	.38	.21

Sources: Columns 1 and 2: Carnegie Foundation for the Advancement of Teaching (1987, table 2). Columns 3–6: Authors' calculations from the College Entrance Examination Board, *1988–89 College Characteristics Tapes*. All proportions are weighted (by faculty size) means of individual institution proportions.

Note: Columns are identified as follows: (1) number of institutions of higher education in 1987; (2) share of institutions of higher education in 1987; (3) share of full-time total faculty employment in 1988–89; (4) proportion of faculty who are full-time in 1988–89; (5) proportion of full-time faculty with Ph.D.s in 1988–89; and (6) proportion of part-time faculty with Ph.D.s in 1988–89.

time faculty at all institutions rarely have such degrees. While some faculty are employed in fields where the terminal degree typically is not a doctorate (e.g., fine arts, physical education), these data suggest that academics without doctorates may be viewed as possible substitutes for academics with doctorates, especially at non-research-oriented institutions, if a "shortage" of doctorates materializes.

How much are academics paid? Table 6.2 contains information obtained by the American Association of University Professors (AAUP) from their annual survey of institutions of higher education on average faculty salaries by institutional category, affiliation (public, private, or church related), and rank for the 1989–90 academic year. The AAUP institutional categories are similar, but not identical, to the Carnegie Foundation classifications used in Table 6.1. Data are presented here for doctoral-level, comprehensive (some masters' programs), general baccalaureate (four-year institutions), and two-year institutions; the latter include only those institutions whose faculty have the standard professional ranks (professor, associate professor, and assistant professor) for which the data are reported in the table.[3]

3. For brevity, data for instructors (employed primarily at two-year institutions), lecturers, and individuals without ranks are omitted from these tables.

Table 6.2   1989–90 Average Faculty Salaries by Institutional Categories, Affiliation, and Academic Rank

| | | | Affiliation | |
| | | | Private | |
Rank and Category	All	Public	Independent	Church Related
Professors:				
Doctoral level	59,920	57,520	68,360	61,210
Comprehensive	49,710	49,610	51,000	48,020
General baccalaureate	42,180	43,270	46,830	37,620
Two-year colleges[a]	42,430	43,000	31,560	26,040
All categories	53,540			
Associate professors:				
Doctoral level	42,830	42,010	46,440	43,810
Comprehensive	39,520	39,690	39,740	38,090
General baccalaureate	34,030	35,850	35,940	31,410
Two-year colleges[a]	35,540	35,990	27,830	25,130
All categories	39,590			
Assistant professors:				
Doctoral level	36,110	35,380	39,110	36,330
Comprehensive	32,640	32,730	32,780	31,900
General baccalaureate	28,210	29,650	29,520	26,390
Two-year colleges[a]	30,080	30,560	24,620	22,490
All categories	32,970			

Source: "The Annual Report on the Economic Status of the Profession, 1989–90," *Academe* 76 (March–April 1990), table 3.

[a]Only two-year colleges where faculty have standard academic ranks are included in these tabulations.

On average, full professors', associate professors', and assistant professors' nine-month academic salaries were $53,540, $39,500, and $32,970, respectively, in 1989–90.[4] As Table 6.2 indicates, however, salaries vary widely across categories of institutions.[5] Among the four-year institutions, doctoral-level institutions pay higher salaries than comprehensive institutions, which in turn pay higher salaries than general baccalaureate institutions. Within each four-year institutional category, private independents tend to pay more than public institutions, which in turn pay more than church-related institutions. While the salary differences across institutional categories and affiliations are most pronounced at the full professor level, they exist at other ranks as well.

Why do such differences exist? In part, research-oriented institutions may compete more aggressively for scholars, and the private independent sector

4. These figures exclude employee benefits (which typically exceed 20 percent of salary), summer earnings paid by the institution for teaching or research (from externally funded grants), and all forms of income earned from other sources (such as consulting and royalties).

5. Average salaries also vary widely within each institutional category. Data on average salary by rank for individual universities and colleges are found in the American Association of University Professors (1990).

may have the most flexibility to adjust salary levels to compete in this academic market. While other factors may also be involved—for example, faculty whose primary interests lie in undergraduate teaching may be willing to accept lower salaries at baccalaureate institutions because of the nonpecuniary advantages such institutions offer them—it is reasonable to assume that, if a shortage of doctorates were to materialize, the institutions that would have the most difficulty attracting faculty would be those with the lowest salaries. In fact, the smaller variability across institutions of average salaries at the assistant professor than at the full professor level suggests that, at the faculty entry level, average salaries are currently set to allow institutions to compete for faculty.

In addition to variation across institutional type and affiliation, salaries also vary across disciplines. Table 6.3 presents data on the average salaries of full professors and new assistant professors in 1989–90 for 21 disciplines obtained from a survey of state universities and land-grant colleges. These institutions are primarily public; hence, they are not representative of the entire

Table 6.3   **Average Salaries for Full Professors and New Assistant Professors by Discipline, 1989–90**

Discipline	(1) Average Full Professor Salary	(2) Average New Assistant Professor Salary	(3) Ratio of Average Full to Average New Assistant Professor Salary
Business	66,492	48,023	1.38
Law	78,875	43,434	1.82
Engineering	65,342	41,845	1.56
Computer information	67,026	40,672	1.65
Physical sciences	59,122	34,003	1.74
Mathematics	57,237	32,858	1.74
Agricultural sciences	51,034	32,246	1.58
Library	56,541	32,056	1.76
Architecture	53,337	32,013	1.67
Biology	53,997	31,994	1.69
Psychology	56,599	31,492	1.80
Public affairs	55,582	31,204	1.79
Home economics	50,420	31,139	1.62
Communications	52,117	30,887	1.69
Social sciences	56,637	30,546	1.85
Education	50,677	29,339	1.73
Area studies	55,799	29,304	1.92
Letters	53,083	27,596	1.92
Interdisciplinary studies	57,562	27,579	2.09
Foreign languages	52,613	26,832	1.96
Fine arts	46,819	26,667	1.76

Source: "The Annual Report on the Economic Status of the Profession, 1989–90," *Academe* 76 (March–April 1990), table III. These data are taken from the 1989–90 Faculty Survey by Discipline of Institutions Belonging to the National Association of State Universities and Land-Grant Colleges, conducted by the Office of Institutional Research, Oklahoma State University.

academic labor market. Nonetheless, these data make clear how large disciplinary differences in salary are, even when one eliminates medical schools (which the data do), where salaries tend to be the highest.

As table 6.3 shows, at the full professor level (col. 1), salaries in the highest-paying discipline in the sample, law, are almost 1.7 times the salaries in the lowest-paying discipline, fine arts ($78,875 vs. 46,819). At the new assistant professor level (col. 2), the differences are even more pronounced. Here, average salaries in the highest-paid discipline, business, are over 1.8 times the average salaries paid in the lowest, fine arts ($48,023 vs. 26,667). Not surprisingly, those disciplines with the highest starting salaries tend to be those in which there are both high student demand for instruction and highly paid nonacademic employment opportunities for faculty. They also tend to be disciplines in which the ratio of the average full to average new assistant professor salaries (col. 3) are relatively low.[6]

Full professors have much more institutional and academic "specific human capital" and also tend to have stronger ties to their communities than do their younger colleagues. As such, their probability of leaving their institutions is relatively low (Ehrenberg, Kasper, and Rees, in press); thus, institutions are under somewhat less pressure to raise their salaries in response to tightening labor market conditions. However, the broad disciplinary differences that exist, even at the full professor level, suggest that labor market conditions do influence faculty salaries and that projections of future shortages must take this into account.

Tables 6.1–6.3 paint a portrait of the academic labor market at one point in time. However, the academic labor market is fluid and has undergone several swings over the last two decades. For example, between academic years 1970–71 and 1980–81, the salary of the average faculty member in the United States fell by about 21.1 percent in real terms. In contrast, between 1980–81 and 1989–90, the salary of the average faculty member rose by about 16.6 percent in real terms (American Association of University Professors 1990, table I). To take another example, between 1970 and 1980, full-time-equivalent employment of faculty in the United States rose from 402,000 to 522,000, an increase of more than 2.6 percent a year. In contrast, by 1987, full-time-equivalent faculty employment had risen only to 547,000, an increase of less than 0.7 percent a year, and was projected to remain constant through 1990 (Anderson, Carter, and Malizio 1989, table 105).

In further contrast to these swings, Table 6.4 indicates that, after a tripling of the production of doctorates between 1960–61 and 1970–71, annual production of new doctorates in the United States has remained roughly constant—in the 32,000–34,000 range throughout the 1970s and 1980s (col. 5). However, this relative stability masks a number of substantial changes that did

6. Formally, the correlation across fields between starting assistant professor salaries and the ratio of full to starting assistant professor salaries is −0.66.

Table 6.4   Earned Degrees Conferred by Institutions of Higher Education in the United States, 1960–61 to 1986–87

Year	Associate's Degrees (1)	Bachelor's Degrees (2)	Master's Degrees (3)	First Professional Degrees (4)	Doctoral Degrees (5)	Ratio of First Professional to Doctoral Degrees (6)	Ratio of Doctoral to Bachelor's Degrees 6 Years Earlier (7)
1960–61	a	369,995	81,690	25,253	10,575	2.39	a
1961–62	a	388,680	88,414	25,607	11,622	2.20	a
1962–63	a	416,928	95,470	26,590	12,822	2.07	a
1963–64	a	466,944	105,551	27,209	14,490	1.88	a
1964–65	a	501,713	117,152	28,290	16,467	1.72	a
1965–66	111,607	520,923	140,548	30,124	18,237	1.65	a
1966–67	139,183	558,852	157,707	31,695	20,617	1.54	.056
1967–68	159,441	632,758	176,749	33,939	23,089	1.47	.063
1968–69	183,279	729,656	193,756	35,114	26,088	1.34	.064
1969–70	206,023	792,656	208,291	34,578	29,866	1.16	.064
1970–71	252,610	839,730	230,509	37,946	32,107	1.18	.064
1971–72	292,119	887,273	251,633	43,411	33,363	1.30	.064
1972–73	316,174	922,362	263,371	50,018	34,777	1.44	.062
1973–74	343,924	945,776	277,033	53,816	33,816	1.59	.053
1974–75	360,171	922,933	292,450	55,916	34,083	1.64	.047
1975–76	391,454	925,746	311,771	62,649	34,064	1.84	.043
1976–77	406,377	919,549	317,164	64,359	33,232	1.94	.040
1977–78	412,246	921,204	311,620	66,581	32,131	2.07	.036
1978–79	402,702	921,390	301,079	68,848	32,730	2.10	.035
1979–80	400,910	929,417	298,081	70,131	32,615	2.15	.034
1980–81	416,377	935,140	295,739	71,956	32,958	2.18	.036
1981–82	434,515	952,998	295,546	72,032	32,707	2.20	.035
1982–83	456,441	969,510	289,921	73,136	32,775	2.23	.036
1983–84	452,416	974,309	284,268	74,407	33,209	2.24	.036
1984–85	454,712	979,477	286,251	75,063	32,943	2.28	.036
1985–86	446,047	987,823	288,567	73,910	33,653	2.20	.036
1986–87	437,137	991,339	289,557	72,750	34,120	2.13	.036

Source: U.S. Department of Education (1989, table 200).

ªNot reported or not calculated.

occur during the latter period. While the production of doctorates remained roughly constant, the number of bachelor's degrees granted in the United States roughly doubled between the mid-1960s and the mid-1970s. As a result, the ratio of doctorates granted to bachelor's degrees granted six years earlier fell from .0064 in 1970–71 to .035 in 1978–79 and has remained roughly constant at the lower level since (col. 7). A much smaller proportion of college graduates are obtaining doctoral degrees now than 20 years ago.[7] Moreover, as will be shown in the next chapter, the proportion of doctorates awarded to foreign residents has increased substantially during the past two decades; thus, the proportion of American citizen college graduates receiving doctorates has actually continued to decline.

Part of the reason that this has occurred is that American college graduates have increasingly turned to other forms of postcollege study. In 1970–71, the ratio of first professional degrees (law, dentistry, medicine, and other professions) to doctoral degrees granted stood at 1.18 (col. 7); approximately the same number of first professional and doctoral degrees were awarded. However, by 1977–78, over twice as many first professional degrees as doctoral degrees were awarded, and this has continued in every year since. The ratio of master's degrees granted (col. 3), which includes MBAs, to doctoral degrees granted (col. 6) has also risen; this stood at 7.18 in 1970–71 but rose to 8.58 in 1974–75 and since then has remained close to or above that level. More college graduates are thus entering terminal master's programs (such as the MBAs) and/or starting study toward a doctoral degree but terminating at the master's level.

7. What is true in the aggregate is not necessarily true in every field. However, the scope of this study precludes detailed analyses by field. For a recent analysis of production of doctorates in the biomedical fields, see National Research Council (1990).

7   A Stock Flow Model of Academic Labor Supply

7.1   A Conceptual Model

Figure 7.1 presents a schematic representation of the various components of academic labor supply.[1] After tracing through the figure to highlight the wide variety of areas at which public policies might be directed, the following section presents data on a number of the component stocks and flows.

The potential flow of American undergraduate students into doctoral study depends initially on the number of undergraduate seniors and the major fields they have chosen to study. Choice of undergraduate major is important because in many fields it is rare for students to enter doctoral study from anything other than an undergraduate major in the same, or a closely related, field. In 1988, for example, 73 percent of new doctorates in physics and astronomy, 80 percent of new doctorates in chemistry, 76.4 percent of new engineering doctorates, 62 percent of new doctorates in economics, and 57 percent of new humanities doctorates had undergraduate majors in their doctorate field (National Research Council 1989d, app. A, table 2).

Once students receive undergraduate degrees, they face a number of options. They can enter graduate study directly and become Ph.D. students at American institutions of higher education, they can search for employment, they can pursue graduate study toward other degrees (e.g., business, law, medicine, or the other professions), or they can pursue foreign study. Some of the individuals who fail to enter doctoral study at American institutions directly after receiving their undergraduate degrees may enter at some later date.

---

1. For expository convenience, Figure 7.1 assumes that all academics have doctoral degrees. I return to a discussion of substituting faculty with for faculty without doctorates in chapter 10. Since the vast majority of faculty at two-year colleges do not have doctoral degrees (Table 6.1), this figure and the discussion that follows should be thought of as applying to the four-year college market.

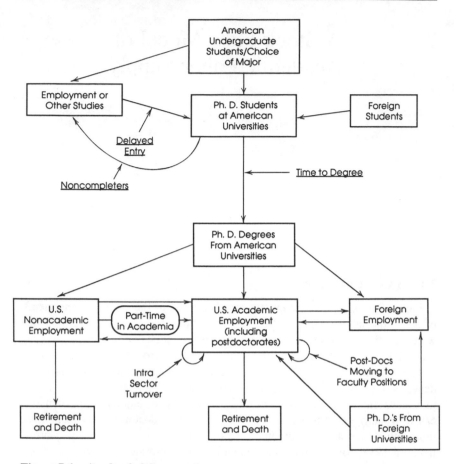

Figure 7.1   Academic labor supply.

The sum of American students who are direct and delayed entrants and of foreign students who both want to pursue doctoral study in the United States and are admitted determines the flow of students into doctoral programs in American universities.

Doctoral study is a risk endeavor, and some students will fail to complete their programs, either because they prove unsuitable academically, because their interests change, or because finances force them to drop out. These students will accept employment in the United States or abroad or enroll in other types of educational programs. The remaining students will ultimately receive doctoral degrees from American universities. Of key concern is the length of time that it takes these students to complete their degrees. Other things being equal, the longer it takes to complete degrees, the less attractive prospective students will find doctoral programs, and the greater noncompletion rates are likely to be.

Students who receive doctorates from American universities face a number of options. Some move directly into academic positions in the United States. Others, especially in the sciences, accept postdoctoral research positions in which they receive additional research experience for one or two years, and then some of these ultimately obtain faculty positions. Others accept nonacademic positions in the United States, and still others accept foreign employment. Some of those initially employed in the nonacademic sector in the United States or in the academic or nonacademic sectors abroad may at a later date find employment in the U.S. academic sector. In addition, American colleges and universities may try to hire new doctorates produced at foreign universities directly as faculty members. Finally, doctorates employed full-time in the nonacademic sector may "moonlight" and also be employed part-time in the academic sector.

Each year, approximately 15 percent of full-time assistant professors and 7–10 percent of the full-time associate and full professors who are employed in American colleges and universities "turn over" and are not employed at the same institution in the next year (Ehrenberg, Kasper, and Rees, in press, tables 1–3). At the assistant professor level, turnover reflects both voluntary movement to other U.S. academic institutions, foreign institutions, or the nonacademic sector and involuntary mobility to these places owing to denial of reappointment or tenure. At the associate professor level, turnover reflects primarily voluntary mobility. Finally, at the full professor level, it reflects voluntary mobility to other positions, retirements, and deaths. The age distribution of the faculty obviously has a major effect on out-mobility from the academic sector: younger faculty are more likely to move to a nonacademic employer, and older faculty are more likely to retire or die.

7.2   Trends in Academic Labor Supply

7.2.1   The Production of Doctorates

During the last two decades, substantial changes have occurred in the distribution of college students' majors. Table 7.1 presents information on the share of bachelor's degrees conferred by U.S. academic institutions in different disciplines for the period 1970–71 to 1987–88. During this period, the proportion of students majoring in business almost doubled, rising to nearly one-quarter of all bachelor's degrees granted. The shares of engineering and other professional degrees increased substantially, while the shares of education and arts and science degrees declined substantially. Within the arts and sciences, the humanities and social sciences were hit the hardest, with the former's share declining by over one-third and the latter's share declining by an even greater amount. Presumably, many students who in previous years would have majored in the social sciences now major in business. More generally, changes in decisions about field of study made by women are an impor-

Table 7.1   Share of Bachelor's Degrees Conferred by U.S. Institutions of Higher
                 Education in Different Disciplines

Category	1970–71	1975–76	1980–81	1985–86	1987–88
Business	.137	.154	.213	.241	.246
Education	.210	.167	.116	.088	.092
Engineering	.059	.050	.081	.097	.099
Other professional	.096	.177	.203	.189	.171
Arts and sciences	.488	.442	.390	.385	.359
Humanities	.147	.118	.097	.090	.095
Life sciences	.043	.059	.046	.039	.037
Physical sciences	.058	.046	.054	.081	.070
Psychology	.045	.054	.044	.041	.045
Social sciences	.185	.136	.107	.095	.101
Interdisciplinary	.010	.030	.042	.040	.041

Sources: Author's computations from data in U.S. Department of Education (1989, table 205)
and unpublished tabulations of the data for 1987–88 provided by the Education Information
Branch, Office of Educational Research and Improvement, U.S. Department of Education.

Table 7.2   Discipline Distribution of Doctorates Awarded by U.S. Colleges and
                 Universities, 1960–88

	Share of Doctorates Awarded in the:						
	Physical Sciences	Engineering	Life Sciences	Social Sciences	Humanities	Education	Professional/ Other
1960	.221	.082	.178	.171	.164	.159	.025
1964	.217	.116	.165	.158	.151	.164	.028
1968	.203	.124	.162	.152	.151	.176	.032
1972	.168	.106	.154	.165	.153	.214	.040
1973	.157	.100	.153	.171	.160	.214	.045
1976	.137	.086	.153	.189	.148	.234	.053
1980	.133	.080	.176	.189	.125	.245	.053
1984	.142	.093	.184	.189	.113	.217	.062
1988	.159	.125	.184	.172	.106	.190	.064

Source: Summary Report 1988: Doctorate Recipients from United States Universities (Washington, D.C.: National Academy Press, 1989), tables A, C.

tant cause of these changing proportions, and, presumably, these reflect, at
least partially, a widening of career options for women (Turner and Bowen
1990).

Some of these trends are reflected in the disciplinary distribution of doctorates awarded by American colleges and universities, which is presented for
the period 1960–88 in Table 7.2. What is most striking is the one-third drop
since the early 1970s in the proportion of doctoral degrees awarded in the
humanities, which reflects the importance influence that an individual's
undergraduate major has on his or her field of graduate study (see the previous

section). The share of doctoral degrees granted in the social sciences has not declined substantially; this apparent divergence from the comparable undergraduate trend may partially reflect the possibility that the shift in students from undergraduate social science to business majors was a shift of students who were unlikely to choose doctoral study.

The shift in the distribution of degrees awarded is also heavily influenced by the inflow of foreign graduate students. As Table 7.3 indicates, over the last 30 years the share of new doctorates from American universities awarded to U.S. citizens and permanent residents has fallen from about 90 to 80 percent. The decline has been most pronounced in the physical sciences and engineering, where foreign students (temporary residents in the United States) represented about 30 and 35 percent, respectively, of new doctorates awarded in 1988. As will be shown below, foreign students are less likely to remain in the United States once they receive their degrees. Thus, given the total number of new doctorates produced, an increase in the proportion who are foreign may reduce the potential academic labor supply to American colleges and universities.[2]

While the number of doctorates produced in American academic institutions has remained roughly constant, the time it takes for students to complete their degrees has lengthened during the past two decades. Data on median years of time spent enrolled as a doctoral student are reported for the period 1968–88 by field and year of degree in Table 7.4. Median *registered time* to degree rose over the period by almost a year and a half, from 5.5 to 6.9 years. The increase in registered time to degree was somewhat smaller in the sciences and engineering but considerably larger in other fields, including the humanities, where registered time to degree rose by three years, from 5.5 to 8.5 years.[3]

2. The distinction made between permanent and temporary residents depends on an individual's immigration status. Permanent residents are noncitizens who have been granted immigrant status or permission to stay in the United States permanently. Temporary residents, or, more precisely, nonimmigrants, are people who have been admitted to the United States for specified purposes (e.g., tourist, student, exchange visitor) for a fixed period of time. As discussed in Chapter 10, temporary residents sometimes subsequently become permanent residents.

3. An important qualification about these time-to-degree data (first recognized by Bowen, Lord, and Sosa, in press) is in order here. The data in Table 7.4 are grouped by year of completion of degree, not by year of entry into doctoral programs. As a result, even if the distribution of times to degree in each entering cohort remains constant over time, these reported average times to degree by year of completion will change if the sizes of entering cohorts are systematically changing over time. In particular, if entering cohorts are increasing in size, average time to degree by year of completion will spuriously appear to decrease, while, if entering cohorts are declining in size, average time to degree by year of completion will spuriously appear to increase. This would occur because, in the former case, those completing degrees in a given year would disproportionately come from "fast" completers from relatively large cohorts, while, in the latter case, those completing degrees in a given year would disproportionately come from "slow" completers from relatively large cohorts.

A simple numerical example illustrates this point. Suppose that all entering students receive degrees, that (unrealistically) half of each year's entering doctoral cohort complete in one year, and the other half complete in two years. Average time to degree by year of entering cohort is thus

Table 7.3   **Share of New Doctorates Going to U.S. Citizens and Permanent Residents**

	Total Doctorates	Physical Sciences	Engineering	Life Sciences	Social Sciences	Humanities	Education	Professional/Other
1960	.907	.896	.836	.852	.910	.970	.953	.898
1964	.896	.886	.837	.822	.907	.962	.949	.871
1968	.899	.888	.850	.840	.909	.955	.954	.871
1972	.923	.886	.845	.874	.914	.959	.960	.903
1973	.904	.869	.850	.872	.908	.953	.959	.887
1976	.894	.840	.813	.863	.909	.951	.954	.885
1980	.879	.829	.705	.867	.914	.945	.931	.880
1984	.839	.770	.646	.853	.887	.925	.918	.826
1988	.801	.702	.654	.815	.865	.895	.919	.801

Source: Summary Report 1988: Doctorate Recipients from United States Universities (Washington, D.C.: National Academy Press, 1989), table C.

Understanding the causes of the lengthening of registered time to degree is important because longer times to degree probably discourage people from entering doctoral study, may increase the likelihood that initial enrollees fail to complete their programs, and increase the length of time it takes new graduate students to enter the academic labor market. Indeed, even if time to degree had no effect at all on the number of people electing graduate study or their completion rates, a reduction in time to degree of one year would create a doubling for one year in the number of doctorates produced and thus contribute to increased academic labor supply.[4]

Data are also presented in Table 7.4 on *total time* to degree, the total length of time between an individual's receipt of the bachelor's degree and his or her receipt of a doctoral degree. Median total time to degree has risen by 2.4 years

---

constant at 1.5 years. Suppose that, in years 0 and 1 (and all previous years), entering cohort size is 100. The top half of the table below shows that reported time to degree by year of completion will decrease from 1.5 to 1.476 years if, starting in year 3, entering cohort size increases by 10 percent per year. Similarly, the bottom half shows that reported time to degree by year of completion will increase from 1.5 to 1.526 years if starting in year 3, entering cohort size decreases by 10 percent per year:

Year	Entering Cohort Size	No. Who Will Complete in t + 1	No. Who Will Complete in t + 2	Average Time to Degree of Completers in the Year
0	100	50	50	1.5 ([50 × 1] + [50 × 2])
1	100	50	50	1.5 ([50 × 1] + [50 × 2])
2	110	550	55	1.5 ([50 × 1] + [50 × 2])
3	121	60.5	60.5	1.476 ([55 × 1] + (50 × 2])
4	133.1	66.55	66.55	1.476 ([60.5 × 1] + [55 × 2])
0	100	50	50	1.5 ([50 × 1] + [50 × 2])
1	100	50	50	1.5 ([50 × 1] + (50 × 2])
2	90	45	45	1.5 ([50 × 1] + [50 × 2])
3	81	40.5	40.5	1.526 ([45 × 1] + [50 × 2])
4	72.9	36.45	36.45	1.526 ([40.5 × 1] + [45 × 2])

While the total number of doctorates awarded in the United States remained roughly constant over the period 1970–88 (Table 6.4), the share and hence the absolute number awarded in the humanities fell substantially (Table 7.2). One can infer from these data that entering cohorts of humanities doctoral students were declining. Bowen, Lord, and Sosa (in press) compute that slightly over half the reported increase in time to degree, reported in Table 7.4, is spuriously due to the declining humanities cohort sizes. This line of reasoning suggests that, while time to degree has increased in the humanities, the increase is not as large is suggested by Tables 7.4 and 7.5 below. Similar studies of how changing cohort sizes affect reported times to degree in other fields have yet to be undertaken.

4. A numerical example illustrates this point. Suppose that it initially takes six years to complete a degree, that 100 students enter the program, and that all complete their degrees. Then, in steady state, there will be 100 first-year, 100 second-year, 100 third-year, 100 fourth-year, 100 fifth-year, and 100 sixth-year students enrolled each year. If time to degree could be reduced to five years in year t, both the fifth- and the sixth-year cohorts would receive degrees that year. Hence, there would be 200 doctorates produced in year t, and median time to degree would be 5.5 years. In year $t + 1$ and all subsequent years, only the fifth-year cohort would receive degrees. Thus, median time to degree would drop to, and thereafter remain at, five years, and doctorate production would return to 100 a year.

Table 7.4   Median Years to Degree for Doctorate Recipients by Broad Field, 1968–88

	All Fields	Physical Sciences	Engineering	Life Sciences	Social Sciences	Humanities	Education	Professional/Other
Registered time:								
1968	5.5	5.1	5.1	5.3	5.1	5.5	5.8	5.1
1970	5.5	5.3	5.2	5.3	5.5	6.1	6.2	5.4
1972	5.7	5.6	5.5	5.5	5.6	6.2	6.1	5.6
1974	5.9	5.6	5.6	5.5	5.7	6.6	6.3	6.0
1976	6.0	5.6	5.6	5.6	5.8	6.9	6.3	6.1
1978	6.1	5.8	5.6	5.7	6.0	7.3	6.5	6.2
1980	6.3	5.8	5.6	5.8	6.4	7.7	6.9	6.4
1982	6.5	5.8	5.7	6.0	6.7	8.0	7.2	6.7
1984	6.8	6.0	5.7	6.3	7.1	8.2	7.6	7.1
1986	6.8	6.0	5.9	6.4	7.2	8.2	7.8	7.3
1988	6.9	6.1	5.9	6.5	7.4	8.5	8.1	7.3
Total time:								
1968	8.1	6.0	7.1	7.1	7.7	9.5	13.9	10.9
1970	7.9	6.1	6.9	6.6	7.3	9.1	12.7	10.2
1972	8.2	6.5	7.5	7.0	7.5	9.0	12.5	9.7
1974	8.5	6.8	7.6	7.2	7.7	9.3	12.4	9.8
1976	8.6	6.7	7.5	7.3	7.8	9.7	12.7	10.3
1978	8.9	7.0	7.5	7.3	8.1	10.2	12.7	10.3
1980	9.3	6.9	7.6	7.4	8.6	10.6	13.2	11.1
1982	9.6	6.9	8.0	7.6	9.2	11.2	13.6	11.6
1984	10.0	7.2	8.0	8.2	9.7	11.5	14.6	12.3
1986	10.4	7.3	8.1	8.7	10.1	12.1	15.7	12.8
1988	10.5	7.4	8.1	8.9	10.5	12.2	16.9	13.0

Source: Summary Report 1988: Doctorate Recipients from United States Universities (Washington, D.C.: National Academy Press, 1989), table I.

Table 7.5   **Mean Number of Years between Receipt of Baccalaureate Degree and Taking of the GREs for Students Planning Doctoral Study[a]**

	Field of Planned Graduate Study											
	(1)	(2)	(3)	(4)	(5)	(6)	(7)	(8)	(9)	(10)	(11)	(12)
1976	2.2	2.1	6.3	2.5	2.0	1.1	1.8	.8	1.8	1.5	1.1	2.2
1977	2.4	2.2	6.2	2.8	2.0	1.2	2.0	1.0	1.8	1.7	1.0	2.3
1978	2.7	2.4	6.8	3.0	2.1	1.3	2.5	1.1	2.0	2.0	.9	2.6
1979	2.9	2.5	7.2	3.2	2.3	1.8	2.7	1.4	2.0	2.1	1.0	2.8
1980	2.8	2.7	7.4	3.3	2.3	1.6	3.1	1.4	2.0	2.2	1.1	2.9
1981	3.2	2.9	8.0	3.9	2.6	1.6	3.2	1.6	2.1	2.5	1.2	3.1
1982	2.8	3.2	8.5	3.5	2.6	1.7	3.6	1.6	2.2	2.6	1.3	3.1
1983	2.9	3.1	8.6	4.1	2.6	1.8	3.6	1.8	2.3	2.7	1.2	3.2
1984	3.3	3.2	8.8	4.4	2.7	2.0	3.8	2.2	2.3	2.8	1.2	3.3
1985	3.9	3.2	9.1	4.6	2.7	2.0	3.9	2.2	2.4	2.8	1.4	3.4
1986	4.3	3.5	9.2	4.7	3.0	2.2	4.4	2.5	2.8	3.0	1.6	3.7
1987	4.5	3.5	9.4	5.0	2.9	2.3	4.5	2.5	2.8	3.0	1.7	3.7

Source: Author's computations from Educational Testing Service (1988), table 42, and the comparable table from the prior years' reports.

[a]Year student took the GRE (e.g., the 1986–87 academic year is treated as 1987 since most students would enter doctoral study in the fall of 1987) minus the year the student reported receiving the bachelor's degree. The fields are as follows: (1) arts; (2) other humanities; (3) education; (4) other social sciences; (5) behavioral sciences; (6) biological sciences; (7) health; (8) applied biology; (9) engineering; (10) mathematical sciences; (11) physical sciences; and (12) total (including fields not reported separately above and intended field not reported by the student).

from 8.1 to 10.5 years; again, much smaller increases are observed for the sciences and engineering, with larger increases for other fields. Total time to degree will be larger than registered time to degree if students delay entry to graduate programs, if they start study in one field and then switch to another at a later date, or if they spend some time not enrolled in graduate study after their initial entry. Evidence presented from the Educational Testing Service in Table 7.5 on the mean number of years between the time students planning doctoral study first take the Graduate Record Examination (which is required for admission by many institutions) and when they received their bachelor's degrees suggests that college graduates are increasingly delaying entry to doctoral study. On average, test takers waited a year and a half longer in 1987 than they did in 1976 (col. 12).

Completion rates for entrants into doctoral programs vary widely across fields and institutions. Data for a set of selected major research universities for periods during the 1970s and early 1980s appear in Table 7.6. These data suggest that completion rates tend to be higher in the sciences than in the humanities and that in most of these programs doctoral completion rates lie in the 40–70 percent range.[5] Even the very best science graduate students, those

5. The rates reported in Table 7.6 may understate the true completion rates slightly because some people who were noncompleters as of the survey dates will ultimately complete their degrees and because one school (University D) reports only those who completed degrees within seven years of their first enrollment.

Table 7.6   Doctoral Completion Rates at Selected Major Research Universities

	University A (1975–77)		University B (1975–80)		University C (1970–82)		University D (1974–80)		University E (1975–77)		University F (1975–77)	
Field	No. of Observations	Completion Rate (%)	No. of Observations	Completion Rate (%)	No. of Observations	Completion Rate (%)	No. of Observations	Completion Rate (%)	No. of Observations	Completion Rate (%)	No. of Observations	Completion Rate (%)
Anthropology	66	43.9	49	43.0	152	39.0	30	33.3	31	51.0	69	55.1
Architecture	24	37.5					28	39.3			25	44.0
Astronomy	15	60.0			65	72.0					10	70.0
Biochemistry and molecular biology	68	77.9			134	75.0	59	64.4			60	75.0
Biology							67	73.1	57	63.0		
Business administration	59	54.2			103	62.0					56	66.1
Chemical engineering	42	83.3			90	53.0	88	85.2			35	60.0
Chemistry	213	83.1	93	87.0	424	68.0	157	75.8	84	60.0	66	74.2
City regional planning	21	42.9			141	51.0					34	61.8
Civil engineering	152	55.9			235	57.0	53	73.6			38	57.9
Classics	28	25.0	23	61.0	47	51.0	41	36.6			21	52.4
Comparative literature	66	19.7	21	71.0	50	52.0	61	50.8			14	50.0
Dramatic art	24	25.0			38	39.0					14	78.6
Economics	97	59.8	66	48.0	247	51.0	41	36.6			21	52.4
Education	230	43.9			385	64.0					707	50.9
Electrical engineering and computer science	211	50.2	26	46.0	502	55.7	102	89.2			106	53.8
English	109	34.9	94	46.0	211	57.0	102	60.8	82	49.0	90	55.6

Entering Class Years

Field	A (N)	A (%)	B (N)	B (%)	C (N)	C (%)	D (N)	D (%)	E (N)	E (%)	F (N)	F (%)
French	20	35.0		52.0	59	52.0			34	50.0	18	50.0
Genetics	23	82.6	23	52.0	118	45.0	65	72.3			14	71.4
Geology & geography	43	60.5	51	61.0								
German	27	33.3	6	17.0	68	37.0	39	48.7	61	52.0	11	36.4
History	105	19.0	54	31.0	153	41.0	111	32.4			88	42.1
Industrial engineering / operational research	51	39.2			152	58.0						
Linguistics	36	47.2	22	55.0	160	47.0	6	100.0			49	40.8
Material science and engineering	57	66.7			137	64.0					9	44.4
Mathematics	199	46.7	47	72.0	169	54.0	116	77.6			68	50.0
Mechanical engineering	122	58.2			123	35.0	70	75.7			35	62.9
Music	24	75.0	6	50.0	84	54.0	64	37.5			111	54.1
Near East studies	26	23.1			25	68.0	55	45.4			31	45.2
Nuclear engineering	32	50.0	37	49.0							49	73.5
Philosophy	30	43.3	102	70.0	80	46.0	64	40.6	42	40.0	35	28.6
Physics	147	67.3			400	60.0	141	79.4	56	71.0	51	58.9
Physiology	21	71.4			44	59.0			7	86.0	15	66.7
Political science	92	51.1			210	45.0	110	29.1			74	40.5
Psychology	72	68.1	31	90.0	165	64.0	76	67.1	57	56.0	165	73.3
Romance language and literature	6				152	50.0	75	38.7			42	42.9
Slavic language and literature	23	21.7	23	52.0	60	32.0					18	33.3
Sociology	70	41.4	63	65.0	135	59.0	63	41.3			72	52.8
Statistics	45	62.2			32	63.0	39	69.2			14	14.3

Source: Unpublished tabulations prepared by the University of California, Berkeley, Graduate Division, dated 3 May 1989.

Note: University A: Completion rate as of May 1988. University C: Completion rate as of May 1988. University D: Completion rate after seven years following the first enrollment for each cohort. University E: Completion rate as of December 1987. University F: Completion rate as of January 1988.

who win prestigious National Science Foundation Graduate Fellowships, had completion rates of 80 percent or less during the period 1962–76 (Harmon 1977, table 1; J. Snyder 1988). These completion rates should be contrasted with completion rates of over 98 percent in the top 20 American law schools, of over 90 percent in major American medical schools, and of 80–95 percent for top MBA programs in the United States.[6] Doctoral study is considerably riskier than its alternatives.

7.2.2   Initial Postdegree Experiences of New Doctorates

Each year, when doctoral candidates submit their dissertations to their graduate schools for final approval, they are asked to respond to the Survey of Earned Doctorates (SED), which is administered by the National Research Council. Among the questions asked in the SED are whether respondents have made definite employment plans in the United States and, if so, whether their employment is in the academic or the nonacademic sector.[7] Data on the sectoral distribution of employment for U.S. citizen and permanent resident new doctorates from the SED are reported in Table 7.7 for 1968, 1978, and 1988. Quite strikingly, the share of these employed new doctorates finding employment in academe has declined in the aggregate from two-thirds in 1968 to about half in 1988. With the exception of the health sciences and business and management fields, the academic share declined in all fields. Indeed, while almost 94 percent of employed new doctorate humanists were employed in academe in 1968, by 1988 slightly less than 80 percent were initially so employed.

Of crucial concern for public policy is whether the declining academic share of employed new doctorates is due to an increasing demand and higher relative salaries for new doctorates in the nonacademic sector or simply due to a scarcity of job openings in the academic sector during the period. While the answer will likely vary across fields, if the former is the case, it will be necessary to increase academic salaries vis-à-vis nonacademic salaries to attract a greater share of new doctorates into academe. If the latter is the case, an expansion of academic job opportunities in itself (without any increase in academic salaries) may lead a greater share of new doctorates to enter aca-

6. The law school data come from *Barrons' Guide to Law Schools* and are for the mid-1980s. The American Medical Association (1988) reports a net attrition rate of 2.6 percent of 1986–87 enrollments at AMA approved medical schools. Since most medical schools have a four-year curriculum, this implies that completion rates exceed 90 percent. Finally, while completion rates of MBA programs are not collected, James Schmotter, associate dean at Cornell's Johnson School of Management, reports that Cornell's MBA completion rate is 98 percent, and other top MBA program rates are also greater than 90 percent, save perhaps Harvard and Virginia. This latter two use the case-study method, and, apparently, test scores and undergraduate records cannot predict which applicants will succeed in these programs, at least not as well as they do for other programs.

7. It is rare for the U.S. citizens holding doctorates to have definite employment plans outside the United States. For example, of those U.S. citizen new doctorates whose future location was known when they returned the SED, 97.6 percent (15,778 of 16,182) had plans in the United States in 1988 (see National Science Foundation 1989e, table 15).

Table 7.7   Sector of Employment of U.S. Citizen and Permanent Resident Doctorate Recipients with Employment Commitments in the United States, 1968, 1978, and 1988 (%)

Field	Academe 1968	Academe 1978	Academe 1988	Industry 1968	Industry 1978	Industry 1988	Government 1968	Government 1978	Government 1988	Other 1968	Other 1978	Other 1988
Total all fields	66.6	56.4	49.8	14.8	15.3	20.4	7.4	12.5	10.8	11.2	15.9	19.1
Physical sciences	50.1	37.9	36.2	34.6	45.2	50.0	9.4	14.4	11.8	5.9	2.4	1.9
Physics/astronomy	52.1	25.9	26.1	25.0	46.9	48.2	16.1	24.1	23.4	6.7	3.1	2.3
Chemistry	29.5	18.4	15.3	58.9	71.4	77.7	4.9	7.7	5.0	6.7	2.5	2.0
Earth, atmospheric, marine	50.7	33.2	39.3	25.9	36.1	30.4	17.8	27.9	29.5	5.6	2.9	.9
Mathematics	79.9	70.8	75.9	12.6	19.1	19.0	3.7	8.2	2.3	3.9	1.9	2.8
Computer sciences	a	58.2	56.6	a	35.8	32.7	a	6.0	8.8	a	.0	1.8
Engineering	33.3	23.5	28.5	47.0	57.1	55.5	10.6	17.5	15.0	9.1	2.0	.9
Life sciences	65.9	59.0	51.9	11.8	20.4	23.7	14.0	16.3	16.8	8.4	4.3	7.6
Biological sciences	68.0	60.9	47.7	9.0	17.7	27.1	13.0	16.4	18.0	9.9	5.0	7.2
Health sciences	56.8	62.9	63.1	23.7	17.2	13.8	6.8	14.5	12.5	12.7	5.5	10.6
Agricultural sciences	62.2	53.7	44.3	16.1	26.7	30.8	19.3	17.3	20.4	2.4	2.4	4.4
Social sciences (including psychology)	75.3	58.5	45.1	4.8	9.6	19.4	10.6	16.0	14.2	9.2	16.0	21.3
Psychology	61.0	40.0	29.6	6.5	12.4	24.6	17.0	20.7	16.5	15.6	26.9	29.3
Other social sciences	85.1	76.2	66.2	3.7	6.9	12.3	6.3	11.4	11.1	4.9	5.5	10.4
Humanities	93.9	82.6	79.3	6.0	4.9	5.8	1.4	3.8	3.7	4.3	8.7	11.2
Education	68.1	51.9	43.8	1.0	3.4	7.3	3.9	12.5	9.0	26.9	32.2	39.8
Professional/other	80.9	74.1	73.8	8.9	7.0	8.2	3.9	7.2	6.4	6.3	11.8	11.6
Business and management	84.6	87.0	90.0	9.1	7.9	7.0	1.9	4.3	2.6	4.4	.8	.4
Communications	88.9	83.9	81.9	8.3	9.3	8.1	.0	4.1	2.0	2.8	2.6	8.1

Source: Summary Report 1988: Doctorate Recipients from United States Universities (Washington, D.C.: National Academy Press, 1989), table R. "Other" includes elementary/secondary schools, nonprofit institutions, self-employment, and other employers.

aNot available.

demic life and may also induce some doctorates currently employed in the nonacademic sector to enter or reenter academe.

Table 7.7 may present a misleading picture of the proportion of new doctorates entering academic careers directly because it focuses on those new doctorates who have accepted employment and ignores the increasing share of new doctorates accepting one- or two-year postdoctoral appointments (postdocs). These positions, found in universities, government, and the private sector, offer doctorates additional opportunities to develop their research skills before moving on to more permanent employment.

Table 7.8 contains data on the share of new doctorates with definite plans in the United States going on to postdocs and academic employment between 1970 and 1988. During this period, the share of new science/engineering U.S. citizen doctorates with definite plans who were starting postdocs rose from 0.22 to 0.39, which was almost equal to the decline from 0.44 to 0.24 in the share accepting academic employment.[8] The trends for permanent residents were very similar. In contrast, in the nonscience/nonengineering fields, very few students accept postdocs, and the small increase that occurred over the last 20 years cannot "explain" the large decline in the share of new doctorates with definite plans accepting academic employment.

When one examines more narrowly defined science/engineering fields, one finds variations in behavior across them. In some of the specific fields listed in Table 7.8, the increase in the share accepting postdocs between 1970 and 1988 was approximately equal to, or greater than, the decrease in the share accepting academic employment (physical sciences, earth and material sciences, life sciences, mathematical sciences, engineering). In other fields, such as the social and psychological sciences, the decline in the share accepting academic employment far exceeded the increase in the postdoc share.

These trends suggest a number of policy issues. Is the increasing share of postdocs in most fields caused by a deepening of knowledge and hence a required longer training period before faculty appointments can be obtained? Or does it represent a response to a relatively loose academic labor market and attempts by doctorates to enhance their attractiveness in the search for permanent academic positions by accepting these lower-paying training positions?[9] Are differences in the growth of postdocs across fields caused at least partially by differences in the strength of the nonacademic labor market across fields? Do postdocs eventually wind up in academic positions so that the net effect on the academic labor supply is simply to lengthen the pipeline? Is the increasing "need" for a postdoc partially responsible for the decline in the

8. In Table 7.8, the social sciences and psychology are included as sciences, and the nonscience/nonengineering fields include the humanities, education, and other professional doctoral fields.

9. As of 1979, the median postdoc stipend was, on average, less than 60 percent of the median salary of full-time-employed new doctorates, although this percentage varied across fields (see National Research Council 1981, table 53).

share of college graduates seeking doctorates? If the increased use of postdocs is a result of a "loose" academic labor market, would a "tight" market lead to an increase in the number of new doctorates directly accepting academic employment? If this occurs, would the decline in the probability that a postdoc is required for academic employment make doctoral study more attractive and increase the flow of college graduates into doctoral programs?

Table 7.8 also contains data on temporary resident (foreign) new doctorates who reported having definite plans in the United States. Although temporary resident new doctorates with definite plans are less likely to remain in the United States than U.S. citizen and permanent resident new doctorates, the share of the former doing so has increased from 0.42 to 0.55 in the total sciences/engineering fields and from 0.22 to 0.30 in the nonscience/nonengineering areas over the period 1970–88. Of those who do stay, a much greater proportion obtain postdocs than do citizen or permanent resident degree holders. Moreover, in 1988, in the total science/engineering area, the share of temporary resident doctorates who stay and find academic appointments was actually as high as the comparable shares of U.S. citizen new doctorates finding academic employment, and, in the nonscience/nonengineering area, it was greater. In part, this may be because temporary resident doctorates may have difficulty obtaining visas to work in the U.S. nonacademic sector. Whether an expansion of temporary resident U.S. academic employment is possible, or desirable, will be discussed in a later chapter.

What do postdocs actually do on completion of their appointments? Every two years, the Office of Scientific and Engineering Personnel of the National Research Council conducts a national probability survey of all doctorates residing in the United States. The Survey of Doctoral Recipients (SDR) is longitudinal in design and allows one to track individuals' changes in status over two-year periods if they respond to the survey in two consecutive periods.

Special tabulations from the SDR presented in Table 7.9 indicate that the percentage of those doctorates who held postdoctoral appointments in 1985 that were employed in the U.S. academic sector in 1987. In the aggregate, 63.6 percent of U.S. citizen and permanent resident postdocs in 1985 were employed in academe in 1987, and over 50 percent were employed in faculty positions. Both these percentages exceed the 49.8 percent of all employed new doctorates in 1988 who were employed in academe (Table 7.7). Indeed, contrasting the percentages of 1985 postdocs employed in the academic sector in 1987 in the physical sciences (54.0), life sciences (67.7), and social sciences and engineering (61.7) with the comparable percentages of new doctorates employed in academe in 1988 (Table 7.7), it is clear that in each field postdocs *are* more likely to enter academe than are new doctorates who accept employment immediately on graduation.

It is somewhat more difficult to use the SDR to draws conclusions about temporary residents because nonresponse rates for temporary residents increase substantially in the SDR with time since degree. Partially, this reflects

Table 7.8   Share of New Doctorates with Definite Plans in the United States Going on to Postdoctorate and Academic Appointments

	Total		U.S. Citizen		Permanent Resident		Temporary Resident		
	SPDOC	SACAD	SPDOC	SACAD	SPDOC	SACAD	SPDOC	SACAD	SDEFU
Total science/engineering:									
1970	.24	.43	.22	.44	.28	.36	.51	.31	.42
1975	.28	.37	.26	.39	.35	.23	.50	.22	.40
1980	.33	.29	.32	.30	.27	.21	.50	.21	.45
1985	.36	.26	.35	.26	.28	.27	.50	.28	.49
1988	.42	.24	.39	.24	.35	.28	.58	.25	.55
Total nonscience/nonengineering:									
1970	.02	.79	.02	.79	.06	.86	.15	.75	.22
1975	.02	.66	.02	.65	.07	.73	.22	.64	.20
1980	.03	.58	.03	.58	.07	.67	.25	.61	.15
1985	.03	.55	.03	.55	.08	.77	.11	.72	.21
1988	.05	.56	.04	.56	.05	.70	.15	.76	.30
Selected fields:									
Physical science (physics/astronomy and chemistry):									
1970	.38	.21	.35	.23	.51	.13	.72	.15	.63
1988	.61	.07	.54	.08	.59	.09	.89	.03	.70

Earth and material sciences:									
1970	.21	.43	.18	.45	.26	.31	.70	.25	.36
1988	.39	.23	.35	.26	.50	.08	.88	.04	.33
Life sciences:									
1970	.46	.37	.43	.39	.57	.26	.81	.14	.35
1988	.74	.12	.72	.13	.76	.09	.92	.06	.47
Social sciences:									
1970	.04	.82	.04	.82	.05	.90	.09	.75	.25
1988	.09	.65	.08	.64	.05	.64	.12	.74	.38
Psychological sciences:									
1970	.14	.52	.14	.52	.35	.42	.25	.56	.35
1988	.21	.24	.21	.24	.14	.32	.52	.32	.60
Mathematical sciences:									
1970	.06	.75	.06	.76	.06	.66	.20	.73	.52
1988	.20	.65	.15	.65	.23	.55	.30	.67	.51
Engineering:									
1970	.07	.27	.05	.27	.12	.21	.27	.28	.48
1988	.20	.26	.11	.26	.12	.29	.40	.27	.59

Source: National Science Foundation (1989e, table 15).

Note: SPDOC = share of doctorates with definite plans in the United States going on to postdoctoral appointments; SACAD = share of doctorates with definite plans in the United States going on to academic appointments; and SDEFU = share of those with definite plans with plans in the United States.

Table 7.9   **Percentage of Postdocs in 1985 Who Were Employed in the U.S. Academic Sector in 1987[a]**

		Field		
	Total	Physical Sciences	Life Sciences	Social Sciences and Engineering
U.S. citizens and permanent residents:				
Total number of postdocs in 1985	6,722	1,551	4,176	965
% in academe in 1987	63.6	54.0	67.7	61.7
% in faculty positions	50.3	41.0	53.1	53.4
% in nonfaculty positions	7.9	9.6	8.6	2.3
% faculty status not reported	5.4	3.4	5.9	6.0
Temporary residents:				
Total number of postdocs in 1985	924	451	277	196
% in academe in 1987	27.3–58.0	23.1–52.0	53.8–92.0	b
% in faculty positions	20.2–42.9	21.7–49.0	32.1–54.9	b
% in nonfaculty positions	2.2– 4.6	.7– 1.5	6.1–10.5	b
% faculty status not reported	5.0–10.6	.7– 1.5	15.5–26.5	b

Source: Special tabulations prepared from the *Survey of Doctorate Recipients* by the Office of Scientific and Engineering Personnel, National Research Council.

[a]Based on respondents to the 1985 *Survey of Doctoral Recipients* who received their doctorates in 1980–84. The figures for U.S. citizens and permanent residents assume that nonrespondents to the 1987 *Survey* were distributed across employment categories in an analogous manner to respondents. The upper-bound estimates for temporary residents similarly assume this, while the lower-bound estimates assume that all temporary resident nonrespondents in 1987 were employed abroad or outside the U.S. academic sector in 1987.

[b]Sample was too small to compute percentages.

a tendency, based on both immigration law and their desires, for temporary resident doctorates to leave the United States and return to their home countries. If one assumes that all nonrespondents in 1987 returned to their home countries, one can compute a lower-bound estimate of the proportion of temporary resident postdocs in 1985 employed in the U.S. academic sector in 1987. If instead one assumes that all nonrespondents in 1987 in fact remained in the United States and were distributed across employment categories in a manner similar to 1987 respondents, one can compute an upper-bound estimate.

Both these estimates are presented in the bottom half of Table 7.9. In both the physical and the life sciences, even the lower-bound estimates of the proportion of 1985 temporary resident postdocs employed in the U.S. academic sector in 1987 exceed the proportion of 1985 and 1988 temporary resident new doctorates directly entering employment in the U.S. academic sector (Table 7.8). While this provides evidence that temporary resident new doctorates contribute to academic labor supply in the United States, both directly on receipt of their doctorates and subsequently to postdoc appointments, no evidence is available on their expected length of academic careers here. However, since their immigration status does directly affect their ability to remain in the United States, one suspects that this expected length is shorter than that of otherwise comparable citizen and permanent resident new academics.

7.2.3 Stocks and Flows of Experienced Doctorates

The age distribution of doctorates employed in academe at a point in time depends on patterns of growth of positions in the past and decisions by experienced doctorates to enter or leave academe and retire from the work force. Over the period 1977–87, the age distribution of doctoral scientists, social scientists, and engineers employed by educational institutions shifted to the right as relatively few new faculty positions were created during the 1980s.[10] As a result, the proportion of these faculty below age 35 fell from 21.7 to 12.2 percent, while the proportion of faculty age 55 and over rose from 15.0 to 21.6 percent (Table 7.10).

As the share of faculty who are age 55 and older increases, so does concern over the impending growth in retirements and thus the increased replacement demand for faculty that will occur. As of 1994, faculty will no longer be subject to mandatory retirement, and concern over whether research and teaching productivity decline, on average, with age leads to discussion of policies that might be pursued to "encourage" older faculty to retire. Alternatively, given projections of future faculty shortages, some wonder whether encouraging older faculty to postpone retirement will have a substantive effect on the magnitude of these shortages.

The changing age distribution also has implications for the mobility pattern of experienced doctorates between the academic and the nonacademic sectors. Table 7.11 presents data (for three age groups) on the share of doctorates employed in either the academic or the nonacademic sector in 1985 who moved to the other sector by 1987. These data, which come from analyses of the SDR, make clear that on average the proportion of faculty who move to the nonacademic sector declines substantially with age while the proportion that move from the nonacademic to the academic sector is much less dependent on age.

There are also substantial differences in these proportions across fields, relating presumably to differences in the relative availability and attractiveness of employment opportunities in the two sectors. In most fields, the proportion of academics moving to the nonacademic sector is greater than the proportion of nonacademics moving to the academic sector for the two age groups under 50, but the inequality is reversed for the older cohorts. A notable exception is the humanities, where for all age groups the proportion of nonacadem-

---

10. Similar trends have been observed in the age distribution of all humanities doctorates (see National Research Council 1989b, tables 2, 9; National Research Council 1986, table 3; National Research Council 1982, table 2.3; and National Research Council 1978, table 2.3).

Table 7.10   Age Distribution of Doctoral Scientists, Social Scientists, and Engineers Employed by Educational Institutions

Category	1977	1979	1981	1983	1985	1987
	% in:					
Under 30	3.3	2.6	2.4	1.8	1.5	1.2
30–34	18.4	16.3	14.9	12.4	12.0	11.0
35–39	22.7	22.8	20.5	18.7	18.1	16.3
40–44	15.8	16.9	19.2	20.9	20.1	18.9
45–49	13.7	13.6	13.1	14.1	15.7	18.5
50–54	11.0	11.2	11.5	11.9	11.6	12.4
55–59	8.1	8.9	9.3	9.7	9.5	10.0
60–64	4.8	5.3	6.0	6.8	7.4	7.5
65 and over	2.1	2.5	3.2	3.6	4.0	4.1
No report	.1	.0	.0	.1	.1	.2

Source: National Science Foundation (1988a, table 3).

Table 7.11   Shares of Doctorates Employed in Both 1985 and 1987 Who Changed Sectors between 1985 and 1987, by Field and 1987 Age

	Age 35 and Under		Age 35–50		Age 50 and Over	
	AN	NA	AN	NA	AN	NA
All fields	.107	.078	.052	.043	.024	.047
Physical sciences	.206	.030	.052	.019	.014	.034
Mathematical sciences	.074	.059	.018	.039	.006	.046
Computer sciences	.064	.000	.071	.025	.000	.267
Environmental sciences	.026	.084	.062	.026	.043	.052
Life sciences	.122	.144	.068	.063	.025	.053
Psychology	.152	.084	.090	.032	.047	.032
Social sciences	.029	.116	.044	.093	.035	.089
Engineering	.069	.038	.041	.023	.032	.030
Humanities	.065	.191	.036	.074	.013	.081

Source: Special tabulations prepared by the Office of Scientific and Engineering Personnel, National Research Council, from the *Survey of Doctorate Recipients*. These computations assume that nonrespondents in 1987 are distributed across sectors in an identical manner to respondents.

Note: AN = share of those employed in the academic sector in 1985 who were employed in the nonacademic sector in 1987; and NA = share of those employed in the nonacademic sector in 1985 who were employed in the academic sector in 1987.

ics moving to academe is substantially greater than the proportion of academics moving to the nonacademic sector.

Of course, the number of people moving from each sector depends not only on the proportions of people leaving the sector but also on the number of people initially in the sector. Table 7.12 presents estimates from the SDR on the number of experienced doctorates (by field in 1985) employed in the academic and nonacademic sectors. On average, the number employed in the

Table 7.12   Estimated Number of Doctorates by Field, Sector of Employment, and Age in 1985

	Age 35 and Under		Age 35–50		Age 50 and Over	
	A	N	A	N	A	N
All fields	30,740	27,697	146,266	134,513	79,673	51,795
Physical sciences	4,062	7,137	17,015	28,673	10,718	13,915
Mathematical sciences	1,822	565	8,378	4,138	3,751	975
Computer sciences	567	351	792	1,267	61	62
Environmental sciences	738	809	3,413	4,642	1,818	1,764
Life sciences	9,699	6,009	33,195	24,462	16,850	9,841
Psychology	3,471	5,005	13,126	19,472	5,630	7,642
Social sciences	4,276	2,050	24,093	12,299	13,088	4,401
Engineering	2,872	4,671	11,964	25,407	6,637	8,322
Humanities	3,233	1,100	34,290	14,153	21,120	4,873

Source: Special tabulations prepared by the Office of Scientific and Engineering Personnel, National Research Council, from the Survey of Doctorate Recipients. Approximately 0.1 percent of doctorates did not report their ages and are excluded from these totals.

Note: A = employed in academic sector; and N = employed in nonacademic sector.

academic sector exceeds the number employed in the nonacademic sector, and, on balance, the net flow of experienced doctorates is from the academic to the nonacademic sector, rather than vice versa, except for the age 50 and over group. There are, of course, substantial differences by field. However, even for the humanities (because of the greater proportion of doctorates employed in the academic sector), the net flow is from the academic to the nonacademic sector. Later chapters will discuss whether the potential exists for these net flows to be reversed and for experienced doctorates currently employed in the nonacademic sector to help avert projected shortages of doctorates.

8　　Decisions to Undertake and Complete Doctoral Study and Choices of Sector of Employment

This chapter beings with a general model of the decision to undertake and complete doctoral study and then summaries what prior studies by economists tell us about the magnitudes of various behavioral relations. The conclusion is that, unfortunately, they tell us very little. The next section then presents data on trends in various variables to see if these can help "explain" the decline in U.S. citizen and permanent resident new doctorates over the past two decades. Given the important role that time to degree likely plays in attracting people to doctoral study, models of and empirical evidence on the determinants of time to degree are then discussed and implications for public policy affecting this outcome and the number of students entering doctoral programs highlighted.

After a brief digression on whether the "quality" of new doctoral students has been declining, the chapter then turns to a discussion of the allocation of new and experienced doctorates between the academic and the nonacademic sectors. It addresses whether the academic sector can hope in the future to attract a greater share of new doctorates, to reduce the proportion of its experienced doctorates who leave, and to increase the proportion of those experienced doctorates employed in the nonacademic sector who move to the academic sector.

8.1　The Decision to Undertake and Complete Doctoral Study

Viewed from the perspective of an economist, the decision to undertake and complete doctorate study is a special case of the theory of occupational choice (Ehrenberg and Smith 1991, chap. 8). Individuals are assumed to evaluate the expected pecuniary and nonpecuniary benefits and costs that will result over their lifetimes if they choose various options and then to choose the option that maximizes their expected well-being. These decisions are made with imperfect information about current and future benefits and costs as well as about an individual's expected productivity in any occupation. As such, these choices involve considerable uncertainty.

What are the theoretical implications of this general approach? First, given an individual's aptitudes, interests, and family background, his or her choice of undergraduate major will depend, at least partially, on a comparison of the expected labor market returns that are available from various majors. Other things being equal, the higher the expected labor market returns available from a major, the greater the share of students who will choose that major. Note that, in principle, the returns available from a major may depend on the option it provides for further study (e.g., majoring in business likely precludes entering a doctoral program in physics) and the benefits and costs (including forgone earnings) of such study.

Second, given an individual's interests, aptitude, family background, and undergraduate major, the decision to enter and ultimately complete doctoral study in a field depends on a number of factors. The expected current and future streams of pecuniary and nonpecuniary benefits from entering the work force directly, from pursuing graduate study in the field, from pursuing graduate study in other fields, and from pursuing study leading to a professional degree and career surely all matter. So does the cost of pursuing each of these options, which depends on the tuition levels charged to students, the levels and availability of financial aid to subsidize each type of study, the completion rates, and the lengths of time (and thus the forgone earnings) it takes to complete each option. Other things being equal, higher benefits (higher earnings, better working conditions) and lower costs (lower tuition, more generous aid policies, higher completion rates, and shorter times to degree) will encourage more people to undertake and complete doctoral study in a field.

Three points are worth stressing here. To the extent that capital markets are imperfect and/or individuals dislike incurring debt, high debt levels accumulated from an individual's undergraduate days may discourage him or her from pursuing graduate study. To the extent that academic positions provide greater nonpecuniary returns (such as tenure, freedom to choose research topics, more freedom to allocate time) than nonacademic positions, a decline in academic employment opportunities in a field may discourage people from pursuing doctoral study in that field, even if the average pecuniary benefits from earning a doctorate do not change. Finally, to say that individuals base decisions partially on expected current and future pecuniary benefits does not provide any insight into how these expectations are formed. Do prospective doctoral students look at starting salaries at the time they are making decisions, or do they try to project what starting salaries are likely to be when they complete their program and how salaries are likely to grow over their work lives?

Empirical studies suggest that the model outlined above can help explain undergraduate students' choices of majors. Some studies use institutional-level data or data for the nation as a whole and show that the flow of students into different majors or the share of degrees granted in each major depends on starting salaries received by graduates in the field (Cebula and Lopes 1982; Fiorito and Dauffenbach 1982). Other studies use individual-level data and find that, other things being equal, an increase in a student's verbal aptitude increases and an increase in his or her mathematical aptitude decreases, the probability of majoring in the humanities (Polachek 1978). One recent study of a national probability sample of American youths found that, after controlling for measures of ability and other personal characteristics, the probability that a student would major in one of five broad fields (business, liberal arts, engineering, science, or education) depended on the individual's expected present value of earnings (over the first 12 years of a career) in each field but *not* on his or her expected starting salary (Berger 1988).[1] Both expected present value of earnings and expected starting salaries in each field were estimated from models that took account of an individual's background characteristics; they were not based solely on published nationwide average salary data. I return to these points in the next section.

Studies of individuals' decisions to enter and complete doctoral study are surprisingly few, and all follow in the tradition of Richard Freeman's (1971) analysis. Table 8.1 summarizes the results of these studies and also of two related studies for MBAs and medical school students. For each study, the author's estimates (or my estimates from the author's results) are reported of the elasticities of the number of new entrants or doctorates awarded in a field with respect to each of nine variables. That is, they report what the effects are, in percentage terms, on the outcome of a 1 percent increase in each of the nine variables. A "dot" in a column indicates that the variable was not included in the analyses performed in the particular study.

The nine variables are listed at the bottom of the table; they are a subset of the variables that the theory outlined above suggests should influence entrance into and completion of doctoral study.[2] It is remarkable that each study took account of three or fewer of the hypothesized important factors and that no study included earnings opportunities and financial aid in closely allied doctoral fields or students' debt levels on graduation from college in its analyses. In part, these omissions reflect data and sample size limitations; most studies use aggregate time-series data for relatively short time spans. However, the omissions suggest that the elasticity estimates presented in the table should be considered quite tentative.

Virtually all studies find that the earnings of doctorates in the field matter. Some find the supply of doctorates very sensitive to earnings, while others

1. None of these studies includes in the analysis the "option" that a particular major provides to pursue doctoral study and the expected earnings if such study is pursued.
2. For brevity, undergraduate loan burdens, the probability of obtaining academic jobs, and completion rates of doctoral and other programs are omitted from Table 8.1. None of the cited studies considers these variables.

find elasticities less than unity. Similarly, while most studies agree that higher earnings in other professions reduce the supply of doctorates, the estimated magnitude of this effect varies across studies.

The three studies that control for the number, or fraction, of doctoral students receiving financial support find that increases in financial support do increase the number of doctoral students, although the magnitude of the response varies across studies. In contrast, the two that control for stipend levels find inelastic responses, and they imply that a 10 percent increase in graduate student stipend levels, other things being equal, would probably result in only a 2–3 percent increase in the number of new doctorates. Finally, only one study has included average time to degree as an explanatory variable. While it finds that longer times to degree tend to reduce the supply of doctorates, it was based on only 12 observations, and the estimated effect was not statistically significantly different from zero.

In the main, then, these studies are of limited use for policy simulations. While both doctorates' relative earnings and financial support for graduate students clearly influence the supply of doctorates our knowledge of the magnitude of these responses is too imprecise to be useful. Furthermore, the studies summarized in Table 8.1 are in the main based on analyses of science or social science fields. It may well be the case that the responses of potential humanities doctorates to economic variables are different than those of potential scientists and social scientists.

8.2 Underlying Trends

8.2.1 Choice of Major

Data on average starting salaries of college graduates, by major, for the period 1973–88 appear in Table 8.2. These data come from annual surveys conducted by the College Placement Council, save for the education salaries, which are collected by the American Federation of Teachers and are averages for beginning teachers (not all beginning teachers are education majors, and many have master's degrees or some postgraduate course work). In addition to the salary levels, the ratio of each major's average salary to the average salary in engineering (the highest paid major in the set) is included in the table.

Given the swings in the distribution of majors across fields that occurred during the 1970s and 1980s (Table 7.1), it is somewhat surprising to observe that the dramatic decline in the shares of humanities and social science majors was not accompanied by a substantial decline in relative starting salaries in these fields. Similarly, the dramatic growth in business majors was apparently not due to a rise in their relative starting salaries. While the starting salary in education fell substantially relative to engineering during the period 1974–

Table 8.1   Estimated Elasticities of Doctoral and Other Postgraduate Educational Outcomes with Respect to Various Variables

Study	Years	Coverage	Outcome	(1)	(2)	(3)	(4)	(5)	(6)	(7)	(8)	(9)
Freeman (1971)	1956–64	52 fields (changes across fields)	New Ph.D.s	.	.	.	.	.18*	.23**	.	.	.
Sloan (1971)	1934–66	Medical schools	Applicants	.	.	[a]	[b]	.	.	.	.	[c]
Freeman (1975)	1956–72	Physics	New Ph.D.s, entrants grad school	.	.	.82*	−.42	.	.	.	.	.
						.87	−1.04*					
Scott (1979)	1965–74, 1961–74	Economics	New Ph.D.s, entrants grad school	.	.	1.25*d	.	.16*	.	.	.	.
Kuh and Radner (1980)	1967–76	Mathematics	New Ph.D.s	.	.	.44	−1.67*	.	.	.	.	.
Hoffman and Low (1983)	1962–76	Economics	Entrants grad school	.	.	2.6*e	−1.2*e	.	.	.	.	.
						4.8*f	−4.0*f					
Alexander and Fry (1984)	13 years	MBAs	Ratio MBAs/pool potential applicants	.	.	1.44*g	.	.	.	.	.	−.48

Study	Years	Field	Sample	(1)	(2)	(3)	(4)	(5)	(6)	(7)	(8)	(9)
Hoffman and Orazem (1985)	1962–82	Agricultural economics	New Ph.D.s, entrants grad school	·	·	3.0*	−2.80*	·	.33*h	·	·	·
Baker (1989)	1975–87	Biomedical sciences	Entrants grad school	·	·	.43	−.70	·	.57*h	·	·	·
Stapleton (1989)	1961–85	Economics	New Ph.D.s	·	·	.59**	.91*	.64	1.36*	·	·	−.50

Source: Author's interpretations of the original studies.

Note: Columns represent the following: (1) current earnings opportunities if do not go on to graduate school; (2) debt level upon graduation from college; (3) earnings opportunities with degree; (4) earnings opportunities with alternative professional degrees; (5) number or fraction of graduate students with aid; (6) average stipend level; (7) earnings opportunities with degree and financial aid in closely allied doctoral fields; (8) average time to get degree; and (9) tuition. A dot in a column indicates that the variable was not included in the analyses performed in the particular study.

[a] Computation of elasticity not possible. Estimate suggests an additional 0.4–1.3 individuals apply per dollar increase in salary.

[b] Computation of elasticity not possible. Estimate suggests that, if biologist earnings increase by 10 percent, there would be 1,002 fewer medical school applicants.

[c] A dollar increase in the direct cost of medical school (tuition-stipends) generates 6 to 14 applicants.

[d] Elasticity with respect to ratio of starting salary to median professional salary.

[e] Rational expectations model estimate.

[f] "Naive" model estimate.

[g] Elasticity with respect to ratio of MBAs' salaries to undergraduates' salaries.

[h] Elasticity with respect to teaching/research assistants' salaries.

Table 8.2   Average Starting Salaries for College Graduates, by Major, Selected
                   Fields

Year of Graduation	Humanities	Social Sciences	Chemistry	Engineering	Business	Education
1973	7,968	8,280	9,912	11,022	9,036	a
	(.72)	(.75)	(.90)		(.82)	
1974	8,292	8,844	10,608	11,967	9,636	8,058
	(.69)	(.74)	(.89)		(.81)	(.67)
1975	8,676	9,240	11,422	13,386	10,116	a
	(.65)	(.69)	(.85)		(.76)	
1976	9,300	9,840	12,336	14,169	10,464	9,085
	(.66)	(.69)	(.87)		(.74)	(.64)
1977	9,720	10,356	13,224	15,351	11,124	a
	(.63)	(.67)	(.86)		(.72)	
1978	10,452	10,716	14,292	16,710	11,916	10,062
	(.63)	(.64)	(.86)		(.71)	(.60)
1979	11,796	11,664	15,984	18,210	13,224	a
	(.65)	(.64)	(.88)		(.73)	
1980	12,888	12,864	17,508	20,139	14,616	11,676
	(.64)	(.64)	(.87)		(.73)	(.58)
1981	14,448	15,992	19,644	22,674	16,555	a
	(.64)	(.71)	(.87)		(.73)	
1982	15,396	15,432	21,012	24,906	18,040	13,539
	(.62)	(.62)	(.84)		(.72)	(.54)
1983	16,560	15,840	20,504	24,723	18,217	a
	(.67)	(.64)	(.83)		(.74)	
1984	17,724	17,424	21,072	25,424	18,997	15,482
	(.70)	(.69)	(.83)		(.75)	(.61)
1985	17,532	18,540	22,764	26,364	19,861	a
	(.66)	(.70)	(.86)		(.75)	
1986	19,296	19,980	23,376	27,075	20,705	17,667
	(.71)	(.74)	(.86)		(.77)	(.65)
1987	20,256	21,876	25,572	27,504	21,341	18,657
	(.74)	(.80)	(.93)		(.78)	(.68)
1988	19,828	21,715	26,004	28,614	23,358	19,683
	(.69)	(.76)	(.91)		(.82)	(.69)

Sources: College Placement Council, Inflation and the College Graduate: 1962–1985 (Bethlehem, Pa., 1986), and CPC Salary Survey (various issues). The figures for engineering and business are unweighted averages each year of more detailed occupations. Beginning teachers' salaries are from American Federation of Teachers, Survey and Analyses of Salary Trends, 1988
(Washington, D.C., July 1988), table III-2.

Note: Numbers in parentheses are the category's average salary relative to the average salary of
engineering majors. All salaries are in current dollars.

aNot available.

82, it has risen back to its initial level since then. The share of education
majors, which fell through the mid-1980s has in fact increased slightly in
more recent years (Table 7.1).

For the most part, the major shifts in the distribution of college majors that
have occurred do not appear to be supply responses to changing relative start-

ing salaries. What, then, might explain these shifts? One possibility is that, as noted above, it is not starting salaries but rather the expected present value of career earnings that influence choice of major (Berger 1988). If the steepness of age/earnings profiles has increased for majors in fields like business and engineering and declined for majors in fields like the humanities and the social sciences, this might explain the shift. No evidence is currently available, however, on this point.

Alternatively, it is possible that the changing distribution of college majors represents not a supply response of a given population to changes in economic variables but rather a change in the nature of the population of college graduates. Despite well-publicized concerns by academic institutions about the decline in the college age population, the number of bachelor's degrees awarded by American colleges and universities has either remained roughly constant or risen in every year since 1974–75, and, by 1986–87, it was over 10 percent higher than it was in 1971–72 (Table 6.4). This growth in degrees was due to a number of factors, including small increases in high school graduation rates, small increases in college attendance rates of new high school graduates, and an increased likelihood that older adults were enrolled in colleges (Anderson, Carter, and Malizio 1989, tables 11, 15; Bowen and Sosa 1989, table 3.1).

Some of the growth in high school graduation rates and college attendance rates of new high school graduates came about because of an expansion in opportunities for underrepresented minorities with high ability levels. However, some may have simply reflected high schools' increased propensity to graduate and colleges' increased propensity to enroll more marginal students. To the extent that the increased college enrollments thus come from "lower-quality" and older students, these student's interests are likely to be more pragmatic in nature, which may help explain the shift in majors toward business and away from the arts and sciences.

Finally, as noted by Turner and Bowen (1990), to a large extent recent shifts in the distribution of college graduates by major reflect shifts in the curriculum decisions of women. In part, they view these shifts as a consequence of the removal of culturally imposed constraints, which has led to a greatly widened range of career alternatives for women.

8.2.2 Doctoral and Professional Degrees

Table 6.4 illustrated the dramatic growth in the ratio of first professional to doctoral and master's to doctoral degrees that has occurred since the early 1970s. Are fewer American college graduate students entering doctoral programs because earnings opportunities in the professions are now so much better? Some suggestive evidence is found in Table 8.3, which contains starting salary information for the period 1970–88 for new assistant professors in mathematics (col. 1), physics (col. 2), and economics (col. 3) as well as for MBAs (col. 4), new lawyers in non-patent-law firms (col. 5), and new graduates with master's degrees in engineering (col. 6). Presumably, individuals contemplating doctoral study in economics might also consider getting MBAs

Table 8.3   **Average Starting Salaries for Ph.D. Economists, Mathematicians, Physicists, MBAs, Lawyers, and Master's Degree in Engineering Graduates**

Year of Degree	Ph.D.s (1)[a]	(2)[b]	(3)[c]	MBAs (4)[d]	Lawyers (5)[e]	Engineers (6)[f]
				12,528		12,057
1970	11,000	e	11,897	(.95)	e	(.91)
				12,528		12,210
1971	11,000	e	12,112	(.97)	e	(.90)
				12,684		12,324
1972	11,500	e	12,481	(.98)	e	(.93)
				13,308		12,753
1973	11,600	e	12,659	(.95)	e	(.91)
				14,172		13,400
1974	12,100	e	13,319	(.94)	e	(.90)
				15,000	15,688	15,123
1975	12,800	e	14,044	(.94)	(.90)	(.85)
				15,876	16,188	16,020
1976	13,300	e	14,875	(.94)	(.92)	(.83)
				16,920	17,688	17,181
1977	14,000	14,760	15,482	(.92)	(.88)	(.81)
				17,976	17,813	18,702
1978	14,500	13,930	16,605	(.92)	(.93)	(.78)
				19,332	19,063	20,418
1979	15,700	15,960	17,880	(.92)	(.94)	(.77)
				21,540	20,875	22,458
1980	17,100	16,800	19,529	(.91)	(.94)	(.76)
				24,000	22,688	25,470
1981	19,000	20,400	21,917	(.91)	(.97)	(.75)
				25,620	23,938	28,116
1982	20,600	23,880	24,074	(.94)	(1.01)	(.73)
				25,580	24,938	27,738
1983	21,700	23,880	25,750	(1.01)	(1.03)	(.78)
				28,500	30,688	29,487
1984	23,000	26,520	26,930	(.95)	(.87)	(.78)
				28,584	32,438	30,603
1985	25,000	29,400	29,340	(1.03)	(.90)	(.82)
				30,348	34,188	31,647
1986	26,900	29,400	31,320	(1.03)	(.92)	(.85)
				31,524	36,875	32,688
1987	28,000	28,920	34,670	(1.10)	(.94)	(.86)
				39,024	39,438	33,231
1988	29,300	29,400	35,700	(.91)	(.90)	(.88)

Sources: Columns 4 and 6: College Placement Council, *Inflation and the College Graduate: 1962–85* (Bethlehem, Pa., 1986), and *CPS Salary Survey* (various issues). Column 5: *Student Lawyer's* "Annual Salary Survey" (various issues). Column 2: American Institute of Physics, *Graduate Student Survey* (various issues). Column 3: American Economic Association, *Annual Salary Survey* (data prior to 1985 provided by David Stapleton at Dartmouth). Column 1: annual AMS-MAA Survey, *Notices of the American Mathematical Society* (various issues).
Note: All salaries are in current dollars. Numbers in parentheses are, for col. 4, SALE/SALB; for col. 5, SALE/SALL; and for col. 6, SALM/SALG.

Table 8.3   **(continued)**

[a]Median nine-month academic salary for new assistant professors in mathematics department (SALM).
[b]Median monthly academic salary for new physics assistant professors employed in universities multiplied by 12.
[c]Average nine-month salary for new assistant professors in economics (SALE).
[d]Average starting salary of new MBAs with nontechnical undergraduate degrees (SALB).
[e]Average starting salary across eight cities (unweighted) of lawyers entering non-patent-law firms (SALL).
[f]Average starting salary of graduates with master's degrees in engineering (average across subfields) (SALG).
[g]Not available.

or law degrees, while those people considering doctoral training in mathematics and physics might also consider engineering programs. As such, the focus is on these comparisons.

The ratios of average starting salaries of assistant professors in economics to average starting salaries of MBAs and lawyers are found in parentheses in columns 4 and 5, respectively. These data do *not* suggest that the average starting assistant professor salary in economics declined relative to that of MBAs or lawyers during the period. Column 6 presents the ratio of starting mathematics assistant professors' salaries to starting master's of engineering graduates' salaries, and here there is some evidence of a decline. Between 1972 and 1982, the ratio declined form 0.93 to 0.73, a substantial drop; however, since 1982, it has risen back to near its initial level. For brevity, the ratio of new assistant professors of physics to new master's of engineering graduates' salaries is omitted from the table; however, no trends in that ratio were apparent during the period.

While declining relative starting salaries may have thus discouraged people from entering doctoral programs in mathematics during part of the period, they do not appear to be responsible for the decline in economics or physics doctorates. However, average starting salaries do not capture all aspects of compensation, and two other factors may have mattered.

First, as Table 6.3 indicates, in virtually all academic fields, the ratio of full professor to new assistant professor salaries is less than two. That is, the typical full professor earns less than twice as much as his or her new assistant professor colleagues. In contrast, the professions offer much more opportunity for earnings growth over a career. It is quite common, for example, for partners in law firms to earn four to six times as much as starting attorneys.[3] While the ratio of full professor to assistant professor salaries in the aggregate has remained roughly constant during the 1970s and 1980s (Hamermesh 1988), it is possible that the return to seniority in the professions may have increased during the period, and this would serve to increase the relative at-

3. See, e.g., the annual salary survey in the November issue of *Student Lawyer.*

traction of the professions vis-à-vis doctoral study. Some evidence in fact exists that this did occur between 1982 and 1989 for lawyers.[4]

This line of reasoning suggests that, to increase the flow of new doctorates, academic institutions must be concerned about raising the salaries of their full professors as well as of their entry-level faculty. Only if potential doctorates view career earnings profiles in academe as sufficiently attractive will the supply of doctorates increase (Kasper 1990b).

Second, the average salary data in professional fields may give a misleading impression of the earnings opportunities of individuals contemplating doctoral study and subsequent careers in these professions. Focusing on economics, for example, to the extent that potential doctoral students' intelligence and aptitude would make them among the "better" applicants to business and law schools, one might expect that the potential earnings of graduates from top professional and business schools would be a better measure of their alternatives.[5] Although "hard" data on this point are not readily available, one senses that the dispersion of earnings between graduates of top and lesser professional programs may have widened over time and thus that the relative economic attractiveness of professional schools may well have risen vis-à-vis doctoral study, even though the comparisons of average starting salaries presented above do not indicate this.

8.2.3. Financial Support for Graduate Students and Undergraduate Loan Burdens

The lengthening of median years of registered time to degree (Table 7.4) and the increased proportion of science/engineering graduate students taking postdoctoral (postdoc) appointments (Table 7.5) have surely discouraged potential students from undertaking doctoral study. Even if the direct costs of doctoral study and then postdocs were financed fully, first through fellowships and assistantships and then through postdoc stipends, a lengthening of the period before regular employment is possible implies increased costs in terms of forgone earnings. Hence, even if the earnings of new doctorates via-à-vis professional degree holders had not changed, the lengthening "training period" for new doctorates should lead to a reduction in doctoral enrollments.

---

4. See Ehrenberg (1989, table 10), where evidence is presented that the ratio of salaries of lawyers with four years of experience relative to those just starting practices rose between 1982 and 1986 in four of six large cities and was roughly constant in the other two. Data presented in the November 1989 issue of *Student Lawyer* indicate that results between 1982 and 1989 were similar.

5. Some evidence to support this conjecture was found by Hartnett (1987, table 4), who contrasted the undergraduate SAT scores of graduates from doctoral programs in the arts and sciences and from professional programs in business, law, and medical schools. The median math and verbal SAT scores in 1981 of his sample of professional school graduates were *each* 30 points *lower* than the comparable median scores for his sample of doctoral recipients. One caution, however, is that response rates for doctoral programs (72 percent) was much higher than response rates for the professional schools (36–45 percent) in the study, so it is not obvious how far the findings can be generalized.

Table 8.4   Percentage of Full-Time Science/Engineering Graduate Students in Doctorate-Granting Institutions by Major Source of Support

	% Federal	% Institutional	% Other Outside Support	% Self-Support
1974	24.6	38.5	8.4	28.6
1975	22.9	36.7	8.0	32.4
1976	22.7	37.0	8.3	32.0
1977	23.2	37.0	8.4	31.5
1978	23.7	36.8	8.9	30.6
1979	23.7	37.1	9.0	30.3
1980	23.0	37.6	9.1	30.3
1981	21.7	38.5	9.6	30.2
1982	19.9	39.4	10.0	30.8
1983	19.4	39.5	10.0	31.0
1984	19.3	40.6	10.0	30.1
1985	19.6	41.0	10.6	28.9
1986	19.8	41.6	10.2	28.4
1987	20.2	41.9	9.5	28.4
1988	20.4	42.2	9.5	27.8

Sources: Author's computations from National Science Foundation, *Academic Science/Engineering: Graduate Enrollment and Support, Fall 1988* (Washington, D.C., 1990), table C15, and *Academic Science/Engineering: Graduate Enrollment and Support, Fall 1981* (Washington, D.C., 1983), table C14.

All that is in question is the magnitude of the response; unfortunately, as described above, the econometric literature provides little guidance on this point.

Have the direct costs of doctoral study been fully subsidized? Table 8.4 presents data on the percentage of full-time science/engineering graduate students enrolled in doctorate-granting institutions by major source of support. The percentage self-supported (primarily non-university-related employment, loans, and support from other family members) was about the same in 1974, the first year data were available, as it was in the last year, 1988. The composition of support did change, however, with students receiving proportionately less federal support but more institutional and other outside (foundation, state government, foreign) support. Unless graduate stipend levels fell relative to individuals' opportunity costs of time, it appears at first glance that the direct costs of graduate study were as well subsidized in 1988 as they were in 1974.[6]

6. National data on average doctoral student stipends are not available; however, data for one university provides some evidence on this point. From 1974–75 to 1987–88, the average graduate student stipend at Cornell rose from $2,950 to $6,400, a 117 percent increase. During the same period, the average starting salaries of new assistant professors in math, new assistant professors in economics, MBAs, new lawyers in non-patent-law firms, and graduates with master's degrees in engineering rose by 129, 154, 160, 151, and 174 percent, respectively (table 8.3). So, at least for one university, graduate stipends did not keep pace over the period with earnings in some fields or with earnings in alternative professions.

Table 8.5   Percentages of Full-time Science/Engineering Graduate Students in Doctorate-Granting Institutions, by Field and Major Source of Support, 1974 and 1988

Field	1974	1988	Field	1974	1988
Total:			Agriculture:		
Fellowship	19.7	14.0	Fellowship	10.1	5.8
RA	20.3	27.4	RA	45.8	51.1
TA	23.6	22.9	TA	7.8	9.6
Other	36.4	35.7	Other	36.3	33.4
Engineering:			Biology:		
Fellowship	14.3	8.7	Fellowship	25.7	23.4
RA	33.0	37.8	RA	20.3	36.4
TA	15.4	17.7	TA	26.5	21.6
Other	37.3	35.8	Other	27.5	18.6
Physical Science:			Health:		
Fellowship	11.6	8.5	Fellowship	39.6	27.3
RA	30.1	42.6	RA	5.5	12.1
TA	47.3	40.4	TA	11.0	9.2
Other	10.9	8.5	Other	43.9	51.4
Environmental Science:			Psychology:		
Fellowship	10.8	9.1	Fellowship	24.2	11.0
RA	32.0	38.6	RA	12.1	14.9
TA	24.2	24.6	TA	20.8	22.0
Other	33.1	27.7	Other	42.9	52.1
Math and CIS:			Social Sciences:		
Fellowship	9.5	7.5	Fellowship	21.0	17.4
RA	10.3	15.6	RA	11.0	11.8
TA	46.5	40.2	TA	17.5	20.2
Other	33.7	36.9	Other	50.5	50.6

Sources: Author's computations from National Science Foundation, *Academic Science/Engineering: Graduate Enrollment and Support, Fall 1988* (Washington, D.C., 1990), table C16, and *Academic Science/Engineering: Graduate Enrollment and Support, Fall 1981* (Washington, D.C., 1983), table C23.

Note: RA = research assistantship; TA = teaching assistantship; CIS = computer and information sciences.

This would be an erroneous conclusion, however, for two reasons. First, as Table 8.5 indicates, the proportion of these full-time students on fellowships declined in all fields, as increasingly students' graduate training was financed (depending on the field) either through research or through teaching assistantships. Because students increasingly had to "work" for their graduate support, time to devote to studies, and thus the desirability of doctoral study, may well have decreased.[7]

---

7. Both teaching and research assistantships contribute to a doctoral candidate's development as a teacher and a researcher. However, time spent preparing to teach classes, talking with students, and grading exams is time that could have been spent on studies. Similarly, while in some disciplines and some situations a research assistantship may permit a student to work on his or her own dissertation research, in other cases it again diverts time from the student's own research.

Table 8.6   Percentage of Science/Engineering Doctoral Students
               Enrolled Part-Time

Field	1974	1977	1980	1983	1988
Total	26.3	29.1	30.9	32.0	31.5
Engineering	40.5	43.6	40.2	38.1	36.4
Physical science	13.3	12.3	12.4	11.7	11.0
Environmental science	16.8	18.2	19.8	19.6	23.7
Math and computer and information science	33.3	33.7	39.7	41.0	39.2
Agriculture	14.8	15.0	17.2	18.4	16.0
Biology	14.4	16.2	16.1	15.3	14.5
Health	24.7	35.3	38.7	46.1	48.1
Psychology	24.0	24.2	26.6	26.6	28.5
Social sciences	28.0	31.1	35.8	37.0	34.4

Sources: Author's computations from National Science Foundation, *Academic Science/Engineering: Graduate Enrollment and Support, Fall 1988* (Washington, D.C., 1990), tables C2, C5, and *Academic Science/Engineering: Graduate Enrollment and Support, Fall 1981* (Washington, D.C., 1983), tables C6, C41.

Second, these data refer only to full-time students. However, as Table 8.6 shows, on balance the percentage of science/engineering graduate students who were enrolled on a part-time basis rose from 26.3 to 31.5 percent during the period 1974–88. This percentage actually declined in well-funded fields, such as engineering and the physical sciences, but it rose substantially in other fields, such as health and the social sciences. An increase in the share of students enrolled on a part-time basis may be due to an inadequate total number of fellowships and assistantships. Lengthening the average time needed to complete degrees contributes to reduced doctoral enrollments.

Of course, not only has median registered time to degree increased substantially over the last 20 years, but the median length of time between an individual's receipt of a bachelor's degree and his or her doctorate has increased by an even greater amount (Table 7.4). In part, this reflects individuals' increasingly delaying their initial entry into doctoral programs (Table 7.5). Other things being equal, the later the age at which new doctorates start their careers, the fewer the number of years that they will have to reap the "return" on their investments and thus the smaller the incentive potential doctoral students have to undertake doctoral study.[8]

What role may have undergraduate loan burdens played in both delaying and discouraging entry into doctoral study? Loans as a percentage of total financial aid awarded to undergraduate students declined from 28.9 in 1970–71 to 16.9 in 1975–76 but then rapidly grew to 48.0 in 1982–83 and have

---

8. Of course, other things are not equal. Federal legislation, namely, the 1978 and 1986 amendments to the Age Discrimination in Employment Act, precluded academic institutions from requiring tenured faculty to retire prior to age 70 as of 1 July 1982 and eliminated all mandatory retirement as of 1994. This lengthening of faculty members' potential work lives may partially offset their increasingly delayed career starts.

Table 8.7   Grants, Loans, and Work as a Percentage of Aid Awarded to
                   Postsecondary Students

	Share of:		
	Grants	Loans	Work
1970–71	66.1	28.9	5.1
1975–76	80.3	16.9	2.8
1977–78	74.2	21.6	4.3
1979–80	63.5	32.3	4.2
1980–81	55.3	40.9	3.9
1981–82	52.3	44.2	3.5
1982–83	51.4	44.9	3.7
1983–84	48.2	48.0	3.9
1984–85	47.7	49.0	3.3
1985–86	49.4	47.5	3.1
1986–87	50.1	47.0	2.9
1987–88	47.1	50.4	2.6
1988–89	48.3	49.4	2.3
1989–90[a]	48.7	48.5	2.8

Sources: Gillespie and Carlson (1983, table 6); Gillespie and Carlson (1990, table 4).
[a]Estimated/predicted share.

remained in that range ever since (Table 8.7). Moreover, the rapid rise in undergraduate tuitions since the late 1970s has substantially increased the proportion of undergraduate students who receive some form of financial aid. As a result, the number of students receiving support under various federally subsidized or guaranteed loan programs more than tripled between 1970–71 and 1989–90 and over one-third of American undergraduate students now have debts on graduation (Table 8.8; Hansen 1990). While the number with debts has increased, as Table 8.8 shows, average levels of debt have remained roughly constant in recent years in nominal terms and declined somewhat in real terms.[9]

Evidence on the effects of undergraduate debt on career choice and the decision to undertake doctoral study is in the main impressionistic or based on tabulations of responses to surveys; there has been only one econometric study on the subject. A study of 2,000 borrowers under the Massachusetts Guaranteed Student Loan Program found that 35 percent of those who decided not to go on to graduate school said that concern over borrowing was "very or extremely important" in their decision (Baum and Schwartz 1988a, 1988b). Other studies reported that individuals with high undergraduate debt burdens

9. Partially, this reflects the fact that, throughout the period, the Guaranteed Student Loan (GSL) annual limit for undergraduates was capped at $2,500 in nominal terms. The 1985 Higher Education Act Reauthorization raised this limit to $4,000 per year for students in their junior and senior years, effective the fall of 1987. The data in Table 8.8 do not permit us to ascertain if the number of individuals with loans from more than one program has increased in recent years. If it has, debt levels per borrower may have increased.

Table 8.8   Number of Recipients and Aid per Recipient, Various Postsecondary
                       Loan Programs

	No. of Recipients (000s)	% of Undergrads	Loan per Recipient	
			In Current Dollars	In 1989 Dollars
NDSL/Perkins loans:				
1970–71	452	6	532	1,660
1975–76	690	7	667	1,491
1980–81	813	8	853	1,221
1981–82	684		848	1,118
1982–83	675		884	1,119
1983–84	719	6	949	1,156
1984–85	697	6	971	1,140
1985–86	701	6	1,003	1,143
1986–87	716	6	1,067	1,189
1987–88	674	6	1,145	1,280
1988–89	692	6	1,263	1,293
1989–90	826	7	1,022	998
GSL/Stafford loans:				
1970–71	1,017	13	998	3,115
1975–76	922	9	1,374	3,070
1980–81	2,904	27	2,135	3,057
1981–82	3,135		2,280	3,005
1982–83	2,942		2,208	2,789
1983–84	3,147	28	2,307	2,810
1984–85	3,546	33	2,297	2,694
1985–86	3,536	33	2,355	2,684
1986–87	3,499	31	2,381	2,655
1987–88	3,595	32	2,537	2,716
1988–89	3,626	32	2,570	2,632
1989–90	3,696	33	2,614	2,552
Plus Programs:[a]				
1980–81	1	< 1	2,509	3,592
1981–82	21		2,544	3,352
1982–83	47		2,501	3,157
1983–84	65	< 1	2,597	3,163
1984–85	92	< 1	2,636	3,093
1985–86	91	< 1	2,650	3,021
1986–87	91	< 1	2,761	3,079
1987–88	147	1	2,966	3,176
1988–89	212	2	3,075	3,148
1989–90	256	2	3,128	3,054

Sources: Gillespie and Carlson (1983, table 7); Gillespie and Carlson (1990, table 5); and *1989–
90 Fact Book on Higher Education* (New York: Macmillan, 1989), table 45.
[a]Parental Loans for Undergraduate Students.

are more likely to choose careers or undergraduate majors that promise high earnings opportunities (American Council on Education 1985; Mohrman 1987). It is unclear from these latter studies, however, as to which way causation runs; individuals planning to enter relatively high-paying careers may be more willing to incur high debt levels to finance their education. Still other studies, reported in a comprehensive review of the literature (Hansen 1987), find no evidence that debt levels affect postgraduate plans.

The econometric study by Schapiro, O'Malley, and Litten (in press) used survey data collected from graduating seniors in 1982, 1984, and 1989 at institutions belonging to the Consortium on Financing Higher Education (COFHE), a group of elite private research universities and liberal arts colleges. The probability that a student planned to enroll in graduate school in the arts and sciences in the next fall was seen *not* to depend on his or her having a high debt level on graduation, after holding constant other individual and family characteristics. This study arbitrarily defined cutoff points for having high (e.g., $12,500 or higher in 1989) and low debt, and all students who planned to enroll in professional programs (e.g., law, medicine, business) were included in the "not enrolled in graduate school" group. The issues raised above about the direction of causality apply to this study as well.

Whether growing undergraduate debt burdens have, on average, caused individuals to delay, or not consider, graduate school entry is thus an open question. Of course, it is possible that growing debt burdens may have different effects on minority students from low-income families; this point is discussed in the next chapter.

8.3 Time to Degree

An economic model of the doctorate production process was developed by Breneman (1976), who sought to explain why registered time to degree, the attrition rate, and the timing of attrition varied widely across doctoral fields at the University of California, Berkeley, during the 1950s and 1960s. Rather than focusing on differences in the intrinsic nature of the disciplines studied, Breneman stressed optimizing behavior on the part of graduate students and faculty.

At the risk of overly simplifying his approach, from the perspective of students, opportunity costs were postulated to be the key variable. Other things being equal, better job market opportunities, as measured by higher starting salary levels and the availability of nonacademic alternatives (when academic positions were in short supply) for doctorates, were postulated to lead to shorter times to degree. Similarly, greater availability of financial support for graduate students in the form of fellowships or assistantships was assumed to lead to shorter times to degree.

From the perspective of faculty, the key variable that Breneman emphasized was the desire to maximize faculty members' prestige in the scholarly community and the resources flowing to their department. To the extent that, in the 1950s and 1960s, faculty members' prestige depended on the quality of their students placed in academic jobs, fields in which few nonacademic job alternatives exist for new doctorates would tend to "flunk out" their weaker students. In contrast, fields in which substantial nonacademic job opportunities exist could place their "lemons" in this sector, and attrition rates would thus be lower in these fields.[10]

Finally, the time at which attrition occurred would depend on the nature of the financial support available to graduate students and faculty members' demand for graduate students. In fields such as the sciences and engineering, in which graduate students are supported primarily by research assistantships (Table 8.5), a weak student may potentially have a substantially negative effect on a faculty member's research. As such, attrition is likely to occur early in these fields, to minimize adverse effects on faculty research. In contrast, in fields such as the humanities, graduate students are supported primarily by teaching assistantships, and relatively low flows of new graduate students suggest the need for long times to degree to provide "bodies" to serve as teaching assistants and enrollees in graduate courses; attrition is therefore likely to take place later in the program.

While formal econometric models were not estimated, Breneman found that on balance his approach explained quite well the patterns of time to degree, attrition rates, and when attrition occurred in doctoral programs across 28 fields at Berkeley during the period 1947–68. His analysis was strictly cross-sectional, and no attempt was made to explain changes in time to degree within fields over the 20-year period his data covered.

Subsequent empirical studies of time to degree have been surprisingly few and quite limited. Abedi and Benkin (1987) studied the determinants of time to degree for 4,225 doctorates from the University of California, Los Angeles, during the period 1976–85. Using stepwise regression methods, they found that individuals whose primary source of support was their own earnings (*not* assistantships) on average took longer to complete their degrees than others. In contrast, other things being equal, doctoral students supported by assistantships had unexpectedly shorter total times to degree than those on fellowships.

Abedi and Benkin's analysis had a number of shortcomings. It failed to control for individuals' ability levels (which presumably are correlated with whether they received financial support), for changing market opportunities for doctorates in different fields over time (constant field-specific effects were

---

10. Given that the share of newly employed doctorates accepting nonacademic employment has risen from roughly 30 to 50 percent over the last 20 years (Table 7.7), it is not obvious that faculty members' prestige in many fields is still derived from the quality of their academic placements. Thus, there should be no presumption that doctorates taking positions in the nonacademic sector today are on average of lower "quality" than their counterparts taking jobs in the academic sector. Empirical evidence that bears on this issue is discussed below.

permitted), for possible sample selection bias (only students who completed doctorates were included in the sample; see Table 7.6 for evidence on how completion rates vary across fields), or for the likelihood that the effect of having an assistantship depends on both the type of assistantship held and the field.

This latter point was emphasized by Tuckman, Coyle, and Bae (1990) in their time-series study of why median time to degree, by field, increased over the period 1968–87.[11] While teaching assistantships, which take time away from study, should presumably slow down degree progress vis-à-vis those with fellowships, research assistantships may actually speed up completion. The latter would occur if activities involved in research assistantships increase holders' research skills (by more than fellowship holders can achieve on their own) or are on or directly related to holders' dissertation topics.

Tuckman, Coyle, and Bae estimate median time-to-degree equations for each of 11 fields using national data for the 20-year period, with doctorate recipients grouped by year of degree. Explanatory variables experimented with included measures of the doctorates' personal characteristics (e.g., percentage with undergraduate degrees in the same field), financial support (e.g., percentage with *any* support from research assistantships during their doctoral study), institutional variables (e.g., percentage receiving doctoral degrees from Research I institutions), and economic and social variables (e.g., starting doctoral salaries). In all, almost 20 variables were experimented with in the various analyses; given the small sample sizes, only a subset of these could appear in any equation.

Unfortunately, these authors do not find consistent patterns of results across the 11 fields. The types of financial support matter in some fields but not in others and not always in the manner expected. One *cannot* conclude from their findings that increasing federal support for graduate students would be an effective way to shorten time to degree. Moreover, while in some cases changes in market variables, such as starting salaries or unemployment rates, appear to influence changes in time to degree, again these variables do not consistently matter across fields.

One must caution, however, against drawing negative conclusions about the effects of graduate support and market variables from such an aggregate level of analysis. As the authors note, small sample sizes in the aggregate data, coupled with high multicollinearity among the variables, surely decreased the likelihood of finding significant effects. In addition, their financial support variables related to the percentages of doctorates who received any support

11. Tuckman, Coyle, and Bae (1990) also studied changes in total time to degree and the lag between graduation from college and entry into doctoral programs. They found no trend in the latter, which is in sharp contrast to the data reported above in Table 7.5. Their data, however, covered people who *entered* doctoral programs probably, on average, between 1962 and 1980, while the data reported in Table 7.5 cover entrants between 1976 and 1987. The positive trend in the latter period is quite clear.

from various sources because data on the percentages who received their *primary* support from the various sources were not collected in the Survey of Earned Doctorates (SED) until the later years of the period. Finally, as Bowen, Lord, and Sosa (in press) have stressed, changes in median times to degree for degree recipients grouped by year of degree are subject to aggregation biases if entering doctoral student cohort sizes are systematically changing over time.

Future econometric analyses of the determinants of time to degree surely must use individual data, be institutionally based, separate out the effects of financial support from ability, and take account of noncompleters as well as completers. Nonetheless, although the prior econometric literature provides little basis for arguing that increased federal support for doctoral study would decrease times to degree, it is interesting simply to contrast the data for the period 1974–88 on changes in time to degree by field found in Table 7.4 with the data for the same period on changes in the proportion of full-time science/engineering graduate students who are receiving various forms of major financial support and of science/engineering graduate students enrolled part-time found in Tables 8.5 and 8.6, respectively.[12]

Between 1974 and 1988, median registered time to degree rose by 0.5 years or less for both the physical sciences and engineering (Table 7.4). While both fields saw the share of full-time graduate students on fellowship support decline over the period, the share of research assistants grew in both to compensate for most of these declines. Indeed, the growth in research assistants was so large that the share of full-time students on teaching assistantship actually declined by almost 7 percentage points in the physical sciences (Table 8.5). In both fields, the percentage of part-time students also declined during the period (Table 8.6).

In contrast, between 1974 and 1988, median registered time to degree rose by 1.7 years in the social sciences (which in Table 7.4 is defined to include psychology). The substantial decline in the shares of full-time students in psychology and the social sciences whose major source of support was fellowships was accompanied by increases in the share of those with teaching assistantship and self-support (Table 8.5) and increases in the share of all doctoral students in the field who were enrolled part-time (Table 8.6).

These comparisons are only suggestive, as they do not control for changing labor market conditions and personal characteristics of doctoral students. However, they do hint that increased fellowship and research assistantship support can lead to reduced median registered time to degree, or at least slow down the increase. Unfortunately, they provide little guidance about the magnitudes of likely responses.

Furthermore, even if one knew with certainty what the effect of increased

---

12. Unfortunately, data on the types of financial support received by doctoral students in the humanities were not separately reported in the volumes on which Tables 8.5 and 8.6 are based.

fellowship and research assistantship support would be on median time to degree and what the direct effects of increased support and reduced time to degree would be on students' decisions to enter and complete doctoral study, it would not necessarily follow that increased governmental support for doctoral students would be an effective way of expanding doctorate production. Often absent from the policy debate has been any concern for the possibility that increased federal support may simply induce institutions to redirect their own financial resources in a way that at least partially frustrates the intent of such a policy.

For example, increased federal support for science/engineering graduate students could lead institutions to cut back somewhat on (or not increase as rapidly as they had planned) their own internal support for these students and use the funds saved either to support graduate students in other disciplines or for other purposes (nongraduate student expenditures or tuition increase reductions). Conversely, cutbacks in federal support may lead institutions to attempt partially to offset the cutbacks by increasing their own expenditures. Indeed, as Table 8.4 indicates, the fall between 1974 and 1988 in the percentage of full-time science/engineering graduate students supported by federal funds was accompanied by an increase in the percentage of these full-time students supported by institutional funds. While causation should not be inferred from these aggregate time-series data, the changes are suggestive.

To the extent that changes in federal financial support for graduate education lead institutions to redirect and/or reduce their own expenditures, changes in the field composition and total number of doctorates that are produced may be different than policymakers intended.[13] To analyze the likely effects of an increase in federal support for doctoral students fully thus requires an analysis of the extent to which federal funds displace institutional funds. No existing study has addressed this issue, and research is clearly warranted on it. About all that one can currently say is that analyses that ignore potential displacement effects will likely overstate the effects of increased federal support.

8.4   Has the Quality of New Doctoral Students Declined?

Has the decline over the last two decades in the annual number of American citizen doctorates produced been accompanied by a decline in their average quality? Put another way, are our most talented undergraduates increasingly pursuing study in law, business, and medicine rather than doctoral programs?

13. The issue being raised here is very similar to one confronted by policymakers in the 1970s and early 1980s, when concern was expressed that the net job creation effects of public-sector employment programs (programs in which the federal government gave state and local governments funds to increase their employment levels) were considerably less than the number of positions funded. Empirical studies of what became known as the "displacement effect" or "fiscal substitution effect," of public-sector employment programs did indeed find that, on average, an increase in program positions typically led to a smaller increase in public-sector employment levels (Ehrenberg and Smith 1991, chap. 13).

The issue was recently raised by Bowen and Schuster (1986, chap. 2), but the evidence is inconclusive.

On the one hand, Rosovsky (1990) reports that the proportion of those Harvard undergraduates graduating summa cum laude (roughly the top 5 percent of the class) who after graduation attended graduate school in the arts and sciences fell from 77 percent in 1964 to 25 percent in 1981 before rebounding to 32 percent in 1987. Kasper (1990a) surveyed nine highly selective liberal arts institutions and found that, over the last two decades, the number and average quality (as measured by grade-point averages relative to those of the college as a whole) of their undergraduate economics majors had increased but that both the share and the absolute number of their majors choosing to pursue graduate study in economics had fallen substantially. Both these "case studies" suggest that a falloff may have occurred in the number of "high-quality" doctoral students coming from leading research universities and selective liberal arts colleges. Focusing on exceptional undergraduates nationwide, namely, those elected to Phi Beta Kappa or receiving a Rhodes Scholarship, Bowen and Schuster similarly find slight declines in the proportion of each entering academic careers between 1970–74 and 1975–79 (Bowen and Schuster 1986, fig. 11.1).

In contrast, other evidence is mixed or less supportive of the "decline in quality" view. Bowen and Schuster's interviews with faculty at 15 institutions revealed concern that doctoral student quality was declining in the humanities and arts and sciences, but a questionnaire mailed to the chairs of 404 departments (which were among the highest-ranked departments in each of 32 fields) found more support for the notion that graduate students were "better" in 1983–84 than they were in 1968–72 (Bowen and Schuster 1986, table 11.1). A study of graduate admissions at 20 leading research institutions covering the period 1972–80 found that, in the humanities and the social sciences, the number of applicants fell and acceptance rates rose (Garet and Butler-Nalin 1982). While at first glance this may seem to imply declining average quality of graduate students, such a conclusion would necessarily be valid only if the quality distribution of applicants did not improve during the period.

Schapiro, O'Malley, and Litten's (in press) study of graduates of 27 elite private research universities and liberal arts colleges found that the percentage of graduating seniors planning to enter graduate school in the arts and sciences was 11 percent in 1982, rose to 13 percent in 1984, and then fell back to 10 percent in 1989. When the analyses were confined to the top 5 percent of all undergraduates, namely, those students who reported straight A averages, the comparable percentages were 25, 29, and 24. So, even among this elite group of students, propensities to attend graduate school in the arts and sciences did not appear to fall during the 1980s.

Evidence from objective test scores is also less supportive of the declining quality view. Hartnett (1987) contrasted undergraduate Scholastic Aptitude

Test (SAT) scores for individuals who received doctoral and professional degrees (law, business, and medicine) in 1966, 1971, 1976, and 1981 from a set of surveyed institutions and found that the ratio of SAT scores for those who earned doctoral degrees relative to the ratio of scores for those who earned professional degrees did not decline during the period. Thus, it did not appear that better students were increasingly entering professional rather than doctoral programs over the period.

Of course, students who received doctorates in 1981 entered graduate school, on average, in the early to mid-1970s. What has happened to the quality of doctoral students nationwide since then? Some evidence can be obtained from data reported annually between 1975–76 and 1986–87 by the Educational Testing Service on the mean Graduate Record Examination (GRE) Verbal and Quantitative test scores of students *planning* doctoral study (see, e.g., Educational Testing Service 1988).

These data can be used to estimate the annual trends in the mean test scores of students planning doctoral study, by field, as well as the trends that exist after one controls for changes in the SAT scores of undergraduates. The former trends indicate what has been happening absolutely to the quality of students planning doctoral study, while the latter indicate how their quality has been changing relative to that of undergraduate students. The data can similarly be used to estimate the annual trends by field in the sum of the mean GRE score plus two standard deviations in GRE scores during the period 1977–78 to 1986–87. If GRE scores were normally distributed, these would represent the trends in GRE test scores for the upper 2.5 percent of test takers contemplating doctoral study in each field.

The estimates obtained when this was done do not suggest a substantial decline in the average quality of applicants to doctoral programs over the period.[14] The results for all fields combined show declines in the mean or upper-tail verbal scores of less than one point a year, which are more than offset by annual increases in quantitative scores of over three points a year. When SAT scores of undergraduate students are controlled for, on balance no evidence is found of trends in the mean or upper-tail GRE scores. Of course, results do differ by field. Those that show the greatest annual decline in verbal scores are, in the main, fields that have exhibited a large growth in foreign enrollments (e.g., the physical and life sciences).

Since these GRE data refer to all test takers, not solely American citizen and permanent resident test takers, they cannot, in any case, provide firm evidence as to how the quality of American doctoral students has increased. Hence, this is yet another area in which our knowledge is very imprecise. Moreover, given the evidence presented in Table 8.3 that the average starting salaries of doctorates in some fields have not declined relative to average starting salaries in professional alternatives, one might wonder where the specu-

---

14. These estimates are available from the author.

lation that the average quality of doctorates has declined has come from. That is, why do many people believe that the "better" students are now increasingly attracted to nondoctoral study alternatives?

One possible explanation for this speculation can be illustrated by focusing on potential applicants to doctoral programs in economics. Suppose that, as Table 8.3 shows, the average starting salary of doctorate economists has not changed relative to the average starting salary of lawyers in recent years. Suppose also, however, that the dispersion in starting salaries for economists has remained constant while the dispersion of starting salaries of lawyers has widened considerably (i.e., suppose that the ratio of big city, large law firm salaries has risen relative to other lawyers' salaries). If the higher-paying employers in both fields attract the graduates with the highest ability, the return to ability will in effect have risen in law relative to that in economics. Holding constant the average salary in each, this would encourage the more able students to choose law over economics more frequently.[15]

This line of reasoning can easily be applied to other fields. It emphasizes that decisions to enroll in doctoral programs will be based, not only on expected earnings from doctoral study and other options, but also on the return to ability in each. Prior empirical studies of doctorate labor supply have not taken the return to ability in each option into account.

8.5 Choice of Sector of Employment

8.5.1 New Doctorates

Decisions by new doctorates to accept employment in either the academic or the nonacademic sectors appear to be sensitive to the compensation offered in each sector. Studies that focus on economists (Hansen et al. 1980; Stapleton 1989) or on all new doctorates as a group (Freeman 1975b) find, on average, that an increase of a given percentage in starting academic salaries vis-à-vis starting nonacademic salaries will increase the ratio of new doctorates accepting employment in the academic sector to those accepting employment in the nonacademic sector by an equal percentage. So, for example, a 10 percent increase in starting academic salaries relative to starting nonacademic salaries would likely lead to an increase in the number of new doctorates accepting

---

15. This, of course, assumes that individuals with potentially high ability as economists would also potentially have high ability as lawyers. The discussion of how individuals are sorted among different alternatives according to their abilities is derived from Roy (1951). The approach has recently been applied to explain why the "quality" of immigrants coming to the United States from various countries differs (Borjas 1987). Whether the assumed changes have occurred in law is an open question and warrants empirical testing. Some of the increase in big city, large law firm salaries represents compensation for more rapid increases in living costs and longer hours of work (Kramer 1989). Many of the highest-ability law students also take relatively low-paying judicial clerkships, although these often lead to high-paying professorial positions (relative to economists) or high-paying practices.

academic employment relative to the number accepting nonacademic employment of about 10 percent, if all other factors remain unchanged.

Have academic relative salaries begun to adjust to existing, and projected, shortages of doctorates? Table 8.9 presents median salary data for new doctoral scientists, social scientists, and engineers employed in the academic and nonacademic sectors for the period 1973–89. These data were obtained from the biennial Survey of Doctoral Recipients (SDR); new doctorates are defined as those with five years' experience or less since receiving their doctorates. Unfortunately, such data are available only since 1973. However, when one looks at how the ratios by field of median new doctorate academic salaries to median new doctorate nonacademic salaries have changed (Table 8.10), some interesting patterns arise.

In most fields, relative academic starting salaries declined through the early 1980s but have been increasing in recent years. An exception is in engineering, where the relative academic salary reached its low point in 1977 and then increased thereafter. Engineering is one of the few fields that experienced an increase in the share of newly employed doctorates entering the academic sector between 1978 and 1988 (going from 23.5 to 28.5 percent; Table 7.7). The increase in the relative academic salary from 0.82 to 0.99 during the period 1977–89 obviously contributed to inducing more new engineering doctorates to enter the academic sector.[16] In contrast, the life, psychological, and social sciences saw their academic shares of new doctorate employment continue to fall between 1978 and 1988 (Table 7.7), and the relative academic salaries in these fields did not begin to rise until 1985 or 1987 (Table 8.10).

Given this evidence that relative academic starting salaries have begun to rise and that the share of new doctorates accepting employment in the academic sector is responsive to the academic relative starting salary, one might expect to observe an increasing share of new doctorates accepting academic employment in more fields in the future. However, several caveats, which relate to the fact that other factors are not likely to remain unchanged, are in order.

First, as nonacademic employment opportunities have expanded for new doctorates, there is evidence (at least for economics) that the share of new doctorates accepting nonacademic employment has increased, other things (including relative earnings) held constant (Stapleton 1989). To the extent that nonacademic employment opportunities for doctorates will continue to expand, increasing relative academic salaries may simply slow down the rate of decline in the share of new doctorates accepting academic employment rather than reversing it. Projections of the growth of nonacademic employment op-

16. I say "contributed to" since the increase in the employment share of 21.3 percent ({[28.5 − 23.5]/23.5} × 100) exceeds the 14.6 percent increase {[.94 − .82]/.82} × 100) in the academic relative salary. This implies that an elasticity of around 1.5, which is somewhat larger than the previous studies have found, would be required to "explain" the changing academic share of employment.

Table 8.9   Median Salaries of New Doctoral Scientists, Social Scientists, and Engineers Employed Full-Time in the Academic and Nonacademic Sectors

Field	1973	1975	1977	1979	1981	1983	1985	1987	1989
Physical sciences:									
A	15,181	16,831	18,390	19,967	23,258	26,004	29,482	34,150	36,709
NA	18,091	20,553	22,588	25,930	31,642	36,637	40,797	43,291	46,633
Mathematical sciences:									
A	15,809	17,190	18,100	19,783	22,534	26,473	30,212	33,732	36,839
NA	[a]	21,985	22,996	25,889	30,635	37,647	39,792	43,307	45,846
Computer sciences:									
A	18,236	19,367	19,612	22,157	27,454	32,760	41,625	46,320	51,896
NA	[a]	21,525	23,206	26,669	32,914	35,804	42,321	50,239	55,012
Environmental sciences:									
A	15,649	17,365	18,567	20,417	23,250	26,724	30,207	34,210	36,615
NA	[a]	21,717	22,761	27,129	32,454	37,197	40,061	40,829	42,134
Life sciences:									
A	15,658	17,342	18,996	20,980	24,225	27,275	29,983	33,316	36,569
NA	17,071	20,079	21,618	24,679	29,411	33,038	35,793	39,314	42,441
Psychology:									
A	16,289	17,598	18,396	20,347	22,486	26,082	29,312	32,112	35,534
NA	18,039	20,143	21,580	23,624	27,192	32,316	33,867	37,963	41,552
Social sciences:									
A	16,592	18,007	19,172	20,623	24,106	27,383	29,779	35,332	36,190
NA	20,450	22,485	24,223	27,123	31,097	25,803	39,075	41,639	45,156
Engineering:									
A	17,875	19,767	20,784	23,738	29,028	34,450	40,146	44,558	50,331
NA	20,668	22,873	25,340	28,495	34,727	40,689	45,273	47,387	50,763

Source: Special tabulations prepared from the *Survey of Doctorate Recipients* by the Office of Scientific and Engineering Personnel, National Research Council.

Note: A = academic sector; NA = nonacademic sector. New doctorates are those with five or less postdoctoral years of experience at the survey date.

[a]Not available.

Table 8.10   Relative Median Salaries for New Doctorate Scientists, Social Scientists, and Engineers

Field	1973	1975	1977	1979	1981	1983	1985	1987	1989
Physical sciences	.839	.819	.814	.770	.735	.710	.723	.789	.787
Mathematical sciences	a	.782	.787	.764	.736	.703	.759	.779	.803
Computer sciences	a	.898	.845	.831	.834	.915	.984	.922	.943
Environmental sciences	a	.800	.816	.753	.716	.718	.754	.838	.869
Life sciences	.917	.864	.879	.850	.824	.826	.838	.847	.862
Psychology	.903	.874	.852	.861	.827	.807	.866	.846	.851
Social sciences	.811	.801	.791	.760	.775	.765	.762	.849	.801
Engineering	.865	.864	.820	.833	.836	.847	.887	.940	.991

Source: Special tabulations prepared from the *Survey of Doctorate Recipients* by the Office of Scientific and Engineering Personnel, National Research Council.

Note: Figures represent ratio of median academic to median nonacademic salaries of doctorates with five or less years postdoctoral experience who are employed full-time in the field.

aNot available.

portunities for scientists and engineers are often based on projections of government and industry research and development expenditures (National Science Foundation 1989d; Forest 1990); uncertainty about proposed reductions in military expenditures, coupled with the existence of persistent budget deficits, makes such projections highly uncertain.

A second caveat is that the relative attractiveness of entering academic versus nonacademic employment depends on more than relative starting salaries. Expected future earnings matter, yet we have little evidence on how doctorates' expected age/earnings profiles in the academic and nonacademic sectors contrast at a point in time or how they have changed over time. Surely, the "quality" of academic jobs available, the time it takes to achieve tenure, and the difficulty of achieving tenure also matter. When the academic labor market is "loose" and more new doctorates are searching for academic jobs than are needed, most doctorates' probabilities of finding positions at better-quality teaching and research institutions will be lower, and publication standards for tenure will increase, as will the time it takes to achieve tenure (Kuh 1977; Kuh and Radner 1980; Perrucci, O'Flaherty, and Marshall 1983; Moore, et al. 1983; Willis 1990). Together these forces reduce the attractiveness of academic careers. In contrast, in tight labor markets, with "shortages" of doctorates (as are projected for the future), these patterns are reversed, the relative attractiveness of academic careers is increased, and this adds to the likelihood that the share of new doctorates choosing academic careers would increase.

Working conditions in both the academic and the nonacademic sectors also surely matter. While it is difficult to measure all these, it is well-known that student/doctorate faculty ratios have been falling over the past two decades (Bowen and Sosa 1989, chap. 5). In addition, while data from three national surveys of faculty conducted by the Carnegie Foundation for the Advancement of Teaching in 1975, 1984, and 1989 do not indicate that substantial changes have occurred in the number of hours per week that professors spend in classroom instruction (Tables 8.11 and 8.12), they do suggest that faculty members spent considerably less time in scheduled office hours per week in 1989 then they did in 1975 (Table 8.13). Lower student/faculty ratios and fewer scheduled office hours (which provides faculty with more flexibility in how they can allocate their time) surely increase the relative attractiveness of academic careers. While academic institutions might hope to respond to projected future shortages of doctorates by increasing faculty work loads, increased competition for scarce faculty will make it difficult for them to do so.

Hand in hand with concern about the reduced share of new doctorates choosing academic careers, concern is often expressed that the academic sector may be (increasingly) losing the highest-quality new doctorates to the nonacademic sector. However, evidence to confirm that this is occurring is not very strong. One detailed study of all students receiving doctorates in economics between June 1972 and June 1978 found that a new doctorate's probability of obtaining a first job in the academic sector was higher the higher the

Table 8.11   **Typical Hours per Week Spent in Undergraduate Classroom Instruction by American Academics**

	Hours				
Category	None	1–5	6–10	11–20	> 20
All respondents:					
1989 (N = 4,923)	6.1	21.1	29.0	39.2	4.6
1984 (N = 4,731)	11.2	24.6	25.3	35.1	3.8
1975 (N = 2,232)	10.0	23.2	25.9	36.0	5.0
Four-year institutions:					
1989 (N = 3,069)	9.5	29.3	35.2	24.8	1.3
1984 (N = 3,552)	13.8	29.1	30.2	25.2	1.7
1975 (N = 1,847)	10.6	24.5	32.9	28.9	3.1
Research institutions:					
1989 (N = 1,011)	18.0	46.1	27.8	7.3	.7
1984 (N = 1,080)	26.4	43.3	21.6	8.0	.7
1975 (N = 1,201)	23.1	38.7	25.2	11.5	1.6
Doctoral institutions:					
1989 (N = 463)	9.2	35.5	40.1	13.3	1.8
1984 (N = 561)	13.9	32.9	32.2	18.9	2.1
1975 (N = 206)	7.0	24.1	52.1	14.6	2.2
Comprehensive institutions:					
1989 (N = 1,256)	4.7	17.6	38.1	38.3	1.3
1984 (N = 1,530)	7.5	20.5	33.9	36.2	1.9
1975 (N = 355)	5.4	17.1	30.1	43.2	4.2
Libreral arts institutions:					
1989 (N = 338)	2.2	13.5	39.4	42.9	2.0
1984 (N = 382)	3.5	18.1	37.1	38.5	2.9
1975 (N = 85)	3.1	15.8	33.6	43.2	4.2

Source: Author's computations from unpublished tabulations provided by the Carnegie Foundation for the Advancement of Teaching from their 1989 (question 9A), 1984 (question 6A), and 1975 (question 8A) National Surveys of Faculty. In 1975 and 1984, a five- to six-hour interval was reported, and the people in this interval were split equally between the one- to five- and the six- to ten-hour categories in this table.

quality of the individual's graduate department (as measured by surveys of reputation or faculty publication counts) and the higher the selectivity (as measured by *Barron's Profiles of American Colleges* 1986) of the individual's undergraduate institution (Willis 1990, chap. 4). To the extent that students who graduate from both highly selective undergraduate schools and highly ranked graduate departments represent our "best and brightest," this suggests that, at least during the 1970s, academe was more likely to attract the most able new doctorate economists, at least initially. More recently, however, a survey conducted in 1988–89 of doctoral candidates from the top 50 graduate programs in economics found that a slightly higher percentage of students from the top 15 programs were accepting jobs in the nonacademic sector than were graduates of the lesser-rated programs (Barbezat 1989b).

Evidence for doctorates in general is more sketchy. We know that, in the

Table 8.12   **Typical Hours per Week Spent in Graduate or Professional Student Classroom Instruction by American Academics**

	Hours				
Category	None	1–5	6–10	11–20	> 20
All respondents:					
1989 (N = 4,923)	44.5	41.4	11.2	2.4	.5
1984 (N = 4,731)	57.9	31.5	8.0	2.4	.3
1975 (N = 2,232)	47.4	35.9	12.0	3.8	1.0
Four-year institutions:					
1989 (N = 3,069)	34.1	50.0	13.3	2.3	.2
1984 (N = 3,552)	48.6	38.8	9.8	2.6	.3
1975 (N = 1,847)	41.9	40.5	12.9	3.9	.8
Research institutions:					
1989 (N = 1,011)	24.1	59.5	14.6	1.7	.1
1984 (N = 1,080)	32.6	53.5	12.0	2.4	.6
1975 (N = 1,201)	27.7	50.7	15.8	4.6	1.1
Doctoral institutions:					
1989 (N = 463)	27.7	54.0	15.4	2.4	.4
1984 (N = 561)	40.8	43.2	12.5	3.2	.3
1975 (N = 206)	30.9	48.8	15.4	4.2	.8
Comprehensive institutions:					
1989 (N = 1,256)	43.1	41.2	12.1	3.1	.5
1984 (N = 1,530)	57.2	32.4	8.1	2.4	.1
1975 (N = 355)	49.7	34.3	11.4	4.0	.6
Liberal arts institutions:					
1989 (N = 338)	75.1	17.3	5.1	2.5	.0
1984 (N = 382)	81.5	10.5	5.3	2.3	.5
1975 (N = 85)	84.6	11.1	3.1	.9	.4

Source: Author's computations from unpublished tabulations provided by the Carnegie Foundation for the Advancement of Teaching from their 1989 (question 9B), 1984 (question 6B), and 1975 (question 8B) National Surveys of Faculty. In 1975 and 1984, a five- to six-hour interval was reported, and the people in this interval were split equally between the one-to five- and the six- to ten-hour categories in this table.

mid-1950s, doctorates who accepted postdocs, who often represent the very best graduate students in the sciences, were more likely to take a first job in academe than were other doctorates who accepted employment immediately on graduation (Tables 7.7 and 7.9).[17] Special tabulations prepared from the SED by the National Research Council also allow us to ascertain how the percentage of new doctorates in 1988 with employment plans in the U.S. academic sector varied (by field) between Research I and all other doctorate-granting institutions and, within institutional category, by the doctorates' major sources of financial support during their studies.

These tabulations, presented in Table 8.14, suggest that, in psychology, the

17. Postdocs were also more likely (at least during the early 1970s) to wind up in tenure-track positions in major research universities (National Research Council 1981).

Table 8.13   Typical Scheduled Office Hours per Week of American Academics

Category	Hours				
	None	1–5	6–10	11–20	> 20
All respondents:					
1989 (N = 4,923)	4.2	66.1	22.7	5.4	1.6
1984 (N = 4,731)	8.2	43.5	33.4	9.9	5.2
1975 (N = 2,232)	8.9	38.7	30.3	11.8	10.5
Four-year institutions:					
1989 (N = 3,069)	4.8	64.9	24.0	4.8	1.5
1984 (N = 3,552)	9.5	47.7	30.3	7.9	4.6
1975 (N = 1,847)	8.7	40.0	29.5	11.2	10.7
Research institutions:					
1989 (N = 1,011)	9.1	70.6	15.9	3.1	1.2
1984 (N = 1,080)	17.0	54.3	20.1	5.2	5.6
1975 (N = 1,201)	14.3	42.1	21.6	8.3	13.6
Doctoral institutions:					
1989 (N = 463)	4.6	63.6	24.9	5.0	1.8
1984 (N = 561)	7.9	46.3	32.6	8.2	4.9
1975 (N = 206)	7.7	39.6	29.5	11.6	11.5
Comprehensive institutions:					
1989 (N = 1,256)	1.7	64.5	27.2	5.3	1.3
1984 (N = 1,530)	5.9	46.0	35.9	8.6	3.8
1975 (N = 355)	4.8	39.9	34.5	11.8	8.9
Liberal arts institutions:					
1989 (N = 338)	2.4	49.7	36.6	8.1	3.1
1984 (N = 382)	4.3	40.4	37.9	13.4	4.1
1975 (N = 85)	7.4	35.6	33.8	15.5	7.7

Source: Author's computations from unpublished tabulations provided by the Carnegie Foundation for the Advancement of Teaching from their 1989 (question 9E), 1984 (question 6C), and 1975 (question 8C) National Surveys of Faculty. In 1975 and 1984, a five- to six-hour interval was reported, and the people in this interval were split equally between the one- to five- and the six- to ten-hour categories in this table.

social sciences, the humanities, and the professional fields, students from Research I institutions and, within institutional type, students with financial support (teaching assistantships, research assistantships, or fellowships) tend to be more likely to obtain initial employment in the academic sector. Again to the extent that these students represent the "best and the brightest," the academic sector still appears to be holding on at the entry level to high-quality doctorates. Results for the sciences, also reported in Table 8.14, are less clear because in some of the sciences many of the best new doctorates accept postdocs and are thus not counted as accepting academic employment.

8.5.2 Experienced Doctorates

Data on the age distribution of employed doctorates in the academic and nonacademic sectors, by field, were presented in Table 7.12, and data on mo-

Table 8.14   Percentage of New Doctorates with Employment Plans in the U.S. Academic Sector, 1988

	Physical Science		Computer Science		Engineering		Biological Science		Agricultural Science		Health Science	
	Research I	Other	Research I	Other	Research I	Other	Research I	Other	Research I	Other	Research I	Other
All	33.4	39.1	54.6	63.6	28.7	34.7	43.8	54.8	39.8	45.1	61.4	66.4
U.S. citizen	30.0	36.7	53.7	58.7	26.5	31.3	42.8	54.2	42.1	49.4	61.0	69.5
U.S. citizen/support:												
Own/family	27.1	29.7	45.2	57.1	27.5	44.4	42.9	59.0	45.0	58.3	68.1	72.0
Teaching assistantship	43.7	55.3	66.7	87.5	28.8	60.9	65.8	76.9	30.8	66.7	68.8	60.0
Research assistantship	22.7	34.4	53.7	57.1	27.5	27.3	34.2	56.3	40.0	45.5	40.0	a
Fellowship	41.9	35.3	50.0	50.0	34.1	23.1	40.0	47.8	83.3	100.0	64.3	66.7
State loans	28.6	50.0	50.0	50.0	37.5	25.0	57.1	80.0	50.0	a	63.6	100.0
Other	20.0	18.9	33.3	27.3	12.5	25.0	36.7	31.3	29.4	37.5	48.1	58.8

	Psychology		Social Science		Humanities		Professional Fields		Total	
	Research I	Other	Research I	Other	Research I	Other	Research I	Other	Research I	Other
All	37.5	24.6	68.5	59.4	82.4	71.9	83.9	66.9	54.3	49.0
U.S. citizen	36.7	24.7	68.1	58.5	82.0	71.6	83.3	65.8	54.0	48.3
U.S. citizen/support:										
Own/family	29.3	20.7	58.9	51.5	73.3	66.7	83.6	59.5	55.0	46.8
Teaching assistantship	54.8	54.1	81.1	74.6	90.0	80.7	91.6	96.8	72.0	72.2
Research assistantship	38.9	37.0	71.8	65.4	80.0	60.0	75.6	90.9	35.0	40.9
Fellowship	55.6	17.4	75.3	64.7	88.9	74.2	89.5	64.7	66.5	48.1
State loans	28.3	18.9	64.5	93.3	87.0	84.0	76.9	70.4	57.2	38.9
Other	29.4	28.1	43.6	36.4	74.4	66.7	63.4	54.1	35.6	35.8

Source: Special tabulations prepared by the Office of Scientific and Engineering Personnel, National Research Council, from the 1988 Survey of Earned Doctorates.

a Not available.

bility rates between sectors, by age and field, were presented in Table 7.11. These data can be combined to provide quantitative estimates of the extent to which changes in mobility rates can lead to changes in the number of experienced doctorates employed in the academic sector.

In the aggregate, the stock of employed doctorates in each sector age 35 and under in 1985 was approximately equal to the annual number of new doctorates awarded (all in the range of 30,000), while the stock of employed doctorates in each sector age 35–50 was approximately equal to four to five times the annual flow of new doctorates. In the aggregate, the percentage of those initially employed in academe who had moved to the nonacademic sector two years later was roughly 11 and 5, respectively, for the two age groups, while the percentage initially employed in the nonacademic sector who were employed in the academic sector two years later was 8 and 4, respectively. If one could reduce the out-migration rates from the academic sector by 2 percentage points, over 3,500 more doctorates would remain in the academic sector by the end of the two-year period. If one could increase the in-migration rates to the academic sector by 3 percentage points, over 4,800 more experienced doctorates would be employed in the academic sector by the end of the two-year period. Are changes of such magnitude realistic possibilities?

The literature on sectoral mobility of experienced doctorates is quite limited. There are no studies that address how changing relative earnings prospects in the two sectors influence sectoral mobility. However, several studies do suggest that experienced doctorates' mobility to and from academe depends on the availability of jobs in the academic sector and the general level of tightness in the academic labor market.

Crowley and Chubin (1976) found that considerable movement back to the academic sector of young doctorates in sociology occurred during the 1960s, when academic employment opportunities in sociology were expanding. Rosenfeld and Jones (1988) studied the decisions of over 600 doctorates in psychology with initial appointments in academe on whether to exit from academe during the first six years of their careers and, if so, whether subsequently to return. An excess supply of new psychology doctorates was seen to increase the probability of young academic doctorates moving to the nonacademic sector, as colleges and universities respond to the excess supply by increasing tenure standards and thus increasing the involuntary mobility of young faculty out of the sector.[18] Such an excess supply of new doctorates also made it more difficult for experienced doctorates to return to the academic sector after they had left. Conversely, tighter academic labor markets, as have been predicted for the mid-1990s would lead to less out-migration from and more in-migration to the academic sector.

18. Kuh (1977) found similar changes in tenure probabilities and time to tenure with market conditions for mathematicians.

Table 8.15   Sources of Appointments to Full-Time Academic Positions in
Engineering Schools in 1985 and 1987

	1985		1987	
Status Prior to Accepting Position	*T*	*N*	*T*	*N*
Full-time graduate or postdoctoral student (%)	43.5	45.5	44.6	46.4
Full-time faculty at another institution (%)	31.0	26.7	30.4	17.7
Full-time employee in industry/government (%)	20.6	18.4	19.6	22.6
Other or unknown (%)	4.9	9.4	5.3	13.2
Total no. of appointments	936	a	973	265

Source: "ASEE Survey of Engineering Faculty and Graduaate Students, Fall 1985," *Engineering Education* (October 1986), table 8; and "Who Are We? Engineering and Engineering Faculty Survey, Fall 1987, Part II," *Engineering Education* (November 1988), table 2.
Note: T = tenure track; N = non-tenure track.
ªNot reported.

Of course, one must be careful about generalizing from these two studies of social science fields. The substantial current differences across fields (Table 7.11) in the probabilities of moving to and from the academic sector reflect both field-specific differences in job opportunities and the transferability of skills between the academic and the nonacademic sectors.

In the humanities, for example, it seems clear that an increase in the availability of academic positions would draw nonacademic doctorates back to the academic sector and reduce (involuntary) mobility out of the sector, for even during the tight humanities labor market conditions of the mid-1980s, the probabilities that nonacademic doctorates moved to the academic sector during the two-year period covered by the data far exceeded the probabilities that academic economists moved to the nonacademic sector during the same time. A halving of the out-migration rates from the academic sector and a doubling of the in-migration rates from the nonacademic sector would have resulted in 2,511 more experienced humanities doctorates being employed at the end of the period in the academic sector. Alternatively, holding out-migration rates constant but simply increasing each in-migration rate by 2 percentage points would have led to an increase in academic employment of 604 by the end of the period.[19] These numbers should be contrasted to the total of 3,553 humanities doctorates that were awarded in 1988 (National Research Council 1989d).

In some fields, a substantial share of academic appointments is currently made to experienced doctorates employed in the nonacademic sector. For example, Table 8.15 shows that, in recent years, approximately 20 percent of full-time appointments in engineering on both tenure and non-tenure tracks went to doctorates who were previously full-time employees in industry and

19. These increases are computed using the data in Table 7.10 and 7.11.

Table 8.16   Sources of New Mathematics Faculty for U.S. Colleges and Universities

	Nontenured						Tenured					
	T	g	a	n	f	o	T	g	a	n	f	o
Doctorate-granting departments:												
1986	381	.467	.367	.010	.136	.018	52	0	.750	.000	.096	.156
1985	342	.389	.471	.020	.088	.032	62	0	.710	.000	.177	.113
1984	396	.452	.367	.023	.121	.035	41	0	.805	.024	.171	.000
1983	347	.432	.378	.040	.104	.046	25	0	.800	.040	.160	.000
1982	377	.459	.393	.050	.082	.016	42	0	.714	[a]	[a]	[a]
1981	371	.431	.402	.003	.113	.051	47	0	.809	[a]	[a]	[a]
1980	278	.429	.410	.029	.082	.050	35	0	.686	[a]	[a]	[a]
1979	380	.447	.421	.039	.066	.026	40	0	.750	[a]	[a]	[a]

	Doctorate-Holding						Nondoctorate					
	T	g	a	n	f	o	T	g	a	n	f	o
All four-year institutions:												
1984	1,336	.338	.477	.049	.086	.049	910	.381	.229	.091	.025	.274
1983	1,276	.334	.472	.064	.067	.063	724	.420	.124	.133	.019	.304
1982	1,371	.386	.451	.058	.058	.047	880	.377	.247	.115	.000	.261
1981	1,366	.343	.467	.070	.059	.061	739	.429	.179	.143	.015	.234
1980	1,355	.330	.444	.065	.089	.073	620	.479	.131	.100	.010	.276
1979	1,135	.335	.485	.053	.066	.062	550	.455	.164	.127	.036	.236
1978	1,080	.407	.417	.074	.046	.056	490	.510	.184	.082	.020	.204
1977	1,140	.404	.439	.035	.061	.061	435	.575	.126	.067	.025	.207

Source: Author's calculations from data found in the "Annual AMS-MAA Surveys (Second Reports)," *Notices of the American Mathematical Society* (various issues).

Note: T = total number of faculty hired; g = share of new hires that are new Ph.D.'s; a = share of new hires from other U.S. or Canadian institutions' faculty; n = share of new hires from the nonacademic sector; f = share of new hires from foreign countries; and o = share of new hires from other sources.

[a]Data not reported.

government. Given the large number of experienced doctorate engineers employed in the nonacademic sector, one would suspect that this group can provide an increased share of future academic appointments.

In other fields, for example, mathematics, experienced nonacademic doctorates currently make up only a small share of academic appointments. Annual data collected by the American Mathematical Society and reported in Table 8.16 show that experienced nonacademic doctorates make up less than 5 percent of the new faculty hired at doctorate-granting institutions during the period 1979–86 and 3.5–7.5 percent of the new appointments at all four-year institutions.

Given that a large stock of experienced nonacademic doctorates exists in mathematics and many other scientific fields (Table 7.12) but that in some fields (e.g., mathematics) they currently rarely return to the academic sector, the question arises as to whether nonacademic doctorates have retained the types of skills that academe demands. Only if they do is it important to consider how they might respond to increased job opportunities and an increased ratio of academic to nonacademic salaries. While one can only speculate about nonacademic doctorates' interest in teaching and their ability to do so, there is evidence that many nonacademic scientists do have active research programs.

Specifically, Stephan and Levin (1987) studied the publishing performance of physicists, earth scientists, biochemists, and plant and animal physiologists, using data from the 1973, 1975, 1977, and 1979 waves of the SDR, merged with publication data from the *Science Citation Index*. While scientists at highly rated academic institutions published the most, a substantial number of publishing scientists employed in business and industry, government, and federally funded research-and-development centers had publication records that were comparable to those employed in lesser academic institutions (Table 8.17). Although the types of research conducted in academic and nonacademic settings may well differ, there do appear to be many nonacademic scientists in these fields whose research records would qualify them for consideration for academic appointments.

Of course, one must caution that these results on publishing performance are only for selected science fields. Similar evidence is required for other science fields, the social sciences, and the humanities before one can conclude that, in general, a large stock of nonacademic doctorates have retained the skills that academe demands. In addition, to the extent that there is a much greater dispersion of compensation in the nonacademic than in the academic sector and the most talented doctorates command the highest salaries in both sectors, the financial cost of returning to the academic sector may often be highest for the most talented nonacademic doctorates. As such, the very people academe wants to attract back the most may well be the people who are least likely to want to return.[20]

20. I am indebted to Albert Rees for this point.

Table 8.17   Publishing Performance of Academic and Nonacademic Doctoral Scientists in the Stephan/Levin Sample

		Those That Publish					
	All	All	ACE	NON-ACE	BUS/IND	FFRDC	GOVT
Physicists:							
PUB1	1.72	3.67	4.26	2.98	3.57	3.87	3.23
PUB2	.74	1.58	1.77	1.39	1.59	1.55	1.50
PUB3	4.25	9.04	12.06	7.09	8.13	8.99	7.19
PUB4	1.71	3.66	4.69	3.15	3.55	3.34	3.11
PPUB	.47	a	a	a	a	a	a
N	7,231	3,399	854	517	418	695	184
Earth scientists:							
PUB1	1.00	2.71	3.25	2.58	1.95	2.71	2.28
PUB2	.53	1.43	1.71	1.43	1.11	1.22	1.19
PUB3	1.76	4.78	6.80	4.06	2.64	4.98	3.64
PUB4	.91	2.46	3.51	2.09	1.47	2.22	1.90
PPUB	.37	a	a	a	a	a	a
N	3,649	1,350	412	315	119	61	306
Biochemists:							
PUB1	3.91	6.09	6.89	6.07	4.69	4.87	6.62
PUB2	1.53	2.38	2.80	2.41	1.70	2.02	2.43
PPUB	.64	a	a	a	a	a	a
N	4,685	2,998	517	733	169	92	296
Plant and animal physiologists:							
PUB1	3.39	5.56	5.52	6.27	3.97	5.14	4.47
PUB2	1.38	2.26	2.44	2.55	1.71	1.95	1.75
PPUB	.61	a	a	a	a	a	a
N	3,344	2,040	355	508	29	81	161

Source: Stephan and Levin (1987).

Note: PUB1 = mean number of publications in the two years following the survey year; PUB2 = adjusted (for coauthors) mean number of publications in the two years following the survey year; PUB3 = mean number of publications adjusted for "impact" in the two years following the survey year; PUB4 = adjusted (for coauthors and "impact") mean number of publications in the two years following the survey year; PPUB = proportion of doctorates that published at all during the period; N = sample size; All = entire sample; ACE = those employed in the field in academic institutions ranked by the American Council on Education; NON-ACE = those employed in the field in nonranked institutions; BUS/IND = those employed in the field in business and industry; FFRDC = those employed in federally funded research-and-development centers; and GOVT = those employed in government.

aNot available.

9 The Demographic Distribution of American Doctorates

9.1 Faculty Age Structure, Productivity, and Retirement

The supply of academics depends not only on the supply of new doctorates and the sector of employment choices of new and experienced doctorates but also on the age structure of faculty and their retirement behavior. As Table 7.10 indicates, the percentage of doctoral scientists, social scientists, and engineers employed by academic institutions who were age 60 and older rose from 6.9 in 1977 to 11.6 in 1987. A similar increase, in the share of academic doctorates age 45–60 also occurred.[1] As such, the proportion of faculty who are nearing retirement will remain high over the next 20 years. High levels of faculty retirements, which lead to high levels of replacement demand for faculty, contribute to projections of faculty shortages.[2]

Of course, as of 1994, faculty will no longer be subject to mandatory retirement at age 70. If an appreciable number of older faculty can be induced to stay on beyond age 70, would this substantially reduce projected shortages? Is it likely that a substantial number could be induced to stay on? Finally, is it the case that, after some age, on average, teaching and research productivity of faculty begin to decline so that, rather than trying to induce older faculty to remain, universities might more profitably think about ways to "encourage" them to retire?

Bowen and Sosa (1989, chap. 8) have answered the first question, at least for faculty in the arts and sciences. They show that, if the expected retirement rate of faculty in the 65–69 age range could have been cut in half as of 1987, the effect in their projection model would have been to reduce the replacement

1. Changes in the age distribution of doctorate humanists, the vast majority of whom are academics, are quite similar (National Research Council 1989b, 1986, 1982, 1978).
2. As noted in Chapter 6, Bowen and Sosa (1989) have emphasized that the primary cause of projected faculty shortages is the increased demand for new faculty, not the increased replacement demand caused by increased retirements.

demand for faculty by 8 percent during the period 1987–92. This reduction would be equivalent to a 6.5 percent increase in the supply of new doctorates, and, while in itself such an increase would only partially close the shortage they project, it would be a step in the right direction.

Unfortunately, the net effect of delayed retirements on the replacement demand for faculty projected in their model would be much smaller in subsequent five-year periods, as the reduced retirements from the 65–69 age group in each of these periods would be partially offset by an increased number of faculty ages 70 and older who would retire during each period. Indeed, they project that, over the period 1997–2012, the net effect of halving the retirement rates of faculty in the 65–69 age range would be equivalent to only about a 2 percent reduction in the replacement demand for faculty.

With respect to the second question, several recent studies suggest that the uncapping of mandatory retirement in 1994 is unlikely to have effects on retirement rates of even the above magnitudes. Rees and Smith (1990) contrasted arts and sciences faculty retirement behavior at 12 public research universities and private liberal arts colleges that have already eliminated mandatory retirement (owing to state laws or institutional decisions) with faculty retirement behavior at 22 similar public and private research universities and private liberal arts colleges that currently require mandatory retirement at age 70. They found no differences in mean retirement ages between capped and uncapped institutions, even after controlling for institutional type and discipline (humanities, social science, sciences). Mean retirement ages at elite private research universities were seen to be higher than at other institutions, and only at elite public and private research institutions do an appreciable number of faculty currently wait until age 70 to retire. Since very few private research universities have eliminated mandatory retirement yet, this suggests that uncapping might potentially lead to delayed faculty retirement in this set of institutions.

A second study (Lozier and Doris 1990), which focused on a broader set of 101 institutions, also concluded that changes in mandatory retirement laws have little short-run effects on retirement rates. A survey of over 500 retired professors from these institutions found that 80 percent claimed that mandatory retirement rules had not been a significant determinant of when they retired. Since many of the other 20 percent retired at age 70 and many of these people claimed that they would have preferred to retire at age 75 or later, the authors concluded that the uncapping of mandatory retirement will lead to a gradual small shift in retirement patterns.

In contrast, two earlier studies that tried to predict the effect of the increase in the mandatory retirement age from 65 to 70, which was legislated in 1978 and went into effect in 1981 for most colleges and universities, found somewhat larger effects on professors' expected ages of retirement. Holden and Hansen (1989) conducted a survey in 1980 of a sample of faculty age 50 and over from a stratified national sample of institutions and found, after holding other factors constant, that those employed in institutions that had already raised the mandatory retirement age to 70 planned to retire about one year later than those who faced mandatory retirement at age 65. Montgomery (1989; cited in Holden and Hansen 1989) summarized research contrasting retirement ages in 1980 in Consortium on Financing Higher Education (COFHE) institutions with mandatory retirement ages of 65 and 70 and concluded that faculty facing mandatory retirement at 70 retired, on average, some two years later.

Neither of these earlier studies controlled for the possibility that faculty members may have chosen employment at institutions whose mandatory retirement ages were consistent with their preferences. Such self-selection (faculty who want to retire late choosing institutions with later mandatory retirement ages) would distort their comparisons and cause them to overstate the effects of relaxing mandatory retirement laws. Moreover, there is no reason to suspect that the effect on retirement ages of the movement of mandatory retirement from age 70 to no mandatory retirement would be the same as the effect of the movement of mandatory retirement from age 65 to age 70.

Would increases in retirement ages lead to a decline in faculty productivity? The issue of how faculty productivity varies with age has been addressed for both teaching and research, using proxy measures for productivity in both cases. Feldman's (1983) meta-evaluation of over 100 previous studies concluded that half found no relation and half found a weak negative relation between professors' ages and their students' evaluations of their teaching effectiveness. However, all these studies were cross-sectional in nature and thus do not permit one to identify how a given professor's teaching effectiveness varies over his or her career. In addition, none focused on the teaching effectiveness of professors near the ends of their careers.

More recently, Kinney and Smith (1989) studied the relation between students' evaluations of teaching effectiveness and professors' ages for tenured arts and sciences professors at a single selective research institution. They found that, in cross sections, teaching effectiveness seemed to increase for tenured professors in the humanities and social sciences as they neared age 70 while for professors in the physical and biological sciences there seemed to be a very slight decline.[3] These findings suggest that, at least for this one institution, the uncapping of mandatory retirement should not lead to a dramatic decline in faculty teaching effectiveness.

Similarly, studies of the relation between faculty research productivity and age leave one with the impression that uncapping will not have a major effect on faculty research productivity. Reskin (1985) surveyed the prior literature

3. Kinney and Smith (1989) also emphasize that cross-sectional age–teaching effectiveness relations may be distorted if retirement ages vary systematically with teaching effectiveness. For the institution they studied, they find that there is a slight tendency for the most effective teachers to retire earlier in the humanities and the physical and biological sciences and later in the social sciences.

on how publications and citations vary with faculty members' ages. Although results differ across disciplines, typically she found that, while peak research productivity occurs when faculty members are 10 to 20 years out of graduate school, those faculty who are 40 years out of graduate school publish as much on average as relatively young faculty.

Related evidence is presented by Biedenweg and Shelley (1988), who found that, while the average indirect cost recovery (the amount of external research funding) of Stanford University faculty peaks in the 46–50 age range, average indirect cost recovery of faculty age 66–70 is *higher* than that of faculty who are younger than 40. Similar findings for another major research university are reported in Howe and Smith (1990).

Levin and Stephan's (1989a) study of the publishing performance of biochemists, earth scientists, physicists, and plant and animal physiologists similarly suggests that, while publication counts tend to decline starting somewhere between ages 40 and 55 (depending on the field), older doctorate scientists often publish as much as doctorate scientists below the age of 40. Finally, preliminary results from a Barnard College study of faculty research productivity at 13 elite liberal arts colleges indicate that the fraction of faculty age 60 and above who are in the top quartile of researchers (as measured by recent publications and citations) is about the same as the fraction of all faculty who are in this top quartile (25 percent).[4]

All the studies discussed above are cross-sectional in nature. Levin and Stephan's (1989b) longitudinal study of six subfields of physics and earth science finds that, with the exception of particle physics, scientists in these subfields do appear to publish somewhat less after a point as they age. A second longitudinal study of male sociologists and psychologists found a very high correlation between faculty members' career publications and their publications between the ages of 59 and 70 (Havighurst 1985). Apparently, those faculty who are relatively productive among their cohort when they are young remain relatively productive at the later stages of their careers.

Taken as a group, these results suggest that the uncapping of mandatory retirement is not likely to lead to a substantial decline, on average, in faculty research productivity. Rather, the problem it may create is that some relatively unproductive researchers, who previously could be mandatorily retired at age 70, may now be "attached" to major research universities for longer periods of time. One suspects that the selective use of retirement incentives can help "encourage" relatively unproductive older faculty to retire.[5]

4. I am grateful to Dean Robert McCaughey of Barnard College, director of the Higher Education and College Faculty Study, which is being funded by the Spencer Foundation, for providing me with these results.

5. For example, for a number of years, Stanford University has been alleged to have a retirement incentive plan in which only "below average" productivity faculty have been allowed to participate. Given the result cited above that relatively productive people tend to be so throughout their lifetimes, having a low salary relative to salaries of similarly aged faculty in one's department has been used to measure "below average" productivity.

Of course, some people assert that the relations between publication counts, research grants, and citations, on the one hand, and faculty age, on the other, do not fully convey the importance of having a constant stream of new young faculty entering academe. Young faculty are needed to introduce new research methodologies, new ideas, and new lines of research as well as to serve as role models and mentors for potential new doctorates (National Research Council 1979; Hansen 1985). While this might suggest to some that retirement incentives be given to encourage all faculty to retire at age 70, recent simulations suggest that, even if one doubles the fraction of faculty staying on beyond age 70, the proportion of faculty below age 40 will increase in the United States over the next two decades (Rees and Smith 1990). Projected growth in faculty positions (because of increasing enrollments and an increased share of faculty near retirement age) much more than offsets any projected decline in faculty positions that might occur because of delayed retirements.

9.2 Female Doctorates

As Table 9.1 indicates, between 1973 and 1988, the share of new doctorates awarded by U.S. universities to women rose in the aggregate from 0.18 to 0.35. This almost doubling of the aggregate female share was accompanied by substantial increases in the female shares in all fields. These increases, however, did not eliminate female underrepresentation in many fields. So, for example, while over half of new doctorates in education went to women in 1988, reflecting the opening to women of career options in educational administration, substantial underrepresentation of women remains among physical science and engineering new doctorates, where shares of approximately 0.17 and 0.07, respectively, were observed in 1988.

The rapid growth in the female share of new doctorates might lead one to conclude that the proportion of female college graduates who complete doctoral study has increased substantially since the early 1970s. In fact, this has *not* been the case. Table 9.2 contains information on the number of doctoral degrees awarded to women relative to the number of bachelor's degrees awarded to women six years earlier. This ratio hovered around 0.025 during the entire period 1971–72 to 1987–88, and 0.025 is considerably smaller than the comparable ratio of 0.036 reported in Table 6.4 in recent years for all college graduates (regardless of gender). Put another way, as of 1988, the probability that a female college graduate will receive a doctorate was only about two-thirds the comparable probability for males.

The increase in the female share of doctorates that has occurred was caused by two factors. First, the share of bachelor's degrees received by women increased from 0.424 in 1971–72 to 0.502 in 1987–88 (Table 9.2, col. 2); more female college graduates means more potential female applicants for doctoral study. Second, the absolute number of doctorates awarded to males fell from

Table 9.1 Share of New Doctorates Awarded by U.S. Universities to Women

	Total Doctorates	Physical Sciences	Engineering	Life Sciences	Social Sciences	Humanities	Education	Professional/Other
1973	.180	.072	.014	.181	.210	.286	.246	.127
1978	.270	.105	.022	.230	.308	.377	.397	.205
1979	.286	.115	.025	.243	.334	.384	.421	.239
1980	.303	.122	.036	.259	.349	.396	.446	.266
1981	.315	.121	.039	.274	.358	.413	.472	.283
1982	.324	.134	.047	.287	.370	.424	.488	.304
1983	.338	.139	.045	.310	.395	.437	.504	.294
1984	.341	.148	.052	.311	.409	.450	.510	.316
1985	.343	.158	.063	.323	.412	.434	.518	.321
1986	.354	.161	.067	.340	.426	.452	.543	.339
1987	.353	.165	.065	.353	.431	.449	.551	.332
1988	.352	.166	.068	.368	.450	.443	.552	.320

Source: Summary Report 1988: Doctorate Recipients from United States Universities (Washington, D.C.: National Academy Press, 1989), table E.

Table 9.2   Female Earned Degrees Conferred by U.S. Institutions of
                   Higher Education

	(1)	(2)	(3)
1971–72	.024	.424	.51
1972–73	.026	.422	.57
1973–74	.023	.434	.82
1974–75	.023	.437	.96
1975–76	.023	.431	1.25
1976–77	.022	.434	1.47
1977–78	.022	.436	1.69
1978–79	.023	.438	1.75
1979–80	.023	.442	1.79
1980–81	.025	.453	1.89
1981–82	.025	.455	1.89
1982–83	.026	.461	2.00
1983–84	.026	.471	2.08
1984–85	.025	.482	2.17
1985–86	.026	.490	2.08
1986–87	.026	.498	2.17
1987–88	.025	.503	2.08

Source: Author's calculations from data in U.S. Department of Education (1989, table 200).

Note: Figures in columns represent (1) ratio of doctoral degrees awarded to women to bachelor's degrees awarded to women six years earlier; (2) share of bachelor's degrees awarded to women six years earlier; and (3) ratio of first professional degrees awarded to women to doctoral degrees awarded to women.

over 28,000 to about 22,000 during the period (U.S. Department of Education 1989, table 200). To a large extent, recent increases in the share of female doctorates reflect a substantial decrease in the likelihood that male college graduates enter and complete doctoral study, not an increased likelihood for female college graduates.

Women are increasingly likely, however, to go on to other forms of post-graduate study, in particular to professional degree programs. In 1971–72 approximately half as many women received first professional degrees as received doctoral degrees (Table 9.2, col. 3). With the opening of the professions to women, female enrollments in medicine, law, and other professional degree programs soared, and, each year since 1982–83, the number of female new first professional degrees has been more than twice the number of female new doctoral degrees. While the ratio of new first professional to doctoral degrees increased somewhat for the population at large during the period 1971–72 to 1986–87 (Table 6.4, col. 6), the increase in the ratio was much more pronounced for females.

One can only speculate about the factors that have induced female college graduates to "flood" into professional rather than doctoral programs. In part, it may reflect the opening up of career opportunities for women in the professions. In part, it may reflect that the lengthening of time to degree, particularly in the nonscience/nonengineering fields (Table 7.4), has a greater effect on women's than men's decisions because longer times to degree require some women to contemplate either postponing childbirth or undertaking doctoral study while they are parents of young children. In part, for similar reasons, the growing need to accept postdoctoral (postdoc) positions in the physical sciences (Table 7.8), which further postpones entry into a permanent academic position, may discourage women from entering doctoral study in the physical sciences. If the latter two hypotheses are correct, and if tightening academic labor markets reduce both time to degree and the need for postdocs (as hypothesized in Chapter 8), one might expect these forces to make doctoral study both in the aggregate and in the physical sciences more attractive to women in the future.

The nature of academic careers may also influence the types of institutions in which new female doctorates locate. "Up or out" tenure decisions are made during the sixth or seventh years of an individual's initial tenure-track appointment, and, especially in doctoral institutions, substantial efforts are required to begin research programs and bring them to fruition. These demands often come at a time when family formation decisions have already been postponed by young female doctorates or young children are already present in their households. As a result, new female academics may often feel pressured to "choose" between their families and their careers.[6]

It is probably not surprising, then, that one observes that women constitute a greater share of the full-time assistant professors at undergraduate institutions than they do at doctoral institutions (Table 9.3). In addition, female new doctorates are much more likely to be employed part-time and on non-tenure-track positions than are male new doctorates (Heath and Tuckman 1989). While some might argue that such patterns reflect discrimination against female new doctorates, especially by research universities, a recent survey of new job market applicants from top economics doctoral programs concluded that females rated employment in a liberal arts college as being preferable to employment in a top-tier graduate department while males ranked the two choices in reverse order (Barbezat 1989b). Similarly, the survey concluded that a higher proportion of females expected to work part-time during part of their careers or to withdraw from the labor force temporarily. Females stressed maternity leaves and family responsibilities as the reasons for these actions.

Even if the tendencies of female faculty to be employed disproportionately at undergraduate institutions or in non-tenure-track positions were the result of voluntary choice, these choices have implications for the attractiveness of academic careers and hence doctoral study for women. It is difficult to move from primarily undergraduate to more research-oriented (Youn and Zelterman

---

6. New male academics also face such pressures. However, considerable research shows that the vast majority of household and parental responsibilities fall on females in two-earner households, although younger males are increasingly assuming more important roles (Blau and Ferber 1986, chap. 5).

Table 9.3   **Proportion of Female Faculty and Female/Male Salary Ratios by Rank, Institutional Category, and Affiliation in 1989–90**

	Proportion Female[a]				Female/Male Salary Ratio[b]			
Affiliation	A	Pu	Pr	C	A	Pu	Pr	C
Professors:								
Doctoral level	.09	.09	.08	.17	.90	.90	.88	.90
Comprehensive	.15	.15	.15	.11	.96	.97	.95	.91
General baccalaureate	.16	.15	.18	.16	.94	.96	.93	.93
Associate professor:								
Doctoral level	.23	.22	.24	.29	.94	.96	.93	.92
Comprehensive	.26	.26	.25	.30	.95	.96	.93	.93
General baccalaureate	.30	.31	.33	.30	.95	.99	.94	.97
Assistant professors:								
Doctoral level	.35	.36	.30	.40	.90	.91	.91	.91
Comprehensive	.40	.41	.42	.40	.94	.94	.93	.93
General baccalaureate	.43	.40	.44	.46	.96	.95	.97	.96

Source: Author's calculations from "The Annual Report on the Economic Status of the Profession, 1989–90," *Academe* 76 (March–April 1990), tables 4, 16,
Note: A = all four-year institutions; Pu = public; Pr = private independent; and C = church related.
[a]Share of full-time faculty members in the rank who are female.
[b]Weighted (by institution size) average salary of full-time female faculty in the rank divided by the weighted average salary of full-time male faculty members in the rank.

1988); as a result, it is not surprising that the female share of associate and full professors at doctoral institutions tends to be less than their share at comprehensive institutions, which in turn tends to be less than their share at general baccalaureate institutions (Table 9.3). Salaries, especially at the senior levels, tend to be higher at doctoral than at comprehensive institutions and higher at comprehensive than at baccalaureate institutions (Table 6.2). Hence, on average, female full-time faculty are disproportionately found teaching in lower-paying institutions and thus can expect to have lower career earnings than male full-time faculty. Studies also suggest that part-time non-tenure-track academic positions rarely lead to tenure-track positions, tend to receive smaller salary increases than full-time positions, and have limited opportunities for promotion (Tuckman and Pickerill 1988).

Within institutional categories and academic ranks, the average full-time female faculty member also receives a lower salary than the average full-time male faculty member (Table 9.3). For example, in doctoral institutions in 1989–90, the typical female professor received 90 percent, the typical associate professor 94 percent, and the typical assistant professor 90 percent of her male counterpart's salary. In part, but only in part, this reflects the fact that females in senior ranks tend to have somewhat less seniority than males (Kasper 1990b). In part, this reflects the fact that females represent a greater share of doctorates in such fields as the humanities (Table 9.1), which tend to be relatively low paying (Table 6.3), than they do in such fields as engineering and the physical sciences, which, because of market conditions, tend to be higher paying. In part, some might argue that this reflects salary discrimination against female faculty.[7] Save for the gender differences that are due to seniority differences, lower within-institution pay for females will also discourage women from entering doctoral study and academe.

Clearly, policies that increase the attractiveness to women of employment at higher-paying research-oriented universities would increase the attractiveness to them of academic careers and doctoral study. Provision for "tenure clocks" to be slowed or temporarily stopped for a year when children are born or adopted—an alternative that some institutions are beginning to experiment with—may prove useful, as would provisions for reduced teaching loads for new assistant professors, another alternative that many economics departments and business schools are now adopting (Stromsdorfer 1989).[8] Of course, to increase the flow of women into doctoral study in the sciences and engineering requires policies to increase precollege mathematics and science training for women, to increase the flow of women into undergraduate science and engineering majors, to provide women with incentives and encouragement to enter and complete doctoral study, and then to facilitate the start of their research careers (National Science Foundation 1988d, 1989e).

9.3 Minorities

Table 9.4 presents data on the race and ethnicity of U.S. citizen and permanent resident new doctorates during the period 1978–88. While there have been increases in both the absolute number and the share of new doctorates awarded to native Americans, Asians, and Hispanics, in contrast the number and share of new doctorates awarded to blacks declined over the period. Indeed, in 1988, only 3.8 percent of new doctorates were awarded to blacks, even though they represent over 13 percent of the 18- to 24-year-old population in the United States. Similarly, although Hispanic doctorate production has been increasing, in 1988 only 2.8 percent of new doctorates were awarded to Hispanics, even though they represent over 10 percent of the 18- to 24-year-old population in the United States (Carter and Wilson 1989, table 1).

In fact, these data do not fully convey the extent of the underrepresentation in many fields of blacks and Hispanics in the new doctorate population. Table 9.5 presents data on the field distribution of U.S. citizen doctorates in 1988 by race and ethnicity. Quite strikingly, 46 percent of new black doctorates

---

7. For a comprehensive study of gender-based salary differences in academe over the period 1968–84, see Barbezat (1989a).

8. Of course, while reduced teaching loads for new assistant professors would increase the attractiveness of academe to new doctorates, they would lead to increased work loads for other faculty or an increase in the demand for new faculty.

Table 9.4   Doctorates Received by U.S. Citizens and Permanent Residents by Race and Ethnicity (share of the total)

	Total	Native Americans	Asian	Black	Hispanic	White	Unknown Race/Ethnicity
1978	26,635	60	1,032	1,106	538	22,342	1,557
		(.002)	(.039)	(.041)	(.020)	(.839)	(.058)
1979	26,784	81	1,102	1,114	539	22,396	1,552
		(.003)	(.042)	(.042)	(.020)	(.836)	(.058)
1980	26,512	75	1,102	1,106	485	22,461	1,283
		(.003)	(.042)	(.042)	(.018)	(.847)	(.048)
1981	26,342	85	1,073	1,110	526	22,470	1,078
		(.003)	(.041)	(.042)	(.020)	(.853)	(.041)
1982	25,616	77	1,044	1,143	614	22,140	638
		(.003)	(.041)	(.045)	(.024)	(.864)	(.025)
1983	25,633	82	1,043	1,005	608	22,244	651
		(.003)	(.041)	(.039)	(.024)	(.868)	(.025)
1984	25,250	74	1,019	1,055	607	21,863	632
		(.003)	(.040)	(.042)	(.024)	(.859)	(.025)
1985	24,687	95	1,069	1,043	634	21,291	555
		(.004)	(.043)	(.042)	(.026)	(.862)	(.022)
1986	24,513	99	1,059	949	679	21,222	505
		(.004)	(.043)	(.039)	(.028)	(.866)	(.021)
1987	24,569	115	1,167	906	710	21,124	547
		(.005)	(.047)	(.037)	(.029)	(.860)	(.022)
1988	24,783	93	1,233	951	693	21,353	460
		(.004)	(.050)	(.038)	(.028)	(.862)	(.019)

Source: Summary Report 1988: Doctorate Recipients from United States Universities (Washington, D.C.: National Academy Press, 1991), table F.

Table 9.5   Race and Ethnicity of U.S. Citizen Doctorates Awarded in 1988 (share of field total/share of race/ethnic group total)

Field	Native Americans	Asians	Blacks	Hispanics	Whites
Total	93	612	805	594	20,685
	(.004/1.00)	(.027/1.00)	(.035/1.00)	(.026/1.00)	(.91/1.00)
Physical science:	11	111	32	69	2,913
	(.004/.118)	(.035/.181)	(.010/.039)	(.022/.116)	(.93/.014)
Physics & astronomy	1	19	11	13	645
Chemistry	5	47	17	43	1,231
Earth, atmos., & mar. sci.	2	8	2	8	476
Mathematics	2	17	1	3	308
Computer science	1	20	1	2	253
Engineering	4	141	19	43	1,527
	(.002/.043)	(.081/.230)	(.011/.024)	(.025/.072)	(.881/.074)
Life sciences:	18	127	71	84	4,019
	(.004/.194)	(.029/.208)	(.016/.088)	(.019/.141)	(.931/.197)
Biological science	6	100	36	61	2,867
Health science	5	16	25	10	586
Agricultural science	7	11	10	13	586
Social sciences:	12	85	158	133	3,864
	(.003/.129)	(.020/.134)	(.037/.196)	(.031/.224)	(.909/.187)
Psychology	7	37	96	89	2,382
Anthropology	2	3	5	10	234

Economics	0	22	11	8	380
Pol. sci. & int. rel.	0	4	7	6	244
Sociology	2	8	14	13	274
Other social sci.	1	11	25	7	350
Humanities:	7	37	77	94	2,528
	(.003/.075)	(.013/.060)	(.028/.096)	(.034/.158)	(.922/.122)
History	1	10	8	13	456
Amer. & Eng. lang. & lit.	3	11	26	21	845
Foreign lang. & lit.	0	5	3	46	219
Other humanities	3	11	40	14	1,008
Education:	35	82	370	152	4,575
	(.007/.376)	(.016/.134)	(.071/.460)	(.029/.256)	(.88/.221)
Teacher educ.	3	8	31	10	323
Teaching fields	2	10	49	25	690
Other educ.	30	64	290	117	3,562
Professional/other:	6	29	78	19	1,259
	(.004/.066)	(.006/.047)	(.056/.097)	(.014/.002)	(.905/.061)
Bus. & management	4	16	16	4	558
Communications	0	1	10	2	171
Other prof. fields	2	12	52	13	503
Other fields	0	0	0	0	27

Source: Summary Report 1988: Doctorate Recipients from United States Universities (Washington, D.C.: National Academy Press, 1989), table G.

Note: Includes only doctorates whose citizenship and race/ethnic group are known.

were in the field of education. As a result, while blacks represented 3.5 percent of the American citizen doctorates awarded in 1988, they represented only 1.0 percent of those awarded in the physical sciences, 1.1 percent in engineering, 1.6 percent in the life sciences, and 2.8 percent in the humanities. The small absolute number of black and other underrepresented minority doctorates produced in most fields should make clear the difficult task that American institutions of higher education face in trying to achieve increased minority representation on their faculties.

Given current levels of production of minority doctorates, an institution can succeed in improving its minority representation primarily by inducing minority faculty from other institutions to move to it (Mooney 1989). One would suspect that the net result of this competition will be to redistribute minority faculty toward higher-paying doctorate-granting institutions (Table 6.2), which will benefit minority faculty economically in the short run and may also help increase the flow of future minority doctorates in the longer run.[9]

Understanding why minority doctorate production is currently so low and ascertaining what policies might more directly increase the number of minority doctorates are of utmost importance both for equity reasons and because the share of these groups in the youth population is increasing. Put another way, unless we can substantially increase the share of doctorates received by minorities, other things being equal, the total number of new American doctorates will decline.

The factors responsible for the underrepresentation of minority doctorates can be identified early in the educational pipeline. The black and Hispanic shares of the 18- to 24-year-old population rose during the period 1976–88 from 0.123 to 0.139 and from 0.058 to 0.103, respectively, but the white share fell from 0.859 to 0.826 (Carter and Wilson 1989, table 1).[10] While high school completion rates rose substantially for blacks, remained roughly constant for whites, and began and ended at roughly the same level for Hispanics during the period, the 1988 rate of 0.823 for whites exceeded the 0.754 rate for blacks, which in turn exceeded the 0.552 rate for Hispanics (Carter and Wilson 1989, table 3). The latter is equivalent to a 45 percent Hispanic high school dropout rate.

The fraction of students who graduate from high school that ever enroll in

9. An unresolved issue is what effect such competition will have on the historically black colleges and universities in the United States. In 1987, 97 of these institutions granted 20,291 bachelor's degrees, 4,064 master's degrees, 194 doctoral degrees, and 853 first professional degrees. Assuming that these degrees were all awarded to blacks, they represent, respectively, 35.8, 29.7, 25.2, and 24.9 percent of the degrees awarded to black Americans (Carter and Wilson, 1989, tables 4–7, 12). These institutions tend to be relatively low paying ones, and, if they are weakened by losing some of their better faculty to other institutions, this may have an adverse effect on black doctorate production.

10. Unlike other statistics reported in this chapter, those for whites and blacks discussed in this paragraph include Hispanics of those races. While they exclude Asians and native Americans (they are not broken out separately in these data), the double counting of Hispanics leads the sum of the shares of the three groups to exceed one.

Table 9.6   Degree Attainment by Race/Ethnicity, Selected Years

	1976	1981	1985	1987
White:				
BS	.884	.864	.853	.849
MS	.850	.820	.797	.791
DS	a	.877	.888	.890
PS	.907	.905	.890	.875
Black:				
BS	.064	.065	.059	.057
MS	.066	.058	.050	.048
DS	a	.040	.039	.033
PS	.043	.041	.043	.048
Hispanic:				
BS	.020	.023	.027	.027
MS	.017	.022	.024	.024
DS	a	.019	.024	.027
PS	.017	.022	.027	.029
Asian American:				
BS	.012	.020	.026	.033
MS	.013	.021	.028	.030
DS	a	.019	.022	.024
PS	.015	.020	.026	.032

Source: Carter and Wilson (1989, tables 4, 5).

Note: BS = share of all bachelor's degrees awarded; MS = share of all master's degrees awarded; DS = share of all U.S. citizen doctoral degrees awarded; and PS = share of all first professional degrees awarded.

aNot reported.

a two-year or four-year college also varied over time and across groups. During the period 1976–88, it rose from 0.535 to 0.586 for whites but fell from 0.504 to 0.466 for blacks and from 0.489 to 0.472 for Hispanics (Carter and Wilson 1989, table 1). Not only are blacks and Hispanics less likely to graduate from high school than whites, but, if they graduate, they are also less likely ever to be enrolled in college. Nonetheless, because of the growing shares of blacks and Hispanics in the youth population and the increasing black high school graduation rates. Blacks and Hispanics represent a growing share of the 18- to 24-year-olds who have ever been enrolled in college.

However, enrollment shares do not necessarily translated into degree-attainment shares. While the white share of all bachelor's degrees awarded in the United States since 1976 has roughly tracked the white share of ever-enrolled students, in recent years both the black and the Hispanic shares of bachelor's degrees granted have been less than their enrollment shares (Table 9.6).[11] For example, in 1987, the black and Hispanic shares of bachelor's

11. The sums across the five groups in Table 9.6 of the bachelor's degree, master's degree, and professional degree shares are each less than one because of the omission of nonresident degree shares from the table.

degrees granted were 0.057 and 0.027. Moreover, while the Hispanic bachelor's degree share has risen since 1976, the black degree share has actually fallen.

What factors explain the difference between the bachelor's degree attainment and the ever-enrolled-in-college statistics? Blacks enrolled in two-year colleges are less likely to graduate from them than are white enrollees. If they do graduate, they are less likely to enroll in four-year colleges than are white two-year college graduates. Once enrolled in four-year colleges, they are also less likely to graduate (see Part I). Some similar patterns are observed for Hispanic students, who are also more likely to be enrolled in two-year colleges than white students (Olivas 1986).

Moreover, on receiving bachelor's degrees, blacks are less likely to attain subsequent degrees than are whites, Hispanics, Asian Americans, or native Americans. The white share of doctoral and first professional degrees exceeds their share of bachelor's degrees. The Hispanic and native American shares of all graduate degrees are approximately equal to their bachelor's degree share, and the former have been increasing over time.[12] In contrast, the black shares of all graduate degrees are less than the black bachelor's shares and, save for first professional degrees, have been declining over time (Table 9.6).

Another way to look at the data is to contrast, as has been done earlier for the entire population (Table 6.4) and for females (Table 9.2), the number of doctorates awarded to a group relative to the number of bachelor's degrees awarded to the group six years earlier. Using 1980–81 bachelor's degree data and 1986–87 doctoral degree data, the ratios for white non-Hispanics, black non-Hispanics, Hispanics, Asians or Pacific Islanders, and native Americans/ Alaskan natives are 0.030, 0.017, 0.034, 0.056, and 0.029, respectively. The 0.017 figure for blacks stands out quite clearly.

The underrepresentation of most minority groups in the pool of new doctorates reflects primarily their underrepresentation among the pool of college graduates; save for blacks, minority groups' doctorate/bachelor's ratio is about the same as or greater than that of whites.[13] As such, policies to increase the flow of doctorates from most minority groups should probably focus on increasing the flow of college graduates. These include policies to increase high school graduation rates, increase four-year college participation rates for

12. These bachelor's shares, however, are substantially less than their population shares and thus remain a matter of serious social concern. While Asian-Americans share of doctorates in each year is less than their bachelor's share, this is an artifact of the rapid growth in their bachelor's share. In fact, the 1987 doctorate share for the group (0.24) exceeds its 1981 share of bachelor's degrees, 0.21.

13. One qualification is in order here. Some Hispanic citizen new doctorates are individuals who were previously foreign residents, were schooled (through college) abroad, came to the United States for graduate study, and then achieved permanent resident and subsequent citizenship status by marrying American citizens. To the extent that a large number of Hispanic citizen doctorates are obtained this way, I may well be overstating the doctorate/bachelor's ratio for Hispanic American citizens who grew up in the United States. I am grateful to Michael Olivas for stressing this point to me.

high school graduates, and then increase retention rates of college enrollees. In contrast, black college graduates are much less likely to receive doctorates than are graduates from all the other minority groups. Hence, policies designed to increase both the flow of blacks into doctoral programs and their retention are needed, as are policies designed to increase the flow of black college graduates.

Potential policies to increase the flow of low-income black college graduates are discussed in Clotfelter (see Part I). Here, the focus is on factors that may currently limit the flow of black college graduates into doctorate programs. One study of graduating seniors from elite private COFHE institutions found that, after controlling for grades, family income, father's education, and college debt levels, black graduates were in fact as likely to pursue graduate study as white graduates (Schapiro, O'Malley, and Litten, in press). Moreover, neither high debt levels nor low family income levels negatively affected these students' probabilities of attending graduate school, and black/white differences in grades and parental education levels were sufficiently small that graduate school attendance probabilities for blacks and whites were the same in the raw data as well.

Unfortunately, most black undergraduates do not attend, or graduate from, elite COFHE institutions. Indeed, full-time black undergraduates enrolled in four-year institutions are much less likely than comparable whites to attend selective four-year colleges and universities (see Part I). As is demonstrated in the next chapter, graduates of the best research universities (Research I and Research II) and the selective liberal arts colleges (Liberal Arts I) earn a disproportionate share of doctorates. Hence, the distribution of black undergraduates across institutional types has an adverse effect on black students' propensity to attend graduate school.

The distribution of black college graduates by broad category of major is quite similar to the distribution of white college graduates by major, so differences in undergraduate fields of study per se probably do not contribute to black/white differences in the propensity to attend graduate school.[14] In contrast, black students who take the GRE score, on average, more than 100 points lower on both the quantitative and the verbal aptitude tests (Educational Testing Service 1988, tables 59, 60) than white test takers, and such performance differences may adversely affect their interest or opportunity to enter graduate programs.[15]

As noted above, black college students tend to come from lower-income

14. For example, the shares of bachelor's degrees awarded by U.S. institutions in 1986–87 to whites (blacks) were 0.24 (0.26) in business, 0.09 (0.08) in education, 0.09 (0.06) in engineering, 0.18 (0.20) in other professional fields, and 0.39 (0.40) in arts and sciences (U.S. Department of Education 1989, table 215).

15. No normative judgment should be drawn from this statement as to whether these differences reflect "cultural bias" in the GREs or differences in the backgrounds of black and white students that leave the former less prepared to enter and complete doctoral programs.

families than white college students. While there is no evidence nationally that low family income levels affect the probability of entering graduate school and only mixed evidence that debt burdens do (see Chapter 8), evidence on racial and ethnic differences in the probability of having college loans suggests that financial variables may adversely affect black graduate school attendance.

Table 9.7 presents information on college loan burdens for full-time four-year college students in 1986–87 by race/ethnicity and family income class. Black dependent students from each family income class are much *less* likely to have taken out college loans than students from other race/ethnic groups.[16] Whether this reflects a lower willingness of black families to borrow to finance higher education or a greater concentration of black students in lower-priced public institutions (which reduces their need to borrow) cannot be ascertained from these data. Black independent students in each income class are also less likely to have loans than all other independent students in an income class (save for Asians in a few income classes). However, the loan burdens that these black students acquire are a much higher share of their income (0.637) than are the loan burdens of any other group. Taken together, these results suggest that a lower willingness to borrow for black dependent students and higher loan burdens for black independent students may contribute to the lower probability that black college graduates enroll in graduate school.

The ways that black students finance graduate education once they do enter graduate school serve to exacerbate this problem. As Table 9.8 indicates, in 1988, black doctorates were less likely to have received their degrees from Research I universities than white doctorates for all fields except psychology. In most fields, a smaller proportion of doctorates were self-supporting (family support, loans, nonacademic earnings) in Research I than in other institutions. Hence, on balance, a greater share of black than white doctorates were self-supporting.[17]

These data suggest that increased financial support for black students contemplating doctoral study may prove to be an effective way of expanding the number of black doctorates. Both the federal and state governments and a number of universities and private foundations have, in fact, recently expanded, or introduced, doctoral fellowship programs for minority groups.[18]

It is also important to stress that Schapiro, O'Malley, and Litten (in press) found that having a precollege interest in a career in higher education signifi-

---

16. Dependent students are those who can be claimed as dependents on their parents', or other adult's, income-tax returns. Independent students are heads of households.

17. Within fields and institutional type, black doctorates were less likely to be self-supporting in some cases.

18. For example, the National Science Foundation sponsors a special minority graduate fellowship program, and the Ford Foundation provides doctoral and postdoctoral fellowship for minorities.

Table 9.7 Percentage of All Four-Year College Full-Time Students Receiving Loan Aid and Average of Loans (for those with loans), 1986–87 Academic Year

Family Income Class	All %	All $	Asian %	Asian $	Black %	Black $	Hispanic %	Hispanic $	White %	White $
Dependent students:										
All	33.5	2,341	42.6	2,592	22.8	2,348	49.3	2,177	32.7	2,364
0–7,500	40.3	2,150	71.7	1,157	23.0	2,307	53.7	2,054	38.5	2,225
7,501–15,000	50.9	2,215	28.5	2,011	34.1	2,720	48.8	2,079	53.4	2,217
15,001–25,000	50.9	2,295	54.1	1,776	27.8	2,053	60.1	2,220	52.6	2,316
25,001–40,000	39.3	2,343	32.1	3,162	26.6	2,330	49.5	2,209	39.6	2,351
40,001 and over	20.9	2,474	48.8	3,095	14.0	2,416	30.0	2,395	20.7	2,479
Independent students:										
All	51.5	2,403	35.9	2,537	44.7	2,230	51.5	2,406	52.4	2,416
0–5,000	58.1	2,340	29.2	2,908	51.9	2,229	52.6	2,275	62.0	2,372
5,001–10,000	62.3	2,423	52.6	2,545	33.7	1,847	57.0	2,626	65.5	2,421
10,001–15,000	55.5	2,433	44.1	1,500	21.6	2,500	40.9	2,237	57.7	2,473
15,001 and over	33.4	2,500	.0		24.2	2,934	47.7	2,590	32.7	2,454
Dependent students:										
1. Average loan		2,341		2,592		2,348		2,177		2,364
2. Average family income of families with loans		31,026		32,026		28,313		21,009		33,464
3. (1) divided by (2)		.074		.080		.083		.104		.071
Independent students:										
1. Average loan		2,405		2,537		2,230		2,406		2,416
2. Average family income of families with loans		9,157		6,651		3,500		8,075		
3. (1) divided by (2)		.263		.381		.637		.297		.247

Source: Tabulations prepared by Dr. Daniel Sherman of Pelavin Associates, Inc., from the U.S. Department of Education, *1987 National Post Secondary Student Aid Study.*

Table 9.8 Primary Sources of Financial Support for Black (B) and White (W) Graduate Students Receiving Doctorates in 1988, by Field and Institution Type

| | | | | | Agricultural and Biological Sciences | | Social Sciences | | | | | | Nonscience/ Engineering | |
| | Total Science | | Physical Sciences | | | | | | Psychology | | Engineering | | | |
Primary Source	B	W	B	W	B	W	B	W	B	W	B	W	B	W
All institutions (N)	(241)	(10,339)	(28)	(1,880)	(44)	(3,367)	(68)	(1,648)	(99)	(2,403)	(19)	(1,529)	(553)	(8,902)
University teaching assistant	11.4	17.8	26.9	21.6	7.5	14.6	10.7	22.1	6.0	12.5	.0	7.7	7.7	14.3
University research assistant	12.3	18.8	26.9	33.6	20.0	22.7	7.1	9.5	8.3	7.8	17.6	32.7	1.7	2.9
University other[a]	11.4	6.4	3.8	4.4	17.5	7.8	12.5	7.6	10.7	6.0	17.6	7.2	10.0	6.1
Total university[b]	35.1	43.0	57.7	59.6	45.0	45.0	30.4	39.3	25.0	26.3	35.3	47.7	19.4	23.3
Total federal[c]	17.1	17.8	19.2	23.7[a]	32.5	29.0	10.7	7.9	13.1	5.0	17.6	21.3	6.9	3.5
Total personal[d]	42.7	36.6	3.8	13.8	17.5	23.9	53.6	50.0	60.7	67.3	17.6	19.8	68.5	68.9
Total other[e]	5.2	2.5	19.2	2.9	5.0	2.1	5.4	2.9	1.2	1.4	29.4	11.3	5.2	4.2
Research I institutions (N):	(138)	(6,411)	(17)	(1,363)	(26)	(2,212)	(36)	(1,121)	(57)	(993)	(14)	(1,165)	(251)	(4,588)
University teaching assistant	15.0	18.0	18.8	18.5	12.5	12.6	17.2	23.6	10.2	17.0	.0	6.8	8.3	19.2
University research assistant	12.5	21.8	31.3	37.5	16.7	23.2	10.3	10.1	6.1	9.7	25.0	34.8	1.4	4.0
University other	12.5	6.1	.0	4.0	12.5	6.7	17.2	9.0	14.3	6.0	16.7	6.7	13.9	7.4

Total university[b]	40.0	46.0	50.0	60.0	41.7	42.4	44.8	42.7	30.6	32.7	41.7	48.3	23.6	30.5
Total federal	18.3	22.3	18.3	22.1	37.5	34.7	6.9	8.6	16.3	7.4	25.0	21.9	9.7	4.3
Total personal	35.0	29.4	6.3	11.7	16.7	20.8	41.4	46.1	51.0	58.5	.0	19.4	61.6	61.5
Total other	6.7	2.4	25.0	2.5	4.2	2.1	6.9	2.6	2.0	1.4	33.3	10.4	5.1	3.7
Other institutions (N):	(103)	(3,928)	(11)	(517)	(18)	(1,155)	(29)	(527)	(42)	(1,410)	(5)	(384)	(302)	(4,314)
University teaching assistant	6.6	17.4	40.0	30.0	.0	18.4	3.7	19.2	.0	9.3	.0	10.5	7.2	9.2
University reaearch assistant	12.1	14.0	20.0	23.3	25.0	21.8	3.7	8.4	11.4	6.6	.0	26.8	1.9	1.8
Other university	9.9	6.8	10.0	5.4	25.0	9.9	7.4	4.7	5.7	5.9	20.0	8.6	6.8	4.8
Total university[b]	28.6	38.1	70.0	58.6	50.0	50.0	14.8	32.2	17.1	21.8	20.0	45.9	16.0	15.9
Total federal	15.4	10.9	20.0	17.9	25.0	18.1	14.8	6.3	8.6	3.3	.0	19.3	4.6	2.8
Total personal	52.7	48.3	.0	19.6	18.8	29.8	66.7	58.0	74.3	73.6	60.0	21.0	74.1	76.6
Total other	3.3	2.7	10.0	3.9	6.3	2.1	3.7	3.5	.0	1.3	20.0	13.8	5.3	4.8
Proportion of group receiving degrees from Research I institutions	.57	.62	.39	.73	.59	.66	.55	.68	.58	.41	.74	.76	.45	.51

Source: Special tabulations prepared by the Office of Scientific and Engineering Personnel, National Research Council, from the 1988 Survey of Earned Doctorates.

[a] Primarily fellowships and college work study.

[b] Sum of three previous categories.

[c] Primarily fellowships.

[d] Primarily family support, loans, and nonuniversity earnings.

[e] Primarily grants from other organizations and foreign support.

cantly increased the probability that graduates from COFHE institutions enrolled in graduate school. While no analyses were conducted of how such interest varies by race and ethnicity, it is likely that, because the socioeconomic distribution of black families differs from that of white families and because of the paucity of black (and other minority) "role models" among the professoriate, black students will have less interest in and familiarity with academic careers. This suggests that programs that widen their exposure to academic life, such as targeted minority undergraduate research experiences, may also prove useful.[19]

19. An example is a program sponsored by the Dana Foundation that is providing 150 undergraduates at black colleges with both funds to eliminate their college debts and research apprenticeships with senior researchers at Duke University (Teltsch 1989).

10   Should Policies Be Pursued to Increase the Flow of New Doctorates?

10.1   Would a Shortage of American Doctorates Really Matter?

Suppose that a "shortage" of American doctorates does occur in the future. Would this have a substantial negative effect on academe? To answer this question, one needs to know which types of institutions would be hurt the most by a shortage and the extent to which such a shortage would have an adverse effect on undergraduate education, on the flow of future generations of students into doctoral programs, and on the research productivity of faculty at American colleges and universities.

To the extent that doctorates value both their economic well-being and the nonpecuniary conditions of their employment, such as research opportunities and opportunities to teach bright students, the hardest-hit institutions are likely to be those that are relatively low-paying and nonselective. The average faculty salary data presented in Table 6.2 indicate that salaries are lower in comprehensive and baccalaureate institutions than they are in doctoral-level institutions and about the same in two-year and baccalaureate institutions. Within the comprehensive and baccalaureate categories, salaries are lowest at Liberal Arts II and Comprehensive II institutions.[1] Taken together, this sug-

---

1. As the following tabulations from the 1989–90 American Association of University Professors (AAUP) salary survey indicate, among four-year institutions, salaries tend to be lowest at Liberal Arts II and Comprehensive II institutions:

Institution Type	Professor	Associate Professor	Assistant Professor
Research I	59,803	41,698	35,448
Research II	52,953	39,477	32,720
Doctorate-Granting I	51,790	39,099	32,547
Doctorate-Granting II	48,283	37,363	31,906
Comprehensive I	46,222	36,925	30,344
Comprehensive II	37,217	31,079	26,141
Liberal Arts I	47,067	35,812	29,051
Liberal Arts II	33,813	28,476	24,314

gests that the institutions that will have the greatest difficulty recruiting new doctorates if a shortage materializes will be two-year institutions and Liberal Arts II and Comprehensive II institutions. Together, these institutions currently employ about 27 percent of all full-time faculty, but only about 12.3 percent of full-time doctorate faculty (Table 6.1).

Would this result in a substantial reduction in the research produced by faculty in American institutions of higher education? As Table 10.1 indicates, both federally funded and total college and university research expenditures are heavily concentrated in the major research universities. In 1988, research expenditures at the top 200 institutions (which are primarily Carnegie category research and doctorate-granting institutions) represented 97 percent of the total research expenses of American colleges and universities. Hence, only a very small share of our nation's research is currently being undertaken in the potentially hard-hit institutions.

Furthermore, research output appears to be as highly concentrated as research expenditures. For example, in a recent year, 80 percent of the highly competitive National Science Foundation research awards to economists went to faculty employed at only 30 institutions (Nelson 1989). Similarly, among the economists with the largest number of citations to their works over the period 1971–85, 96 percent of the top 25 were at 12 institutions, and 77 percent of the top 150 were at 16 institutions (Medoff 1989). This concentration of top scholars in a small number of economics departments is in fact typical of many science and social science disciplines (Fox 1983).

More striking, perhaps, is the concentration of publishing scholars among graduates of a small number of graduate departments. Again, using economics as an example, 65 percent of the individuals who contributed articles to

Table 10.1   Concentration of Federal Research-and-Development Expenditures at Major Research Universities

Institutions	(1) Share of All Colleges' and Universities' Federally Financed R&D Expenditures in Fiscal Year 1987	(2) Share of All Colleges' and Universities' Total R&D Expenditures in Fiscal Year 1987
Top 10	.24	.21
Top 20	.40	.35
Top 30	.48	.45
Top 40	.56	.54
Top 50	.63	.60
Top 100	.84	.83
Top 150	.93	.92
Top 200	.97	.97

Source: Author's calculations from National Science Foundation (1989b, table B-30).

Note: Total R&D expenditures include federal, state, and local government, industry, institutional, and other sources of support.

the *American Economic Review* during the period 1960–72 received their doctorates from just 10 highly rated programs, while 88 percent of the contributors received their degrees from 25 top departments (Sun 1975). More recent studies, which focus on publications in wider numbers of journals, find heavy (although not as high) representation from graduates of the top 25 departments (Hirsch et al. 1984; Hogan 1986). Studies from other disciplines confirm that graduates of top programs are disproportionately represented among publishing scientists and social scientists (Fox 1983).

Together, the results outlined above suggest that, if a shortage of new doctorates were felt primarily by the relatively nonselective Liberal Arts II, Comprehensive II, and two-year institutions, it would not have a substantial effect on research productivity. Indeed, since research grants, research expenditures, and publications are so heavily concentrated among faculty from and graduates of top graduate departments, even if the shortage adversely affected the ability of lesser departments (say those in the Doctorate-Granting II category) to attract new doctorates to their faculty and to enroll new graduate students, this too would not substantially affect American institutions' research productivity.

Of course, assuming that the "quality" distribution of doctorates did not change (see Chapter 8) and that the highest-quality doctorates seek to go to the very best departments, the average quality of new doctorates employed at all but the very best institutions would fall because of a doctorate shortage. Intuitively, if the top institutions were forced to reach deeper down into the quality distribution to fill their positions, the quality of applicants available to fill other positions would decline. All but the very top research universities and teaching colleges would find themselves hiring lower-quality applicants, and the resulting decline in average doctorate faculty quality at doctorate-producing, liberal arts, and comprehensive institutions would lead to some decline in aggregate faculty research productivity.

Would a reduction in the number of doctorates teaching at the Liberal Arts II and Comprehensive II institutions have an adverse effect on the flow of undergraduates into doctoral programs? Table 10.2 presents information for 1988 on the percentage of doctorates whose undergraduate degrees came from various Carnegie categories of institutions, by field and Carnegie category of graduate institution. The column labeled "Other Four Year" contains data on percentages of new doctorates whose undergraduate degrees were from Liberal Arts II or Comprehensive II institutions.

In the aggregate, only 3.2 percent of new doctorates from Research I institutions and 7.0 percent of new doctorates from other doctorate-granting institutions (Research II, Doctorate I, and Doctorate II) received their undergraduate degrees from Liberal Arts II or Comprehensive II institutions. Since 65 percent of new doctorates were awarded by the Research I institutions, this implies that, in total, only about 4.5 percent of new doctorates in 1988 received their undergraduate degrees from Liberals Arts II and Comprehensive

Table 10.2   Percentage of Ph.D.s from Various Categories of Undergraduate
                  Institutions, by Field and Carnegie Category of Graduate School, 1988

Field[a]	Research I	Other Research/ Doctorate	Comprehensive I	Liberal Arts I	Other Four Year	Specialty and Other[b]
Physical science:						
Research I (70)	29.8	12.1	10.9	8.7	3.0	35.4
Other (30)	12.1	19.3	15.4	7.6	5.1	40.5
Computer science:						
Research I (74)	29.4	10.5	6.6	3.4	3.1	47.0
Other (26)	14.3	22.6	9.8	3.0	5.3	45.1
Engineering:						
Research I (73)	29.7	9.9	4.6	1.7	.7	53.4
Other (27)	10.1	22.5	6.5	1.2	1.2	58.5
Biological science:						
Research I (65)	39.6	15.1	10.9	10.1	3.2	21.1
Other (35)	19.9	23.6	17.8	8.1	7.7	22.9
Agricultural science:						
Research I (70)	28.6	13.8	7.8	3.3	2.5	44.0
Other (30)	18.4	23.4	7.1	.8	3.7	46.6
Health science:						
Research I (72)	28.0	16.6	14.5	5.8	4.7	30.5
Other (28)	15.9	24.9	20.0	3.7	7.8	27.8
Psychology:						
Research I (42)	35.2	17.9	18.2	11.9	4.7	12.0
Other (58)	20.0	25.4	21.7	9.2	6.9	16.8
Social science:						
Research I (66)	27.2	14.0	10.1	10.4	3.3	35.0
Other (34)	14.1	23.3	16.8	6.4	4.8	34.5
Humanities:						
Research I (67)	29.2	15.1	14.6	15.5	5.2	20.4
Other (33)	13.8	21.7	18.1	11.9	13.6	20.9
Professional fields/other:						
Research I (56)	21.2	15.0	14.3	6.6	4.5	38.3
Other (44)	14.2	21.5	19.5	4.3	11.7	28.8
Total arts/sciences/professional/engineering:						
Research I (65)	30.6	13.6	10.9	8.4	3.2	33.3
Other (35)	15.5	22.7	16.5	6.9	7.0	31.4

Source: Special tabulations prepared by the Office of Scientific and Engineering Personnel, National Research Council, from the 1988 Survey of Earned Doctorates.

[a]Numbers in parentheses are the percentage of degrees in the field granted by that type of graduate school.

[b]Includes students from foreign institutions.

II institutions. The percentage was somewhat higher in the humanities, professional fields, psychology, and health sciences, about the same in the biological sciences, but substantially lower in all other fields.[2]

2. In the humanities, Bowen and Sosa's (1989) primary concern, about 8 percent of new doctorates received their degrees from these institutions.

Table 10.3   **National Science Foundation Graduate Fellowship Programs for Fiscal Year 1989, Three-Year Fellowship Awards**

Field (No. of Winners)	% of Winners Attending Graduate School at: Research I Universities	% of Winners Who Went to Undergraduate School at:			
		Research I Universities	Liberal Arts I Colleges	Comprehensive II Universities	Liberal Arts II Colleges
Regular program:					
Physical sciences (130)	96.9	68.5	12.3	.8	1.5
Earth, atmospheric, and marine sciences (25)	84.0	64.0	16.0	4.0	4.0
Life sciences (192)	93.2	60.9	18.2	.5	2.0
Social sciences (97)	92.8	63.9	18.6	.0	1.0
Psychology (46)	95.7	65.2	17.4	.0	.0
Mathematics and computer/ information sciences (98)	94.9	79.6	5.1	1.0	.0
Engineering (172)	94.8	69.8	2.3	.0	1.7
Total Regular program (760)	94.2	67.4	11.8	.6	1.6
Total minority programs (100)	95.0	66.0	7.0	2.0	1.0

Source: Author's calculations from award data in *National Science Foundation Graduate Fellowship Program for Fiscal Year 1989 Three-Year Fellowship Awards* (Washington, D.C., 1989); *National Science Foundation Minority Graduate Fellowship Program for Fiscal Year 1989 Three-Year Fellowship Awards* (Washington, D.C., 1989); and institutional classification data in Carnegie Foundation for the Advancement of Teaching (1987).

The small number of new doctorates whose undergraduate degrees came from Liberal Arts II and Comprehensive II institutions suggests that, even if these institutions have difficulty recruiting new doctorates to their faculties, the flow of undergraduates to subsequent doctoral study will not be substantially affected. Indeed, even if the flow from these institutions were cut by one-quarter, this would reduce the total flow into doctoral study by only 1.1 percent.

Furthermore, the share of these institutions in the total number of doctorates produced probably overstates their share of the very best entering doctoral students. Table 10.3 shows the percentage of prestigious National Science Foundation (NSF) Graduate Fellowship winners in fiscal year 1989 who attended undergraduate school at various Carnegie categories of institutions. In the aggregate, only 2.2 percent of the regular fellowship winners and 3.0

percent of the minority fellowship winners attended Comprehensive II and Liberal Arts II institutions. Only in the earth, atmospheric, and marine sciences did these institutions produce a substantial share (8 percent) of fellowship winners; however, in absolute terms, this represented only two awards.[3]

A shortage of doctorates that affected primarily two-year, Comprehensive II, and Liberal Arts II institutions would thus be unlikely to have major adverse effects on the research productivity of faculty at American colleges and universities (although it would likely lead to a reduction in the average quality of faculty in all but the top departments) or on the flow of students, especially the most talented ones, into doctoral study. The remaining issue to address is the likely effect of such a shortage on the quality of undergraduate education.

In beginning this discussion, it is useful to point out that many institutions used the relatively loose academic labor markets of the last two decades to upgrade their faculty substantially. To illustrate this point, data on the percentage of mathematics department faculty with doctorates for the period 1970–71 to 1988–89 are presented in Figure 10.1. During these two decades, the percentage of mathematics faculty with doctorates in doctorate-granting institutions rose from 86.8 to 94.0, in master's degree–granting institutions from 54.6 to 75.0, and in bachelor's degree–granting institutions from 42.0 to 66.2. Virtually all the increase occurred during the 1970s; the percentages remained roughly constant throughout the 1980s.

Assuming that mathematics is typical of other disciplines, did these increases lead to an improvement in the quality of undergraduate education?[4] If, as is postulated above, a shortage of doctorates would be felt primarily by less selective institutions among the bachelor's- and master's-granting categories and by two-year colleges, and if the percentage of faculty members with doctorates in these institutions would decline, would this lead to a decline in the quality of undergraduate education at these institutions?

There is a voluminous literature on the correlates of teacher ratings and students' performance on standardized tests, which unfortunately does not provide unambiguous answers to these questions. Some studies find that a faculty member's rank per se does not affect student evaluations of his or her performance, while others find a weak positive correlation (Centra 1981; Feldman 1983; Marsh and Overall 1981). Other studies find no difference in the final examination scores of introductory economics students taught by faculty and graduate students (nondoctorates), although these studies tend to take place at major doctorate-producing institutions, which will probably not be

3. It is interesting to note that almost three-quarters of the minority fellowship winners were undergraduates at Liberal Arts I colleges or Research I universities. Very few minority NSF fellowship winners were undergraduates at historically black institutions.

4. As noted by Bowen and Sosa (1989), data from the 1975 and 1984 Carnegie surveys of faculty (Anderson, Carter, and Malizio 1989, table 107) show no increase between 1975 and 1984 in the percentage of faculty holding doctorates. Figure 10.1 suggests that most of the increase for mathematicians occurred prior to 1975 and that mathematics may well be typical of other disciplines.

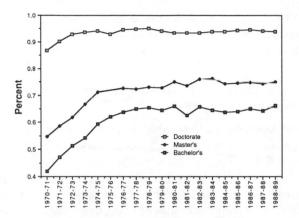

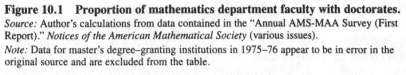

Figure 10.1   Proportion of mathematics department faculty with doctorates.
Source: Author's calculations from data contained in the "Annual AMS-MAA Survey (First Report)." *Notices of the American Mathematical Society* (various issues).
Note: Data for master's degree–granting institutions in 1975–76 appear to be in error in the original source and are excluded from the table.

affected that much by projected doctorate shortages (Siegfried and Fels 1979; Siegfried and Walstad 1990; Watts and Lynch 1989).

Still other studies find a weak positive correlation between the research productivity of faculty and their teaching evaluations (Feldman 1987). Moreover, this correlation tends to be strongest at institutions at which research does not appear to be valued very highly. To the extent that Comprehensive II and Liberal Arts II institutions fall in this category and that faculty with doctorates have higher research outputs than faculty without doctorates, these studies suggest that there may be a cost, in terms of lower-quality instruction, of a shortage of doctorates.

Studies that focus directly on the relation between faculty members' educational backgrounds and their teaching ratings are limited, and their findings vary across institutional types. Studies of major research institutions and elite public teaching colleges (where the vast majority of faculty have doctorates) tend to find that students rank faculty with doctorates as being better teachers, or being higher-quality lecturers, or knowing their subject matter better (Alciatore and Alciatore 1979; Metz 1970; Riley, Ryan, and Lifshitz 1950). In contrast, early studies of teacher evaluations at less prestigious teaching colleges (where many faculty did not have doctorates) found that faculty with doctorates tended to score more poorly than or about the same as nondoctorate faculty on teaching evaluations (Hudiburg 1965; Rader 1968; Metz 1970).

Most of these studies of the doctorate/teaching evaluation relation are dated and suffer from not controlling for factors other than degree that might affect teaching ratings. This is an area that clearly warrants new research. At best, one must remain agnostic—one cannot really say if a reduction in the percentage of the faculty with doctorates at Liberal Arts II, Comprehensive II, and two-year institutions would have an adverse effect on the quality of instruction at these institutions.

10.2 Foreign Scholars and American-Trained Doctorates from Foreign Countries

One noted American academic administrator has recently asserted that two-thirds to three-quarters of the world's top institutions of higher education are located in the United States (Rosovsky 1990, chap. 2). Foreign students flock to the United States for doctoral study. Given the academic freedom that American institutions of higher education offer as well as the relatively good research facilities and high standards of living that academics have here vis-à-vis academics in most other countries, it is reasonable to ask if an increased supply to U.S. institutions of foreign academics and newly trained temporary resident doctorates from U.S. universities could help avert projected doctorate shortages in the United States.

It is natural to start this discussion by focusing on current statistics on these flows. The first three rows of Table 10.4 contain information from the 1988 Survey of Earned Doctorates on the number of doctorate recipients from American universities, the number of these who had made definite future plans as of the date they received their degrees, and the number in the latter group with definite plans in the United States. These data are reported separately for all new doctorates and temporary resident new doctorates and for those with definite plans in the United States who are entering academic employment and postdoctoral (postdoc) positions. The approximately one-third of new doctorates who did not have definite plans as of the survey date as well as the small number with definite plans who did not report their location are ignored in the simulations that follow. Thus, these simulations understate the total number of new doctorates entering the U.S. academic sector.

Information on the shares of U.S. citizen and permanent and temporary resident postdocs in 1985 who held academic appointments in the United States in 1987 were presented earlier (Table 7.9) and are recorded in the fourth row.[5] Assuming that the share of postdocs accepting academic employment remains roughly constant over time, as do the number of postdocs, one can compute an estimate of the number of U.S. academic positions that were filled by new doctorates and recently completed postdocs in 1988. That estimate is 9,877, of which 898, or 9.1 percent, were temporary resident doctorates (rows 5 and 6).

Suppose one were to double the share of temporary resident new doctorates with definite plans in the United States—0.316 in 1988 (row 7). Such an

5. These simulations assume that the "lower-bound" estimates in Table 7.9 for temporary residents are the correct ones. The figure .59 in row 4, col. 1, of Table 10.4 is a weighted average of the temporary resident and U.S. citizen and permanent resident figures from Table 7.9.

Table 10.4   **Simulated Effects of Increasing the Number of Temporary Resident New Doctorates Who Remain in the United States on U.S. Academic Labor Supply**

	All New Doctorates, N	Temporary Resident New Doctorates, T
1. Total in 1988	33,456	6,176
2. Total with definite plans in 1988	22,089	3,911
3. Total with definite plans in the United States in 1988:	18,455	1,952
A. Academic employment	6,952	623
B. Postdoctoral study	4,958	1,019
4. Estimated share of postdocs in U.S. academic positions two years later	.59	.27
5. Estimated steady-state flow into U.S. academic employment (row 3A) + [(row 3B)(row 4)]	9,877	898
6. Share of temporary resident new doctorates in new doctorate academic employment (row 5, col. T)/(row 5, col. N)		.091
7. Share of temporary resident new doctorates with definite plans in the United States (row 3, col. N)/(row 1, col. N)		.316
8. Simulated effect on total flow into U.S. academic employment of doubling share of temporary resident doctorates with definite plans in the United States (100)(row 6, col. N)		9.1[a]
9. Simulated effect on total flow into U.S. academic employment of doubling the share of temporary resident postdocs in U.S. academic positions two years later [(1,019)(.27)/9,877](100)		2.8[a]

Source: Rows 1–3: National Science Foundation (1988e, table 15). Row 4: author's calculations from data in Table 7.9.

[a]Percentages.

increase, other things held constant, would be equivalent to a 9.1 percent increase in the flow of doctorates into U.S. academic positions (row 8). Alternatively, suppose one were to double the share of temporary resident new doctorates in postdoc positions who wind up in U.S. academic positions two years later. Such a doubling, ceteris paribus, would lead to a 2.8 percent increase in the flow of new doctorates into U.S. academic positions. Increases of these magnitudes would be significant contributions to the supply of academics to U.S. institutions.

Several qualifications are, however, in order. First, not all new doctorates or postdocs accepting academic employment wind up in faculty positions; some wind up in research associate or administrative positions. Temporary resident doctorates accepting academic appointments may well be disproportionately represented in the research associate category (see below). Second, unless temporary residents (nonimmigrants) can convert to permanent resident (immigrant) status, their expected tenure at American institutions will be shorter than their American citizen and permanent resident counterparts. Thus, the estimates given above may be overestimates. Finally, temporary resident doctorates constituted a smaller share of the new doctorates accepting academic employment or postdocs in the nonscience/nonengineering fields than in the science/engineering fields. Hence, doubling the share of nonscience/nonengineering temporary resident doctorates accepting American academic appointments would have a smaller percentage effect on the flow of new doctorates into U.S. nonscience/nonengineering faculty positions than the stimulation above suggests. Since it was the humanities where projections of shortages by Bowen and Sosa (1989) were the largest, such changes would thus have a much smaller effect on projected humanities faculty shortages.

Data on the flow of experienced foreign scholars into U.S. academic positions are harder to come by. In spite of well-publicized stories in the press about increases in the number of experienced British scholars moving here, no hard data on the number of foreign scholars in the United States really exist (Walker 1989).

As is well known, U.S. immigration policy is based primarily on family reunification criteria. While some foreign academics may enter the United States this way or as refugees seeking asylum, the vast majority enter as nonimmigrants who are temporarily admitted to the country for specific purposes. By far the vast majority, perhaps 90 percent, are employed under the H-1 and J-1 classifications of Section 101(a)(15) of the Immigration and Nationality Act (Farley 1988).[6]

The H-1 classification provides for the temporary admission of workers of "distinguished merit and ability." Determination of whether an individual is eligible for such a classification is made by the Immigration and Naturalization Service (INS) on submission of an application filed by an employer. Once approved, the individual may be employed for up to five years by the employer and may, under circumstances described below, have his or her status adjusted to that of a permanent resident (immigrant to the United States) without first having to leave the country. Colleges and universities that conduct

---

6. The 90 percent estimate comes from Michael Olivas of the University of Houston Law Center's Institute for Higher Education, Law, and Governance (private correspondence, 18 June 1990).

international job searches and can document that the qualifications of a foreign academic exceed those of domestic applicants usually have little difficulty obtaining H-1 classifications.

The J-1 (exchange visitor) classification permits foreign visitors to work for up to three years in approved "exchange visitor programs" sponsored by (among others) educational institutions. Individuals in the United States under J-1 visas are required in many cases to leave the country for two years before they can obtain permanent resident status. As a result, although this classification is used frequently for visiting scholars (e.g., Fulbright exchanges), explicit visiting appointments, or term research associate appointments, it is used only infrequently for faculty appointments that are meant to be permanent. As such, attention is limited to individuals on H-1 visas below.

Data on the number of H-1 workers admitted by occupation is sketchy and incomplete. The INS does not keep records of the number of doctorate college and university faculty members admitted; rather, it records the number of "postsecondary teachers" admitted. The latter include some nondoctorate faculty as well as faculty at postsecondary proprietary vocational training institutions. In 1978, 193 H-1 "postsecondary teachers" were admitted to the United States. This number grew to 531 in 1984 and then to 1,133 in 1986 (Farley 1988, table 5.2). One senses from these data that a trend toward increased reliance on foreign scholars for faculty may have already begun at American institutions of higher education.

More recent data, presented in Table 10.5, for 10 elite private universities suggest that this is true. Over the period 1986–87 to 1989–90, the number of foreign scholars employed under H-1 visas rose substantially at most of these institutions. Indeed, for the seven that reported comparable data in 1986–87 and 1989–90, total H-1 visa employment rose from 381 to 659 during the period. These institutional-level data are *not* restricted to faculty, and one institution estimates that half to two-thirds of its H-1 employees were research associates.[7] However, if in each institution half *were* faculty, foreign scholars under H-1 visas would have already represented, on average, almost 6 percent of these institutions' full-time faculty in 1989–90.[8] Foreign scholars may also be more important as a share of new hires. For example, one institution reported that, of the 63 full-time tenure-track faculty it hired in 1988–89, seven, or 11 percent, were foreign scholars.[9]

Of course, in order for foreign scholars temporarily admitted to the United States on H-1 visas to stay here permanently, they must convert their status to that of permanent resident. An unknown number do so by marrying U.S. cit-

7. Private communication with Jerry Wilcox, director of Cornell's International Students and Scholars Office, 20 June 1990.

8. This estimate uses institutional full-time faculty employment data reported in American Association of University Professors (1990).

9. These figures are for Cornell and were reported by David Fontenau of Cornell's Office of Institutional Planning and Research, 20 June 1990.

Table 10.5 Foreign Scholars Employed at Selected Elite Private Universities under H-1 Visas and Number of Labor Certifications Filed by These Institutions

	Foreign Scholars under H-1 Visas				No. of Labor Certifications Filed			
	1989–90	1988–89	1987–88	1986–87	1988–89	1987–88	1986–87	1985–86
Harvard	192	162	106	95	52	a	a	a
Stanford	176	87	a	a	a	31	a	a
MIT	125	121	100	94	15	14	24	23
Cornell	127	117	114	68	17	28	13	11
Yale	129	93	76	67	17	12	22	8
Penn	97	a	40	30+	14	a	23	23
Princeton	28	35	25	18	30	9	4	6
Columbia	60	a	a	a	14	a	a	a
Brown	38	30	23	22	8	5	a	a
Dartmouth	20	16	18	17	3	4	4	2

Source: Cornell University, International Students and Scholars Office.

[a]Data not reported.

izens or permanent residents or by qualifying under other family reunification provisions of the current immigration system.[10] Still others achieve permanent resident status by being classified as members of the professions, as persons of exceptional ability in the sciences or the arts, or as skilled workers who are in occupations that are in short supply. To achieve permanent residency by the latter routes requires an employer to seek and receive a certification from the U.S. Department of Labor of the individual's eligibility and then to sponsor his or her application for permanent residency.

In fiscal years 1988 and 1989, respectively, 1,570 and 1,681 submissions for certification by colleges and universities were approved by the Department of Labor.[11] These numbers are equivalent to a roughly 5 percent increase in new doctorate production.[12] If institutions carefully document their needs and their recruitment efforts during the prior six months, approval rates are quite high (in the range of 95 percent). Table 10.5 also contains data on the number of labor certifications filed by the 10 private universities. The number of certifications filed is considerably less in most cases than the number of foreign scholars present under H-1 visas. Furthermore, these institutional data are again not restricted to faculty. One institution reported that, of the 164 certifications it filed over the period 1980–90 in support of permanent residency applications, only about 52 percent were for faculty.[13]

If more widespread shortages of new doctorates do emerge, colleges and universities should be able to obtain labor certificates more easily and increase

10. A brief primer on immigration law as of 1990 (U.S. Department of State 1990) is in order here. Individuals who marry U.S. citizens are eligible for permanent resident status without limit, as are refugees. Section 201(a) of the Immigration and Nationality Act (INA) sets an annual limit of 270,000 for others, with no more than 20,000 coming from each foreign country (refugee limits are specified by the president under different legislation). Section 203(a) of the INA prescribes the following order of preference: (i) unmarried sons and daughters of U.S. citizens and their children (up to 20 percent); (ii) spouses and unmarried sons and daughters of permanent residents and their children (up to 26 percent plus any unused spaces from i); (iii) members of the professions or persons of exceptional ability in the sciences and arts, spouses, and children (up to 10 percent); (iv) married sons and daughters of U.S. citizens and their spouses and children (up to 10 percent plus any unused spaces from i, ii, and iii); (v) brothers and sisters of U.S. citizens 21 years of age or older and their spouses and children (up to 24 percent plus unused spaces from i, ii, iii, and iv); (vi) skilled and unskilled workers in short supply and their spouses and children (up to 10 percent); and (vii) any spaces not used up by the first six categories (in practice, this category is no longer used). The overall annual limit was raised in 1991 and several of the individual categories altered (Pear 1990).

11. Telephone communication from Dennis Gruskin, Division of Foreign Labor Certification, U.S. Department of Labor, June 1990. Individuals so certified may have doctorates from American or foreign universities, or they may not have doctorates.

12. This calculation ignores those foreign scholars who achieve permanent residency in other ways. While the numbers of these are unknown, data are collected on the fraction of all scientists and engineers who achieve permanent resident status without a labor certification; in 1987, this fraction was 0.56 (National Science Foundation 1988d, table B.2). These data are not restricted to individuals with doctorates, and they exclude individuals who cited their occupation as teacher. If one assumes that 0.5 is the approximate fraction for professors, then the flow of foreign scholars is currently equivalent to a roughly 10 percent increase in new doctorate production.

13. Cornell University International Student and Scholars Office, 20 April 1990.

the flow of foreign scholars on H-1 visas to permanent resident status.[14] This assumes, however, that immigration rules will not be changed in a way that makes it more difficult for foreign professors to move here. In fact, the Immigration Act of 1990 more than doubled the number of permanent visas available that are based on job skills and thus, in the short run, should make it easier for outstanding foreign scholars to move to the United States (Pear 1990; National Association for Foreign Student Affairs 1990).

While the possibility that increased reliance on foreign scholars may partially offset future shortages of American doctorates exists, it is by no means certain. Increased reliance would require continued accommodating immigration policies in the United States and accommodating emigration policies abroad. It would require that the relative attractiveness of academic employment in the United States, both economically and professionally, not substantially diminish, for, if mobility is voluntary, academics can flow out of the United States as rapidly as they flow in. Finally, it would require that foreign scholars have both the required academic background and abilities and sufficient proficiency in English to serve as effective teachers.

Although some concern has been expressed that individuals for whom English is a second language are on average less effective instructors, empirical evidence to this effect is limited. One study found such evidence for introductory economics courses (Watts and Lynch 1989). That study focused on graduate student instructors, not doctorate faculty, and it emphasized the importance of assessing the English competence of foreign graduate students and providing training for them in classroom instruction. A number of states have passed legislation requiring that teaching assistants and faculty be proficient in English.[15]

10.3 Will a Shortage of Doctorates Actually Materialize?

Will a shortage of American doctorates actually materialize? Bowen and Sosa (1989, table 8.5) project shortages of 43 percent or more, 57 percent or more, and 66 percent or more of new doctorates in the arts and sciences overall, in mathematics and the natural sciences, and in the humanities and social

14. One caution: there is already a backlog for fully processed visas under the third (exceptional ability) and sixth (skilled worker in short supply) preferences of Section 203(a) of the INA. For example, as of 1 June 1990, individuals with fully processed approved visas from 1 February 1989 were first being admitted as permanent residents under the third preference and first being admitted from 15 January 1987 under the sixth preference from most parts of the world. For applicants from some countries (e.g., the Philippines), delays were even longer (U.S. Department of State 1990). In 1990, a total of 54,000 individuals could be admitted under these two preferences each year; hence, doubling or tripling the number of certifications requested by colleges and universities (1,681 in fiscal year 1989) should not add to the backlog substantially. Furthermore, the Immigration Act of 1990 more than doubled the number of visas granted on the basis of job skills to 140,000 as of 1991 (Pear 1990).

15. For a discussion of a recent Pennsylvania law, see "Fluency in English Required of Faculty" (1990).

sciences, respectively, during the period 1997–2002. However, their projections do not fully account for a number of behavioral reactions of college students, new doctorates, experienced doctorates, and institutions that, independent of public policy, *may* potentially offset at least part of the projected shortfall. Possible magnitudes for various responses are summarized in Table 10.6 and discussed below.[16]

As academic labor markets tighten and academic jobs become more plentiful, one should expect to observe an increase in academic salaries for both new and experienced doctorates, an easing of tenure standards, a reduction in the time it takes to complete doctorates, and a decrease in the need for holding postdoctoral appointments in some of the sciences prior to regular academic employment. All these forces should encourage college seniors to enter and complete doctoral programs and new college freshmen to major in fields that lead to doctoral study.

The empirical studies summarized in Table 8.1 do not yield sufficiently precise parameter estimates to enable one to predict how even a given change in new doctorate salaries will translate into a change in new doctorate supply. However, it is probably reasonable to assume that the net effect of all the forces described above will likely increase new doctorate production by at least 10 percent. What such an increase would translate into, in terms of total U.S. citizen and permanent resident new doctorates and the number of these going on to academic employment, using 1988 levels as the base, is found in the first row of Table 10.6.

The tightening of academic labor markets should cause academic salaries for new doctorates to rise relative to nonacademic salaries for new doctorates. This, as well as the increased availability of academic jobs, should slow down and perhaps reverse (as has already occurred in engineering and several other fields—see Table 7.7) the decline in the share of new doctorates choosing academic employment. Table 8.10 suggests that the ratios of new doctorate academic to new doctorate nonacademic salaries have already begun to increase, and in many fields the increase has already been more than 10 percent. Given estimates that the elasticity of the share of new doctorates who find employment in academe with respect to the relative academic/nonacademic salary is in the range of unity and the likelihood that relative academic salary will continue to rise, one might project that the share of new doctorates entering academe might "rebound" by 0.05. As the second row of Table 10.6 indicates, this would have the same effect on academic labor supply as a 9.4 increase in the number of new citizen and permanent resident doctorates produced.

As noted in Table 7.11, about 11 percent of doctorates age 35 and under

---

16. Details of the calculations underlying Table 10.6 are found in the appendix to this chapter. Bowen and Sosa's (1989) projections allow all of the forces discussed below to reduce the demand for new American doctorates by at most 5 percent.

Table 10.6   Simulated Effects of Various Changes

	(A) Effect on U.S. Citizen and Permanent Resident Doctorate Supply	(B) Effect on U.S. Citizen and Permanent Resident Academic Doctorate Supply
1. Increasing U.S. citizen permanent resident new doctorate supply by 10 percent	2,680 (10)	1,431 (10)
2. Increasing the share of U.S. citizen and permanent resident new doctorates entering academie, both directly and after postdocs, by 0.05	a	1,340 (9.4)
3. Reducing out-migration to the nonacademic sector of experienced academic doctorates age 50 and under by 2 percentage points	a	1,750 (12.2)
4. Increasing in-migration to the academic sector of experienced nonacademic doctorates, age 50 and under by 3 percentage points	a	2,400 (16.8)
5. Increasing the share of temporary resident new doctorates who enter academic employment in the United States, both directly and after postdocs, by 0.05	a	334 (2.3)
6. Doubling the annual flow of experienced foreign scholars entering with labor certifications	1,691 (6.3)	1,691 (11.8)
7. Halving the retirement rate of faculty age 65–69 (steady state)	509 (1.9)	509 (3.6)
8. Increasing the proportion of female college graduates receiving doctorates from 0.026 to 0.030	1,250 (4.6)	673 (4.7)
9. Decreasing the number of faculty with doctorates by 5 percent (one-time change)	11,130 (42.0)	11,130 (77.8)

Note: See the appendix for details. Numbers in parentheses are what the change is equivalent to in terms of a percentage increase in American citizen and permanent resident new doctorates.
aNot applicable.

and 5 percent of those between the ages of 35 and 50 who were employed in academe in 1985 had moved to the nonacademic sector by 1987. Increasing relative academic salaries and the availability of academic jobs as well as an easing of tenure standards should reduce both voluntary and involuntary outmobility from the academic sector. If each of the rates given above could be reduced by 2 percentage points, approximately 3,500 more doctorates, or 1,750 annually, would remain in the academic sector over a two-year period. This would be equivalent to a 12.2 percent increase in the flow of new citizen and permanent resident doctorates to academe (row 3).

Similarly, about 8 and 4 percent of doctorates in the two age groups, respectively, who were employed in the nonacademic sector in 1985 had moved to the academic sector by 1987. Each of the factors mentioned above should encourage increased mobility of experienced doctorates from the nonacademic to the academic sector. If the two rates each increased by 3 percentage points, approximately 4,800 more doctorates, or 2,400 annually, would move to the academic sector over a two-year period. Such a flow would be equivalent to a 16.8 percent increase in the annual flow of new citizen and permanent resident doctorates to academe (row 4).[17]

Currently, approximately 20 percent of new doctorates are temporary residents of the United States. Approximately one quarter of these obtain academic employment in the United States, either directly after receiving their degrees or after holding a postdoctoral appointment in the United States. The number of temporary resident doctorates seeking positions here appear greatly to exceed the number who achieve such positions, and shortages of U.S. citizen and permanent resident doctorates would provide universities and colleges with an incentive to expand their hiring of temporary resident doctorates. If the proportion receiving academic appointments here rose by 0.05, this would yield 334 more appointments, which is equivalent to a 2.3 percent increase in U.S. academic doctorate supply (row 5).

Of course, as described in the previous section, temporary residents can accept employment in the United States only for a limited time, unless their residency status changes. Thus, their expected academic job tenure is shorter than that of American citizen and permanent resident new doctorates, unless they eventually receive permanent resident status. In fiscal year 1989, 1,691 experienced foreign scholars and new temporary resident doctorates became permanent residents of the United States via the labor certification route, and perhaps an equal number achieved permanent resident status by other mean (primarily, family reunification). If American colleges and universities were able to double the number of such foreign scholars admitted to the United States via the labor certification route each year, this would be equivalent to an 11.8 percent increase in the flow of U.S. citizen and permanent resident new doctorates to academe.

The abolition of mandatory retirement for faculty as of January 1994 will likely have some effect on faculty retirement ages. As noted in Chapter 9, the existing literature suggests that, on balance, these effects will not be very large. Moreover, Bowen and Sosa's (1989) analysis suggests that, even if the retirement rate of 65- to 69-year-old faculty were cut in half, the long-run effect of this change would be to reduce the number of retirements only by about 2 percent. This would be equivalent to about a 1.9 percent increase in U.S. citizen and permanent resident new doctorate supply and a 3.6 percent increase in the supply of these new doctorates to academe. While these num-

17. These mobility calculations ignore the existence of a pool of doctorates who are not currently employed. For example, over 6 percent of the individuals who received doctorates in the humanities between 1979 and 1984 were not employed in 1985 (National Research Council 1986, table 5). While some of these individuals may have been out of work for family-related reasons, almost half were actively seeking employment. This pool of nonemployed doctorates is another potential source of academic labor supply. They also ignore the possibility that older (age 50 and up) doctorates employed in the nonacademic sector may opt for early retirement from their nonacademic jobs and move to the academic sector.

bers should be viewed as upper-bound estimates of the likely effect of the abolition of mandatory retirement per se (see Rees and Smith 1990), institutions can influence their faculty members to postpone retirement by pursuing institutional policies that provide faculty with incentives to stay on.

The proportion of American female college graduates who ultimately receive doctorates is currently about 0.026; this is lower than the aggregate proportion of American college graduates who ultimately receive doctorates, which is around 0.030. As noted in Chapter 9, a shortening of time to degree and a reduced need for holding postdocs may well influence women's educational decisions above and beyond these variables' effects on men's. If these forces, plus policies that institutions may begin to pursue to attract and retain female faculty (e.g., family leave policies that delay tenure "clocks" after childbirth, sabbatical leaves for nontenured faculty), succeed in raising the proportion of female college graduates who receive doctorates to 0.030 (holding constant the proportion of male college graduates who receive doctorates), the increase in the number of female doctorates choosing academic careers that will result will be in the range of 4.7 percent of the current new doctorate academic labor supply.[18]

The magnitudes of all the effects postulated above are, at best, "guestimates." There is no assurance that any one will occur, nor are most rigorously supported by precise evidence on the magnitudes of behavioral relations. Indeed, one role of this essay has been to point out the many areas in which there is little or no empirical evidence on the size of the behavioral relations. Furthermore, one may question how plausible the magnitudes and signs of some of these postulated effects are—some changes may actually go in the direction of worsening doctorate shortages.

For example, economic expansion and social changes in European and Asian nations could conceivably lead to an increased attractiveness of academic careers abroad and a decline (rather than an increase) in the U.S. employment share of new nonresident doctorates. To take another example, increased nonacademic demand for Ph.D.s might prevent the share of doctorates entering academe from increasing. Nonetheless, if we perform the exercise of simply summing up these effects, in total they are equivalent to a 68.5 percent increase in the supply of U.S. citizen and permanent resident new doctorates to academe.[19] If, on balance, two-thirds of these effects were to result, the shortages projected by Bowen and Sosa would vanish, on average.

Of course, Bowen and Sosa (1989, chap. 9) and others have emphasized the time it takes for the flow of new doctorates to be increased. Because of the

18. This increase in female doctorate production should be thought of as being above and beyond the proportionate increase in male and female doctorate production that is reflected in row 1 of Table 10.6.

19. This summation omits the 2.3 percent figure in row 5 of Table 10.6, assuming that the long-run effect of keeping more temporary resident doctorates here is included under row 6.

length of the doctorate pipeline (see Table 7.4), students first enrolling in doctoral programs in the fall of 1990 will not emerge as new doctorates, on average, until the spring of 1997. To wait for the academic market to respond to projected shortages in the mid-1990s and beyond is almost to guarantee that the shortages will occur, at least in the short run. As such, they and others argue for increased federal financial support for doctoral students now, in the form of increased fellowships and research assistantships, as a way of increasing the output of new doctorates in time to head off the projected shortages.

The discussion above suggests that the academic labor market has, in fact, already begun to respond to current and projected shortages of doctorates, although whether the response will actually prove sufficient to prevent these shortages is not known. Moreover, as Chapter 8 stressed, we have virtually no empirical evidence on what the effects of increased federal financial support for doctoral students would likely be on students' average time to degree or on what the direct effects of changes in the latter and increased financial support for doctoral students would be on the number of students who enroll in, and complete, doctoral programs.

We also have no sense of whether institutions of higher education would respond to increases in federal funding of doctoral students by reducing their own support of doctoral students by an equal, or smaller, amount. If such displacement effects occur, the net effect of the increased federal funding on doctoral supply would be less than what policymakers expected (assuming that they knew the effect of increased aid on doctorate supply). In sum, although increased federal support of doctoral students may be desirable, we really cannot predict with any accuracy what the effects of any given increase would be on doctorate supply.

As is well known, student/doctorate faculty ratios have been declining during the 1980s, in both the arts and sciences and other fields, as institutions have sought to upgrade their status (Bowen and Sosa 1989, chap. 5). Bowen and Sosa's and most other projections of future doctorate shortages assume either that this trend will continue, albeit somewhat more slowly, or that student/doctorate faculty ratios will level off.[20] They, and others, argue that, in a period of tight academic labor markets, it would be difficult for institutions to increase student/doctorate faculty ratios by increasing class sizes or teaching loads of doctorate faculty (Bowen and Sosa 1989, chap. 8). Such actions would decrease the attractiveness of academe as a career option and would likely adversely affect the flow of new doctorates.[21]

20. At one point, Bowen and Sosa (1989, chap. 7) do allow for a 7.5 percent increase in the arts and science student/faculty ratio over the period 1987–2002. However, this increase is allowed for only in projections that call for arts and science enrollments to increase. That is, they allow for reduced faculty replacement demand only when increased demand for new faculty owing to enrollment increases is occurring.

21. Increasing average class size and faculty teaching load may also influence the quality of undergraduate instruction.

This line of reasoning ignores the increased pressures that institutions of higher education are facing because tuition increases far outpaced inflation, rising at almost twice the rate of inflation during the 1980s (Hauptman 1990a; see also Part I). Increasingly, pressure is being brought to bear on higher educational institutions to limit tuition increases and to improve productivity. Rising salaries for doctorate faculty will invariably put pressure on institutions to limit overall cost increases, and, if work loads of doctorate faculty are not permitted to rise, other ways to limit cost increases must be found. One way of limiting cost increases is to allow student/doctorate faculty ratios to rise, without increasing the work load of doctorate faculty, by substituting nondoctorate for doctorate faculty. As discussed earlier in this chapter, the effects on research productivity are likely to be minimal. The prior literature does not provide strong evidence, however, as to what the effects of increased usage of nondoctorate faculty would be on faculty teaching effectiveness.

The effect of even a small increase in the student/doctorate faculty ratio, caused by the substitution of nondoctorate for doctorate faculty, on the demand for new doctorates is extraordinary. For example, a one-time 5 percent reduction in the number of doctorate faculty at each institution is equivalent to increasing the supply of citizen and permanent resident new doctorates entering academe by almost 78 percent (Table 10.6, row 9). A reduction of this magnitude alone would be sufficient to offset several years of projected shortages and would give the other behavioral responses time to kick in.

Others have argued that a larger increase in the student/doctorate faculty ratio is both desirable and possible and that an increase to the late 1970s level in the ratio would effectively eliminate projected doctorate shortages (Cheney 1989). Such an increase seems both unlikely and unrealistic. If caused by increased work loads for doctorate faculty, it would decrease the attractiveness of academic careers just at the time when attempts are being made to increase the flow of people into doctoral study. If caused by the widespread substitution of nondoctorate for doctorate faculty, it might substantially affect the aggregate research productivity of American colleges and universities. Nonetheless, there is room for American colleges and universities to economize somewhat on their use of doctorate faculty. Reductions in the range of 5 percent would probably not have a major effect on aggregate faculty research and teaching productivity or on college graduates' decisions to pursue doctoral study.

As noted in Chapter 6, all categories of institutions of higher education currently employ a significant share of faculty without doctoral degrees (Table 6.1). Whether a further substitution of nondoctorate for doctorate faculty will materialize depends, in part, on how institutions feel the increased usage of nondoctorate faculty would affect their institutional objectives. How important is it to various types of institutions to maintain the prestige that accrues from having a higher proportion of doctorates on their faculty (Garvin 1980)? Put another way, will the increased salaries that are likely to be commanded by new doctorates actually induce the institutions that used the relatively loose academic labor markets of the last two decades to increase the share of their faculty with doctorates (Figure 10.1) now to decrease the share of their faculty with doctorates.

Furthermore, what may be true in the aggregate is not necessarily true in any one field. One of the major strengths of Bowen and Sosa's analyses was their focus on the arts and sciences and their further disaggregation by field of study. They projected vast differences across fields, with substantial shortages emerging in the late 1990s in humanities, social sciences, mathematics, and physical sciences but much smaller (or no) shortages in the life sciences and psychology. The simulations conducted in Table 10.6 are, for the most part, for doctorates in the aggregate, not solely for those in the arts and sciences.

As noted in Chapter 8, most studies of doctorate labor supply focus on the sciences or social sciences; we have no estimates, for example, of supply elasticities in the humanities. It is not obvious that the sensitivity of supply to variables like salaries, stipend levels, and time to degree will be the same across fields. Moreover, luring a substantial number of individuals back to academe from fields such as engineering, where there are substantial stocks of doctorates employed in the nonacademic sector, may also prove easier than luring individuals back in fields such as the humanities, where the stock of doctorates employed in nonacademic settings is much smaller (but see n. 17 above). Similarly, temporary resident new doctorates are much more likely to be found in the sciences than they are in fields like American history, and thus they are unlikely to be a major source of increased academic labor supply in the latter area.

As such, public policies with regard to doctorate production clearly need to be based on detailed field-specific analyses. The variation of market conditions, as well as the likely variation in behavioral responses, across fields suggests that broadly based policies will probably not be in order.

Finally, it must be stressed that the simulations presented in Table 10.6 do not deal explicitly with increasing the probabilities that minorities receive doctorates. Since minority groups represent a growing share of American youths and most are underrepresented among new doctorates, unless policies are pursued to increase the flow of minorities doctorates, more severe doctorate shortages than those projected could result. As discussed in Chapter 9, while some policies can be directed at minority college graduates, it is even more important to increase the likelihood that minorities enter, and ultimately complete, four-year college programs.

10.4   Implications for Future Research

Policy decisions aimed at increasing the supply of doctorates should be guided by the findings of academic research. Yet I have here repeatedly emphasized how imprecise our knowledge of key relations is. I have also stressed the need for further research on a wide variety of topics. Rather than cataloging all these needs, I conclude with a brief discussion of four important examples. These are the determinants of enrollments in doctoral programs, the determinants of time to degree and completion rates, the responsiveness of academic institutions to changes in federal financial support of doctoral students, and the substitutability of nondoctorates for doctorates in the undergraduate educational process.

Some 20 years after Freeman's (1971) seminal work on doctorate labor supply, virtually all researchers studying the topic persist in analyzing aggregate time-series data for relatively short time spans, by field, or pooled across fields. As discussed in Chapter 8, such studies do not permit one to include many important variables that likely influence postgraduate decisions into the analyses, their small sample sizes do not permit precise estimates to be obtained, and the limited aggregate data on the humanities have not permitted them to analyze responses in the humanities to policy variables. The aggregate data also do not permit analyses of how responses by students of different ability levels and different race/ethnic groups vary (key policy questions) and of the extent to which loan burdens deter, or postpone, entry into doctoral study.

It is time for scholars pursuing research on doctoral study decisions to shift methodological approaches and utilize individual-level data. Existing representative national data sets, such as the National Longitudinal Survey of Youths, the National Longitudinal Survey of the Class of 1972, and High School and Beyond have proved extremely useful in analyzing college-going behavior (see Part I). However, these data sets are of less use in analyzing doctoral study decisions because each contains in its sample relatively few individuals who ultimately graduate from college and enter doctoral study. Rather, what is required is a national sample survey of college graduates that is repeated periodically. Such an approach would allow analyses of the effects of individuals, family, and institutional characteristics on doctoral study decisions. Moreover, since the survey would be periodicaly repeated, one could merge into the data variables reflecting labor market conditions and the characteristics of doctoral programs (e.g., availability of financial support, time to degree).

Schapiro, O'Malley, and Litten's (in press) study (discussed in Chapter 8), which analyzed data collected from graduating seniors in 1982, 1984, and 1989 from elite Consortium on Financing Higher Education (COFHE) institutions, is a step in the right direction. However, its analyses failed to include any labor market conditions or doctoral program characteristics as explanatory variables. In addition, this type of study needs to be extended to encompass a wider range of institutions and a larger number of years.

Both long times to degree and low probabilities of degree completion presumably discourage entry to doctoral programs. For policy purposes, we need to know the determinants of both. As with studies of doctorate supply, prior studies of the determinants of time to degree have, in the main, also tended to use aggregate time-series data (e.g., Tuckman, Coyle, and Bae 1990). The numerous problems associated with such an approach were discussed in Chapter 8.

Surely, future studies in this area must also use individual data, be field and institutionally based, separate out the effects of financial support from those of student ability and labor market conditions, and take account of noncompleters as well as completers. The latter point is important because labor market conditions and financial support variables may well influence *both* dropout rates and time to degree for completers. Failure to take account of the former when analyzing data on degree time for completers will lead to inaccurate estimates of the effects of labor market conditions and financial support variables on time to degree.

The importance of having information on noncompleters limits the usefulness of the annual Survey of Earned Doctorates (SED) for studies of time to degree. To increase its usefulness would require extending it to include data on noncompleters, possibly by surveys administered by departments. The SED also contains no information on students' ability levels (as measured by GRE scores), without which its usefulness is further limited.

Knowledge of the effects of the level and types (fellowship, research assistant, teaching assistant) of financial support on the number of students entering doctoral programs, their completion rates, and their average times to degree is not sufficient to analyze fully the likely effects of an increase in federal support for doctoral students on doctorate labor supply. One also needs to know the extent to which changes in external funding for doctoral student support induce institutions to alter their own support levels. Do institutions respond to changes in federal support by redirecting their own financial resources in a way that partially frustrates the intent of policy changes? Are the magnitude of such responses different for changes in fellowship, research assistant, and teaching assistant support?

To answer such questions requires access to institutionally based data sets that contain information by field on institutional and external support for graduate students as well as on other factors that influence each field's demand for graduate students. To control for differences in unobserved variables across institutions and changes in federal policies over time, one would need data for a number of years for each institution. Fortunately, such data are available, and research on those issues is already underway.[22]

Finally, as discussed in the previous section, projections of doctorate shortages depend heavily on the assumption that student/doctorate faculty ratios, which declined during the 1980s, will not increase in the future. One way to economize on doctorate faculty is to substitute more nondoctorate faculty in the undergraduate educational process.

22. For a description, see Ehrenberg (1990).

While economists are equipped to study how changing relative prices of doctorate and nondoctorate faculty have influenced their relative usage, the key issue here is not solely economic. Institutions must come to grips with how increasing their usage of nondoctorate faculty would affect their institutional objectives? How important to them is the "prestige" that accrues from having more doctorate faculty (Garvin 1980)? What would be the effect on the quality of the undergraduate education being provided of reductions in the number of doctorate faculty in some institutions?

Prior studies of faculty teaching effectiveness have not adequately analyzed the influence of having a doctorate degree per se, holding constant other factors such as course level (e.g., freshman, sophomore), course type (e.g., lecture, discussion), instructor experience, and field of study. Extensive research is clearly required in this area, along with serious rethinking by institutions, about whether undergraduate education, especially in less selective institutions, needs to be as doctorate-faculty intensive as it has been in the recent past. A conclusion that not as many doctorates are required might actually serve to increase the number of people entering graduate school, for, if the academic demand for noncompleters ("ABDs") and people terminating graduate study with master's degrees went up, this would reduce the costs of embarking on, but failing to complete, doctoral study.

Appendix
Details of the Calculations in Table 10.6

Increasing the U.S. Citizen and Permanent Resident (CPR) New Doctorate Supply

This calculation takes the total 1988 new doctorate production of 33,456 and assumes that individuals who fail to report their citizenship or residency status are distributed in the same manner as those who do report; thus, 0.199 of new doctorates are temporary residents (National Research Council 1989d, tables A, C). It also makes all the assumptions listed below (in the next section) to reach the conclusion that, as of 1988, 53.4 percent of new CPR doctorates entered academe either directly on receiving their degrees or after completing postdocs.

Increasing the Share of CPR New Doctorates Entering Academe

This calculation assumes that individuals without definite plans at the survey date wind up distributed across employment and study categories in a manner similar to those with definite plans (National Research Council 1989d, table N, R). The proportion of CPR postdocs who wind up in academic appointments two years later is obtained from Table 7.9 in the text.

Reduced Out-Migration to the Nonacademic Sector of Experienced Academic Doctorates

Increased In-migration to the Academic Sector of Experienced Nonacademic Doctorates

These two calculations use the data presented in Tables 7.11 and 7.12 in the text on mobility rates and the age distribution of doctorates in each sector.

Increasing the Share of Temporary Resident New Doctorates Accepting Academic Employment in the United States

This calculation assumes that the individuals without definite plans at the survey date are distributed across employment and study categories in a manner similar to those with definite plans (National Research Council 1989d, table 0 and p. 40), that the share of temporary resident new doctorates is 0.199 (see above), and that the share of temporary resident postdocs who wind up in U.S. academic appointments two years later is the lower-bound estimate of 0.27, obtained from Table 7.9 in the text.

Doubling the Annual Flow of Experienced Foreign Scholars Entering with Labor Certifications

This calculation uses the fiscal year 1989 figure of 1,691 provided by the U.S. Department of Labor, Division of Foreign Labor Certification.

Halving the Retirement Rate of Faculty Age 65–69

Bowen and Sosa (1989, table 8.4) estimate that a halving of the retirement rate for those arts and science faculty age 65–69 would reduce the replacement demand for arts and science faculty by 8 percent during the period 1987–92 and that this would be equivalent to about a 6.5 percent increase in new doctorate supply. For later periods, when retirements of those age 70 and over would increase, replacement demand would be reduced only by about 2 percent. The 2 percent figure is used as a "steady-state" value in the computation, and, following Bowen and Sosa, it is assumed that this would be equivalent to a 1.9 percent increase in new doctorate supply. This is assumed to apply to all faculty, not solely those in arts and science.

Increasing the Proportion of CPR Female College Graduates Receiving Doctorates

This calculation assumes that 0.801 of the 33,456 doctorates went to CPR, that 0.35 of these went to women, and that the number of female CPR doctorates would increase by $(0.4/.26) \times 100$ percent (National Research Council 1989d, tables A, C, E).

Reducing the Number of Doctorate Faculty by 5 Percent

This calculation uses the data in Table 6.1 to compute the fraction of full-time faculty with doctorates and an estimate that 459,000 full-time faculty were employed in 1987 in American institutions of higher education (Anderson, Carter, and Malizio 1989, table 104).

III

Costs and Productivity in American Colleges and Universities

Malcolm Getz and
John J. Siegfried

11   Cost Inflation

Are institutions of higher education increasing tuition charges unnecessarily, unfairly, or, worse, because of incompetence? Is there a bias toward higher costs and so higher charges by institutions of higher education in the United States? Bowen (1980) suggests that costs expand to absorb whatever revenues become available to higher education. Tuition and fees at both public and private institutions increased at an average of over 9 percent per annum from 1980 to 1987, a rate about 4.5 percentage points faster than the consumer price index (CPI) rose over the same period (Hauptman 1990a, p. 4, table 1; see also Table 3.4 above). Even though the experience of the 1970s was quite different, with the average annual rate of increase of tuition lagging the CPI by about 1 percent, tuition increases exceeding advances in the CPI are nothing new. For almost a century, from 1905 through 1989, tuition charges increased an annual rate of 2.5 percentage points in excess of the CPI for three private universities tracked by Bowen (1969) and the College Savings Bank (1989).

Critics conclude that higher education costs got out of control in the 1980s, that university presidents and their faculties are taking a larger share of the national income while producing less, and that high cost is putting college education beyond the financial reach of many low - and, especially, middle-income households.[1] The *Washington Post Weekly* (21–27 August 1989, p. A18) has gone as far as to characterize higher education as a machine with no brakes. Defendants of higher education call attention to declines in federal support, to the overhang of the long-deferred maintenance of buildings and the more rapid obsolescence of increasingly sophisticated equipment, and to the desirability of increasing faculty salaries so as to attract the most able

---

1. For example, William Bennett, "Our Greedy Colleges," *New York Times,* 18 February 1987, p. A31.

people to the professoriate (e.g., Hauptman 1990a). Others mention the increased expenditures on marketing, student services, and support operations that have become necessary to attract students in this more status-conscious and comfort-demanding era, when the number of people in the prime college-attending population age groups is declining.

Tuition is the price charged to students for higher education. Total expenditures by colleges and universities are much higher than tuition revenues, even at institutions with the highest tuitions. Colleges and universities depend on other sources of revenue as well, including state and federal governments, endowment earnings, philanthropy, and the sale of ancillary services. For all institutions of higher education, tuition and fees combined are less than one-quarter of total revenues. In 1985–86, tuition and fees covered only 36 percent of direct educational expenditures (what we subsequently call adjusted educational and general (AE&G) expenditure, less scholarships from unrestricted university funds) at all colleges and universities in America (Anderson, Carter, and Malizio 1989). From a social perspective, the problem of high cost is larger than the problem of high tuition. Tuition increases alone, however, do *not* imply rampant cost inflation because increases may be caused by shifts in the relative proportion of different revenue sources.

This part of the volume examines the changing patterns of costs at colleges and universities in light of these claims. We do not purport to measure outputs, so our discussion of productivity is tangential. In this chapter, we describe six theories of why college costs surged in the 1980s, and we describe the data we will use in the following chapters to explore these theories. Chapter 12 examines changes in aggregate expenditures, expenditures per student, and expenditures per degree at different types of colleges and universities. Chapter 13 reveals how enrollment growth affects costs and assesses scale economy estimates in higher education. Finally, Chapter 14 decomposes the cost increases of the last decade into changes in the student/faculty ratio, changes in faculty compensation, changes in nonfaculty instructional costs, and changes in the cost of higher education's support functions.

11.1   Why Do College Costs Rise?

The real cost of educational expenditures per student at U.S. colleges and universities rose about 2.7 percent annually from 1978–79 and 1987–88,[2] less than the rate at which real tuition rose, but high enough for concern nevertheless. The increased costs in higher education might be explained in several ways. Six broad points of view reveal the diversity of opinion about rising costs in higher education.

One explanation holds that the market is competitive and that institutions

---

2. The 2.7 percent per year growth in expenditures per student is calculated from an increase of $1,752 on a 1978–79 base of $6,370 per student (all figures expressed in 1987–88 constant dollars). See Table 12.2.

must therefore meet market tests to survive and prosper. Under these constraints, colleges must provide the range of services that students wish to purchase. Naturally, the level of costs follows from the level of services. Prospective students may be attracted by faculties with stronger reputations, better facilities, a stronger marketing program, and services that improve students' chances of success or that enhance their experience. Where the market for prospective students is strongly competitive, cost increases might reflect product improvements that differentiate a single institution in ways that prospective students find worth the cost, which is passed along accordingly as higher tuition. Colleges, then, must spend more on computers, wider curricula, international programs, and attractive grounds and charge accordingly or risk losing students to institutions who do respond to these student demands. Thus, rising costs of higher education may reflect a change in preferences of students toward a more expensive educational experience with enhanced services. A critical issue is whether institutions of higher education sell their services in workably competitive markets.

A special case of increased costs due to changing student tastes arises from shifts among degree programs. Student interests shifted noticeably in the 1980s. Bowen and Sosa (1989, 47) report that, "between 1970–71 and 1984–85, the number of degrees conferred in the arts and sciences dropped from 40.0 percent of all degrees to 24.9 percent," as students and their parents became concerned about job prospects and the relevance of the arts and sciences. The number of students earning degrees in education also fell substantially. Over the same period, a striking increase occurred in the number of engineering and business degrees awarded.[3]

3. The mix of degrees awarded by American colleges and universities changed substantially in the 1980s. The percentage of total degrees awarded by the institutions in our sample in each of 10 broad categories in 1978–79 and 1985–86 is as follows:

Degree	1978–79 (%)	1985–86 (%)
Two-Year	26.3	26.8
Natural science	6.8	4.6
Social science	10.4	9.6
Humanities	6.8	6.2
Health & allied fields	4.1	3.4
Engineering	4.3	5.1
Business	12.7	17.1
Education	14.8	10.5
Professional (law, medicine, dentistry)	2.1	3.8
Other (including graduate)	11.7	16.2

Source: Authors' calculations based on HEGIS/IPEDS data, (see n. 14 below).
Note: All degrees are four-year except the categories, two-year, professional (which are postbaccalaureate), and other (which includes graduate).

As can be seen from this table, the percentage of degrees awarded in the arts and sciences (the categories natural science, social science, and humanities combined) fell from 24.0 in 1978–79 to 20.4 in 1985–86.

If engineering and business degrees are more costly than arts and sciences and education degrees, the shift in student interests alone can account for some of the rise in the average cost of higher education. In order to evaluate the importance of this explanation of college and university cost inflation in the 1980s, one might identify the relative costs of enrollment in different disciplinary programs and simulate the aggregate cost increase resulting from the actual change in degree mix that occurred over the period, holding constant the costs in each discipline. In view of the shift away from arts and sciences and education toward engineering and business programs, this explanation probably would account for some of the rising aggregate costs. In essence, costs increase because students select more expensive educational programs.[4] Changes in costs due to enrollment shifts would occur in a competitive environment.

A second point of view also considers the market for higher education to be competitive but recognizes that increased prices of inputs faced by all colleges and universities will pass through to consumers in higher charges even if the students see no improvement in the product. For example, a shortage of qualified faculty might increase instructional salaries industry wide. The increased cost of library materials, utilities, and building maintenance would be reflected in total costs and so in tuition charges and claims on legislatures. Again, a critical issue is the degree of competition because it affects the extent to which factor price increases are passed to consumers.

To explore the issue of competition further, consider whether institutions in higher education operate in workably competitive markets. Although institutions differ in character, mix of programs, size, and location, many institutions may operate in market segments that force them to compete for students. For institutions with strong national or regional reputations, the competition may be among institutions at some distance from one another but with a correspondingly large number of competitors. For other institutions, particularly those whose students commute daily from home, the relevant market may be very local, and a given institution may hold a near monopoly on certain services. Yet the next relevant alternative for students may be more hours of employment; hence, these schools may have little ability to increase their tuition without significant loss in enrollment. An important consideration, then,

4. Sufficient data on relative cost differences among disciplines and enrollments (not degrees) by discipline are not available to conduct such a simulation. Furthermore, the effect of changing degree mix alone on the cost inflation of higher education might be overstated by such a stimulation analysis. First, short-run effects of changes in student preferences among disciplines are likely to have relatively little effect, as they will be absorbed as changes in the student/faculty ratio across disciplines. Second, to the extent possible, there will be some substitution of resources (e.g., space, supplies, support staff) from disciplines losing enrollments to those gaining them. Third, the distribution of enrollments across departments is likely to be less responsive to changing preferences than the distribution of degrees since a significant proportion of enrollments in many disciplines consists of "service courses" that form part of general education requirements. Thus, while the changing degree mix probably accounts for some of the cost inflation of the 1980s, it is unlikely to be the sole or even the primary culprit.

is the size of the relevant market for each school and the nature of the programs offered. A critical issue for understanding increased costs is the nature of competition in higher education.

As a third explanation for the rising costs of higher education, the competitive view might be modified if colleges and universities have little opportunity to substitute other inputs for labor in the face of the rising relative cost of their labor inputs. This idea was articulated initially by Baumol and Bowen (1966; Baumol 1967), who applied it first to the live performing arts and then to other service industries. If a certain amount of labor is required to produce higher education, that is to say, if student/faculty ratios are fixed, then, as faculty salaries rise, costs must rise. Productivity gains in the rest of the economy will tend to allow average wage levels to increase with the general price level plus the rate of increase in average productivity. Faculty salaries must increase at the same rate as other wages in the economy if an academic career is to remain attractive. Yet higher education may have smaller gains in productivity if student/faculty ratios are difficult to change. That would be the case if the personal interaction between students and faculty is the product itself, akin to hearing the Boston Symphony perform in Symphony Hall. Therefore, costs and charges in higher education will tend to increase at the same rate as other salaries in the economy and faster than the general price level. At the heart of this argument is the issue of whether there is any prospect of changing the student/faculty ratio and sufficient scope for institutions to adopt innovative methods that increase productivity.[5]

A fourth possible explanation focuses on the central position of faculty and administrators within a college or university. Under the constraints of a not-for-profit organization, it seems plausible to assume that the compensation[6] of those in control, as well as the prestige of being associated with the institution, may play a prominent role among the institution's objectives (Newhouse 1970, 65). The trustees and administration, as well as the faculty, may give considerable weight to the quality of their product as a means to pursue status. Under such circumstances, and with limitations on free entry into the market, institutions are likely to provide greater quality (smaller classes, higher admission standards, greater emphasis on research) than would accommodate consumer tastes in a competitive for-profit market (Newhouse 1970). Al-

5. On the basis of a sample of 37 institutions, Getz and Siegfried (1990) identify and document 30 significant innovations in higher education over the past 50 years. The innovations range from curriculum to finances to student life. It appears that innovations diffuse less rapidly in higher education than in manufacturing. Innovations that use electronic devices seem to diffuse faster than others; innovations involving faculty decision making or that require significant capital outlays seem to diffuse more slowly. The evidence suggests that opportunities exist for institutions of higher education to innovate. Productivity need not remain stagnant. For a positive program to enhance productivity in Research and Doctorate-Granting universities, see Massy (1989).

6. Faculty compensation is not restricted to pecuniary rewards. Job characteristics such as status, control, and hours of work are important to all workers; noncompetitive rents may be extracted through increased status, control over the amount of time faculty spend doing research instead of teaching, the number and distribution of hours worked, and other nonpecuniary means.

though one might argue that management's responsibility is to limit faculty tendencies in this direction, administrators in higher education are frequently drawn from faculty ranks, and many dream that they will eventually return to the classroom. In view of their experience as faculty and their possible return to the ranks, they may act, not as the representatives of trustees or public officials, but rather as agents for the faculty, adopting policies that enhance their salaries, comfort, and status. For institutions where competition is intense, the outcome may be the same as with a competitive process. However, for institutions having succeeded in establishing reputations with distinctive programs and other advantages over rivals, the advantage may be captured by the faculty in the form of increased compensation, improved working conditions, and featherbedding or strategies that promote and display the status of the faculty (e.g., lower teaching loads or a greater emphasis on research). In order for this explanation to bear on the increasing costs of higher education in the 1980s, however, faculty and administrators must either have become more effective in manipulating institutions to their personal advantage or have experienced a change in their preferences, for example, taking greater pride in working at a prestigious institution than they did a decade earlier.[7]

A fifth view of the rising costs of higher education considers the quality of management and decision making in colleges and universities. If institutions do not carefully assess costs and benefits when making decisions, if purchase decisions are not made in a way that induces vendors to give attractive prices, and if rewards are little associated with performance, then indeed costs will be higher without the college's services being more attractive to students or improving faculty welfare. In short, the institution may fail to achieve its goals, whatever they are, at minimum cost. The weak management view is consistent with presidents and other administrators rising through the ranks as successful academics but with limited experience and skill at management. Alternatively, managers imported from outside higher education may fail for lack of experience in higher education. Of course, when an institution is in a competitive market, it will lose students and faculty if management is sufficiently poor. To account for *rising* college and university costs in the 1980s, however, the quality of management must have deteriorated vis-à-vis earlier periods. Critical questions here are the extent to which market forces discipline institutions to perform efficiently and whether institutions have become less adept at attracting and sustaining skilled managers.

A sixth view points to a series of government regulations that create new expectations for higher education. Occupational Safety and Health Administration regulations, Affirmative Action programs, requirement for access and services for the handicapped, requirements for coequal facilities for intercol-

---

7. On the success of faculty extracting rents from universities, especially at larger, research-oriented institutions, see Hoenack (1983). For an argument that status is an important component in modern consumers' utility functions, see Frank (1985). For arguments that the weight placed on status and "winning" has increased over recent decades, see Frank and Cook (1990).

legiate athletics for females, and increased requirements for cost sharing in many research, training, and other program grants might be cited as examples of regulations that impose cost burdens on institutions, usually without commensurate revenue offsets. Of special note in this view are changing federal government policies with respect to indirect cost recovery rates. Federal grants bear direct costs of the time, equipment, and supplies used by investigators and their research time. However, the direct costs do not include rent for the space, access to library and computing resources, the accounting and oversight functions of the university, and many other functions necessary to operating a research enterprise. Universities have been allowed to aggregate all such costs and to charge an appropriate fraction of such costs as an add-on to grants called "indirect cost recovery." In recent years, however, the federal agencies responsible for reviewing indirect cost recovery rates have sought to lower them even when the cost basis is well established by detailed accounting information. If the allowed indirect cost recovery declines relative to the costs incurred, other sources of revenue, including tuition and appropriations from state legislatures must cover more of the shared costs. Changes in federal programs and in regulations, then, can affect the level and mix of costs on campuses, especially where federal grants are a significant source of revenue. It is worth noting, however, that many of the regulations that affect higher education affect other sectors of our society as well.

In the six explanations of rising costs just given, the rising costs benefit different groups. In the competitive product story, the advantages of higher cost accrue to the students who are simply shopping with their dollars from a long menu for the bundle of services they wish. In the input price story, increasing costs reflect events in input markets beyond the control of higher education. No one in higher education benefits, not even the faculty whose compensation rises (because their opportunity costs rise as well). In Baumol and Bowen's view, higher education is disadvantaged relative to the rest of the economy by its inherently labor-intensive technology of instructors teaching students in groups of relatively fixed size. By contrast, in the management utility maximization view, the faculty and administrators pocket the higher costs as salary and prestige, using market power to impose higher charges on students so they can earn more than they would make in their best alternative employment and enjoy a preferred work environment.[8] In the poor management story, presidents and administrators, students, and faculty all lose through poor decision making. In the government-as-culprit view, congressional and social goals take precedence. These views are not necessarily mutually exclusive, and there may be other explanations as compelling on a priori grounds as some of these (Hauptman 1990a; Kirshstein et al. 1990).

In this study, we present empirical evidence that, in some cases, lends support to some of these explanations and, in other cases, seems inconsistent with

---

8. Sykes (1988) argues this view forcefully, to the point of exaggeration.

some of them. The study may generate new points of view as well. We hope the result will be a better understanding of the nature of changes in the cost of higher education and, by inference, improved insight into the nature of the institutions. Before we delve into our data, however, we need to address the issue of service quality in higher education, after which we describe the data used in this part of the volume.

11.2   Product Quality and Diversity

Do higher-cost colleges and universities produce better education? If an automobile plant produces superior cars, we may expect those cars to be more costly and to bear higher sticker prices. If consumers buy the more expensive cars when less expensive ones are available, we may conclude that consumers value the additional quality in excess of the cost of the additional resources required to create it and that the automobile plant is more "productive" even though it incurs higher costs per unit. Can the case be made that the quality of output from higher education has increased sufficiently to make the higher-priced product worth the extra cost? Has higher education become more valuable as its costs have risen? Or have costs increased even as the quality of college education has stagnated or, worse, declined?

Quality in higher education is nearly impossible to define (Solmon 1973). One might take the earnings differential between college and high school graduates as an index of the contribution of college education,[9] but growth in the differential can be ascribed to numerous factors other than improved quality in higher education, for example, shifts in the demand for the labor of high school and college graduates or a decline in the quality of secondary education.

It is tempting to conclude that improved knowledge of the various disciplines implies an ever-increasing quality of college education, but such a conclusion may be far from correct. First, it can be argued that the steady flow of new scholarly research does not always improve faculty knowledge. There is a limit to what the human mind can store, process, and understand. Faculty knowledge progresses only if better ideas and improved understanding replace inferior ideas and understanding. Thus, progress depends on the character of competition for ideas and the process by which science and art advance. There is no assurance against temporary setbacks, no guarantee that each discipline moves closer to "truth" each decade.

A more fundamental flaw in the argument that scholarly progress guarantees improved quality in higher education is the implicit premise that the purpose of higher education is to impart "truth" to students. Many would challenge that premise, arguing instead that the primary purpose of a liberal arts

---

9. For a survey of empirical studies of the value of a college education based on earnings differentials, see Cohn and Geske (1990, 106–10). See also Table 3.2 above.

education is—at the least—to help individuals develop their capacity to think clearly and critically about issues and problems in a variety of ways. If that is the purpose of higher education, scholarly progress among the disciplines in discerning "truth" may have little, if any, effect on the primary output of higher education.

Higher education benefits students through a sequence of events. First, students and their families spend money on tuition, but, more important, they invest their time, time that alternatively they could have devoted to earning income. The forgone earnings of most studen. s still larger than tuition at all but the most expensive private institutions.[10] Second, the institution provides a set of experiences that transform the students. Among the experiences will be contact with faculty in classes of varying size, association with other students of differing interests, backgrounds, talents, and aspirations, a range of social experiences, and, perhaps, religious, athletic, cultural, political, and other influential experiences. Third, these education experiences have influence throughout the rest of the student's life. The influences may be on career choice, on earnings, on the likelihood of changing careers, on choice of mate, on participation in politics, on health, on enjoyment of the arts, and so on. An assessment of the performance of an institution of higher education would establish the connections between the three links of the chain: student commitment, institutional experiences, and life prospects. Although a few studies have followed a cohort of students through the process and some analysts have drawn inferences from cross-sectional comparisons, all the studies fall short of offering a comprehensive view of the influence of various experiences in higher education on the life prospects of participants (Jacobi, Astin, and Ayala 1987).

Productivity studies of higher education are particularly difficult to conduct. Traditional productivity studies of manufactured products relate output to inputs. Productivity is then judged on the basis of trends over time or on comparisons of the amount of output produced per input unit across producers at a point in time. In most cases output can be measured directly in physical units.

For higher education, on the other hand, there is substantial disagreement about both what output is and what it should be (Pascarelli and Terenzini 1991). One source of the dispute is the practice of funding America's higher education with contributions from various sources. As a result, students, their parents, foundation officials, alumni, government agencies, and taxpayers all believe that they have a role in defining the goals of higher education. Add to

10. Following Table 3.5 above, average nine-month earnings (after taxes and discounted by the probability of unemployment) for a 25- to 34-year-old high school graduate with no college experience in 1987–88 were $12,925 for males and $9,128 for females. Average tuition at private universities was $8,770 in 1987–88. However, some institutions charged much more: tuition and fees at Bennington College, Rensselaer Polytechnic Institute, and Tulane University were $14,850, $11,850, and $11,280, respectively, in 1987–88 (College Entrance Examination Board, *The College Handbook 1987–88* [New York, 1987]).

this faculty and administrators, who argue that their professional judgments are essential to directing the mission of such a complex enterprise as higher education, and considerable conflict occurs about output mix and priorities.

Colleges and universities in America produce a vast array of goods and services. For undergraduates, colleges contribute to cognitive and affective development, sorting and screening, helping individuals develop a sense of responsibility and self-esteem, social development, citizenship, and even entertainment (e.g., on Saturday afternoon in the university football stadium). A large fraction of our universities are also heavily involved in graduate and postbaccalaureate professional education and research, the products of which include future lawyers, physicians, business leaders, and faculty—and new ideas. Many of our colleges and universities also provide public services, such as the agricultural extension and experimentation services of land-grant universities or the job retraining assistance provided by many two-year colleges.

The problems of measuring the productivity of colleges and universities, however, go beyond multiple outputs valued differently by different constituents.[11] By its very nature, the output of higher education includes substantial intangible elements that are not traded in markets. Few would argue that the sole purpose of higher education is to enhance the subsequent earnings of students. But how is one to measure the benefits of self-discovery, socialization, maturation, and improved reasoning and judgment beyond their effects on labor market achievement? How is one to measure the value of friendships and memories? In short, so many of the services of higher education cannot be measured in physical units and escape formal valuation in markets that there is little prospect ever to pin down even a rough approximation of their value.

The problems go even further than multiple, intangible, and unpriced outputs. Productivity analysis in higher education faces additional measurement problems because many of the outputs are jointly produced with inputs that are not hired by the institutions, for example, students' intrinsic talents, and because the production process for learning is so poorly understood and varies so much across individuals. Furthermore, output includes both consumption and investment components, and many people consider the process itself to be an essential component of output.

A great deal of what individuals gain from a college experience may, in fact, be impossible to measure. Many years ago, James A. Garfield spoke of the ideal college as a log with Mark Hopkins on one end and a student on the other.[12] We may suppose that Hopkins imparted a set of skills that might be

---

11. Multiple outputs can be related to multiple inputs with sophisticated econometric techniques. For illustrations of this practice applied to higher education, see Cohn, Rhine, and Santos (1989) and de Groot, McMahan, and Volkwein (1989).

12. Garfield articulated this view of college during a speech at his alma mater, Williams College, before he was inaugurated as the twentieth president of the United States. At the time of the speech, Hopkins was president of Williams College.

measured directly. But we may also suppose that Hopkins responded to student puzzles, instilled a spirit of responsibility, nurtured intellectual curiosity, and offered a measure of inspiration that could not be measured directly. We expect the professor to appeal differently to different students; some need context, some need discipline, some need courage. We expect students to respond differently: some value the poetry, some the logic, and some the power of the same idea. We can imagine a student of accounting learning in one setting that the debits are on the window side of the ledger, in another why firms may (honestly) keep three sets of books (one for the shareholders, one for the tax collector, and one for the managers), and in a third why accountants seldom become chief executive officers of large corporations. Higher education may be as important in socialization, matching interest to opportunity, and developing a coherent worldview as in developing specific skills. Social science needs more powerful tools if it is to offer insight into the full breadth of influence of higher education on those who invest in it.

Finally, higher education may affect our society on a scale far beyond the consequences measured for each individual student. Colleges and universities produce ideas expressed in books, music, art, patents, and medical, managerial, and legal techniques. Professors advise senators and presidents, often creating and interpreting the vocabulary by which the public debates the issues of the day. The full consequences of having a literate and cultured society may not be measured even approximately by the experiences of individuals taken one at a time. Measuring such purely social consequences of higher education is beyond available techniques.

Realistic estimates of educational production functions have been limited by the obstacles outlined above (Schapiro 1987; Gilmore 1988). Because the task of measuring outcomes is so difficult (some argue impossible), our focus here is on inputs and costs rather than results. Any insight about outcomes and productivity offered here comes indirectly and cautiously. Even if we are unable to measure and value outcomes, however, if they have remained about the same over the past decade, we can still learn something from changes in costs over the period.[13]

11.3 Higher Education in the 1980s

It is useful to begin our analysis of costs with a review of the institutions constituting higher education in the United States in the 1980s. Institutions

---

13. The difficulties measuring outputs and assigning inputs to these outputs may make productivity analysis in higher education difficult, but they do not make it impossible. In a study conceived out of the project that led to this book, Getz and Siegfried (1990) look at productivity in higher education in terms of the rate at which ultimately successful innovations diffuse through educational institutions. By restricting the analysis to "successful" innovations, the speed with which colleges and universities adopt new ideas can be used to measure their "productivity" because the failure to adopt improvements promptly forces society to incur unnecessary opportunity costs. Characteristics of institutions that appear to be leaders in innovation can then be identified.

Table 11.1   **Sample Institutions Compared with Population**

	(1) No. of Institutions per Carnegie Foundation, 1987	(2) No. of Institutions in Our Sample, 1978–79 to 1987–88	(3) Coverage [(2)/(1)] × 100 (in %)
Research	104	90	86.5
Doctoral	109	96	88.1
Comprehensive	595	522	87.7
Liberal Arts I	142	131	92.2
Other-Four-Year[a]	430	353	82.1
Two-Year	1,367	853	62.4
Specialized	642	0	.0
Total	3,389	2,045	60.3

Sources: Carnegie Foundation for the Advancement of Teaching (1987, table 2); and U.S. Department of Education HEGIS/IPEDS data for 1978–79, 1983–84, 1985–86, and 1987–88.
[a]Called "Liberal Arts II" by the Carnegie Foundation.

are a proper focus of the analysis of costs because in most cases the critical decisions are made by officials of individual institutions. Moreover, the Department of Education collects data about institutions, and so analysis of institutional behavior with a broad sample is possible. The few studies of costs at the department level have almost always looked at a single institution or a small group of institutions (Hoenack et al. 1986; Tierney 1980a; Brovender 1974; Razin and Campbell 1972; Borgman and Bartram 1969; Gibson 1968; Buckles 1978), thus limiting the extent to which their findings can be generalized.

There are about 3,400 institutions of higher education in the United States offering at least a two-year associate or four-year degree program, as shown in Table 11.1. At least two hundred of these were founded during the 1980s, more than the total number of colleges existing in America in 1850 (Harris 1972, table 5.2–1, p. 924). The institutions serve diverse missions; well over one-third of them offer only two-year programs, and about one-fifth offer four-year programs exclusively. Approximately one-third of the institutions offer postbaccalaureate programs in addition to undergraduate programs, and about one-fifth have programs confined to specialties such as freestanding medical or law schools. Over 400 institutions award doctoral degrees. Other institutions engage in postsecondary training programs that are not generally viewed as part of higher education; most important among these are the proprietary vocational schools. These usually offer vocational training (e.g., data processing, cosmetology, truck driving).

Our analysis relies on the HEGIS/IPEDS[14] survey of institutions of higher education undertaken annually by the U.S. Department of Education. We use

14. The annual "census" of colleges and universities was called the Higher Education General Information Survey (HEGIS) through 1985–86. At that time, the survey was revised and expanded and its name changed to the Integrated Postsecondary Education Data System (IPEDS).

survey data from 1978–79, 1983–84, 1985–86, and 1987–88 to examine the finances and enrollments of 2,045 institutions over time.[15] Our sample includes over 80 percent of the institutions identified by the Carnegie Foundation in all categories except the Two-Year group, where our coverage is slightly over 60 percent, and specialized institutions, which we exclude entirely (see Table 11.1)[16] Eight-six percent of the colleges and universities that award a bachelor's degree are included in our data base. In the remainder of this part of the volume, we draw conclusions from the sample of 2,045 as though it were all of higher education.[17] For expositional convenience, we will occasionally refer to the period 1978–79 to 1987–88 as though it were coterminous with the decade of the 1980s.

The HEGIS/IPEDS responses are unaudited. When an institution's own accounting system uses categories that are incongruent with the HEGIS/IPEDS categories, the institution may make arbitrary choices in deciding on a response. The institution may make one choice in one year and respond differently in a subsequent year. The Department of Education, which collects the survey, does not verify the information, test for consistency from one year to the next, or require that the information be complete. We have excluded from our statistics institutions with wildly implausible figures by checking for certain kinds of internal consistency. We do not provide independent verification of the data. *Caveat lector.*

The flagship state universities, leading private universities, and other doc-

---

15. Our sample consists of 2,045 colleges and universities that operated continuously in the United States from 1978–79 to 1987–88. We omitted specialized institutions (e.g., freestanding medical and law schools) and any other schools that did not have any full-time undergraduate students. Only institutions reporting at least some expenditures for instruction, student services (e.g., admissions, registrar), institutional support (president, provost), and plant operations (maintenance, utilities) are included. In short, a college is a college in our view only if it reports spending at least one dollar on each of these four fundamental services; a few dozen institutions were eliminated on the basis of this criterion. Reports of zero expenditures for sponsored research, public service, and unrestricted scholarships appear for some institutions that surely have such expenditures. We concluded that those institutions reported such expenditures in other accounts. If the reporting appears consistent (e.g., a category was zero for all four years), we accepted it, understanding that some of the expenditures in other categories are for research, public service, and/or scholarship purposes. If the reporting standard appears inconsistent (e.g., Columbia University's public service expenditures increased from zero in 1984 to $126,000,000 in 1988), we assumed that there had been a change in accounting practice that would invalidate comparisons over time, and the institution was deleted from our sample. We also eliminated five colleges that reported implausible enrollment fluctuations, probably caused by data-processing errors. Reported library expenditure data for many institutions on the IPEDS 1987–88 data tape are implausible (e.g., we do not believe that Harvard spent nothing on its 50 libraries in 1988). Because library expenditures are included in academic support, we do not report library expenditures separately.

16. For a description of each Carnegie classification, see Table 2 of the introduction to this volume.

17. Based on enrollment shares reported in Table 2 of the introduction to this volume and coverage ratios reported in Table 11.1, we estimate that our sample includes 68.5 percent of total enrollments and 87.2 percent of enrollments at four-year undergraduate colleges in 1987–88. The largest share of total enrollments missing from the sample is two-year colleges (22.9 percent). We exclude specialized institutions, which account for only 3.8 percent of total enrollments. Thus, only 4.8 percent of the enrollments missing from our survey come from four-year institutions.

Table 11.2   Sample Institutions and Enrollment by Carnegie Classification

Carnegie Classification	No. of Institutions	% of Instititutions	No. of FTE Students[a]	% of FTE Students
Research	90	4.4	1,660,920	23.2
Doctoral	96	4.7	895,051	12.5
Comprehensive	522	25.5	2,174,478	30.4
Liberal Arts I	131	6.4	185,754	2.6
Other-Four-Year	353	17.3	265,190	3.7
Two-Year	853	41.7	1,975,801	27.6
Total	2,045	100.0	7,157,194	100.0

Source: Calculations by authors based on HEGIS/IPEDS data.
[a]Full-time-equivalent (FTE) students = full-time students + ⅓ part-time students averaged over 1978–79, 1983–84, 1985–86, and 1987–88.

toral institutions that the Carnegie Foundation labels "Research" and "Doctoral" constitute fewer than 10 percent of the institutions of higher education but account for 36 percent of the total enrollment in full-time equivalents, as shown in Table 11.2.[18] They dominate graduate education, public service, research, big-time college athletics, and name recognition by the general public; these are the conglomerates of higher education. Conversely, the smaller institutions in the Liberal Arts I and Other-Four-Year categories account for 24 percent of institutions in our sample, but only 6 percent of enrollment.

The Research and Doctoral institutions have a special importance because their graduate programs produce future professors for all of higher education and their research efforts are an integral part of basic research in America. The Liberal Arts I schools graduate a disproportionate share of the baccalaureates who later become professors[19] and a large fraction of our country's cultural, political, and business leaders. There is something of a pecking order of influence and prestige, with Research universities training faculty for most of the other sectors. Yet the Comprehensive institutions and the Two-Year colleges together enroll more than half of all students. All the institutions play different roles and therefore have different characteristics, which are reflected as much in their finances as in their catalogs.

The great importance of the private sector in higher education in the United States is unique in the world. Private colleges and universities account for 41 percent of the institutions of higher education, as shown in Table 11.3. The private institutions ("privates," for short) in every Carnegie classification are smaller than the public institutions ("publics"), and so the privates account for

18. Following the convention of others (e.g., Bowen and Sosa, 1989, 32), we define full-time-equivalent enrollment as full-time plus one-third part-time enrollment.
19. Although a high proportion of the baccalaureate graduates of Liberal Arts I colleges have traditionally continued their education to earn a Ph.D. in economics, this fraction appears to have declined in the 1980s (Kasper 1990a).

Table 11.3   Sample Institutions and Enrollment by Institutional Control

Control	No. of Institutions	% of Instititutions	No. of FTE Students[a]	% of FTE Students
Public	1,203	58.8	5,643,032	78.8
Private	842	41.2	1,514,162	21.2
Total	2,045	100.0	7,157,194	100.0

Source: Calculations by authors based on HEGIS/IPEDS data.
[a]Full-time-equivalent (FTE) students = full-time students + ⅓ part-time students averaged over 1978–79, 1983–84, 1985–86, and 1987–88.

only 21 percent of enrollment. Private institutions are somewhat more important in graduate education than undergraduate, they are much less important in Two-Year education than four-year, and they wholly dominate the Liberal Arts I and Other-Four-Year categories. The private sector includes many schools with a strong religious emphasis or with ethnic identifications. About 100 private institutions have endowments that are large enough to be important in the financial life of the schools.[20] The philanthropic tradition in America sustains many of the private schools with current giving as well as in periodic capital campaigns.[21]

Private colleges and universities charge tuitions that are many multiples of tuitions in the public sector, yet, in the aggregate, they continue to thrive. The privates must offer services that students find worth the price difference. As we will see, the privates do not, on average, pay their faculties more than public institutions. They have pursued a variety of strategies to distinguish themselves, including different student/faculty ratios, a religious emphasis, and distinctive social milieus. That privates are, on average, much smaller than their public competitors should not be accepted as coincidental. The smaller scale may well be critical in providing a distinctive experience that some students value highly.

Public higher education is primarily a responsibility of the several states, education not having been mentioned in the federal constitution. Each state operates one or more systems of higher education, often with grand research university campuses as centerpieces flanked by regional comprehensive universities (many of whom had former lives as teacher-training academies).

20. For fiscal year 1986, Harvard reported the largest endowment, $3.4 billion; Colorado College was ranked 100 among the 3,400 colleges and universities, with an endowment of $87.5 million. The largest 100 endowments accounted for 72 percent of the endowments of all colleges and univerisites (U.S. Department of Education 1988, table 148, p. 282). Endowment income constitutes less than 3 percent of revenues of all colleges and universities combined. It is relatively more important at private institutions, where it accounted for 5 percent of revenues in 1985–86 (Anderson, Carter, and Malizio 1989, tables 95, and 97).

21. Endowment income plus private gifts, grants, and contracts accounted for about 15 percent of the revenues of private colleges and universities in 1985–86 (Anderson, Carter, and Malizio 1989, table 97).

These are complemented by an array of Two-Year colleges that offer terminal vocational programs or specialized professional training (e.g., dental hygiene, mortuary science) or serve as the lower division (i.e., freshman- and sophomore-level programs) of the state university system (e.g., the Pennsylvania State University has numerous two-year campuses that feed its University Park campus).

The national government began support for higher education with the Morrill Act during the Lincoln administration, awarding grants of land to universities in each state for promoting agriculture and industry. The federal government continues to support university-based agricultural research, education, and extension programs. Early in this century, the federal government began to support university-based medical research, with funding awarded on a competitive basis for specific projects. This model was adapted for the support of scientific research as the Cold War induced the federal government to sponsor defense-related research in the 1950s. Recently, the agricultural community has called for moving its federal support programs toward the competitive project grant regime as a way of improving quality and productivity (National Research Council 1989c). In the 1960s, the federal government added support to higher education through grants and loans to students. To a degree, aid flows to students and allows them to shop for what they perceive to be the "best values" in higher education (Hansen and Weisbrod 1971). The national government directly supports its five service academies and a few institutions in the District of Columbia. There is no national university.

The financing of private and public colleges and universities differs substantially. In Chapter 12 we show that, on average, private institutions (without a medical school) spent about $3,400 more per full-time-equivalent student than did comparable public universities in 1987–88. In the same year, however, the difference in tuition between them was closer to $5,700 (see Table 3.4 above). Although students at public institutions do not enjoy the same level of expenditures as those at the privates, they receive a price discount that more than compensates for the lower level of spending. The difference, of course, is covered by direct appropriations from (mostly) state governments. In essence, *all* students at public institutions receive a partial scholarship roughly equivalent to the difference between their tuition and expenditures per student at their school.

Students at the same institution also often make different contributions to revenues, reflecting differences in scholarship awards. The variation is greater at private than at public schools. According to the sample used in this part of the volume, the sum of external and institutionally supported scholarship aid per student averaged $533 at publics and $1,769 at privates in 1987–88. Thus, the average *net* tuition difference between privates and publics was about $4,500 in 1987–88. The average tuition level, however, means less at private than at public colleges and universities because scholarship aid is distributed much less uniformly across students than is state aid at public universities. At private institutions, many students pay the "sticker price," while others receive scholarships based on need, academic or athletic merit, or other criteria. In short, public universities in America are similar to discount stores, offering "everyday low prices" to their customers, while private colleges and universities are like full-service stores, competing on the basis of service and carefully distributed discount coupons (which they call financial aid).

Federal grants to support research and development are an important source of revenue for Research and Doctoral institutions, and the research activities of colleges and universities account for a significant proportion of the total research and development produced in the United States. Total federal obligations to universities and colleges for research and development summed to $6.5 billion in 1986.[22] The 100 institutions earning the largest amounts received 85 percent ($5.6 billion) of the total. Johns Hopkins University received the largest amount at $446 million, Yale was tenth with $112 million, and Georgetown University was one hundredth with $15 million.[23] Research funds are consequential to research universities.

The National Science Foundation reports the total national expenditure on research and development in 1986 at $51.4 billion, of which colleges and universities received or managed $9 billion (about 17 percent) when federally funded research-and-development centers are added to grants.[24] Federal intramural research facilities and industrial labs account for most of the rest. Note that the National Science Foundation survey omits university-based investigation that is not sponsored by external funds. In basic research, the role of colleges and universities is even more important. Higher education spent or managed $4.8 billion of the $8.1 billion the nation spent on basic research in 1986. The three agencies accounting for the largest amounts of research-and-development funds to universities and colleges are as follows: Health and Human Services, $3.3 billion (58 percent of the agency's total R&D effort); Defense, $1.1 billion (3 percent of the agency's R&D effort); and the National Science Foundation, $0.9 billion (73 percent of the agency's R&D effort). The research productivity of the nation depends critically on the activities of colleges and universities.

22. National Science Foundation, *Federal Support to Universities, Colleges, and Selected Nonprofit Institutions, Fiscal Year 1986* (Washington, D.C.: U.S. Government Printing Office, 1986), table B-5, p. 15.
23. Many of the research grants are awarded by competition. For example, the *National Science Foundation Annual Report, 1988* ([Washington,D.C.: U.S. Government Printing Office, 1988], inside cover) reports that the NSF received 37,500 proposals and awarded more than 16,000 grants in 1988. A telephone call revealed that the National Institutes of Health received 20,080 proposals in fiscal year 1990 and funded 4,845.
24. National Science Foundation, *Federal Funds for Research and Development, Fiscal Years 1986, 1987, and 1988* (Washington, D.C.: U.S. Government Printing Office, 1988), vol. 36, tables C-1, p. 16, and C-7, pp. 28–29.

Table 11.4   Sample Institutions and Enrollment by Size Class

Enrollment Size Class[a]	No. of Institutions	% of Institutions	No. of FTE Students[b]	% of FTE Students
0–999	635	31.1	398,083	5.6
1,000–2,999	750	36.7	1,310,661	18.3
3,000–9,999	500	24.4	2,721,851	38.0
10,000–19,000	119	5.8	1,635,688	22.9
20,000+	41	2.0	1,090,911	15.2
Total	2,045	100.0	7,157,194	100.0

Source: Calculations by authors based on HEGIS/IPEDS data.

[a]Based on average number of full-time-equivalent students in 1978–79, 1983–84, 1985–86, and 1987–88.

[b]Full-time-equivalent (FTE) students = full-time students + ⅓ part-time students averaged over 1978–79, 1983–84, 1985–86, and 1987–88.

Institutions differ widely in size, as reported in Table 11.4. More than two-thirds of our colleges have enrollments of under 3,000. Many of these small colleges are in rural areas, conveniently located for commuting students. Some of the small schools limit enrollment by design. They are small enough for the president to know each faculty member by name, if not each student. Some institutions are small because their enrollments have declined as their programs have lost favor. We will be interested in observing whether costs differ systematically with size. Can larger institutions offer education at lower cost per student than smaller ones? We will turn to the financial data in Chapter 13 with this question among others.

Enrollments grew over the 1980s, and they grew in almost every subcategory, both full- and part-time at both four- and two-year schools and at both graduate and undergraduate levels, as shown in Table 11.5. This growth occurred despite unfavorable demographic trends. The size of the birth cohort peaked in 1962. Eighteen years later, the number of 18-year-olds reached a peak, so the pool of candidates in the prime age bracket for higher education started its slide at the beginning of the decade. For a time, the shrinking college age cohort did not affect enrollment levels, owing mainly to an increase in the enrollment rate of 18- to 24-year-olds and increased enrollment of older students, as the baby-boom cohort moved above age 30. At the beginning of the 1990s, however, it appears that college enrollments will finally begin to decline, and projections are that they may decline until at least 1995 (Bowen and Sosa 1989, 37).

Both the public and the private sectors gained enrollment during the 1980s, as shown in Table 11.6. Graduate education became somewhat more important for the private sector but became a slightly smaller share of the public sector. Part-time students are especially important at public Two-Year col-

Table 11.5   **Enrollment Trends in American Colleges and Universities, 1978–79 to 1987–88**

	1978–79	1983–84	1985–86	1987–88	Annual Rate of Change
Four-year institutions (N = 1,192):					
Full-time enrollment	4,341,522	4,593,297	4,553,614	4,655,940	.7
Part-time enrollment	1,801,380	1,935,139	1,955,227	2,051,850	1.4
Full-time undergraduate	3,995,998	4,232,819	4,181,844	4,279,523	.7
Part-time undergraduate	1,228,668	1,378,310	1,391,353	1,454,502	1.8
Full-time graduate	345,524	360,478	371,770	385,417	1.2
Part-time graduate	572,712	556,829	563,874	597,348	.3
Two-Year institutions (N = 853):					
Full-time enrollment	1,215,934	1,346,643	1,226,788	1,251,164	.2
Part-time enrollment	1,907,809	2,205,820	2,156,162	2,318,237	2.0
Full-time undergraduate	1,215,836	1,346,541	1,226,661	1,251,080	.2
Part-time undergraduate	1,906,933	2,205,316	2,155,379	2,317,727	2.0
Full-time graduate	98	102	127	84	− .3
Part-time graduate	876	504	783	510	− 4.6

Source: Calculations by authors based on HEGIS/IPEDS data.

leges, and their importance grew throughout the 1980s. Interestingly, the private Two-Year colleges attract part-time students at about the same rate as private four-year schools. In this respect, as in quite a number of others, the private Two-Year colleges are more like private four-year colleges than they are like public Two-Year colleges.

Table 11.7 reports enrollment data by Carnegie classification. Research institutions and Liberal Arts I colleges grew somewhat more slowly than Doctoral and Comprehensive institutions, perhaps by design and perhaps in response to the accelerating tuition levels of Research and Liberal Arts I institutions in the 1980s. Many institutions consciously limit enrollments so as to retain the human attributes of a particular scale of operation. By restricting enrollment, institutions can limit admission to particular students. The selective schools can then offer the promise of a certain exclusivity to future students. If the attitudes, skills, and motivation of peers is an important ingre-

Table 11.6   Full-Time-Equivalent Enrollment Trends in American Colleges and Universities, 1978–1979 to 1987–88, by Control

Control	1978–79	1983–84	1985–86	1987–88	Annual Rate of Change
Four-year institutions (N = 1192):					
Public (N = 453):					
FTE enrollment	3,541,469	3,768,440	3,740,166	3,846,166	.9
Average FTE enrollment	7,818	8,319	8,256	8,491	
% part-time	29.5	29.2	29.9	30.6	
% graduate	14.5	13.2	13.5	13.7	
Private (N = 739):					
FTE enrollment	1,400,513	1,469,903	1,465,191	1,493,497	.7
Average FTE enrollment	1,895	1,989	1,983	2,021	
% part-time	29.0	30.8	30.5	30.5	
% graduate	16.2	16.1	16.7	17.2	
Two-Year institutions (N = 853):					
Public (N = 750):					
FTE enrollment	1,800,058	2,020,908	1,887,864	1,966,827	.9
Average FTE enrollment	2,400	2,695	2,517	2,622	
% part-time	61.8	62.8	64.4	65.6	
% graduate	.0	.0	.0	.0	
Private (N = 103):					
FTE enrollment	51,812	61,008	57,644	57,082	1.1
Average FTE enrollment	503	592	560	554	
% part-time	22.3	30.8	32.0	32.0	
% graduate	.0	.0	.0	.0	

Source: Calculations by authors based on HEGIS/IPEDS data.

[a]Full-time-equivalent (FTE) students = full-time students + ⅓ part-time students.

dient in the educational process, or if the screening accomplished by the admissions process is relied on by employers and graduate and professional schools, then the fact of selection may increase the attractiveness of the school to subsequent students. We have kept the number of schools and their classification by mission unchanged over the interval of study (they are all classified on the basis of their 1987 Carnegie classification) so that the reported enrollment and financial figures are not affected by possible changes in mission or entrances and exits of institutions. Although some institutions may be misclassified (Breneman 1990), each category represents a consistent set of institutions.

Institutions of all size groups experienced growth, but, on average, smaller institutions grew slightly faster than larger institutions, as Table 11.8 reveals. Among Two-Year colleges, the schools with fewer than 3,000 students grew

Table 11.7   **Enrollment Trends in American Colleges and Universities by Type of Institution, 1978–79 to 1987–88**

	1978–79	1983–84	1985–86	1987–88	Annual Rate of Change
Research institutions (N − 90):					
FTE enrollment	1,595,578	1,671,114	1,671,630	1,705,360	.7
Average FTE enrollment	17,729	18,568	18,574	18,948	
% part-time	22.6	22.9	22.8	23.5	
% graduate	20.5	19.8	20.3	20.7	
Doctoral institutions (N = 96):					
FTE enrollment	854,653	907,456	898,783	919,312	.8
Average FTE enrollment	8,903	9,453	9,362	9,576	
% part-time	32.0	32.3	32.4	32.8	
% graduate	17.9	16.7	17.0	17.4	
Comprehensive institutions (N = 522):					
FTE enrollment	2,049,591	2,211,077	2,188,874	2,248,369	1.0
Average FTE enrollment	3,926	4,236	4,193	4,307	
% part-time	35.2	34.9	35.8	36.2	
% graduate	12.1	11.0	11.1	11.3	
Liberal Arts I institutions (N = 131):					
FTE enrollment	182,627	184,869	185,385	190,133	.4
Average FTE enrollment	1,394	1,411	1,415	1,451	
% part-time	12.8	12.9	12.1	12.2	
% graduate	3.4	3.6	4.0	4.0	
Other-Four-Year institutions (N = 353):					
FTE enrollment	259,533	263,828	260,684	276,716	.5
Average FTE enrollment	735	747	738	784	
% part-time	20.1	24.6	26.1	27.7	
% graduate	26.3	31.1	38.9	45.2	
Two-Year institutions (N = 853):					
FTE enrollment	1,851,870	2,081,916	1,945,509	2,023,910	.9
Average FTE enrollment	2,171	2,441	2,281	2,373	
% part-time	61.1	70.6	63.7	64.9	
% graduate	.0	.0	.0	.0	

Source: Calculations by authors based on HEGIS/IPEDS data.
Note: FTE = full-time-equivalent.

twice as fast as the schools with 3,000 or more students. Among four-year institutions, growth appears to be concentrated in medium-sized schools. Those with enrollments under 1,000 and over 20,000 grew at about half the rate of schools with enrollments between 1,000 and 20,000. These patterns reflect the enrollment targets set by selective schools and the investments in campuses made by state systems, but probably are dominated by the selection of schools by prospective students.

Full-time-equivalent enrollments have grown at slightly less than 1 percent annually from 1978–79 to 1987–88. But growth has not been uniform at all

Table 11.8   **Full-Time-Equivalent Enrollment Trends in American Colleges and Universities, 1978–1987, by Size Class**

Average Enrollment	Sample Size	1978–79	1983–84	1985–86	1987–88	Average Annual Rate of Change
Four-year institutions:						
0–999	333	208,000	212,724	209,544	221,009	.5
1,000–2,999	412	687,599	727,980	727,954	755,131	1.0
3,000–9,999	303	1,613,668	1,739,820	1,715,915	1,745,711	.9
10,000–19,999	103	1,377,774	1,460,463	1,453,308	1,505,327	.9
20,000+	41	1,054,941	1,097,356	1,098,636	1,112,713	.6
Total	1,192	4,941,982	5,238,343	5,205,357	5,339,891	
Two-Year institutions:						
0–999	302	171,706	190,713	184,279	194,357	1.3
1,000–2,999	338	536,253	623,402	577,976	606,349	1.2
3,000–9,999	197	976,157	1,070,396	1,000,191	1,034,546	.5
10,000–19,999	16	176,754	197,405	183,062	188,658	.6
Total	853	1,860,870	2,081,916	1,945,508	2,023,910	

Source: Calculations by authors based on HEGIS/IPEDS data.

institutions. One-third of our sample institutions experienced growth rates exceeding 1.8 percent annually over the period, while enrollments at about another third (36.5 percent) actually declined. The different enrollment experiences of various categories of institutions are reported in Tables 11.9 and 11.10.

Because the public sector has grown slightly faster than the private sector over the decade, it is no surprise to find that public Comprehensive and public Two-Year colleges contain the highest proportion of institutions whose enrollments grew in excess of 1.8 percent annually. Of the institutions with declining enrollments, a disproportionate share are private Other-Four-Year (less selective liberal arts and smaller comprehensives) and Two-Year colleges. Both these categories appear to contain institutions in the midst of transition. Over 78 percent of the institutions in each category are experiencing either rapidly rising or declining enrollments. Both categories contain mostly institutions that enroll under 1,000 students (267 of 330 private Other-Four-Year and 93 of 103 private Two-Year), and the two categories together account for 57 percent of the 635 institutions in our sample with fewer than 1,000 students. This, and further evidence we uncover later, suggests that such small institutions are not in stable equilibrium. Most of these institutions will either grow to enrollment levels beyond 1,000 or eventually close their doors.

With this description of the environment of American higher education in the 1980s, we turn in subsequent chapters to an analysis of the patterns and trends in costs. In Chapter 12, we look at how cost structures and changes in costs over time are related to institutional mission and control. In Chapter 13,

Table 11.9 Distribution of Institutions with Fastest-Growing Enrollments[a] (percentage among top third enrollment growth, 1978–79 to 1987–88)

Carnegie Classification	Public			Private			Total		
	Sample Size	No. Growing	% Growing	Sample Size	No. Growing	% Growing	Sample Size	No. Growing	% Growing
Research	66	8	12.1	24	3	12.5	90	11	12.2
Doctoral	60	14	23.3	36	8	22.2	96	22	22.9
Comprehensive	301	114	37.9	219	72	32.9	520	186	35.8
Liberal Arts I	2	1	50.0	129	16	12.4	131	17	13.0
Other-Four-Year	22	9	40.9	331	105	31.7	353	114	32.3
Two-Year	750	296	39.5	103	36	35.0	853	332	38.9
Total	1,203	442	36.7	842	240	28.2	2,045	682	33.3

Source: Computations by authors based on HEGIS/IPEDS data for 1978–79, 1983–84, 1985–86, and 1987–88.

[a]The lowest annual rate of enrollment growth 1978–79 to 1987–88 among the fastest-growing one-third of institutions is 1.8 percent.

Table 11.10   Distribution of Institutions with Fastest-Declining Enrollments[a] (percentage among lowest third enrollment growth, 1978–79 to 1987–88)

Carnegie Classification	Public			Private			Total		
	Sample Size	No. Declining	% Declining	Sample Size	No. Declining	% Declining	Sample Size	No. Declining	% Declining
Research	66	17	25.8	24	0	0.0	90	17	18.9
Doctoral	60	11	18.3	36	13	36.1	96	24	25.0
Comprehensive	301	79	26.1	219	71	32.4	520	150	28.8
Liberal Arts I	2	1	50.0	129	38	29.5	131	39	29.8
Other-Four-Year	22	6	27.3	331	154	46.5	353	160	45.3
Two-Year	750	243	32.4	103	49	47.6	853	292	34.2
Total	1,203	357	29.7	842	325	38.6	2,045	682	33.3

Source: Computations by authors based on HEGIS/IPEDS data for 1978–79, 1983–84, 1985–86, and 1987–88.

[a]The highest annual rate of enrollment growth 1978–79 to 1987–88 among the slowest-growing third of institutions is −0.1 percent. Of the 2,045 institutions in the sample, 747 experienced declining enrollments.

we look more closely at the effect of growth and decline on per-student expenditures and examine how per-student costs vary with the size of an institution. Finally, in Chapter 14, we investigate the link between the student/ faculty ratio and the cost per student in an effort to learn precisely what is driving up college costs. Our goal throughout is to see what we can learn about recent developments in the costs of higher education that might shed light on the different theories of why tuition has increased so rapidly.

12   Where Does the Money Go?

The rising costs of higher education fall into different categories of expenditures. The U.S. Department of Education survey of higher education, HEGIS/IPEDS, uses 11 categories to describe the different activities constituting the core of colleges and universities.[1] The main function is instruction, followed by plant operations and student services. By comparing the survey accounts for 1978–79 with those for 1987–88, we can learn how rapidly costs increased in the different categories. Did all the categories of expenditures increase faster than the general price level? Yes. Did instructional expenditures increase faster or slower than average? Slower. Was the rate of increase in the several categories the same for different kinds of institutions? No. Was the pattern of change the same for comprehensive universities as for liberal arts colleges, for publics as for privates? No, and no. This type of evidence will not allow us to conclude that the institutions are either highly competitive and efficient or noncompetitive and inefficient. But knowing where the funds go will make clear what functions have had priority among college presidents and their boards over the last decade and how the institutions adapted to a changing environment. We may then be able to draw inferences about how the institutions respond to changes in their environments.

12.1   Education and General Expenditure

Current (as opposed to capital) expenditures on the core functions of a college or university are called educational and general (E&G) expenditures.

---

1. HEGIS/IPEDS purports to classify expenditures by function rather than by type of input (e.g., cost of goods sold, salaries, utilities, etc.). To complicate matters, it actually does some of both, aggregating all interest expenditures into a single category and all utility expenditures into a single category but allocating payroll and supplies across several categories on the basis of their purpose. The result is considerable discretion in the classification of expenditures by respondents.

They cover teaching, research, and public service. Four categories of expenditures beyond the E&G core complete the total annual spending by colleges and universities.

First, most capital expenditures are treated separately from E&G. Indeed, because few colleges or universities charge annual depreciation to their current accounts, annual E&G expenditures reflect little in the way of capital costs, either initial investment or the annual flow of services from buildings and equipment. In this sense, the annual flow of expenditures we analyze here understates costs and will understate costs relatively more at more capital intensive institutions. During a period of relatively stable aggregate enrollments, such as the 1980s, depreciation charges might be expected to remain fairly stable; thus, their exclusion may not undermine cost comparisons over time. On the other hand, some institutions invested substantial resources in repair and maintenance of facilities during the 1980s, while others have not (Rush and Johnson 1989).[2] Whether major repair expenditures show up in annual plant operations costs or are treated as capital costs is unknown to us and likely varies by institution.

Second, auxiliary enterprises, including housing, food service, bookstores, and intercollegiate athletics, are generally excluded from E&G expenditures.[3] Auxiliary enterprise expenditures are roughly 10 percent of current fund expenditures (which include all expenditures except capital investments). But auxiliary enterprises are undergoing substantial change on many campuses, as food services and bookstores, in particular, are increasingly contracted out to private for-profit companies.[4] In such cases, the college or university usually negotiates the return of a percentage of gross revenue for the use of its facilities and access to its student customers. Such an arrangement, of course, removes considerable gross expenditures and revenues from the books of colleges and universities, in the same way that notebook paper purchased at a private stationery store or a personal computer purchased through an electronics dealer never appears as part of college and university expenditures. To the

---

We rely on the first principle of accounting—consistency is more important than accuracy—to give us confidence that apparent changes in expenditures in certain categories over times are real changes rather than reflections of arbitrary shifts in the classification of expenditures.

2. A 1988 survey of physical facilities on American college campuses reported $60 billion of deferred maintenance, $20.5 billion of which was classified as in "urgent" need of repair (Rush and Johnson 1989). This amounts to more than $1,500 for every enrolled student. The problem is worst at Research and Doctoral institutions (see also Kaiser 1989). The run-down campuses of the 1970s and 1980s will require substantial attention in the coming decades, making the issue of how to account for capital improvements a more important matter in the future.

3. One of 12 institutions in a survey we use subsequently to disaggregate E&G expenditures includes intercollegiate athletics in its E&G accounts.

4. In a 1990 survey of 31 mostly Research and Doctoral universities, respondents reported that 67 percent of institutionally provided meals on their campuses were produced by a private for-profit contractor and that 17 percent of on-campus textbook sales were made by a private contractor leasing the bookstore (see Siegfried, Getz, and Dunn 1991, table 2). For a detailed discussion of the issues, see Bookman (1989).

extent that expenditures on food and housing would be incurred whether or not an individual is enrolled in college, their exclusion from the accounts may be a good thing, as they do not represent an opportunity cost. Some auxiliary services, however, such as textbook sales, clearly represent resources consumed *because* the consumers are enrolled in college. For the present, the situation is discomforting as the proportion of student expenditures for services provided by auxiliaries appearing in the financial records of colleges and universities is unknown.[5]

Third, hospitals, whether integral to the teaching missions of medical schools, as at Duke, or simply community service facilities, as at the University of the South, are excluded from E&G expenditures, being a special case of an auxiliary service. Hospitals, in aggregate, account for almost 10 percent of total current fund expenditures. Of course, a much greater share of expenditures goes to hospitals at the relatively few institutions with medical centers. Again, if university hospitals simply substitute for non-university hospital services, the expenditures are not additions attributable to higher education, and they do not reflect resources that would be conserved if colleges and universities did not exist. Surely, only a minuscule fraction of the patients at university hospitals are students who got sick or were injured because they were studying!

Finally, other independent operations, primarily federally funded research and development centers, are excluded from E&G expenditures. This category is very small compared to E&G.

E&G expenditure categories define a set of functions that are reasonably common and central to the educational missions of most colleges and universities. E&G represents roughly 80 percent of total current fund spending by colleges and universities (Anderson, Carter, and Malizio, 1989, table 99, p. 155) and accounts for most of the added expenditures that are incurred because students are enrolled in a college or university.

12.2 Adjusted Educational and General Expenditures

The 11 functional categories of E&G used by HEGIS/IPEDS encompass broad areas of the educational enterprise. Table 12.1 reports expenditures separately in eight of these categories as the share of adjusted educational and general (AE&G) expenditure. One E&G category, libraries, is included in a broader category, academic support. Two E&G categories, sponsored research and restricted scholarships, are excluded from AE&G and are not reported here. Table 12.2 reports the average expenditure per student in each functional category for 1978–79 and 1987–88 for all institutions combined and for four-year and Two-Year colleges separately.

5. To the extent that an institution leases access to it students and space on its campus to private suppliers of auxiliary services, some gross revenues (i.e., the lease payments) continue to show up in the accounting records.

Table 12.1   Distribution of Adjusted Educational and General (AE&G) Expenditures, 1978–79 and 1987–88

Carnegie Classification	Instruction and Self-Supported Research	Public Service[a]	Academic Support[b]	Student Services[c]	Institutional Support[d]	Plant Operations	Internal Scholarships[e]	Mandatory Transfers[f]	Total AE&G[g]
All institutions (N = 2,045):									
1978–79	.491	.046	.102	.067	.127	.120	.026	.021	1.000
1987–88	.476	.046	.105	.073	.134	.108	.040	.018	1.000
Change	–.015	.000	+.003	+.006	+.007	–.012	+.014	–.003	.000
Four-year institutions (N = 1,192):									
1978–79	.486	.052	.106	.063	.122	.121	.030	.020	1.000
1987–88	.471	.051	.109	.067	.129	.107	.046	.019	1.000
Change	–.015	–.001	+.003	+.004	+.007	–.014	+.016	–.001	.000
Two-Year institutions (N = 853):									
1978–79	.515	.017	.079	.086	.151	.117	.005	.029	1.000
1987–88	.498	.023	.086	.103	.159	.117	.007	.009	1.000
Change	–.017	+.006	+.007	+.017	+.008	.000	+.002	–.020	.000

Source: Computations by authors based on HEGIS/IPEDS data.

[a]Includes extension services.

[b]Computers, libraries, and deans.

[c] Admissions, registrars, counseling, student health, and recreation.

[d]Administration, accounting, security, alumni, and development.

[e]Scholarships from internal funds.

[f]Debt service.

[g]Total E&G expenditures under control of chief executive officer.

Table 12.2 Adjusted Educational and General (AE&G) Expenditures per Full-Time-Equivalent Student in Constant 1987–88 Dollars,[a] 1978–79 and 1987–88

Carnegie Classification	Instruction and Self-Supported Research	Public Service[b]	Academic Support[c]	Student Services[d]	Institutional Support[e]	Plant Operations	Internal Scholarships[f]	Mandatory Transfers[g]	Total AE&G[h]
All institutions (N = 2,045):									
1978–79	3,126	294	647	427	809	767	164	136	6,370
1987–88	3,863	376	855	594	1,088	881	323	142	8,122
Change	+737	+82	+208	+167	+279	+114	+159	+6	+1,752
Share of increase	42.1	4.7	11.9	9.5	15.9	6.5	9.1	.3	100.0
Share of AE&G expenditures, 1987–88	47.6	4.6	10.5	7.3	13.4	10.8	4.0	1.8	100.0
Four-year institutions (N = 1,192):									
1978–79	3,539	379	772	460	890	881	217	144	7,282
1987–88	4,432	478	1,025	633	1,215	1,006	432	180	9,401
Change	+893	+99	+253	+173	+325	+125	+215	+36	+2,119
Share of increase	42.1	4.7	11.9	8.2	15.3	5.9	10.1	1.7	100.0
Share of AE&G expenditures, 1987–88	47.1	5.1	10.9	6.7	12.9	10.7	4.6	1.9	100.0
Two-year institutions (N = 853):									
1978–79	2,026	68	312	340	593	462	21	114	3,936
1987–88	2,362	108	407	489	753	554	35	41	4,749
Change	+336	+40	+95	+149	+160	+92	+14	−73	+813
Share of increase	41.3	4.9	11.7	18.4	19.7	11.3	1.7	−9.0	100.0
Share of AE&G expenditures, 1987–88	49.8	2.3	8.6	10.3	15.9	11.7	.7	.9	100.0

Source: Computations by authors based on HEGIS/IPEDS data.

[a] Current dollars are converted to constant dollars with the GNP implicit price deflator in this and all subsequent tables.

[b] Includes extension service.

[c] Computers, libraries, and deans.

[d] Admissions, registrars, counseling, student health, and recreation.

[e] Administration, accounting, security, alumni, and development.

[f] Scholarships from internal funds.

[g] Debt service.

[h] Total AE&G expenditures under control of chief executive officer.

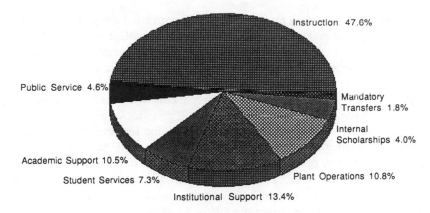

Figure 12.1   Allocation of AE&G Expenditures, 1987–88.
Source: Table 12.1.

The AE&G figures exclude externally funded research (e.g., National Science Foundation grants) and restricted (and mostly externally funded) scholarships (e.g., Pell grants). We exclude these two categories from our base total because each category contains largely earmarked funds, that is, funds not subject to the discretion of the institution's management. Our primary concern in this part of the volume is with resource allocation decisions made by colleges and universities, and these two categories are largely beyond that purview.

Libraries are reported separately in HEGIS/IPEDS but are also included with academic support expenditures. We do not report them separately. Therefore, there are actually eight categories across which AE&G expenditure patterns can vary in this study. These are described in detail below. A recent study of most of these categories (Cambridge Associates 1990) for 12 private research universities improves our understanding of what constitutes each. Figure 12.1 depicts the allocation of AE&G among the eight categories in 1987–88.

12.2.1   Instruction

Instruction accounts for nearly half of AE&G expenditures (see Table 12.1). Instruction includes salaries and fringe benefits for faculty and support staff, both full-time and part-time, and materials and supplies for general academic instruction, including faculty travel, communications, and personal computers. Expenditures for all types of instruction (occupational and vocational, community education, adult basic education, remedial, and tutorial) are included. This category also includes expenditures for public services that are not separately budgeted and all "departmental research," which is the cost of research not supported externally.[6] This departmental research is the part-time research that many faculty do routinely as part of their work. Much of it is an essential ingredient of teaching excellence. Thus, a great deal of research activity of colleges and universities, as well as some public service expenditures, is lumped together with direct instructional expenditures in this category. The relative importance of research in the instruction expenditures category will undoubtedly vary by type, control, and size of institution. James (1978) used a faculty questionnaire to estimate the importance of teaching within the instructional budget at research universities. She found it was slightly less than 50 percent in the mid-1970s and had declined from about 70 percent in the early 1960s.[7] Continued change in this fraction complicates the interpretation of cost changes. Although real instructional expenditures per student continued to rise during the 1980s, instruction's share of AE&G expenditures declined by about 1.5 percentage points, as shown in table 12.1. Teaching's share of instruction may have also declined over the period if the trend detected by James has not been reversed.

12.2.2   Public Service

Public service accounts for about 5 percent of AE&G in four-year institutions and about 2 percent in Two-Year colleges. It accounts for about 11 percent of AE&G at public Research universities and about 5 percent at public Doctoral universities but no more than 3 percent in any category of private institutions or in the remaining categories of public colleges and universities. Public service includes funds expended for activities established primarily to provide noninstructional services beneficial to groups external to the institution. Agricultural experimentation stations and extension services are an obvious example. At a sample of seven public Research universities that we surveyed by telephone, agricultural experimentation and extension services accounted for 62 percent of the public service category; continuing education was the second most important type of public service expenditure at these institutions, accounting for 5 percent of the category.[8] Some medical center expenditures may account for a significant portion of public service expenditures (e.g., unreimbursed hospital services or overhead expenses for public

---

6. Over time, improvements in college and university accounting systems will probably reduce instruction costs because instruction is the category used to collect residual expenditures—those expenditures that are not specifically identified and assigned to their most appropriate account. The importance of this bias in the trends of category shares depends on the rate at which accounting systems in higher education are refined.

7. If half the instruction budget is devoted to university-supported research, America's 98 Research universities alone (excluding the many Doctoral, Comprehensive, and Liberal Arts I institutions that engage actively in research) spent $5.9 billion on research in 1987–88. This is over 10 percent of the total federal expenditure on research and development (see Chapter 11, n. 24).

8. The public Research universities we queried about the composition of their 1987–88 public service expenditures were the Universities of Arkansas, Florida, Georgia, Kentucky, and North Carolina, Clemson University, and Michigan State University.

medical clinics). Public policy institutes, conference programs, science fairs, and cultural programs are also usually included in this category. Public service expenditures at Two-Year colleges seem to be primarily for cooperative (with government) job retraining programs under the Job Training Partnership Act.[9] Public service expenditures grew at the same rate as aggregate AE&G from 1978–79 to 1987–88.

12.2.3 Academic Support

Academic support accounts for about 10 percent of AE&G. Academic support includes expenditures for libraries, museums, galleries, audiovisual services, academic computing support, academic administration, personnel development, and course and curriculum development. For the 12 private research universities in the Cambridge Associates study, 93 percent of academic support is allocated to libraries (40 percent),[10] academic computing (10 percent), and administration (43 percent). Academic support expenditures grew at the same rate as aggregate AE&G from 1978–79 to 1987–88.

12.2.4 Student Services

Student services account for about 7 percent of AE&G at four-year institutions and slightly over 10 percent at Two-Year colleges. Student services include expenditures for admissions, registrar activities, and activities whose primary purpose is to contribute to students' emotional and physical well-being and to their intellectual, cultural, and social development outside the context of the formal instructional program. It includes career guidance and placement, counseling, financial aid administration, and student health services. It also includes the administrative allowance for Pell grants. For the 12 institutions in the Cambridge Associates study, this category consists primarily of admissions (22 percent), vice president for campus life (13 percent), student health services (9 percent), registrar (9 percent), student activities (8 percent), financial aid administration (8 percent), intramural sports (4 percent), counseling (3 percent), and student union (3 percent). The remaining 20 percent of student services goes to such diverse activities as band, college chaplain, fraternity/sorority assistance, and learning support services. Student services expenditures are growing faster than other expenditures at all types of institutions, but they are particularly high and increasing rapidly at private liberal arts colleges.

9. The public Two-Year colleges we queried about the composition of their 1987–88 public service expenditures were Jackson State and Columbia State Community Colleges.

10. Reliable HEGIS/IPEDS data on libraries are available for 1978–79. The percentage of academic support accounted for libraries in Research, Doctoral, Comprehensive, Liberal Arts I, Other-Four-Year, and Two-Year colleges is 41, 48, 46, 59, 52, and 43, respectively. For the 12 private research universities in the Cambridge Associates study, 54 percent of library expenditures was for salaries, and 33 percent was for the acquisition of books and serials.

12.2.5 Institutional Support

Institutional support accounts for about 13 percent of AE&G, but much more in Two-Year colleges and four-year liberal arts colleges (where it is close to 20 percent), and noticeably less in Research universities (where it is about 10 percent). Institutional support includes expenditures for general administrative services, executive direction and planning, legal and fiscal operations, accounting, public relations, alumni and development, and, often, police and security. For the 12 private research universities in the Cambridge Associates study, the majority of institutional support was for administration and finance: the office of the president and provost accounted for 13 percent, and other administrative and finance offices accounted for 40 percent (personnel, legal affairs, affirmative action, vice president finance, controller, budget, internal audit, purchasing, treasurer). The offices of governmental relations, public relations, and alumni and development averaged 25 percent of the total. The remaining important components of institutional support include administrative computing (6 percent), academic support other than the provost (e.g., dean of graduate school, facilities planning, emeriti center, sponsored research administration; 6 percent), police and security (3 percent), and other miscellaneous, which includes such items as telecommunications, mail service, bus service, printing, risk management, and child-care center (6 percent). The share of expenditures going to institutional support is growing at all types of institutions, but it is rising most rapidly at Doctoral and Comprehensive universities.

12.2.6 Operation and Maintenance of Plant

Plant operations expenditures account for about 11 percent of AE&G. Plant operations includes expenditures for operations established to provide service and maintenance related to grounds and facilities. It includes utilities, fire protection, housekeeping, grounds maintenance, carpentry, electrical, plumbing, heating and ventilating repair, and property insurance premiums. Plant and grounds maintenance is the largest component of plant operations, accounting for 38 percent in the Cambridge Associates study. Utilities is the next largest component at 34 percent, followed by housekeeping and janitorial expenses (11 percent), plant administration (5 percent), and fire, security, and safety (4 percent). Thus, about half of plant operations costs are devoted to the purchase of services in local labor markets, while about one-third goes to purchase energy.[11] Campus security expenditures are often included in plant operations if they are not part of institutional support. Plant operations expenditures increased more slowly than overall AE&G expenditures at all types

---

11. The Association of Physical Plant Administrators periodically collects data from member institutions about their plant operations expenditures. Based on their sample of 520 institutions for 1987–88, we can subdivide the plant operations category and report the percentage distribution of expenses across subcategories by Carnegie classification:

of institutions during the 1980s, at least in part as a result of only modest increases in the cost of utilities over the period.

12.2.7 Unrestricted Scholarships

Unrestricted scholarships now account for about 4 percent of AE&G. Unrestricted scholarships include grants and stipends paid to individuals enrolled in formal course work and tuition and fee remissions. Unrestricted scholarships are scholarships for which no stipulation has been made by an external agency or donor as to the disposition of funds; these are funds that are allocated to scholarships at the discretion of the institution. Scholarship aid is, in effect, a price discount offered to selected students, often those who could not otherwise afford the college they attend or those with unusual academic or athletic talent. It can be argued that scholarship aid is not an expenditure but rather a reduction in revenues. On the other hand, concern about the level of tuition has largely focused on tuition before taking account of scholarship grants, on the "sticker price." The many students receiving no scholarship assistance view the list price tuition as the relevant base. To the extent that their tuition rises to produce revenue to fund scholarships, these students and their families would view unrestricted scholarships as a "cost." This cost may provide nonscholarship students with a richer peer environment and, thus, augment their college experience. In such a context, it makes sense to view scholarships as an expenditure. Furthermore, the scholarship budget competes, to a degree, with other expenditure categories for resources. Therefore, we elected to treat it as an expenditure category in spite of its fundamental ambiguous nature. Unrestricted scholarships, although a relatively small proportion of total AE&G, is the single fastest-growing category of expenditures in higher education. Growth has been fastest at Liberal Arts I and Other-Four-Year colleges.

12.2.8 Mandatory Transfers

The mandatory transfers category includes expenditures that must be made in order to fulfill binding legal obligations. It is primarily interest expense on debt.

Carnegie Classification	Sample Size	Administration & Engineering	Building Maintenance	Custodial	Grounds Maintenance	Utilities
Research	87	7.2	23.4	20.6	5.5	43.3
Doctoral	35	6.9	22.1	25.3	6.0	39.6
Comprehensive	69	7.8	21.8	25.6	7.3	37.5
Liberal Arts[a]	61	9.8	26.8	24.4	8.6	30.4
Two-Year	158	12.9	25.7	22.9	7.2	31.2
Totals	410[b]	10.0	24.5	23.1	6.9	35.5

Source: Association of Physical Plant Administrators (1989, table 3).
[a]Liberal Arts = Liberal Arts I plus Liberal Arts II.
[b]Specialized and professional institutions are not reported.

12.3   Other Current Account Expenditures

Three categories of E&G expenditures in HEGIS/IPEDS are excluded from our AE&G expenditures. They are sponsored research, restricted scholarships, and libraries. Library expenditures are included in academic support, described above.

12.3.1   Sponsored Research

Externally supported research is very important at Research universities, modestly significant at Doctoral institutions, and relatively insignificant at other types of colleges and universities. Expenditures for sponsored research are equal to about 30 percent of AE&G at Research universities,[12] although they are not part of AE&G as we have figured it. Sponsored research includes expenditures for research commissioned by an agency either external to the institution or separately budgeted by an organizational unit within the institution. It is primarily research supported by noninstitutional funds. Externally funded research has been growing faster than AE&G expenditures at Research universities, about kept pace at Doctoral institutions, and is lagging behind the growth in overall AE&G in all other types of institutions. The result is an increase in the concentration of sponsored research at Research institutions.

12.3.2   Restricted Scholarships

Restricted scholarships account for 6.6 percent of AE&G.[13] Restricted scholarships include grants paid to individuals enrolled in formal course work where the source of funds is an external agency or donor who has stipulated the precise use of the funds. The institution has no discretion in their use. Federal Pell grants are the largest component of restricted scholarships. Need-based and merit-based scholarships are commingled in this account.

Both externally sponsored research and restricted scholarships are, in a sense, "flow-through" expenditures. They are administered by colleges and universities but funded externally. In both cases, the income is expected to match the expenditures for such purposes, and such funds may not be diverted to alternative uses. This approach, in the case of externally funded research, presumes that indirect costs realistically represent actual (long-run incremental) costs incurred by the institution in the performance of sponsored research (Massy 1990).[14] In the case of restricted scholarships, this approach presumes

12. At Doctoral, Comprehensive, Liberal Arts I, Other-Four-Year, and Two-Year colleges in 1987–88, sponsored research accounted for 9.9, 2.4, 1.4, 0.6, and 0.0 percent of AE&G respectively.

13. Restricted scholarships as a percentage of AE&G expenditures varied by Carnegie group as follows: Research 5.6, Doctoral 5.9, Comprehensive 8.0, Liberal Arts I 7.9,Other-Four-Year 13.9, and Two-Year Colleges, 8.2. The value of need-based scholarship aid depends, in part, on the tuition level of the institution a student attends. Thus, relatively high-priced colleges and universities with need-blind admissions will enroll students who are eligible for large restricted scholarships, especially federal Pell grants.

14. Considerable controversy exists about whether the indirect costs of sponsored research

that the costs of administering the scholarships are covered separately by the external agency, which is the way that Pell grants are organized if the administrative allowance for Pell grants accurately represents the added cost of handling them. It also presumes that an institution's expenditures are not affected, in general, by financial aid programs.[15]

For some purposes, it is also desirable to exclude *unrestricted* scholarships from E&G expenses. Unrestricted scholarships are a return of tuition money to students, albeit after a redistribution. In order to gauge the rise in the real cost of higher education accurately, we periodically report on AE&G expenditures *less* unrestricted scholarships, which is a rough measure of the value of the resources consumed directly in the production of higher education services. It would be roughly equivalent to long-run opportunity costs if factors of production were all hired in competitive markets (Hoenack 1990)[16] and capital costs were included.

12.4   Cost Trends among Functional Categories

Most of the analysis that follows compares expenditures for separate expenditure categories to AE&G expenditures. The adjusted figure excludes sponsored research and restricted scholarships. Library expenditures are included among academic support expenditures. This procedure should permit us to identify changes in the pattern of expenditures under the direct control of the management of higher education. But, as a result of this convention, direct comparisons of expenditure shares from our analysis to similar prior studies (e.g., Bowen 1980; Snyder 1988; Hauptman 1990a) are not possible.

A word of caution about HEGIS/IPEDS data is necessary. Changes in accounting practices or teaching methods over time can cause some changes in expenditure patterns to be little more than a mirage. For example, if throughout the 1980s institutions of higher education systematically began to develop separate accounts for public service as their accounting systems matured,

match the expenditures incurred as a result of the research projects. Much of the debate centers on what expenditures would be incurred by the college or university in the absence of sponsored research. The answer undoubtedly varies with the intensity of the institution's sponsored research program. Although a single externally funded grant might be accommodated with otherwise existing facilities at a small college, massive sponsored research programs undoubtedly call for additions to an institution's infrastructure.

15. Some would argue, e.g., that need-based aid formulas, which establish need on the basis of tuition less ability to pay, reduce the sensitivity of higher education management to increased cost because the costs can be recovered through tuition hikes that do not affect the amount *all* students or their families must pay.

16. Expenditures represent opportunity costs only if resources are acquired at competitive prices, i.e., at prices that reflect their opportunity cost accurately. Although some important inputs to college and university education seem to be sold in fairly competitive markets (e.g., faculty, construction work, housekeeping and groundskeeping services, personal computers, law enforcement, and fund-raising services), the extent of competition in other input markets is less clear (e.g., mainframe computers, library books and serials, electricity, and communication services).

much of the public service that was reported in the instruction category in 1978–79 would have moved to a separate public service category by 1987–88. Not only will the rise in reported public service expenditures therefore be misleading, but the decline in instruction will also not reflect any real change in the use of resources.

As colleges and universities shift their emphasis from mainframe academic computers to personal computers, expenditure patterns will also change. Mainframe computers are included in academic services, while most personal computers are included in the instruction account. It is possible that category shares may shift while in reality computing retains a stable share of AE&G expenditures.

Looking at the period 1978–79 to 1987–88 as a whole, the most obvious trend in expenditure patterns is the declining importance of the core areas of a college or university—instruction, academic support, and plant operations. The share of AE&G accounted for by these three areas combined declined from 71.3 to 68.9 percent over the period, continuing a trend evident from at least 1967–68 (Cheit 1971, table 2, pp. 32–33). Though not dramatic, this decline is certainly meaningful if the trend should continue.

Where has this money gone? The most rapid increase has been in internal (unrestricted) scholarships. Also increasing at a noticeable rate over the period is the share of expenditures devoted to student services (about 9 percent) and institutional support (about 6 percent).

The decline in the share of expenditures going to the core areas is less in Two-Year institutions than in four-year institutions, primarily because the plant operations expenditures of Two-Year institutions have kept pace with total expenditures. Two-Year institutions do not spend much on internally funded scholarships, nor has this category increased nearly as rapidly as it has in four-year institutions. Expenditures devoted to student services, on the other hand, have increased significantly as a share of the total over the decade at Two-Year institutions, rising from 8.6 to 10.3 percent.

The effect of excluding sponsored research and external scholarships from E&G expenses can be assessed. Because both categories increased relative to total AE&G for both four-year and Two-Year institutions, their inclusion in AE&G would cause the share of each of the other categories either to increase less or to decline more over the period. With sponsored research and external scholarships in the picture, the core areas would have lost an even greater share of expenditures.

Responsibility for the increase in the cost of higher education, however, may be hidden by changes in expenditure shares because a great deal of the increase in costs may arise from a large expenditure category that is increasing at slightly less than the rate of increase in total AE&G costs. Furthermore, the real value of almost *all* expenditure categories increased over the period 1978–79 to 1987–88.

12.5 Expenditures per Student

Expenditures per student for each cost category will help identify responsibility for the real cost increases over the decade. Our expenditures are in 1987–88 dollars, deflated by the gross national product (GNP) implicit price deflator (U.S. Council of Economic Advisers 1990, 298), a broad representation of input prices. We use the GNP implicit price deflator rather than either the consumer price index (CPI) or the higher education price index (HEPI) (Research Associates of Washington 1989) because the GNP deflator provides a standard economywide production cost index against which to evaluate changes in the costs of higher education. The CPI is more appropriately used to evaluate tuition inflation because it reflects the prices of goods and services that students and their families might have purchased instead of a college education. Using the HEPI to deflate expenditures could overstate or understate the extent to which inflationary price increases for inputs have put higher education cost inflation beyond the control of colleges and universities. The prices of certain inputs with large weights in the HEPI (e.g., faculty salaries)[17] are determined, in part, by the behavior of colleges and universities themselves. If they compete more vigorously for faculty, attempting to "raid" rivals, the HEPI will rise. Thus, the HEPI does not represent the uncontrollable increase in the cost of higher education because, to some degree, colleges and universities can influence its level.

Our measure of full-time-equivalent students is the sum of full-time students and one-third the number of part-time students. We combine baccalaureate, master's, Ph.D., and postbaccalaureate professional degree students as if each were equally costly. A more sophisticated analysis would sort out the effects of enrollment mix on college costs. Degree-mix data for our sample are available, but degree mix does not reflect enrollment mix. Some departments, such as English, history, and mathematics, account for a substantially higher fraction of enrollments than degrees. Furthermore, costs vary by level of instruction in undergraduate education (Brinkman 1989; Berg and Hoenack 1987) as well as between undergraduate and graduate students. Thus, it would be fairly complicated to construct a more accurate measure of full-time-equivalent enrollment. We adopted the simpler approach, at the risk of some inaccuracy. The important differences in cost per student between undergraduate and graduate education are controlled, in part, by our separation of insti-

---

17. Faculty salaries constituted 33.3 percent of the E&G expenditures of colleges and universities in 1983. The demand for certain other professional occupations is also dominated by colleges and universities, e.g., graduate assistants, extension and public service personnel, and college and university administrators. These professionals accounted for an additional 13.0 percent of 1983 E&G. Thus almost half the HEPI consists of salaries and wages that are determined in markets dominated by colleges and universities. These salaries and wages are unlikely to be determined independently of the behavior of the institutions (see Research Associates of Washington 1989, pp. 11–12 and table 10).

tutions by Carnegie classification. Table 12.2 above reports expenditures per student for all institutions and separately for four-year and Two-Year colleges.

For the 2,045 institutions in our sample, AE&G expenditures increased by $1,752 (1987–88 dollars) per student over the period 1978–79 to 1988–89. This is a 27.5 percent increase in real expenditures per student, or 2.7 percent per year over and above the general rate of price increase of the GNP. Removing all scholarships from AE&G expenditures reduces the increase to $1,593 per student, or 2.5 percent per year over and above the general rate of price increase of gross national product (GNP).

The GNP implicit price deflator increased at an average annual rate of 5.2 percent during our period of analysis. The HEPI increased at an average annual rate of 7.2 percent over approximately the same period (Research Associates of Washington 1989). Thus, about 2 percentage points of the 2.7 percent per year increase in real expenditures per student can be accounted for by the especially high inflation in inputs used intensively by colleges and universities. From this perspective, the real cost increase over the period is more modest, exceeding the HEPI by only 0.7 percent annually. Over 70 percent of the real rate of increase in higher education expenditures per student can be attributed to the especially high price increases experienced by inputs used heavily in higher education. This, however, does not diminish the importance of the cost inflation because those paying additional revenues to cover the elevated costs may take little comfort in knowing that the source of their burden is higher prices for inputs rather than additional input purchases. Furthermore, at least some of the input cost inflation may have been caused by the behavior of colleges and universities themselves.

The increase of $1,752 per student over the period is decomposed in row 4 of Table 12.2. There we report the share of the $1,752 accounted for by increases in the real cost per student for each expenditure category. Row 5 repeats the 1987–88 expenditure shares of each function in order to facilitate interpretation of the decomposed increase. Categories contributing more than their expenditure share to the increase have experienced growth in real expenditure per student exceeding the rate of increase of total expenditures. Those contributing less than their expenditure share grew slower than overall AE&G.

Instructional expenditures rose at a rate of 2.4 percent annually in excess of the GNP implicit price deflator for all colleges and universities in our sample. Although this is a hefty rate of increase, it is not unprecedented. In a study of the tuition and costs of three private research universities since the beginning of the century, Bowen (1968) found that, during normal peacetime periods, instructional costs per student increased at about 6 percent above the GNP deflator. From 1949 through 1966, the difference was slightly more than 5 percent. In contrast, instructional costs for Research universities increased only 2.6 percent per year faster than the GNP deflator over the period 1978–79 to 1988–89.

Although instruction and self-supported research expenditures account for the largest share of increased expenditures per student, 42.1 percent, these expenditures have not been growing as rapidly as total AE&G. Thus, real expenditures on some other college and university functions must have increased more rapidly over the period. Those categories with faster increases are institutional support (general administration), internal scholarships, student services, and, to a lesser degree, academic support. In sum, the evidence points to college-supported financial aid, general administrative expenses, and student services as the fastest-growing cost components. Instruction, however, still deserves considerable attention because it accounts for over 40 percent of the increase in costs.

AE&G expenditures rose at an annual clip of 2.9 percent at four-year institutions and 2.1 percent at Two-Year colleges. The pattern, as well as the rate, of cost increases also differs between four-year and Two-Year institutions, primarily because of a large decline in interest expenses over the period for Two-Year colleges. The increase in institutional support and student services was larger in Two-Year colleges than at four-year schools. Historically, Two-Year colleges allocated little unrestricted money to scholarships, and that policy did not change during the 1980s.

12.6 Cost Trends by Carnegie Classification

We expect the pattern of expenditures by function to vary depending on the institution's mission. The Carnegie classifications usefully distinguish institutions with different missions. Within the Carnegie classifications, however, there is at least one very important difference in the output mix of institutions, namely, the presence or absence of an on-campus medical school. Research universities can be used to illustrate the problem.

Expenditure shares and expenditures per student for each functional category are reported in Table 12.3 for Research universities with medical schools and those without, looking separately at public and private institutions. Institutions with medical schools exhibit quite different patterns than those without. The public universities with medical schools spend 34 percent more per student than their public counterparts without medical schools. The difference in total AE&G expenditures per student for private research universities with and without a medical school parallels that for the public institutions, but the composition of the cost elevation differs. For both public and private institutions, instructional costs per student are 44 percent higher at universities with medical schools. In Chapter 14, we show that these higher instructional costs at universities with medical schools are caused by greater expenditures on instructional resources other than full-time faculty salaries (e.g., fringe benefits, support staff, and equipment), rather than by differences in average faculty salaries or student/faculty ratios. For categories other than instruction, the pattern of cost differences at public universities diverges from the pattern

Table 12.3   Distribution of Adjusted Educational and General (AE&G) Expenditures and AE&G Expenditures per Full-Time-Equivalent (FTE) Student, Research Universities by Medical School Status, 1987–88

Carnegie Classification	Instruction and Self-Supported Research	Public Service[a]	Academic Support[b]	Student Services[c]	Institutional Support[d]	Plant Operations	Internal Scholarships[e]	Mandatory Transfers[f]	Total AE&G[g]
Public research universities:									
Distribution of AE&G:									
Without med school (N = 36)	.464	.112	.118	.054	.098	.112	.022	.021	1.000
With med school (N = 30)	.502	.088	.136	.044	.095	.098	.022	.014	1.000
AE&G expenditures per FTE student:									
Without med school (N = 36)	4,468	1,074	1,136	516	945	1,074	208	206	9,627
With med school (N = 30)	6,456	1,138	1,744	567	1,228	1,261	289	181	12,864
Private research universities:									
Distribution of AE&G:									
Without med school (N = 7)	.462	.008	.112	.066	.159	.115	.069	.010	1.000
With med school (N = 17)	.502	.026	.104	.041	.120	.099	.086	.022	1.000
AE&G expenditures per FTE student:									
Without med school (N = 7)	8,441	143	2,046	1,200	2,899	2,095	1,252	188	18,264
With med school (N = 17)	12,130	626	2,515	994	2,892	2,388	2,065	535	24,145

Source: Computations by authors based on HEGIS/IPEDS data.

[a]Includes extension services.

[b]Computers, libraries, and deans.

[c]Admissions, registrars, counseling, student health, and recreation.

[d]Administration, accounting, security, alumni, and development.

[e]Scholarships from internal funds.

[f]Debt service.

[g]Total E&G expenditures under control of chief executive officers.

at privates. The presence of a medical school seems to elevate expenditures for academic support, student services, and institutional support more at public than at private Research universities. Indeed, expenditures per student for student services and general administration are lower at those private Research universities with medical schools than at those without. In contrast, public service commitments and self-supported scholarship expenditures leap upward as a private university acquires a medical school on campus but rise only moderately as one turns from public institutions without a medical school to those with one.

Because the institutions with medical schools have a substantially different pattern and level of costs, we exclude the 72 universities that include medical schools in their HEGIS/IPEDS statistics from most of the analysis in this chapter. Universities with medical schools are examined again in parts of Chapters 13 and 14. Note, however, that some universities with medical schools report figures for the medical campuses separately (e.g., Cornell, Texas, Tennessee, and Penn State). Thus, their main campus figures may be compared fairly with other campuses that do not have medical schools.

Expenditure shares can be expected to vary depending on the emphasis that various institutions place on different goals. We should expect public institutions to accept a relatively greater public service responsibility, for example, and Research and Doctorate-Granting institutions to place greater emphasis on research and graduate education. The implications of different missions for expenditures on the various functions of a college or university, however, are not obvious. What effect, if any, does an emphasis on research have on the share of expenditures committed to general administration (i.e., institutional support)? How does the relative importance of student services differ between liberal arts colleges that enroll primarily full-time undergraduate students and either Research universities, which have a much larger proportion of graduate and professional students, or Two-Year colleges, which have a much larger number of part-time students?

Tables 12.4 and 12.5 help answer such questions by reporting expenditure shares and expenditures per student in 1978–79 and 1987–88 for institutions (without a medical school) by Carnegie classification. As disclosed in table 12.5, among the four-year institutions, the rate of increase in expenditures per student is highest at Liberal Arts I institutions (4.7 percent annually) and lowest at Comprehensives (2.4 percent annually). At Research, Doctoral, and Other-Four-Year institutions, AE&G grew at annual rates of 2.8, 2.6, and 2.7 percent, respectively, over the period.

Instruction takes a larger relative share of expenditures at Two-Year colleges than at any of the types of four-year institutions, which is to be expected in view of their primary teaching mission. Research, Doctoral, and Comprehensive institutions allocate almost half of AE&G to instruction, although one must interpret these proportions carefully. If Research and Doctoral institutions allocate relatively more discretionary resources to research (James 1978), the actual fraction of expenditures that directly supports teaching will

Table 12.4   Distribution of Adjusted Educational and General (AE&G) Expenditures, Four-Year Institutions without On-Campus Medical Schools, 1978–79 and 1987–88, by Carnegie Classification

Carnegie Classification	Instruction and Self-Supported Research	Public Service[a]	Academic Support[b]	Student Services[c]	Institutional Support[d]	Plant Operations	Internal Scholarships[e]	Mandatory Transfers[f]	Total AE&G[g]
Research (N = 43):									
1978–79	.473	.107	.115	.049	.099	.117	.023	.016	1.000
1987–88	.464	.099	.117	.055	.106	.112	.027	.020	1.000
Change	−.009	−.008	+.002	+.006	+.007	−.005	+.004	+.004	.000
Doctoral (N = 81):									
1978–79	.500	.045	.101	.066	.118	.118	.031	.020	1.000
1987–88	.480	.040	.110	.069	.131	.106	.046	.018	1.000
Change	−.020	−.005	+.009	+.003	+.013	−.012	+.015	−.002	.000
Comprehensive (N = 513):									
1978–79	.489	.019	.095	.081	.134	.127	.026	.029	1.000
1987–88	.474	.024	.097	.087	.147	.112	.040	.020	1.000
Change	−.015	+.005	+.002	+.006	+.013	−.015	+.014	−.009	.000
Liberal Arts I (N = 131):									
1978–79	.407	.009	.088	.097	.175	.138	.064	.023	1.000
1987–88	.372	.008	.087	.108	.184	.113	.110	.019	1.000
Change	−.035	−.001	−.001	+.011	+.009	−.025	+.046	−.004	.000
Other-Four-Year (N = 352):									
1978–79	.382	.013	.078	.105	.203	.138	.058	.023	1.000
1987–88	.344	.011	.076	.116	.209	.119	.105	.020	1.000
Change	−.038	−.002	−.002	+.011	+.006	−.019	+.047	−.003	.000

Source: Computations by authors based on HEGIS/IPEDS data.

[a]Includes extension services.

[b]Computers, libraries, and deans.

[c]Admissions, registrars, counseling, student health, and recreation.

[d]Administration, accounting, security, alumni, and development.

[e]Scholarships from internal funds.

[f]Debt service.

[g]Total E&G expenditures under control of chief executive officer.

be less than the 46 or 48 percent reported for instruction by Research and Doctoral institutions, respectively. The HEGIS/IPEDS data cannot detect changes in faculty time allocation between teaching and research. Consequently, we cannot shed additional light on the validity of accusations (Sykes 1988) that faculty have reduced their commitment to teaching in order to devote greater attention to research in recent years.

What is most surprising about the instructional budget is the relatively low proportion of total expenditures allocated to it at liberal arts colleges. Instruction's share of expenditures has declined steadily at both Liberal Arts I and Other-Four-Year (Liberal Arts II) institutions. With an AE&G base excluding internally funded scholarships, instruction's share at Liberal Arts I colleges has declined from 53.5 percent in 1967–68 (Cheit 1971, table 2, pp. 32–33) to 43.5 percent in 1978–79 and only 41.8 percent in 1987–88.[18] Comparable fractions for Other-Four-Year colleges are 50.1 percent (1967–68), 40.6 percent (1978–79), and 38.4 percent (1987–88). This modest role for instructional expenditures occurs in spite of the fact that the liberal arts colleges have the lowest student/faculty ratio (and thus the most faculty per student), as we demonstrate in Chapter 14.

If liberal arts colleges spend a smaller share of their budgets on instruction and self-supported research, what accounts for a larger share of their budgets? The answer is not public service or deans, computers, and libraries, on which they also spend relatively little. It is, rather, student services, institutional support, and unrestricted scholarships. Liberal arts colleges, almost all of which are private, allocate relatively more to admissions, counseling, placement, student health and recreation, central administration, alumni relations and fund-raising, security, and scholarships than do other types of colleges and universities. These are student-oriented institutions, and it is apparent in their pattern of expenditures.[19]

Public service expenditures are significant only for Research and Doctoral institutions, the two Carnegie categories that include most large state universities. Academic support is relatively more important at the Research and Doctoral universities and least important in the less selective liberal arts colleges and Two-Year colleges. The more sophisticated library and academic computing requirements of large research-oriented universities apparently outweigh any scale economy advantages in these areas that such institutions may enjoy from their size.

18. The calculations for instruction divided by AE&G minus internal scholarships for 1978–79 and 1987–88 are based on data in Table 12.4.

19. In some cases, the demand for additional student services comes directly from students in the form of protests and requests by activist student groups. Relatively small but vocal groups can obtain favored benefits by pressuring administrators. They can raise the cost to administrators of failing to comply with the requests by threatening action (e.g., confrontation) that will occupy a great deal of administrators' time. At the same time, the costs of the added services are spread sufficiently over the entire student body that it is not in the interest of other students to oppose the added services. Little by little, services directed at various small constituencies accumulate and raise the overall cost of student services.

Table 12.5 Adjusted Educational and General (AE&G) Expenditures per Full-Time-Equivalent Student in Constant 1987–88 Dollars, Institutions without On-Campus Medical Schools, 1978–79 and 1987–88, by Carnegie Classification

Carnegie Classification	Instruction and Self-Supported Research	Public Service[a]	Academic Support[b]	Student Services[c]	Institutional Support[d]	Plant Operations	Internal Scholarships[e]	Mandatory Transfers[f]	Total AE&G[g]
Research (N = 43):									
1978–79	3,774	853	920	390	786	934	184	130	7,792
1987–88	4,739	1,011	1,198	563	1,078	1,144	279	205	10,216
Change	+965	+158	+278	+173	+292	+210	+95	+75	+2,244
Share of increase	43.0	7.0	12.4	7.7	13.0	9.4	4.2	3.3	100.0
Share of AE&G expenditures, 1987–88	46.4	9.9	11.7	5.5	10.6	11.2	2.7	2.0	100.0
Doctoral (N = 81):									
1978–79	3,148	280	638	417	744	741	198	128	6,294
1987–88	3,790	318	866	548	1,031	834	366	145	7,898
Change	+642	+38	+228	+131	+287	+93	+168	+17	+1,604
Share of increase	40.0	2.4	14.2	8.2	17.9	5.8	10.5	1.1	100.0
Share of AE&G expenditures, 1987–88	48.0	4.0	11.0	6.9	13.1	10.6	4.6	1.8	100.0
Comprehensive (N = 513):									
1978–79	2,647	103	515	436	724	688	140	156	5,409
1987–88	3,156	160	643	577	980	748	266	130	6,661
Change	+509	+57	+128	+141	+256	+60	+126	−26	+1,252
Share of increase	40.7	4.6	10.2	11.3	20.4	4.8	10.1	−2.1	100.0

Share of AE&G expenditures, 1987–88	47.4	2.4	9.7	8.7	14.7	11.2	4.0	2.0	100.0
Liberal Arts I (N = 131):									
1978–79	3,452	74	743	821	1,482	1,172	539	198	8,482
1987–88	4,787	98	1,114	1,386	2,365	1,447	1,421	240	12,858
Change	+1,335	+24	+371	+565	+883	+275	+882	+42	+4,376
Share of increase	30.5	.5	8.5	12.9	20.2	6.3	20.2	1.0	100.0
Share of AE&G expenditures, 1987–88	37.2	.8	8.7	10.8	18.4	11.3	11.0	1.9	100.0
Other-Four-Year (N = 352):									
1978–79	2,432	80	499	666	1,291	876	372	146	6,362
1987–88	2,781	89	611	940	1,690	965	848	162	8,086
Change	+349	+9	+112	+274	+399	+89	+476	+16	+1,724
Share of increase	20.2	.5	6.5	15.9	23.1	5.2	27.6	.9	100.0
Share of AE&G expenditures, 1987–88	34.4	1.1	7.6	11.6	20.9	11.9	10.5	2.0	100.0

Source: Computations by authors based on HEGIS/IPEDs.

[a]Includes extension services.
[b]Computers, libraries, and deans.
[c]Admissions, registrars, counseling, student health, and recreation.
[d]Administration, accounting, security, alumni, and development.
[e]Scholarships from internal funds.
[f]Debt service.
[g]Total E&G expenditures under control of chief executive officer.

Student services are least important at the large Research and Doctoral universities. Institutional support, or general administrative expenses, increase as a share of the total budget as one moves from Research and Doctoral institutions to Comprehensive universities, to liberal arts colleges, and on to Two-Year colleges. This is somewhat surprising in view of the typical stereotype of the administrative bureaucracy of large research universities and the image of a personalized, streamlined administration at liberal arts colleges, where there is often only one layer of management between faculty members and the president.

Unrestricted scholarships, a form of private redistribution of income among students, are most important at private liberal arts colleges and are growing rapidly. The rapid growth in scholarship aid from unrestricted funds at the Liberal Arts I colleges may be a response to the growing tuition difference between private and public colleges. It may be a matter of survival for many of the Other-Four-Year colleges. In many cases of need-based aid, it permits an institution to "cut prices" to students who otherwise might not enroll.

Changes in expenditure shares by Carnegie classification over the decade are reported in table 12.4. The reduced relative emphasis on the core activities of colleges and universities is most pronounced at private liberal arts colleges. Collectively, the share of expenditures accounted for by instruction, academic support, and plant operations declined by 6.1 percentage points for Liberal Arts I colleges and 5.9 percentage points for Other-Four-Year institutions from 1978–79 to 1987–88. An almost equal increase in share occurs in student services and internal scholarships, two categories that reflect efforts to recruit students.

The pinnacle of the college age cohort in America occurred early in the period covered by this study. By 1990, however, the downturn in the number of college-age Americans did not result in declining aggregate enrollments (Evangelauf 1991). The shrinking college age cohort had been widely predicted, and the increasingly intense competition for students resulting from anxiety about it undoubtedly helped mitigate its effect on enrollments. Heavy recruiting, creative program design, and generous financial aid assistance all helped increase the enrollment rate of students during the 1980s sufficiently to delay the inevitable day, probably in the early 1990s, when the absolute number of students enrolled in American colleges and universities will decline.

As the gap in tuition between public and private colleges widens, it becomes increasingly difficult for private colleges to maintain enrollment levels if students and their families are price sensitive. Recruiting efforts have focused on high school students, who usually have a role in the decision about which college they attend but often do not shoulder the financial responsibility for tuition and fees directly (they do, of course, bear the burden of forgone earnings). As a result of intense competition for students, campuses have been spruced up with bark mulch and pine needles, remodeled dormitory rooms are fitted with telephones and cable television connections, and student recreation centers and health clinics are expanded to meet increasing demand by students.[20] The costs of these added amenities and intensified recruitment efforts eventually show up as tuition increases.[21] Because the students who make the enrollment decisions pay little tuition directly, the (expected negative) effect of tuition hikes on enrollments may be quite modest.[22] Thus, there may have been little downside risk to many institutions for undertaking considerable expense to improve the comfort and type of life experienced by their students.

Most important in recruiting is financial aid. What clearly occurred in the (almost exclusively private) liberal arts colleges throughout the decade is a redistribution of the tuition burden among college students, from those who are able to pay and who have strong or ordinary academic qualifications to those who cannot pay (need-based aid) and to those who can pay but who have outstanding academic qualifications (academic merit aid). Competition for students via merit scholarships and the quest for a diversified student body intensified over the decade, and the results are evident in the proportion of expenditures these schools allocate to need-based and merit scholarships. The institutions hardly have a choice if they wish to maintain their image. If they do not offer sufficiently tempting financial aid packages to attract a diversified class of academically strong students, they will lose their image (and perhaps the reality) of being selective and equally desirable to students of all economic backgrounds, and the demand for places at them may dry up as less expensive public Comprehensive universities begin to attract their prospective high-quality students.

The net effect of the intensifying scholarship competition is that real resource costs are not increasing as much at liberal arts colleges as it first appears (3.9 percent annually if both restricted and unrestricted scholarships are excluded from AE&G). Scholarships are expenditures that are recycled as tuition payments. Nevertheless, even after accounting for the fact that unrestricted scholarships do not represent the sacrifice of real resources, there has been a substantial reallocation from instruction to student services and institutional support in liberal arts colleges, and costs have risen sufficiently rap-

20. Ernest Boyer (1987) reports that more than 60 percent of prospective college students responding to a recent Carnegie Foundation survey considered the appearance of the campus to be most crucial in their choice of college. Boyer concludes that "the facilities of a college are vitally important in the recruitment of its students . . . [and that the] director of facilities is more important to the survival of the institution than the academic dean" (p. 25). To the extent that competition among colleges for a shrinking college age population has been manifested in buildings-and-grounds improvements, however, the effect has not been sufficiently large to dislodge plant operations as the *slowest*-growing cost category for almost all types of institutions. Improved management, modest increases in the costs of plant operations inputs, and neglect of less visible maintenance needs have all likely contributed to the stability of plant operations costs.

21. The costs of added amenities show up in tuition unless, of course, they are extracted from other budget categories or are covered by nontuition revenue sources earmarked exclusively for the amenities.

22. The responsiveness of enrollment to tuition increases has generally been found to be "inelastic." That is, the percentage decline in enrollment is less than the percentage increase in tuition that precipitated it (see Chapter 3).

idly that scholarships do not account for more than one-fifth of the increase in expenditure per student at those institutions. Increased scholarship aid is far from the sole answer to why costs have been rising so fast at private liberal arts colleges.

Over the decade, AE&G expenditures per student outpaced the rate of input inflation, as measured by the GNP implicit price deflator, by 2.7 percent annually for all types of colleges and universities and grew almost 1 percentage point (0.7, to be precise) per year above the HEPI. Because the rate of increase in expenditures per student at Liberal Arts I colleges has been so much greater (4.7 vs. 2.7 percent for all institutions), however, even after accounting for the growth in unrestricted scholarships at those institutions (a 3.9 vs. a 2.6 percent growth rate for all colleges and universities), there must be something unusual happening at our selective private liberal arts colleges. Whatever the problems that such institutions face in maintaining revenues from nontuition sources (e.g., endowment income, gifts, and grants) that may be forcing tuition to bear relatively more of the revenue burden, and beyond the increased financial aid that they have made available to their students, real expenditures per student are rising very rapidly at these colleges.

12.7   The Extremes of Expenditure Changes

At all types of institutions, student services and institutional support have been increasing more rapidly and plant operations expenditures less rapidly than total AE&G. The control of plant operations expenses at all but the Research universities and Liberal Arts I colleges is remarkable.

The stability of energy costs from 1978–79 to 1987–88 contributed substantially to the control of plant operations costs over the decade. Periodic surveys by the Association of Physical Plant Administrators (1980, 1989) report utility costs per square foot. Surveys were conducted for both 1978–79 and 1987–88. The *nominal* average annual percentage rates of increase in utility costs per square foot for a sample of institutions reporting in both years are as follows: Research (6.0 percent), Doctoral (3.8 percent), Comprehensive (4.0 percent), Liberal Arts I (6.1 percent), Other-Four-Year (7.3 percent), and Two-Year institutions (5.1 percent). The GNP implicit price deflator increased at an average annual rate of 5.2 percent over the period. Utility expenses account for roughly 30–40 percent of plant operations expenditures. Thus, it is clear that the trend in energy prices over the period (or, more precisely, the particularly high energy prices in 1978–79) explains a good deal of the stability of plant operations expenditures.

Further savings in plant operations may have been achieved by deferring needed maintenance. The accumulation of deferred maintenance could eventually necessitate repair and replacement expenditures even larger than the net present value of those that would be required to maintain the physical plant of colleges and universities in a timely fashion. Between 1950 and 1975, the physical space in higher education tripled (Rush and Johnson 1989, 6). As a result, a great deal of physical plant and equipment is now at an age when refurbishing is required. The 1988 physical facility renewal and replacement needs of colleges and universities were estimated at $60 billion, with $20.5 billion of that representing "urgent" repairs and renovations (Rush and Johnson 1989). How much is really urgent is difficult to judge.

The increased expenditures on student services and institutional support are more difficult to evaluate. They may reflect a market response to changing demands from students, whose values shifted toward increased counseling and health services, and they could reflect increased demand for campus security. The increase in institutional support could reveal an acceleration in private fund-raising efforts of colleges and universities in reaction to the diminished tax incentive to contribute to colleges and universities caused by declining marginal income tax rates (Clotfelter 1990) or the increased cost of complying with government regulations and responding to private litigation. Likewise, these increases might reflect an increase in self-canceling marketing efforts of colleges chasing a shrinking population of college age students or simply a proliferation of administrators (Hansen and Guidugli 1990; Galambos 1988).

The HEGIS/IPEDS data are not sufficiently detailed to disentangle these hypotheses. In a recent survey of 428 colleges and universities, a majority of financial officers singled out five detailed categories of expenditures as growing faster than the rate of inflation: insurance, marketing and recruiting, computing equipment and facilities, administrative computing, and complying with government regulations (Chaney and Farris 1990). Fund-raising was the sixth most frequently mentioned category. Although it would be useful to compare these university administrators' perceptions with the facts, cost allocation problems imply that such a time-series analysis will be both difficult and costly to perform (Cambridge Associates 1990).

12.8 Disaggregation

The primary danger in attempting to draw conclusions from differences in expenditure patterns and expenditures per student across Carnegie classifications is that institutions differ systematically in more ways than one. For example, there are very few public liberal arts colleges in our sample (only two of 131 in Liberal Arts I and only 22 of 430 Other-Four-Year colleges).[23] Thus,

23. The primary criterion for identifying liberal arts colleges in the Carnegie classification is the proportion of undergraduate degrees awarded in the liberal arts (vis-à-vis professional programs). A minimum of 50 percent is required to qualify for the Liberal Arts I category. The Liberal Arts II category, which we relabel "Other-Four-Year," has a similar standard, except for institutions with a total enrollment of fewer than 1,500. All four-year institutions with an enrollment of less than 1,500 that do not qualify for the Research, Doctoral, or Liberal Arts I categories are placed in Liberal Arts II. The two public Liberal Arts I colleges in our sample are the State University of New York at Purchase and the Virginia Military Institute. Large numbers of students

a comparison between Comprehensive and Liberal Arts I institutions risks attributing financial differences to an institution's mission when in reality they reflect differences between publicly and privately controlled schools. Likewise, only one Liberal Arts I college in our sample has more than 3,000 full-time-equivalent students (Bucknell). Thus, a comparison by Carnegie classification may reveal as much about the effects of size as of mission.

Consequently, we reclassified the 2,045 institutions in our sample into 24 separate categories, which we believe are fairly homogeneous groups. In no case do we combine public with private institutions, and in only a few cases do we combine colleges into different Carnegie codes. These few cases involve the public Liberal Arts I and Liberal Arts II (which we call Other-Four-Year) institutions. A careful examination of the 24 public institutions[24] in the liberal arts categories convinced us that all but a few are actually small comprehensive institutions (Breneman 1990).[25] For simplicity, therefore, we moved the 24 public liberal arts colleges into the public Comprehensive classification for subsequent analysis. An examination of expenditure patterns of institutions with and without medical schools in each of our groups convinced us of the necessity to segregate those universities in our sample which have on-campus medical schools. This created six additional categories, as there are both public and private Research, Doctoral, and Comprehensive institutions with medical schools on campus. Finally, to keep the number of cells in our distribution manageable, we sometimes combined institutions of different sizes into a single group, especially when a finer disaggregation left relatively few observations in individual cells.

The 24 resulting categories are identified in Table 12.6. The table provides examples of institutions in each category. The structure of the combinations can be understood better with the help of Table 12.7, which shows the grouping that we used to form the categories and also reveals the cells that contain no institutions (e.g., private liberal arts colleges with 20,000 or more students).

This new grouping of institutions enables us to focus more clearly on the important differences among colleges and universities. For example, in Table 12.8 and 12.9, we report the distribution of expenditure shares and the expenditure per student for four of the Carnegie classifications, holding approximately constant control (they are all public), medical school status (none has a medical school), enrollment size, and the growth rate of enrollment (re-

---

are educated in colleges of liberal arts, letters and science, or arts and sciences at Research, Doctoral, and Comprehensive universities. The undergraduate liberal arts program at those institutions, however, either is surrounded by a major research or doctoral program or awards fewer than half the institution's undergraduate degrees.

24. It is purely coincidental that both our number of institutional categories and the number of public liberal arts colleges are 24.

25. Most are called "comprehensive" universities in *Peterson's Guide to Four Year Colleges,* and most appear to have significant professional degree programs, the primary criterion that distinguishes them from liberal arts colleges.

Table 12.6   **Twenty-Four Categories of Higher Education Institutions, Cross-Classified by Type, Size, and Control**

Category No.	Category	Enrollment Range	No. of Institutions	Examples
1	Public Research: no med school	8,000–33,000	36	Rutgers, Oregon
2	Public Research: with med school	11,000–38,000[a]	30	West Virginia, Wisconsin
3	Private Research: no med school	3,000–17,000[b]	7	Princeton, Carnegie-Mellon
4	Private Research: with med school	4,000–22,000	17	Harvard, Vanderbilt
5	Public Doctoral: no med school	4,000–20,000[c]	50	Mississippi, Clemson
6	Public Doctoral: with med school	6,000–20,000	10	Vermont, Louisville
7	Private Doctoral: no med school	2,000–15,000[d]	31	Fordham, Baylor
8	Private Doctoral: with med school	4,000–10,000	5	Tufts, Dartmouth
9	Public Comprehensive & Other-Four-Year: no med school	Under 1,000	17	Western Montana, Laredo State
10	Public Comprehensive & Other-Four-Year: no med school	1,000–2,999	101	Citidel, Evergreen State
11	Public Comprehensive & Other-Four-Year: no med school	3,000–9,999	170	Florida A&M, James Madison
12	Public Comprehensive: no med school	10,000–25,000	33	George Mason, San Diego State
13	Public Comprehensive: with med school	7,000–14,000	6	East Carolina, Marshall
14	Private Comprehensive: no med school	Under 3,000	160	Whittier, Rollins
15	Private Comprehensive: no med school	3,000–10,000	56	Bradley, Seton Hall
16	Private Comprehensive: with med school	1,000–7,000	4	Mercer, Wake Forest
17	Private Liberal Arts I: no med school	Under 1,000	40	Mills, Bennington
18	Private Liberal Arts I: no med school	1,000–3,000[e]	89	Williams, Grinnell
19	Private Other-Four-Year: no med school	Under 1,000	267	Transylvania, Hawaii Loa
20	Private Other-Four-Year: no med school	1,000–3,000[f]	63	Spellman, Wittenberg
21	Public Two-Year: no med school	Under 1,000	209	Penn State (Allentown), State Fair Community College
22	Public Two-Year: no med school	1,000–2,999	328	Eastern Arizona, Kilgore
23	Public Two-Year: no med school	3,000–16,000	213	Pasadena City, Milwaukee Area Technical
24	Private Two-Year: no med school	Under 3,000	103	College of Boca Raton, Chatfield

Source: Computations by authors based on HEGIS/IPEDS data.

[a]Except University of California, San Francisco, 3,700.

[b]Except California Institute of Technology, 1,800.

[c]Except State Univeristy of New York Environmental Science Campus, 1,400, and Colorado School of Mines, 2,500.

[d]Except Northeastern University, 24,000.

[e]Except Bucknell, 3,200.

[f]Except Columbia College (Chicago), 3,600.

Table 12.7   **Counts of Institutions in Sample, Grouped into Twenty-Four Categories**

Carnegie Code and Medical School Status	Enrollment				
	0–999	1,000–2,999	3,000–9,999	10,000–19,999	20,000+
Public institutions:					
Research, no medical school[C1]			2	18	16
Research, medical school[C2]			1	13	16
Doctoral, no medical school[C5]		2	24	24	
Doctoral, medical school[C6]			5	3	2
Comprehensive, no medical school	2[C9]	93[C10]	169[C11]	30[C12]	3[C12]
Liberal Arts I, no medical school		2[C10]			
Other-Four-Year, no medical school	15[C9]	6[C10]	1[C11]		
Comprehensive, medical school[C13]			3	3	
Two-Year	209[C21]	328[C22]	197[C23]	16[C23]	
Private institutions:					
Research, no medical school[C3]		1	4	2	
Research, medical school[C4]			9	5	3
Doctoral, no medical school[C7]		5	21	4	1
Doctoral, medical school[C8]			4	1	
Comprehensive, no medical school	8[C14]	152[C14]	56[C15]		
Liberal Arts I, no medical school	40[C17]	88[C18]	1[C18]		
Other-Four-Year, no medical school	267[C19]	62[C20]	1[C20]		
Comprehensive, medical school[C16]	1	1	2		
Two-Year[C24]	93	10			
Count of institutions by size class	635	750	500	119	41

Source: Computations by authors based on HEGIS/IPEDS data.

Note: The twenty-four categories are described in Table 2.6. They are identified here by "C" numbers (e.g., C1 = category 1). Categories that comprise only one Carnegie classification are identified by "C" numbers in the stub column. If a category comprises more than one Carnegie classification, or if a Carnegie classification has been divided into one or more categories, the "C" numbers are given in the body of the table.

Table 12.8 Distribution of Adjusted Educational and General (AE&G) Expenditures by Carnegie Classification, Holding Control, Medical School Status, Enrollment Size, and Enrollment Growth Rate Constant[a]

Carnegie Classification	Instruction and Self-Supported Research	Public Service[b]	Academic Support[c]	Student Services[d]	Institutional Support[e]	Plant Operations	Internal Scholarships[f]	Mandatory Transfers[g]	Total AE&G[h]
Research (N = 36):									
1978–79	.473	.119	.116	.047	.092	.117	.020	.016	1.000
1987–88	.462	.112	.118	.054	.098	.112	.022	.021	1.000
Change	−.009	−.007	+.002	+.007	+.006	−.005	+.002	+.005	.000
Doctoral (N = 50):									
1978–79	.509	.059	.106	.064	.107	.119	.016	.020	1.000
1987–88	.500	.053	.116	.069	.114	.110	.021	.018	1.000
Change	−.009	−.006	+.010	+.005	+.007	−.009	+.005	−.002	.000
Comprehensive (N = 203):									
1978–79	.514	.020	.100	.077	.114	.129	.014	.030	1.000
1987–88	.510	.028	.100	.081	.130	.116	.017	.018	1.000
Change	−.004	+.008	.000	+.004	+.016	−.013	+.003	+.012	.000
Two-Year (N = 213):									
1978–79	.524	.017	.075	.085	.150	.113	.004	.033	1.000
1987–88	.512	.021	.084	.102	.154	.115	.004	.008	1.000
Change	−.012	+.004	+.009	+.017	+.004	+.002	.000	−.025	.000

Source: Computations by authors based on HEGIS/IPEDS data.

[a]Includes only publicly controlled institutions without a medical school; enrollment ranges 8,000–33,000, 4,000–20,000, 3,000–25,000 and 3,000–16,000 respectively; annual enrollment growth rates 0.79, 0.91, 0.98 and 0.64 respectively.

[b]Includes extension services.

[c]Computers, libraries, and deans.

[d]Admissions, registrars, counseling, student health, and recreation.

[e]Administration, accounting, security, alumni, and development.

[f]Scholarships from internal funds.

[g]Debt service.

[h]Total E&G expenditures under control of chief executive officer.

Table 12.9 Adjusted Educational and General (AE&G) Expenditures per Full-Time-Equivalent Student by Carnegie Classification, 1978–79 and 1987–88, Holding Control, Medical School Status, Enrollment Size, and Enrollment Growth Rate Constant[a]

Carnegie Classification	Instruction and Self-Supported Research	Public Service[b]	Academic Support[c]	Student Services[d]	Institutional Support[e]	Plant Operations	Internal Scholarships[f]	Mandatory Transfers[g]	Total AE&G[h]
Research (N = 36):									
1978–79	3,609	907	888	362	706	891	152	121	7,636
1987–88	4,468	1,074	1,136	516	945	1,074	208	206	9,628
Change	+859	+167	+248	+154	+239	+183	+56	+85	+1,992
Share of increase	43.1	8.4	12.4	7.7	12.0	9.2	2.8	4.3	100.0
Share of AE&G expenditures, 1987–88	46.4	11.2	11.8	5.4	9.8	11.2	2.2	2.1	100.0
Doctoral (N = 50):									
1978–79	3,094	357	644	390	650	725	97	123	6,080
1987–88	3,523	376	817	471	804	778	149	124	7,041
Change	+429	+19	+173	+81	+154	+53	+52	+1	+961
Share of increase	44.6	2.0	18.0	8.4	16.0	5.5	5.4	.1	100.0
Share of AE&G expenditures, 1987–88	50.0	5.3	11.6	6.9	11.4	11.0	2.1	1.8	100.0
Comprehensive (N = 203):									
1978–79	2,705	110	526	407	601	677	75	160	5,261
1987–88	3,109	171	609	491	789	709	104	109	6,092

Change	+404	+61	+83	+84	+188	+32	+29	−51	+831
Share of increase	48.6	7.3	10.0	10.1	22.6	3.9	3.5	−6.1	100.0
Share of AE&G expenditures, 1987–88	51.0	2.8	10.0	8.1	13.0	11.6	1.7	1.8	100.0
Two-Year (N = 213):								
1978–79	1,963	64	281	318	561	425	13	123	3,749
1987–88	2,289	94	374	458	690	516	17	34	4,472
Change	+326	+30	+93	+140	+129	+91	+4	−89	+723
Share of increase	45.1	4.1	12.9	19.4	17.8	12.6	.6	−12.3	100.0
Share of AE&G expenditures, 1987–88	51.2	2.1	8.4	10.2	15.4	11.5	.4	.8	100.0

Source: Computations by authors based on HEGIS/IPEDS data.

[a] Includes only publicly controlled institutions without a medical school; enrollment ranges 8,000–33,000, 4,000–20,000, 3,000–25,000, and 3,000–16,000, respectively; annual enrollment growth rates 0.79, 0.91, 0.98, and 0.64, respectively.

[b] Includes extension services.

[c] Computers, libraries, and deans.

[d] Admissions, registrars, counseling, student health, and recreation.

[e] Administration, accounting, security, alumni, and development.

[f] Scholarships from internal funds.

[g] Debt service.

[h] Total E&G expenditures under control of chief executive officer.

ported in the tables). What we learn from these comparisons for the most part confirms our earlier findings about changes in expenditures by Carnegie classification. Instruction accounts for the largest share of the increased expenditures per student at each type of institution, although its rate of increase is less than the rate of increase of total AE&G. We examine the instruction category in more detail in Chapter 14, where we continue to use this new grouping of institutions. Student services and institutional support grew faster than all AE&G in each group, and plant operations grew slower (except at Two-Year colleges). Growth in the academic support category of Doctoral institutions is more pronounced when the public institutions are examined separately.

12.9   Historically Black Colleges

The percentage of black Americans who achieved four or more years of college education increased from 4.8 in 1960 to 12.3 in 1988 (see Table 2.3 above). While white student college enrollment rates also increased since the Civil Rights Act was passed in 1964, black college enrollment rates increased faster. The result has been a modest rise in the proportion of all college students who are black and a significant increase in the number of black college students.

Before the 1960s, most black college students were served by a select group of institutions that catered especially to them. Seventy-one of these historically black institutions are among the 2,045 colleges and universities in our sample. Thirty-three of them are public Comprehensive universities enrolling between 1,000 and 3,000 students. Twenty-seven are private Other-Four-Year colleges (less selective liberal arts colleges) with 3,000 or fewer students. Five are private Comprehensive universities, and six are Two-Year colleges.

Ironically, these historically black colleges and universities did not thrive during the years of rising black student enrollments. Not only did more black students attend college, but also many blacks enrolled in what had traditionally been almost exclusively white institutions. The substitution away from historically black colleges was so strong that it overpowered the effect of an overall increase in black enrollments. Thirty-nine of the 71 historically black colleges in our sample actually lost enrollments from 1978–79 to 1987–88, and only 11 experienced average annual enrollment growth above 1.8 percent.[26] As we will argue more generally in the next chapter, declining enrollments cause expenditures per student to rise. This, coupled with the lower

26. Although many colleges and universities reported sharp declines in enrollment in fall 1990, the historically black colleges seem to have bucked the trend. Several reported a surge in enrollments, with increases in the 10–15 percent range. For some, this upward trend has been in place for several years. It appears that historically black colleges may have reached their lowest enrollments in the late 1980s (Wilson 1990, 1) and have entered a period of recovery.

income levels of many black families, has placed many of these historically black colleges in a severe financial squeeze.

We compare expenditures per student in 1987–88 at historically black colleges with all other colleges for three of our disaggregated categories of institutions in Table 12.10. These three groups contain 54 of the 71 historically black institutions in the sample.

For the public Comprehensive institutions, AE&G expenditures per student are higher at the historically black colleges. Each functional category contributes to the difference. On the other hand, the historically black private Other-Four-Year colleges spend less per student than their non-historically black counterparts. Here the pattern is not consistent across functions. The historically black colleges spend more per student on public service, institutional support, and plant operations, but they spend substantially less on instruction, libraries, student services, and internally funded scholarships. Although the financial need of the students attending these colleges in undoubtedly high, revenues from full-price students to fund unrestricted scholarship aid are limited.

12.10   Cost Trends by Institutional Control

Expenditure shares and expenditures per student are reported separately by public and private control in Tables 12.11–12.14. The declining role of instructional expenditures is predominantly a private school phenomenon. The larger public service responsibility of public colleges and universities is evident, but public service does not account for much of the increased costs in public institutions. The rising costs of student services and institutional support transcend control, but the sharp increase in internally funded scholarships shows up only at the private schools. Plant operations loses share at both public and private institutions.

Tables 12.13 and 12.14 contain several public/private comparisons for groups of institutions that are otherwise similar. Private Comprehensive universities are experiencing a much faster increase in costs than public Comprehensive institutions. In 1978–79, the privates were spending almost $500 less per student than their public counterparts, but, by 1987–88, they were spending almost $1,000 more. The public Comprehensives seem to have held the line on all expenditure categories except the instructional budget, while the privates experienced large increases in instruction, student services, institutional support, and unrestricted scholarships.

A similar pattern occurred in Two-Year colleges, where publics and privates spent about the same amount per student in 1978–79, but, by 1987–88, the privates were spending $900 more per student. The public Two-Year colleges experienced a significant increase in student services and institutional support expenditures—however, not nearly as large as the increase in those functional

Table 12.10   Adjusted Educational and General (AE&G) Expenditures per Full-Time Equivalent Student, Selected Institutions without On-Campus Medical Schools, 1987–88, Historically Black versus Other Institutions

	Instruction and Self-Supported Research	Public Service[a]	Academic Support[b]	Student Services[c]	Institutional Support[d]	Plant Operations	Internal Scholarships[e]	Mandatory Transfers[f]	Total AE&G[g]
Public Comprehensive:									
1,000–3,000 students:									
Historically black schools (N = 18)	3,387	339	801	761	1,405	1,055	238	81	8,066
Other schools	2,974	158	647	567	931	812	92	99	6,279
3,000–10,000 students:									
Historically black schools (N = 15)	3,303	256	759	563	1,225	1,007	221	–1	7,334
Other schools	2,890	205	613	453	752	712	117	149	5,892
Private Other-Four-Year under 1,000 students:									
Historically black schools (N = 24)	2,298	96	569	780	2,004	1,189	558	136	7,629
Other schools	2,661	69	564	1007	1,762	941	925	187	8,116

Source: Computations by authors based on HEGIS/IPEDS data.

[a]Includes extension services.

[b]Computers, libraries, and deans.

[c]Admissions, registrars, counseling, student health, and recreation.

[d]Administration, accounting, security, alumni, and development.

[e]Scholarships from internal funds.

[f]Debt service.

[g]Total E&G expenditures under control of chief executive officer.

Table 12.11 Distribution of Adjusted Educational and General (AE&G) Expenditures, Institutions without On-Campus Medical Schools, 1978–79 and 1987–88, by Control

	Instruction and Self-Supported Research	Public Service[a]	Academic Support[b]	Student Services[c]	Institutional Support[d]	Plant Operations	Internal Scholarships[e]	Mandatory Transfers[f]	Total AE&G[g]
Public (N = 1,157):									
1978–79	.503	.046	.098	.072	.121	.122	.013	.025	1.000
1987–88	.494	.049	.102	.080	.130	.115	.015	.015	1.000
Change	−.009	+.003	+.004	+.006	+.009	−.007	+.002	+.010	.000
Private (N = 816):									
1978–79	.430	.012	.085	.089	.175	.124	.061	.025	1.000
1987–88	.395	.012	.089	.098	.183	.106	.096	.021	1.000
Change	−.035	−.000	+.004	+.009	+.008	−.018	+.035	−.004	.000

Source: Computations by authors based on HEGIS/IPEDS data.

[a]Includes extension services.

[b]Computers, libraries, and deans.

[c]Admissions, registrars, counseling, student health, and recreation.

[d]Administration, accounting, security, alumni, and development.

[e]Scholarships from internal funds.

[f]Debt service.

[g]Total E&G expenditures under control of chief executive officer.

Table 12.12 Adjusted Educational and General (AE&G) Expenditures per Full-Time-Equivalent Student, Institutions without On-Campus Medical Schools, 1978–79 and 1987–88, by Control

	Instruction and Self-Supported Research	Public Service[a]	Academic Support[b]	Student Services[c]	Institutional Support[d]	Plant Operations	Internal Scholarships[e]	Mandatory Transfers[f]	Total AE&G[g]
Public (N = 1,157):									
1978–79	2,614	241	510	374	629	636	66	129	5,199
1987–88	3,054	303	631	492	801	712	93	95	6,182
Change	+440	+62	+121	+118	+172	+76	+27	−34	+983
Share of increase	44.8	6.3	12.3	12.0	17.5	7.7	2.7	−3.5	100.0
Share of AE&G expenditures, 1987–88	49.9	4.9	10.2	8.0	13.0	11.5	1.5	1.5	100.0
Private (N = 816):									
1978–79	2,853	76	565	588	1,158	823	401	165	6,627
1987–88	3,782	113	847	935	1,749	1,019	922	199	9,567
Change	+929	+37	+282	+347	+591	+196	+521	+34	+2,940
Share of increase	31.6	1.3	9.6	11.8	20.1	6.7	17.7	1.2	100.0
Share of AE&G expenditures, 1987–88	39.5	1.2	8.9	9.8	18.3	10.6	9.6	2.1	100.0

Source: Computations by authors based on HEGIS/IPEDS data.

[a]Includes extension services.

[b]Computers, libraries, and deans.

[c]Admissions, registrars, counseling, student health, and recreation.

[d]Administration, accounting, security, alumni, and development.

[e]Scholarships from internal funds.

[f]Debt service.

[g]Total E&G expenditures under control of chief executive officer.

areas experienced by the privates. Almost everything except public service and interest expense rose for private Two-Year colleges over the period.[27]

The story is repeated with Doctoral institutions. The increase in expenditures per student was twice as large at private as at public Doctoral universities. Unrestricted scholarships, interest expense, and student services account for a disproportionate share of the increase.

Overall, real expenditures per student at public institutions increased 1.9 percent annually from 1978–79 to 1987–88, while they increased 4.2 percent annually at private colleges and universities. Expenditures per student increased much faster in private Doctoral, Comprehensive, and Two-Year institutions than in their public counterparts. This is consistent with the very high rate of increase in expenditures per student at private liberal arts colleges, for which there is no comparable public reference group.

12.11 When Did Costs Accelerate Most?

The pattern of cost inflation over the period 1978–79 to 1987–88 is not constant. Over the first five years (1978–79 to 1983–84), AE&G per student for the whole industry increased at an average rate of only 1.1 percent above the GNP implicit price deflator.[28] But, between 1983–84 and 1987–88, the average rate of increase rose to 4.8 percent per year (averaging 2.7 percent over the entire period). The greatest increase in costs occurred over the years 1983–84 to 1985–86, when AE&G per student rose at 7.0 percent per year above the GNP deflator. (This was followed by a more modest 2.6 percent average annual rate from 1985–86 to 1987–88). The forces driving higher education's cost inflation in the 1980s appear to have been most effective in the middle of the decade.

What apparently exacerbated the rate of increase in costs in the mid-1980s is public institutions joining the privates in experiencing rapid cost increases. Over the first five years of the period, the rate of increase in average costs for privates was 3.3 percent, which rose to 5.4 percent from 1983–84 to 1987–88. Public colleges and universities, on the other hand, held the line on costs over the first half of the period (0.3 percent per year) but then joined the privates, experiencing an average annual rate of increase of 4.5 percent from 1983–84 to 1987–88.

27. For an interesting analysis of the allocation of Alabama state education funds between two-year and four-year institutions and among two-year colleges and four-year institutions, see Long (1987). Long concludes that Alabama has too many state-supported colleges (53 in 1987), many enrolling far too few students to make effective use of facilities. He notes that Alabama's two-year colleges average only one-fifth the size of those in neighboring Florida (pp. iv-1).

28. The figures reported in this section are based on samples that include institutions with medical schools. The rates of change are only slightly different if the 72 institutions with medical schools are excluded. The only growth rates that differ by more than 0.2 percent are those for Research universities without medical schools whose AE&G per student increased at an average annual rate of 1.4 percent from 1978–79 to 1983–84 and 5 percent from 1983–84 to 1987–88.

Table 12.13 Distribution of Adjusted Educational and General (AE&G) Expenditures, by Control, 1978–79 and 1987–88, Holding Carnegie Classification, Medical School Status, Enrollment Size, and Enrollment Growth Rate Constant

Carnegie Classification	Instruction and Self-Supported Research	Public Service[a]	Academic Support[b]	Student Services[c]	Institutional Support[d]	Plant Operations	Internal Scholarships[e]	Mandatory Transfers[f]	Total AE&G[g]
Comprehensive institutions, no medical school:[h]									
Public (N = 118):									
1978–79	.452	.022	.101	.086	.156	.151	.013	.020	1.000
1987–88	.463	.028	.103	.091	.154	.130	.018	.014	1.000
Change	+.011	+.006	+.002	+.005	-.002	-.021	+.005	-.006	.000
Private (N = 160):									
1978–79	.424	.011	.072	.098	.184	.119	.062	.030	1.000
1987–88	.397	.009	.076	.110	.183	.104	.101	.020	1.000
Change	-.027	-.002	+.004	+.012	-.001	-.015	+.039	-.010	.000
Two-Year institutions:[i]									
Public (N = 209):									
1978–79	.501	.020	.102	.084	.151	.125	.006	.012	1.000
1987–88	.478	.023	.100	.105	.160	.119	.010	.005	1.000
Change	-.023	-.003	-.002	-.021	+.009	-.006	+.004	-.007	.000
Private (N = 103):									
1978–79	.361	.006	.074	.123	.217	.138	.039	.042	1.000
1987–88	.344	.004	.074	.139	.230	.131	.052	.026	1.000
Change	-.017	-.002	.000	+.016	+.013	-.007	+.013	-.016	.000

Doctoral institutions, with medical school:[j]

Public (N = 10):									
1978–79	.502	.077	.121	.045	.105	.113	.010	.026	1.000
1987–88	.478	.086	.122	.043	.120	.101	.024	.026	1.000
Change	−.024	+.009	+.001	−.002	+.015	−.012	+.014	.000	.000
Private (N = 5):									
1978–79	.469	.029	.138	.050	.153	.110	.039	.011	1.000
1987–88	.454	.010	.142	.062	.147	.095	.058	.032	1.000
Change	−.015	−.019	+.004	+.012	−.006	−.015	+.019	+.021	.000

Source: Computations by authors based on HEGIS/IPEDS data.

[a] Includes extension services.

[b] Computers, libraries, and deans.

[c] Admissions, registrars, counseling, student health, and recreation.

[d] Administration, accounting, security, alumni, and development.

[e] Scholarships from internal funds.

[f] Debt service.

[g] Total E&G expenditures under control of chief executive officer.

[h] Enrollments less than 3,000 students; annual enrollment growth rates of 1.40 and 1.21 percent, respectively.

[i] Enrollments less than 1,000 students; annual enrollment growth rates of 1.42 and 1.13 percent, respectively.

[j] Enrollment ranges of 6,000–20,000 and 4,000–10,000, respectively; annual enrollment growth rates of 0.98 and 0.68, respectively.

Table 12.14 Adjusted Educational and General (AE&G) Expenditures per Full-Time-Equivalent Student by Control, 1978–79 and 1987–88, Holding Carnegie Classification, Medical School Status, Enrollment Size, and Enrollment Growth Rate Constant

Carnegie Classification	Instruction and Self-Supported Research[h]	Public Service[a]	Academic Support[b]	Student Services[c]	Institutional Support[d]	Plant Operations	Internal Scholarships[e]	Mandatory Transfers[f]	Total AE&G[g]
Comprehensive institutions, no medical school:[h]									
Public (N = 118):									
1978–79	2,686	130	601	511	926	898	79	116	5,947
1987–88	3,036	184	673	597	1,013	852	116	92	6,562
Change	+350	+54	+72	+86	+87	−46	+37	−24	+615
Share of increase	56.9	8.8	11.7	14.0	14.1	−7.5	6.0	−3.9	100.0
Share of AE&G expenditures, 1987–88	46.3	2.8	10.3	9.1	15.4	13.0	1.8	1.4	100.0
Private (N = 160):									
1978–79	2,321	61	394	538	1,007	650	339	163	5,474
1987–88	2,988	65	570	830	1,380	783	759	150	7,526
Change	+667	+4	+176	+292	+373	+133	+420	−13	+2,052
Share of increase	32.5	.2	8.6	14.2	18.2	6.5	20.5	−.6	100.0
Share of AE&G expenditures, 1987–88	39.7	.9	7.6	11.0	18.3	10.4	10.1	2.0	100.0
Two-Year institutions:[i]									
Public (N = 209):									
1978–79	2,271	89	463	381	683	566	27	52	4,531
1987–88	2,633	128	549	580	880	654	54	26	5,505
Change	+362	+39	+86	+199	+197	+88	+27	−26	+974
Share of increase	37.2	4.0	8.8	20.4	20.2	9.0	2.8	−2.6	100.0
Share of AE&G expenditures, 1987–88	47.8	2.3	10.0	10.5	16.0	11.9	1.0	.5	100.0
Private (N = 103):									
1978–79	1,654	26	340	564	994	630	180	191	4,578
1987–88	2,201	24	475	892	1,473	837	331	164	6,397

Change	+547	−2	+135	+328	+479	+207	+151	−27	+1,819
Share of increase	30.1	−.1	7.4	18.0	26.3	11.4	8.3	−1.5	100.0
Share of AE&G expenditures, 1987–88	34.4	.4	7.4	13.9	23.0	13.1	5.2	2.6	100.0
Doctoral institutions, with medical school:[j]									
Public (N = 10):									
1978–79	4,139	639	996	375	863	933	84	216	8,247
1987–88	4,887	883	1,244	441	1,230	1,035	246	262	10,229
Change	+748	+244	+248	+66	+367	+102	+162	+46	+1,982
Share of increase	37.7	12.3	12.5	3.3	18.5	5.1	8.2	2.3	100.0
Share of AE&G expenditures, 1987–88	47.8	8.6	12.2	4.3	12.0	10.1	2.4	2.6	100.0
Private (N = 5):									
1978–79	5,688	358	1,669	612	1,856	1,330	468	139	12,120
1987–88	7,609	175	2,374	1,040	2,458	1,590	977	546	16,770
Change	+1,921	−183	+705	+428	+602	+260	+509	+407	+4,650
Share of increase	41.3	−3.9	15.2	9.2	12.9	5.6	10.9	8.8	100.0
Share of AE&G expenditures, 1987–88	45.4	1.0	14.2	6.2	14.7	9.5	5.8	3.2	100.0

Source: Computations by authors based on HEGIS/IPEDS data.

[a] Includes extension service.

[b] Computers, libraries, and deans.

[c] Admissions, registrars, counseling, student health, and recreation.

[d] Administration, accounting, security, alumni, and development.

[e] Scholarships from internal funds.

[f] Debt service.

[g] Total E&G expenditures under control of chief executive officer.

[h] Enrollments less than 3,000 students; annual enrollment growth rates of 1.40 and 1.21 percent, respectively.

[i] Enrollments less than 1,000 students; annual enrollment growth rates of 1.42 and 1.13, percent respectively.

[j] Enrollment ranges of 6,000–20,000 and 4,000–10,000, respectively; annual enrollment growth rates of 0.98 and 0.68, respectively.

The increases in average costs seem to have hit private liberals arts colleges first. Liberal Arts I colleges experienced average increases of 4.6 percent over the first five and 4.9 percent over the latter four years of the period. The comparable numbers for Other-Four-Year colleges are 2.3 and 3.2 percent, respectively. Most of the other categories of institutions held the line pretty well until 1983–84. The average annual rates of increase for Research, Doctoral, and Comprehensive universities from 1978–79 to 1983–84 were 1.8, 1.6, and 1.0 percent, respectively. Average costs at Two-Year colleges even declined relative to the GNP deflator over the period (by 0.4 percent annually). But the experience of these institutions from 1983–84 to 1987–88 was not much different from that of private liberal arts colleges, as their average annual rates of increase skyrocketed to 5.0, 3.9, 4.2, and 5.4 percent, respectively. Thus, one might ask what happened to private liberal arts colleges from 1978–79 to 1983–84 that eventually also infected public Research, Doctoral, Comprehensive, and Two-Year institutions a few years later.

12.12   Expenditures per Degree

By using the growth in AE&G expenditures per full-time-equivalent student in this analysis, we have assumed implicitly that a year's experience in college is equally productive regardless of the degree program or type of institution in which the student is enrolled. In addition, AE&G per full-time-equivalent enrollment treats each year of college equally; thus, the freshman experience is equated with the senior year (or even a year in law school or a Ph.D. program). It also implies that there is no special value to completing a degree. This assumption is not supported by the literature on screening, in which some of the benefits of education take the form of reduced costs to employers of evaluating and comparing prospective workers (Berg 1970; Taubman and Wales 1973).

Although some writers question the relevance of the screening function of higher education (Layard and Psacharopoulos 1974), most of the empirical evidence supports the idea that, among other things, higher education produces valuable credentials for its students. In particular, evidence exists that the internal rate of return to investment in a degree relative to two years of college is greater than the return to the first two years of postsecondary education (Becker 1964, 92–93). Although this observation could result from a more valuable educational experience during the last two years of a four-year degree than during the first two, it is also consistent with the credentialism hypothesis.

If we accept degrees as a measure of the output of higher education, the analysis can be recast in terms of the average annual rate of growth in AE&G expenditures per degree awarded. These calculations are reported in Table 12.15 for both samples, including and excluding institutions with on-campus medical schools. The sample is 2,023 rather than 2,045 because a few insti-

Table 12.15   Average Annual Growth Rate of Adjusted Educational and General (AE&G) Expenditures per Full-Time-Equivalent (FTE) Student and per Degree, 1978–79 to 1985–86

Institutions	Including Institutions with Medical Schools				Excluding Institutions with Medical Schools			
	Sample Size	% Growth AE&G per FTE Enrollment	% Growth AE&G per Degree	Ratio[a]	Sample Size	% Growth AE&G per FTE Enrollment	% Growth AE&G per Degree	Ratio[a]
All	2,023	2.8	2.9	.97	1,951	2.5	2.6	.96
Four-Year	1,180	2.9	3.1	.94	1,108	2.7	3.0	.90
Two-Year	843	2.0	1.6	1.25	843	2.0	1.6	1.25
Research	89	3.2	3.3	.97	42	2.7	2.9	.93
Doctoral	96	2.7	3.0	.90	81	2.6	2.9	.90
Comprehensive	517	2.5	3.0	.83	508	2.5	2.8	.89
Liberal Arts I	131	4.8	4.3	1.12	131	4.8	4.3	1.12
Other-Four-Year	347	2.9	2.6	1.12	346	2.9	2.6	1.12
Public	1,188	2.2	2.5	.88	1,142	2.0	2.3	.87
Private	835	4.1	3.8	1.08	809	4.0	3.6	1.11

Source: Calculations by authors based on HEGIS/IPEDS data.

[a]Ratio of average annual growth rate of AE&G per FTE enrollment to average annual growth rate of AE&G per degree.

tutions did not report degrees awarded. The period covers seven years, 1978–79 to 1985–86, because degree data for 1987–88 were frequently not reported. Average annual rate of growth calculations for AE&G expenditures per full-time-equivalent student for the same sample and period are shown for comparison with the cost per degree figures.

Table 2.15 reveals modest differences in cost inflation when degrees rather than enrollment levels are used as a measure of output. In Research, Doctoral, and Comprehensive universities, costs per degree rose faster than costs per full-time-equivalent student. This implies that, over the period 1978–79 to 1985–86, either students at these institutions enrolled for more years before obtaining a degree (see Chapter 5, sec. 5.3, above) or retention rates deteriorated (see Table 5.4 above), or both. At Liberal Arts I, Other-Four-Year colleges, and Two-Year colleges, costs per degree increased more slowly than costs per student. By improving either retention rates or the rate of progress toward degree, Liberal Arts I, Other-Four-Year colleges, and Two-Year colleges contained cost inflation more per degree than per student enrolled. Viewing degrees as a measure of output, the cost inflation problem in higher education looks slightly worse than the picture developed with AE&G expenditures per full-time-equivalent enrollment. The situation at private Liberal Arts I colleges is better (i.e., costs per degree increased at an average annual rate of 4.3 percent vis-à-vis 4.8 percent for costs per student), and the situation at public Comprehensive universities is worse. Retention and time-to-degree problems appear to be most severe at public institutions, especially Comprehensive universities.

12.13 Summary

Expenditures per student for educational services at America's colleges and universities increased 2.7 percent per year faster than the general rate of inflation (as reflected by the GNP implicit price deflator) over the 1980s. The increases were greatest for student services, general administration, and institutionally supported scholarships. Because scholarships are recirculated as tuition income, they do not represent the consumption of real resources with valuable alternative uses. Even excluding scholarships, however, the rate of cost increase per student in American higher education outstripped inflation by 2.6 percent annually from 1978–79 to 1987–88.

Costs increased least for the central functions of a college—instruction (faculty), academic services (including libraries), and plant operations (classrooms). These three categories combined accounted for 2.4 fewer percentage points of adjusted educational and general (AE&G) expenditures in 1987–88 than they did in 1978–79. There was a discernible shift away from instructional expenditures to ancillary and administrative services. Although instructional expenditures declined as a proportion of total costs, they are still the largest single category by a considerable margin and represent an important source of potential cost savings. We therefore examine this category of costs more closely in chapter 14.

The rate of increase in expenditures per student was three times larger in private institutions than in public colleges and universities. The trend away from the central functions of higher education was also less severe in public institutions. Selective private liberal arts colleges exhibit the most pronounced increases in both costs per student and shifts in budget shares away from instruction, academic services, and plant operations.

In Chapter 13, we compare the increase in cost per student across institutions of different size, looking for economies of scale, and across institutions that experienced different trends in their enrollment, looking for evidence that enrollment shifts affect reported costs per student.

13   Costs and Enrollments

College enrollments grow, sometimes rapidly, as new programs are launched, as population in an area surges, and as institutions gain reputation. Enrollments may remain stable because demand for particular programs in a particular place remains steady. Enrollment may also remain stable by design. Institutions may decide to limit enrollment to a particular level in order to become more selective in admissions. Enrollment may also decline, sometimes precipitously, as population shifts, student tastes for particular programs wane, or an institution loses reputation. Significant numbers of institutions were in each of these three sets of circumstances in the 1980s. The pattern of change in enrollments has important effects on costs. Changes in costs per student as a consequence of recent changes in enrollment can also cloud understanding of how costs vary with the size of an institution, the second principal subject of this chapter. Taking recent changes in enrollment into account will help us understand the pattern of costs per student in higher education.

13.1   Adjusting to Changing Enrollment

In a dynamic market economy, resources are constantly reallocated in response to price signals about the value consumers place on various products and services. Price increases entice suppliers to expand production of those products and services currently in favor. As consumer demand for college and university attendance changes, we would expect the management of these institutions to adjust supply accordingly, increasing faculty, classroom space, and academic support services when more students enroll and cutting back on inputs when enrollments decline.

A few hundred colleges and universities differentiate their services by maintaining and emphasizing their selectivity. These institutions appeal to a selective group of students who have been successful in high school and who thrive on competition. The demand for selectivity has other bases as well. Students learn from their peers, and one can expect to learn more from peers who know more themselves. In addition, the screening process of highly selective institutions may be valuable in itself. Prospective employers and graduate and professional school admissions committees may acknowledge admission to a highly selective institution as an indicator of likely success in a career (Arrow 1973).

When selective colleges experience an increase in demand, they have the option of expanding enrollments or further increasing their selectivity. Greater selectivity will benefit both current students and alumni and may also enhance the stature of the institution's faculty and administrators if their prestige is connected to the academic quality of their students. Thus, some selective colleges may enforce a rigid ceiling on enrollments even as their applications grow, forcing more applicants to attend slightly less selective institutions. In such circumstances, the increased demand for places will manifest itself through expanded enrollments in less selective colleges, as students work their way down the pecking order.

The academic labor market operates with particularly long lead times. Faculty are usually hired in the spring of a year to begin work in September. The personnel policies of many colleges and universities require at least a full year's notice to untenured faculty prior to termination. And, of course, institutions usually retain tenured faculty for the rest of their lives if they do not resign or retire. Because of these institutional characteristics, adjustment to unexpected changes in enrollments can be slow in academe, and we might therefore observe a weaker relation between enrollment and cost than would be expected in for-profit firms.

To examine the effect of changing enrollment rates on expenditures, we computed the annual growth rate of full-time-equivalent enrollment for each institution in our sample of 2,045 over the period 1978–79 to 1987–88. The growth rate is based on an ordinary least squares regression of the natural logarithm of enrollments on time. The coefficient on time in the estimated equation is the best single estimate of the average annual growth rate of enrollment over the period, based on the four years of data we had available: 1978–79, 1983–84, 1985–86, and 1987–88.[1]

The average annual growth rates of enrollment vary from a low of −18 percent per year (Spertus College) to a high of 20 percent per year (Hawaii Pacific College). Forty-seven institutions in our sample lost enrollments at an average rate of 5 percent or more annually, while 174 grew at an average annual rate of 5 percent or more. Over a nine-year period, an annual growth

1. A growth rate of enrollment calculated on the basis of the best general relation between enrollment and time over the period is preferred to a simple comparison of enrollments in 1978–79 with enrollments in 1987–88 because it is less sensitive to the possibility that 1978–79 or 1987–88 is an aberration.

rate of 5 percent would convert a college with 3,000 students into one enrolling 4,654 students and could easily change the character of the institution.

The median growth rate of enrollment across all institutions is 0.8 percent per year. About one-third of our institutions experienced enrollment growth rates exceeding 1.8 percent annually, and another third actually suffered a decline in enrollments over the period. We divided the institutions into three equal size groups, those whose enrollments rose by 1.8 percent or more annually, those that experienced relatively stable enrollments, their growth rate varying from zero to 1.8 percent annually, and those that experienced declining enrollments. Comparisons among these groups may reveal how quickly colleges and universities are able to adapt to enrollment fluctuations, that is, how flexible they are.[2]

How well did the management of the institutions whose enrollments changed substantially adapt to the change? Were they able to cut costs quickly in the face of declining enrollments, and did they expand resources adequately when enrollment increased?

Clues to these questions are revealed in Tables 13.1–13.4, which report changes in the distribution of adjusted educational and general (AE&G) expenditures, AE&G expenditures per full-time-equivalent student, and their functional composition from 1978–79 to 1987–88. Over the period, instruction accounted for an increasing share of the expenditures of four-year institutions whose enrollments were growing at 1.8 percent annually or more and a declining share of the expenditures of four-year institutions whose enrollments were falling. There appears to be little difference in the expenditure pattern over time between rapidly growing and declining Two-Year colleges.

Changes in expenditures per full-time-equivalent student at four-year institutions, shown in Table 13.3, disclose what is happening. Expenditures per student at the 350 four-year colleges that grew faster than 1.8 percent annually over the period and the 390 four-year institutions whose enrollments actually declined over the period were similar in 1978–79. But AE&G expenditures per student increased more than twice as fast at the contracting schools as at the growing institutions. This pattern holds for all categories of expenditures, but it is especially pronounced for public service, academic support, and plant operations, where expenditures per student increased three times as fast at contracting as at rapidly expanding institutions.

The institutions with stable enrollments experienced cost increases almost as large as those of the contracting schools, but they seem to have been able to control expenditures per student marginally better in the "overhead" categories of academic support, student services, institutional support, and plant operations. The biggest difference in the growth of expenditures per student is between the rapidly growing institutions and the others. Indeed, the annual

2. We are here implicitly assuming that each institution was in equilibrium at the beginning of the period. This assumption will clearly be inaccurate for some colleges, whose enrollment fluctuations over the 1980s helped them adjust to an existing disequilibrium in 1978–79.

rate of growth of expenditures per student was only 1.8 percent per year for the growing institutions compared to 2.9 percent for the stable enrollment colleges and 3.8 percent for the schools whose enrollment was dropping. These differences reveal the important role of the denominator in cost per student calculations. Expenditures obviously change less rapidly than enrollments.

13.2 Changes within Groups

The comparisons displayed in Tables 13.1–13.4 can be misleading if a systematic relation exists between enrollment growth rates and some other characteristic that is highly correlated with the rate of cost increase. For example, if most of the shrinking institutions are Liberal Arts I and Other-Four-Year colleges, we may inadvertently attribute to different growth rates those cost differences that are more accurately traced to differences in institutional mission and their corresponding output mixes.

A comparison of cost increases between contracting and rapidly growing institutions that holds some of the other important characteristics of colleges and universities constant can be accomplished with the use of the 24 categories of institutions delineated in Chapter 12 (Table 12.6). Those categories distinguish institutions by control, Carnegie classification (mission), and medical school status and, where sample size permits, also separate institutions by size. They also segregate institutions with on-campus medical schools. In Table 13.5, we report the change in AE&G expenditures per full-time-equivalent student for the declining enrollment, stable enrollment, and rapidly growing enrollment institutions for nine selected groups from among the 24 categories. The criterion for selection was primarily sample size. We also tried to select both some public and some private institutions and groups from different Carnegie classifications. None of the groups contain institutions with on-campus medical schools.

The results in Table 13.5 confirm the conclusion that rapidly growing colleges and universities experienced much smaller increases in expenditures per student over the 1980s than institutions who were losing students. There are no exceptions to this conclusion. The average annual growth rate of AE&G per student for declining institutions is 3.7, compared to 1 percent for growing schools, a dramatic difference. Contracting colleges experienced larger increases in expenditures per student than did rapidly growing institutions for all functional categories (except mandatory transfers) for all nine groups of colleges and universities.[3] Clearly, expenditures respond to shifts in enrollment with a noticeable lag.

---

3. For our entire sample, the elasticity of the growth in AE&G per student with respect to the growth in enrollment is − 0.041 and, while very inelastic, is statistically significantly different from zero. This estimate was computed using enrollment and dummy variables for the Carnegie classifications as independent variables, using ordinary least squares. The sign of each coefficient

Table 13.1   **Adjusted Educational and General (AE&G) Expenditure Distribution Trends for Four-Year Institutions, 1978–79 and 1987–88, by Enrollment Trends**

Distribution of AE&G	Instruction and Self-Supported Research	Public Service[a]	Academic Support[b]	Student Services[c]	Institutional Support[d]	Plant Operations	Internal Scholarships[e]	Mandatory Transfers[f]	Total AE&G[g]
Growing enrollments (N = 350):									
1978–79	.472	.051	.107	.066	.131	.128	.026	.019	1.000
1987–88	.477	.045	.105	.071	.137	.106	.040	.018	1.000
Change	+.005	−.006	−.002	+.005	+.006	−.022	+.014	−.001	.000
Stable enrollments (N = 452):									
1978–79	.493	.050	.109	.060	.118	.119	.031	.021	1.000
1987–88	.477	.052	.111	.064	.122	.106	.047	.020	1.000
Change	−.016	+.002	+.002	+.004	+.004	−.013	+.016	−.001	.000
Declining enrollment (N = 390):									
1978–79	.482	.056	.100	.067	.125	.121	.029	.019	1.000
1987–88	.451	.054	.109	.071	.138	.111	.048	.017	1.000
Change	−.031	−.002	+.009	+.004	+.013	−.010	+.019	−.002	.000

Source: Computations by authors based on HEGIS/IPEDS data.

[a]Includes extension services.

[b]Computers, libraries, and deans.

[c]Admissions, registrars, counseling, student health, and recreation.

[d]Administration, accounting, security, alumni, and development.

[e]Scholarships from internal funds.

[f]Debt service.

[g]Total E&G expenditures under control of chief executive officer.

Table 13.2 Adjusted Educational and General (AE&G) Expenditure Distribution Trends for Two-Year Colleges, 1978–79 and 1987–88, by Enrollment Trends

Distribution of AE&G	Instruction and Self-Supported Research	Public Service[a]	Academic Support[b]	Student Services[c]	Institutional Support[d]	Plant Operations	Internal Scholarships[e]	Mandatory Transfers[f]	Total AE&G[g]
Growing enrollments (N = 332):									
1978–79	.517	.021	.078	.087	.148	.119	.006	.025	1.000
1987–88	.502	.025	.085	.103	.154	.114	.009	.010	1.000
Change	−.015	+.004	+.007	+.016	+.006	−.005	+.003	−.015	.000
Stable enrollments (N = 229):									
1978–79	.517	.015	.086	.085	.147	.122	.005	.024	1.000
1987–88	.494	.023	.090	.096	.166	.117	.006	.009	1.000
Change	−.023	+.008	+.004	+.011	+.019	−.005	+.001	−.015	.000
Declining enrollment (N = 292):									
1978–79	.511	.016	.075	.087	.156	.113	.005	.036	1.000
1987–88	.497	.020	.083	.108	.159	.119	.007	.007	1.000
Change	−.014	+.004	+.008	+.021	+.003	+.006	+.002	−.029	.000

Source: Computations by authors based on HEGIS/IPEDS data.

[a]Includes extension services.

[b]Computers, libraries, and deans.

[c]Admissions, registrars, counseling, student health, and recreation.

[d]Administration, accounting, security, alumni, and development.

[e]Scholarships from internal funds.

[f]Debt service.

[g]Total E&G expenditures under control of chief executive officer.

Table 13.3 Adjusted Educational and General (AE&G) Expenditure per Full-Time-Equivalent (FTE) Student, Trends for Four-Year Institutions, 1978–79 and 1987–88, by Enrollment Trends

AE&G per FTE Student	Instruction and Self-Supported Research	Public Service[a]	Academic Support[b]	Student Services[c]	Institutional Support[d]	Plant Operations	Internal Scholarships[e]	Mandatory Transfers[f]	Total AE&G[g]
Growing enrollments (N = 350):									
1978–79	3,244	352	735	454	903	878	178	127	6,871
1987–88	3,842	365	844	572	1,103	853	326	147	8,052
Change	+598	+13	+109	+118	+200	−25	+148	+20	+1,181
Share of increase	50.6	1.1	9.2	10.0	16.9	−2.1	12.5	1.7	100.0
Share of AE&G expenditures, 1987–88	47.7	4.5	10.5	7.1	13.7	10.6	4.0	1.8	100.0
Stable enrollments (N = 452):									
1978–79	3,850	394	849	471	920	927	245	160	7,816
1987–88	4,844	525	1,124	651	1,240	1,073	480	208	10,146
Change	+994	+131	+275	+180	+320	+146	+235	+48	+2,330
Share of increase	42.7	5.6	11.8	7.7	13.7	6.3	10.1	2.1	100.0
Share of AE&G expenditures, 1987–88	47.7	5.2	11.1	6.4	12.2	10.6	4.7	2.0	100.0
Declining enrollment (N = 390):									
1978–79	3,190	373	660	445	826	799	195	125	6,612
1987–88	4,174	500	1,005	660	1,286	1,026	444	159	9,255
Change	+984	+127	+345	+215	+460	+227	+249	+34	+2,643
Share of increase	37.2	4.8	13.1	8.1	17.4	8.6	9.4	1.3	100.0
Share of AE&G expenditures, 1987–88	45.1	5.4	10.9	7.1	13.8	11.1	4.8	1.7	100.0

Source: Computations by authors based on HEGIS/IPEDS data.

[a] Includes extension services.

[b] Computers, libraries, and deans.

[c] Admissions, registrars, counseling, student health, and recreation.

[d] Administration, accounting, security, alumni, and development.

[e] Scholarships from internal funds.

[f] Debt service.

[g] Total E&G expenditures under control of chief executive officer.

Table 13.4 Adjusted Educational and General (AE&G) Expenditure per Full-Time-Equivalent (FTE) Student, Trends for Two-Year Colleges, 1978–79 and 1987–88, by Enrollment Trends

AE&G per FTE Student	Instruction and Self-Supported Research	Public Service[a]	Academic Support[b]	Student Services[c]	Institutional Support[d]	Plant Operations	Internal Scholarships[e]	Mandatory Transfers[f]	Total AE&G[g]
Growing enrollments (N = 332):									
1978–79	2,187	88	328	366	626	501	24	107	4,227
1987–88	2,241	110	379	461	688	508	39	42	4,467
Change	+54	+22	+51	+95	+62	+7	+15	−65	+240
Share of increase	22.5	9.2	21.3	39.6	25.8	2.9	6.3	−27.1	100.0
Share of AE&G expenditures, 1987–88	50.2	2.5	8.5	10.3	15.4	11.4	.9	1.0	100.0
Stable enrollments (N = 229):									
1978–79	1,999	58	335	328	567	471	19	93	3,868
1987–88	2,310	109	421	451	765	549	28	44	4,678
Change	+311	+51	+86	+123	+198	+78	+9	−49	+810
Share of increase	38.4	6.3	10.6	15.2	24.4	9.6	1.1	−6.0	100.0
Share of AE&G expenditures, 1987–88	49.4	2.3	9.0	9.6	16.6	11.7	.6	.9	100.0
Declining enrollment (N = 292):									
1978–79	1,935	61	285	331	591	429	21	135	3,785
1987–88	2,554	105	425	555	817	612	35	38	5,141
Change	+619	+44	+140	+224	+226	+183	+14	−97	+1,356
Share of increase	45.6	3.2	10.3	16.5	16.7	13.5	1.0	7.2	100.0
Share of AE&G expenditures, 1987–88	49.7	2.0	8.3	10.8	15.9	11.9	.7	.7	100.0

Source: Computations by authors based on HEGIS/IPEDS data.

[a] Includes extension services.

[b] Computers, libraries, and deans.

[c] Admissions, registrars, counseling, student health, and recreation.

[d] Administration, accounting, security, alumni, and development.

[e] Scholarships from internal funds.

[f] Debt service.

[g] Total E&G expenditures under control of chief executive officer.

Table 13.5   Change in Adjusted Educational and General (AE&G) Expenditures per Student from 1978–79 to 1987–88 by Enrollment Trends for Homogeneous Groups of Institutions, All without Medical Schools

Category Number[a]	Carnegie Classification	Control	Size	Change in AE&G per Student ($)			Average Annual % Change in AE&G per Student		
				Growing	Stable	Declining	Growing	Stable	Declining
5	Doctoral	Public	4,000–20,000	+519 (N = 12)	+917 (N = 27)	+1,660 (N = 11)	.8	1.7	2.6
10	Comprehensive & Other-Four-Year	Public	1,000–3,000	+37 (N = 46)	+615 (N = 29)	+1,635 (N = 26)	.1	1.1	2.9
11	Comprehensive & Other-Four-Year	Public	3,000–10,000	+314 (N = 59)	+557 (N = 67)	+1,584 (N = 44)	.6	1.1	3.0
14	Comprehensive	Private	0–3,000	+1,405 (N = 57)	+2,144 (N = 56)	+2,798 (N = 47)	2.6	3.6	4.8
19	Other-Four-Year	Private	0–1,000	+503 (N = 86)	+1,793 (N = 57)	+2,608 (N = 24)	.8	2.7	4.0
21	Two-Year	Public	0–1,000	+582 (N = 101)	+913 (N = 51)	+1,902 (N = 57)	1.4	2.0	4.0
22	Two-Year	Public	1,000–3,000	+200 (N = 127)	+1,084 (N = 97)	+1,299 (N = 104)	.5	2.6	3.3
23	Two-Year	Public	3,000–16,000	+140 (N = 68)	+647 (N = 63)	+1,273 (N = 82)	.4	1.8	3.4
24	Two-Year	Private	0–3,000	+1,017 (N = 36)	+1,553 (N = +18)	+2,617 (N = +49)	2.0	3.5	5.4

Source: Calculations by authors based on HEGIS/IPEDS data.

[a]For category descriptions, see Table 12.6.

[b]In constant 1987–88 dollars, deflated by GNP implicit price deflator.

Institutions with growing enrollments are the only category of colleges and universities we uncovered in this study for which instruction and self-supported research account for a greater share of the increase in expenditures per student than their share of AE&G. The data suggest the following scenario. As enrollments rise, expenditures in most functional categories do not respond much. Deans and faculty are asked to provide services to the additional students, but their budgets are augmented only marginally. The rising enrollments force down expenditures per student as more students are accommodated with the same computers, deans, library, recreation hall, registrar, admissions office, president, and grounds crew.

More students quickly place pressure on class sizes in certain departments, particularly those where the institution's culture requires smaller classes (e.g., writing and mathematics courses). If the institution is to maintain smaller class sizes in freshman English, calculus, and foreign languages, it must accommodate the rising enrollments with additional faculty. Many of these faculty may be part-time teachers at first, but, once the institution acknowledges the change in enrollment to be permanent, they are converted to full-time positions. Instruction rises as a fraction of total expenditures for institutions with rising enrollments because there is some response in the number of full-time faculty to growing enrollments, at least over our nine-year period. Even though instructional expenditures per student rise less at growing institutions than at stable and declining ones, they rise relatively faster than other types of expenditures at the rapidly growing institutions, primarily because the other expenditures rise hardly at all.

The substantial difference in cost increases between growing and declining institutions suggests considerable sluggishness in resource adjustments to shifts in demand. The differences are clear and large over the period of analysis.

A similar pattern of cost increases occurred in Two-Year colleges over the period, as shown in Table 13.4. At Two-Year colleges whose enrollments grew 1.8 percent or more annually, AE&G per student increased only 0.7 percent annually compared to 3.4 percent for Two-Year colleges with declining enrollments. It appears that having more students at Two-Year colleges does not generate additional instructional or plant operations expenditures. Class size must simply be allowed to rise in the existing classrooms.

The pattern of cost increases for institutions experiencing different enrollment trends suggests that changes in the college age cohort and enrollment rates have a noticeable effect on costs per student. The college and university business appears to be one in which adjustment to change is slow. In the mean-

---

was plausible, and each was statistically significantly different from zero. Twenty-eight percent of the linear variation in AE&G per student was explained by the linear variation in the independent variables. The elasticity was computed at the mean values of AE&G per student and the growth rate of enrollment.

time, the resources on hand are used to serve whatever number of students show up at registration. As difficult as they are, predictions of aggregate college student enrollment are easier to pin down than estimates of future enrollments at specific institutions. Changes in student tastes and the attraction of different institutions weaken the accuracy of forecasted enrollments at specific institutions, even over a period as short as a decade. This phenomenon may have helped control costs during the 1960s and 1970s, when enrollments rose rapidly at two-thirds of all colleges and universities and existing expenditures were perpetually being spread over an ever increasing student population. It also suggests that, as the shrinking college age cohort finally overtakes rising enrollment rates and the absolute number of students in higher education declines in the early 1990s, costs per student may rise even faster than we have seen so far because more institutions may contract.

13.3   Estimating Economies of Scale

Scale economies allow the production of goods or services at a lower per-unit cost when the scale of operation is enlarged. Knowledge about the relation between average cost and enrollment can usefully guide management or government policy decisions about enrollment growth and the number of colleges required to serve students at the lowest possible cost. There are scores of empirical estimates of scale economies in higher education (Brinkman and Leslie 1986; Brinkman 1990). Substantial variation in the size of colleges and universities, ranging from multiversity campuses so large that bus transportation is essential to colleges so small that all students are on a first-name basis, facilitates studies of scale economies in higher education. Unfortunately, most of the studies illustrate the various pitfalls surrounding attempts to identify the minimum long-run average cost at various enrollment levels from cross-sectional data.

Most of the studies are statistical cost analyses (Johnston 1960) conducted by relating the cost per unit of "output" (usually measured as annual educational and general [E&G] expenditures per full-time-equivalent student) to the scale of operation (usually measured in terms of annual full-time-equivalent enrollment). A number of (frequently implicit) assumptions are made when such an effort consists of regressing E&G per student on various specifications of annual enrollment.

First, it is usually assumed that all institutions in the analysis have similar objectives and produce a homogeneous "output" that is, annual student enrollments. The homogeneous output assumption may be appropriate for those colleges and universities that do not emphasize faculty research and that have few, if any, postbaccalaureate programs. But it is clearly invalid for Research, Doctoral, and Comprehensive universities, where, among other differences, some institutions have on-campus medical schools. Liberal Arts I, Other-

Four-Year colleges, and Two-Year colleges probably produce as workably homogeneous an output as can be found among the Carnegie classifications.

When output is measured by enrollment, each year of higher education is valued equally. No premium is attributed to graduation beyond the learning acquired during the final year of baccalaureate study. But the proportion of students graduating differs across institutions. Using enrollment to measure output also values a year's college experience equally, whether at a more or less selective institution, whether it consists of intimate honors seminars or mass lectures delivered via closed-circuit television, or whether it involves more or less effective pedagogical methods.

Second, the nonprofit status of colleges and universities calls into question a related assumption critical to estimating the minimum long-run cost curve, namely, that all institutions strive equally to minimize costs (Newhouse 1970). Hoenack (1990) argues that the organizational character of colleges and universities permits units within them to capture varying amounts of rents by exerting local "market power." Individual units within colleges and universities may not share with the institution's central management the goal of producing a given quality of product at minimum cost. Because monitoring and enforcement costs grow with an organization's size, one would expect subunits in larger universities to be more effective in achieving their own goals. Furthermore, one might question whether the objectives of the central management of nonprofit organizations embrace cost minimization at all.

Third, statistical cost studies of higher education scale economies implicitly assume that the technology and factor prices faced by each institution in the sample were similar when each selected its factor proportions and production methods. If the observed institutions selected their production methods from menus available to them at different points in time, and if technology has changed over time, cross-sectional analysis will be unable to disentangle scale economies from shifts in the long-run scale curve caused by technological improvement (or long-run adjustments in factor prices). It can be argued that, on these grounds, higher education is particularly well suited to estimating scale economies because its technology is stagnant. In other work, however, we gather evidence that calls that conclusion into question (Getz and Siegfried 1990).

Fourth, Friedman (1955) argued long ago that statistical cost analyses are destined to reveal horizontal long-run average cost curves because institutions of the most efficient size will command a premium in the secondary asset market, thus increasing their measured costs under new ownership, and vice versa for inefficiently sized institutions. Because few colleges or universities are sold, this problem does not appear to plague scale economies estimates in higher education.

What is a problem with college and university accounting data, however, is the absence of uniform capital accounts. Almost all colleges and universities operate exclusively on a current account basis, with no allowance for the depreciation of long-lived assets.[4] The E&G data of the U.S. Department of Education measure annual direct educational operating expenses. Excluded are expenditures on auxiliary operations (e.g., food service, bookstores, housing), hospitals, and federally funded research centers as well as the annual depreciation related to the flow of services from plant and equipment.[5] This implies that scale economy estimates based on current account data are likely to understate the importance of scale economies in higher education and understate the enrollment level at which costs are minimized because average capital costs usually decline with size.[6]

Fifth, the financing of public higher education in America may eliminate, or at least obscure, any real relation between average cost and size. Funding formulas at many public universities depend on enrollments (Caruthers and Marks 1988; Lyddon 1986; Tennessee Higher Education Commission 1990). In addition, tuition revenues are approximately proportional to enrollments. If one views legislative funding of public institutions as a residual, in which the state provides resources sufficient to cover the excess of costs over tuition at state colleges and universities, and if "needed" revenue per student is established exogenously through negotiations among the institutions, higher education commissions, and the state legislatures, then state universities will want to spend all their state revenues. Thus, expenditures per student will track revenues per student. Even if the marginal cost of additional enrollments in reality declines to a point where it is quite low, the institution will report a constant average cost because an incentive exists to spend "excess" revenues on "slack," to use Williamson's (1975) term. Slack consists of expenditures over and above what is necessary to attract and retain the necessary resources to accomplish an assigned task.[7] In higher education, slack may take the form of expenditures on recruitment, expenditures to improve the quality of the student body and enhance the reputation of faculty and administration, expenditures on secretaries, new microcomputers, and library acquisitions to foster research, or expenditures on the working environment, for example, new furniture or campus beautification projects. In this view, expenditures per

4. Accepted accounting practices as promulgated by the National Association of College and University Business Officers do not call for recognition of the annual cost of depreciation. In recent years, however, some institutions, particularly private universities, began recording some depreciation costs.

5. The HEGIS/IPEDS data (see Chapter 11, n. 14, above) do include information on the book value of buildings, equipment, and land, but they do not contain a measure of the annual flow of depreciation of these assets.

6. If the technology that permits lower unit costs at larger scales of operation involves a substantial substitution of capital for labor, it is possible for average capital costs to rise with size. Scale economies can exist under such circumstances so long as the savings in variable inputs per unit outweigh the increased capital costs per unit at larger scales of operation.

7. Whether such "slack" represents inefficiency or whether it creates alternative leisure value of equivalent or greater value to the management or workers who "capture" it is controversial (see Leibenstein 1978; and Stigler 1976; a summary of the debate is contained in Siegfried and Wheeler 1981).

student may be constant across a wide variety of enrollment levels even if minimum required costs decline with enrollment. Public universities will identify other expenditures, presumably "unnecessary," in order to avoid returning revenues to the state legislature, and expenditures per student will then be determined by revenue formulas rather than by minimum necessary costs.

Sixth, attempts to estimate the long-run scale curve from cross-sectional data implicitly assume that each institution is in long-run cost-minimizing equilibrium, that it is on, not above, the long-run scale curve. But, as we documented earlier in this chapter, some colleges and universities operate temporarily at lower than planned enrollment levels, while others periodically operate beyond their planned enrollment levels. Even sophisticated estimates of scale economies in higher education (e.g., Cohn, Rhine, and Santos 1989) treat all institutions as if they are in long-run equilibrium, although several take care to argue specifically that their estimates describe the average behavior of colleges and universities rather than the minimum cost frontier (Brinkman 1985, 341; Cohn and Geske 1990, 167). As Brinkman (1990) noted, failure to control for the rate of change in enrollment will lead to understatements of cost during periods of enrollment growth and overstatements during periods of decline, which may generate false evidence of scale economies.

13.4 Disequilibrium and the Estimation of Economies of Scale

Economies of scale estimates are supposed to disclose the lowest average cost of producing each of many different possible output levels when all inputs can be varied. In the short run, a large proportion of college and university costs are fixed, or at least quasi-fixed, in the sense that they cannot be adjusted quickly to accommodate the actual enrollment level optimally. In the long run, institutions have more flexibility to adjust "plant" size (here including quasi-fixed factors such as tenured faculty) to accommodate the realized output level.

If the long-run scale curve declines over the relevant range of output, costs likely will be higher than expected for institutions experiencing declining enrollments and lower than expected for institutions growing modestly faster than expected (because, as output expands beyond the equilibrium level, the short-run average cost curve first declines before eventually rising). The cost disadvantage of operating in disequilibrium will appear to be more for institutions experiencing declining enrollments because the short-run average cost curve rises immediately as output falls below the long-run equilibrium level. Of course, the divergence of short-run from long-run cost curves at output levels above expected enrollment might actually be greater or less than the divergence at enrollment levels comparably below the planned level, and it is doubtful that instructional quality, at least as reflected in the student/faculty ratio, remains constant in the face of unexpected enrollment outcomes.

If an institution is growing or declining rapidly, it is likely to find itself operating on a short-run cost relation, making due with the relatively "fixed" inputs of full-time faculty and physical facilities selected for a different enrollment level and adjusting the few inputs over which it has immediate control (e.g., part-time faculty) in order to accommodate the unexpected level of enrollments.

The evidence presented in Tables 13.1–13.4 suggests a much greater cost disadvantage for institutions with declining enrollments than for those with growing enrollments. If anything, expanding colleges appear to enjoy much smaller increases in costs than stable or declining institutions, suggesting that students at growing institutions are accommodated with existing resources. This implies that the short-run marginal cost of additional students is modest, although a decline in the quality of education is also likely to accompany spurts in enrollment if resources have any effect on the quality of education.

To evaluate the importance of the equilibrium assumption for estimates of scale economies, we assume that each institution expects its own enrollment to grow at approximately the average rate over the period. The average rate can be predicted by institutions with reasonable accuracy on the basis of demographic trends, even if it is more difficult to predict enrollment growth for specific institutions.[8]

To illustrate the possible consequences for scale economies estimates of including data from colleges and universities operating in disequilibrium, we estimate average cost functions for the private four-year institutions in each of the Carnegie classifications. For each category, we estimate 1987–88 AE&G expenditures per full-time-equivalent student as a quadratic function of enrollment, first using only those institutions experiencing enrollment growth rates between zero and 1.8 percent annually from 1978–79 to 1987–88 (the middle third of the enrollment growth rates), which we call "stable." Limiting the observations to institutions with relatively stable enrollment growth rates should eliminate from the sample those institutions most likely to be operating off their long-run cost curve. We then compute the estimated minimum efficient scale for the entire sample so as to compare with results obtained when the declining and rapidly growing institutions are excluded.

Estimates are computed only for private institutions because the average cost-size relation of public institutions is likely skewed by the institutional character of funding higher education in the various states. Under such conditions, it is difficult, if not impossible, to identify minimum average cost for different enrollment levels.

Decision making could be improved if the source of scale economies could be identified. That is, scale economies in, say, library and computer functions, as opposed to plant operations functions, suggest specific strategies to minimize costs. Nevertheless, we do not estimate scale economies for the functional categories in the HEGIS/IPEDS accounting system because we believe

---

8. Changes in enrollment *rates*, however, can lead to errors in predicting enrollments from demographic trends alone, as was experienced during the 1980s.

that the classification of costs among categories may be systematically related to institutional size. At larger institutions, management is more specialized and often more sophisticated; accounting categories are more refined, and greater care is given to developing an accurate accounting system. It is more difficult for top management at larger institutions to learn about their college or university informally. Therefore, accounts are more important for management of larger institutions. For example, HEGIS/IPEDS indicates that public service and sponsored research expenditures should be reported separately, if possible. Many smaller colleges (and a few larger institutions) did not report these categories separately, including relevant expenditures, instead, in instruction. Thus, instructional expenditures may appear to decline with size of institution because of the accounting treatment of public service and sponsored research.

In addition, many inputs are used in more than one function, necessitating joint cost allocations. How these are done may also be related to institutional size. Consequently, we estimate scale economies only for total AE&G expenditures per student.[9]

The relation between average costs and size may be estimated a number of different ways. First, one must decide whether to estimate how total costs vary with enrollment and from that estimate derive computationally the average cost-enrollment relation or whether instead to estimate the average cost-enrollment relation directly. The decision hinges primarily on econometric considerations.[10] An examination of the alternatives indicates that a better estimate is obtained by relating average cost directly to enrollment.

Second, one must decide what functional specification best describes the relation between cost and size. The traditional specification, consistent with average cost first declining and eventually rising with size, is a quadratic form. We adopted this form (illustrated in Figure 13.1).[11]

---

9. The fear is that cross-sectional comparisons of expenditures per student in various functional categories are invalid. The analysis in Chapter 12 also relied on functional categories. However, most of the comparisons in Chapter 12 were in terms of the change in expenditures over time in different categories and were essentially time-series comparisons. We, of course, rely on the principle of accounting consistency, and, where individual institutions refined or altered their accounting practices, the comparisons in Chapter 12 also may be subject to error.

10. The choice, in part, depends on the extent to which the "tightness" of the estimated relation varies with the size of the institution. A test for heteroskedasticity revealed that the error terms are correlated with enrollment size for all Carnegie classifications when estimating total cost as a function of enrollment. When estimating average cost directly, only two of the five equations estimated for Carnegie classifications suffered from this defect.

11. Estimating average total cost with a quadratic implies that all costs vary, to some degree, with output. That is, if the quadratic equation for average total cost were multiplied through by enrollment, there would be no term independent of enrollment, thus no term expressing fixed costs. We experimented with an alternative form that explicitly allowed for fixed costs:

$$\text{average total cost} = \frac{\alpha_i}{E} + \alpha_2 + \alpha_3 E + \alpha_4 E^2,$$

where E = enrollment. Estimates of the alternative form suffered from severe heteroskedasticity; we therefore abandoned it.

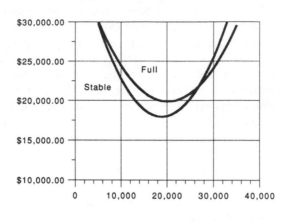

AE&G per Student

Figure 13.1   Economies of scale in private research universities.
Source: Authors' calculation from HEGIS/IPEDS data.
Note: The curve marked "Full" is estimated with 1987–88 data for all 24 private Research universities in the survey, as reported in Table 13.7. The minimum AE&G expenditure per student occurs at 20,227 students. The curve marked "Stable" is estimated with data from the 21 private Research universities with stable enrollment from 1978–79 to 1987–88 (Table 13.6). The minimum AE&G expenditure per student occurs at 18,934 students when the relation is estimated using only universities with stable enrollment.

We followed procedures used in other studies in several other respects as well, for example, using full-time-equivalent students as a measure of "output." A number of past studies distinguished between undergraduate and graduate enrollments as outputs, and a few even distinguished between upper- and lower-division undergraduate courses (Brinkman 1981b). We do not make such a distinction; instead, we treat all student enrollments as equivalent, without distinction among instructional levels. Thus, our estimates are subject to some of the same criticisms that we leveled earlier against prior studies of scale economies in higher education.

To address the output mix problem, most cost functions for colleges and universities have been estimated for groups of institutions, frequently Carnegie classifications. This minimizes some of the potential distortion, but the mix of outputs at different Research and Doctoral universities, in particular, still varies considerably, complicating interpretation of the results. We adopt the standard approach.

13.5   Scale Economies in Research, Doctoral, and Comprehensive Universities

Statistically estimated cost functions began appearing in the late 1960s (Brinkman and Leslie 1986; Brinkman 1990). Most focused on either instructional costs (including self-supported research) or E&G expenditures.

Output in the cost studies is usually measured by enrollments, sometimes delineated by level of instruction. A few studies (e.g., Verry and Davies 1976; Cohn, Rhine, and Santos 1989) also attempt to measure research outputs. None, to our knowledge, has attempted to measure and include public service outputs, and few have made any attempt to *value* student enrollments (but see Verry and Davies 1976). Thus, a student enrolled in a course is said to create the same "output" no matter the size or character of the course and no matter the type, size, or control of the institution. A year's experience in small seminars at Davidson or Princeton is equivalent to a year's worth of lectures held in the gymnasium of a large state university. Likewise, a full-time-equivalent student year at Berkeley or Michigan is valued equally to a year spent at a tiny private liberal arts college with eight full-time faculty, not one of whom has a Ph.D.

A number of studies of cost functions estimate marginal and average costs at the average-size institution. If average costs exceed marginal costs, economies of scale exist at that output level. If marginal costs exceed average costs, diseconomies of scale exist. Using this method of analysis, Tierney (1980a), Brovender (1974), and Brinkman (1981b, 1984) discovered economies of scale for departments in selective private liberal arts colleges, a large public research university, and less selective liberal arts colleges.

The most common method used to identify scale economies has been to estimate average costs as a function of enrollment. The literature based on this methodology reports mixed findings about economies of scale in research universities (Brinkman 1990; Hoenack 1990). For example, Broomall et al. (1978) found no evidence for scale economies in public research and doctoral universities, while Cohn, Rhine, and Santos (1989), using a multiple output production function, found evidence of scale economies for the simultaneous expansion of undergraduate, graduate, and research programs up to about 5,000 students and for research alone up to the size of all but the largest public research universities. They applied an econometric estimation method that captures the independent and joint effects on cost of expanding any of three outputs: undergraduate enrollment, graduate enrollment, and research. In an extension of this analysis, de Groot, McMahon, and Volkwein (1989) also discovered strong evidence of scale economies in producing teaching and research at research universities. The lowest-cost research university turns out to be quite large, according to their evidence, with cost minimizing undergraduate enrollment even larger than in any of the existing institutions.

Brinkman (1981a) found no evidence of instructional cost advantages to larger public research institutions. This finding might be due to the institutional environment of public institutions' revenue formulas. When Brinkman combined public and private universities, scale economies appeared to surface, but these could be an illusion based on differences in the output mix and quality of instruction between public and private institutions. Of course, quality differences in the education provided at different size institutions may undermine all the efforts to detect scale economies. Verry and Davies (1976), in a study of British universities excluding Oxford, Cambridge, and London, attempted to control for the quality of teaching across institutions by using graduation rates and improvements in examination scores. They found some evidence that the value of education may improve with institutional size. If their conclusion is correct, scale economies studies may systematically underestimate the "output" of larger institutions and understate the advantages of size in higher education. Even without using such a correction for quality, Corrallo (1970) discovered that expenditures per student were lower at larger research universities. In his classic study of college and university costs, Bowen (1980) found an irregular relation between "educational costs" (a concept very close to our AE&G) and enrollment. In sum, the evidence of scale economies for research universities is mixed.

Our empirical results based on 1987–88 data are reported in Tables 13.6 (for stable-growth private colleges and universities only) and 13.7 (for all private institutions). For private Doctoral and Comprehensive institutions, there is no evidence of a relation between average cost and enrollment. Indeed, for the estimates based on the sample of institutions that we expect to be closest to operating on the minimum long-run average cost curve (Table 13.6), the signs of the coefficients are not even "correct." The usual (U-shaped) cost curve, as shown in Figure 13.1, requires a negative sign on the enrollment coefficient and a positive sign on the coefficient of enrollment squared.

For the private Research universities, we obtain different results, depending on the sample used. This illustrates the importance of excluding institutions in the midst of large enrollment change and ensuring that institutions in the sample share a common mission. The results based on all 24 private Research universities in our sample, reported in Table 13.7, reveal a flat average cost curve. Because neither of the coefficients related to enrollment is statistically different from zero, it is proper to interpret the results as indicating no relation between AE&G per student and enrollment. Although the scale curve estimated with the full sample appears in Figure 13.1 to exhibit declining unit costs until an enrollment level of 20,000 students, the relation is too uncertain to draw such a conclusion.

In contrast, the private Research universities display a declining average cost curve up to an enrollment level around 19,000 students, when only the 21 (of 24) private Research universities with stable enrollments are used in the estimation. These results are shown in Table 13.6 and Figure 13.1. The relation appears sufficiently consistent to lend confidence to the conclusion that average costs do decline in private Research universities up to an enrollment level of about 19,000. That only three universities could change the results so much indicates the importance of rapidly declining or growing institutions.[12]

Although the coefficient on enrollment squared is not statistically signifi-

---

12. The three private Research universities in our sample that did not experience stable enrollments from 1978–79 to 1987–88 were Carnegie-Mellon, Harvard, and Johns Hopkins. All three experienced average annual enrollment growth exceeding 1.8 percent per year.

Table 13.6   **Estimated Scale Economies for Private Four-Year Colleges and Universities, 1987–88, by Carnegie Classification, Stable-Growth Institutions Only**

Carnegie Classification	Sample Size	Estimated Average Cost (E = enrollment)	$\bar{R}^2$	Minimum Efficient Scale (MES)	% Cost Elevation at E = ½ MES
Research	21	$\dfrac{AE\&G}{E} = 39{,}786 - 2.31E + .000061E^2$ $(-1.70)^*$ (1.24)	.19	18,934[a]	30.5
Doctoral	15	$\dfrac{AE\&G}{E} = 14{,}563 + .67E - .000103E^2$ $(.25)$ (-0.56)	.11	[b]	[b]
Comprehensive	76	$\dfrac{AE\&G}{E} = 6{,}841.3 + .46E + .000021E^2$ $(.89)$ $(.36)$	.11	[b]	[b]
Liberal Arts I	75	$\dfrac{AE\&G}{E} = 14.105 - .77E + .000170E^2$ $(-.24)$ $(.20)$	-.03	[b]	[b]
Other-Four-Year	72	$\dfrac{AE\&G}{E} = 11{,}610 - 6.82E + .003057E^2$ $(-2.31)^*$ $(1.94)^*$	.06	1,100	11.9

Source: Computations by authors based on HEGIS/IPEDS data.

[a]See text for proper interpretation of Research university results.

[b]Not available.

*Statistically significant at the 90 percent confidence level, using a one-tailed test.

Table 13.7   Estimated Scale Economies for Private Four-Year Colleges and Universities, 1987–88, by Carnegie Classifications, All Institutions

Carnegie Classification	Sample Size	Estimated Average Cost (E = enrollment)	$\bar{R}^2$	Minimum Efficient Scale (MES)	% Cost Elevation at E = ½ MES
Research	24	$\dfrac{AE\&G}{E} = 37{,}834 - 1.78E + .000044E^2$ $(-1.14)\qquad(.77)$	.08	a	a
Doctoral	36	$\dfrac{AE\&G}{E} = 15{,}067 - .54E + .000008E^2$ $(-1.04)\qquad(.36)$	.08	a	a
Comprehensive	219	$\dfrac{AE\&G}{E} = 7{,}223 + .34E + .000008E^2$ $(.91)\qquad(.18)$	.04	a	a
Liberal Arts I	129	$\dfrac{AE\&G}{E} = 14{,}848 - 3.06E + .000965E^2$ $(-1.56)^*\qquad(1.62)^*$	.01	1,600	5.0
Other-Four-Year	331	$\dfrac{AE\&G}{E} = 12{,}302 - 6.00E + .001391E^2$ $(-5.72)^*\qquad(3.95)^*$	.09	2,150	27.6

Source: Computations by authors based on HEGIS/IPEDS data.

*Statistically significant at the 90 percent confidence level, using a one-tailed test.

aNot available.

cantly different than zero at the conventional 90 percent confidence level, we nevertheless calculate the enrollment size that would minimize costs for private Research universities as if the declining cost curve *did* eventually begin to rise at larger enrollment levels.[13] So calculated, minimum efficient scale occurs at about 19,000 students, well above the average size of the private Research universities (11,250 students). Costs per student are about 30 percent higher for a private Research university of 9,500, a substantial "cost penalty" to pay for operating at half the minimum efficient scale.[14]

The appearance of scale economies here is deceiving. The 21 private Research universities with stable enrollments over the period include 15 with medical centers on their campuses and six without. As demonstrated in Chapter 12 (Table 12.3), Research universities with and without medical schools have different cost structures. The average 1987–88 AE&G expenditure per full-time-equivalent student at the 17 private Research universities with medical centers was $24,145, compared to $18,264 at the seven private Research universities without medical schools. The private Research universities without on-campus medical schools are, on average, much smaller (7,550 full-time-equivalent students) than their counterparts with medical schools (12,750 full-time-equivalent students). Under these circumstances, depending on the cost levels of individual universities, it is possible to observe scale economies for the combined institutions (grouping together those with and without medical schools) when, in fact, for each group separately the scale relation is flat. Thus, estimated scale economies based on a combined sample may portray an illusion of declining costs because the average cost levels of characteristically different types of institutions are being inadvertently compared. Further statistical analysis of our data verifies this account. If private Research universities with medical schools are appropriately considered as different from those without medical schools in ways that affect their average costs, they should be analyzed separately. When analyzed separately, evidence of scale economies for private Research universities evaporates, regardless of the sample used (the 21 stable-growth universities or all 24 institutions). We conclude that estimates of scale economies for private Research universities that lump together those with and those without medical schools produce a misleading conclusion. In contrast to most of the previous findings about cost differences between large and small Research universities, we find no evidence of any systematic relation between average cost and size for private Research universities.[15]

13. Formally, because the negative coefficient on enrollment is statistically significantly different from zero and the positive coefficient on enrollment squared it not statistically significantly different from zero, the scale curve for private Research universities continues to decline at higher and higher enrollment levels, never attaining an enrollment level beyond which average costs rise.

14. We estimated the scale economies relations for 1978–79, 1983–84, and 1985–86 too. The results are virtually the same for each category of institution.

15. This conclusion helps explain an anomaly between the behavior of the prestigious Research universities and an implication of the usual finding in the literature—that scale economies exist

13.6 Scale Economies in Liberal Arts Colleges

In their comprehensive summary of scale economies studies on liberal arts colleges, Brinkman and Leslie (1986, 18) conclude that these institutions "typically seem to achieve most of their scale-related economies by the time enrollment reaches 1,500 to 2,000 full-time-equivalent students . . . , or even a little sooner." Whether E&G expenditures per student actually rise at liberal arts colleges after reaching their minimum is unknown. Maynard (1971) and Bowen (1980) point to evidence of diseconomies of scale of the largest liberal arts colleges, but Brinkman (1981b), Carlson (1972), and Metz (1964) report a flat unit cost curve after scale economies are exhausted.

We were able to detect no relation between expenditures per student and enrollment levels for stable-enrollment private Liberal Arts I colleges (see Table 13.6). The difference between our results and past studies, which usually report a declining long-run average cost curve, may be caused by restricting our sample to only those institutions whose enrollments were relatively stable over the nine prior years.[16] Using the stable-enrollments criterion eliminated 27 of the 40 Liberal Arts I colleges with fewer than 1,000 students from the sample; 20 of the 27 experienced declining enrollments over the period, while enrollments at seven grew faster than 1.8 percent annually. Only 13 of the 40 were "stable." For the 89 Liberal Arts I colleges enrolling more than 1,000 students (all but one of which had fewer than 3,000), 62 experienced stable enrollments, 18 had declining enrollments, and the enrollments at nine grew faster than 1.8 percent per year. Based on these facts, we would expect to observe scale economies if the long-run average cost curve were estimated with the entire sample, including the vast majority of relatively smaller institutions that experienced declining enrollments. Including all the smaller colleges overstates their long-run equilibrium costs. By comparing the (higher) short-run disequilibrium costs of smaller schools that recently lost enrollment to the long-run equilibrium costs of larger colleges, it is possible to infer evidence of scale economies when none exist. The results reported in Table 13.7

---

up to an enrollment level of about 20,000 students. Only three of the 24 private Research universities in our sample are larger than 20,000 students, and those three by only a slight amount (Boston University, New York University, and the University of Southern California each enrolled about 23,000 full-time-equivalent students in 1987–88). If scale economies were possible up to an enrollment level of, say, 19,000, and if institutions of half that size suffered a 30 percent cost disadvantage (see Table 13.6), why would a majority of these institutions (14 of 24) operate at less than half the size necessary to minimize their costs? The answer is that in all likelihood the apparent scale economies are a mirage.

16. An alternative explanation for the difference is that we estimated separate scale curves for Liberal Arts I and Other-Four-Year institutions while most of the previous attempts to identify scale effects for liberal arts colleges combined the two categories. Because Liberal Arts I colleges are, on average, larger and more expensive than Other-Four-Year colleges, a scale curve estimated for the combined categories is likely to be flatter than one estimated for either group of institutions separately. Therefore, this is not likely the reason we find an absence of scale effects for Liberal Arts I colleges while "the literature" reports declining unit costs with enrollment.

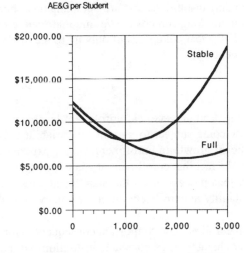

AE&G per Student

Figure 13.2   **Economies of scale in Other-Four-Year colleges.**
Source: Authors' calculation from HEGIS/IPEDS data.
Note: The curve marked "Full" is estimated with 1987–88 data for all 331 Other-Four-Year colleges in the survey, as reported in Table 13.7. The minimum AE&G expenditure per student occurs at 2,150 students. The curve marked "Stable" is estimated with data from the 72 Other-Four-Year colleges with stable enrollment from 1978–79 to 1987–88 (Table 13.6). The minimum AE&G expenditure per student occurs at 1,100 students when the relation is estimated using only data from colleges with stable enrollment.

confirm this story; using *all* the data to estimate the average cost curve, it (incorrectly) appears that institutions of fewer than 1,600 students suffer a unit cost disadvantage, just as is generally found in the literature (Brinkman and Leslie 1986). Using only those Liberal Arts I colleges with stable enrollment (Table 13.6) yields a horizontal unit cost curve.

The evidence from the private Other-Four-Year colleges reveals an analogous (but opposite) effect of disequilibrium. The estimates of the cost per student relation for private Other-Four-Year colleges using the full sample and stable-enrollment institutions are illustrated in Figure 13.2. Table 13.6 shows that, for the stable enrollment Other-Four-Year colleges (only about 22 percent of the category), economies of scale are evident until an enrollment level of about 1,100. There is a cost disadvantage of about 12 percent for operating at half this size.[17] With the entire sample included, the estimated minimum efficient scale enrollment rises to 2,150, closer to the 1,500–2,000 range observed in the literature (Brinkman and Leslie 1986). The usual conclusion from past studies is suspect because it is derived from statistical cost analyses

17. The average enrollment of the 72 Other-Four-Year colleges with stable enrollment growth was 800 in 1987–88. Only 17 of them were as small as 550 students, half the lowest cost scale.

that are based on many institutions that are operating on a short-run cost curve that is *above* minimum long-run costs. We find that scale economies do exist for private Other-Four-Year colleges, but only up to the modest annual enrollment of 1,100 students.[18]

13.7 Summary

For many colleges and universities, enrollment level is not fixed by policy but rather is an outcome subject to significant variability. Some institutions experience significant growth in enrollment; others experience sustained declines. In view of the fact that enrollment at some institutions is controlled by a selective admissions process or by the state agency responsible for higher education, the volatility in enrollment among so many institutions is remarkable.

The variation in enrollment has important consequences for costs. In particular, holding other characteristics constant, institutions with declining enrollments tend to exhibit higher current operating costs per student. Institutions with increasing enrollments tend to have lower costs per student. Colleges and universities, then, appear to be slow to adjust their operations to changing enrollment levels. If the accounting records included the costs of space and facilities, that is, the cost of the capital used, the disparity in cost per student between declining, stable, and expanding institutions would be all the more striking.

The effect of changes in enrollment on cost per student has important consequences for efforts to measure economies of scale. When enrollment change is taken into account in a simple way, estimates of minimum cost scale change. When ignoring enrollment fluctuations, our estimates of scale economies are similar to those of many other investigators. When we take account of changes in enrollment, however, estimated scale effects differ. Because rates of change in enrollments vary widely across higher education, controlling for enrollment change in estimating scale effects is important. Until cross-sectional studies of scale economies account for recent trends in enrollment, the numbers that are derived from them should be used only with considerable caution.[19]

---

18. Although we believe that unrestricted scholarships should be viewed as a cost of college (see Chapter 12, sec. 12.2), it can be argued that they are better treated as a revenue offset and, thus, should not be included in costs. We excluded unrestricted scholarships from AE&G and reestimated the scale economies equations; the results were virtually the same.

19. Even if the disequilibrium problem can be overcome, the output mix, nonprofit incentives, different cohorts, absence of capital costs, and public funding formula problems may be so severe that we are unlikely to obtain scale economies estimates that are of sufficient quality to inform higher education managers or public policy about optimal college size.

14   Costs per Student over Time

Instructional expenditures in higher education can be linked to the student/ faculty ratio in a way that reveals important differences in the structure of costs in higher education. To what extent do costs differ because of differences in the student/faculty ratio or differences in faculty salaries or perhaps differences in other instructional costs? The student/faculty ratio is viewed sometimes as a shortcut measure of educational quality (lower ratios imply better quality) and sometimes as a measure of efficiency (higher ratios imply more efficiency). Changes in the student/faculty ratio over time reveal how higher education responds to a changing environment (O'Neill 1976). The salaries of faculty are the most important cost in higher education, and so a concern for trends in costs must of necessity address trends in student/faculty ratios and in faculty salaries.

Over the last 120 years in higher education in the United States, the aggregate student/faculty ratio has changed substantially. Figure 14.1 shows that, in 1869, the student/faculty ratio for all of higher education was just under 10 and stayed essentially unchanged through 1909, even as the number of colleges nearly doubled, the average size of institutions increased nearly fourfold, and total enrollment increased over sevenfold. As depicted in the accompanying table (Table 14.1), the ratio rose over 20 percent from 1909 to 1919 and showed modest further increase to 1929. It fell nearly to 10 again by 1939 and remained in that vicinity through 1959. In the 1960s, the ratio increased by 86 percent to 17.8. There was a modest decline from the 1969 peak in the succeeding years. Clearly, the 1960s were an era of rapid change in higher education. Enrollment grew by about 120 percent, the number of institutions grew by just over 25 percent, and the number of faculty grew by only 18 percent. This was an era of rapid increase in institutional size and change in production relations. Whether the change reflected a deterioration in quality

Students/Institution

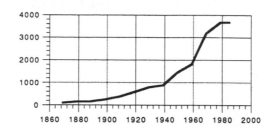

Students/Faculty

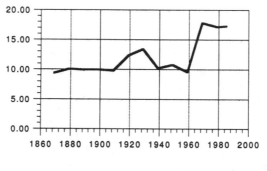

Figure 14.1   Students per institution and student/faculty ratio, 1869–1985.
Source: U.S. Department of Education (1988, table 116, p. 141).

Table 14.1   **Students, Faculty, and Institutions from 1869 to 1985**

	Students (in 1,000s)	Faculty (in 1,000s)	Institutions	Students per Institution	Students per Faculty
1869	52	5.6	563	93	9.35
1879	116	11.5	811	143	10.05
1889	157	15.8	998	157	9.92
1899	238	23.9	977	243	9.95
1909	355	36.5	951	374	9.74
1919	598	48.6	1,041	574	12.30
1929	1,101	82.4	1,409	781	13.36
1939	1,494	149.9	1,708	875	10.17
1949	2,659	247.7	1,851	1,437	10.78
1959	3,640	380.6	2,008	1,813	9.56
1969	8,005	450.0	2,525	3,170	17.79
1979	11,570	675.0	3,152	3,671	17.14
1985	12,247	710.0	3,340	3,667	17.25

Source: U.S. Department of Education (1988, table 116, p. 141).

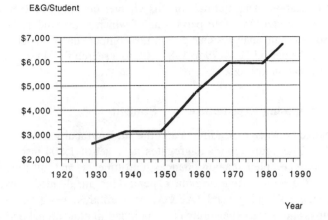

Figure 14.2   E&G expenditures per student, 1929–30 to 1985–86, in 1987–88 dollars.
Sources: U.S. Department of Education (1988, table 116, p. 141); Bureau of the Census, *Historical Statistics of the United States, Colonial Times to 1970* (Washington, D.C.: U.S. Government Printing Office, 1975), 197; U.S. Bureau of the Census, *Statistical Abstract of the United States* (Washington, D.C.: U.S. Government Printing Office, various years).

or an increase in productivity requires a more powerful analysis. We can conclude, however, that higher education in the aggregate has been capable of rapid change in its fundamental character.

Information about educational and general (E&G) expenditures is available in the aggregate from 1929–30, as shown in Figure 14.2. Expenditures per student, inflated to dollars of 1987–88 purchasing power by the GNP implicit price deflator over 50 years, have more than doubled. The increase, however, has occurred in episodes of very rapid change interspersed with eras of little change. Expenditure per student in constant dollars changed little from 1929–30 to 1949–50. The 1950s and 1960s were periods of very rapid increase. The stability of the 1970s was followed by another interval of rapid expansion in the 1980s.

This chapter looks in detail at the period 1978–79 to 1987–88 as reported in the HEGIS/IPEDS survey (see Chapter 11, n. 14, above) about expenditures, number of faculty, and enrollment at four points in time. Our sample is limited to 1,804 institutions because some colleges and universities did not report either the number of faculty or faculty salaries in one or more of the surveys used.[1] The institutions in the sample come from all the major sectors

1. This chapter uses data from the HEGIS/IPEDS reports of 1978–79, 1983–84, 1985–86, and 1987–88. The data on the number of faculty are for 1982–83 instead of 1983–84. American Association of University Professors (AAUP) data on faculty salaries are not used because we do not have them for the same set of institutions over time. AAUP data may be individually more accurate both because the AAUP asks institutions to verify the data reported and because the AAUP compares current year with previous year reports in order to identify irregularities.

of higher education. The first half of this chapter decomposes 1987–88 expenditures per student into four parts, one of which is the student/faculty ratio. The second half analyzes changes in the components of expenditure per student over the period 1978–79 to 1987–88, in a search for clues to solve the recent cost inflation mystery.

14.1   Decomposing Expenditures per Student

The linkage between expenditures and the student/faculty ratio is shown in Figure 14.3. The figure reports aggregates for a set of 1,804 institutions for which we have complete data on finances, enrollments, and full-time faculty. At Level I, the total current account expenditures are divided between adjusted educational and general (AE&G) expenditures, research, restricted scholarships, and other expenditures not included in educational and general (E&G). For the 1,804 institutions, the total AE&G was $54.7 billion in 1987–88. Level II shows that $26.1 billion of AE&G flowed to instruction, leaving $28.6 billion to noninstructional functions. The ratio of instructional expenditure (Level II) to AE&G (Level I) is 0.48 (labeled A in Figure 14.3). Level III shows that 44 percent (B in Figure 14.3) of the instructional expenditure, or $11.3 billion, flowed to the salaries of the full-time faculty. HEGIS/IPEDS reports information only for full-time faculty, so this investigation is limited to a discussion of full-time faculty.[2] The fringe benefits for the full-time faculty and compensation for all other instructional staff, as well as all noncompensation expenditures in instruction, are excluded from the $11.3 billion. The $11.3 billion salary bill was paid to 315,719 full-time faculty members at the 1,804 institutions. Thus, $35,889 was the average salary per full-time faculty member in 1987–88 (labeled C in Figure 14.3). This average salary figure is slightly lower than that shown in AAUP data reported in Table 6.2 above. The HEGIS/IPEDS data include a larger set of two-year colleges, and they include data for faculty below the rank of assistant professor, for example, instructors and lecturers, categories that the AAUP data exclude. Level V shows that the institutions enrolled 6.6 million full-time-equivalent

---

2. Counts of full-time and part-time senior instructional faculty are reported in U.S. Department of Education (1989, table 190, p. 212) as follows (in thousands):

	Total	Full-Time	Part-Time	% Part-Time
1970	474	369	104	21.9
1973	527	389	138	26.2
1977	678	448	230	33.9
1983	724	471	254	35.1
1988	741	467	275	37.1

The increase in percentage part-time is consistent with the subsequent evidence reported in this chapter.

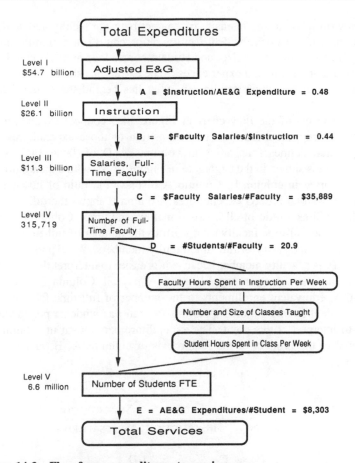

Figure 14.3   Flow from expenditures to services.
Source: Authors' calculation from HEGIS/IPEDS data.
Note: Figures are aggregates for 1,804 institutions, 1987–88.

students. On average, then, these 1,804 colleges and universities had a per-student expenditure (AE&G) of $8,303 (labeled E in Figure 14.3) and a student to full-time faculty ratio of 20.9 (labeled D in Figure 14.3).[3]

Figure 14.3 shows three additional connections between faculty and students, links that define the nature of the contact between the two. Faculty members may differ in the number of hours per week devoted to class, lab, and office hours. The faculties may teach different numbers of classes of different sizes. Students may spend different numbers of hours per week in class. The HEGIS/IPEDS surveys do not document these three extra links. How-

3. Rates of flow for the 2,045 institutions used in Chapter 12 are similar to the rates shown here for the 1,804 subset. At level B, 47.6 percent of AE&G flows to instruction. Expenditure per student is $8,122 for the 2,045 institutions in 1987–88.

ever, they do relate to the intensity of contact between faculty and students. Institutions with identical student/faculty ratios could differ significantly in faculty teaching load, class size, and student course load and, so, could yield quite dissimilar educational experiences.[4] The extra links should be examined for a more complete understanding of what lies behind the student/faculty ratio.

The five levels of the flow chart in Figure 14.3 connect expenditures to students and suggest a four-part decomposition of those expenditures. The decomposition defines four ratios in columns A–D of Table 14.2 (which match the ratios shown in the aggregate in Figure 14.3), with expenditures per student reported in column E. Column A displays the ratio of instructional expenditure to total AE&G expenditures. Column B shows the full-time faculty salary bill as a ratio of all instructional expenditures. Column C reports the ratio of the full-time faculty salary bill to the number of full-time faculty, so it is the average salary of full-time faculty members. We express this ratio as the salary per faculty member because it is easier to interpret than the number of faculty members per, say, \$100,000 of payroll. Column D is the ratio of full-time-equivalent enrollments to the number of full-time faculty members, a student/faculty ratio. Expressing the ratio as students per faculty is easiest to interpret at this point. The expenditure per student in column E is then equal to the product of the reciprocals of columns A, B, and D times column C:

$$E \quad = \quad 1/A \quad \cdot \quad 1/B$$

$$\frac{\$\text{AE\&G}}{\#\text{STUDENTS}} = \frac{\$\text{AE\&G}}{\$\text{INSTRUCTION}} \cdot \frac{\$\text{INSTRUCTION}}{\$\text{FACSALARIES}}$$

$$\cdot \quad C \quad \cdot \quad 1/D$$

$$\cdot \frac{\$\text{FACSALARIES}}{\#\text{FACULTY}} \cdot \frac{\#\text{FACULTY}}{\#\text{STUDENTS}}.$$

Differences in expenditure per student from one group of institutions to another can be investigated in terms of variation in the four ratios of the de-

---

4. Tables 8.11, 8.12, and 8.13 above report average student contact hours for faculty members. If the midpoint number of hours in each cell in each table applies to all faculty, faculty members on average spent about 12 hours per week in class and just under five hours per week in office hours. Office hours show some downward trend, but class time does not exhibit a trend.

In the High School and Beyond survey data set used in Part I of this volume, students report the number of hours per week they spend in class, laboratories, and recitations for a single year. The authors accumulated the hours reported by students for each school. On average, students spend about 15.9 hours in contact with faculty each week, with students at private institutions spending somewhat more time (16.2 hours) than those at public institutions (15.7 hours). Because the High School and Beyond survey is for a single point in time, we cannot use it to identify trends in student class hours.

We have no information on class size and know of no survey that gathers this information across a significant number of colleges and universities.

Table 14.2   Ratios of Dollars to Students, 1987–88 Aggregates

Group	(A) $INSTRUCTION $AE&G	(B) $FACSALARIES $INSTRUCTION	(C) $FACSALARIES #FACULTY	(D) #STUDENTS #FACULTY	(E) $AE&G #STUDENTS	Sample Size
All institutions	.48	.44	35,889	20.9	8,303	1,804
By control:						
All public	.50	.45	36,272	22.0	7,424	1,078
All private	.43	.40	34,703	17.4	11,748	726
By Carnegie classification:						
Research	.49	.36	42,728	19.0	12,816	87
Doctoral	.48	.45	37,501	20.5	8,578	88
Comprehensive	.48	.51	34,471	20.7	6,739	485
Liberal Arts I	.37	.53	35,173	13.9	12,958	122
Other-Four-Year	.35	.53	24,660	16.7	8,068	306
Two-Year	.50	.46	29,875	27.0	4,903	716
By size group[a]						
Under 1,000	.38	.49	24,625	18.5	7,116	557
1,000 to 2,999	.43	.49	30,330	19.9	7,147	671
3,000 to 9,999	.48	.45	35,192	21.8	7,487	426
10,000 to 19,999	.50	.42	39,619	21.2	8,877	111
20,000 up	.50	.38	42,948	20.6	10,974	39

Source: Authors' calculations from HEGIS/IPEDS data.
Note: For definitions of variables, see the text.
[a]Size is measured by 1987–88 full-time-equivalent enrollment.

composition. Institutions might have higher costs per student because they spend more on noninstructional functions (A), because they spend more on non-full-time faculty instructional items (B), because they pay higher average full-time faculty salaries (C), or because they have a lower student/faculty ratio (D). A comparison of the four ratios of the decomposition across groups of institutions with different expenditures per student can help us understand why certain institutions have different costs. This decomposition, then, should reveal the role of the student/faculty ratio as a determinant of cost.

14.2   Cost Comparisons across Aggregate Groups

Table 14.2 provides a first look at the decomposition by comparing institutions classified by control, Carnegie group, and size. The last column reports the number of institutions in each group. The cost per student in public institutions was 63 percent of the cost per student in private institutions in 1987–88. The difference arises because student/faculty ratios are 21 percent lower in the privates, because privates devote only 43 percent of their AE&G expenditures to instruction compared to 50 percent for publics, and because only 40 percent of the instructional expenditures in the private institutions goes to full-time faculty salaries compared with 45 percent in the publics. Private institutions employ relatively more noninstructional and nonfaculty inputs than public colleges and universities. These three differences more than overcome the fact that the publics, on average, pay 4 percent higher faculty salaries.

Even stronger contrasts appear in the comparison of the six Carnegie classifications, reported in the middle of Table 14.2. Figure 14.4 shows the expenditures per student in a chart. As might be expected, Liberal Arts I colleges and Research universities show the highest cost per student, $12,816 and $12,958, respectively.[5] The Liberal Arts I colleges' costs are highest primarily because their student/faculty ratios are low (about two-thirds of the others) and because they devote a smaller fraction (37 percent) of AE&G expenditures to instruction than do Research (49 percent), Doctoral (48 percent), or Comprehensive (48 percent) institutions. As we reported in Table 12.5, the selective liberal arts institutions spend more than twice as much per student on student services, institutional support, and internal scholarships as do Research, Doctoral, or Comprehensive universities. These two factors more than overcome the facts that non-full-time faculty instructional expenditures are relatively less and that the average faculty salary at Liberal Arts I colleges is slightly below the national average.

Research universities' costs are high because they pay the highest faculty salaries and because they devote a smaller fraction of instructional expenditures to full-time faculty, by implication employing relatively more non-full-

5. These figures differ from those reported in Table 12.5 above because we are using the 1,804 rather than the 2,045 sample institutions and because the cost per student reported in Table 12.5 for Research universities excludes institutions with on-campus medical schools.

Expenditures per FTE Student, 1987-88

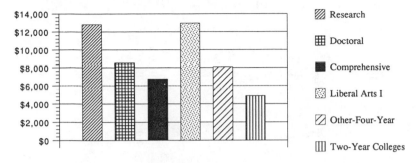

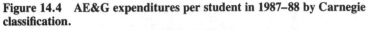

Figure 14.4   AE&G expenditures per student in 1987–88 by Carnegie classification.
Source: Authors' calculation from HEGIS/IPEDS data.

time faculty and other instructional resources. Their student/faculty ratio is only slightly below the national average. At the other extreme, the Two-Year colleges have low expenditures per student, averaging but $4,903 in 1987–88. The Two-Year schools have low costs primarily because student/faculty ratios are 29 percent higher than the average and because faculty salaries are about 17 percent below the average.

In similar aggregate fashion, we can compare costs across institutions of different size (see Table 14.2). Cost per student is smallest in the under-1,000 size class and rises with enrollment. Faculty salaries increase monotonically with size and the fraction of the instructional budget devoted to full-time faculty salaries falls uniformly with size. These two factors account for most of the strong positive association of cost per student and size. The student/faculty ratio is highest for the 3,000–9,999 size class, where Comprehensives dominate. Non-full-time faculty instructional inputs are relatively more important for larger institutions. The relative importance of noninstructional costs is smaller among the institutions of larger size and so tends to reduce costs at larger institutions, primarily the Research, Doctoral, and Comprehensive institutions. The strong association between size and costs in the aggregate groups primarily reflects the fact that institutions with different missions are clustered at different size levels: liberal arts colleges are small, doctoral universities are large.

14.3 Cost Comparisons across Smaller Groups

The differences in cost patterns among Carnegie classifications, among size classes, and by public/private control, however, may disguise underlying patterns because mission, size, and control often change together. Table 14.3

Table 14.3   Ratios of Dollars to Students, 1987–88, for 24 Groups of Institutions

		(A) $INSTRUCTION	(B) $FACSALARIES	(C) $FACSALARIES	(D) #STUDENTS	(E) $AE&G	
	Group No.	$AE&G	$INSTRUCTION	#FACULTY	#FACULTY	#STUDENTS	Sample Size
Research institutions:							
Public, no medical school	1	.46	.47	41,172	19.6	9,628	36
Public, medical school	2	.50	.33	42,433	19.9	12,865	30
Private, no medical school	3	.46	.41	47,545	13.7	18,264	7
Private, medical school	4	.51	.23	47,500	16.1	24,754	14
Doctoral:							
Public, no medical school	5	.50	.49	36,406	21.0	7,090	47
Public, medical school	6	.48	.36	37,210	21.0	10,229	10
Private, no medical school	7	.44	.45	40,006	19.5	10,272	27
Private, medical school	8	.45	.31	41,067	17.6	16,655	4
Public Comprehensives:							
Under 1,000	9	.45	.50	28,478	18.9	6,778	17
1,000–2,999	10	.46	.54	31,339	19.2	6,537	97

3,000–9,999	11	.49	.56	33,875	20.8	5,980	168
10,000+	12	.56	.53	40,893	22.0	6,320	32
With medical school	13	.55	.27	33,854	22.8	9,975	6
Private four-year:							
Comprehensive under 3,000	14	.40	.49	28,792	19.8	7,527	138
Comprehensive over 3,000	15	.41	.47	34,606	19.8	8,994	49
Comprehensive, medical school	16	.63	.16	36,139	18.0	20,003	2
Liberal Arts I under 1,000	17	.35	.54	30,573	13.2	12,391	35
Liberal Arts I over 1,000	18	.37	.53	35,984	13.9	13,122	85
Other-Four-Year under 1,000	19	.33	.53	23,022	16.5	8,020	227
Other-Four-Year over 1,000	20	.36	.53	26,884	16.5	8,717	57
Public Two-Year:							
Under 1,000	21	.48	.44	25,707	22.1	5,501	198
1,000–2,999	22	.50	.46	27,931	24.4	4,973	288
3,000+	23	.51	.46	33,153	30.6	4,659	149
Private Two-Year:							
All under 3,000	24	.35	.44	22,039	22.5	6,375	81

Source: Authors' calculations from HEGIS/IPEDS data.

Note: Size is measured by 1987–88 full-time-equivalent enrollment. For definitions of variables, see the text.

reports more useful contrasts in costs among groups because it looks at narrower (thus more homogeneous) groups of institutions. The groups here are the same 24 categories described in Table 12.6, here categorizing the sample of 1,804 institutions for which we have faculty and salary data by Carnegie classification, control, size, and presence or absence of a medical school.

The presence of a medical school has a significant effect on cost per student. Among public Research universities, expenditures per student are 34 percent higher for institutions with medical schools compared to those without. Among private Research universities, costs are 36 percent higher where a medical school is present. The difference is even more pronounced among private Doctoral schools, where the presence of a medical school is associated with 62 percent higher costs per student. Costs are higher when medical schools are present primarily because a much smaller fraction of the instructional expenditure goes to full-time faculty salaries, for example, 33 percent with medical versus 47 percent without medical among public Research universities. That is to say, there is a particularly large instructional budget for things *in addition to* full-time faculty at institutions with medical schools. Surprisingly, average faculty salaries, the student/faculty ratio (defined in terms of full-time faculty), and the proportion of AE&G expenditures going to instruction do not differ systematically with the presence or absence of a medical school.

Among Research universities, private institutions have costs per student that average 90 percent higher than their public counterparts without a medical school and 92 percent higher given a medical school. This difference arises because the student/faculty ratio is lower in the privates, because the average faculty salary is higher in the privates, and because the privates use relatively more non-full-time faculty instructional resources. The privates do have a significantly different cost structure than the publics. The public-private cost differences are somewhat less pronounced within the Doctoral category.

Among the public Comprehensive universities, cost is remarkably similar across size classes. Only the six institutions with medical schools have unit costs much above $7,000 per year. Those with enrollments of 10,000 and over have higher salaries, but they also have somewhat higher student/faculty ratios and devote a significantly higher proportion of AE&G expenditures to instruction, apparently economizing on noninstructional expenditures.

The private four-year colleges divide into three groups. First, the Comprehensives have costs that are somewhat above their public counterparts, $7,527 for the smaller privates versus $6,537 for the smaller publics (averaging all the publics under 3,000 students). The privates devote somewhat less of AE&G to instruction and a somewhat smaller fraction of the instructional budget to full-time faculty salaries. Faculty salaries and student/faculty ratios are similar for the private and public Comprehensives. The higher cost of the privates occurs because of the higher use of non-full-time faculty and other instructional resources and relatively more expenditures on student services, institutional support, and scholarships. Second, the Liberal Arts I group has high costs, averaging $13,122 per student for those institutions enrolling 1,000 or more students. Liberal Arts I schools have high costs because of their much lower student/faculty ratio, much lower than any other group, and because they commit a larger fraction of AE&G expenditures to student services, institutional support, and internal scholarships (see Table 12.4). Third, the private Other-Four-Year colleges, including less selective liberal arts colleges and small (under 1,500 students) comprehensives, are much lower in cost than are Liberal Arts I institutions, primarily because faculty salaries are about 25 percent lower. Many institutions in the private Other-Four-Year group have strong religious affiliations. For each of the three groups of privates, costs are somewhat lower for the smaller schools because faculty salaries are lower at the smaller schools. The other elements of costs differ little with size within the private four-year school groups.

Among public Two-Year colleges, costs decline moderately with enrollment. The student/faculty ratio rises with enrollment faster than does the average full-time faculty salary. The proportion of AE&G expenditure devoted to instruction rises slightly with enrollment.

Private Two-Year colleges, most of which have enrollments under 1,000 (see Table 12.7), have the lowest faculty salaries of all the groups. The student/faculty ratios are comparable to small, public Two-Year schools. Interestingly, the proportion of AE&G expenditure devoted to instruction is much lower than for the public Two-Year schools. Indeed, the ratio for the private Two-Year colleges is similar to the instruction ratio for the private Liberal Arts I and the private Other-Four-Year groups. The private Two-Year colleges, then, have cost structures that are in some measure like other private institutions and in some measure like public Two-Year schools.

Costs differ remarkably across the different subsectors of higher education in ways that reflect the different missions and markets of the institutions. All four elements of the decomposition are relevant to understanding the differences in costs, but different ratios are important in different comparisons. The broad differences suggest that higher education is not one market but many and, therefore, that different subsectors will likely respond to changing circumstances differently. From the student's point of view, the variety means that consumers have a diverse menu available and can choose higher- or lower-cost institutions offering different levels and combinations of services.

14.4 Behind the Ratios

Decomposing the cost per student into ratios helps explain why costs differ across institutions. The ratios, however, are good guides only when there is little variation in them within the groups, that is, when they truly represent most of the institutions in the group. The usefulness of the ratios can be

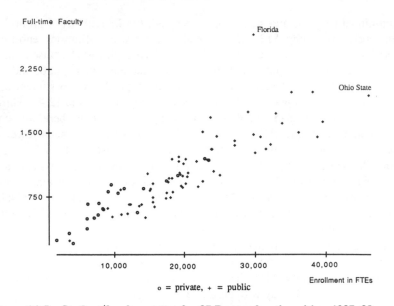

Figure 14.5   Student/faculty scatter for 87 Research universities, 1987–88.
Source: Authors' calculation from HEGIS/IPEDS data.
Note: Each point in the figure represents the number of full-time faculty and the full-time-equivalent enrollment of an individual university. The slope of the ray from the origin to the point is the ratio of faculty to students.

checked by examining scatter plots of the numerators against the denominators of the ratios. Consider first the ratio of full-time faculty to students.

A plot of full-time faculty versus full-time-equivalent enrollment reveals the variation in the ratio of faculty to students across institutions. Figure 14.5 shows the pattern for public and private Research universities. Here we plot faculty on the vertical axis and express the ratio as faculty to students because it makes better sense to view the faculty as the "dependent" variable, faculty being hired to accommodate the number of enrolled students. The ratio of faculty to students is the slope of a ray drawn from the origin to any point. Each point in the diagram represents one of the 87 Research universities among the sample of 1,804 institutions. The circles indicate the private universities. The private universities are generally smaller than the publics. The higher faculty/student ratio for the privates seems to be related to their relatively smaller size. They fit within the overall pattern, which implies that some faculty requirements persist even if enrollment approaches zero.[6] A sim-

6. Regressing full-time faculty on full-time-equivalent enrollment for Research universities in 1987–88 yields:

$$\text{FACULTY} = \underset{(3.91)}{203.17} + \underset{(17.0)}{0.041} \text{ ENROLLMENT}$$

$R^2 = 0.773$, df = 85, and $s = 210.7$. The coefficient implies an incremental student/faculty ratio of 24.4 with a minimum faculty of 203 at zero enrollment. (The numbers in parentheses in this and the following notes are *t*-ratios. Because only bivariate regressions are reported, the R^2's are not adjusted for degrees of freedom.)

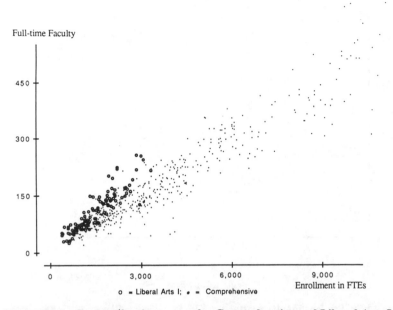

Figure 14.6   Student/faculty scatter for Comprehensive and Liberal Arts I institutions, 1987–88.
Source: Authors' calculation from HEGIS/IPEDS data.
Note: Each point in the figure represents the number of full-time faculty and the full-time-equivalent enrollment of an individual college or university. The slope of a ray from the origin to any point indicates the ratio of faculty to students. The figure is limited to institutions with enrollment under 10,000 for clarity.

ilar scatter for Doctoral institutions (not shown) indicates that private institutions dominate the smaller end of the group and that the privates fit well within the overall pattern.[7]

When private Liberal Arts I colleges are compared with the Comprehensive institutions in Figure 14.6, a significant difference appears.[8] The diagram is

7. Regressing full-time faculty on full-time-equivalent enrollment for 88 Doctoral universities yields:

$$\text{FACULTY} = \underset{(5.51)}{105.154} + \underset{(21.4)}{0.0379} \text{ ENROLLMENT}$$

$R^2 = 0.842$, df $= 86$, $s = 79.90$. The coefficient implies an incremental student/faculty ratio of 26.4 with 105 faculty members at zero enrollment.

8. Regressing full-time faculty on full-time-equivalent enrollment for 122 Liberal Arts I colleges yields:

$$\text{FACULTY} = \underset{(0.926)}{4.435} + \underset{(23.4)}{0.0688} \text{ ENROLLMENT}$$

$R^2 = 0.820$, df $= 120$, $s = 22.01$. The coefficient implies an incremental student/faculty ratio of 14.5 with four faculty members at zero enrollment. Regressing full-time faculty on full-time-equivalent enrollment for 485 Comprehensive universities yields:

$$\text{FACULTY} = \underset{(6.41)}{21.806} + \underset{(72.9)}{0.0434} \text{ ENROLLMENT}$$

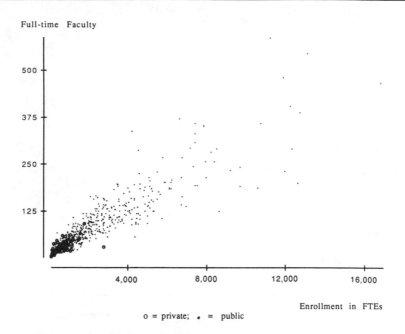

Full-time Faculty

o = private; . = public

Figure 14.7   Student/faculty scatter for 716 Two-Year colleges, 1987–88.
Source: Authors' calculation from HEGIS/IPEDS data.
Note: Each point in the scatter represents the number of full-time faculty and the full-time-equivalent enrollment of an individual Two-Year college. The slope of a ray from the origin to the point indicates the ratio of faculty to students.

limited to enrollments under 10,000 so that the differences will be clear. The small Liberal Arts I schools have similar enrollments and faculty size as the comparably sized (mostly public) Comprehensives, but, for larger institutions, faculties of the selective liberal arts colleges are proportionately larger than those of Comprehensives.

The scatter for Two-Year colleges in Figure 14.7 tells a different story. The private Two-Year colleges are small and have quite a range of faculty/student ratios. The small public Two-Year colleges have faculty/student ratios that are comparable to the privates; however, the range of the ratio becomes extremely wide for larger-size public Two-Year colleges.[9] The Milwaukee Area Technical College reported enrollment of 11,227 full-time-equivalent students with

---

$R^2 = 0.917$, df $= 483$, $s = 47.64$. The coefficient implies an incremental student/faculty ratio of 23 with 22 faculty members at zero enrollment.

9. Regressing full-time faculty on full-time-equivalent enrollment for Two-Year colleges yields:

$$\text{FACULTY} = 15.473 + 0.0297 \text{ ENROLLMENT,}$$
$$(9.61) \qquad (55.4)$$

$R^2 = 0.811$, df $= 714$, $s = 30.63$. The coefficient implies an incremental student/faculty ratio of 33.6 with a faculty of 15 at zero enrollment.

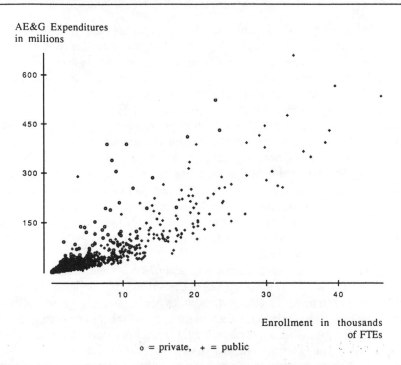

AE&G Expenditures
in millions

Enrollment in thousands
of FTEs

o = private, + = public

**Figure 14.8   AE&G expenditure and enrollment for 1,804 institutions,
1987–88.**
Source: Authors' calculation from HEGIS/IPEDS data.
Note: Each point in the figure reppresents the total expenditure and the full-time-equivalent
enrollment at an individual college or university. The slope of a ray from the origin to a point
indicates the expenditure per student. Dollar values are in 1987–88 dollars.

586 full-time faculty, while Pima County Community College in Arizona reported 11,977 students with only 231 full-time faculty. The variation in the
faculty/student ratio is much wider among Two-Year colleges than in the other
groups.

The scatter of faculty against enrollment for all 1,804 schools together (not
shown here) also reveals substantial variation.[10] The vast majority of schools
are relatively small, and the pattern is linear in the aggregate, with some significant variation. Figures 14.5–14.8 show that private schools generally have
lower enrollments and higher faculty/student ratios and that these two facts
are linked. The private Liberal Arts I colleges, which seem to have no direct

10. Regressing full-time faculty on full-time-equivalent enrollment for all 1,804 institutions
yields:

$$\text{FACULTY} = 1.831 + 0.0474 \text{ ENROLLMENT,}$$
$$(0.891) \quad (146.0)$$

$R^2 = 0.922$, df = 1,802, $s = 71.22$. The coefficient implies an incremental student/faculty ratio
of 21 with two faculty members at zero enrollment.

public counterparts, have a distinct pattern, with higher faculty/student ratios (i.e., lower student/faculty ratios) than any other group. Similarly, the public Two-Year colleges have lower faculty student ratios, although the variation among the Two-Year schools is striking. Note, however, that part-time faculty and graduate teaching assistants, both of which are least prevalent in selective liberal arts colleges, are countervailing forces.

Scatter diagrams also reveal the variation in the other ratios of the decomposition. The total instructional expenditure in each school plotted against AE&G expenditures shows (diagram omitted for brevity) a scatter radiating from the origin clustered tightly along a line.[11] The ratio here is a good summary of the relation. In contrast, the aggregate plot of the full-time faculty salary bill against instructional expenditures shows a wide scatter. The ratio here summarizes the relation less well.[12] The plot of total salary bill against the number of faculty shows a tight linear relation.[13] The salary bill tracks the number of faculty quite well.

The decomposition comes together in Figure 14.8, where AE&G expenditure is plotted against full-time-equivalent enrollment. The slope of a ray from the origin to each point indicates expenditures per student. This scatter shows wide variation.[14] The variation in each of the ratios of the decomposition combines to create substantial dispersion in total expenditure per student. Cost per student varies widely because faculty/student ratios vary and because the faculty salary bill is a widely varying proportion of instructional expenditures. The proportion of AE&G expenditures devoted to instruction shows a degree of constancy over institutions of different sizes and missions, as does the average salary per faculty member. It appears that differences in student/faculty

---

11. Regressing instructional expenditures on AE&G expenditures for the 1,804 institutions yields:

$$\text{\$INSTRUCTION} = -803,517 + 0.503 \text{ \$AE\&G},$$
$$(-7.24) \quad (306.0)$$

$R^2 = 0.981$, df = 1,802, $s = 4,207,652$.

12. Regressing the salary bill for full-time faculty on the total instructional expenditures for the 1,804 institutions yields:

$$\text{\$FACSALARIES} = 1,514,842 + 0.333 \text{ \$INSTRUCTION},$$
$$(13.9) \quad (103)$$

$R^2 = 0.854$, df = 1,802, $s = 417,664$.

13. Regressing the full-time faculty salary bill on the number of full-time faculty for the 1,804 institutions yields:

$$\text{\$FACSALARIES} = -1,134,608 + 42,372.6 \text{ FACULTY},$$
$$(-23.6) \quad (273)$$

$R^2 = 0.976$, df = 1,802, $s = 1,681,320$.

14. Regressing AE&G expenditure on enrollment for the 1,804 institutions yields:

$$\text{\$AE\&G} = -7,044,495 + 10,232.7 \text{ ENROLLMENT},$$
$$(-8.39) \quad (132.9)$$

$R^2 = 0.767$, df = 1,802, $s = 29,093,083$.

ratios and differences in the use of non-full-time faculty and other instructional resources have more to do with differences in the level of expenditure per student than do either faculty salaries or the allocation of resources between instruction and the other functions of colleges and universities. In short, the two main reasons why costs per student differ across categories of institutions are (1) differences in student/faculty ratios and (2) differences in non-full-time faculty and other instructional resources.

The extent of this variation would seem to be consistent with broad, competitive markets. Colleges and universities are differentiated by location, mission, and size and in other ways that induce each of them to develop a different production structure. The wide variation in faculty/student ratio seems inconsistent with the Baumol/Bowen fixed factor proportion theory, at least in its simple formulation. The wide variation in the proportion of instructional expenditure devoted to full-time faculty salaries also suggests that institutions have found different combinations of inputs that meet particular needs. The high degree of variation in the structure of costs might be consistent with institutions fitting themselves into niches, each with a unique demand curve and cost structure. A better understanding, however, will come from examining changes in the elements of cost over time.

14.5   What Caused Costs to Change over the 1980s?

How did the elements of the cost decomposition change over the last decade? Our HEGIS/IPEDS data provide observations on each of the 1,804 institutions at four points in time: 1978–79, 1983–84, 1985–86, and 1987–88. From these data, we compute an average annual growth rate for each of the five elements of the decomposition:[15] AE&G expenditure, instructional expenditures, full-time faculty salary bill, number of full-time faculty, and full-time-equivalent enrollment. The three elements measured in dollars are deflated by the gross national product (GNP) implicit price deflator[16] so that the discussion will be in terms of dollars of constant 1987–88 purchasing power. The average annual rates of change are computed in the aggregate for each group of schools shown in the tables.[17]

The average annual rates of change from 1978–79 to 1987–88 for the five aggregates are shown in Table 14.4 by control, Carnegie classification, and enrollment size class. From 1978–79 to 1987–88, AE&G expenditures grew by an average of 3.6 percent per year in real dollars at all institutions, 3.2

15. Estimating the trend growth rates via a semilogarithmic regression uses all four years of survey data we have available. The estimated trend is less dependent on the specific values in the earliest and latest years than if we simply calculated the trend from the end points.

16. In Chapter 12 above, we discuss the selection of GNP implicit price deflator.

17. The aggregate change in a category can be thought of as the geometric mean of the rates of change (more properly, one plus the rate of change) in the individual schools in the category. It weights institutions according to their size; thus, larger schools play a role in the analysis proportional to their size.

Table 14.4   **Average Annual Real Growth Rates, 1978–79 to 1987–88**[a]

Group	(A) $INSTRUCTION	(B) $FACSALARIES	(C) #FACULTY	(D) #STUDENTS	(E) $AE&G	Sample Size
All institutions	3.20	2.10	.53	.89	3.60	1,804
By control:						
All public	2.89	1.89	.36	.92	3.16	1,078
All private	4.11	2.78	1.06	.78	4.78	726
By Carnegie group:						
Research	3.53	2.33	.42	.67	3.76	87
Doctoral	2.91	2.26	.59	.86	3.41	88
Comprehensive	3.06	2.11	.66	1.05	3.42	485
Liberal Arts I	3.75	2.65	.82	.40	5.02	122
Other-Four-Year	2.24	1.25	.65	.74	3.41	306
Two-Year	2.88	1.46	.32	.99	3.32	716
By size group[b]						
Under 1,000	2.89	1.49	.72	1.02	3.69	557
1,000–2,999	3.31	2.13	.79	1.06	3.99	671
3,000–9,999	3.19	1.96	.51	.86	3.56	426
10,000–19,999	3.40	2.35	.58	.97	3.57	111
20,000+	2.95	2.12	.12	.61	3.38	39

Source: Authors' calculations from HEGIS/IPEDS data.
Note: For definitions of variables, see the text.
[a]All dollar values were deflated to 1987–88 with the GNP implicit price deflator.
[b]Size is measured by 1987–88 full-time-equivalent enrollment.

percent at public institutions, and 4.8 percent at private institutions. Instructional expenditures grew less quickly than AE&G. Colleges and universities were committing a larger proportion of AE&G to functions other than instruction by the end of the period. The shift was more pronounced among private institutions. The bill for full-time faculty salaries (in real terms) grew more slowly than instructional expenditures. Instructional expenditures other than the salary of full-time faculty took up the slack. The GNP deflator increased by 5.2 percent per year over this period. Faculty salaries grew more slowly at public schools than at privates. The number of faculty grew by 1.1 percent annually at privates and by 0.4 percent per year at public schools, on average. Enrollments, however, grew slightly faster at public institutions: 0.9 versus 0.8 percent per year. The ratio of students to faculty went up at the publics and down at the privates because enrollment grew faster than faculty in the publics but more slowly than faculty in the privates. Table 14.5 reports the rates of change for the 24 detailed groups of institutions.

The rate of change in a ratio is the rate of change of the numerator minus the rate of change of the denominator. Thus, the rates of change of the five elements reported in Table 14.4 can be used directly to compute the rates of change in the associated ratios of the decomposed expenditures per student. Using the rates of change of the components as the starting point makes clear the sources of change in each ratio. For example, the student/faculty ratio may change because of change in the number of students, change in the number of faculty, or both. Tables 14.6 and 14.7 report the annual rate of change in the ratios used in the decomposition of costs for the various groups of colleges and universities over the period 1978–79 to 1987–88.

Table 14.6 shows the annual rate of change in each of five ratios. The rate of change in the cost per student (AE&G/full-time-equivalent enrollment) is the negative of the sum of the rate of change in the four ratios of the decomposition (counting the rate of change in salary per faculty member negatively). The letters in the equation correspond to the columns of table 14.6 and 14.7, where lower-case letters represent changes:

$$e = c$$

$$\%\Delta[\frac{\$\text{AE\&G}}{\text{STUDENTS}}] = \%\Delta[\frac{\$\text{FACSALARIES}}{\text{FACULTY}}]$$

$$- \quad a \quad - \quad b \quad - \quad d,$$

$$- \%\Delta[\frac{\$\text{INSTRUCT}}{\$\text{AE\&G}}] - \%\Delta[\frac{\$\text{FACSALARIES}}{\$\text{INSTRUCT}}] - \%\Delta[\frac{\text{STUDENTS}}{\text{FACULTY}}],$$

where $\%\Delta$ refers to the annual percentage rate of change in the ratio.

Overall, AE&G expenditure per student increased on average by 2.7 percent per year over the period for the 1,804 institutions examined here. In the aggregate, the student/faculty ratio increased by 0.4 percent annually, a modest increase that would tend to reduce costs.[18] The average real salary increased by 1.6 percent per year on average in the aggregate, a rate three-fifths of the rate of increase in expenditure per student. The decrease in the proportion of AE&G going to instruction has increased costs somewhat. This represents added noninstructional expenditures and just about balances the cost savings derived from higher student/faculty ratios.

A larger source of cost increases is the decrease in the proportion of instructional expenditures going to the salaries of full-time faculty. This is consistent with the popular belief that institutions began relying more on part-time faculty during the 1980s. Included in this category are fringe benefits, the salaries of part-time faculty,[19] and instructional costs other than the compensation of faculty (e.g., secretarial, technical, and support staff, personal computers, travel, communications, duplicating, and supplies).[20] In the aggregate during

18. A detailed investigation of student/faculty ratios in the 1950s and 1960s also found a positive trend at that time (Radner 1976, 415–44).

19. If fringe benefits for faculty are about 20 percent of salaries, fringe benefits of the full-time faculty might account for 15 percent of the instructional expenditures other than the salary of full-time faculty. That part-time faculty have played an important and growing role in instruction is made clear in n. 2 above.

Table 14.5   **Average Annual Real Growth Rates, 1978–79 to 1987–88 for 24 Groups of Institutions**

	Group No.	(A) $INSTRUCTION	(B) $FACSALARIES	(C) #FACULTY	(D) #STUDENTS	(E) $AE&G	Sample Size
Research institutions:							
Public, no medical school	1	3.11	2.02	.30	.79	3.37	36
Public, medical school	2	3.09	2.42	.39	.42	3.40	30
Private, no medical school	3	4.82	3.09	.50	1.17	5.23	7
Private, medical school	4	4.98	3.35	.93	1.10	4.98	14
Doctoral:							
Public, no medical school	5	2.59	2.01	.51	1.01	2.75	47
Public, medical school	6	2.84	1.89	.36	.98	3.40	10
Private, no medical school	7	3.50	2.99	.95	.32	4.50	27
Private, medical school	8	3.82	3.22	.78	1.13	4.74	4
Public Comprehensives:							
Under 1,000	9	4.03	1.88	1.01	1.55	3.66	17
1,000–2,999	10	2.83	1.55	.36	1.37	2.61	97
3,000–9,999	11	2.41	1.65	.44	1.09	2.50	168

10,000+	12	2.96	2.44	.32	.86	3.25	32
With medical school	13	4.34	1.94	.29	2.00	5.15	6
Private four-year:							
Comprehensive under 3,000	14	4.08	2.95	1.67	1.36	4.83	138
Comprehensive over 3,000	15	3.94	3.04	1.43	.38	5.18	49
Comprehensive, medical school	16	6.78	4.57	2.89	1.79	6.52	2
Liberal Arts I under 1,000	17	3.15	1.80	.54	-.11	4.21	35
Liberal Arts I over 1,000	18	3.87	2.79	.88	.46	5.22	85
Other-Four-Year under 1,000	19	2.11	1.02	.59	.72	3.29	227
Other-Four-Year over 1,000	20	2.33	1.65	.79	.46	3.89	57
Public Two-Year:							
Under 1,000	21	3.31	1.72	.61	1.41	3.79	198
1,000–2,999	22	2.87	1.61	.48	1.10	3.26	288
3,000+	23	2.72	1.25	.02	.81	3.14	149
Private Two-Year:							
All under 3,000	24	4.42	2.64	1.67	1.50	4.94	81

Source: Authors' calculation from HEGIS/IPEDS data.

Note: Size is measured by 1987–88 full-time-equivalent enrollment.

[a] All dollar values were deflated to 1987–88 with the GNP implicit price deflator.

Table 14.6   Average Annual Real Rate of Change in Ratios of Decomposition, 1978–79 to 1987–88[a]

Group	(a) $INSTRUCTION / $AE&G	(b) $FACSALARIES / $INSTRUCTION	(c) $FACSALARIES / #FACULTY	(d) #STUDENTS / $FACULTY	(e) $AE&G / #STUDENTS
All institutions	− .40	− 1.10	1.57	.36	2.71
By control:					
All public	− .26	− 1.00	1.53	.55	2.24
All private	− .67	− 1.33	1.73	− .28	4.00
By Carnegie group:					
Research	− .23	− 1.20	1.91	.25	3.08
Doctoral	− .50	− .65	1.67	.27	2.55
Comprehensive	− .36	− .95	1.45	.40	2.37
Liberal Arts I	− 1.27	− 1.10	1.83	− .42	4.62
Other-Four-Year	− 1.17	− .99	.60	.09	2.67
Two-Year	− .44	− 1.42	1.14	.67	2.33
By size group[b]					
Under 1,000	− .80	− 1.41	.77	.30	2.67
1,000–2,999	− .68	− 1.18	1.34	.27	2.93
3,000–9,999	− .38	− 1.23	1.45	.35	2.71
10,000–19,999	− .18	− 1.05	1.77	.39	2.61
20,000 +	− .43	− .83	1.99	.48	2.77

Source: Difference in rates calculated from Table 14.4.

Note: Columns here provide the *rates of change* in the ratios given in equivalent columns in Table 14.2.

[a]All dollar values were deflated to 1987–88 with the GNP implicit price deflator.

[b]Size is measured by 1987–88 full-time-equivalent enrollment.

this period, faculty salaries led the increase in expenditure per student, with instructional costs other than the salaries of full-time faculty second and non-instructional expenditures third.

Rates of growth in expenditure per student by Carnegie group are displayed in Figure 14.9. The highest rate of increase was in the Liberal Arts I colleges, with Research universities being a distant second. There is no systematic association between the rate of change in cost and the size of the institutions (see Table 14.6). Costs increased at the Liberal Arts I colleges in part because of a decrease in the student/faculty ratio, which is consistent with a view that selective liberal arts colleges were attempting to differentiate themselves further during the 1980s by offering more quality (at a higher price). The decline in the student/faculty ratio at selective liberal arts colleges occurred as both the number of students and the number of faculty grew; the number of faculty

20. Hansen and Guidugli (1990, 157) report an increase in the ratio of nonfaculty professional employees to faculty members at colleges and universities from 1975 to 1983. Their data, however, do not distinguish between those nonfaculty professionals counted in instructional expenditures and those who fill other functions such as computer center and library employees.

Average Annual Rate of Growth

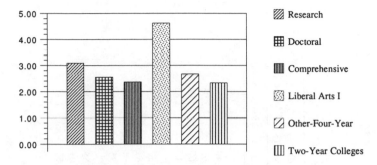

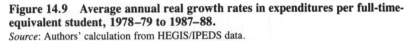

Figure 14.9   Average annual real growth rates in expenditures per full-time-equivalent student, 1978–79 to 1987–88.
Source: Authors' calculation from HEGIS/IPEDS data.

just grew faster. The privates, led by the Research universities and the Liberal Arts I colleges, experienced a large shift toward non-full-time-faculty expenditures in the instructional budget, an important source of increase in costs in all types of institutions. Two-Year colleges experienced the largest rate of increase in the student/faculty ratio, 0.7 percent per year.

The average salary per full-time faculty member grew in all categories even when viewed in constant dollars. Clearly, salaries for full-time faculty have been a significant element in the overall increase in expenditures per student. This result is consistent with the view of universities as clubs, captured and operated for the benefit of the incumbent faculty and administration. However, the outcome is equally consistent with competition in the labor markets for faculty. The growth in real salaries in the 1980s countered the decline in real faculty salaries in the 1970s.[21] Hansen attributes the decline in real faculty salaries during the 1970s primarily to institutional factors in the public sector. It is not clear how or why those institutional forces may have reversed in the period 1978–79 to 1987–88 (Hansen 1990, 80–112). If the faculty and administrators utility-maximization explanation is to hold up, it must explain both the decline and the increase in real salaries. Viewing salaries as determined

21. Faculty salaries declined in real terms through the 1970s and rose through the 1980s, as reported in U.S. Department of Education (1989, table 192, p. 213). We deflate the average salary of full-time instructional faculty by the GNP implicit price deflator:

	Average Nominal Salary	Salary in 1987–88 Dollars
1972–73	13,850	34,437
1975–76	16,634	32,072
1979–80	21,367	29,757
1984–85	30,447	33,247
1987–88	36,011	36,011

Table 14.7   Average Annual Real Rates of Change in Ratios of Decomposition, 1978–79 to 1987–88[a]

	(a) $INSTRUCTION / $AE&G	(b) $FACSALARIES / $INSTRUCTION	(c) $FACSALARIES / #FACULTY	(d) #STUDENTS / $FACULTY	(e) $AE&G / #STUDENTS
Group No.					
Research institutions:					
Public, no medical school	1	−.26	−1.09	1.72	.49	2.58
Public, medical school	2	−.31	−.67	2.03	.03	2.98
Private, no medical school	3	−.40	−1.74	2.59	.67	4.06
Private, medical school	4	.00	−1.63	2.42	.17	3.88
Doctoral:					
Public, no medical school	5	−.16	−.57	1.50	.50	1.74
Public, medical school	6	−.56	−.95	1.53	.62	2.42
Private, no medical school	7	−1.00	−.50	2.04	−.64	4.18
Private, medical school	8	−.92	−.60	2.43	.35	3.61
Public Comprehensives:					
Under 1,000	9	.37	−2.15	.88	.55	2.11
1,000–2,999	10	.22	−1.29	1.18	1.01	1.24
3,000–9,999	11	−.09	−.76	1.21	.65	1.41

10,000+		−.30	−.52	2.12	.54	2.39
With medical school		−.81	−2.39	1.66	1.71	3.15
Private four-year:						
Comprehensive under 3,000	14	−.75	−1.13	1.28	−.32	3.47
Comprehensive over 3,000	15	−1.24	−.90	1.61	−1.05	4.80
Comprehensive, medical school	16	.26	−2.21	1.68	−1.10	4.74
Liberal Arts I under 1,000	17	−1.07	−1.35	1.26	−.66	4.33
Liberal Arts I over 1,000	18	−1.34	−1.09	1.90	−.42	4.76
Other-Four-Year under 1,000	19	−1.18	−1.09	.43	.13	2.57
Other-Four-Year over 1,000	20	−1.57	−.68	.86	−.33	3.44
Public Two-Year:						
Under 1,000	21	−.48	−1.59	1.11	.80	2.38
1,000–2,999	22	−.39	−1.26	1.13	.62	2.16
3,000+	23	−.41	−1.47	1.24	.80	2.32
Private Two-Year:						
All under 3,000	24	−.52	−1.78	.97	−.18	3.45

Source: Differences in rates calculated from Table 14.5.

Note: Size is measured by 1987–88 full-time-equivalent enrollment. Columns here provide the *rates of change* in the ratios given in equivalent columns in Table 14.3.

[a]All dollar values were deflated to 1987–88 with the GNP implicit price deflator.

by markets can explain both increases and decreases. (See the discussion of the market for faculty in Part II of this volume.) The highest rate of increase in salary per faculty member occurred among the Research universities, a finding consistent with institutions oriented toward prestige, bidding up salaries for "brand name" faculty members. The lowest rate of increase in faculty salaries was among the Other-Four-Year group. These colleges invested relatively more heavily in noninstructional services and held student/faculty ratios nearly steady over the period.

Looking at the more disaggregated groups of institutions reported in Tables 14.5 and 14.7 reveals that enrollment in the private Research universities grew more rapidly than the number of full-time faculty, so the student/faculty ratio increased even in the private Research universities. Student/faculty ratios fell in private Doctoral universities without medical schools, in all but one of the groups of private four-year colleges, and in the private Two-Year schools. The character of instruction at many private schools seems to differ from that in the publics, and the gap is widening.

Although the structure of costs is significantly different in universities with medical schools, the rates of change in costs do not appear to be systematically different. Cost per student increased at about the same rate in institutions with medical schools as in those without.

Cost per student increased least at mid-sized public Comprehensive universities, those with enrollments between 1,000 and 9,999. In those institutions, the student/faculty ratio increased much faster than average, and real salary per faculty member grew relatively more slowly than in many other groups. It appears that, in mid-sized Comprehensives, class sizes grew and faculty salaries lagged behind.

Public Two-Year colleges with enrollments over 1,000 had relatively low rates of increase in costs per student during the period. Student/faculty ratios rose by about 0.7 percent per year, and faculty salaries grew by 1.2 percent annually in real terms, a rate well below average. To a degree, these changes offset the decline in the proportion of the instructional budget going to full-time faculty salaries. Two-Year colleges, like all other groups, shifted expenditures within the instructional category away from salaries for full-time faculty.

Our overall impression of the changes in costs is one of institutions responding to environmental pressures. Faculty salaries grew significantly in real terms but at different rates in different groups of institutions. Student/faculty ratios rose, except in that part of the private sector where they are an important element in the quality that attracts students. Institutions seem to have shifted resources toward instructional expenditures other than full-time faculty. The number of nonfaculty professional employees grew relative to the number of faculty at colleges and universities from 1975 to 1983 (Hansen and Guidugli 1990). Computer professionals and laboratory staff are examples of categories of employees that increased more quickly than faculty. The number of part-time faculty also grew faster than the number of full-time faculty (see n. 2 above). The substitution of other professional employees and part-time faculty for full-time faculty seems counter to the Baumol/Bowen hypothesis that factor proportions are fixed in service industries like higher education. Expenditures other than instruction increased for most categories of institutions. Colleges and universities displayed a significant degree of flexibility in adapting the production methods over the period 1978–79 to 1987–88.

14.6   Behind the Change in Ratios

A scatter diagram of the rate of growth of the numerator of a ratio against the rate of growth of the denominator reveals how well the aggregate rate of change in the ratio describes the behavior of the individual institutions. Consider first the rate of change in the student/faculty ratio for Research universities shown in Figure 14.10. The average annual rate of growth of the faculty is plotted on the vertical axis, and the average annual rate of growth in enrollment is shown on the horizontal. If the student/faculty ratio remained constant, the scatter of points would fall along an upward-sloping 45-degree line through the origin. (The scales on the two axes are the same for the line of stable change to be literally at 45 degrees; when the scales differ, our reference is to a figurative 45-degree line.) Institutions with rising student/faculty ratios will be below the 45-degree line; those with declining student/faculty ratios will be above. Looking at the scatter diagram of rates of change allows us to see whether institutions collectively exhibit a particular pattern of change in the student/faculty ratio.

The rates of change in student/faculty ratio shown for Research universities in Figure 14.10 do not conform to a single pattern.[22] Some of the schools fall along the 45-degree line through the origin, with Wayne State, at the bottom left, having experienced significant declines in both faculty and enrollment; Kansas State had nearly stable faculty and enrollment, and North Carolina State University had significant growth in both enrollment and faculty. These three and many others kept the student/faculty ratio nearly constant. In contrast, Oklahoma State had growth in faculty and declines in enrollment, while Nebraska had growing enrollments and declines in faculty.[23] Taken together, the overall pattern shows a wide variety of experience. Changes in the size of

22. Regressing the average annual growth rate in faculty on the annual growth rate in enrollment for 87 Research universities yields:

FACULTY GROWTH RATE $=$ 0.000332 $+$ 0.572 ENROLLMENT GROWTH RATE,
                         (0.248)   (6.12)

$R^2 = 0.306$, df $= 35$, $s = 0.0104$.

23. An optimist would say that the quality of instruction has increased at Oklahoma State while Nebraska got more efficient. A pessimist might say that Oklahoma State became less efficient while the quality of instruction at Nebraska deteriorated.

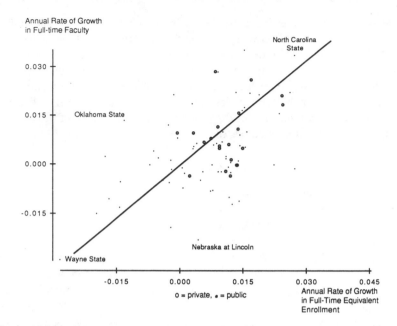

Figure 14.10   Average annual growth rates of faculty and enrollment for 87 Research universities, 1978–79 to 1987–88.

Source: Authors' calculation from HEGIS/IPEDS data.

Note: Each point represents the average annual rate of growth from 1979 to 1988 in number of full-time faculty and in full-time-equivalent enrollment at an individual university. The slope of a ray from the origin to a point indicates the rate of change in the ratio of faculty to students. The 45-degree line indicates those points where the ratio of faculty to students remains constant.

the faculty do not seem to be tightly linked to changes in enrollments among Research universities. Private universities show somewhat less variation than publics. Because Research universities receive so much revenue from federal grant programs, attract so many philanthropic dollars, and generally have significant endowments, the lack of strong association between faculty and enrollment should be expected and may indeed be desirable. These are, generally, not enrollment-driven universities.

The rates of change in the student/faculty ratio for Doctoral institutions (not shown) exhibit little pattern.[24] About as many institutions are above the 45-degree line as below. More institutions had growth than decline in both enrollment and faculty, but the association between the growth rates of the two is not strong. In distinct contrast, the rate of change in faculty is closely asso-

---

24. Regressing the annual growth rate in faculty on the annual growth rate in enrollment for 88 Doctoral universities yields:

$$\text{FACULTY GROWTH RATE} = 0.00374 + 0.473 \text{ ENROLLMENT GROWTH RATE},$$
$$(2.38) \quad (5.61)$$

$R^2 = 0.268$, df $= 86$, $s = 0.0136$.

ciated with the rate of change in enrollments among Comprehensive universities (diagram not shown).[25] Except for a few outliers who experienced sharp declines in faculty, the Comprehensives show a relatively compact pattern that sticks close to the 45-degree line. The rate of change in full-time faculty is associated with rates of change in full-time-equivalent enrollments. The Comprehensive universities are enrollment driven, and the funding formulas used by state legislatures likely enforce that characteristic.

The Liberal Arts I group (diagram not shown) exhibits a much more disperse pattern, with little association between growth in enrollment and growth in faculty. More than half the Liberal Arts I colleges are above the 45-degree line, indicating that they generally experienced falling student/faculty ratios.[26] The Two-Year colleges also show remarkable variation in the rates of change in enrollments, from schools with enrollments falling at 5 percent per year to institutions with enrollments growing at over 10 percent per year (diagram not shown).[27] Because the geographic market for individual Two-Year colleges is small, such colleges may be particularly sensitive to local demographic change, as when a military base closes. The rates of change for faculty also show considerable variation. The number of faculty and students seems to be much more volatile at Two-Year institutions than at the other types.

Having examined the changes in student/faculty ratios in some detail, we use the same approach to examine changes in all the ratios used to decompose costs per student. The rate of change in AE&G expenditures is plotted against the rate of change in enrollments for all 1,804 institutions in Figure 14.11. The scatter is dispersed but generally has a positive slope; total costs have tended to rise where enrollments are rising.[28] The slope is less than one, how-

25. Regressing the average annual growth rate in faculty on the average annual growth rate in enrollment for 485 Comprehensive universities yields:

> FACULTY GROWTH RATE = 0.00333 + 0.557 ENROLLMENT GROWTH RATE
> (3.70)   (19.3)

$R^2 = 0.437$, df $= 483$, $s = 0.0182$.

26. Regressing the average annual growth in faculty on the average annual growth rate in enrollment for 122 Liberal Arts I colleges yields:

> FACULTY GROWTH RATE = 0.00706 + 0.353 ENROLLMENT GROWTH RATE
> (4.82)   (3.99)

$R^2 = 0.117$, df $= 120$, $s = 0.0158$.

27. Regressing the average annual growth in faculty on the average annual growth rate in enrollment among 716 Two-Year colleges yields:

> FACULTY GROWTH RATE = 0.00082 + 0.489 ENROLLMENT GROWTH RATE
> (0.790)   (15.7)

$R^2 = 0.256$, df $= 714$, $s = 0.0260$.

28. Regressing the average annual growth rate in AE&G expenditures on the average annual growth rate in enrollment for the 1,804 institutions yields:

> \$AE&G GROWTH RATE = 0.0235 + 0.676 ENROLLMENT GROWTH RATE
> (35.4)   (31.4)

$R^2 = 0.354$, df $= 1,802$, $s = 0.0266$.

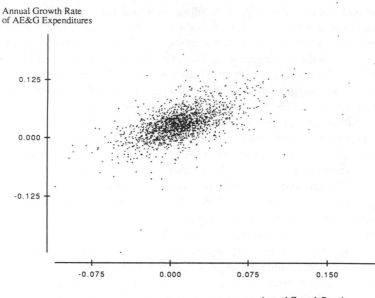

Annual Growth Rate
of AE&G Expenditures

Annual Growth Rate in
Full-Time-Equivalent Enrollment

Figure 14.11   Average annual real growth in AE&G expenditure and enrollment in 1,804 institutions, 1978–79 to 1987–88.
Source: Authors' calculation from HEGIS/IPEDS data.
Note: Each point represents the average annual growth rate in AE&G expenditures and in full-time-equivalent enrollment for an individual college or university. The slope of a ray from the origin to the point indicates the rate of change in expenditures per student. Points falling along a 45-degree line indicate no change in the expenditure per full-time-equivalent student. Dollar values are in 1987–88 dollars.

ever, showing that AE&G expenditures per student are increasing less rapidly at the growing institutions and more rapidly at institutions experiencing enrollment declines.[29] The relation between the rate of change in instructional expenditures and AE&G expenditures is tighter and more strongly positive (diagram not shown).[30] This is consistent with the tighter relation seen in the *levels* of instructional expenditures and the level of AE&G. In contrast, the relation between the rate of change in instructional expenditures and the rate of change in the salary bill for full-time faculty shows no strong pattern (dia-

29. See the discussion of enrollment change in Chapter 13.
30. Regressing the average annual growth rate in instructional expenditures on the average annual growth rate in AE&G expenditures for all 1,804 institutions yields:

$INSTRUCTION GROWTH RATE $=$ 0.0164 + 0.665 $AE&G GROWTH RATE
                                    (31.3)   (57.2)

$R^2 = 0.645$, df $= 1,802$, $s = 0.0164$.

gram not shown).[31] The greatest diversity among colleges and universities is in this cost element, revealing considerable variability in how institutions deliver instructional services.

The growth in the number of full-time faculty and the growth in the total deflated salary bill show a very clear relation. The tight scatter is only slightly steeper than a 45-degree line (diagram not shown).[32] The salary bill is growing slightly faster than the number of faculty over the period for all the institutions taken together.

Finally, the rate of change in the student/faculty ratio for all 1,804 institutions appears in Figure 14.12.[33] Although the variation is wide, the pattern shows some significant positive association. The rate of change in enrollments has some association with the rate of change in number of faculty. The relation between enrollment and faculty is much sharper within Carnegie groups than in the aggregate.

14.7 Summary

At the beginning of Part III, we asked why costs in higher education increased so rapidly. We found that costs per student increased by 2.7 percent per year faster than the general price level from 1978–79 to 1987–88, among all the 2,045 colleges and universities examined in Part III, as well as among the 1,804 institutions examined in this chapter. This rate of increase is significant, so our initial question is a compelling one.

We described six among many possible hypotheses about why costs in higher education may increase faster than the general price level. Having reviewed the structure and pattern of change in costs, we return to address this question directly.

Two of the hypotheses concern whether the market for higher education is

31. Regressing the average annual growth rate in the full-time faculty salary bill on the average annual growth rate in instructional expenditures for the 1,804 institutions yields:

$FACSALARIES GROWTH RATE $=$ -0.0054 $+$ 0.688 $INSTRUCTION GROWTH RATE
$\qquad\qquad\qquad\qquad\qquad$ (-5.46) $\qquad$ (32.0)

$R^2 = 0.363$, df $= 1,802$, $s = 0.0251$.

32. Regressing the average annual growth rate in the full-time faculty salary bill on the average annual growth rate in the number of faculty for the 1,804 institutions yields:

$FACSALARIES GROWTH RATE $=$ 0.0112 $+$ 1.027 # FACULTY GROWTH RATE,
$\qquad\qquad\qquad\qquad\qquad$ (37.7) $\qquad$ (101)

$R^2 = 0.851$, df $= 1,802$, $s = 0.0121$.

33. Regressing the average annual growth rate in faculty on the average annual growth rate in full-time-equivalent enrollment for the 1,804 institutions yields:

#FACULTY GROWTH RATE $=$ 0.0028 $+$ 0.545 ENROLLMENT GROWTH RATE,
$\qquad\qquad\qquad\qquad\qquad$ (4.77) $\qquad$ (29.0)

$R^2 = 0.318$, df $= 1,802$, $s = 0.0233$.

Annual Rate of Growth
in Full-time Faculty

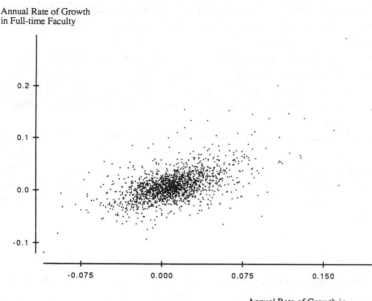

Annual Rate of Growth in
Full-Time-Equivalent Enrollment

Figure 14.12   Average annual growth in number of faculty and enrollment for 1,804 institutions, 1978–79 to 1987–88.
Source: Authors' calculation from HEGIS/IPEDS data.
Note: Each point represents the rate of growth in full-time faculty and in full-time-equivalent enrollment for an individual college or university. The slope of a ray from the origin to a point indicates the rate of change in the faculty/student ratio. Points along a 45-degree line show no change in the ratio.

competitive, the hypothesis concerning faculty and administrators' quest for salary and status and the hypothesis concerning the quality of management. The most striking finding here is that one-third of the institutions suffered declines in enrollment even as overall enrollment in higher education grew. That so many institutions could lose enrollment gives strong indication that market forces bear heavily on institutions of higher education. Where institutions fall out of favor with their customers, or where demographic shifts lead students elsewhere, institutions face loss of revenues both from tuition and, for public institutions, from state grants, which are often linked by formulas to enrollment level. The marketplace, then, imposes its discipline. Institutions that do not deliver services that a sufficient number of students find attractive must change course or suffer decline. The very evident prospect of enrollment decline limits the opportunity for faculty and administration to capture the institutions or for institutions to tolerate weak management.

Three hypotheses assumed competition. During the 1980s, demand for higher education increased, leading to a larger number of students served and to an increase in the cost per student, as would be expected with a demand increase in a competitive market with an upwardly sloped supply curve. The supply may slope upward because some important input, like faculty, is relatively scarce. As the demand for higher education increases, the derived demand for the most important input, faculty, also increases, causing a rise in average salaries. The evidence here found that faculty salaries increased by 1.6 percent per year above the rate of increase in the general price level over the period 1978–79 to 1987–88, so the finding is consistent with the supply of higher education having an upward slope because faculty salaries increase to draw more people into the professoriate.[34]

The supply of higher education might be yet more steeply sloped and cause an increase in demand to push costs still higher because of the difficulty of substituting less expensive for more expensive inputs, the Baumol/Bowen hypothesis. That is to say, if other inputs could be substituted for full-time faculty as their salaries increased, total cost per student need not increase quite as fast as faculty salaries. We find that some substitution away from full-time faculty occurred during the 1980s, as real faculty salaries rose. In the aggregate, the student/faculty ratio increased by 0.4 percent per year. The proportion of the instructional budget devoted to the salaries of full-time faculty declined by 1.1 percent per year. These findings show a degree of substitutability, presumably manifested through changes in class sizes and use of part-time faculty and teaching assistants. We conclude that some substitution for faculty did occur, so the increase in faculty salaries and the cost of higher education were mitigated to a degree.

A final competitive hypothesis suggests that consumers are seeking a higher-quality product and that the extra cost reflects the higher quality. We find that elements of AE&G expenditures other than instruction grew faster than instructional expenditure. These cost elements include institutional support, student services, and academic services. Cost increases in these areas could be associated with efforts to enrich the educational experience and so yield improved product. Of course, increased fund-raising, marketing and recruiting efforts, and self-funded financial aid also affect this ratio, so the proper interpretation is ambiguous. Among the private four-year schools, we see decreases in the student/faculty ratio that contribute to well-above-average rates of increase in costs. These changes are readily interpretable as institutions supplying a demonstrably higher-quality service at a higher cost.

When demand is increasing for both quantity and quality, cost in higher education will be likely to continue to increase. The demand for higher education is considered in detail in Part I of this volume, and a decrease in demand is possible in the 1990s (see Chapter 5). If demand were to decrease, the implication for cost may not be entirely symmetric. We would expect the rate of increase in faculty salaries to be less than the rate of increase in the

---

34. Table 10.6 above, along with the associated discussion, makes clear the many ways in which the supply of faculty adjusts to changing relative scarcity as reflected in salaries.

general price level, as occurred during the 1970s. The rate of increase in total costs would thus be damped. However, we observed that individual institutions with declining enrollments tend to have higher costs per student than other similar institutions. Colleges and universities have many fixed costs, obligations that persist for some considerable period of time even when enrollments decline. To avoid these fixed costs, institutions must restructure significantly, including, for some, closing down. Such adjustments are slow and difficult, especially in the public sector, where political decisions are involved. Therefore, we expect that a decrease in demand, as might be caused by demographic shifts, recession, or declines in the relative returns to a college education, will cause the rate of growth in higher education costs to be only modestly slower.

References

Abedi, J., and E. Benkin. 1987. The Effects of Students, Academic, Financial and Demographic Variables on Time to Doctorate. *Research in Higher Education* 17 (1): 3–14.

Abowd, John M. 1977. An Econometric Model of the U.S. Market for Higher Education. Ph.D. diss., University of Chicago.

Adams, Henry. [1918] 1946. *The Education of Henry Adams: An Autobiography*. Boston: Houghton Mifflin.

Alciatore, Robert, and Pegge Alciatore. 1979. Consumer Reactions to College Teaching. *Improving College and University Teaching* 27(Spring): 94–95.

Alexander, E., and D. Frey. 1984. An Econometric Estimate of the Demand for MBA Enrollments. *Economics of Education Review* 3(2): 97–103.

Allison, P. D. 1980. Inequality and Scientific Productivity. *Social Studies of Science* 10(May): 163–79.

Allison, P. D., et al. 1982. Cumulative Advantage and Inequality in Science. *American Sociological Review* 47(October): 615–25.

Alwin, Duane F. 1976. Socioeconomic Background, Colleges, and Post-Collegiate Achievements. In *Schooling and Achievement in American Society,* ed. William H. Sewell et al., 343–72. New York: Academic.

American Association of University Professors. 1990. The Annual Report on the Economic Status of the Profession, 1989–1990. *Academe* 76(March/April): 1–84.

American Council on Education. 1985. *Fact Sheet: Student Borrowing Has Implications for Career Choice*. Washington, D.C.

———. 1988. *Minorities in Higher Education: Seventh Annual Status Report, 1988*. Washington, D.C.

American Medical Association. Undergraduate Medical Education. 1988. *Journal of the American Medical Association* 260(26 August): 1063–71.

Anderson, C. Arnold, Mary Jean Bowman, and Vincent Tinto. 1972. *Where Colleges Are and Who Attends*. New York: McGraw-Hill.

Anderson, Charles J., Deborah J. Carter, and Andrew G. Malizio. 1989. *1989–90 Fact Book on Higher Education*. New York: Macmillan.

Anderson, Kristine L. 1984. Race Differences in the Effects of College Characteristics on Educational Attainment. Florida Atlantic University. Typescript.

Arrow, Kenneth J. 1973. Higher Education as a Filter. *Journal of Public Economics* 2(July): 193–216.

Association of Physical Plant Administrators of Universities and Colleges. 1980. *1978–1979 Comparative Costs and Staffing Report.* Washington, D.C.

———. 1989. *1987–1988 Comparative Costs and Staffing Report.* Washington, D.C.

Astin, Alexander W., et al. Various years. *The American Freshman: National Norms.* Los Angeles: Cooperative Institutional Research Program.

Astin, Alexander W. 1985. Selectivity and Equity in the Public Research University. In *The Future of State Universities,* ed. Leslie W. Koepplin and David A. Wilson. New Brunswick, N.J.: Rutgers University Press.

Astin, Alexander W., and Carolyn J. Knouye. 1988. How Public Policy at the State Level Affects Private Higher Education Institutions. *Economics of Education Review* 7(1): 47–63.

Atkinson, Richard C. 1990. Supply and Demand for Scientists and Engineers: A National Crisis in the Making. Presidential address delivered to the American Association for the Advancement of Science, New Orleans.

Baird, L. L. 1984. Relationships between Ability, College Attendance and Family Income. *Research in Higher Education* 21(4): 373–95.

Baker, Joe G. 1989. The Ph.D. Supply Crisis: A Look at the Biomedical Sciences. Washington, D.C.: National Research Council, Office of Scientific and Engineering Personnel. Mimeo.

Barbezat, Debra. 1989a. Affirmative Action in Higher Education: Have Two Decades Altered Salary Differentials by Sex and Race? *Research in Labor Economics* 10:107–56.

———. 1989b. The Market for New Ph.D. Economists. Amherst College. Mimeo.

Barnes, Gary T. 1977. An Economist's View of the Uniform Methodology. Special Report no. 21. Iowa City, Iowa: American College Testing Program.

Barron's Guide to Law Schools. 1986. 7th ed. New York: Barron's Educational Services.

Barron's Profiles of American Colleges. Various years. New York: Barron's Educational Services.

Baum, Sandy, and Saul Schwartz. 1988a. The Impact of Student Loans on Borrowers. Boston: New England Loan Marketing Corp.

———. 1988b. The Impact of Student Loans on Borrowers' Consumption Patterns and Attitudes. Tufts University. Mimeo.

———. 1988c. Merit Aid to College Students. *Economics of Education Review* 7(1): 127–34.

———. 1989. What Strategy for the Education President? *Challenge* 32:44–50.

Baumol, William J. 1967. The Macroeconomics of Unbalanced Growth: The Anatomy of Urban Crisis. *American Economic Review* 57(June): 415–26.

Baumol, William J., and William G. Bowen. 1966. *Performing Arts: The Economic Dilemma.* New York: Twentieth Century Fund.

Becker, Gary S. 1964. *Human Capital.* New York: National Bureau of Economic Research.

Becker, William E. 1990. The Demand for Higher Education. In *The Economics of American Universities,* ed. Stephen A. Hoenack and Eileen L. Collins, 155–88. Albany: State University of New York Press.

Behrman, J. R., Z. Hrubec, P. Taubman, and T. J. Wales. 1980. *Socio-Economic Success.* New York: North-Holland.

Behrman, Jere R., Robert A. Pollak, and Paul Taubman. 1989. Family Resources, Family Size, and Access to Financing for College Education. *Journal of Political Economy* 97(2): 398–419.

Berg, David J., and Stephen A. Hoenack. 1987. The Concept of Cost-Related Tuition and Its Implementation at the University of Minnesota. *Journal of Higher Education* 58(May/June): 276–305.

Berg, Ivar. 1970. *Education and Jobs: The Great Training Robbery.* New York: Praeger.

Berger, Mark. 1988. Predicting Future Earnings and Choice of College Major. *Industrial and Labor Relations Review* 41(April): 418–29.

Biedenweg, Rick, and Dana Shelley. 1988. *1986–87 Decanal Indirect Cost Study.* Stanford, Calif.: Stanford University.

Bishop, John. 1977. The Effect of Public Policies on the Demand for Higher Education. *Journal of Human Resources* 12(3): 285–307.

Black, MacKnight. 1989. *Minority Student Issues: Racial/Ethnic Data Collected by the National Center for Educational Statistics since 1969.* Washington, D.C.: National Center for Educational Statistics.

Blakemore, A. E., and S. A. Low. 1983. Scholarship Policy and Race-Sex Differences in the Demand for Higher Education. *Economic Inquiry* 21(October): 504–19.

———. 1985. Public Expenditures on Higher Education and Their Impact on Enrollment Patterns. *Applied Economics* 17(April): 331–40.

Blau, Francine D., and Marianne A. Ferber. 1986. *The Economics of Women, Men, and Work.* Englewood Cliffs, N.J.: Prentice-Hall.

Bok, Derek. 1986. *Higher Learning.* Cambridge, Mass.: Harvard University Press.

Bookman, Mark. 1989. *Contracting Collegiate Auxiliary Services.* Houston: Bookman Educational and Non-Profit Consulting.

Borgman, C. W., and J. W. Bartram. 1969. *Mineral Engineering Education in the West.* Boulder, Colo.: Western Interstate Commission for Higher Education.

Borjas, George J. 1987. Self-Selection and the Earnings of Immigrants. *American Economic Review* 77(September): 531–53.

Bowen, Howard R. 1980. *The Costs of Higher Education: How Much Do Colleges and Universities Spend per Student and How Much Should They Spend?* San Francisco: Jossey-Bass.

Bowen, Howard R., and Jack H. Schuster. 1986. *American Professors: A National Resource Imperiled.* New York: Oxford University Press.

Bowen, William G. 1968. *The Economics of the Major Private Universities.* Berkeley, Calif.: Carnegie Commission on Higher Education.

———. 1969. Economic Pressures on the Major Private Universities. In *The Economics and Financing of Higher Education in the United States.* Washington, D.C.: Joint Economic Committee of Congress.

———. 1977. Admissions and the Relevance of Race. *Educational Record* 58(Fall): 333–49.

Bowen, William G., Graham Lord, and Julie Ann Sosa. In press. Measuring Time to the Doctorate: A Reinterpretation of the Evidence. *Proceedings of the National Academy of Sciences.*

Bowen, William G., and Julie Ann Sosa. 1989. *Prospects for Faculty in the Arts and Sciences.* Princeton, N.J.: Princeton University Press.

Boyer, Ernest. 1987. Buildings Reflect Our Priorities. *Educational Record* 70(Winter): 25–27.

Breneman, David W. 1976. The Ph.D. Production Process. In *Education as an Industry,* ed. J. T. Fromkin, D. T. Jamison, and R. Radner. Cambridge, Mass.: Ballinger.

———. 1981. The Labor Market for Doctorates: Issues for the 1980s. Washington, D.C.: Brookings. Mimeo.

———. 1990. Are We Losing Our Liberal Arts Colleges? *College Board Review* 156(Summer): 16–21, 29.

Breneman, David W., and Chester E. Finn, eds. 1978. *Public Policy and Private Higher Education.* Washington, D.C.: Brookings.

————. 1978. An Uncertain Future. In *Public Policy and Private Higher Education*, ed. David W. Breneman and Chester E. Finn. Washington, D.C.: Brookings.

Brinkman, Paul T. 1981a. Factors Affecting Instructional Costs at Major Research Universities. *Journal of Higher Education* 52(May/June): 265–79.

————. 1981b. Marginal Costs of Instruction in Public Higher Education. Ph.D. diss., University of Arizona.

————. 1984. A Comparison of Expenditure Patterns in Four-Year Public and Private Institutions. Boulder, Colo.: National Center for Higher Education Management Systems.

————. 1985. The Financial Impact of Part-Time Enrollments on Two-Year Colleges: A Marginal Cost Perspective. *Journal of Higher Education* 56(May/June): 338–53.

————. 1989. Instructional Costs per Student Credit Hour: Differences by Level of Instruction. *Journal of Education Finance* 18(Summer): 34–52.

————. 1990. Higher Education Cost Functions. In *The Economics of American Universities*, ed. Stephen A. Hoenack and Eileen L. Collins. Albany: State University of New York Press.

Brinkman, Paul T., and Larry L. Leslie. 1986. Economies of Scale in Higher Education: Sixty Years of Research. *Review of Higher Education* 10(Fall): 1–28.

Broomall, L. W., B. T. Mahan, G. W. McLaughlin, and S. S. Patton. 1978. *Economies of Scale in Higher Education*. Blacksburg: Virginia Polytechnic Institute and State University.

Brovender, S. 1976. On the Economics of a University: Toward the Determination of Marginal Cost of Teaching Services. *Journal of Political Economy* 82(May/June): 657–64.

Buckles, Stephen. 1978. Identification of Causes of Increasing Costs in Higher Education. *Southern Economic Journal* 45(July): 258–65.

Cambridge Associates. 1990. *Preliminary Comparative Financial Data Survey*. Boston.

Carlson, D. E. 1972. *The Production and Cost Behavior of Higher Education Institutions*. Berkeley, Calif.: Ford Foundation Program for Research in University Administration.

Carnegie Foundation for the Advancement of Teaching. 1987. *A Classification of Institutions of Higher Education: 1987 Edition*. Princeton, N.J.: Princeton University Press.

————. 1989. *The Condition of the Professoriate: Attitudes and Trends, 1989*. Princeton, N.J.: Princeton University Press.

Carter, Debra, and Reginald Wilson. 1989. *Minorities in Higher Education: Eighth Annual Status Report*. Washington, D.C.: American Council on Education.

Cartter, Allan M. 1976. *Ph.D.'s and the Academic Labor Market*. New York: McGraw-Hill.

Caruthers, J. Kent, and Joseph L. Marks. 1988. *State Funding Formulas for Higher Education in the SREB States*. Atlanta: Southern Regional Education Board.

Cebula, R. J., and J. Lopes. 1982. Determinants of Student Choice of Undergraduate Major Field. *American Educational Research Journal* 19(Summer): 303–12.

Centra, John. 1981. *Determining Faculty Effectiveness*. San Francisco: Jossey-Bass.

Chaney, Bradford, and Elizabeth Farris. 1990. *The Finances of Higher Education*. Higher Education Survey Report no. 8. Washington, D.C.: Westat.

Cheit, Earl F. 1971. *The New Depression in Higher Education*. New York: McGraw-Hill.

Cheney, Lynne. 1989. The Phantom Ph.D. Gap. *New York Times*, 28 September.

Clark, Burton R. 1985. Conclusions. In *The School and the University*, ed. Burton R. Clark. Berkeley and Los Angeles: University of California Press.

Clotfelter, Charles. 1990. The Impact of Tax Reform on Charitable Giving: A 1989

Perspective. In *Do Taxes Matter? The Impact of the Tax Reform Act of 1986*, ed. Joel Slemrod. Cambridge, Mass.: MIT Press, 1990.

Clowes, D. A., D. E. Hinkle, and J. C. Smart. 1986. Enrollment Patterns in Postsecondary Education, 1961–1982. *Journal of Higher Education* 57(March/April): 121–33.

Cohn, Elchanan, and Terry G. Geske. 1990. *The Economics of Education*. 3d ed. Oxford: Pergamon.

Cohn, Elchanan, Sherrie L. W. Rhine, and Maria C. Santos. 1989. Institutions of Higher Education as Multi-Product Firms: Economies of Scale and Scope. *Review of Economics and Statistics* 71(May): 283–90.

Coleman, James S. 1973. The University and Society's New Demands upon It. In *Content and Context*, ed. Carl Kaysen. New York: McGraw-Hill.

College Entrance Examination Board. 1989. *Trends in Student Aid: 1980 to 1989*. New York.

College Savings Bank. 1989. *A Century of College Cost Inflation*. Princeton, N.J.: College Savings Bank, Research Division.

Cook, Philip J., and Robert H. Frank. 1991. Ahead of the Curve: The Growing Concentration of Top Students at Elite Schools. Paper presented at National Bureau of Economic Research Conference on the Economics of Higher Education, 17–19, May.

Corazzini, Arthur J., Dennis J. Dugan, and Henry G. Grabowski. 1972. Determinants and Distributional Aspects of Enrollment in U.S. Higher Education. *Journal of Human Resources* 7(Winter): 39–59.

Corman, Hope. 1983. Postsecondary Education Enrollment Responses by Recent High School Graduates and Older Adults. *Journal of Human Resources* 17(2): 247–67.

Corrallo, S. B. 1970. An Analysis of Instructional Expenditures for Institutions of Higher Education in the Northeast United States. Ph.D. diss., State University of New York at Buffalo.

Cox, Raymond, and Kee Chung. N.d. Patterns of Research Output in the Economics Literature. Central Michigan University. Mimeo.

Crowley, C., and D. Chubin. 1976. The Occupational Structure of Science: A Log-Linear Analysis of the Intersectoral Mobility of American Sociologists. *Sociological Quarterly* 17(Spring): 197–217.

de Groot, Hans, Walter W. McMahon, and J. Fredericks Volkwein. 1989. The Cost Structure of American Research Universities. Bureau of Economic and Business Research Faculty Working Paper no. 89-1597. Champaign-Urbana: University of Illinois.

Doyle, Denis P., and Terry W. Hartle. 1985. Facing the Fiscal Chopping Block. *Change* 17(July/August): 8–10.

Dresch, Stephen P. 1975. Demography, Technology, and Higher Education: Toward a Formal Model of Educational Adaptation. *Journal of Political Economy* 83(3): 535–69.

Educational Testing Service. 1988. *A Summary of Data Collected from Graduate Record Examinations Test Takers during 1986–87: Data Summary Report no. 12.* Princeton, N.J., June.

Ehrenberg, Ronald G. 1989. An Economic Analysis of the Market for Law School Students. *Journal of Legal Education* 39(suppl.): 627–54.

———. 1990. How Would Universities Respond to Increased Support for Graduate Education. Cornell University. Mimeo.

Ehrenberg, Ronald G., Hirschel Kasper, and Daniel Rees. In press. Faculty Turnover at American Colleges and Universities. *Economics of Education Review.*

Ehrenberg, Ronald G., and Rebecca A. Luzadis. 1986. The Social Security Student

Benefit Program and Family Decisions. *Economics of Education Review* (5(2): 119–28.

Ehrenberg, Ronald G., and Alan J. Marcus. 1982. Minimum Wages and Teenagers' Enrollment-Employment Outcomes: A Multinomial Logit Model. *Journal of Human Resources* 17(1): 39–58.

Ehrenberg, Ronald G., and Daniel R. Sherman. 1984. Optimal Financial Aid Policies for a Selective University. *Journal of Human Resources* 19(Spring): 202–30.

———. 1987. Employment While in College, Academic Achievement, and Postcollege Outcomes. *Journal of Human Resources* 22(Winter): 1–23.

Ehrenberg, Ronald G., and Robert S. Smith. 1991. *Modern Labor Economics*. 4th ed. New York: Harper Collins.

Ethington, C., and J. Smart. 1985. Persistence to Graduate Education. *Research in Higher Education* 24(3): 287–303.

Evangelauf, Jean. 1991. A Record 13,951,000 Students Enrolled in College Last Fall, Education Department Survey Shows. *Chronicle of Higher Education* 37(27 February): 1.

Fallows, James. 1980. The Tests and the "Brightest": How Fair Are the College Boards? *Atlantic Monthly* (February): 37–48.

———. 1985. The Case against Credentialism. *Atlantic Monthly* (December): 49–67.

———. 1990. Wake Up, America! *New York Review of Books*, 1 March, pp. 14–19.

Farley, Ann T. 1988. U.S. Immigration Policy: An Assessment of the Provision for the Admission of Temporary Workers of Distinguished Merit and Ability. M.S. thesis, Cornell University.

Feldman, Kenneth A. 1983. Seniority and Experience of College Teachers as Related to Evaluations They Receive from Students. *Research in Higher Education* 18(1): 3–121.

———. 1987. Research Productivity and Scholarly Accomplishments of College Teachers as Related to Their Instructional Effectiveness: A Review and Exploration. *Research in Higher Education* 26(3): 227–98.

Fiorito, J., and R. C. Dauffenbach. 1982. Market and Nonmarket Influences on Curriculum Choice by College Students. *Industrial and Labor Relations Review* 36(October): 88–101.

Fiske, Edward. 1989. Shortages Seen for Faculties for the 1990s. *New York Times*, 13 September, p. A1.

Fluency in English Required of Faculty. 1990. *New York Times*, 11 July, p. A13.

Forest, Lawrence R. 1990. A Model of the Science and Engineering Ph.D. Labor Market. Report. Washington, D.C.: DRI McGraw-Hill.

Fox, M. F. 1983. Publication Productivity among Scientists: A Critical Review. *Social Studies of Sciences* 13(May): 285–305.

Frank, Robert H. 1985. *Choosing the Right Pond*. Oxford: Oxford University Press.

Frank, Robert H., and Philip J. Cook. 1990. Collaborative Research on Winner-Take-All Markets. Cornell University. Typescript.

Freeman, Richard B. 1971. *The Market for College-Trained Manpower*. Cambridge, Mass.: Harvard University Press.

———. 1975a. Overinvestment in College Training? *Journal of Human Resources* 10(Summer): 287–311.

———. 1975b. Supply and Salary Adjustments to the Changing Science Manpower Market: Physics, 1948–73. *American Economic Review* 65(March): 27–39.

———. 1986. Demand For Education. In *Handbook of Labor Economics*, ed. Orley Ashenfelter and Richard Layard. Amsterdam: North-Holland.

Friedman, Milton. 1955. Survey of the Empirical Evidence of Economies of Scale: Comment. In *Business Concentration and Price Policy*. Princeton, N.J.: Princeton University Press, for the National Bureau of Economic Research.

———. 1962. *Capitalism and Freedom*. Chicago: University of Chicago Press.

Fuller, W. C., C. F. Manski, and D. A. Wise. 1982. New Evidence on the Economic Determinants of Postsecondary Schooling Choices. *Journal of Human Resources* 17(Fall): 477–98.

Galambos, Eva C. 1988. Higher Education Administrative Costs and Staffing. In *Higher Education Administrative Costs: Continuing the Study,* ed. Thomas P. Snyder and Eva C. Galambos. Washington, D.C.: Office of Educational Research and Improvement.

Galper, Harvey, and Robert M. Dunn. 1969. A Short-Run Demand Function for Higher Education in the United States. *Journal of Political Economy* 77(September/October): 765–77.

Garet, Michael S., and Paul Butler-Nalin. 1982. *Graduate and Professional Education: A Review of Recent Trends.* Cambridge, Mass.: Consortium on Financing Higher Education.

Garvin, David. 1980. *The Economics of University Behavior.* New York: Academic.

Gee, Helen Hofer. 1989. Productivity. In *Biomedical and Behavioral Scientists: Their Training and Supply.* Vol. 3, *Commissioned Papers.* Washington, D.C.: National Academy Press.

Getz, Malcolm, and John J. Siegfried. 1990. Adoption of Innovations in Higher Education. Vanderbilt University. Typescript.

Gibson, T. T. 1968. Unit Costs of Higher Education: A Study of the University of Colorado. Ph.D. diss., University of Colorado.

Gillespie, Donald A., and Nancy Carlson. 1983. *Trends in Student Aid: 1963 to 1983.* Washington, D.C.: College Board.

Gillespie, Donald A., and Nancy Carlson. 1990. *Trends in Student Aid: 1980–90.* Washington, D.C.: College Board.

Gilmore, Jeffrey L. 1988. *Studies of Productivity in Higher Education.* Washington, D.C.: U.S. Department of Education, Office of Educational Research and Improvement.

Girves, J. E., and V. Wemmerus. 1988. Developing Models of Graduate Student Degree Progress. *Journal of Higher Education* 59(March/April): 163–89.

Gladieux, Lawrence E. 1985. Federal Student Aid and the Goal of Equal Opportunity: The Record and the Future. Address to the Indiana Student Financial Aid Association, 4 December, Indianapolis.

———. 1989. *Radical Reform or Incremental Change? Student Loan Policy Alternatives for the Federal Government.* New York: College Entrance Examination Board.

Gladieux, Lawrence E., and Gwendolyn L. Lewis. 1987. *The Federal Government and Higher Education.* New York: College Entrance Examination Board.

Gladieux, Lawrence E., and Thomas R. Wolanin. 1978. Federal Politics. In *Public Policy and Private Higher Education,* ed. David W. Breneman and Chester E. Finn. Washington, D.C.: Brookings.

Glenny, Lyman A. 1980. Demographic and Related Issues for Higher Education in the 1980s. *Journal of Higher Education* 51(July/August): 363–80.

Haines, Richard W. 1984. The Debate over No-Need Scholarships: Wrong for Society, Wrong for Institutions, and Wrong for Students. *Change* 16(6): 24–31.

Hamermesh, Daniel. 1988. Salaries: Disciplinary Differences and Rank Injustices. *Academe* 74(May/June): 20–24.

Hansen, Janet. 1987. *Student Loans: Are They Overburdening a Generation?* New York: College Entrance Examination Board.

———, ed. 1990. *College Savings Plans.* New York: College Entrance Examination Board.

Hansen, W. Lee. 1984. Economic Growth and Equal Opportunity: Conflicting or Complementary Goals in Higher Education? In *Education and Economic Productivity,* ed. Edwin Dean. Cambridge, Mass.: Ballinger.

———. 1985. Changing Demography of Faculty in Higher Education. In *Faculty Vi-*

tality and Institutional Productivity, ed. Shirley Clark and Darrell Lewis. New York: Teachers College Press.

———. 1986. Changes in Faculty Salaries. In *American Professors: A National Resource Imperiled,* ed. Howard R. Bowen and Jack H. Shuster. Oxford: Oxford University Press.

———, ed. 1970. *Education, Income, and Human Capital.* New York: National Bureau of Economic Research.

Hansen, W. Lee, and Thomas F. Guidugli. 1990. Comparing Salary and Employment Gains for Higher Education Administrators and Faculty Members. *Journal of Higher Education* 61(March/April): 142–59.

Hansen, W. Lee, and M. S. Rhodes. 1988. Student Debt Crisis: Are Students Incurring Excessive Debt? *Economics of Education Review* 7(1): 101–12.

Hansen, W. Lee, and Jacob O. Stampen. 1987. The Economics and Financing of Higher Education: The Tension between Quality and Equity. In *New York State Higher Education Services Corporation, Fourth Annual NASSGP/NCHELP Research Conference on Student Financial Aid Research.* Saint Louis: Washington University.

Hansen, W. Lee, and Burton A. Weisbrod. 1969. The Distribution of Costs and Direct Benefits of Public Higher Education: The Case of California. *Journal of Human Resources* 4(Spring): 176–91.

———. 1971. A New Approach to Higher Education Finance. In *Financing Higher Education,* ed. Mel W. Orwig. Iowa City: American College Testing Program.

Hansen, W. Lee, et al. 1980. Forecasting the Market for New Ph.D. Economists. *American Economic Review* 70(March): 49–63.

Harford, Jon D., and Richard D. Marcus. 1986. Tuition and U.S. Private College Characteristics: The Hedonic Approach. *Economics of Education Review* 5(4): 415–30.

Harmon, Lindsey. 1977. *Career Achievement of NSF Graduate Fellows: The Awardees of 1952–72.* Washington, D.C.: National Research Council.

———. 1979. *Career Patterns of Doctoral Scientists and Engineers, 1973–77.* Washington, D.C.: National Academy of Science.

Harrington, Paul E., and Andrew M. Sum. 1988. Whatever Happened to the College Enrollment Crisis? *Academe* 74(September/October): 17–22.

Harris, Seymour E. 1972. *A Statistical Portrait of Higher Education.* New York: McGraw-Hill.

Hartman, Robert W. 1970. A Comment on the Pechman-Hansen-Weisbrod Controversy. *Journal of Human Resources* 5(Fall): 519–23.

———. 1978. Federal Options for Student Aid. In *Public Policy and Private Higher Education,* ed. David W. Breneman and Chester E. Finn. Washington, D.C.: Brookings.

Hartnett, Rodney. 1987. Has There Been a Graduate Student Brain Drain in the Arts and Sciences? *Journal of Higher Education* 58(September/October): 562–85.

Hauptman, Arthur M. 1982. *Financing Student Loans: The Search for Alternatives in the Face of Federal Contraction.* Washington, D.C.: College Board.

———. 1990a. *The College Tuition Spiral.* Washington, D.C.: American Council on Education.

———. 1990b. *The Tuition Dilemma.* Washington, D.C.: Brookings.

Hauser, Robert M. 1990. The Decline in College Entry among African Americans: Findings in Search of Explanations. University of Wisconsin. Typescript.

Hauser, Robert M., and William H. Sewell. 1986. Family Effects in Simple Models of Education, Occupational Status, and Earnings: Findings from the Wisconsin and Kalamazoo Studies. *Journal of Labor Economics* 4(3): S83–S115.

Haveman, Robert. 1989. *Starting Even.* New York: Simon & Schuster.

Havighurst, Robert. 1985. Aging and Productivity: The Case of Older Faculty. In *Faculty Vitality and Institutional Productivity*, ed. Shirley Clark and Darrell Lewis. New York: Teachers College Press.

Hearn, James C. 1988. Attendance at Higher-Cost Colleges: Ascribed, Socio-Economic, and Academic Influences on Student Enrollment Patterns. *Economics of Education Review* 7(1): 65–76.

Hearn, James C., Robert H. Fenske, and Denis J. Curry. 1985. Unmet Financial Need among Postsecondary Students: A Statewide Study. *Journal of Student Financial Aid* 15:31–44.

Hearn, James C., and D. Longanecker. 1985. Enrollment Effects of Alternative Post-Secondary Pricing Policies. *Journal of Higher Education* 56(September/October): 485–508.

Hearn, James C., and Sharon L. Wilford. 1985. A Commitment to Opportunity: The Impacts of Federal Student Financial Aid Programs. University of Minnesota. Typescript.

Heath, J. A., and H. P. Tuckman. 1986. The Effect of Tuition Level and Financial Aid on the Demand for Advanced Terminal Degrees. *Economics of Education Review* 6 (3): 227–38.

———. 1989. The Impact on Labor Markets of the Relative Growth of New Female Doctorates. *Journal of Higher Education* 60(November/December): 704–15.

Hirsch, B. T., R. Austin, J. Brooks, and B. Moore. 1984. Economics Departmental Rankings: Comment. *American Economic Review* 74:822–26.

Hoenack, Stephen A. 1983. *Economic Behavior within Organizations*. Cambridge: Cambridge University Press.

———. 1990. An Economist's Perspective on Costs within Higher Education Institutions. In *The Economics of American Universities*, ed. Stephen A. Hoenack and Eileen L. Collins. Albany: State University of New York Press.

Hoenack, Stephen A., and Eileen L. Collins, eds. 1990. *The Economics of American Universities*. Albany: State University of New York Press.

Hoenack, Stephen, and William Weiler. 1975. Cost-Related Tuition Policies and University Enrollments. *Journal of Human Resources* 19(Summer): 332–60.

Hoenack, Stephen A., W. C. Weiler, R. O. Goodman, and D. J. Pierro. 1986. The Marginal Costs of Instruction. *Research in Higher Education* 24(4): 335–418.

Hoffman, Dennis, and Stuart Low. 1983. Rationality and the Decision to Invest in Economics. *Journal of Human Resources* 18(Fall): 480–96.

Hogan, Timothy D. 1986. The Publishing Performance of U.S. Ph.D. Programs in Economics during the 1970s. *Journal of Human Resources* 21(Spring): 217–29.

Holden, Karen, and W. Lee Hansen. 1989. Eliminating Mandatory Retirement: The Effects on Retirement Age. In *The End of Mandatory Retirement: Effects on Higher Education*, ed. Karen Holden and W. Lee Hansen. San Francisco: Jossey-Bass.

Howe, Alan, and Sharon Smith. 1990. Age and Research Activity. Princeton, N.J.: Project on Faculty Retirement. Mimeo.

Hudiburg, George E. 1965. The Relationship of Degrees Held by College Instructors and Teaching Effectiveness. Ph.D. diss., University of Arkansas.

Huffman, W. E., and P. Orazem. 1985. An Econometric Model of the Market for New Ph.D.'s in Agricultural Economics in the United States. *American Journal of Agricultural Economics* 67(December): 1207–14.

Iwai, Stanley I., and William D. Churchill. 1982. College Attrition and the Financial Support Systems of Students. *Research in Higher Education* 17(2): 105–13.

Jackson, G. A. 1988. Did College Choice Change during the Seventies? *Economics of Education Review* 7(1): 15–27.

Jacobi, Maryana, Alexander Astin, and Frank Ayala. 1987. *College Student Outcomes Assessment*. College Station, Texas: Association for the Study of Higher Education.

James, Estelle. 1978. Product Mix and Cost Disaggregation: A Reinterpretation of the Economics of Higher Education. *Journal of Human Resources* 13(Spring): 157–86.

―――. 1990. Decision Processes and Priorities in Higher Education. In *The Economics of American Universities,* ed. Stephen A. Hoenack and Eileen L. Collins. Albany: State University of New York Press.

James, Estelle, et al. 1988. College Quality and Future Earnings: Where Should You Send Your Child to College? Washington, D.C.: U.S. Department of Education, Office of Research. Typescript.

Jensen, Eric L. 1984. Student Financial Aid and Degree Attainment. *Research in Higher Education* 20(1): 117–27.

Johnston, J. 1960. *Statistical Cost Analysis.* New York: McGraw-Hill.

Johnstone, D. Bruce. 1986. *Sharing the Costs of Higher Education.* New York: College Entrance Examination Board.

Kaiser, Harvey. 1989. Rebuilding the Campus. *Educational Record* 70(Winter): 4–7, 49–52.

Kane, Thomas J. 1989. Black Educational Progress since 1970: Policy Lessons. Cambridge, Mass.: Kennedy School of Government. Mimeo.

―――. 1990. College Entry by Blacks since 1970: The Role of Tuition, Financial Aid, Local Economic Conditions and Family Background. Cambridge, Mass.: Kennedy School of Government. Mimeo.

Karabel, J. 1972. Community Colleges and Social Stratification: Submerged Class Conflict in American Higher Education. *Harvard Educational Review* 42:521–62.

Kasper, Hirschel. 1990a. The Education of Economists: From Undergraduate to Graduate Study. Report of the Committee of College Faculty. Oberlin College. Typescript.

―――. 1990b. Some Dynamic Aspects of Academic Careers: The Urgent Need to Match Aspirations with Compensation. *Academe* 76(March/April): 1–10.

Katz, Lawrence F., and Kevin M. Murphy. 1990. Changes in Relative Wages, 1963–87: Supply and Demand Factors. Cambridge, Mass: National Bureau of Economic Research, April. Typescript.

Kerr, Clark. 1982. *The Uses of the University.* Cambridge, Mass.: Harvard University Press.

King, Vereda J. 1984. Admissions Policies for a Non-Selective Institution: An Economic Analysis. Ph.D. diss., Duke University.

Kinney, Daniel, and Sharon P. Smith. 1989. Age and Teaching Performance. Princeton, N.J.: Project on Faculty Retirement. Mimeo.

Kirshstein, Rita J., Daniel R. Sherman, Valentina K. Tikoff, Charles Masten, and James Fairweather. 1990. *The Escalating Cost of Higher Education.* Washington, D.C.: Pelavin Associates.

Klitgaard, Robert E. 1985. *Choosing Elites.* New York: Basic.

Kramer, John. 1989. Who Will Pay the Piper or Leave the Check on the Table for the Other Guy? *Journal of Legal Education* 39(suppl.): 655–96.

Kuh, Charlotte. 1977. Market Conditions and Tenure for Ph.D's in U.S. Higher Education. Report to the Carnegie Council on Policy Studies in Higher Education, Berkeley. Typescript.

Kuh, Charlotte V., and Roy Radner. 1980. *Mathematicians in Academia: 1975–2000.* Washington, D.C.: Conference Board of the Mathematical Sciences.

Laband, David. 1985. An Evaluation of 50 "Ranked" Economics Departments. *Southern Economic Journal* 52(July): 216–40.

―――. 1986. A Ranking of U.S. Economics Departments by Research Productivity of Graduates. *Journal of Economic Education* 17(Winter): 70–76.

Layard, Richard, and George Psacharopoulos. 1974. The Screening Hypothesis and the Returns to Education. *Journal of Political Economy* 82(September/October): 985–98.

Lee, John B. 1985. *The Distribution of Student Financial Aid: Trends among the Post-secondary Sectors.* Washington, D.C.: American Council on Education.

———. 1987. The Equity of Higher Education Subsidies. In *Fourth Annual NASSGP/NCHELP Research Conference on Student Financial Aid Research,* sponsored by the New York State Higher Education Services Corp. Saint Louis: Washington University.

Leibenstein, Harvey. 1978. X-Efficiency Xists: Reply to a Xorcist. *American Economic Review* 68(March): 203–11.

Leslie, Larry L. 1984. Changing Patterns in Student Financing of Higher Education. *Journal of Higher Education* 55(May/June): 313–46.

Leslie, Larry L., and Paul T. Brinkman. 1987. Student Price Response in Higher Education: The Student Demand Studies. *Journal of Higher Education* 58(March/April): 181–204.

———. 1988. *The Economic Value of Higher Education.* New York: Macmillan.

Levin, Sharon, and Paula Stephan. 1989a. Age and Research Productivity of Academic Scientists. St. Louis: University of Missouri. Mimeo.

———. 1989b. Research Productivity over the Life Cycle: Evidence from Academic Scientists. St. Louis: University of Missouri. Mimeo.

Lewis, Gwendolyn L. 1988. *Trends in Student Aid, 1980 to 1988.* New York: College Entrance Examination Board.

Lewis, Lionel S., and Paul William Kingston. 1989. The Best, the Brightest, and the Most Affluent: Undergraduates at Elite Institutions. *Academe* 75(November/December): 28–33.

Litten, L. H., and A. E. Hall. 1989. In the Eyes of Our Beholders. *Journal of Higher Education* 60(May/June): 302–24.

Long, James E. 1987. An Economic Analysis of State Appropriations for Higher Education in Alabama. Auburn, Ala.: Auburn University. Mimeo.

Lozier, G. Gregory, and Michael J. Doris. 1990. Faculty Retirement Projections beyond 1994: Effects of Policy on Individual Choice. Boulder, Colo.: Western Interstate Commission for Higher Education. Mimeo.

Lyddon, Jan W. 1986. *State Financing of Higher Education under Changing Conditions.* Ann Arbor: University of Michigan, Center for the Study of Higher Education.

McCormick, R. E., and M. Tensley. 1987. Athletics versus Academics? Evidence from SAT Scores. *Journal of Political Economy* 95(October): 1103–16.

McGinnis, Robert, and Scott Long. 1988. Entry into Academia: Effects of Stratification, Geography and Ecology. In *Academic Labor Markets and Careers,* ed. David Breneman and Ted Youn. New York: Falmer.

McGuinness, Aims C., and Christine Paulson. 1990. A Survey of College Prepayment and Savings Plans in the United States. In *College Savings Plans,* ed. Janet S. Hansen, 44–72. New York: College Entrance Examination Board.

McPherson, Michael S. 1978. The Demand for Higher Education. In *Public Policy and Private Higher Education,* ed. David W. Breneman and Chester E. Finn. Washington, D.C.: Brookings.

———. 1988a. *How Can We Tell If Federal Student Aid Is Working?* New York: College Entrance Examination Board.

———. 1988b. On Assessing the Impact of Federal Student Aid. *Economics of Education Review* 7(1): 77–84.

McPherson, Michael S., and Morton Schapiro. 1991. Does Student Aid Affect College Enrollment? New Evidence on a Persistent Controversy. *American Economic Review* 81 (March): 309–18.

McPherson, Michael S., Morton Schapiro, and Gordon C. Winston. 1989a. The Impact of Federal Student Aid on Institutions: Toward an Empirical Understanding. In *Studying the Impact of Student Aid on Institutions*, ed. R. H. Fenske. San Francisco: Jossey-Bass.

———. 1989b. Recent Trends in U.S. Higher Education Costs and Prices: The Role of Government Funding. *American Economic Review* 79(May): 253–57.

Manski, Charles F. 1989. Schooling as Experimentation: A Reappraisal of the Postsecondary Dropout Phenomenon. *Economics of Education Review* 8(4): 305–12.

Manski, Charles F., and David A. Wise. 1983. *College Choice in America*. Cambridge, Mass.: Harvard University Press.

Marsh, Herbert, and J. U. Overall. 1981. The Relative Influence of Course Level, Course Time and Instructor on Students' Evaluations of College Teaching. *American Educational Research Journal* 18 (Spring): 103–12.

Massy, William F. 1989. Productivity Improvement for College and University Administration: Stanford University. Typescript.

———. 1990. Financing Research. In *Financing Higher Education in a Global Economy*, eds. Richard E. Anderson and Joel W. Meyerson. New York: Macmillan.

Maynard, James. 1971. *Some Microeconomics of Higher Education: Economies of Scale*. Lincoln: University of Nebraska Press.

Medoff, Marshall H. 1989. The Ranking of Economists. *Journal of Economic Education* 20(Fall): 405–46.

Metz, G. E. 1964. *Current Fund Expenditures*. Atlanta: Southern Association of Colleges and Schools, Commission on Colleges.

Metz, Joseph. 1970. A Study of the Relationship between Student Evaluation of Teaching and Selected Faculty Characteristics. Ph.D. diss., University of Maryland.

Miller, Scott E., and Holly Hexter. 1985a. *How Low-Income Families Pay for College*. Washington, D.C.: American Council on Education.

———. 1985b. *How Middle-Income Families Pay for College*. Washington, D.C.: American Council on Education.

Mohrman, Kathryn. 1987. Unintended Consequences of Federal Student Aid Policies. *Brookings Review* 5(Fall): 24–30.

Moline, Arlett. 1987. Financial Aid and Student Persistence: An Application of Causal Modeling. *Research in Higher Education* 26(2): 130–47.

Montgomery, Sarah. 1989. Findings from the COFHE Studies. In *The End of Mandatory Retirement: Effects on Higher Education*. (Cited in Holden and Hansen 1989.)

Mooney, Carolyn. 1989. Affirmative Action Goals Coupled with Tiny Number of Minority Ph.D.'s, Set Off Faculty Recruiting Frenzy. *Chronicle of Higher Education* 35(2 August): Al.

Moore, William J., Robert J. Newman, John Raisian, and R. William Thomas. 1983. A Quality Adjustment Model of the Academic Labor Market: The Case of Economists. *Economic Inquiry* 21(April): 241–54.

Mortenson, Thomas G. 1988a. *Attitudes of Americans toward Borrowing to Finance Educational Expenses, 1959–1983*. Student Financial Aid Research Report no. 88-22. Iowa City: American College Testing Program.

———. 1988b. *Pell Grant Program Changes and Their Effects on Applicant Eligibility, 1973–74 to 1988–89*. Student Financial Aid Research Report no. 88-1. Iowa City: American College Testing Program.

———. 1990. *The Impact of Increased Loan Utilization among Low Family Income Students*. Student Financial Aid Research Report no. 90-1. Iowa City: American College Testing Program.

Mortenson, Thomas G., and Zhijun Wu. 1990. *High School Graduation and College Participation of Young Adults by Family Income Backgrounds, 1970 to 1989*. Student Financial Aid Research Report no. 90-3. Iowa City: American College Testing Program.

Murphy, Kevin, and Finis Welch. 1989. Wage Premiums for College Graduates: Recent Growth and Possible Explanations. *Educational Researcher* 18(May): 17–26.

Nairn, Allan, et al. 1980. *The Reign of ETS.* Washington, D.C.: Ralph Nader.

National Association for Foreign Student Affairs and the Association of International Educators. 1990. The Immigration Act of 1990 (S358): Summary of Provisions Relevant to U.S. Colleges and Universities. Washington, D.C. Mimeo.

National Research Council. 1978. *Science, Engineering and Humanities Doctorates in the United States: 1977.* Washington, D.C.: National Academy of Sciences.

———. 1979. *Research Excellence through the Year 2000.* Washington, D.C.: National Academy of Sciences.

———. 1981. *Postdoctoral Appointments and Disappointments.* Washington, D.C.: National Academy Press.

———. 1982. *Science, Engineering and Humanities Doctorates in the United States, 1981 Profile.* Washington, D.C.: National Academy Press.

———. 1986. *Humanities Doctorates in the United States, 1985 Profile.* Washington, D.C.: National Academy Press.

———. 1989a. *Common Destiny: Blacks and American Society.* Washington, D.C.: National Academy Press.

———. 1989b. *Humanities Doctorates in the United States, 1987 Profile.* Washington, D.C.: National Academy Press.

———. 1989c. *Investing in Research: A Proposal to Strengthen the Agricultural, Food and Environmental System.* Washington, D.C.: National Academy Press.

———. 1989d. *Summary Report, 1988: Doctorate Recipients from United States Universities.* Washington, D.C.: National Academy Press.

———. 1990. *Biomedical and Behavioral Research Scientists: Their Training and Supply.* Vol. 1, *Findings.* Washington, D.C.: National Academy Press.

National Science Foundation. 1988a. *Characteristics of Doctoral Scientists and Engineers in the United States: 1987.* Washington, D.C.

———. 1988b. *Doctoral Scientists and Engineers: A Decade of Change.* Washington, D.C.

———. 1988c. *Federal Support to Universities, Colleges and Selected Non-Profit Institutions: Fiscal Year 1987.* Washington, D.C.

———. 1988d. *Immigrant Scientists and Engineers: 1987.* Washington, D.C.

———. 1988e. *Women and Minorities in Science and Engineering.* Washington, D.C.

———. 1989a. *Academic Science/Engineering: Graduate Enrollment and Support, Fall 1987.* Washington, D.C.

———. 1989b. *Academic Science/Engineering: R&D Funds, Fiscal Year 1987.* Washington, D.C.

———. 1989c. *Achieving Full Participation of Women in Science and Engineering.* Washington, D.C.: Report of the Task Force on Women in Science and Engineering.

———. 1989d. Future Scarcities of Scientists and Engineers: Problems and Solutions. Washington, D.C.: National Science Foundation, Division of Policy Research and Analysis, Directorate for Scientific, Technological, and International Affairs. Mimeo.

———. 1989e. *Science and Engineering Doctorates: 1960–88.* Washington, D.C.

Nelson, Charles. 1989. Grant Funding from the National Science Foundation during Fiscal Year 1987. Discussion Paper no. 89-10. University of Washington, Department of Economics.

Nerlove, Marc. 1972. On Tuition and the Costs of Higher Education: Prolegomena to a Conceptual Framework. *Journal of Political Economy* 80(May/June): S178–S218.

Newhouse, Joseph F. 1970. Toward a Theory of Nonprofit Institutions: An Economic Model of a Hospital. *American Economic Review* 60(March): 64–74.

Newman, Frank. 1985. *Higher Education and the American Resurgence*. Princeton, N.J.: Carnegie Foundation for the Advancement of Teaching.

Nichols, M. Gene. 1967. A Study of the Influence of Selected Variables Involved in Student Evaluations of Teaching Effectiveness. Ph.D. diss., University of South Dakota.

Olivas, Michael. 1986. Research on Latino College Students: A Theoretical Framework and Inquiry. In *Latin College Students,* ed. Michael Olivas. New York: Teachers College Press.

Olson, Lorayn, and Rachael A. Rosenfeld. 1984. Parents and the Process of Gaining Access to Student Financial Aid. *Journal of Higher Education* 55 (July/August): 455–80.

O'Neill, June. 1976. Productivity Trends in Higher Education. In *Education as an Industry,* ed. Joseph T. Froomkin, Dean T. Jamison, and Roy Radner. Cambridge, Mass.: National Bureau of Economic Research.

Pascarella, Ernest T., and Patrick T. Terenzini. 1991. *How College Affects Students.* San Francisco: Jossey-Bass.

Pear, Robert. 1990. Major Immigration Bill Is Sent to Bush. *New York Times,* 29 October.

Pechman, Joseph. 1970. The Distributional Effects of Public Higher Education in California. *Journal of Human Resources* 11(Summer): 343–53.

Peltzman, Sam. 1973. The Effect of Government Subsidies-in-Kind on Private Expenditures: The Case of Higher Education. *Journal of Political Economy* 81(January/February): 1–27.

Pencavel, John. 1989. Schooling, Productivity, and the Efficient Allocation of Resources. Paper presented for the symposium on Increasing Productivity in Higher Education, sponsored by the Forum for College Financing Alternatives, Stanford University.

Peng, Samuel S. 1977. Trends in Entry to Higher Education: 1961–1972. *Educational Researcher* 6(1): 15–19.

———. 1983. Changes in Access to Postsecondary Education: 1972–1980. Washington, D.C.: National Center for Educational Statistics, 14 April. Typescript.

Peterson's Guide to Four-Year Colleges: 1990. 1990. Princeton, N.J.: Peterson's Guides.

Perrucci, R., K. O'Flaherty, and H. Marshall. 1983. Market Conditions, Productivity and Promotion among University Faculty. *Research in Higher Education* 19(4): 431–49.

Polachek, Solomon. 1978. Sex Differences in College Major. *Industrial and Labor Relations Review* 31(July): 498–508.

Rader, Nicholas. 1968. College Student Ratings of Instructors. *Journal of Experimental Education* 37(Winter): 76–81.

Radner, Roy. 1976. Faculty-Student Ratios in U.S. Higher Education. In *Education as an Industry,* ed. Joseph T. Froomkin, Dean T. Jamison, and Roy Radner. Cambridge, Mass.: National Bureau of Economic Research.

Radner, Roy, and Leonard S. Miller. 1975. *Demand and Supply in U.S. Higher Education.* New York: McGraw-Hill.

Razin, A., and J. Campbell. 1972. Internal Allocation of University Resources. *Western Economic Journal* 10(September): 308–20.

Rees, Albert, and Sharon P. Smith. 1990. *Faculty Retirement in the Arts and Sciences.* Princeton, N.J.: Project on Faculty Retirement.

Research Associates of Washington. 1989. *Higher Education Prices and Price Indexes.* Washington, D.C.

Reskin, Barbara F. 1985. Aging and Productivity: Careers and Results. In *Faculty Vitality and Institutional Productivity,* ed. Shirley Clark and Darrell Lewis. New York: Teachers College Press.

Riesman, David. 1980. *On Higher Education.* San Francisco: Jossey-Bass.

Riley, J., B. Ryan, and M. Lifshitz. 1950. *A Student Looks at His Teacher.* New Brunswick, N.J.: Rutgers University Press.

Rivlin, Alice M. 1961. *The Role of the Federal Government in Financing Higher Education.* Washington, D.C.: Brookings.

Rosenfeld, Rachel, and Jo Ann Jones. 1986. Institutional Mobility among Academics: The Case of Psychologists. *Sociology of Education* 59(October): 212–26.

———. 1988. Entry and Reentry in Higher Education. In *Academic Labor Markets and Careers,* ed. David W. Breneman and Ted I. K. Youn. New York: Falmer.

Rosovsky, Henry. 1990. *The University: An Owner's Manual.* New York: Norton.

Roy, Andrew D. 1951. Some Thoughts on the Distribution of Earnings. *Oxford Economic Papers* 3(June): 80–93.

Rush, Sean C., and Sandra L. Johnson. 1989. *The Decaying American Campus: A Ticking Time Bomb.* Joint Report of the Association of Physical Plant Administrators of Universities and Colleges and the National Association of College and University Business Officers in Cooperation with Coopers & Lybrand.

St. John, Edward P., and Charles Byce. 1982. The Changing Federal Role in Student Aid. In *Meeting Student Aid Needs in a Period of Retrenchment,* ed. M. Kramer. San Francisco: Jossey-Bass.

Schapiro, Morton O. 1987. The Concept of Productivity in Institutions of Higher Education. Paper presented at the conference of the Organization for Economic Cooperation and Development, University of Quebec.

Schapiro, Morton O., Michael P. O'Malley, and Larry H. Litten. In press. Progression to Graduate School from the "Elite" Colleges and Universities: Understanding the Past and Influencing the Future. *Economics of Education Review.*

Schultz, Theodore W. 1972. Optimal Investment in College Instruction: Equity and Efficiency. *Journal of Political Economy* 80(May/June): S2–S30.

Schwartz, J. Brad. 1985. Student Financial Aid and the College Enrollment Decision: The Effects of Public and Private Grants and Interest Subsidies. *Economics of Education Review* 4(2): 129–44.

———. 1986. Wealth Neutrality in Higher Education: The Effects of Student Grants. *Economics of Education Review* 5(2): 107–17.

Scott, Charles. 1979. The Market for Ph.D. Economists: The Academic Sector. *American Economic Review* 69(May): 137–42.

Sewell, William H., and Robert M. Hauser. 1975. *Education, Occupation, and Earnings.* New York: Academic.

Sharpe, Russell T. 1933. College and the Poor Boy. *Atlantic Monthly* 151 (January/June): 696–705.

Sharpe, Russell T., et al. 1946. *Financial Assistance for College Students.* Washington, D.C.: American Council on Education.

Siegfried, J. J. 1986. The Effects of Student Higher Education Grants. *Economics of Education Review* 5(2): 129–33.

Siegfried, John, and Rendig Fels. 1979. Research on Teaching College Economics: A Survey. *Journal of Economic Literature* 17(September): 923–69.

Siegfried, John J., Malcolm Getz, and Lori Dunn. 1991. To Make or Buy Auxiliary and Business Services. *College Services Administration* 14(June): 40–44.

Siegfried, John, and William Walstad. 1990. Research on Teaching College Economics. In *The Principles of Economics Course: A Handbook for Instructors,* ed. Phillip Saunders and William Walstad. New York: McGraw-Hill.

Siegfried, John J., and Edwin H. Wheeler. 1981. Cost Efficiency and Monopoly Power: A Survey. *Quarterly Review of Economics and Business* 21(Spring): 25–46.

Sloan, F. 1971. The Demand for Higher Education: The Case of Medical School Applicants. *Journal of Human Resources* 6(Fall): 466–89.

Smith, James F. 1984. Race and Human Capital. *American Economic Review* 74:685–98.

Smith, Marshall S., and Jennifer O'Day. 1990. Educational Equality: 1966 and Now. Stanford University. Typescript.

Snyder, Joan. 1988. Early Career Achievement of National Science Foundation Graduate Fellows, 1967–76. Washington, D.C.: National Research Council. Mimeo.

Snyder, Thomas D. 1988. Recent Trends in Higher Education Finance, 1976–77 to 1985–86. In *Higher Education Administrative Costs: Continuing the Study,* ed. Thomas P. Snyder and Eva C. Galambos. Washington, D.C.: U.S. Department of Education, Office of Educational Research and Improvement.

Solmon, Lewis C. 1973. The Definition and Impact of College Quality. In *Does College Matter?* ed. Lewis C. Solmon and Paul J. Taubman. New York: Academic.

Solmon, Lewis C., and Paul J. Taubman, eds. 1973. *Does College Matter?* New York: Academic.

Spies, Richard R. 1978. *The Effect of Rising Costs on College Choice: A Study of the Application Decisions of High-Ability Students.* New York: College Entrance Examination Board.

Stafford, K. L., S. B. Lundstest, and A. D. Lynn, Jr. 1984. Social and Economic Factors Affecting Participation in Higher Education. *Journal of Higher Education* 55(September/October): 590–608.

Stampen, Jacob O., and Alberto F. Cabrera. 1986. Exploring the Effects of Student Aid on Attrition. *Journal of Student Financial Aid* 16(Spring): 28–40.

———. 1988. The Targeting and Packaging of Student Aid and Its Effect on Attrition. *Economics of Education Review* 7(1): 29–46.

Stampen, Jacob O., Roxanne W. Reeves, and W. Lee Hansen. 1988. The Impact of Student Earnings in Offsetting "Unmet Need." *Economics of Education Review* 7(1): 113–26.

Stapleton, David C. 1989. Cohort Size and the Academic Labor Market. *Journal of Human Resources* 24(Spring): 221–52.

Stapleton, David C., and Douglas Young. In press. Educational Attainment and Cohort Size. *Journal of Labor Economics.*

Stedman, James B. 1988. *Financing Postsecondary Education Attendance: Current Issues Involving Access and Choice.* Washington, D.C.: Congressional Research Service.

Stephan, Paula, and Sharon Levin. 1987. Demographic and Economic Determinants of Scientific Productivity. Georgia State University. Mimeo.

———. 1989. Cohort Effects and the Publishing Productivity of Physicists. Georgia State University. Mimeo.

Stigler, George J. 1976. The Xistence of X-Efficiency. *American Economic Review* 66(March): 213–16.

———. 1989. The Future of Higher Education: An Economic Perspective. Working Paper no. 56. University of Chicago: Center for the Study of the Economy and the State.

Stromsdorfer, Ernst W. 1989. Final Report on the 1989–90 Salary Survey for New Assistant Professors. Washington State University. Mimeo.

Sun, Emily. 1975. Doctoral Origins of Contributors to the *American Economic Review, 1960–72. Journal of Economic Education* 65(Fall): 50–55.

Sykes, Charles J. 1988. *Profscam.* Washington, D.C.: Regnery Gateway.

Taubman, Paul J., and Terrence J. Wales. 1973. Higher Education, Mental Ability, and Screening. *Journal of Political Economy* 81(January/February): 28–55.

Teltsch, Kathleen. 1989. Dana Foundation to Help Blacks Become College Teachers. *New York Times,* 12 April.

Tennessee Higher Education Commission. 1990. *Appropriations Formula: Academic Formula Units, Fiscal Year 1990–91.* Nashville.

Tierney, M. L. 1980a. An Estimate of Departmental Cost Functions. *Higher Education* 9(July): 453–68.

———. 1980b. The Impact of Financial Aid on Student Demand for Public/Private Higher Education. *Journal of Higher Education* 51(September/October): 527–45.

———. 1983. Student College Choice Sets: Toward an Empirical Characterization. *Research in Higher Education* 18(3): 271–84.

Tinto, Vincent. 1975. Dropout from Higher Education: A Theoretical Synthesis of Recent Research. *Review of Educational Research* 45(Winter): 89–125.

Trends in Student Aid. 1989. Washington, D.C.: College Board.

Tuckman, Howard, Susan Coyle, and Yupin Bae. 1990. *On Time to the Doctorate.* Washington, D.C.: National Academy Press.

Tuckman, Howard, and D. Katz. 1984. Displacement of Full-Timers by Part-Timers— a Model for Projection. *Economics of Education Review* 3 (1): 85–90.

Tuckman, Howard, and Karen Pickerill. 1988. Part-Time Faculty and Part-Time Academic Careers. In *Academic Labor Markets and Careers,* ed. David Breneman and Ted Youn. New York: Falmer.

Turner, Sarah E., and William G. Bowen. 1990. The Flight from the Arts and Sciences: Trends in Degrees Conferred. *Science* 250(26 October): 517–21.

U.S. Bureau of the Census. 1988. *Current Population Reports,* Series P-20, *Educational Attainment in the United States: March 1981 and 1986.* No. 428. Washington, D.C.: U.S. Government Printing Office.

———. 1989. *Current Population Reports,* Series P-25, *Projections of the Population of the United States, by Age, Sex and Race: 1988 to 2080,* No. 1018. Washington, D.C.: U.S. Government Printing Office.

———. 1990. *Current Population Reports,* Series P-25, *State Population and Household Estimates: July 1, 1989.* No. 1058. Washington, D.C.: U.S. Government Printing Office.

———. Various years. *Current Population Reports,* Series P-20, *School Enrollment— Social and Economic Characteristics of Students.* Washington, D.C.: U.S. Government Printing Office.

———. Various years. *Current Population Reports,* Series P-25, *Estimates of the Population of the U.S. by Age, Sex and Race.* Washington, D.C.: U.S. Government Printing Office.

———. Various years. *Current Population Reports,* Series P-60, *Money Income of Households, Families and Persons in the United States.* Washington, D.C.: U.S. Government Printing Office.

U.S. Congressional Budget Office. 1988. *Trends in Family Income: 1970–1986.* Washington, D.C.: U.S. Government Printing Office.

U.S. Council of Economic Advisers. Various years. *Economic Report of the President.* Washington, D.C.: U.S. Government Printing Office.

U.S. Department of Education. Various years. *Digest of Education Statistics.* Washington, D.C.: U.S. Government Printing Office.

U.S. Department of State. 1990. *Visa Bulletin,* vol. 6 (9 May).

Van Dusen, William D., and Hal F. Higginbotham. 1984. *The Financial Aid Profession at Work: A Report on the 1983 Survey of Undergraduate Need Analysis Policies, Practices, and Procedures.* New York: College Entrance Examination Board.

Venti, S. F., and D. A. Wise. 1983. Individual Attributes and Self-Selection of Higher Education: College Attendance versus College Completion. *Journal of Public Economics* 21(June): 1–32.

Verry, D., and B. Davies. 1976. *University Costs and Outputs*. Amsterdam: Elsevier.

Veysey, Laurence R. 1965. *The Emergence of the American University*. Chicago: University of Chicago Press.

———. 1973. Stability and Experiment in the American Undergraduate Curriculum. In *Content and Context*, ed. Carl Kaysen, 1–63. New York: McGraw-Hill.

Viehland, Dennis W., Norman S. Kaufman, and Barbara M. Krauth. 1982. Indexing Tuition to Cost of Education: The Impact on Students and Institutions. *Research in Higher Education* 17(4): 333–43.

Voorhees, Richard A. 1985. Financial Aid and Persistence: Do the Federal Campus-Based Aid Programs Make a Difference? *Journal of Student Financial Aid* 15:21–30.

Walker, David. 1989. Philosophy Professors Are Leaving Britain for American Campuses. *Chronicle of Higher Education* 35(8 May): A1.

Watts, Michael, and Gerald Lynch. 1989. The Principles Course Revisited. *American Economic Review* 79(May): 236–41.

Weiler, William C. 1986. A Sequential Logit Model of the Access Effects of Higher Education Institutions. *Economics of Education Review* 5(1): 49–55.

———. 1987. Enrollment Demand with Constrained Supply in a Higher Education Institution. *Research in Higher Education* 27(1): 51–61.

Williamson, Oliver E. 1975. *Markets and Hierarchies: Analysis and Antitrust Implications*. New York: Free Press.

Willis, Rachel A. 1990. Academic Labor markets: A Study of Academic Placement and Tenure for Doctoral Economists. Ph.D. diss., Northwestern University.

Willis, Robert J., and Sherwin Rosen. 1979. Education and Self-Selection. *Journal of Political Economy* 87(5): 7–36.

Wilson, Robin. 1990. Many Institutions Report Sharp Drops in Freshman Rolls. *Chronicle of Higher Education* 37(3 October): A1, A35.

Wish, John R., and William D. Hamilton. 1980. Replicating Freeman's Recursive Adjustment Model of Demand for Higher Education. *Research in Higher Education* 12(1): 83–95.

Youn, Ted, and Daniel Zelterman. 1988. Institutional Career Mobility in Academia. In *Academic Labor Markets and Careers*, ed. David Breneman and Ted Youn. New York: Falmer.

Author Index

Subject Index

AAUP. *See* American Association of University Professors

Academic support, 293

Acceptance letter as commodity, 83

Accounting practices, 297–98, 343–44

Admission policies, college: criteria for admission, 82–86; discrimination in, 85; selectivity differences in, 80–82. *See also* Rationing, price and non-price; Selectivity, college and university

AE&G. *See* Expenditures, education and general, adjusted

Affirmative action, 85

Age Discrimination in Employment Act (1978, 1986), 187n8

Aid, student. *See* Assistance, financial; Assistance programs, federal

American Association for the Advancement of Science, 143

American Association of University Professors (AAUP), 147–48

American Council on Education, 89

American Federation of Teachers, 177

Applications, college: effect of increased costs on, 73–75; as measure of demand, 60; self-selection factor in, 81–82

Aptitude/ability: as characteristic of enrolled students, 42–44, 47; as criterion for assistance, 106

Assistance, financial: changes in federal, 194; changing composition of, 98–105; College Board methodology for calculating, 96–98; by colleges and universities, 92–93, 100, 104; and college completion,

121–23; criteria shaping distribution of, 106–7; for doctoral study, 184–90; effect of, 105–13, 127, 177; for minorities, 228; forms of, for undergraduates, 90–95; proposals to reform, 120–21; proposed increase of, for doctoral stuudents, 251; sources of, 90–95. *See also* Need, financial; Scholarship aid

Assistance programs, federal: creation and expansion of, 98–105; decline in value of loans from, 100, 124–26; for dependents of social security recipients, 101; formula for calculating, 95–98; grants and loans as, 91–95, 100; objectives for existing public policy, 118–20. *See also* Congressional Methodology; Pell grants; Perkins loans; Stafford Student Loans; Subsidies

Assistance programs, state, 100, 114

Association of Physical Plant Administrators surveys, 310

Attainment, educational: advance in, 57–58; association with income and social status, 40–42, 132–37; economic payoff of, 64–69; in male population, 131–32; patterns of, 48–57; racial differences in, 133; rise in level of, 30; of whites and minorities, 34–37. *See also* Completion, college; Completion, doctoral degree

Basic Educational Opportunity Grants (BEOG). *See* Pell grants

Baumol/Bowen fixed factor proportion theory, 375, 384, 391